Medical Care Output and Productivity

Studies in Income and Wealth
Volume 62

National Bureau of Economic Research
Conference on Research in Income and Wealth

Medical Care Output and Productivity

Edited by **David M. Cutler and Ernst R. Berndt**

The University of Chicago Press

Chicago and London

DAVID M. CUTLER is professor of economics at Harvard University and a research associate of the National Bureau of Economic Research. ERNST R. BERNDT is professor of applied economics at the Sloan School of Management of the Massachusetts Institute of Technology and director of the NBER's Program on Technological Progress and Productivity Measurement.

The University of Chicago Press, Chicago 60637
The University of Chicago Press, Ltd., London
© 2001 by the National Bureau of Economic Research
All rights reserved. Published 2001
Printed in the United States of America

10 09 08 07 06 05 04 03 02 01   1 2 3 4 5

ISBN: 0-226-13226-9 (cloth)

Library of Congress Cataloging-in-Publication Data

Medical care output and productivity / edited by David M. Cutler and Ernst R. Berndt.
   p. cm.   (Studies in income and wealth ; v. 62)
   Includes bibliographical references and index.
   ISBN 0-226-13226-9 (cloth : alk. paper)
   1. Medical care—Cost effectiveness—Econometric models—Congresses.   2. Medical care, Cost of—Congresses.   I. Cutler, David M.   II. Berndt, Ernst R.   III. Series.

RA410.5 .M425 2001
338.4'33621—dc21   00-067235

Contents

Prefatory Note

This volume contains revised versions of most of the papers and discussion presented at the Conference on Research in Income and Wealth entitled "Medical Care Output and Productivity," held in Bethesda, Maryland, on 12–13 June 1998. It also contains some material not presented at that conference.

Funds for the Conference on Research in Income and Wealth are supplied by the Bureau of Labor Statistics, the Bureau of Economic Analysis, the Federal Reserve Board, and the Bureau of the Census; we are indebted to them for their support.

We thank David M. Cutler and Ernst R. Berndt, who served as conference organizers and editors of the volume, and the NBER staff and University of Chicago Press editors for their assistance in organizing the conference and editing the volume.

Executive Committee, July 2000

Ernst R. Berndt	Charles R. Hulten, chair
Carol S. Carson	Lawrence F. Katz
Carol A. Corrado	J. Steven Landefeld
Edwin R. Dean	Robert H. McGuckin III
Robert C. Feenstra	Brent R. Moulton
John Greenlees	Matthew Shapiro
John C. Haltiwanger	Robert Summers

Volume Editors' Acknowledgments

Many individuals assisted in putting together this volume. Substantial funding for the volume, as well as for many of the research projects, was provided to the National Bureau of Economic Research by the Bureau of Labor Statistics, the Bureau of Economic Analysis, the National Institute on Aging, the National Science Foundation, and Eli Lilly and Company. We are grateful to each for their support. We are also grateful to the authors and discussants who so ably brought forward the intricacies of this issue.

The NBER Conference Department, under the able direction of Kirsten Foss Davis, superbly organized the conference at which these research papers were presented. We are also grateful to Helena Fitz-Patrick, who provided extensive support in coordinating the publication of this volume.

Introduction

David M. Cutler and Ernst R. Berndt

Measuring the output of the medical sector has been a long-standing policy concern. With the United States and other developed countries spending so much on medical care (7 to 14 percent of GDP), health care analysts invariably ask what one obtains for all these expenditures. Answering this question requires measuring the output of the medical care sector. National income accountants face the same problem. National income accounts divide nominal spending growth into changes in prices and changes in quantities. But neither prices nor quantities can be estimated without an accurate measure of the medical care industry output.

At the conceptual level, an appropriate measure of medical care output is clear—the health gains resulting from medical care. If increased medical spending leads to health improvements worth more than their cost, then medical care productivity is increasing. If spending increases lead to less valuable increases in health, medical care productivity is falling.

The difficulty rests in implementing this framework. Measuring health status is difficult, and attributing changes in health status to a particular factor such as medical care is even more challenging. Thus, productivity estimation for medical care has necessarily been infrequent and tentative.

Substantial research has recently been directed at this issue, however. The "outcomes movement" in health economics is an attempt to measure the health impact of medical care. Research conducted at and supported by public agencies such as the Bureau of Labor Statistics (BLS), the Bu-

David M. Cutler is professor of economics at Harvard University and a research associate of the National Bureau of Economic Research. Ernst R. Berndt is professor of applied economics at the Sloan School of Management of the Massachusetts Institute of Technology and director of the NBER's Program on Technological Progress and Productivity Measurement.

reau of Economic Analysis (BEA), and the National Institute on Aging, as well as by private pharmaceutical firms such as Eli Lilly and Company, have investigated the pricing of medical services. In 1996, the National Bureau of Economic Research, drawing together many of its own research efforts in this field, organized a study team on the Economics of Medical Treatments.

After several years of research, and in consultation with the Bureau of Labor Statistics, the Bureau of Economic Analysis, the National Institute on Aging, and Eli Lilly and Company, it was decided to take stock of where we are. This volume is the result of that assessment.

The chapters in this volume cover a very wide range, from theoretical discussions of how medical care productivity ought to be measured, to empirical analyses of prices and productivity for different illnesses and medical conditions, to nonmedical factors that affect health status and mortality. The chapters in this volume make a substantial contribution to the measurement of medical care prices, output, and productivity. Together, they illustrate where we are now, what can be done in the near future, and where price index measurement in this vital field can move feasibly and fruitfully in years to come.

This volume is organized around four thematic areas, which we now briefly summarize.

Conceptual Issues in Medical Care Prices and Productivity

The first topic is the methodology for measuring productivity in medical care. Medical care is not the only sector of the economy where productivity measurement is difficult, of course. Productivity measurement is difficult in many of the service sectors. The first section of the volume compares and contrasts the theoretical issues in productivity measurement in medical care with those in other sectors.

In his chapter "What's Different about Health? Human Repair and Car Repair in National Accounts and in National Health Accounts," Jack E. Triplett argues that health care is not in fact wholly different from other services, such as car repair. Both markets, for example, have characteristics of asymmetric information and moral hazard.

Triplett takes as a starting point in the human repair framework that the focal point of expenditures is that for treating diseases and conditions, and not, for example, expenditures for hospitals. This implies that national health accounts must be organized and integrated into cost-of-disease accounts. Moreover, instead of looking just at market transactions, for human repair one must consider what medical resources actually do for health. This means assessing the "production function" for health status outcomes. The integration of economic and outcomes research distinguishes, at least in degree, human repair from car repair accounting.

In his chapter "Theoretical Foundations of Medical Cost-Effectiveness Analysis: Implications for the Measurement of Benefits and Costs of Medical Interventions," David Meltzer explores the theoretical foundations underlying measures of medical care outcomes. The difficulty in measuring the costs and benefits of medical treatments is one of the most salient differences between medical care and other industries. Meltzer notes two key dimensions along which the literature has had substantial debate: how to measure the quality of life for individuals with particular health states, and how cost-effectiveness analysis should deal with costs occurring in the future, after the initial medical treatment has been provided.

On the first point, Meltzer argues that ideally quality of life should be measured with revealed preference analysis—using the choices that individuals actually make between different treatment options to infer their value of different health states. An example is treatment for diabetes. In comparing therapies with different levels of intensity and long-run quality of life gains, Meltzer argues that the choices that diabetic patients make are a reasonable guide to the underlying utility they receive. He shows how this insight can be turned into an estimate of quality of life useful for outcome valuation purposes.

On the second point, Meltzer argues that productivity measurement in medical care must consider the future costs resulting from medical treatments provided today. If medical intervention lengthens an individual's life by ten years, for example, Meltzer shows that the costs of sustaining that person for the ten additional years must be attributed to the intervention, just as the benefits of the ten years of additional life are. Meltzer shows that treating future costs and benefits consistently can have a large effect on our perception of the relative ranking of different interventions.

Another way in which health care differs from many (but not all) other service industries is that most production takes place in nonprofit organizations. Yet relatively little is known about the economic forces affecting productivity in this industry. In their chapter "Medical Care Output and Productivity in the Nonprofit Sector," Tomas Philipson and Darius Lakdawalla specify medical service provider objective functions that allow for productivity differences between for-profit and nonprofit producers to be interpreted as evidence for differences in preferences, rather than in costs. Their model predicts that when both coexist, nonprofits are larger and less efficient in input use ("input preferrers"), but nevertheless become more numerous than for-profit firms, even though the nonprofits exhibit higher average and marginal costs. The nonprofits thrive because of their dependence on donations and tax advantages. The authors interpret empirical evidence from the nursing home industry as supportive of their framework, although discussant Richard G. Frank interprets this evidence as being more ambiguous.

This thematic section on conceptual issues ends with a chapter by Ernst

Berndt, David Cutler, Richard Frank, the late Zvi Griliches, Joseph New-house, and Jack Triplett, "Price Indexes for Medical Care Goods and Services: An Overview of Measurement Issues," summarizing the NBER methodology to price and productivity measurement. The Berndt et al. chapter has two goals. First, it discusses the conceptual and measurement issues that underlie construction of medical care price indexes in the United States, particularly the medical care consumer price indexes (MCPIs) and medical-related producer price indexes (MPPIs). The prob-lems in price measurement are multiple: Insurance makes the cost of medi-cal care to consumers lower than its cost to society; physicians may not do exactly what well-informed patients would want; technological progress makes the basket of goods different over time; and organizational changes such as managed care change the basis of pricing in the market. Because of these various factors, market outcomes are not likely to be efficient, and therefore market transactions data cannot be relied upon to reveal mar-ginal valuations. This implies that productivity measurement must go be-yond the method of hedonic analysis that is now standard in other markets or industries.

The second part of the Berndt et al. chapter describes procedures cur-rently used by the BLS in constructing MCPIs and MPPIs, including re-cent revisions, and then considers alternative notions of medical care out-put. Whereas historical BLS methods relied on pricing all of the detailed services that a patient used, the authors argue instead that the focus should be on more aggregated pricing of an episode of treatment. The authors outline features of a proposed new experimental price index—a medical care expenditure price index—that is more suitable for evaluation and analyses of medical care cost changes than are the current MCPIs and MPPIs. They propose that, in addition to the MCPIs and MPPIs, some federal statistical agency publish an experimental medical care expendi-ture price index.

Current State of Measurement

In the second section of the volume, the current state of official govern-ment measurement regarding price and productivity measurement in med-ical care is summarized and reviewed. The first two chapters discuss the current BLS methodology for the consumer and producer price indexes in medical care, respectively.

In "Medical Care in the Consumer Price Index," Ina Kay Ford and Daniel H. Ginsburg provide details and discuss implications of changes introduced into the January 1998 major revision of the Consumer Price Index (CPI). Item weights are of course changed in this revision. Because the scope of the CPI is limited to consumers' direct out-of-pocket pay-ments plus the employee-paid share of employer-provided health insurance, the expenditure share of medical care in the CPI (7.4 percent in 1995) is much less than its share in the personal consumption expenditure component of GDP (17.9 percent). The Laspeyres fixed quantity basis of the CPI also resulted in the 1997 relative importance weight for medical care of about 7.5 percent being considerably larger than the new weight of 5.6 percent embodied in the 1998 revision.

Other CPI revisions introduced in 1998 include rotating the sample of categories of commodities rather than subsets of the pricing areas, which permits more frequent updating of selected item strata. To capture possible inpatient-outpatient substitution, the new hospital CPI incorporates hospital room expenses, charges for other inpatient services, and the cost of outpatient services all under one umbrella, rather than as distinct item strata. The authors note continuing conceptual and implementation challenges in pricing medical insurance, and conclude with a discussion of input versus outcomes approaches to the choice of what it is that is being priced by the medical CPI.

For quite some time now, the BLS has expanded the scope of its producer price indexes (PPIs) to include service sector industries, not just goods producing sectors. In their chapter, "Health Care Output and Prices in the Producer Price Index," BLS economists Dennis Fixler and Mitchell Ginsburg provide a very detailed and thorough description of how PPIs are now being constructed for the main industries composing the health care sector of the economy. By linking price quotes to patient diagnoses and procedural codes, these health care PPIs now attempt to price much more closely episodes of typical treatments, rather than just pricing discrete medical inputs such as hospital days. These developments in the PPI are very significant. A major continuing difficulty, however, is that the PPI program has as its organizing structure the Standard Industrial Classification (SIC) system, and many medical procedures combine outputs from several SIC industries. For example, the treatment of outpatient mental health combines inputs from psychiatrists and pharmaceuticals, the latter being classified within the SIC manufacturing sector.

The third paper in this section examines one of the long-standing issues in medical care measurement—the differences between different federal health care accounts in the United States. Both the Health Care Financing Administration and the Bureau of Economic Analysis produce and publish a set of national health accounts, where they track medical spending in the economy as a whole. But the two accounts differ by a considerable amount—3 to 4 percent in 1996, for example. With multiple measures of medical care spending, it has been difficult for users to obtain an accurate handle on the scope of the medical sector. Arthur Sensenig and Ernest Wilcox report on an attempted reconciliation between these two accounts in their chapter "National Health Accounts/National Income and Product Accounts Reconciliation." Sensenig and Wilcox highlight both conceptual and data differences between the two accounts. Conceptually, the two accounts differ in their use of revenues versus expenditures. The data used also differ, depending on whether they are benchmarked to other industry surveys. In a changing industry such as medical care, where revenues and costs may differ considerably (as they do, for example, in not-for-profit hospitals), these differences can be quite significant. Tracking these differences might therefore have a substantial impact on output and productivity estimates in the industry.

Recent Developments

The third section of this volume presents new empirical analyses of price, output, and productivity measurement in medical care. The authors of these papers generally focus on treatment of a particular condition, such as heart attacks or acute phase depression. The reason for this narrow focus was detailed in the earlier conceptual section of the volume: Because productivity analysis requires direct measurement of health outcomes, it needs to be done at the level of a specific disease or illness.

In their chapter "Pricing Heart Attack Treatments," David Cutler, Mark McClellan, Joseph Newhouse, and Dahlia Remler estimate price indexes for heart attack treatments, demonstrating the techniques that are currently used in official price indexes and presenting several alternatives. Cutler et al. consider two types of prices indexes: a service price index, which prices specific treatments provided, and a cost-of-living index, which prices the health outcomes of patients. Both indexes are complicated by price measurement issues. For example, list prices and transactions prices are fundamentally different in the medical care marketplace. The development of new or modified medical treatments further complicates the comparison of "like" goods over time. Furthermore, the cost-of-living index is hampered by the need to determine how much of health improvement results from medical treatments in comparison to other factors, such as lifestyle changes.

Cutler et al. describe methods to address each of these obstacles. They employ national data on treatments and outcomes for Medicare beneficiaries who have had a heart attack to measure the cost of living for medical care. Cutler et al. conclude that, while traditional price indexes when applied to heart attack treatments are rising at roughly 3 percent per year above general inflation, a corrected service price index is rising at perhaps 1 to 2 percent per year above general inflation, and the cost-of-living index is falling by 1 to 2 percent per year relative to general inflation.

An alternative method for measuring the impact of medical care involves use of clinical trial evidence on medical treatments. Meta-analyses based on clinical trials can be used to infer the impact of medical treatments on outcomes. The more medically oriented chapter by Paul Heidenreich and Mark McClellan, "Trends in Heart Attack Treatment and Outcomes, 1975–1995," demonstrates this methodology. Heidenreich and McClellan summarize the voluminous medical literature on the efficacy of treatment for myocardial infarction (heart attacks). They conclude that over the 1975–1995 period, medical treatments played a large role in improving heart attack survival rates. Specifically, they conclude that about two thirds of increased survival resulted from medical advances, most notably the diffusion of pharmaceutical therapies such as aspirin, beta blockers, and thrombolytics. Invasive technologies such as primary angioplasty also contributed significantly to increased survival. Heidenreich and McClellan's analysis thus complements the findings of Cutler et al. on the efficacy of medical treatments for myocardial infarction.

The next chapter, "Measuring the Value of Cataract Surgery," provides a dramatic example of the impact of changing medical technologies on reducing the burden of an ophthalmic condition, namely cataracts. The authors, Irving Shapiro, Matthew D. Shapiro, and David W. Wilcox begin by documenting changes in the last half-century for surgically extracting cataracts. Incisions and suturing have improved, intraocular lens implants have eliminated the need for cataract eyeglasses or contact lenses, and surgery is now done largely on an outpatient basis, resulting in greatly improved quality of outcomes. Patients have much faster ambulation, face lower rates of complications, and have better postoperative visual outcomes. Because of these cost reductions and quality improvements, patients with less severe disease are now increasingly having cataract surgery, earlier in the course of the disease, with more long-lived benefits. While precise measurement is still challenging, it is clear that although monetary costs have been relatively flat over time, in any reasonable quality-adjusted world the real price of cataract extraction has fallen sharply with time. The authors conclude with a discussion about the generalizability of their findings, and urge that future research focus on taking into account how the population of patients receiving treatment changes endogenously in response to changes in cost.

In their chapter "Hedonic Analysis of Arthritis Drugs," Iain Cockburn and Aslam Anis focus on measuring price indexes for pharmaceuticals used in the treatment of rheumatoid arthritis. Although this is a widespread and debilitating disease with very substantial impacts on the health of patients and on the economy, currently the available drugs have limited efficacy and serious side effects. Clinical research conducted since these products were approved has resulted in substantial revisions to the body of scientific information available to physicians. The relative quality of these drugs (as represented by efficacy and toxicity measurements reported in peer-reviewed clinical trials) has changed markedly over the past fifteen years. Cockburn and Anis examine how prices relate to quality. Somewhat surprisingly, they find that in this therapeutic class, prices are only weakly related to quality. They do, however, find a relationship between changes in reported efficacy and toxicity, and the evolution of quantity shares within this therapeutic class. Thus the Cockburn-Anis research reminds us that generalization across diverse medical conditions is hazardous, and that disease-by-disease analysis is instead necessary.

The chapter by Ernst Berndt, Susan Busch, and Richard Frank, "Treatment Price Indexes for Acute Phase Major Depression," focuses on alternative price indexes for acute phase unipolar (major) depression. Making use of results from the published clinical literature and from official federal government treatment guideline standards, Berndt et al. begin by identifying therapeutically similar treatment bundles. These bundles can then be linked and weighted to construct price indexes for specific forms of major depression. In doing so, Berndt et al. construct CPI- and PPI-like medical price indexes that deal with prices of treatment episodes rather than prices of discrete inputs, that are based on transaction rather than list prices, that take quality changes and expected outcomes into account, and that employ current, time-varying expenditure weights in the aggregation computations. Berndt et al. find that, regardless of which index number procedure is employed, the treatment price index for the acute phase of major depression has hardly changed, remaining at 1.00 or falling slightly to around 0.97. This index grows considerably less rapidly than the various official PPIs. Thus, relative to overall inflation, the price index for the treatment of the acute phase of major depression has fallen over the period 1991–95.

Berndt et al. further find that a hedonic approach to price index measurement yields broadly similar results. These results imply that given a budget for treatment of depression, more could be accomplished in 1995 in terms of outcomes than in 1991. The results suggest that at least in the case of acute phase major depression, aggregate spending increases are due primarily to a larger number of effective treatments being provided, rather than being the result of price increases.

Extensions of the Frontier

The final section of the volume tackles more exploratory issues in output measurement—previously unstudied issues or extensions to other methodologies. Sherry Glied focuses on nonmedical sources of health improvements for children and adolescents. In her chapter, "The Value of Reductions in Child Injury Mortality in the United States," Glied notes that childhood mortality rates have declined steadily over time and across causes of death. She investigates alternative explanations for this decline. Glied focuses on several potential factors in improved health: changes in children's living circumstances, changes in the professional child injury knowledge base, changes in the information imparted to parents, and changes in the regulations surrounding childhood behavior. Using data from the National Mortality Detail Files on the number of child deaths by age, cause, and state, combined with information from the Current Population Survey on the characteristics of children and their families by state, Glied finds that changes in children's living circumstances can explain little, if any, of the change in child health. There is limited evidence that regulatory interventions intended to change behavior have been important. Most important is evidence suggesting that changes in the knowledge available to parents about child health have become increasingly important. Over time, parents' time has become less important in producing health. These results provide a first effort in understanding the dramatic reduction in child injury mortality and also illustrate how the development of scientific information, a public good, is translated into private outcomes. However, this scientific information can generate growing inequality in those outcomes.

In their chapter, "Patient Welfare and Patient Compliance: An Empirical Framework for Measuring the Benefits from Pharmaceutical Innovation," Paul Ellickson, Scott Stern, and Manuel Trajtenberg develop an empirical framework for evaluating the patient welfare benefits arising from pharmaceutical innovations. Ellickson et al. extend previous studies of the welfare benefits from innovation, unpacking the separate choices made by physicians and patients in pharmaceutical decision making. They develop an estimable econometric model which reflects these choices. The proposed estimator for patient welfare depends on whether patients comply with the prescriptions they receive from physicians, and the motives of physicians in their prescription behavior. By focusing on compliance behavior, the proposed welfare measure reflects a specific economic choice made by patients, and thereby addresses to some extent the principal-agent relationship that confounds analysis of medical care.

Ellickson et al. review evidence that the rate of noncompliance ranges up to 70 percent, suggesting an important gulf between physician prescription behavior and realized patient welfare. Because physicians act as imperfect but interested agents for their patients, the welfare analysis based on compliance must account for the nonrandom selection of patients into drugs by their physicians. The paper integrates the choices made by both physicians and patients into a unified theoretical framework and suggests how the parameters of such a model could be estimated from health claims data.

The final chapter is by Frank Lichtenberg, entitled "The Allocation of Publicly Funded Biomedical Research." Lichtenberg develops a simple theoretical model of the allocation of public biomedical research expenditure and presents selected empirical evidence about the determinants of this allocation. Lichtenberg notes that the composition of expenditures should depend on the relative costs as well as the relative benefits of different kinds of research. Analysts of technical change typically have data on neither of these, but Lichtenberg argues that the burden of illness is indicative of the potential benefit of achieving advances against different diseases, allowing him to infer how closely disease costs and benefits are aligned.

In his empirical work, Lichtenberg calculates distributions of government-funded biomedical research expenditure, by disease, from records of all research projects supported by the U.S. Public Health Service. To obtain a reasonably complete accounting of disease burden, he utilizes data on both the dying (from the Vital Statistics–Mortality Detail file) and the living (from the National Health Interview Survey). Lichtenberg finds a very strong positive relationship across diseases between total life years lost before age sixty-five and public R&D expenditures. He also finds that the amount of publicly funded research on a disease decreases with the share of life years before age sixty-five lost to the diseases by nonwhites. This could reflect the fact that lack of scientific knowledge is a less important cause of premature mortality among nonwhites than it is among whites. The number of research grants mentioning a chronic condition is uncorrelated with the number of people with the condition, but is very strongly positively related to the number of people whose activities are limited by that condition. Finally, Lichtenberg finds that there tends to be more research about chronic conditions that are prevalent among people living in low-income households, and that are prevalent among the youngest (under age eighteen) and the oldest (above age seventy-five).

Concluding Observations

Although the chapters in this volume are diverse, two themes predominate—one expected, and the other a surprise to many. First, accounting for changes in medical outcomes is difficult but essential—particularly as outcomes improvements increasingly involve the quality rather than the length or quantity of life. While current measurement methods are not entirely satisfactory, progress is being made and additional enhancements to measuring medical care productivity are very likely in the near future. Second, the conventional wisdom that technological advances in medicine are a driving force of increasing health care costs is much too simplistic and deserves much more careful empirical scrutiny.

Some technological developments, such as those involving treatment for cataracts and for acute phase depression, enable a larger proportion of the affected population to tolerate and benefit from treatment. In turn, the greater treatment effectiveness creates incentives for more intensive and more frequent diagnoses. While the number of patients receiving effective treatment may increase as a result of the technological developments, and total treatment expenditures may increase, in many cases the treatment cost per patient episode has fallen. Treatment quantity rather than treatment price may well be the largest driver of expenditure escalation.

Finally, the chapters in this volume were written several years ago, and one might ask, why publish them now? There are several compelling reasons. First, the issues addressed in this volume—the reliable measurement of medical care sector output and productivity—continue to persist and frustrate private and public sector analysts, in the United States and elsewhere. As the population age structure becomes older in the coming decades in much of the world, benefits from being able to measure more reliably the efficiency and productivity of a growing medical care sector will be increasingly valuable. In brief, issues involving medical care output measurement are persistent and increasingly important. Second, the literature on measuring medical care output and productivity is still unsettled and in flux, and it is important to understand the diverse and wide-ranging natures of the alternative approaches. This allows us to take stock of where we are. It also allows statistical agencies to evaluate changes in price and productivity measurement for medical care. Third, to facilitate future research, it is particularly valuable and useful to assemble and put into one volume a diverse collection of conceptual and empirical analyses, authored by leading researchers. That goal, we believe, is achieved in this volume.

I

Conceptual Issues in Medical Care Prices and Productivity

What's Different about Health?
Human Repair and Car Repair in National Accounts and in National Health Accounts

Jack E. Triplett

The American patient is likely to . . . regard doctors as
technicians who are periodically called on to repair his
physical machinery.
—Aaron and Schwartz (1983)

Measuring the output of services industries has long been considered difficult. "The conceptual problem arises because in many service sectors it is not exactly clear what is being transacted, what is the output, and what services correspond to the payments made to their providers" (Griliches 1992, 7). Among the hard-to-measure services, no task has been perceived as more difficult than measuring the output of the health care sector.

Why is measuring health care output so hard? The medical economics literature contains a long list of intimidating and discouraging difficulties. In this paper, I propose to cut through this mostly defeatist list by posing what at first might seem a narrowly focused question: Why is health care different from any other analogous service, such as car repair?

Comparing measurement issues in human repair and car repair is instructive. It is not merely the straightforward analogies: Replacing a shock absorber and replacing a hip are both repairs to a suspension system, diagnostic activity is a crucial part of both production processes, the frequency of costly diagnostic errors is a concern in both types of repairs, and the outputs of both repair industries are enhanced by new technologies for

Jack E. Triplett is a visiting fellow at the Brookings Institution.

A grant from the Eli Lilly Company to the National Bureau of Economic Research supported part of this research. The author is greatly indebted to B. K. Atrostic, Ernst R. Berndt, Richard Frank, John Goss, Zvi Griliches, and Thomas Hodgson for valuable discussions and comments on the substance and the exposition of this paper, and to Helen Kim and Jane Kim for research assistance. The paper has also benefited from seminar presentations at the National Bureau of Economic Research, the Health Care Financing Administration, the Australian Bureau of Statistics, the Australian Institute of Health and Welfare, the Brookings Institution, and the International Symposium on National Health Accounts, Rotterdam, June 1999.

diagnosis and for installation of the part and are also embodied in the part installed. As Vaupel (1998) suggests, the subjects of both repair industries are complicated systems, which is why human and automobile mortality functions look remarkably similar.

More importantly, asking why health is different facilitates asking how health is similar. What can we learn from the way we measure the output of car repair that can be applied to the measurement of human repair and can simplify the health care measurement problem? Health care *is* different, but is it so different that we have to start over with a new paradigm?

I contend that health is not *that* different: The paradigm we use for car repair can be applied, with suitable modification, to health care. Emphasizing the similarities in human repair and car repair paradigms makes it easier to design operational measurement strategies. The similarities may also make it easier for national income accountants and users of economic statistics to understand and accept the sometimes controversial extensions to the paradigm that are necessary because health is indeed, in some respects, different.

1.1 Background

Although one might expect that measuring health care output would entail in some manner measuring "health," most prior economic measurement in health care has been conducted without explicit reference to medical care outcomes. Because output measures in the national accounts of most countries are typically produced through deflation—that is, by dividing health expenditures by a price index—medical care price index methodology has determined the concepts embodied in medical care output measures (except of course in national accounts for countries in which medical care is part of the public sector).

Historically in the United States, the Consumer Price Index (CPI) component for medical care has been used for deflating medical expenditures. This CPI medical care index was until recently constructed from a sample of medical care transactions: a hospital room rate, the price for administering a frequently prescribed medicine, or the charge for a visit to a doctor's office (see Berndt et al., chap. 4 in this volume). Such transactions, which are effectively medical inputs, are sufficiently standardized that the same transaction can be observed repeatedly, which is required for a monthly price index.

The health outcomes of those CPI transactions were never considered explicitly. It is, of course, true that when a consumer paid for an influenza shot, the consumer wanted to reduce the probability of contracting influenza. If an influenza shot that was more effective in preventing influenza became available, a "quality adjustment" would in principle be made in the CPI to allow for the value of the improvement.

In practice, however, such quality adjustments were seldom carried out in the medical care price indexes, for lack of the required information. A quality adjustment in the CPI requires more than just a measure of health care "quality," which may itself be difficult to obtain. The CPI quality adjustment requires valuation, an estimate of "willingness to pay"—what would a consumer be willing to pay for the improved influenza shot, relative to the unimproved one? For health care, the willingness-to-pay question was hard to answer.

Thus, for two reasons, health outcome measures were ignored. First, the primary focus in constructing the price index was on collecting information on transactions, not on medical outcomes. A collection system that focuses on transaction prices for medical inputs does not routinely yield medical outcomes. Second, when improved medical outcomes did come into the picture (in the form of a CPI quality adjustment), it was not the outcome itself but the consumer's willingness to pay that was relevant.

It was widely noted, even thirty-five years ago, that the CPI methodology did not adequately account for improvements in medical care. As the influenza shot example suggests, an improvement in medical procedures that raised the cost of treatment but also improved efficacy frequently showed up as an increase in the CPI. When this CPI was used as a deflator, the improved medical care procedure was thereby inappropriately deflated out of the medical output measure.

Two alternatives to CPI methodology surfaced in the 1960s. The first was the idea of pricing the "cost of a cure," estimating the cost of a medical procedure (the treatment of appendicitis, for example). This contrasted with the CPI's focus on hospital billing elements for a medical procedure, such as the hospital room rate and the administration of a pain medication.[1]

Scitovsky (1964, 1967) estimated cost trends for treating selected medical conditions, including appendicitis and otitis media. She reported that the cost of treating illnesses increased faster than the CPI, a result that most economists found puzzling (because the CPI error that it implied went in the opposite direction from what was expected). Scitovsky suggested that the CPI had understated the rate of medical inflation in the 1950s and 1960s because actual charges had advanced relative to the "customary" charges that presumably went into the CPI.[2]

Scitovsky raised some problems with the cost-of-illness approach that had not previously been considered: What should be done about potential

---

1. George Stigler, in testimony on the "Stigler Committee Report," remarked: "we were impressed by some of the preliminary work that has been done . . . on problems such as the changing cost of the treatment of a specific medical ailment. . . . We think it would be possible . . . to take account of things such as the much more rapid recovery and the much shorter hospital stay . . ." (U.S. Congress 1961, 533).

2. In recent years, it has been asserted that the error from "list" prices goes the other way; see Newhouse (1989).

adverse side effects of a new treatment that was better in some respects (or for some care recipients), but worse in others (or for other recipients)? Her example was a new drug treatment for appendicitis that lowered average hospital stay, reduced recovery time, and was far less painful, but increased the chance of a ruptured appendix, with potentially fatal consequences. Though it was not recognized at the time, the Scitovsky study showed that all the outcomes of a medical procedure must be considered, not just any single one, nor just the principal or primary outcome measure. The study said that looking only at the cost of a unidimensional "cure" (appendicitis treatment) without considering the multidimensional attributes or characteristics of a medical procedure could produce its own bias. Though this problem was intractable with the analytic tools that were available in the 1960s, it has been addressed in the cost-effectiveness research of the past ten to fifteen years (see the discussion below).

It is a bit perplexing that, in intervening years since Scitovsky's work, few other estimates of the cost of treating an illness have been made. Cutler et al. (1998), Shapiro and Wilcox (1996), and Frank, Berndt, and Busch (1999) followed Scitovsky by three decades.

As a second alternative to the CPI medical care price index, Reder (1969, 98) proposed to bypass the medical pricing problem altogether by pricing medical insurance: "If medical care is that which can be purchased by means of medical care insurance, then its 'price' varies proportionately with the price of such insurance." Barzel (1969) estimated an insurance measure of medical price inflation, using Blue Cross–Blue Shield plans.

The medical insurance alternative has not been without critics. Feldstein (1969, 141) objected that the cost-of-insurance approach "is almost certain to be biased upward" because "average premiums will rise through time in reflection of the trend toward more comprehensive coverage" and because the insurance plans will purchase "more services or services of higher quality." Moreover, if an epidemic occurred which raised the cost of insurance, it would inappropriately show up as an increase in the cost of medical care, and therefore not an increase in its quantity, unless the medical premium were calculated net of utilization rates. Thus, implementing the insurance alternative requires solving two quality-adjustment problems—adjusting for changes in the quality of medical care and in the quality of insurance plans. Additionally, measuring the output of insurance is conceptually difficult (see Sherwood 1999).

Little empirical work on medical insurance has followed Barzel in the intervening thirty years. Pauly (1999) has recently revived the proposal. He argues that improved methods for measuring willingness to pay make the medical insurance alternative a more attractive option now than it was in the past. In principle, Pauly contends, one could ask how much a consumer would be willing to pay for an insurance policy that covered an expensive medical innovation, compared with one that did not. Weisbrod (1999) noted that no "constant-technology" health insurance contracts exist, no plans promise to pay for yesterday's technology at today's prices, which in itself suggests that the improved technology was worth the increased cost to insurance buyers. Even if the logic of Pauly's proposal suggests an empirical approach, no empirical work exists, so its applicability to measuring medical price and output has not been tested.

As these references from the 1960s suggest, the major issues on health care output were joined years ago. Until recently, debate on measuring the output of the medical sector largely repeated those thirty-year-old arguments. Neither the empirical work nor the data had advanced much beyond the mid-1960s (Newhouse 1989).

Several things have changed recently in the United States. First, the Bureau of Labor Statistics, initially in the Producer Price Index (PPI) and more recently in the CPI, has introduced new medical price indexes that are substantial improvements on what existed before (Catron and Murphy 1996; Berndt et al., chap. 4 in this volume; U.S. Department of Labor 1996). Second, a major new research initiative on health care price indexes, using new approaches and new sources of data, has been created by a research group centered at the National Bureau of Economic Research (these studies are described later). Third, information on health care outcomes has been enhanced greatly by recent research on "cost-effectiveness analysis" within the medical establishment itself (Gold et al. 1996).

A task as yet unexplored is the building of these new price indexes and health outcome measures into an output measure for the medical care sector. The remainder of this paper will develop an approach (which I call the "human repair model"); contrast it with approaches that are used in other parts of national economic accounts and national health accounts; explore the reasons why health care output requires a modification to the measurement conventions typically used for nonmedical services, such as car repair; and, in the last section, present an empirical example of a health account computed from such information.

1.2   The Conceptual Framework for the Human Repair Model

How do we measure the output of nonmedical services in national accounts? Taking as an example car repair, most countries do something like the following. First, one gathers the total expenditure on car repairs (expenditures on brake jobs, water pump and fuel pump replacements, engine overhauls, and so forth). Next, a government statistical agency takes a sample of car repairs (brake jobs and water pump replacements, say); it computes the price change for brake jobs and the price change for water pump replacements, and from these constructs a price index for auto repair.[3] When the price index is used as the deflator for automobile repair

---

3. This describes, very generally, the Bureau of Labor Statistics methodology for the "auto repair" component of the CPI. See U.S. Department of Labor 1992.

expenditures, the result is the (real) expenditures on the output of the auto repair industry (see U.S. Department of Commerce 1989).

Thus, we have

(1)
$$I_{0t} = \frac{\sum_i P_{it} Q_{i0}}{\sum_i P_{i0} Q_{i0}},$$

(2a)
$$Z_{0t} = \frac{\sum_i P_{it} Q_{it}}{\sum_i P_{i0} Q_{i0} / I_{0t}}$$

(2b)
$$= \frac{\sum_i P_{it} Q_{it}}{\sum_i P_{it} Q_{i0}}$$

$$= \text{real expenditure on car repair.}$$

The subscript i in these equations refers to individual car repairs (replacing brake pads, for example). Equation (1) is the car repair price index, weighted in principle by the quantities of the different kinds of repairs. The first term on the right-hand side of equation (2a) is the change in expenditure on auto repair, and equation (2b) gives the expression for the change in real output or expenditure on auto repair.[4]

Constructing a measure of health care output can proceed in ways that are in some respects similar to methods used for nonmedical services. That is, we can assemble data on expenditures on treating groups of diseases, such as, for example, expenditures on treating mental conditions or circulatory diseases, or, if more detailed data are available, on treating heart attacks or depression. If we can construct price indexes by disease, then these disease-specific measures of medical inflation can be used as deflators to obtain measures of the real quantity of medical services by disease, in a manner that is described exactly by equations (1)–(2b). In the rest of this paper, this approach to obtaining real output of the medical care sector is called the "human repair model."

4. Note that equation (1) is a Laspeyres price index number, and equation (2b) is a Paasche quantity index, which is not the usual national accounts index number system. However, at the lowest level of aggregation in the accounts, the price indexes used for deflation come from price statistics agencies in Laspeyres form in most countries. At the detailed level, the resulting deflated output series is therefore Paasche (or worse, a chained series of changes in Paasche quantity indexes). In the United States, the Bureau of Economic Analysis now uses a Fisher index number system for aggregating over components of GDP, and also for aggregating output in gross product originating by industry data (see Landefeld and Parker 1997; Lum and Yuskavage 1997). BLS has announced that most CPI components were converted to geometric mean indexes in January 1999 (but not medical services, which remain Laspeyres). No similar announcement has been made so far for the PPI. Currently, PPI medical care price indexes are used for deflation in the medical care components of the NIPA and in the U.S. NHA. At the detailed level, therefore, equation (2b) describes the calculation that is presently in the real medical care components of the U.S. NIPA and NHA.

There are great advantages to proceeding by the human repair model. However, there are also some necessary differences between human repair and car repair. The following sections highlight some of those differences.

1.2.1   What Is the Output of the Health Care Sector?

When a human repair expenditure is incurred, it must in some sense add to the stock of health, just as car repair adds to the stock of functioning cars.[5] But how should we think about that increment?

There is little disagreement that health is produced by many factors, and not solely by the activities of the medical sector. Diet, lifestyles, environmental factors, genetic endowments, and other influences determine an individual's, or a society's, level of health. It might even be true, as sometimes asserted, that nonmedical influences on health are more important than the medical ones (McKeown 1976; Mokyr 1997).

Medical and nonmedical influences on the "production" of health can be represented in a very general way as

(3)   health = H(medical, diet, lifestyle, environmental, genetic, etc.).

"Health" is thus the ultimate output of a "production process" in which medical interventions are one of a number of contributing inputs.

Using equation (3), it is natural to measure the contribution of the health care sector to the production of health by the incremental contribution to health caused by medical interventions. That is,

$$
\text{(4)   effectiveness of the health sector} = \frac{\partial\,(\text{health})}{\partial\,(\text{medical})},
$$

other influences constant,

where ∂(health) is the change in health that is attributable to ∂(medical), the incremental resources put into medical care interventions. Equation (4) describes a relation between medical procedures and health, *all other influences on health constant.*

To do this right, ∂(medical) should include the increments of all the resources required by a medical intervention, which may include direct and indirect costs (unpaid caregiving by the patients family, for example), and ∂(health) should be a comprehensive measure that incorporates all of the effects on health of a medical intervention, including unwanted side effects if any. Equation (4) implies that the *health outcomes associated with medical interventions define the output of the health care sector.* Let us call this the "medical interventions perspective" on health care output.

The medical interventions perspective on health care output requires

---

5. Many medical procedures or expenditures are preventive in nature; they are not strictly speaking human repairs nor are they disease related. However, car repair expenditures also include preventive maintenance.

scientific information on the relation between medical interventions and health status. The information that economists need for measuring health care output is the same as the information needed to determine whether a medical intervention is an effective treatment. The nature of this medical data is discussed more fully in a subsequent section on cost-effectiveness studies.

Notice that equation (4) does not imply that a society's *level* of health is determined by its health expenditures or by the level of medical interventions it supports. Neither does it imply that a society with a higher level of health expenditures necessarily has a higher level of health than another society with lower health expenditures. One often reads or hears statements such as the following: U.S. spending on health care, which amounts to around 14 percent of GDP, must not be productive (says the speaker), because life expectancy in the United States is lower than it is in some other countries that spend a smaller amount on health care. This "total health" view of the output of the medical sector is widely expressed. An example is the following: "Available estimates generally indicate that medical care has been accountable for only about 10% to 15% of the declines in premature deaths that have occurred in this century—the remainder attributable to factors that have helped prevent illness and injury from occurring. This suggests that the promise implicit in many technological inventions may exceed their ability to deliver genuine health gains, at least on a population-wide basis. However, they certainly consume resources" (McGinnis 1996, vi).

The total health view implies that one can judge a health care system's effectiveness by comparing a society's level of health with the health sector resources that presumably produce it. I believe this is not a useful way to look at the matter. The "other factors" in equation (1) are not necessarily constant in international comparisons of health and health expenditures, or in comparisons over time.

Distinguishing between the total health and medical interventions perspectives (between a society's level of health and the health implications of its medical interventions) is particularly important where a medical intervention is undertaken to correct the health consequences of unhealthy lifestyles. A car repair analogy may be helpful. Suppose a car owner with a taste for stoplight drag races. Severe acceleration has "unhealthy" consequences for the life expectancies of the clutch, transmission, and tires of his car. One would not assess the output of the car repair industry by the life expectancy of clutches on cars used for stoplight drag races, nor deduct from the output of the car repair industry an allowance for the low life expectancy of clutches on cars so used. The car mechanic repairs the consequences of the owner's lifestyle. The medical care sector also repairs, to an extent, the consequences of owners' lifestyles, and repairs as well the consequences of other sources of health problems.

Stoplight drag races, in the car-repair example, and fatty diets, smoking, sedentary lifestyles, and so forth in the human-repair example, are utility-generating activities—people like them, even though they may fully recognize that they are harmful to health or to cars. Although individuals get utility from better health, they also get utility from consumption activities that may have adverse health consequences. The way we want to model the output of health care is not independent of the demand for health care, and the demand for health care (or the demand for "health") is one of a set of demands for different commodities, of which some have positive and some negative implications for health. These demands, moreover, are complicated by intertemporal considerations, both in the production process for health and in consumers' decision making.

The future level of health is a consequence, at least in part, of actions today—of expenditures for health care and of diet, environmental, and lifestyle influences. Thus, we might modify equation (3) into the intertemporal production process:[6]

(3a)   health($t + n$) = H[medical(t), diet(t), lifestyle(t),

environmental(t), genetic(t), etc.].

Some consumption goods that yield current utility (smoking and fatty diets can serve as examples) have adverse consequences for health in subsequent periods. That is, there are some components of diet where ∂[health $(t + n)$]/∂[diet(t)] < 0, and similarly for some components of lifestyles and of environmental influences.

On the demand side, however, the current level of utility depends on current health (which depends, in part, on lagged values of the right-hand-side variables in equation [3a]) and on the current level of consumption of normal consumption goods, including lifestyle components such as restful leisure pursuits. Thus

(5)   utility(t) = U[health(t), diet(t), other consumption goods

and services(t), lifestyle(t), environmental(t), etc.],

where health(t) is determined by the lagged values in equation (3a).

For some of the goods in equation (5)—goods that I henceforth designate w—∂[h($t + n$)]/∂[w(t)] < 0, but ∂[U(t)]/∂[w(t)] > 0. These are goods whose consumption makes a positive contribution to present utility, but which have an adverse effect on future health. Grossman (1972) emphasized that abstaining from consumption of such goods is like an invest-

6. This specification is not intended to deny that current levels of health care expenditure and current diet or lifestyle affect current utility, but rather to emphasize the time paths of the effects and the fact that individuals' decisions are intertemporal and have intertemporal effects.

ment, in the sense that current consumption (utility) is reduced in order to have greater consumption in the future. The future periods may be a long way off, so the adverse consequences of current unhealthy behavior will be discounted by a rational consumer. The future health consequences are normally changes in probabilities, rather than deterministic. Discount rates, assessments of probability changes, and—because of genetic factors, for example—the actual risks of adverse effects may differ greatly across individuals. Thus, their willingness to undertake "investments" in future health—to reduce current unhealthy, but utility-generating, consumption activities—may differ greatly.[7] Indeed, Garber and Phelps (1992) remark that a drastic reduction in fatty diets will only increase life expectancy by four days for men and two days for women.

As incomes rise and as consumers as a group become more wealthy, consumption of, for example, rich diets and more sedentary lifestyles may increase because these are luxury goods.[8] Because expensive medical procedures are also more readily available in a more wealthy society, income affects health in two ways: It may encourage less healthy behavior, leading to lower health (Grossman 1972 presents empirical evidence of this), but income also permits more resources to be devoted to medical care, which increases health.

Thus, the effects of fatty diets, sedentary behavior, and smoking on heart disease might merely be offset by the development of expensive treatments, such as heart bypass surgery. If so, the overall death rate from heart disease might be the same as the rate in a society with healthier living and a smaller amount of expensive surgery. Equality of the expected incidence of heart disease in the two cases, however, tells us nothing about the value of the output of the medical sector.[9]

The empirical question that needs exploring is not whether more medical expenditure gives "more" health, in the sense that a society's level of health is positively correlated with its level of medical expenditures. In the specification of equation (3), the levels might not be closely correlated if other influences on health changed adversely. The task is, rather, to compute the marginal value of a medical intervention on health, holding constant or abstracting from nonmedical influences on health. To measure the output of the health sector we need to model the health consequences of medical interventions, not to compare the aggregate level of health with the resources employed in the health care sector.

7. There is a remark attributed to the late Mickey Mantle (a famous American athlete): "If I'd known I would live so long, I'd have taken better care of myself."

8. Smoking apparently has a low income elasticity, but automobile transportation has a high income elasticity almost everywhere, leading to the observation that automobiles kill more people through reduced exercise than they do in accidents.

9. It might tell us a great deal about the allocation of public expenditures between, for example, medical expenditures and education expenditures that are intended to make individuals more aware of the trade-offs between lifestyles and disease, but that is a different matter.

On the other hand, lifestyle and other unhealthy behaviors will severely complicate the empirical work necessary to estimate health sector output. It might not be clear whether the clutch failed because the owner continued to indulge his taste for stoplight drag racing or because the mechanic installed it improperly. If heart bypass recipients change their lifestyles in more healthful directions, it will lengthen the apparent effect of the medical intervention. Conversely, if they revert to unhealthy lifestyles, it will shorten the apparent effect on life expectancy of the medical intervention.

In summary, in this subsection I considered the appropriate conceptual way to think about health care output. I conclude that we should measure it by the health implications of medical interventions, not by the society's level of health.

The medical interventions approach also implies the following: To find the incremental impact of interventions on health, one cannot proceed by trying to estimate some aggregate of medical interventions.[10] Interventions are, by their nature, specific, and they relate to specific diseases. Measuring the health implications of medical interventions inevitably implies a strategy of examining these interventions on an intervention-by-intervention basis, that is, on a human repair–by–human repair basis.

1.2.2 Cost-Effectiveness Studies and Medical Outcomes

In the previous section, I proposed that the output of the health care sector be measured, conceptually, by the health impacts of medical interventions. In the cost-effectiveness literature, such an impact is called a "health outcome." Gold et al. (1996, 83) define a health outcome as the end result of a medical intervention, or the change in health status associated with the intervention over some evaluation period or over the patient's lifetime.

A typical cost-effectiveness study compares alternative health care procedures for a particular disease or condition. The numerator of the cost-effectiveness ratio is the total cost difference between two alternatives, including all direct costs and indirect costs such as family-provided care during convalescence. The denominator is the difference in health outcomes for the same two alternatives.

U.K. Department of Health (1994) provides a tabulated review of cost-effectiveness studies that existed at that time. Garber and Phelps (1992) provide a theoretical framework for cost-effectiveness studies and show that medical cost-effectiveness studies can be interpreted as willingness to pay for medical interventions. Gold et al. (1996) provide a common protocol for carrying out such studies.

Health outcomes may be specific to a disease. Gold et al. (1996, 85–87,

---

10. An example of what I have in mind here are studies that regress international expenditures on pharmaceuticals on measures of health or longevity. The argument of this section suggests that such regressions are not useful as indicators of the effectiveness of pharmaceutical interventions.

table 4.1) present examples of health outcome measures that have appeared in the cost-effectiveness literature. For critical diseases (a heart attack, for example, or cancer), survival probabilities or changes in life expectancy may be used as the health outcome that measures the effect of an intervention (bypass surgery, for example).

Yet survival is an inadequate measure, because other aspects of health also matter in treatment of life-threatening diseases. For this reason, Gold et al. (1996) recommend as the denominator of the cost-effectiveness ratio a relatively new health outcome measure called the quality-adjusted life year (QALY), a health outcome measure that combines morbidity and mortality into a single measure of health outcome.

QALY is not without controversy. Gold et al. (1996) discuss some of its shortcomings, the assumptions required to implement the measure, and the substantial data that it requires. Others have amplified on the shortcomings, arriving at less favorable assessments, at least with respect to its present level of development. Triplett (1999) discusses the relation between cost-effectiveness studies of health care and price index studies and explains how medical outcome measures such as QALY can be used as adjustments for improvements in medical technology for measuring medical inflation and the real output of medical care services.

1.2.3 The National Health Accounts Production Boundary, Health Care Output, and Car Repair

Market transactions have traditionally provided the production boundary that defines price and output measurement in national accounts and national health accounts. Putting a value on health outcomes crosses this traditional production boundary. Crossing the production boundary has been, and remains, controversial in national accounts and in national health accounts.

Gilbert (1961, 290) asserted that "the production boundary must be fixed at the point at which transactions take place between buyer and seller because that is the only point at which value, output and price are settled for things that are bought and paid for. Recovering from an illness is not a unit of output nor its cost a price." In this view, improvements in mortality or in morbidity are not relevant to measuring the output of the medical care sector because they are not "charged for" explicitly; a measure that combines the two, such as QALY, is doubly condemned. The view expressed by Gilbert is still very much a part of the intellectual heritage of both national accounts and national health accounts.

In this respect, the health output proposal is not strictly analogous to the way car repair output is measured in national accounts. One can think of car repair as a production process that combines a broken car and a repair to produce a functioning automobile, yet no national statistical agency computes in national accounts the increment that car repair makes to the stock of functioning cars, nor calculates explicitly the benefit of the repair to the car owner. In national accounts, the output of the car repair industry equals the quantity or number of, for example, (constant quality) brake jobs and other repairs—output is measured by deflating car repair expenditures by a price index for brake jobs and so forth. No one tries to assess the output of the car repair industry by some measure of the quality or operational effectiveness of the functioning stock of cars.

Why not just measure the number of health care procedures, as we do for car repair? Doing so preserves the transaction as the unit of observation, which has practical advantages. Alternatively, doing so in a government-provided health care system preserves government expenditures as the relevant resource measure, which has comparable advantages.

One part of the answer is, What we do for car repair is not all that satisfactory if there are significant improvements in the quality of car repair procedures, because the price indexes may not allow for those quality changes very well. Quality change may bias the price and output measures of the car repair industry. Some may think that quality changes in car repair are not a measurement problem (though they probably are).[11] Nearly everyone agrees, however, that improvement in medical procedures is substantial and that quality improvement in medical care is a major part of what we want to include in an output measure for health care. Thus, though both car repair and human repair pose similar price and output measurement problems, the "quality-change problem" looms larger in measuring health care output, which justifies, or at least suggests, more radical solutions.

The other part of the answer involves two aspects in which health care differs from car repair or most other services: In car repair, we are willing to assume that the more expensive repair procedure must be better if the consumer chooses it. The consumer could, after all, sell the repaired car (or the unrepaired one). Accordingly, the very fact that the car repair occurred means that it meets a "willingness-to-pay" test.[12]

Economists, and the medical profession, are less convinced of the equivalent assumption in the case of human repair—there are serious doubts that the price of a more expensive medical procedure necessarily measures its greater contribution to health. The consumer has inadequate basis for making informed choices among medical care providers and among options for treatment.

That consumer ignorance makes health care special is frequently as-

---

11. Zvi Griliches notes in his comment to this chapter that the statistics on car repair productivity look peculiar, and suggests that car repair may not be measured very well. See also Levy et al. (1999).

12. Generally, a representative consumer's willingness to pay guides the determination of how quality improvements should be treated in the CPI. Fisher and Shell (1972) and Triplett (1983) provide theoretical rationales.

serted, but one can make too much of it. Charging for unnecessary repairs, or for the wrong repair, is also notorious in car repair. A very large proportion of brake pad replacements are coupled with replacing brake disks as well, which should not be the case. Those Cambridge authorities, Click and Clack,[13] recently reported the reason: It is easier to overcharge for the brake repair than to explain the harmless initial noise that normally accompanies replacement of brake pads alone. In car repair, as in human repair, the choice of treatments is largely in the hands of professionals, rather than the consumer, and agent problems potentially interfere with the welfare-maximizing outcome in both cases.

Additionally, medical economists often emphasize that insurance drives a wedge between payment and valuation. A standard result in medical economics is that insurance causes more demand for medical care than would otherwise be the case. "For many people . . . [medical care is] paid for through health insurance, and the existence of moral hazard combined with reasonably generous health insurance policies can call into strong question the validity of the simple proposition that prices represent consumers' marginal willingness to pay for the relevant products" (Keeler 1996, 189).

However, many car repairs are also paid by insurance, and it is a commonplace observation that car insurance also causes more car repair than would otherwise occur. It is not so clear that insurance makes a fundamental difference between human repair and car repair, although it might be true that the magnitude of its effects are larger in human repair. More likely, insurance gets more attention in the medical industry case because human repair is more important than car repair, both as a share of the economy and in consumer welfare.

Thus, neither consumer ignorance nor insurance creates a fundamental difference between human repair and car repair. The most important difference between human repair and car repair is the fact that the owner can sell the car.

For a car repair, a consumer routinely asks, Considering what the car is worth, should I repair it? Could I get auto transportation services more cheaply by selling the unrepaired car and buying another? Should I do without a car? If we were to collect the values of the unrepaired and repaired car, we presume that we would find that the repaired car's change in value justified the cost of the repair. But we do not do that, largely because it is not necessary. Because the car could always have been sold, we assume that the car repair meets the willingness-to-pay test.

Suppose, for example, that for a brake job the car owner had to choose between two different types of brake pads, one which claimed 20 thousand miles of life and the other 30 thousand. In principle, one could evaluate

---

13. Click and Clack are hosts of a popular American radio program on car repair. They were the 1999 commencement speakers at MIT.

the owner's choice by obtaining "outcome" data (did the more expensive pads actually give longer life or more stopping effectiveness?). This would be analogous to measures of medical effectiveness used in cost-effectiveness studies (see the definition at the beginning of the previous section, or Gold et al. 1996). We could then ask, additionally, whether the improved outcome was worth it. We could calculate (value of repaired car) − (value of unrepaired car) and ask whether this difference exceeded the cost of the repair, again in parallel with medical cost-effectiveness studies.

We do not consider carrying out these calculations for valuing the output of car repair. We assume that the car repair was undertaken because it was economically appropriate for the owner, and for this reason the calculation of cost-effectiveness ratios is unnecessary.[14]

Obviously, in the case of health care expenditure the consumer's decision is different. If the consumer were paying the full cost, the medical expenditure might meet the willingness-to-pay test, in some sense. Because the analogy to selling the unrepaired car is not normally among the consumer's options, however, ability to pay for medical care influences the result in a way that is not the case in car repair. Even if individuals' willingness-to-pay did dominate medical decision making, this is generally abhorred for ethical reasons. Additionally, in a government-provided health care system, the consumer's decision on payment is not the element that matters in deciding whether the human repair is "worth it," and will be provided at public expense.

Thus, in the case of medical care output, it is necessary to estimate societal willingness to pay or something that looks like it. We cannot assume (as in the case of car repair) that because someone undertakes or approves a medical procedure it meets the consumer willingness-to-pay test. In health care, we need data that show that more resource-intensive medical procedures "work," in a sense that we do not need to show that more resource-intensive car repairs are effective (or cost-effective). We need these data in the medical care case mainly because most health care is provided by third-party payers and because we do not tolerate social systems where individuals have to make a decision that is analogous to scrapping the car because it was not worth its repair cost—even though someone must eventually make that equivalent decision in allocating scarce resources to health care.

1.3   Existing Accounting Systems for Health Care Expenditures

Accounting for health care expenditures occurs in three major places in U.S. statistics—national accounts, national health accounts, and cost-of-

14. We might also ask, but we do not, whether the car owner really "needed" the better brake pads (possibly because the rest of the car would only last 15 thousand miles). Such a calculation would parallel cost-effectiveness analysis for human repair, where it is common to ask of a medical intervention that is effective, "Are the benefits worth the cost?"

disease accounts. Several other countries have a comparable three-part health accounting statistical system.

Past efforts to create real output or real expenditure measures for health care have proceeded within one or the other of the first two accounting systems—national accounts and national health accounts. Real output measures have never been developed for cost-of-disease accounts. In this paper, I propose to reorient work on real output of the health care sector toward cost-of-disease accounts.

Developing the proposals of this paper requires, accordingly, an extended overview of the three existing U.S. health care accounting systems. All major countries share one or more of these health expenditure accounting systems, so the discussion and proposals apply to countries other than the United States. (I consider explicitly in a separate paper the task of constructing real output measures for countries that have public health care systems, for which prices are not available, and where price indexes therefore are not relevant.)

1.3.1 National Accounts

Expenditures on health care are part of the U.S. National Income and Product Accounts (NIPA), whose best known statistic is gross domestic product (GDP). The statistical agencies of most countries follow, to a greater or lesser degree, the international standard for national accounting, the System of National Accounts or SNA (Commission of the European Communities et al. 1993). There are no fundamental differences in the treatment of the health sector in the SNA and the NIPA, although the groupings may not be identical across countries, and in countries that have government medical systems, estimating procedures differ substantially from those of the United States.

In the NIPA, personal health care expenditures are located primarily in personal consumption expenditures (PCE), which means that they are mostly classified as final products. The PCE includes not just consumer out-of-pocket health spending, but also other payments for health care, such as by employer-provided health insurance. In 1995, medical care expenditures in PCE amounted to $872 billion, about 18 percent of personal consumption expenditures and about 12 percent of GDP (table 1.1).

The product and service categories in PCE medical care include drugs and some other medical goods, but also institutional providers of services (hospitals and nursing homes, for example). Medical *goods* that are inputs to medical care are classified by a product classification system, like other parts of the PCE, but medical services are classified by type of *provider.* Another way to put it is to say that medical services are grouped by an industry classification system, rather than by a product classification system. Thus, a particular pharmaceutical will be counted in the same place whether it is sold by a grocery store or a pharmacy; but if a medical proce-

Table 1.1   Comparison of NHA and NIPA Medical Care Expenditure
                   Categories, 1995

NHA		NIPA	
Category	$ billion	Category	$ billion
Personal health care	869.0	Medical care	871.6
Hospital care	346.7	Hospitals	310.6
Physician services	196.4	Physicians	191.4
Dental services	44.7	Dentists	47.6
Other professional services	54.3	Other professional services	104.4
Home health care	28.4	Drug preparations and	
Drugs and other medical		sundries	85.7
nondurables	84.9	Ophthalmic products and	
Vision products and other		orthhopedic appliances	13.1
medical durables	13.1	Nursing homes	65.2
Nursing home care	75.2	Other categories	—
Other personal health care	25.3	Medical care and hospitalization	40.7
Program administration and net		Income loss and workers'	
cost of private health		compensation	12.9
insurance	60.1		
Other categories	—		

Sources: Health Care Financing Administration (HCFA) website, http://www.hcfa.gov/stats/
NHE-OAct/tables/t11.htm; and "Personal Consumption Expenditures by Type of Expenditure," *Survey of Current Business,* 77, no. 8 (August 1997), table 2.4.

dure shifts from a hospital to a doctor's office or clinic, expenditures on it
will show up in a different grouping in the PCE.

The distinction between goods and services classifications in the NIPA
is driven largely by data availability (or at least I have never seen a conceptual argument supporting the distinction).

The inconsistency between goods and services classifications is perhaps
subsidiary to another point about the NIPA classification system: No-
where in the categories used for medical expenditures in the NIPA does
the NIPA distinguish what medical spending is for—the system does not
record what is purchased when medical spending takes place. Expenditures for cosmetic surgery and heart surgery are both (if both are done in
a hospital) grouped together in hospital expenditures, and pharmaceuticals for acne and for angina are combined in the medical goods components. If hospital expenditures are growing, there is little in the national
accounts (or in the national health accounts) that will tell us very much
about the hospital medical procedures that are fueling overall growth, or
about the diseases that are being treated.

Moreover, the NIPA classification naturally orients national accounts
producers and users to a particular specification of the deflation problem:
With the NIPA classification system, it seems natural to look for deflators
for "physicians" and "hospitals" (or even "nonprofit hospitals" and "pro-

prietary hospitals"), for those are the expenditure categories that require deflation. With the NIPA classification system it seems less natural to ask, What is the price index, for example, for coronary disease, or for heart attacks, or for depression, or for eye surgery? With the NIPA system for classifying health care, it is not clear what one would do with price measures for treating diseases, even if they became available. Because price indexes for treating diseases or groups of diseases are in fact becoming available, the fact that the NIPA system has no natural place for them is a severe deficiency.

1.3.2   National Health Accounts

A second U.S. accounting for health care expenditure is National Health Expenditures (NHE), often referred to as the National Health Accounts (NHA). Where the NIPA treat health care as one among many products and services purchased or consumed by households, the emphasis in the NHE is on assembling comprehensive data on total national expenditures on health, and on the sources and recipients of those funds. As noted earlier, total U.S. health spending in the NHA equaled 14 percent of GDP in 1995; total *personal* health expenditures were $869 billion in the NHA in the same year, very close to the 12 percent of GDP total in PCE (table 1.1). The remainder of NHA health expenditures includes health education, investment, and certain other components, which appear in other parts of the NIPA (such as the accounts for government).

The U.S. national health accounts have been produced since 1964 (Rice, Cooper, and Gibson 1982; Lazenby et al. 1992). Rice, Cooper, and Gibson refer to a compatible series for private health expenditure that extends back to 1948, and note even earlier estimates of total U.S. health care spending.[15] Health accounts are also constructed for demographic groups, such as the aged (Waldo et al. 1989).

The national health accounts are organized in the form of a matrix. Table 1.2 presents a condensed form of the accounts as they are now published (see Lazenby et al. 1992; Levit et al. 1996).

The columns of the matrix arrange health care expenditures by major source of funding (e.g., households, private health insurance, government). As table 1.2 shows, 54 percent of U.S. health care expenditures ($536 billion) came from private funding, and 46 percent ($455 billion) from government funding; private insurance and the federal government are the biggest individual funding sources for total national health expenditures and for expenditures on personal health care. In these proportions, the United States, of course, differs from most other industrialized countries. More detail is routinely available in the NHA on federal, state, and local

---

15. According to one of these early studies, health care accounted for 4 percent of U.S. GDP in 1929.

Table 1.2   National Health Expenditures, by Source of Funds and Type of Expenditure, 1995 ($ billions)

	Total	Private					Government		
		All Private Funds	Consumer			Other	Total	Federal	State and Local
			Total	Out-of-Pocket	Private Insurance				
National health expenditures	991.4	536.2	493.6	166.7	326.9	42.6	455.2	328.7	126.5
Health services and supplies	960.7	525.3	493.6	166.7	326.9	31.7	435.4	314.7	120.6
Personal health care	869.0	480.4	449.4	166.7	282.6	31.1	388.5	301.7	86.8
Hospital care	346.7	136.2	121.2	9.6	111.6	15.0	210.5	172.3	38.2
Physician services	196.4	133.1	128.9	29.0	99.9	4.1	63.3	50.7	12.6
Dental services	44.7	42.7	42.5	21.0	21.5	0.2	2.0	1.1	0.9
Other professional services	54.3	41.9	38.1	20.4	17.7	3.8	12.4	9.5	2.9
Home health care	28.4	12.4	9.1	5.9	3.2	3.3	16.0	14.1	1.9
Drugs and other medical nondurables	84.9	73.1	73.1	48.6	24.5	—	11.7	6.3	5.5
Vision products and other medical durables	13.1	7.7	7.7	7.1	0.6	—	5.4	5.3	0.1
Nursing home care	75.2	30.2	28.8	25.1	3.7	1.4	45.1	29.5	15.6
Other personal health care	25.3	3.3	—	—	—	3.3	22.0	12.9	9.1
Program administration and net cost of private health insurance	60.1	44.8	44.2	—	44.2	0.6	15.3	9.2	6.1
Government public health activities	31.5	—	—	—	—	—	31.5	3.8	27.7
Research and construction	30.7	10.9	—	—	—	10.9	19.8	14.0	5.8
Research	16.7	1.3	—	—	—	1.3	15.3	12.9	2.4
Construction	14.0	9.6	—	—	—	9.6	4.5	1.1	3.4

Source: Levit et al. (1997), table 11, "National Health Expenditures, by Source of Funds and Type of Expenditure: Selected Calendar Years 1991–96."

Notes: — denotes less than $50 million. Research and development expenditures of drug companies and other manufacturers and providers of medical equipment and supplies are excluded from "research expenditures," but are included in the expenditure class in which the product falls. Numbers may not add to totals because of rounding.

funding sources, and more detailed estimates are periodically provided for business and households (Levit and Cowan 1991).

The rows of the NHA matrix show the uses of the funds, in the sense that they detail the sectors or economic units that receive the expenditures on health care. The categories are similar to those in the NIPA (see table 1.1). However, the close agreement between NHA personal health care expenditures and PCE medical care expenditures at the aggregate level does not extend to the components of medical care. Hospital expenditures, for example, differ in the two accounts (see tables 1.1 and 1.2), as do "other professional services." Several categories appear in one system but not as a separate entry in the other (home health care is the largest such category). A NIPA–NHA reconciliation is contained in Rice, Cooper, and Gibson (1982); a new one is Sensenig and Wilcox (chap. 7 in this volume).

In the case of health care services, the national health accounts distinguish, again in parallel with the NIPA, the organizational unit that receives the funds, rather than (strictly speaking) the type of service. For example, the same type of service for treating a disease might be performed in a doctor's office or in a hospital; the national health accounts would distinguish whether the expenditure was received by a hospital or by a doctor's office, but would not distinguish the expenditure by the type of service performed, or by the disease category for which treatment was rendered. The classification of individual units receiving payments for medical services is based on the U.S. Standard Industrial Classification (SIC) system (Executive Office of the President 1987).

For drugs, eyeglasses, and other durable and nondurable "therapeutic goods," the national health accounts distinguish, as do the NIPA, the type of goods, using product code classifications from the U.S. Bureau of the Census. Expenditures on therapeutic goods count only those goods that are purchased from retail outlets. Any therapeutic goods that are received by patients in hospitals, for example, will be recorded in the expenditures on hospital care.

Thus, the NHA expenditure classification does not strictly speaking correspond to a "goods-services" distinction, nor does it group expenditures by commodities in the usual sense. It is instead a classification based on the institutional structure of the recipient of the funding. In fact, the category "drugs and other therapeutic goods" is really a classification that groups medical expenditures that are received by the retail trade sector. This classification has implications not only for the interpretation of the published components, but also for other aspects of the NHA. For example, the proper deflator for the pharmaceutical portions of NHA will exclude drugs sold to hospitals because they are not included in the drugs that are counted separately in the NHA "goods" classification scheme.[16]

16. Pharmaceutical price indexes in the PPI are based on all sales by manufacturers, and thus do not provide appropriate deflators for the NHA as the NHA are now constructed.

Because a national health accounts matrix is prepared for each year, it is useful to think of the national health accounts as a three-dimensional matrix. There are the two dimensions shown in table 1.2. This is like one page in a book. Then, because there is an equivalent to table 1.2 for each year, there are a series of pages in the book. One can follow any of the columns, or any of the rows, or any combination of cells from the matrix, through time to construct a time series. The constructors of national health accounts, therefore, pay a great deal of attention to time series comparability (which is not the case for cost-of-disease accounts).

Like the NIPA accounts, the structure of the NHA also orients producers and users toward deflation for institutional units, such as hospitals. Severe problems with past deflation at this level, and with available U.S. price indexes (Berndt et al., chap. 4 in this volume), have led to increased use in the NHA of a broader list of hospital inputs as a proxy for output price measures (Freeland et al. 1991). It is widely recognized in the price index literature that measuring the prices of inputs usually provides a poor proxy for the movement of output prices, unless there is no productivity in the industry, which is surely not the case for medical care.

The U.S. NHA are well known and are widely used for analyzing the economics of the health care sector. Similar health accounts are produced in other countries. For example, France has a system of health accounts, Comptes Nationaux de la Santé (Ministère du Travail et des Affaires Sociales 1996), that is similar to the U.S. NHA in that it provides information on the source of funds in France for health care and health spending and on the institutions receiving the funding. The French system dates from 1976, and is available, as is the U.S. system, in quarterly and annual time series.

The Comptes de la Santé are referred to as a "satellite account," a term that is not generally applied to the U.S. NHA.[17] Despite this, the groupings of data in the Comptes de la Santé are similar to those in the U.S. NHA, with some exceptions, such as the inclusion of expenditures for spas ("cures thermales") in France. The Organization for Economic Cooperation and Development (OECD 1997, 121) lists ten OECD countries where satellite accounts for health have been produced or are "under study"; the U.S. NHA is not included in the OECD list of satellite health accounts, presumably because the U.S. NHA are imperfectly articulated into the U.S. NIPA.

Three properties of national health accounts deserve emphasis. First,

---

Ellison and Hellerstein (1999) found that for one pharmaceutical product (cephalosporins) prices for drugs sold to hospitals moved very differently from those sold to retailers, and so presumably the prices charged to consumers by pharmacies.

17. On satellite accounts, see the description in the SNA (Commission of the European Communities et al. 1993), though the reader is warned that this chapter is not particularly clear. For the development of the concept of the satellite account, see Vanoli (1975, 1986), Teillet (1988), and Pommier (1981).

total national health expenditures, and other NHA aggregates, are built up from the bottom. For the most part, these are not estimates where one starts with a total and distributes the total among the different categories. Rather, one adds up the categories to get the total. Cost-of-disease accounts (described in the next section) distribute totals to categories, and as such cannot be estimated independently of NHA-type accounts.

Second, the fact that the NHA accounts are arranged in a matrix means that there are cross-checks. All the row and column totals must add up. But because estimates for different cells of the matrix come from different data sources, which may be compiled by different methodologies and may not be consistent across different sources, adjustments may have to be made to source data to ensure that all row and column totals in the matrix balance. Though this assures consistency in the matrix and corresponds to good economic accounting principles, it can mean that the entry in a particular cell of the matrix does not agree with the best independent estimate of the value for that cell.

Third, as already noted, NHA accounts preserve time series comparability. They are explicitly designed for use in analyzing time trends in health care expenditures.

Unlike the case of national accounts, for which the SNA provides a standard for producing internationally comparable data, no international standard for health accounts exists at present. The World Bank has set out informal guidelines for NHA development for borrowing countries (Mc-Greevey 1996). However, the OECD, with funding from the U.S. agency that produces the U.S. NHA, has released a proposal for an international standard (OECD 1997). No adequate price index or method for producing real output measures is developed in the OECD report.

1.3.3 Cost-of-Disease Accounts

Overview

In some respects, the concepts and structure of national health accounts resemble "flow of funds" accounts in that they focus on financial flows of health expenditures and on sources and recipients of funds. The two dimensions of the national health accounts matrix—sources of funds and recipients of expenditures—have been useful for many of the analytic tasks for which health expenditure data are required. However, these two dimensions are not the only useful way in which one might array health expenditure data.

Consider the subtotal "personal health expenditures." In the national health accounts this category has the following definition: "Personal health care comprises therapeutic goods or services rendered to treat or prevent a specific disease or condition in a specific person" (Lazenby et al. 1992, 91). As this definition suggests, one can envision disaggregating personal

health care expenditures by expenditures on specific diseases. Such a disaggregation is most commonly performed as part of a cost-of-disease or
burden-of-disease study.

For present purposes, I define a *cost-of-disease study* as one that estimates expenditures for treating disease, sometimes referred to as the direct
costs. A *burden-of-disease study* would also include indirect costs of disease—unpaid care provided by family members and loss or reduction of
earnings; such a study would put a value on the losses from premature
mortality and from the disutility of disease itself. Examples of burden-of-
disease studies are Rice (1966) and Murray and Lopez (1996).

A burden-of-disease study considers all the social and economic costs
of disease, and not just—as in a cost-of-disease study—the direct costs,
or direct monetary expenditures. Put another way, a cost-of-disease study
estimates the cost of treating diseases that are treated; a burden-of-disease
study would additionally include the economic and social costs of diseases
that are not treated, or for which treatment is ineffective.

Burden-of-disease studies correspond to a broader economic accounting that goes beyond the traditional market boundary adhered to in national accounts and in national health accounts (see the earlier section on
the production boundary). Mainly for reasons of space, I will not pursue
any of the implications of this broader accounting in the present paper.
The present inquiry, then, will concern only the direct costs of treating
illness, not because those other costs are without relevance, but because
understanding the implications of direct resources that are put into the
health care sector is a step toward any broader accounting. At present, the
goal is creating real measures of the output of medical treatments for disease, and not, or at least not at present, of the real cost of diseases that
are not treated.

The first systematic U.S. disaggregation of health expenditures by disease appears to be Rice (1966), although she cites predecessors. Subsequent updates include Cooper and Rice (1976), Hodgson and Kopstein
(1984), and Hodgson and Cohen (1998). These accounts are summarized
in table 1.3.

Classification Matters

There are of course thousands of diseases, conditions, and diagnoses.
Some grouping of conditions must be carried out. Classifications systems
provide the building blocks for much of economic statistics—though their
properties are often ignored by the economists and health care analysts
who use them.

The most widely used disease classification system is the International
Classification of Diseases (or ICD), which has gone through a number of
revisions since its inception. The *International Classification of Diseases,
Injuries and Causes of Death, 9th Revision* (ICD-9) was developed by the

Table 1.3   U.S. Health Expenditures by ICD Chapter ($ millions)

ICD Chapter Headings	Estimated Direct Expenditures,[a] 1963	Estimated Direct Costs,[b] 1972	Estimated Amounts of Direct Costs,[c] 1980	Estimated Amount of Personal Health Care Expenditures,[d] 1995
Total expenditures	29,394[e]	78,537[f]	219,443[g]	897,510[h]
All conditions (total allocated expenditures)	22,530	75,231	206,878	787,510
Infectious and parasitic diseases, 001–139	502	1,412	4,300	17,656
Neoplasms, 140–239	1,279	3,872	13,049	42,917
Endocrine, nutritional and metabolic diseases, and immunity disorders, 240–279	903	3,436	7,329	33,825
Diseases of the blood and blood-forming organs, 280–289	156	491	1,155	4,890
Mental disorders, 290–319	2,402	6,985	19,824	74,707
Diseases of the nervous system and sense organs, 320–389	1,416	5,947	17,132	65,847
Diseases of the circulatory system, 390–459	2,267	10,919	32,488	133,196
Diseases of the respiratory system, 460–519	1,581	5,931	16,661	61,481
Diseases of the digestive system, 520–579	4,159	11,100	30,974	89,656
Diseases of the genitourinary system, 580–629	1,210	4,471	12,313	37,462
Complications of pregnancy, childbirth, and the puerperium, 630–676	1,391	2,607	—[i]	3,555
Diseases of the skin and subcutaneous tissue, 680–709	248	1,525	5,940	18,824
Diseases of the musculoskeletal system and connective tissue, 710–739	1,430	3,636	13,124	50,309

Congenital anomalies, 740–759	113	381	1,345	5,046
Certain conditions originating in the perinatal period, 760–779	30	—[j]	—[i]	3,349
Symptoms, signs, and ill-defined conditions, 780–799	624	—[k]	3,815	23,487
Injury and poisoning, 800–999	1,703	5,121	18,684	71,806
Supplementary classifications, V01–V82	966	—	—	49,494
Other	150[l]	7,398[k]	8,746[j]	
Unallocated	6,864[j]	3,306[m]	12,656[n]	110,000

[a]From Rice (1966), tables 1 and 31, pp. 3 and 109. Note that the disease classification used at this time period was the ICD-8 or ICDA.

[b]From Cooper and Rice (1976), table 1, p. 23.

[c]From Hodgson and Kopstein (1984); Rice, Hodgson, and Kopstein (1985), table 5, p. 69.

[d]From Hodgson (1997). $110 billion could not be allocated by diagnosis, and this constitutes 12 percent of personal health care expenditures.

[e]From Rice (1966), table 1, p. 3. Differs from NHA personal health care expenditures by $0.1 billion.

[f]From Cooper and Rice (1976), p. 22: The entry for "Other health services" is understood to be the equivalent of the "unallocated" category in this table. This number is added to the "All conditions" number to give the total expenditure.

[g]Differs from NHA by a factor of two.

[h]Differs from NHA. Original total was taken from a projection to 1995; the initial NHA actual estimate was about 2 percent below the projection and the revised estimate is lower than the projection by 3.2 percent. See Hodgson (1997).

[i]The "Other" category includes complications of pregnancy, childbirth, and puerperium, and certain conditions originating during the perinatal period.

[j]Not given explicitly; calculated as "Total expenditures" less "All conditions" (total allocated expenditures)."

[k]The "Other" category for this year includes certain causes of perinatal morbidity and mortality, symptoms of ill-defined conditions, and special conditions without sickness and symptoms.

[l]The "Other" category for this year was actually labeled "Miscellaneous" in the publication, and includes special conditions and examinations.

[m]From Cooper and Rice (1976), p. 22: "Other health services" is the equivalent of "Unallocated."

[n]Includes $8.3 billion of personal health care expenditures that could not be allocated by age and sex, and $4.265 billion that could not be allocated for other reasons.

World Health Organization (WHO) and issued in 1977. The classification system is intended to produce comparable cross-country health statistics, particularly on causes of death. A later revision (ICD-10) is not yet in general use for U.S. statistics.

Experiments with using the ICD system for producing U.S. hospital statistics began in the 1950s. Experience led to a U.S. modification of ICD-9, known as ICD-9-CM (for Clinical Modification; U.S. Department of Health and Human Services 1989), that is now in extensive use for coding hospital records. The main differences from the international system are more detail (that is, more specific and precise codes for medical conditions), elimination of some ambiguities in pregnancy and childbirth conditions and in some other areas, and changes in the presentation to make the system easier to use by data coders. Despite claims on the latter point, private publishers have introduced their own, more user-friendly editions of the classification manual. The growth of such a publication market underscores the increasing practical utilization of ICD-9.

The ICD-9 classification system conforms consistently neither to an anatomical nor to an etiological or causal principle. It does, however, conform generally to the way diseases are treated and to the way medical specialties are demarcated. This makes the ICD an advantageous and natural system to use to generate economic data on the treatment of disease. It is now used not just for classifying incidences of diseases and causes of death, but also for classifying a wide range of economic data, compiled mainly for administrative purposes.

A second classification system is relevant to this paper—the Diagnosis Related Groups system (DRG) of the U.S. Health Care Financing Administration (HCFA; Averill et al. 1997). This system is used to classify hospital and medical procedures for the purpose of making government reimbursements under Medicare and other government health programs. The third revision of the DRG system was introduced for Medicare hospital services in 1986 and is still in effect. The Australian DRG system is a modification of the U.S. DRG system.

The structure of the DRG system is designed to organize hospital admissions by the resources that would be expected to be spent in the treatment of a particular admission. It is thus a classification system that yields, by its design, economic data on the costs of illness. The coding of principal diagnoses under the DRG system conforms, with certain exceptions, to ICD-9 chapters or, more precisely, to the ICD-9-CM.

The DRG system has, nevertheless, two deficiencies for the purposes of this paper. First, it is not an international system, even though the United States and Australia share similar DRG systems. Second, it is not well suited to recording the incidences and prevalence of diseases because, below the first level of chapter groupings, each DRG is a grouping of diseases which might be rather different but which have similar expected treatment costs.

Cost-of-disease studies use ICD-9 chapters. At the chapter level, ICD-9 and DRG systems are similar. Two of the U.S. studies in table 1.3 use the ICD-8 system and the other two use ICD-9. A certain amount of noncomparability is thereby introduced. Another problem is inconsistency in coding practices. Special problems here are the coding of diseases of infancy, old age, and certain respiratory diseases, and diseases like diabetes that typically have extensive comorbidities.[18] Coding inconsistency is a long-standing problem with medical data. For example, McKeown (1976) notes the long-term decline in "old age" as a cause of death—it has gradually been replaced with more precise coding of a medical condition, which reflects not only increased medical knowledge, but also changes in attitudes and social mores.[19]

Estimating Methods

As noted above, similar cost-of-disease disaggregations have been produced recently for several countries, including the United States (Hodgson and Cohen 1998), Canada (Moore et al. 1997), the United Kingdom (actually, England and Wales—U.K. Department of Health 1996), and Australia (Mathers et al. 1998). This section describes their methodologies.

Cost-of-disease studies typically distribute totals for health care expenditures among disease categories. That is, they are not "bottom-up" estimates, as are the NHA, and in fact they typically start from NHA aggregate health care expenditures. The methodology can best be understood by an example, for which I use the allocation of hospital expenditures. The other components of medical expenditures are calculated in similar ways, but of course the data vary according to the component and, to an extent, according to country. Details for the United States are contained in Hodgson (1997, chap. 5).

Total expenditures for inpatient hospital care are computed and published in the NHA (see table 1.2). This expenditure is allocated to ICD-9 chapters by the following steps. The National Hospital Discharge Survey (NHDS) gives the total number of inpatient hospital days and subtotals by ICD-9 chapter. The average charge per inpatient hospital day, grouped by ICD-9 chapter, is found in the National Medical Expenditure Survey (NMES) for the year 1987; this charge is updated to 1995 by the CPI Hospital Room Price Index. For each ICD-9 chapter, the number of hospital days (NHDS) is multiplied by the average charge per day corresponding to diseases in that chapter (NMES); when each of these products is divided by the total for all ICD-9 chapters, the result is the share of expenditures allocated to each chapter. This share is multiplied by total NHA

18. Hodgson (1997) contains a special chapter on the problems of estimating costs for diabetes.

19. Aaron and Schwartz (1983) quote a British physician who remarked that the body gets "a bit crumbly" after age 55. For a very different view of aging, see Vaupel (1998) and Manton and Vaupel (1995).

hospital expenditures (which are, of course, determined independently of the two data sources used to calculate the share) to determine the hospital inpatient expenditures for each ICD-9 chapter.[20]

Hodgson and Cohen (1998) were able to allocate 88 percent of NHA personal health care expenditures to a medical diagnosis, and 98 percent of major categories such as hospitals, physicians' and dentists' services, and nursing homes (see table 1.4). Although all expenditures for prescription drugs were allocated to an ICD-9 chapter, only 35 percent of nonprescription drugs and related goods could be allocated. It is not entirely clear, for example, for what medical condition aspirin will be used. Information on amounts allocated is contained in table 1.4.

The basic methodology for cost-of-disease studies was developed by Rice (1966). The methodology used in Canada (Moore et al. 1997) is very similar to that used in the United States. Estimates in the United Kingdom (U.K. Department of Health 1996) apply a single average cost of hospitalization across all medical conditions, and thus lack the refinement of the Canadian and U.S. studies, which differentiate cost per day across different classes of illnesses. The Australian study contains unique aspects that reflect that country's health care system.

Though the basic estimating methodologies are similar, that does not mean cost-of-illness studies are exactly comparable over time, or across countries at one point in time. Estimating methods, classifications, data sources, and to some extent medical practice, the diseases themselves and how they are diagnosed, classified, and treated, as well as other considerations have changed over the nearly thirty-five years that are covered by cost-of-disease estimates in the United States. For all of these reasons, intertemporal comparability may be compromised.

Similarly, data sources, national practices, and estimating methods create noncomparabilities in international comparisons. For example, in the U.S. estimates, drugs administered in hospitals are included in hospital expenditures; in Canada, drugs administered in hospitals are removed from hospital expenditures and placed in pharmaceutical expenditures.

1.4   Comparisons and Trends, Cost-of-Disease Accounts

Exactly comparable or not, it is very useful to examine the trends of expenditures by disease category, and to make international comparisons of them. Doing so is problematic: To date, cost-of-disease studies have not been produced with an eye toward time series comparability or toward

---

20. "In effect, HCFA's estimates of inpatient hospital expenditures are distributed by sex, age, and diagnosis, according to the distribution of days of hospital care weighted by the average charge per day" (Hodgson 1997, 6). In the above, I have ignored the demographic parts of the calculation. Catron and Murphy (1996) present a similar disaggregation of U.S. hospital revenue for 1987. In their data, circulatory diseases rank first in hospital revenues, and digestive system diseases second.

Table 1.4   **Personal Health Care Expenditures by Allocation Status and Type of Health Service: United States, 1995 estimates ($ billions)**

Type of Health Service	NHA Total	Hodgson's Allocated Total	Unallocated Amount	Unallocated Percent
All personal health care	897.7	787.5	110.2	12.3
Total hospital care	364.5	360.3	4.2	1.2
Total physical services	198.0	185.3	12.7	6.4
Dental services	42.9	42.9	0.0	0.0
Total other professional services	62.9	21.7	41.2	65.5
Home health care	27.9	27.9	0.0	0.0
Drugs and other medical nondurables	84.7	55.2	29.5	64.8
Total vision products and other medical durables	13.9	13.9	0.0	0.0
Nursing home care	80.2	80.2	0.0	0.0
Other personal health care	22.7	0.0	22.7	100.0

Notes: Estimates are based on Hodgson's (1997); additional information supplied by Thomas Hodgson. NHA total refers to preliminary estimates. Numbers for 1995 are updated in Levit et al. 1997, 191.

international comparability. Though a more comprehensive study would first make adjustments for time series and international comparability, this exceeds the scope of the present study. Accordingly, I content myself with a contribution to the demand for future international and time series comparability in cost-of-disease studies (demand for statistics tends to create its own supply).

1.4.1   International Comparisons of Expenditures by Disease

Table 1.5 compares partitions by chapters of the ICD-9 for total health expenditures in the United States, Canada, England, and Australia. Table 1.6 shows a similar partition for hospital expenditures.[21]

The proportions of health spending by disease differ from country to country; however, there are also broad similarities. For example, circulatory system diseases are the largest expenditure category in U.S. overall health care spending (nearly 15 percent of the total) and in U.S. hospital spending (19 percent); they are also the largest expenditure category in Canada, and the second largest expenditure category in both the United Kingdom (12 percent) and Australia (12 percent). Circulatory diseases are only the fourth largest category of spending in Australian hospitals (however, our preliminary concordance for the classification system for Australian hospitals may have noncomparabilities in it). In the United Kingdom, mental disorders are the largest spending category; in the United States, they are the second largest category of hospital spending, and third in overall expenditure. Endocrine, metabolic, and immunity disorders

---

21. Sources are given in the footnotes to the tables.

Table 1.5   Total Health Expenditures, United States, England, Canada, and Australia, Disaggregated by ICD-9 Chapters

Diagnosis and ICD-9-CM Chapters and Codes	United States, 1995, All Personal Health Care[a]		England, Net Public Expenditure, 1992–93, NHS and PSS Expenditure[b]		Canada, 1993, Total Direct Costs		Australia, 1993–94, Total Health System Costs	
	Millions of U.S. Dollars	% of Total	Millions of U.K. Pounds	% of Total	Millions of Can. Dollars	% of Total	Millions of Aus. Dollars	% of Total
All conditions	787,510	100.0	31,060	99.9	44,130	100.0	31,397	100.0
1. Infectious and parasitic diseases, 001–139	17,656	2.0	311	1.0	787	1.8	849	2.7
2. Neoplasms, 140–239	42,917	4.8	1,273	4.1	3,222	7.3	1,905	6.1
3. Endocrine, nutritional and metabolic diseases, and immunity disorders, 240–279	33,825	3.8	497	1.6	1,334	3.0	966	3.1
4. Diseases of the blood and blood-forming organs, 280–289	4,890	0.5	155	0.5	274	0.6	192	0.6
5. Mental disorders, 290–319	74,707	8.3	5,156	16.6	5,051	11.4	2,634	8.4
6. Diseases of the nervous system and sense organs, 320–389	65,847	7.3	2,609	8.4	2,252	5.1	2,333	7.4
7. Diseases of the circulatory system, 390–459	133,196	14.8	3,758	12.1	7,354	16.7	3,672	11.7
8. Diseases of the respiratory system, 460–519	61,481	6.9	1,926	6.2	3,787	8.6	2,510	8.0
9. Diseases of the digestive system, 520–579	89,656	10.0	2,578	8.3	3,326	7.5	3,712	11.8
10. Diseases of the genitourinary system, 580–629	37,462	4.2	1,118	3.6	2,248	5.1	1,658	5.3

Category							
11. Complications of pregnancy, childbirth, and the puerperium, 630–676	3,555	0.4	1,025	3.3	2,025	4.6	1,051	3.3
12. Diseases of the skin and subcutaneous tissue, 680–709	18,824	2.1	528	1.7	892	2.0	955	3.0
13. Diseases of the musculoskeletal system and connective tissue, 710–739	50,309	5.6	2,423	7.8	2,460	5.6	2,971	9.5
14. Congenital anomalies, 740–759	5,046	0.6	124	0.4	305	0.7	191	0.6
15. Certain conditions originating in the perinatal period, 760–779	3,349	0.4	217	0.7	551	1.2	247	0.8
16. Symptoms, signs, and ill-defined conditions, 780–799	23,487	2.6	1,273	4.1	1,851	4.2	1,336	4.3
17. Injury and poisoning, 800–999	71,806	8.0	1,180	3.8	3,122	7.1	2,607	8.3
Supplementary classifications V01–V82	49,494	5.5	1,553	5.0				
Supplementary (health status)			93	0.3				
Well-patient					2,741	6.2		
Other					549	1.2		
Unallocated							1,607	5.1
Total allocated expenditures (from table 1.3).[a]	110,000	12.3	3,230	10.4				

Sources: Hodgson (1997); U.K. Department of Health (1996), table 6.1; Moore et al. (1997); Mathers et al. (1998), table C.2, p. 34.

[a]Total allocated expenditures (from table 1.3).

[b]The definition of "net public expenditure" is assumed to undertake the explanation provided in U.K. Department of Health (1996, annex A, pt. A.4.1.2, p. 81), that describes expenditure data: "The analysis includes the majority of health and social services expenditure, around 85%. The major exclusions comprise NHS headquarters administration, ambulance and accident and emergency services, day hospital care, services classified in the programme budget as 'other hospital', and social services for children. Department of Health administration costs and centrally financed services (such as, for example, Departmental grants to voluntary organisations) are also excluded. Income support expenditure for residents in independent residential care is included . . . in view of the community care reforms." NHS is the National Health Service and PSS is the Personal Social Service. Total percent for all conditions do not add up to 100.0 percent due to rounding.

Table 1.6   Hospital Expenditures, United States, England, Canada, and Australia, Disaggregated by ICD-9 Chapters

Diagnosis and ICD-9-CM Codes	United States, 1995, Hospital Care[a]		England, 1992–93, NHS Hospital Expenditure[b]		Canada, 1993, Direct Costs, Hospitals		Australia, 1994–95, Private Acute Hospitals[c]	
	Millions of U.S. Dollars	% of Total	Millions of U.K. Pounds	% of Total	Millions of Can. Dollars	% of Total	Millions of Aus. Dollars	% of Total
All conditions	60,341	100	16,200	99.9	26,096	100.0	2,399	100.0
1. Infectious and parasitic diseases, 001–139	9,426	2.6	162	1.0	345	1.3	14	0.6
2. Neoplasms, 140–239	28,104	7.8	1,021	6.3	2,467	9.5	79	3.3
3. Endocrine, nutritional and metabolic diseases, and immunity disorders, 240–279	14,643	4.1	194	1.2	527	2.0	20	0.8
4. Diseases of the blood and blood-forming organs, 280–289	2,641	0.7	113	0.7	157	0.6	3	0.1
5. Mental disorders, 290–319	43,172	12.0	2,770	17.1	3,632	13.9	113	4.7
6. Diseases of the nervous system and sense organs, 320–389	13,247	3.7	810	5.0	793	3.0	210	8.7
7. Diseases of the circulatory system, 390–459	67,604	18.8	1,847	11.4	4,862	18.6	225	9.4
8. Diseases of the respiratory system, 460–519	31,039	8.6	940	5.8	1,788	6.9	97	4.0
9. Diseases of the digestive system, 520–579	28,688	8.0	826	5.1	2,093	8.0	326	13.6
10. Diseases of the genitourinary system, 580–629	18	4.9	778	4.8	1,076	4.1	260	10.8

Category								
11. Complications of pregnancy, childbirth, and the puerperium, 630–676	2,121	0.6	875	5.4	1,650	6.3	217	9.1
12. Diseases of the skin and subcutaneous tissue, 680–709	6,411	1.8	324	2.0	223	0.9	96	4.0
13. Diseases of the musculoskeletal system and connective tissue, 710–739	20,512	5.7	923	5.7	1,286	4.9	486	20.2
14. Congenital anomalies, 740–759	2,728	0.8	113	0.7	232	0.9	—	—
15. Certain conditions originating in the perinatal period, 760–779	2,535	0.7	211	1.3	518	2.0	35	1.5
16. Symptoms, signs, and ill-defined conditions, 780–799	7,682	2.1	761	4.7	845	3.2	10	0.4
17. Injury and poisoning, 800–999	40,433	11.2	940	5.8	2,253	8.6	22	0.9
Supplementary classifications V01–V82	21,572	6.0	810	5.0			63	2.6
Well-patient care					1,349	5.2		
Unallocated	—		1,761	10.9			125	5.2

Sources: Hodgson (1997); U.K. Department of Health (1996), table 6.1; Moore et al. (1997); Mathers et al. (1998).

[a]Total allocated expenditures. Expenditures include services provided in short-term community hospitals, $9 billion of expenditures by the Department of Defense, patients seen in hospital outpatient departments and emergency rooms, and may include those for hospice services. From the data in Hodgson (1997).

[b]NHS is the National Health Service. Total percentages for all conditions do not add up to 100.0% due to rounding.

[c]Australian figures were converted from an alternative classification system by diagnoses; as such, congenital anomalies were not assigned figures, and additional information on the classification will be built into a subsequent revision.

account for a larger proportion of spending in the United States than in the United Kingdom, Canada, and Australia, presumably because of AIDS. Digestive system diseases are relatively more important in the United States and in Australia than in the United Kingdom, with Canada in an intermediate position—closer to the United Kingdom, overall, but close to the United States in hospital spending. Other differences exist.

What accounts for international differences in the composition of health care spending? Several potential causes are topics for future research. First, there are international differences in the incidence of diseases. For example, Australia reportedly has one of the highest rates of skin cancer in the world; that would push up Australia's relative spending on ICD-9 chapter 2 (cancers), which at 6 percent is somewhat higher than the proportion in the United States and England (though lower than in Canada). Second, there are also case-mix effects. For example, skin cancer is a relatively low-cost form of cancer, and it is frequently treated outside of hospitals; possibly for this case-mix reason, the proportion of Australian hospital spending on cancer is substantially lower than in the other three countries. Third, there may be international differences in cost per case, even aside from case-mix considerations. Costs per case may differ because some countries employ less effective treatments (see Aaron and Schwartz 1983 for some examples), or because some countries adopt more cost-effective procedures, or because of international differences in medical industry efficiency. These matters are not pursued here.

International comparisons of costs require information on prices. Cross-country prices for medical care appear in the purchasing power parity (PPP) statistics published by the OECD. However, the adequacy of PPP indexes has been questioned recently (Castles 1997). Additionally, international comparisons of the costs of diseases require price or cost differences by ICD-9 chapter, and not just for an overall medical care aggregate. This point parallels the argument developed in this paper for time series comparisons.

Finally, as already noted, noncomparabilities exist in these data, and these will affect the percentages presented in tables 1.5 and 1.6. The totals do not correspond to exactly the same definitions. For example, Australian hospital data exclude certain hospitals. Though the ICD-9 provides an international standard for classifications, it is sometimes not applied consistently. For example, it appears from tables 1.5 and 1.6 that complications of pregnancy and childbirth account for a considerably smaller proportion of U.S. health care spending than in the other three countries (which is puzzling because birth rates are similar in the United States and Australia, for example). However, an examination of incidence rates suggests that the data for the other three countries include normal pregnancies, which are not treated as a disease in U.S. data. An adjustment for pregnancy and childbirth costs can be made to U.S. data, but there are doubtless other noncomparabilities that have not yet been explored.

1.4.2   Trends in U.S. Health Expenditure by Disease, 1963–95

Tables 1.5 and 1.6 show cost-of-disease accounts for the United States for the four years for which these accounts have been compiled (1963, 1972, 1980, and 1995). To correspond to the "production boundary" of NHA, I tabulate only the direct costs, though the sources also present indirect costs of disease. Table 1.7 shows average annual rates of increase computed between each of the years for which U.S. cost-of-disease accounts exist.

The first caveat to be expressed about these tables is that researchers who have assembled cost-of-disease accounts warn that they are not comparable over time. For one thing, the classification systems have changed. The first two U.S. studies use ICD-8, the second two, ICD-9. Unlike conventional national accounts, in which "bridge" tables would have been constructed to permit moving more or less consistently across changes in classification structures, no such adjustments exist for cost-of-disease accounts.

Another noncomparability arises because the proportion of expenditures that can be allocated to disease changes over time. The effect of this at the aggregate level can be seen from comparing the first two lines of table 1.3: When the proportion of unallocated expenditures falls (true between 1972 and 1980), the rate of growth of allocated expenditures will exceed that of total expenditures. Conversely, when the proportion of unallocated expenditures grows, the rate of growth of allocated expenditures will fall short of the growth rate of total expenditures (as is true for the 1980–1995 comparison).

Changes in unallocated expenditure may affect rates of growth for ICD-9 chapters as well. For example, if data become available to allocate ambulance expenses by disease category, the new allocation would probably affect, disproportionately, ICD-9 chapters "Injury and Poisoning" and "Diseases of the Circulatory System," compared with "Skin Diseases" and "Congenital Anomalies."

Finally, there are other differences in estimating methods, data availability, and presentation conventions that also limit time series comparability. Some of these changes can be discerned and adjustments made by users; but for most of them, only the compilers have sufficient knowledge of the data and estimating methods to construct appropriate bridge tables. Again, it is common practice in national accounting and in national health accounting to link out, so far as possible, the effects of changes in data availability, so as to construct a more nearly comparable time series. Little concern for their time series properties is evident in compilation of cost-of-disease accounts.

Judging from the uses and demands for other economic statistics, the lack of time series comparability for cost-of-disease accounts is puzzling. There is, clearly, some value in knowing that circulatory diseases account

Table 1.7   **Direct Cost or Public Health Expenditure Average Annual Rate of Increase by Disease Category, Various Years**

ICD-9-CM/ICDA Chapter Heading	1963–72[a]	1972–80[b]	1980–95[c]
Total expenditures	11.54	13.71	9.85
All conditions (total allocated expenditures)	14.35	13.48	9.32
Infectious and parasitic diseases	12.18	14.94	9.87
Neoplasms	13.10	16.40	8.26
Endocrine, nutritional and metabolic diseases, and immunity disorders[d]	16.01	9.93	10.73
Diseases of the blood and blood-forming organs	13.60	11.29	10.10
Mental disorders[d]	12.59	13.93	9.25
Diseases of the nervous system and sense organs	17.29	14.14	9.39
Diseases of the circulatory system	19.08	14.60	9.86
Diseases of the respiratory system	15.82	13.78	9.09
Diseases of the digestive system	11.53	13.69	7.34
Diseases of the genitourinary system	15.63	13.50	7.70
Complications of pregnancy, childbirth, and the puerperium[d]	7.23	—	—
Diseases of the skin and subcutaneous tissue[d]	22.36	18.53	7.99
Diseases of the musculoskeletal system and connective tissue[d]	10.93	17.40	9.37
Congenital anomalies[d]	14.46	17.08	9.21
Certain conditions originating in the perinatal period[d]	—	—	—
Symptoms, signs, and ill-defined conditions[d]	—	—	12.88
Injury and poisoning[d]	13.01	17.56	9.39
Supplementary classification (V or E codes)[d]	—	—	—
Other	—	—	—

Note: Calculations of rates were made using $x_1 (1 + r)^{1(n-1)} | = | x_n$. All calculations originate from sources giving direct cost figures, except for the 1995 data set, for which only public health expenditures were available.

[a] Data for 1963 from Rice (1966), table 21, p. 109. Data for 1972 from Cooper and Rice (1976), table 1, p. 23.

[b] Data for 1972 from Cooper and Rice (1976). Data for 1980 from Rice, Hodgson, and Kopstein (1985), table 1, p. 62.

[c] Data for 1980 from Rice, Hodgson, and Kopstein (1985). Data for 1995 from Hodgson (1997). For the "All conditions" category, the original amount used from the 1995 data source is the amount originally cited ($787.5 billion) added to the amount not originally included due to the uncertainty of allocation by diagnosis ($110 billion).

[d] These chapter headings, listed as found in the ICD-9-CM, are listed differently in the ICDA (ICD-8), which affects the 1963 and 1972 data sources, and which may or may not affect comparisons.

for nearly 15 percent of U.S. health care spending in 1995 (table 1.5), and nearly 19 percent of U.S. hospital spending in the same year (table 1.6). However, there is also great interest in the rate of growth of U.S. spending on circulatory diseases or mental diseases. Little direct data on rates of growth for expenditure by disease exist. In the future, meeting time series uses for cost-of-disease accounts should be added to the tasks of their producers.

Leaving aside the noncomparabilities and time series inadequacies of the basic data, and taking the data only for what they present, table 1.7 shows that although diseases of the circulatory system are the largest expenditure category in the United States, growth rates are only marginally above average for recent years (9.9 compared with the average of 9.3 percent between 1980 and 1995). Diseases of the digestive system, once the largest category of U.S. expenditure (table 1.3), show a growth rate that is well below average in recent years (7.3, compared with the 9.3 percent growth of total allocated expenditures—see table 1.7). The growth rate for expenditures on mental disorders (considered at greater length in a subsequent section) is about average for the 1980–1995 interval.

1.5   Implementing the Human Repair Model

For the health sector, national accounts, national health accounts, and health satellite accounts all share an unresolved problem: How does one construct adequate real output measures for medical care? How does one measure the real growth in medical care services?

In the present section, I develop a health accounting structure that is derived from the human repair model, which will yield a real output measure for medical services, using existing and prospective data. The accounting structure is implementable now, in principle. It also facilitates, as I will show, use of new data that are being generated from a variety of sources, including price index studies and cost-effectiveness studies. These new data are difficult to integrate into the existing structure of national health accounts.

However, economic measurement of medical care would be much improved with new data on medical outcomes, prices, and quantities of services. The accounting structure is also intended as a framework that suggests the directions in which we can push data development to improve the measurement of the health care sector's output.

The starting point for estimating real output of medical care using the human repair model is expenditure on diseases. The major existing data that are organized by disease are in cost-of-disease accounts, as discussed in a previous section. Cost-of-disease accounts disaggregate medical expenditures by ICD-9 chapters.

Considering the number of diseases identified in the ICD-9 classification system, disaggregating by ICD-9 chapters is a beginning, but it does not go as far as one might like for empirical work on the human repair model. For example, ICD-9 chapter 7 (Circulatory Diseases) covers ICD-9 codes 390–459; of these, codes 393–429 are heart disease codes, of which codes 410–414 are ischemic heart disease, among which code 410 is acute myocardial infarction, or heart attack.

Cutler et al. (1998) estimate a price index for heart attacks. This is the level at which practical research on price indexes and cost-effectiveness (discussed later) must be carried out. For the circulatory disease chapter of ICD-9, some additional disaggregation of expenditures is available. Hodgson (1997), for example, estimates that coronary (ischemic) heart disease (ICD-9 codes 410–414) accounts for roughly half of total expenditures for all heart disease, and additional detailed estimates may be available in the future.

Although additional disaggregation beyond the ICD-9 chapter is essential, at some point more expenditure detail will be both impossible to obtain and perhaps inappropriate: The greater the detail at which expenditures are disaggregated, the more likely that expenditures on a particular episode of illness encompass multiple individual ICD-9 codes.

Section 1.2 developed the idea that the output model for health care must build in data on the outcomes of health care procedures. Two recent bodies of research make use of or generate health outcomes.

1.5.1 Cost-Effectiveness Studies

An increasing number of cost-effectiveness studies are being carried out within the health care industry itself. The effectiveness part of a cost-effectiveness study requires a measure of health outcomes. The denominator of the cost-effectiveness ratio is the difference in health outcomes for two or more alternative treatments for the same disease. The increasing employment of cost-effectiveness studies in medical decision making means that an increasing number of health outcome measures for different diseases are being generated and also that increased research attention is being given to improving measures of health outcomes. The potential value of this research for measuring the output of the medical care sector is tremendous, even if, as Pauly (1999) and others have suggested, substantial problems with existing measures of health outcomes remain to be resolved.

1.5.2 Price Index Research

A number of recent studies have been undertaken by a group of researchers at the National Bureau of Economic Research that have the explicit objective of measuring a price index for some part of the health care sector. Examples are Cutler et al. (1998) on heart attacks, Frank, Berndt, and Busch (1999) and Berndt, Cockburn, and Griliches (1996) on the treatment of depression and depression pharmaceuticals, and Shapiro and Wilcox (1996) on cataract surgery.

In the heart attack study, the medical outcome measure was the increase in life expectancy associated with more resource-intensive heart attack treatments. In the depression studies, the outcome measure was the elimination of the symptoms associated with a diagnosis of severe depression, without holding constant methods of treatment (or, to put it another way, without necessarily holding constant the characteristics of the transaction, as with traditional price and output measurements). Other similar studies are under way.

A price index study such as Cutler et al. (1998) is similar to a cost-effectiveness study, differing mainly in the following ways (an extended discussion of the relation between cost-effectiveness studies and price index studies is contained in Triplett 1999). First, the health outcome measure in Cutler et al. was life expectancy, not QALY (cost-effectiveness studies have also employed life expectancy in the past; see U.K. Department of Health 1994; Gold et al. 1996). If heart disease treatments had no implications for quality of life (e.g., the ability to exercise or conduct daily living without chest pain), then an increase in life expectancy is an increase in QALY. Use of QALY would extend and enhance the measures in Cutler et al.

Second, Cutler et al. (1998) value the change in life expectancy; that is, they put a dollar value on the medical outcome. Medical cost-effectiveness studies do not do this (see the discussion of this point in Gold et al. 1996). Valuing medical outcomes for price indexes is discussed in Triplett (1999) and in Triplett and Berndt (1999).

1.6 An Example: Implementing the Model on Mental Health Care Expenditures

Treatments for mental disorders account for over 8 percent of total U.S. health care expenditures and about a tenth (9.5 percent) of all allocable U.S. personal health care expenditures (tables 1.5 and 1.8). It is well known that the United States spends about one-seventh of its GDP on medical care (the largest proportion in the world), so mental health care expenditures make up just over 1 percent of GDP.[22]

By international standards, the U.S. mental health care expenditure share is not particularly high. The mental health share of U.S. hospital expenditures is about 12 percent, and for hospitals and nursing homes combined, 13.7 percent. This is about the same as the Canadian share of hos-

---

22. These percentages are based on the important new work of Hodgson and Cohen (1998). As noted above, about 12 percent of personal health care expenditures in 1995 cannot be allocated by disease.

Table 1.8   Estimated Amount of Personal Health Care Expenditures, Total and for Mental Disorders, by Type of Provider: United States, 1995

	All Conditions ($ millions)	Mental Disorders ($ millions)[a]	Mental Disorders, as Percentage of All Conditions
All personal health care	787,510[b]	74,707	9.5
Hospital care	360,341	43,172	12.0
Physician services	185,329	7,761	4.2
Prescription drugs	55,224	6,057	11.0
Nursing home care	80,200	16,968	21.2
Hospital care and nursing home care, combined	440,541	60,140	13.7

Source: Hodgson and Cohen (1998), table 2.

[a]ICD-9-CM codes 290–319.

[b]Excludes $110 billion, 12 percent of personal health care expenditures, that cannot be allocated by diagnosis.

pital expenditures going to treat mental illness (13.9 percent), and considerably lower than the comparable share in the United Kingdom (over 17 percent of hospital expenditures). Even though the Australian hospital share is smaller than that in the United States (under 5 percent), the share of mental health in total Australian health expenditures is about the same as that in the United States (see tables 1.5 and 1.6).

To help understand trends in such a significant portion of health care expenditures, I split U.S. mental health expenditure trends into mental health care inflation and quantity of mental health care services. I then adjust the inflation and real medical services trends to account for new data and recent research. The estimates show how new information on inflation and quantity of medical services can improve national health accounts.

1.6.1   Trends in U.S. Mental Health Expenditures

Complete cost-of-disease accounts have been constructed for the United States for only four years, as noted earlier. However, U.S. mental health expenditures have been estimated much more frequently. For the interval 1954–96, more than twenty different single-year estimates of expenditures on mental health treatment exist. A dozen of them were reviewed in Rice, Kelman, and Miller (1991). A list of studies appears in appendix table 1A.1, which also presents each study's estimate of mental health care expenditures.

Most of these estimates originate with two groups of researchers. Rice and her collaborators at the National Center for Health Statistics have produced a series of estimates of expenditures on mental health, the earliest covering 1963 (Rice 1966) and the last 1995 (Hodgson and Cohen

1998). Mental health expenditure estimates of Rice and her collaborators are generally consistent with the cost-of-disease accounts also initiated by Rice (1966). They are consistent as well as with the NHA, because cost-of-disease accounts disaggregate NHA totals for direct expenditures on the treatment of disease.

Another group of studies originated with Levine and Levine (1975), and proceed through a group of researchers at the Research Triangle Institute (RTI). Other estimates include Fein (1958; actually the first such study, treated here as an antecedent of studies by the Rice group), Frank and Kamlet (1985), Parsons et al. (1986), and Mark et al. (1998; condensed as McKusick et al. 1998).

The cost estimates in these studies often include indirect and social costs of mental illness, because a major part of the cost of having mental illness falls on the patient in the form of lost work time and so forth, and on others (family members, for example, or the victims of violence committed by the mentally ill) who experience the effects of mental illness in friends or strangers. However, I address only the direct treatment costs of mental illness in this section because I want to integrate cost of mental illness data with the NHA, which in principle include only the direct costs of treating an illness, and not the costs of *having* the illness. This does not imply that I think that the NHA could not or should not be extended to encompass indirect costs of illness, only that such an extension is beyond the scope of the present study.

Not surprisingly, methodologies for estimating the cost of treating mental illness have evolved through the years. For example, in the 1963 estimate (Rice 1966) pharmaceutical expenditures were not allocated across diseases; when prescription drug allocations first became available (for 1972), they were around 7 percent of mental health expenditures. From this point on, drug expenditures are included in estimates of mental health care expenditures. As a second example, the earliest estimates exclude from mental health costs the costs of treating alcohol and drug abuse; when data for these mental conditions became available, they were first reported separately, and in the later estimates are folded into the mental health total, without a separate allocation (alcohol and drug related conditions are included in the mental conditions chapter of ICD-9).

Of the two major groups of studies, the RTI studies generally obtain higher *levels* of expenditures for treatment of mental conditions than do the studies of Rice and her colleagues. For example, Harwood et al. (1984) report mental health care expenditures (including substance abuse) of $35.5 billion for 1980, while Rice, Hodgson, and Kopstein (1985) report $19.8 billion for the same year. Similarly, Levine and Willner (1976) estimate 1974 expenditures at $17.0 billion, while Paringer and Berk (1977) got only $9.4 billion for the following year. When the two sets of authors reference each other (which is seldom), they simply note that different methodologies are used.[23] However, the published descriptions of methodologies are remarkably similar.

Rather than attempting to reconcile the levels, I convert mental health treatment cost estimates for various years into annual rates of change by matching published studies on groups of authors (Rice and collaborators, and the RTI group—details are in appendix tables 1A.1 and 1A.2). As noted earlier, successive studies from the same group of authors incorporate methodological and data improvements, so they are not, strictly speaking, comparable over time. Yet research methodology is not chosen randomly, and there is a great amount of commonality among studies by the same group of authors. Matching on groups of authors minimizes the methodological noncomparabilities between groups of authors that result in differences in levels, noted earlier.[24] This matching method necessarily omits studies (like Parsons et al. 1986) that were "one-time" estimates and do not fit into either of the major groups of studies.

Even with matching, it is not straightforward to convert these data into a time series. When changes to estimating procedures were made, or when the authors decided to employ a different tabular presentation or classification, they seldom linked the methodology used in one paper with the one they employed for estimates two or three years previously. For example, early estimates apply average costs for all hospital stays to mental health; later ones use an explicit estimate for daily costs for mental health treatment (which are usually lower). However, undoubtedly because time series comparability was not a research priority, authors of studies generally do not provide an estimate of the effect of such changes in methodology on the estimates. In producing growth rates for mental health care expenditures, I have linked out major changes in estimating methods so that increased scope of the estimates is not inappropriately treated as increased expenditures on treating mental health conditions. These links are noted in appendix table 1A.2, but they do not exhaust changes that have been made between adjacent estimates by the same group of authors.[25]

When cost estimates are grouped by authors, rates of increase among the various estimates look fairly consistent and plausible, in the sense that

---

23. Levine and Levine (1975) present information on the quantitative effects of differences in estimating methodologies that were in use at that time. Mark et al. (1998, chaps. 1 and 8) contains a useful summary of methodological differences between their own study and the methods used by the Rice group and the RTI group.

24. For 1980, I use the estimate of Rice, Hodgson, and Kopstein (1985), who report that total mental health expenditures for 1980 were $19.8 billion. This estimate is derived from Hodgson and Kopstein (1984), with correction of an error (the correction was published in *Health Care Financing Review* [winter 1984]: 128–30—information supplied by Thomas Hodgson).

25. The 1968–71 match probably overstates the rate of increase, because it appears that Conley and Conwell (1970), the source for the 1968 estimate, excluded substance abuse expenditures and that Cooper and Rice (1976) included them. I could not find data to remove the effect of the change in coverage from the estimates.

trends in expenditures are more nearly similar between the two groups of studies than are estimates of levels of expenditures. For example, Harwood et al. (1984) estimate the 1980–81 expenditure growth to be 15.1 percent; combining Rice et al. (1990) with Rice, Hodgson, and Kopstein (1985) suggests an average annual rate of growth between 1980 and 1985 of 19.1 percent (see appendix table 1A.2, rows [i] and [l]). However, the RTI estimate for 1977–80, at 19.1 percent annually, exceeds the five-year Rice group estimate (1975–80, 16.1 percent annually) by almost the same amount, suggesting that the differences may in part reflect the difference in year spans of the two studies, and the great spurt of inflation between 1979 and 1982. Where multiple estimates of expenditure growth rates are available for a given year, as in this case, I take the simple average. Thus, the 1980–81 growth rate obtained by averaging these two studies is 17.1 percent. For the post-1990 period, the two available estimates of expenditure growth differ more than is the case for most earlier periods. Additional discussion of the post-1990 period is presented later.

Table 1.9 summarizes rates of growth of expenditures on treatment of mental conditions over different intervals (which depend on data availability) from 1954 to 1995. Expenditures for the treatment of mental conditions accelerated from their 1950s and 1960s rates, reaching a peak of 17 percent annually between 1980 and 1985. After 1990, mental health care expenditure grows at the lowest rate in three decades.

The expenditure growth rate for the 1990s calls for further comment. Two estimates exist. Mark et al. (1998) is, to my knowledge, the only study of mental health expenditures that actually computes a growth rate—7.2 percent per year, for the ten-year interval 1986–96. Their estimate is higher than the growth rate calculated from other studies. Additionally, informa-

Table 1.9	Mental Health Treatments: Average Annual Increases in Expenditure and Price (percent change)	
	Average Annual Expenditure Growth Rates (1)	Average Annual Price Index Growth, Unadjusted BLS Price Indexes[a] (2)
1954–63	3.76	—
1963–72	12.57	9.96
1972–80	13.11	10.76
1980–85	17.09	10.81
1985–90	7.06	8.78
1990–95	4.94	6.47
1985–95	6.00	7.63

[a]BLS price indexes, matched to expenditure categories for mental health care, and weighted with mental health care treatment costs (see explanation in text). 1954–63 not calculated.

tion from the Rice group suggests that the rate of growth of mental health care expenditures declined over this interval. Incorporating the Mark et al. study dampens the slowdown in the rate of growth of expenditures that is evident in estimates from the Rice group, possibly because the Mark et al. definition of mental health excludes some ICD-9 codes included in the definition used by others (Alzheimer's disease, for example).

The domain of the estimate by Mark et al. (1998) differs from other studies, and from the national health accounts, in two respects. First, Mark et al. include mental health expenditures that go to organizations that are classified in the 1987 U.S. SIC system as social services industries, rather than as part of the medical industries. Because the NHA focus on institutional recipients of expenditures, expenditures received by nonmedical "industries" are not included in the NHA definition. Mental health services provided by institutions outside the NHA definition, and included in the Mark et al. study, amount to about 4 percent of the total. Deinstitutionalization of mental health patients has caused a shift in care toward these outpatient facilities, and their exclusion from other estimates (and from NHA) biases downward rates of growth. Surely we want data on expenditures to treat disease, not solely on expenditures received by medical care industries; thus, the domain chosen by Mark et al. is the appropriate one.

Second, Mark et al. (1998) adopt a definition of mental health care that encompasses a narrower set of ICD-9 codes than the definition of, for example, Hodgson and Cohen (1998). Mark et al. exclude Alzheimer's disease and other dementias from their definition of mental health care. No estimate of the size of this exclusion appears in the study. Different definitions may be appropriate for different purposes, but this definition is not well motivated by the authors. It has the effect of reducing both the level and the rate of growth of mental health expenditures recorded in nursing homes, for example, because the number of patients admitted for nondementia forms of mental conditions has declined, while the number of (and presumably the proportion of expenditures on) dementias has risen.

Why have expenditures grown? Has the United States increased the levels of services to the mentally ill? Or is it inflation in mental health care? The following sections construct data and explore the aggregate evidence.

1.6.2   Deflation Methodology for Mental Health Expenditures

Growth in medical care expenditures has three components. First, there may be an increase in the number of patient-treatments. Because there are many types of patient profiles and of mental disorders, one can think of the patient-treatments component as a change in a constant patient-mix measure, which we would probably want to weight according to the relative costs of care for different conditions.

Second, there may be an increase in the cost or the price of treatments. Parallel to the first component, we could measure the increase in price as the cost change of a constant patient mix, holding constant also the level of treatment efficacy. This is medical care inflation.

Third, there may be changes in the patient mix and in the efficacy of treatment which imply changes in average treatment costs. For example, a shift in the patient mix toward more severe mental disorders implies increasing average treatment costs, even if the cost of no single treatment changes. One would not want an adverse (or a favorable) change in the mix of medical illnesses to influence the measure of the *price* of medical treatments. Additionally, improvements in the efficacy of treatment must be measured and allowed for in some way, for the same reason. One does not want a shift toward more expensive, but more efficacious, care to be confused with medical care inflation.

The standard way to obtain output (quantity) measures in economic statistics is to deflate the change in expenditures on a product (like haircuts) by a price index for that product. It has not been customary to apply exactly the same deflation procedure to health care. No existing health expenditures account, to my knowledge, calculates the quantity of mental health care by dividing expenditures on mental health care by a price index for mental health care. There are, however, great advantages to doing so.

In a subsequent section, I present a new price index, or deflator, for expenditures on mental health treatment. Because the first step is to assemble existing published government price indexes, and to match them to mental health treatment expenditure information, it is worthwhile to consider the results of this intermediate price index calculation here.

Details of the match between price indexes and mental health care expenditures are in a data appendix available from the author; excerpts are reproduced as appendix table 1A.7. As an example, hospital and nursing home expenditures on mental health treatment (80 percent of total expenditures on treatment of mental conditions in 1990) are matched to the CPI hospital price index before 1992. After 1992, two new PPI hospital indexes became available: An index for the treatment of mental conditions in general hospitals and an index for psychiatric hospitals. The match weights changes in these two PPI indexes equally. A nursing home PPI index begins in 1994, and it is brought into the match at that point. These hospital and nursing home indexes are combined with price indexes for other components of mental health care (mental health care professionals and pharmaceuticals), using weights based on various mental health care expenditures estimates by the Rice group, for consistency with NHA. These weights are documented in appendix table 1A.6. I calculate ordinary Laspeyres indexes for more nearly straightforward comparison with existing Bureau of Labor Statistics (BLS) medical care price indexes.[26]

---

26. Mark et al. (1998) suggest very different weights, with hospitals and nursing homes receiving only 40 percent of 1996 mental health care expenditures. As noted above, their exclusion of dementias from their definition of mental conditions biases downward their

Average annual growth rates in prices of mental health services, computed in this manner from available published government price indexes, are presented in column (2) of table 1.9. As the table shows, published price indexes that provide the closest match for mental health expenditures suggest that most of the increase in mental health expenditures has been caused by medical care inflation. Since 1985, mental health care inflation, computed this way, amounts to about 7.5 percent per year. These data suggest that price increases for mental health services have actually outstripped both the overall CPI medical care index (up about 6.5 percent per year over this period) and mental health care expenditures, which grew 6 percent per year. This implies that the quantity of mental health services being provided fell after 1985, and fell even more sharply after 1990. Note that this calculation is a total, economy-wide one, not adjusted for population—or patient population—growth; it is not mental health services per capita (which would fall even more).

In subsequent sections, I consider possible biases in these government price indexes for mental health and estimate new mental health price indexes, which show a very different picture of medical care inflation from those in table 1.9. I then use the new price indexes to compute a mental health account that shows trends in expenditure, inflation, and real quantity of mental health services.

Problems in Estimating a Mental Health Care Expenditures Price Index

It has become commonplace that medical care inflation outstrips the overall inflation rate. For example, between 1985 and 1995, the medical care component of the CPI rose 6.5 percent per year, when the overall CPI rose only 3.6 percent. Until fairly recently, price trends for all types of medical care have been inferred almost exclusively from the medical care component of the CPI. Inflation information that is specific to the treatment of mental conditions and the measurement problems is discussed in this section.

The earliest U.S. price index specific to mental health care is the "psychiatrist office visits" component of the CPI, a price index that was published between 1964 and 1977. As table 1.10 shows, over the 1964–77 period the price of a visit to a psychiatrist's office rose less rapidly (about 5.2 percent per year for the whole period) than did the fees of other medical professionals (a bit over 7 percent per year), or CPI medical care as a whole

---

estimate of the nursing home share of expenditures, but the NHA–SIC definition of the medical industry biases upward the hospital/nursing home share in estimates of the Rice group, because a portion of total expenditures on mental health care (around 4 percent, in the Mark et al. data) are excluded from the total. Even so, it is hard to see why the proportions could differ so much. This is a case where a careful reconciliation of the two estimates—which as a practical matter is best done by the authors—would produce more confidence in the results.

Table 1.10   **Consumer Price Indexes, All Items and Selected Medical Care Services, Average Annual Rates of Change, 1964–77**

	Average Annual Growth Rates (percent), 1964–77
CPI, all items	5.29
Medical care, total	6.68
Medical care services	7.51
Physicians' services	7.03
Psychiatrist, office visits	5.19
Hospital Daily Service Charges	10.79
Semiprivate rooms	11.60

Source: U.S. Department of Labor (1999).

(about 7.5 percent per year). In fact, psychiatrists' fees were rising slightly more slowly than the overall CPI.[27]

The CPI psychiatrist office visit index obviously excludes hospital costs for medical treatment of mentally ill patients. In 1963, 88 percent of total expenditures for mental health went to hospitals and nursing homes; in 1995, the proportion was still 81 percent.[28] Nonhospital mental health professionals account for only a small proportion of the cost of treating mental conditions (in 1995, 11 percent).

A CPI hospital index also existed in the 1960s. It measured hospital costs with a price index for hospital room rates (for example, the cost of a semiprivate room in a hospital). Hospital room rates have risen rapidly throughout the postwar years. Mental health care, however, was not distinguished separately in the CPI, so we do not know whether the cost for a day in the hospital for a mental health patient was advancing more or less rapidly than for other patients.

Most importantly, the cost of a day in the hospital or the cost of a psychiatrist's office visit is an inadequate measure of the cost of treating mental illness, unless there is some way to adjust the costs for changes in medi-

27. The price index for psychiatrist office visits ends in 1977 because it was merged into the physician's fee CPI component, which, though it includes psychiatrists on a probability basis, contains no published detail on medical specialties.

28. The data for 1963 exclude prescription drug expenditures, which are included in the 1995 total. Drugs accounted for 6 percent of mental conditions treatment costs in 1972, the first year for which drug expenditure estimates by disease are available (and 8.5 percent in 1995). Making an allowance for the probable size of drug expenditures in 1963, the proportion of hospital and nursing home expenditures in the mental health total has been remarkably stable through ostensibly major changes in treatment regimens over the last thirty-five years: The hospital expenditure share has fallen (from 86 percent to 58 percent), but the share of nursing home expenditures has increased from 1 percent of the total to 23 percent. The deinstitutionalization of mentally ill in the 1970s reduced expenditures in mental hospitals, but this has been matched, almost exactly, by increased expenditures on forms of mental illness, primarily among the elderly, that are treated by institutionalization in nursing homes.

cal efficacy. Do we want to know the price of an office visit, the cost per patient visit, or the cost per incident of depression? For most analytical purposes, we want to know the cost of treating depression and not (or at least not primarily) the cost of one input in treating depression. A CPI that tells us that the cost per psychiatrist's visit has advanced 10 percent may be accurate in what it tells us, but it is highly misleading in terms of what we want to know.

Ideally, one wants to "adjust" or correct the price index in some fashion for improvements in medical efficacy, and to obtain a price index for the treatment of a disease. Because medical economists generally believe that progress has been made in medical technology—better prognoses, less time spent in the hospital for any given condition, less painful and onerous conditions during treatment, and so forth—they believe that inadequate adjustment for these changes in medical technology creates upward biases in price indexes for medical care.

Merely to state the problem this way underscores the difficulties that statistical agencies face in producing price indexes for medical care. Calculating the change in costs for treating an episode of an illness requires not only the traditional statistical agency skills in gathering prices, but also a great deal of medical knowledge about changes in the efficacy of medical treatments (knowledge which, in many cases, is scientifically uncertain or in contention). It also requires knowledge about patient valuations of changes in treatments, particularly when treatments change in dimensions that involve the patient's time, tolerance for pain, and valuation of the disutility of side effects or of the onerous implications of treatments (such as a frequent treatment regimen for a pharmaceutical).

Improved BLS Price Indexes for Mental Health Care Expenditures

After 1977, BLS made few changes in its CPI methodology for pricing medical care until major improvements were initiated in the 1990s. The focus was still on a visit to the doctor's office, the cost of a hospital room, or the administration of a simple medication or a shot, and not on estimating the cost of treating an illness. Moreover, it was, and to an extent still is, a focus on the institution (the hospital, the nursing home, the doctor's office), rather than on the disease (mental illnesses, respiratory or circulatory illnesses, and so forth). The inherent problems (discussed in the previous section) were not overcome.

Much criticism of the CPI medical price indexes was voiced after 1977 because many economists believed that they overstated inflation in medical care. A milestone in that criticism was Newhouse (1989). For the period 1977–92 we know nothing about trends in medical care prices for mental health treatments, because mental health costs are buried in CPI prices for medical care, which were generally believed to be biased upward.

In 1992, BLS introduced new price indexes for health care in its PPI program. Although the new health care price indexes were still oriented toward the institution or the "industry" (the hospital, the nursing home, the doctor's office or clinic), they introduced a new methodology for measuring the price of medical care.

Rather than pricing the cost of a day in the hospital, the BLS now draws a probability sample of treatments for medical conditions. For example, for the PPI price index for mental health care treatment in a hospital the probability selection might be "major depression." The BLS then collects the monthly change in costs for treating that identical medical condition (see Berndt et al., chap. 4 in this volume, and Catron and Murphy 1996 for more information on BLS procedures).

Overall, the new PPI indexes present a picture of lower medical care inflation, compared to CPI measures, for the period where the two overlap (Catron and Murphy 1996). The BLS subsequently introduced similar methodology into the CPI (Cardenas 1996). PPI hospital price indexes (though not those for physicians and clinics) include detail that is broken down approximately by ICD-9 chapter. For the first time, PPI indexes estimate the cost change for treating mental disorders, and they permit comparison with other medical care costs.

For mental health costs, the new methodology makes a striking difference. For the period 1993–98, the CPI "hospital and other related services" index rose 24 percent (table 1.11). The PPI index for "mental diseases and disorders" treated in general medical and surgical hospitals rose about the same amount (21.5 percent), but the PPI index for psychiatric hospitals rose only 4.6 percent over this same period (table 1.11).[29] Taking the simple average of the two PPI indexes for hospital treatment of mental conditions suggests an increase of 13 percent, which is just over half the rise in the CPI hospital index.

Similarly, the PPI index for "offices of clinics of doctors of psychiatry" rose only 3.9 percent between 1994 and 1998 (this PPI index only began in 1994—see table 1.11). The CPI index for "physicians' services" rose 14.9 percent for the same period.

Adjusted Price Indexes for Mental Health Care

The new medical care PPI indexes introduced in 1992 are great improvements on the previously available CPI medical price information (see the assessment in Berndt et al., chap. 4 in this volume). Evidence from the post-1993 period, when both PPI and CPI medical indexes were available, suggests substantial upward bias in the CPI. The BLS did not compute

---

29. It is not clear why these two indexes for hospital treatment of mental conditions should differ so greatly. Perhaps different diseases are treated in the two types of facilities, perhaps they have different cost structures, or perhaps they provide different treatments. Alternatively, the PPI procedures may produce substantial variance in the estimated price index.

64   Jack E. Triplett

Table 1.11   CPI and PPI Medical Price Indexes, Annual Average Growth Rates

	Total Change	Average Annual Change
Hospitals (1993–98)		
CPI: hospital and other related services	23.98	4.39
PPI: general medical and surgical hospitals	21.52	3.98
PPI: psychiatric hospitals	4.63	0.91
Physicians (1994–98)		
CPI: physicians' services	14.86	3.53
PPI: offices and clinics of doctors of medicine, psychiatry	3.89	0.96
Drugs (1982–92)		
CPI: prescription drugs and medical supplies	138.03	9.06
PPI: psychotherapeutics	264.38	13.80
Drugs (1992–98)		
CPI: prescription drugs and medical supplies	20.45	3.15
PPI: psychotherapeutics	254.61	23.49

Source: U.S. Department of Labor (1999).

historical price indexes when it introduced these improvements. There is great need for better historical measures of medical care prices than the CPI has given.

One approach is to "backcast" estimates of the improvement that the PPI indexes represent. For the period following 1992, I match PPI and CPI components. For example, I combine the mental health subindex in the PPI index for general hospitals with the PPI index for psychiatric hospitals (see the earlier discussion) and match the result to the CPI "hospitals and related services" index. In this case, the ratio of the PPI indexes to the CPI index, from 1993 to 1998, was 0.912.[30] This ratio between the PPI and CPI hospital indexes for the period for which both were published provides a correction factor for the historical CPI hospital index before 1993 to make it more appropriate for measuring cost change in mental health treatment. I adjust the CPI hospital components in this manner for 1972 to 1993.

Similar adjustments are made for doctors' offices—see the CPI physicians and PPI psychiatrists indexes in table 1.11. A PPI index for psychotherapeutics begins in 1982. This index is compared with the CPI prescription pharmaceuticals index for the period 1982–92 (table 1.11), and is used to backcast a correction to the CPI for the years 1972–82. Additional de-

30. That is, from table 1.11: $\frac{1}{2}$(PPI mental conditions, general hospitals + PPI psychiatric hospitals)/CPI hospitals index = $\frac{1}{2}$(1.215 + 1.046)/1.240 = 0.912.

tails of the match and the resulting adjustment factors are available in appendix table 1A.1.[31] The resulting adjusted indexes for components of mental health care are combined with a logarithmic aggregator, rather than the arithmetic one (Laspeyres index) used by the BLS, and for the unadjusted indexes. This logarithmic index is discussed later.

The resulting price indexes are labeled "adjustment 1" in table 1.12. It is important to emphasize specifically what adjustment 1 corrects. It corrects the historical CPI for the following: The old CPI index collected mostly list prices; the new PPI indexes are more nearly transactions prices. The old CPI pertained only to consumer out-of-pocket payments, so prices paid by health insurance and for procedures that are not normally paid by consumers were not adequately represented;[32] the PPI indexes cover both these lacunae. The PPI indexes are specific to mental health; the old CPI was much broader, and therefore could not represent price movements in mental health treatments that differed from those for treating other medical conditions. The PPI moved substantially toward pricing the cost of treating an illness, rather than the cost of, for example, a visit to a psychiatrist's office or hospital room charges. PPI methodology should at least partly pick up changes in medical technology that reduce the cost of treatment, compared with the cost of an office visit or hospital room. Finally, the adjustment 1 indexes contain an approximation for fixed-weight index number bias.

It is also important to emphasize limitations. The backcast will be valid if the joint error from all the above factors is the same for the period of the backcast (1972–93) as it was for the overlap period (1993 or 1994 to 1998). It is unlikely that the backcast is exactly valid, but even given its limitations it is likely to be far better than the historical CPI. The work of Scitovsky (1964) suggests that CPI measurement error might have gone in the opposite direction in the 1950s and early 1960s, which argues against backcasting this far.

Even though it is a great improvement, the new PPI methodology still omits some aspects of the cost of treating disease. It has been difficult for BLS to find data to adjust for changes in the efficacy of treatment (see the earlier discussion). Additionally, some changes in medical treatment cause shifts in expenditures among PPI index categories; the PPI methodology contains no obvious way to take these cost savings into account. As an example, consider increased use of drugs that permit treatment of mental

---

31. There is strong evidence of upward bias in the PPI pharmaceutical indexes in recent years (Berndt, Cockburn, and Griliches 1996). I have not adjusted the historical PPI for the results of this research, because the PPI errors appear to be uniquely associated with particular events and years, but an improvement to the adjustment 1 index computed here would incorporate the findings of this and other research on pharmaceutical price indexes.

32. Some of these charges made their way into the CPI health insurance index, but they do not influence directly the CPI price indexes for hospitals and physicians.

Table 1.12   Growth Rates, Expenditures and Prices, Mental Health Treatments, 1972–95

	Annual Expenditure Growth Rates	Price Indexes (percent increase)			Real Expenditure Growth		
		Unadjusted	Adjustment 1[a]	Adjustment 2[b]	Unadjusted	Adjustment 1[a]	Adjustment 2[b]
1972–80	13.11	10.76	4.22	3.65	2.25	8.65	9.25
1980–85	17.09	10.81	2.32	1.76	5.76	14.61	15.24
1985–90	7.06	8.78	−0.57	−1.11	−1.54	7.72	8.31
1990–95	4.94	6.47	0.51	−0.05	−1.37	4.45	5.02

[a]Adjustment based on ratio of PPI/CPI detailed indexes, 1993–98.
[b]Adjustment based on Berndt, Busch, and Frank (chap. 12 in this volume), table 12.7, row labeled Chained Weights, Fisher Ideal.

conditions on an outpatient basis, rather than in a mental hospital. Substitution of drugs (and clinical visits) for hospital care will reduce the cost of treatment, but this cost reduction will be reflected inadequately in the PPI because the PPI holds the weights for the various expenditure categories (hospitals, doctors' offices, pharmaceuticals, and so forth) constant.

The major research on these problems are the two studies by Frank, Berndt, and Busch (chap. 12 in this volume, 1999)—hereafter referred to as FBB. FBB studied the cost of treating depression by American Psychiatric Association guidelines. Rather than creating a price index for each alternative guideline treatment (for example, treatment by psychotherapy alone), they considered all guideline treatments that had equal clinical outcomes as equivalent.[33] For example, partial substitution of drugs for some time spent in psychotherapy generally reduces the cost of treatment. This cost saving is incorporated into FBB's price indexes.

FBB reported that their price index for treating depression fell over the 1991–95 interval.[34] The new PPI indexes for mental health treatment—hospital and nonhospital care—were fully in place only for 1994–95, when, perhaps fortuitously, their rate of increase matches FBB almost exactly (3 percent). The backcasted index (adjustment 1 index in table 1.13) rose more rapidly than did the FBB index in the other two years. Over the entire interval, the ratio of the FBB index to the adjustment 1 index is 0.978, a difference in growth rates of about 0.2 percentage point per year.

However, the costs of treating depression may not be a good proxy for the costs of treating other forms of mental illness. Depression is more frequently treated outside hospitals than are some other mental diseases, and FBB estimate an index for outpatient care.[35] Their results may not adequately represent the cost experience for disorders that more frequently require institutionalization. Additionally, FBB explore pharmaceutical innovations in mental health care for depression. Even though pharmaceutical advances in medical practice for other mental disorders have taken place (for example, schizophrenia), the technological innovations in the treatments for other disorders may not have the same implications for treatment costs as the experience with treating depression.

On the other hand, BLS price indexes do not generally pick up changes in either the efficacy (or quality) of treatments, or changes—such as those

---

33. They also considered alternative assumptions.

34. For purposes of this paper, I use results in the second FBB study (chap. 12 in this volume), which differ to an extent from the first (1999) in that their depression price index falls less in the second study.

35. I have not located data on hospital expenditures for treating depression. DuPont et al. (1996) report that about 59 percent of expenditures on a group of anxiety disorders was spent in hospitals and nursing homes (almost entirely the latter). These anxiety disorders did not include depression, but all are located next to depression in the coding structure of ICD-9, and comorbidities between these disorders and depression suggest that data on the distribution of expenditures on treating depression might be similar.

Table 1.13   Alternative Estimates of Price Change for Mental Health Treatments

	1992–93	1993–94	1994–95	Average Annual Change 1992–95
Unadjusted[a]	1.076	1.038	1.029	1.047
Adjustment 1 index[a]	0.983	1.021	1.029	1.011
FBB[b]	0.963	0.974	1.030	0.989

Note: Ratio of FBB/Adjustment 1 index = 0.989/1.011 = 0.978.

[a] From table 1A.4.

[b] From Berndt, Busch, and Frank (chap. 12 in this volume), table 12.2; see also table 1A.4.

documented by FBB—that reduce the cost of treating an illness by changing the treatment itself. The BLS method standardizes on the treatment, and collects costs for a given treatment for a specified condition. There is thus merit in using the FBB study to adjust a mental health care price index for improvements in medical practice. The only issue is how to use it.

Two options present themselves. One could apply the FBB study as a correction to the entire BLS mental health care price index, on the grounds that FBB is the only study available. For the reasons given above, the FBB study may overstate the improvement in medical care for other mental health conditions, and may also understate the rate of inflation in other mental disorders.

An alternative is to apply FBB only to the depression portion of the mental health care price index. This alternative implies that *no* comparable gains in medical practice occurred in treating other forms of mental illness. Thus, if applying FBB to the entire mental health expenditures creates error (because of the two assumptions noted above), applying the study's results only to the depression part of the index creates error in the other direction. In any case, unless deterioration of medical practice for other forms of mental illness occurred, both errors are bounded by the adjustment 1 index.

Compilers of national accounts and of national health accounts are typically (but not always) conservative about applying results of one piece of research to another set of data, so I suspect that future compilers of accounts for diseases might prefer the second alternative. I do not know the proportion of mental health care costs made up by the treatment of depression. As an exercise, I assume it is 25 percent.[36]

The next question is the use of FBB to backcast, in order to correct the historical indexes for improvements in medical practice in treating mental

36. Affective disorders (not including depression) account for 28.7 percent of mental health care costs (Rice and Miller 1998). Considerable comorbidity exists between affective disorders and depression.

disease. Applying an adjustment from the FBB study implies that the *rate* of improvement in medical practice for treating depression (that is, in health care outcomes) was the same in earlier years. This is debatable. Nevertheless, I use the FBB results to make an additional backcasting correction to the historical price series.

Table 1.13 shows that the difference in trend between the price index for depression in FBB and weighted PPI mental health indexes, for the period in which both are available, is about 0.2 percentage point. I weight *one-quarter* of the mental health adjustment 1 price index with this additional adjustment. The result appears as the "adjustment 2" price index in the third column of table 1.12.

For the reasons given above, the FBB adjustment (adjustment 2) may overstate the improvement in medical care in other periods, and may also understate their rates of inflation. The alternative, as I noted above, is to assume no improvement in medical practice (other than what is incorporated into the new PPI indexes). The "no improvement" assumption yields the adjustment 1 index, which can then be taken as a bound on the error in the adjustment 2 index.

1.6.3   An Expenditure Account for Mental Health

We are now in a position to form a U.S. health expenditure account for mental health treatment that shows trends in expenditures, prices, and the quantity of mental health services for the years 1972–1995. Years before 1972 are omitted here, but could be added for a longer historical series. The summary of this account is in table 1.12.

Price Index Bias

Backcasting improved price measures shows that the old CPI medical care price indexes overstated inflation in medical care costs for mental health, a result that is consistent with medical economists' presumptions. For mental health, CPI indexes weighted to reflect mental health expenditures (the unadjusted index in table 1.12) show double-digit inflation in the 1970s and early 1980s. An adjustment factor based on the improved post-1992 PPI lowers substantially the medical inflation estimates of the 1970s and early 1980s, so that they are no longer double-digit. Indeed, the adjustment 1 price index for mental health care is essentially flat since 1985.

Of course the adjustment 1 index relies on the validity of the backcasting exercise and its assumption that corrections taken from the period of the 1990s apply to the decades of the 1970s and 1980s. Medical economists have a strong presumption that the unadjusted indexes are biased upward, and available empirical work is consistent with that presumption of upward bias; the adjusted indexes, however, may have their own biases.

Adjusting price change for the FBB research results has a smaller, though not negligible, effect (table 1.12). The adjustment 2 index shows slightly negative inflation in mental health care in the 1990s, because FBB found a declining price for depression in their study, and an even more strongly negative mental health care inflation rate for the late 1980s. These estimates compare to the 6.5 percent and nearly 9 percent rates given by the unadjusted price indexes for these two periods.

Possibly the costs of treating depression have fallen relative to the costs of treating other mental conditions. If not, the adjustments applied to obtain the adjustment 2 index are too small, and the adjusted price indexes for mental health care should fall even more rapidly than the adjustment 2 index of table 1.12. As noted, if the PPI indexes are correct for the remainder of mental health treatments, then the adjustment 1 index bounds the correct index.

I noted earlier that it is commonplace that medical care inflation outstrips the overall CPI inflation rate. The price index numbers in table 1.12 call this generalization into doubt. At least since the mid-1980s, inflation in mental health care was substantially lower than the general CPI inflation rate (3.6 percent per year, 1985–95), and it may have been negative through the whole period. For mental health care, "runaway medical inflation" is a wholly invalid characterization.

Growth in Mental Health Services

I next use the adjusted price indexes to estimate the growth in the quantity of mental health care services (or real expenditure growth). For this stage of the research, I take a short cut. I begin from the index number system in equations (1) and (2b), earlier, which is the inverse of the index number system that is normally used in national health accounts. Equation (2b) specifies a Paasche index number for real expenditures. The conventional NHA system employs a Laspeyres index for real expenditures—that is, the real output index (not the price index) is weighted by base-period expenditures. Producing the conventional system implies an additional computational step that has not been undertaken.

One reason is that the conventional national accounts–national health accounts index number system is subject to substitution bias. A better system for computing price indexes and indexes of real expenditures uses a superlative index number system. The NIPA now uses a superlative index number system; specifically, Fisher index numbers.[37] In principle, the Fisher system provides a better measurement system for NHA also.

---

37. The Fisher price index is $I(P)_{0t} = [(\Sigma_i P_{it} Q_{i0} / \Sigma_i P_{i0} Q_{i0})(\Sigma_i P_{it} Q_{it} / \Sigma_i P_{i0} Q_{it})]^{1/2}$, and the Fisher quantity index, $I(Q)_{0t}$, is obtained by reversing the P and Q terms in the price index formula. A convenient property of the Fisher system is that the product of the Fisher price index and the Fisher quantity index—that is, $I(P)_{0t} \times I(Q)_{0t}$—is the change in total expenditure, the first term on the right-hand side of equation (2a).

However, I have not computed a Fisher system for the data on mental health for technical reasons that could readily be surmounted, but that introduce extraneous issues that are better discussed elsewhere.[38] An alternative that is computationally (and procedurally) simpler is to compute base-weighted logarithmic indexes, which are approximately Cobb-Douglas indexes with shares based on the initial period's expenditures (Moulton 1996 explains the procedure). Table 1.12, then, presents real expenditure trend information produced through deflation by a base-weighted logarithmic price index.[39]

Not surprisingly, the largest growth rate estimate comes from using both the adjustments—the adjustment 2 index that incorporates adjustments based on the new PPI indexes and also on the FBB study (the last column of table 1.12). With this adjustment, growth in mental health care services from 1985 to 1990 was over 8 percent, and from 1990 to 1995 it was about 5 percent. This contrasts with the impression of negative growth in aggregate mental health care services that arises from looking at the unadjusted price indexes (table 1.12). But even without the FBB adjustment, the adjustment 1 indexes also show real growth in mental health care services, not the negative growth suggested by the available historical data without adjustment. Even so, the rate of growth of mental health services, which peaked in the early 1980s at over 15 percent per year, has slowed substantially in the 1990s, to under 5 percent annually. Note again that these are aggregate numbers, the type of estimates that typically appear in NHA; they do not estimate mental health care services per capita.

These are, perhaps, just numbers. What is their importance?

A great deal of effort has been put into medical care cost containment in the United States. The data in table 1.12 suggest that medical care inflation is not the driving force behind the run-up in medical care costs, at least in mental health care. In the case of mental health care, the aggregate level of services has improved, judging from the best picture that can be assembled from U.S. aggregate statistics, but the rate of growth of the real quantity of mental health care services has slowed in the post-1990 period of cost containment. If these numbers are anywhere near correct, they suggest that health care cost containment may have social costs—curtailment

---

38. The essence of the Fisher price index or Fisher quantity index is the application of weights for initial and ending periods to the *same* components. Partly because the available weighting information for mental health expenditures comes from years that are fairly far apart, but also because the detailed information on price indexes, as well as the expenditure components that are available, changes from period to period, calculating a Fisher system from existing data on mental health expenditures and price indexes implies applying different weighting structures to different components, not to the same components. There is no reason why this cannot be done; it in fact occurs in the application of Fisher indexes to the NIPA.

39. Note, however, that the adjustment 2 index incorporates FBB's chain Fisher index. The arithmetic (Laspeyres) form of the adjustment 1 index is presented in appendix table 1A.4.

of health care that has real impacts on health—that are more severe than is generally recognized.

If the numbers are not correct, or if they need refinement before they can be used to inform public debate (the need for refinement in these estimates is hardly debatable), it is also the case that decisions on health policy are being based on statistical trend estimates that are at least as defective, and probably far more misleading, than the ones developed here. The need is strong for aggregate U.S. data on health care that match the price and output information that is routinely available for other portions of the U.S. economy.

1.7   A Note on Measuring Output in Publicly Provided Health Care Systems

The examples in this paper reflect the institutional structure of the U.S. health care system, which is atypical for industrialized countries. Three of the countries for which cost-of-disease accounts are shown in tables 1.5 and 1.6 have government-funded health care systems. However, the general "human repair" accounting framework can be applied to government-provided health care systems, as well as or better than it can be applied to market-provided ones.

For the government-provided health care systems, integration of cost-of-disease accounts into NHA in each country is a first step, just as it is in the United States. After that the steps are different. Rather than developing deflators, as in the U.S. case, the accounts require information on case costs and on case quantities, which is information that a national health system ought to collect (but sometimes does not) for its own purposes. The emphasis is on developing direct quantity measures, with associated costs, rather than on producing the quantity measures indirectly through deflation. Information on medical outcomes performs an analogous role in such an implementation. The details are left for another paper.

1.8   Where Does This Take Us? Conclusions

Medical outcome measures are disease-specific. So are research price indexes of the type discussed in this paper (the heart attack price index of Cutler et al. 1998, or the depression price index of Frank, Berndt, and Busch 1999). There are obviously many human repairs to be considered, even in one ICD-9 chapter, let alone across all of them. Moving through the ICD-9 chapters on a disease-by-disease basis is clearly a very big job.

However, there is no reasonable alternative but to take samples of disease treatments and compute the value of medical interventions on the health of the recipients. Trying to deflate expenditures on "hospitals," for example, without considering the treatment of individual diseases, has a long history of failure. Indeed, the new PPI price indexes for hospital care *begin* from measuring the price change for treatment of individual diseases. The greater the possibility that treatment moves from a hospital setting to outpatient care, or that new pharmaceuticals substitute for hospital or clinician resources, the greater the failure of the conventional focus on the institutional setting for treatment. The new PPI indexes are not immune to deficiencies from this source because they are still "industry" price indexes, albeit industry price indexes with useful "product" detail on the costs of treating diseases.

To put the magnitude of this task in context, however, personal health care accounts for about 12 percent of U.S. GDP in 1995. This is a large share of GDP, much larger than, say, the producers' durable equipment (PDE) portion of investment, which was roughly 7.5 percent of GDP in the same year. The unpublished detail from which U.S. PDE is calculated runs to something on the order of 800 lines. Not all of these lines have their own deflators, but the deflation detail in PDE incorporates some 400 lines, for which in many cases both domestic and imported products are distinguished and deflated separately. Additionally, the Bureau of Economic Analysis computes a capital flow matrix that distributes these investment components to the more than one thousand industries identified in the U.S. industry classification system, though not to every one of them at the finest level of industry detail.

Against this product detail in measuring PDE, the expenditure detail available on "products" in the NHA is minimal. This lack of expenditure detail in NHA (product detail that is actually already present in cost-of-disease accounts) is the great limitation on the potential for creating real output measures from NHA data. Even though creating it will be a great deal of work, it is work well worth doing.

Measuring health is not a smaller job than measuring PDE, nor a less important one. The difference is, rather, that the investment accounts have many years' head start.

Appendix

Table 1A.1   Estimates of Direct Treatment Costs for Mental Conditions

Year	Excluding Substance Abuse ($ millions)	Including Substance Abuse ($ millions)	Group[a]	Source	Notes
1954	1,723[b]		Rice	Fein (1958)[c]	
1963[d]	2,402[b]		Rice	Rice (1966)[c]	No drugs
1968	3,760[b]		Rice	Conley and Conwell (1970)[c]	
1971	11,058[b]		RTI	Levine and Levine (1975)[c]	
1972[d]		6,985[b]	Rice	Cooper and Rice (1976)[c]	Adds drugs
1974	16,973[b]		RTI	Levine and Willner (1976)[c]	
1975		9,411[b]	Rice	Paringer and Berk (1977)[c]	
1977	18,745[b]		RTI	Cruze et al. (1981)[c]	
1980[d]	20,301		Rice	Hodgson and Kopstein (1984), table 1	
1980[d]		19,824[b]	Rice	Rice, Hodgson, and Kopstein (1985)[c]	Presumably no "other related direct costs," since authors compare to 1963 and 1972 estimates[e]
1980	23,558	35,470[b]	RTI	Harwood et al. (1984)[c]	Includes support costs
1980		17,224	Other	Frank and Kamlet (1985)	Includes support costs, Frank and Kamlet's low estimate
1980		16,747	Other	Frank and Kamlet (1985)	Includes support costs, Frank and Kamlet's high estimate
1980	14,070		Other	Parsons et al. (1986)	Total direct costs $153,878 (table A) × proportion of mental health 0.094 (figure 7) excludes expenditures such as nursing homes
1981	27,115	40,828[b]	RTI	Harwood et al. (1984), table G-3	Includes support costs

Year			Group[a]	Source	Notes
1982	30,502	45,928[b]	RTI	Harwood et al. (1984), table G-4	Includes support costs
1983	33,445	50,359[b]	RTI	Harwood et al. (1984)[c]	Includes support costs
1985	42,528[b]	51,420	Rice	Rice et al. (1990)[c]	Includes support costs, reports alcohol and drug abuse for the first time
1985	42,528	51,420[b]	Rice	Rice, Kelman, and Miller (1991), table 1	Includes support costs
1986		39,500	Other	Mark et al. (1998), table 5.1	
1988	55,389	66,774[b]	Rice	Rice et al. (1990), table 8[f]	Includes support costs
1990	67,000		Rice	DuPont et al. (1996), table 1	Presumably only mental, otherwise same as 1988 figure, includes support costs
1990	67,000		Rice	Rice and Miller (1998), table 1	Presumably only mental, otherwise same as 1988 figure, includes support costs
1995[d]		71,348[b]	Rice	Hodgson and Cohen (1998), table 1-1	Includes home health care, alcohol and drug abuse no longer reported separately
1996	66,704	79,280	Other	Mark et al. (1998), table 5.1	
1996		76,312	Other	Mark et al. (1998), table 6.1	Number differs from above because recipients of expenditures are consistent with NHA

Note: Includes hospital and nonhospital treatment costs. Support costs, which include costs such as training costs for physicians and nurses, research costs, program administration costs, and net costs of private health insurance, are included only where noted. "Other related direct costs," which include costs such as crime, transportation, and counseling, have been excluded.

[a] Indicates the research group: Rice (all studies treated as part of the Dorothy Rice/NCHS group), RTI (all studies treated as part of the Research Triangle Group), other (in neither group).

[b] This estimate used in calculating growth rates.

[c] Reviewed in Rice, Kelman, and Miller (1991), table 6.

[d] Years where full cost of disease accounts were estimated.

[e] Rice, Hodgson, and Kopstein (1985) attribute this estimate for 1980 to Hodgson and Kopstein (1984); it incorporates a correction to the published Hodgson and Kopstein estimate.

[f] In Rice, Kelman, and Miller (1991, fig. 2, p. 285), estimates for 1988 are $55,610 and $67,000, respectively.

Table 1A.2   Average Annual Growth Rates for Mental Health Expenditures

Between Years:	Ratio of Costs	Total Increase (percent)	Growth Rate	Sources	Notes
a. 1954–63	2,402/1,723	39.4	0.03760	Rice (1966), Fein (1958)	
b. 1963–68	3,760/2,402	56.5	0.09376	Conley and Conwell (1970), Rice (1966)	
c. 1968–72[a]	6,551/3,760	85.8	0.16747	Cooper and Rice (1976), Conley and Conwell (1970)	Drugs and drug sundries cost taken out of 1972 figure to be comparable with the 1968 figure
d. 1971–74	16,973/11,058	53.5	0.15353	Levine and Willner (1976), Levine and Levine (1975)	
e. 1972–75	9,411/6,985	34.7	0.10448	Paringer and Berk (1977), Cooper and Rice (1976)	
f. 1974–77	18,745/16,973	10.4	0.03366	Cruze et al. (1981), Levine and Willner (1976)	
g. 1975–80	19,824/9,411	110.6	0.16068	Rice, Hodgson, and Kopstein (1985), Paringer and Berk (1977)	
h. 1977–80	31,647/18,745	89.2	0.19074	Harwood et al. (1984), Cruze et al. (1981)	Supports costs taken out of 1980 figure to be comparable with the 1977 figure

i.	1980–81	40,828/35,470	15.1	0.15106	Harwood et al. (1984), Harwood et al. (1984)	
j.	1981–82	45,928/40,828	12.5	0.12491	Harwood et al. (1984), Harwood et al. (1984)	
k.	1982–83	50,359/45,928	9.6	0.09648	Harwood et al. (1984), Harwood et al. (1984)	
l.	1980–85	47,485/19,824	139.5	0.19089	Rice et al. (1990), Rice, Hodgson, and Kopstein (1985)	Support costs taken out of 1985 figure to be comparable with the 1980 figure
m.	1985–88	66,774/51,420	29.9	0.09100	Rice et al. (1990), Rice et al. (1990)	
n.	1986–96	79,280/39,500	50.1	0.07200	Mark et al. (1998), Mark et al. (1998)	
o.	1988–95	70,717/61,956	14.1	0.02681	Hodgson and Cohen (1998), Rice et al. (1990)	Support costs taken out of 1988 figure and home health costs taken out of 1995 to be comparable

Note: Growth rates are based on data in table 1A.1 (see sources for each line).

[a] The 1968 Conley and Conwell (1970) figure does not include alcohol and drug abuse treatment costs. The 1972 Cooper and Rice (1976) figure does. However, the alcohol and drug abuse costs cannot be linked out of the 1972 Cooper and Rice (1976) figure as the costs are not broken down in the study.

Table 1A.3   Annual Growth Rates for Mental Health

Years	Rates	Source(s)[a]	Selected Years	Annual Growth Rates[b]
1954–55	0.03760	a		
1955–56	0.03760	a		
1956–57	0.03760	a		
1957–58	0.03760	a		
1958–59	0.03760	a		
1959–60	0.03760	a		
1960–61	0.03760	a		
1961–62	0.03760	a		
1962–63	0.03760	a	1954–63	0.0376
1963–64	0.09376	b		
1964–65	0.09376	b		
1965–66	0.09376	b		
1966–67	0.09376	b		
1967–68	0.09376	b		
1968–69	0.16747	c		
1969–70	0.16747	c		
1970–71	0.16747	c		
1971–72	0.16050	c, d	1963–72	0.1257
1972–73	0.12900	d, e		
1973–74	0.12900	d, e		
1974–75	0.06907	e, f		
1975–76	0.09717	f, g		
1976–77	0.09717	f, g		
1977–78	0.17571	g, h		
1978–79	0.17571	g, h		
1979–80	0.17571	g, h	1972–80	0.1311
1980–81	0.17098	i, l		
1981–82	0.15790	j, l		
1982–83	0.14369	k, l		
1983–84	0.19089	l		
1984–85	0.19089	l	1980–85	0.1709
1985–86	0.09100	m		
1986–87	0.08150	m, n		
1987–88	0.08150	m, n		
1988–89	0.04940	n, o		
1989–90	0.04940	n, o	1985–90	0.0706
1990–91	0.04940	n, o		
1991–92	0.04940	n, o		
1992–93	0.04940	n, o		
1993–94	0.04940	n, o		
1994–95	0.04940	n, o	1990–95	0.0494

Notes: Computed from data in table 1A.2. The rates of increase for each year are computed from the average rates of increase for matched studies, given in table 1A.2. A letter code keying back to table 1A.2 shows the source or sources on which each annual estimate was based. Growth rates for groups of years are simple averages of rates for the years in the group.

[a] Keyed to lines in appendix table 1A.2.

[b] Entries transferred to tables 1.9 and 1.11 in text for periods indicated.

Table 1A.4   Growth Rates and Price Indexes for Mental Health Care Services

	Annual Expenditure Growth Rate[a]	Annual Increase, Price Indexes				Annual Real Expenditure Growth Rates			
			Adjustment 1				Adjustment 1		
		Unadjusted	Laspeyres[b]	Logarithmic[c]	Adjustment 2[d]	Unadjusted	Laspeyres[b]	Logarithmic[c]	Adjustment 2[d]
1954–55	1.03760								
1955–56	1.03760								
1956–57	1.03760								
1957–58	1.03760								
1958–59	1.03760								
1959–60	1.03760								
1960–61	1.03760								
1961–62	1.03760								
1962–63	1.03760								
1963–64	1.09376	1.04637	1.04637	1.04637	1.04637	1.04529	1.04529	1.04529	1.04529
1964–65	1.09376	1.05434	1.05434	1.05434	1.05434	1.03739	1.03739	1.03739	1.03739
1965–66	1.09376	1.09013	1.09013	1.09013	1.09013	1.00333	1.00333	1.00333	1.00333
1966–67	1.09376	1.17222	1.17222	1.17222	1.17222	0.93307	0.93307	0.93307	0.93307
1967–68	1.09376	1.12238	1.12238	1.12238	1.12238	0.97450	0.97450	0.97450	0.97450
1968–69	1.16747	1.12353	1.12353	1.12353	1.12353	1.03911	1.03911	1.03911	1.03911
1969–70	1.16747	1.11619	1.11619	1.11619	1.11619	1.04594	1.04594	1.04594	1.04594
1970–71	1.16747	1.10865	1.10865	1.10865	1.10865	1.05306	1.05306	1.05306	1.05306
1971–72	1.16050	1.06245	1.06245	1.06245	1.06245	1.09229	1.09229	1.09229	1.09229
1972–73	1.12900	1.04279	0.98875	0.98139	0.97602	1.08267	1.14184	1.15042	1.15674
1973–74	1.12900	1.09629	1.03851	1.03154	1.02590	1.02984	1.08713	1.09448	1.10050
1974–75	1.06907	1.15631	1.09473	1.08776	1.08181	0.92455	0.97656	0.98281	0.98822
1975–76	1.09717	1.12578	1.06653	1.05924	1.05345	0.97458	1.02872	1.03580	1.04150
1976–77	1.09717	1.10700	1.04973	1.04174	1.03604	0.99112	1.04519	1.05321	1.05900

(*continued*)

Table 1A.4 (continued)

	Annual Expenditure Growth Rate[a]	Annual Increase, Price Indexes				Annual Real Expenditure Growth Rates			
		Unadjusted	Adjustment 1		Adjustment 2[d]	Unadjusted	Adjustment 1		Adjustment 2[d]
			Laspeyres[b]	Logarithmic[c]			Laspeyres[b]	Logarithmic[c]	
1977–78	1.17571	1.08446	1.02977	1.02068	1.01509	1.08414	1.14172	1.15189	1.15823
1978–79	1.17571	1.10372	1.04736	1.03877	1.03309	1.06522	1.12254	1.13183	1.13805
1979–80	1.17571	1.14424	1.08804	1.07672	1.07083	1.02750	1.08057	1.09193	1.09793
1980–81	1.17098	1.13821	1.07134	1.06408	1.05826	1.02878	1.09300	1.10046	1.10651
1981–82	1.15790	1.13545	1.06888	1.06145	1.05565	1.01978	1.08328	1.09087	1.09687
1982–83	1.14369	1.11189	1.01841	1.01782	1.01226	1.02859	1.12301	1.12366	1.12984
1983–84	1.19089	1.08802	0.99659	0.99598	0.99053	1.09455	1.19497	1.19570	1.20228
1984–85	1.19089	1.06673	0.97713	0.97646	0.97112	1.11640	1.21876	1.21961	1.22631
1985–86	1.09100	1.06471	0.97368	0.97323	0.96790	1.02469	1.12049	1.12102	1.12718
1986–87	1.08150	1.07248	0.98081	0.98032	0.97496	1.00841	1.10267	1.10321	1.10928
1987–88	1.08150	1.09078	0.99749	0.99705	0.99160	0.99149	1.08423	1.08470	1.09066
1988–89	1.04940	1.10803	1.01318	1.01275	1.00721	0.94709	1.03576	1.03619	1.04189
1989–90	1.04940	1.10303	1.00866	1.00819	1.00267	0.95138	1.04039	1.04088	1.04660
1990–91	1.04940	1.09664	1.0261	1.00194	0.99646	0.95693	1.04667	1.04737	1.05313
1991–92	1.04940	1.08391	0.59073	0.99041	0.98499	0.96816	1.05922	1.05957	1.06539
1992–93	1.04940	1.07555	0.58303	0.98276	0.97738	0.97569	1.06752	1.06782	1.07369
1993–94	1.04940	1.03787	1.02136	1.02071	1.01513	1.01111	1.02745	1.02811	1.03376
1994–95	1.04940	1.02934	1.02934	1.02934	1.02371	1.01949	1.01949	1.01949	1.02510
1995–96		1.03749	1.03749	1.03749	1.03182				
1996–97		1.00310	1.00310	1.00310	0.99761				
1997–98		0.99324	0.99324	0.99324	0.98781				

[a]Taken from table 1A.3.

[b]Adjustment based on ratio of CPI/PPI detailed indexes, 1993–98, indexes combined with Laspeyres formula.

[c]Adjustment based on ratio of CPI/PPI detailed indexes, 1993–98, indexes combined with logarithmic formula.

[d]Adjustment based on Berndt, Busch, and Frank (chap. 12 in this volume), table 12.7, row labeled Chained Weights, Fisher Ideal.

Table 1A.5 Growth Rates and Price Indexes for Mental Health Care Services (for selected years)

	Annual Expenditure Growth Rate[a]	Average Annual Growth Rate, Price Indexes				Average Annual Real Expenditure Growth Rate			
			Adjustment 1				Adjustment 1		
		Unadjusted	Laspeyres[b]	Logarithmic[c]	Adjustment 2[d]	Unadjusted	Laspeyres[b]	Logarithmic[c]	Adjustment 2[d]
1954–63	3.76048								
1963–72	12.57455	9.95842	9.95842	9.95842	9.95842	2.48856	2.48856	2.48856	2.48856
1972–80	13.10648	10.75724	5.04276	4.22295	3.65284	2.24538	7.80356	8.65456	9.25218
1980–85	17.08705	10.80614	2.64695	2.31586	1.75619	5.76198	14.26074	14.60583	15.23618
1985–90	7.05619	8.78090	−0.52376	−0.56916	−1.11306	−1.53889	7.67060	7.71984	8.31231
1990–95	4.94033	6.46625	0.54138	0.50325	−0.04651	−1.37235	4.40724	4.44696	5.02144

[a]Taken from table 1A.3.

[b]Adjustment based on ratio of CPI/PPI detailed indexes, 1993–98, indexes combined with Laspeyres formula.

[c]Adjustment based on ratio of CPI/PPI detailed indexes, 1993–98, indexes combined with logarithmic formula.

[d]Adjustment based on Berndt, Busch, and Frank (chap. 12 in this volume), table 12.7, row labeled Chained Weights, Fisher Ideal.

Table 1A.6   **Weights for Mental Health Price Indexes**

Used in Years	Expenditure Description	Shares of Expenditures	
1963–72	Hospital care + nursing home care + nursing care	s_{H+N}	= 0.8782
	Physicians' services + other professional services	s_P	= 0.1218
1972–80	Hospital care + nursing home care	s_{H+N}	= 0.8385
	Physicians' services + other professional services	s_P	= 0.0994
	Drugs and drug sundries	s_D	= 0.0621
1980–85	Hospital care + nursing home care	s_{H+N}	= 0.8472
	Physicians' services + other professional services	s_P	= 0.1035
	Drugs	s_D	= 0.0493
1985–87	Hospitals + nursing homes	s_{H+N}	= 0.82005
	Office-based physicians + other professional services	s_P	= 0.14297
	Drugs	s_D	= 0.03698
1987–90	Hospitals + nursing homes	s_{H+N}	= 0.8201
	Office-based physicians	s_P	= 0.0547
	Other professional services	s_O	= 0.0882
	Drugs	s_D	= 0.0370
1990–93	Mental health organizations + short-stay hospitals + nursing homes	s_{H+N}	= 0.7987
	Office-based physicians	s_P	= 0.0591
	Other professional services	s_O	= 0.1067
	Drugs	s_D	= 0.0354
1993–95	Short-stay hospitals + nursing homes	s_{H+N}	= 0.4831
	Mental health organizations	s_{MH}	= 0.3156
	Office-based physicians	s_P	= 0.0591
	Other professional services	s_O	= 0.1067
	Drugs	s_D	= 0.0354
1995–98	Hospital care	s_H	= 0.5755
	Physician, other professional services	s_P	= 0.1072
	Prescription drugs	s_D	= 0.0854
	Nursing home care	s_N	= 0.2318

Table 1A.7   **Examples: Calculations for Price Indexes**

Example 1: 1963–64

Calculation of Unadjusted Price Index
From table 2 in Rice (1966): Mental, Psychoneurotic, and Personality Disorders

	1963 Expenditures ($ millions)	Shares (%)
Total mental disorder expenditures	2,401.7	100.00
Hospital care	2,059.7	85.76
Nursing home care	29.7	1.24
Physicians' services	281.5	11.72
Nursing care	19.8	0.82
Other professional services	11.0	0.46

From the U.S. Department of Labor, Bureau of Labor Statistics

	1963	1964	ΔPs
CPI: hospital service charges	69.0	72.4	$\Delta P_1 = 1.04927536$
CPI: physicians' services	23.6	24.2	$\Delta P_2 = 1.02542373$

	1963 Expenditures ($ millions)	Shares
Total mental disorder expenditures	2,401.7	
Hospital care + nursing home care + nursing care	2,109.2	$s_{H+N} = 0.87821127$
Physicians' services + other professional services	292.5	$s_P = 0.12178873$

$I_{63-64} = (\Delta P_1)(s_{H+N}) + (\Delta P_2)(s_P)$
$I_{63-64} = (1.05)(0.88) + (1.03)(0.12)$
$I_{63-64} = 0.9215 + 0.1249$
$I_{63-64} = 1.0464$

Example 2: 1972–73

Calculation of Unadjusted Price Index
From table 1 in Cooper and Rice (1976): Mental Disorders

	1972 Expenditures ($ millions)	Shares (%)
Total mental disorder expenditures	6,985	100.00
Hospital care	5,261	75.32
Physicians' services	685	9.81
Other professional services	9	0.13
Drugs and drug sundries	434	6.21
Nursing home care	596	8.53

From the U.S. Department of Labor, Bureau of Labor Statistics

	1972	1973	ΔPs
CPI: semiprivate rooms	173.9	182.1	$\Delta P_1 = 1.04715354$
CPI: psychiatrist, office visits	129.2	133.6	$\Delta P_2 = 1.03405573$
CPI: prescription drugs and medical supplies	47.2	47.1	$\Delta P_3 = 0.99788136$

(*continued*)

Table 1A.7 (continued)

	1972 Expenditures ($ millions)	Shares
Total mental disorder expenditures	6,985	
Hospital care + nursing home care	5,857	$s_{H+N} = 0.83851110$
Physicians' services + other professional services	694	$s_P = 0.09935576$
Drugs and drug sundries	434	$s_D = 0.06213314$

$I_{72-73} = (\Delta P_1)(s_{H+N}) + (\Delta P_2)(s_P) + (\Delta P_3)(s_D)$
$I_{72-73} = (1.05)(0.84) + (1.03)(0.10) + (1.00)(0.06)$
$I_{72-73} = 0.8780 + 0.1027 + 0.0620$
$I_{72-73} = 1.0428$

Calculation of Arithmetic Adjustment 1 Index

	ΔPs	Adj. factor	Adjusted ΔPs
CPI: semiprivate rooms	(1.0472)	(0.9122)	= 0.95516610
CPI: psychiatrist, office visits	(1.0341)	(0.9044)	= 0.93523138
CPI: prescription drugs and medical supplies	(0.9979)	(1.5308)	= 1.52760403

$I_{72-73} = (\Delta P_1)(s_{H+N}) + (\Delta P_2)(s_P) + (\Delta P_3)(s_D)$
$I_{72-73} = (0.96)(0.84) + (0.94)(0.10) + (1.53)(0.06)$
$I_{72-73} = 0.8009 + 0.0929 + 0.0949$
$I_{72-73} = 0.9888$

Calculation of Logarithmic Adjustment 1 Index
$I_{72-73} = -(0.05)(0.84) + -(0.07)(0.10) + (0.42)(0.06) = -0.0187897$
antilog = 0.9814

Calculation of Adjustment 2 Index
25% of logarithmic adjustment 1 index, with an additional adjustment factor (0.978),
   based on table 2 in Berndt, Busch, and Frank (chap. 12 in this volume)
$I_{72-73} = (0.9814 \times 0.978) \times 0.25 + (0.9814) \times 0.75 = 0.97602$

Example 3: 1978–79

Calculation of Unadjusted Price Index
From table 1 in Cooper and Rice (1976): Mental Disorders

	1972 Expenditures ($ millions)	Shares (%)
Total mental disorder expenditures	6,985	100.00
Hospital care	5,261	75.32
Physicians' services	685	9.81
Other professional services	9	0.13
Drugs and drug sundries	434	6.21
Nursing home care	596	8.53

From the U.S. Department of Labor, Bureau of Labor Statistics

	1978	1979	ΔPs
CPI: hospital and related services	55.1	61.0	$\Delta P_1 = 1.10707804$
CPI: physicians' services	63.4	69.2	$\Delta P_2 = 1.09148265$
CPI: prescription drugs and medical supplies	61.6	66.4	$\Delta P_3 = 1.07792208$

Table 1A.7 (continued)

	1972 Expenditures ($ millions)	Shares
Total mental disorder expenditures	6,985	
Hospital care + nursing home care	5,857	$s_{H+N} = 0.83851110$
Physicians' services + other professional services	694	$s_P = 0.09935576$
Drugs and drug sundries	434	$s_D = 0.06213314$

$I_{78-79} = (\Delta P_1)(s_{H+N}) + (\Delta P_2)(s_P) + (\Delta P_3)(s_D)$
$I_{78-79} = (1.11)(0.84) + (1.09)(0.10) + (1.08)(0.06)$
$I_{78-79} = 0.9283 + 0.1084 + 0.0670$
$I_{78-79} = 1.1037$

Calculation of Arithmetic Adjustment 1 Index

	ΔPs	Adj. factor	Adjusted ΔPs
CPI: hospital and related services	(1.1071)	(0.9122)	= 1.00982652
CPI: physicians' services	(1.0915)	(0.9044)	= 0.98717003
CPI: prescription drugs and medical supplies	(1.0779)	(1.5308)	= 1.65013416

$I_{78-79} = (\Delta P_1)(s_{H+N}) + (\Delta P_2)(s_P) + (\Delta P_3)(s_D)$
$I_{78-79} = (1.01)(0.84) + (0.99)(0.10) + (1.65)(0.06)$
$I_{78-79} = 0.8468 + 0.0981 + 0.1025$
$I_{78-79} = 1.0474$

Calculation of Logarithmic Adjustment 1 Index

$I_{78-79} = (0.01)(0.84) + -(0.01)(0.10) + (0.50)(0.06) = 0.0380362$
antilog = 1.0388

Calculation of Adjustment 2 Index

25% of logarithmic adjustment 1 index, with an additional adjustment factor (0.978), based on table 2 in Berndt, Busch, and Frank (chap. 12 in this volume)
$I_{78-79} = (1.0388 \times 0.978) \times 0.25 + (1.0388) \times 0.75 = 1.03309$

Example 4: 1982–83

Calculation of Unadjusted Price Index
From table 1 in Hodgson and Kopstein (1984): Mental Disorders

	1980 Expenditures ($ millions)	Shares (%)
All personal mental health care	20,301	100.00
Hospital care	12,836	63.23
Physicians' services	2,027	9.98
Nursing home care	4,363	21.49
Drugs	1,001	4.93
Other professional services	74	0.36

From the U.S. Department of Labor, Bureau of Labor Statistics

	1982	1983	ΔPs (%)
CPI: hospital and other related services	90.3	100.5	$\Delta P_1 = 1.11295681$
CPI: physicians' services	92.9	100.1	$\Delta P_2 = 1.07750269$
PPI: psychotherapeutics	118	137.8	$\Delta P_3 = 1.16582064$

(*continued*)

Table 1A.7 (continued)

	1980 Expenditures ($ millions)	Shares
All personal mental health care	20,301	
Hospital care + nursing home care	17,199	$s_{H+N} = 0.84719965$
Physicians' services + other professional services	2,101	$s_P = 0.10349244$
Drugs	1,001	$s_D = 0.04930792$

$I_{82-83} = (\Delta P_1)(s_{H+N}) + (\Delta P_2)(s_P) + (\Delta P_3)(s_D)$
$I_{82-83} = (1.11)(0.85) + (1.08)(0.10) + (1.17)(0.05)$
$I_{82-83} = 0.9429 + 0.1115 + 0.0575$
$I_{82-83} = 1.1119$

Calculation of Arithmetic Adjustment 1 Index

	ΔPs	Adj. factor	Adjusted ΔPs
CPI: hospital and other related services	(1.1130)	(0.9122)	= 1.01518887
CPI: physicians' services	(1.0775)	(0.9044)	= 0.97452613
PPI: psychotherapeutics	(1.1658)	(1.0000)	= 1.16582064

$I_{82-83} = (\Delta P_1)(s_{H+N}) + (\Delta P_2)(s_P) + (\Delta P_3)(s_D)$
$I_{82-83} = (1.02)(0.85) + (0.97)(0.10) + (1.17)(0.05)$
$I_{82-83} = 0.8601 + 0.1009 + 0.0575$
$I_{82-83} = 1.0184$

Calculation of Logarithmic Adjustment 1 Index

$I_{82-83} = (0.02)(0.85) + -(0.03)(0.10) + (0.15)(0.05) = 0.0176658$
antilog $= 1.0178$

Calculation of Adjustment 2 Index
25% of logarithmic adjustment 1 index, with an additional adjustment factor (0.978), based on table 2 in Berndt, Busch, and Frank (chap. 12 in this volume)
$I_{82-83} = (1.0178 \times 0.978) \times 0.25 + (1.0178) \times 0.75 = 1.01226$

Example 5: 1988–89

Calculation of Unadjusted Price Index
From table 1 in Rice, Kelman, and Miller (1991): Mental Illness

	1985 Expenditures ($ millions)	Shares (%)
All direct costs, mental illness	39,289	100.00
Hospitals	21,636	55.07
Office-based physicians	2,151	5.47
Other professional services	3,466	8.82
Nursing homes	10,583	26.94
Drugs	1,453	3.70

From the U.S. Department of Labor, Bureau of Labor Statistics

	1988	1989	ΔPs
CPI: hospital and other related services	143.9	160.5	$\Delta P_1 = 1.11535789$
CPI: physicians' services	139.8	150.1	$\Delta P_2 = 1.07367668$
CPI: services by other professionals	108.3	114.2	$\Delta P_3 = 1.05447830$
PPI: antidepressants	105.5	118.6	$\Delta P_4 = 1.12417062$

Table 1A.7 (continued)

	1985 Expenditures ($ millions)	Shares
All direct costs, mental illness	39,289	
Hospitals + nursing homes	32,219	$s_{H+N} = 0.82005141$
Office-based physicians	2,151	$s_P = 0.05474815$
Other professional services	3,466	$s_O = 0.08821808$
Drugs	1,453	$s_D = 0.03698236$

$I_{88-89} = (\Delta P_1)\,(s_{H+N}) + (\Delta P_2)\,(s_P) + (\Delta P_3)\,(s_O) + (\Delta P_4)\,(s_D)$
$I_{88-89} = (1.12)\,(0.82) + (1.07)\,(0.05) + (1.05)\,(0.09) + (1.12)\,(0.04)$
$I_{88-89} = 0.9147 + 0.0588 + 0.0930 + 0.0416$
$I_{88-89} = 1.1080$

Calculation of Arithmetic Adjustment 1 Index

	ΔPs	Adj. factor	Adjusted ΔPs
CPI: hospital and other related services	(1.1154)	(0.9122)	= 1.01737902
CPI: physicians' services	(1.0737)	(0.9044)	= 0.97106577
CPI: services by other professionals	(1.0545)	(0.9044)	= 0.95370217
PPI: antidepressants	(1.1242)	(1.0000)	= 1.12417062

$I_{88-89} = (\Delta P_1)\,(s_{H+N}) + (\Delta P_2)\,(s_P) + (\Delta P_3)\,(S_O) + (\Delta P_4)\,(S_D)$
$I_{88-89} = (1.02)\,(0.82) + (0.97)\,(0.05) + (0.95)\,(0.09) + (1.12)\,(0.04)$
$I_{88-89} = 0.8343 + 0.0532 + 0.0841 + 0.0416$
$I_{88-89} = 1.0132$

Calculation of Logarithmic Adjustment 1 Index
$I_{88-89} = (0.02)\,(0.82) + -(0.03)\,(0.05) + -(0.05)\,(0.09) + (0.12)\,(0.04) = 0.0126685$
antilog = 1.0127

Calculation of Adjustment 2 Index
25% of logarithmic adjustment 1 index, with an additional adjustment factor (0.978),
  based on table 2 in Berndt, Busch, and Frank (chap. 12 in this volume)
$I_{88-89} = (1.0127 \times 0.978) \times 0.25 + (1.0127) \times 0.75 = 1.00721$

Example 6: 1994–95

Calculation of Unadjusted Price Index
From table 1 in Rice and Miller (1998): Mental Illness

	1990 Expenditures ($ millions)	Shares (%)
All direct costs, mental illness	61,831	100.00
Mental health organizations	19,516	31.56
Short-stay hospitals	13,392	21.66
Office-based physicians	3,655	5.91
Other professional services	6,599	10.67
Nursing homes	16,478	26.65
Drugs	2,191	3.54

From the U.S. Department of Labor, Bureau of Labor Statistics

(continued)

Table 1A.7 (continued)

	1994	1995	ΔPs
PPI: general medical and surgical hospitals	106.0	109.9	$\Delta P_1 = 1.03679245$
PPI: psychiatric hospitals	107.9	110.4	$\Delta P_2 = 1.02316960$
PPI: offices and clinics of doctors of medicine, psychiatry	102.9	104.7	$\Delta P_3 = 1.01749271$
CPI: services by other professionals	141.3	143.9	$\Delta P_4 = 1.01840057$
PPI: antidepressants	186	193	$\Delta P_5 = 1.03540773$

	1990 Expenditures ($ millions)	Shares
All direct costs, mental illness	61,831	
Short-stay hospitals + nursing homes	29,870	$s_{H+N} = 0.48309101$
Mental health organizations	19,516	$s_{MH} = 0.31563455$
Office-based physicians	3,655	$s_P = 0.05911274$
Other professional services	6,599	$s_O = 0.10672640$
Drugs	2,191	$s_D = 0.03543530$

$I_{94-95} = (\Delta P_1)(s_{H+N}) + (\Delta P_2)(s_{MH}) + (\Delta P_3)(s_P) + (\Delta P_4)(s_O) + (\Delta P_5)(s_D)$
$I_{94-95} = (1.04)(0.48) + (1.02)(0.32) + (1.02)(0.06) + (1.02)(0.11) + (1.04)(0.04)$
$I_{94-95} = 0.5009 + 0.3229 + 0.0601 + 0.1087 + 0.0367$
$I_{94-95} = 1.0293$

Calculation of Arithmetic Adjustment 1 Index

	ΔPs	Adj. factor	Adjusted ΔPs
PPI: general medical and surgical hospitals	(1.0368)	(1.0000)	= 1.03679245
PPI: psychiatric hospitals	(1.0232)	(1.0000)	= 1.02316960
PPI: offices and clinics of doctors of medicine, psychiatry	(1.0175)	(1.0000)	= 1.01749271
CPI: services by other professionals	(1.0184)	(1.0000)	= 1.01840057
PPI: antidepressants	(1.0354)	(1.0000)	= 1.03540773

$I_{94-95} = (\Delta P_1)(s_{H+N}) + (\Delta P_2)(s_{MH}) + (\Delta P_3)(s_P) + (\Delta P_4)(s_O) + (\Delta P_5)(s_D)$
$I_{94-95} = (1.04)(0.48) + (1.02)(0.32) + (1.02)(0.06) + (1.02)(0.11) + (1.04)(0.04)$
$I_{94-95} = 0.5009 + 0.3229 + 0.0601 + 0.1087 + 0.0367$
$I_{94-95} = 1.0293$

Calculation of Logarithmic Adjustment 1 Index

$I_{94-95} = 0.0361(0.48) + 0.0229(0.32) + 0.0173(0.06) + 0.018(0.11) + 0.035(0.04)$
$I_{94-95} = 0.0289$
antilog = 1.0293

Calculation of Adjustment 2 Index
25% of logarithmic adjustment 1 index, with an additional adjustment factor (0.978), based on table 2 in Berndt, Busch, and Frank (chap. 12 in this volume)
$I_{94-95} = (1.0293 \times 0.978) \times 0.25 + (1.0293) \times 0.75 = 1.02371$

References

Aaron, Henry J., and William B. Schwartz. 1983. *The painful prescription: Rationing hospital care.* Washington, D.C.: Brookings Institution.

Averill, Richard F., Robert L. Mullin, Barbara A. Steinbeck, Norbert Goldfield, and Enes D. Elia. 1997. *Diagnosis related groups, definitions manual,* version 15.0. Washington, D.C.: 3M Health Information Systems.

Barzel, Yoram. 1969. Productivity and the price of medical services. *Journal of Political Economy* 77 (6): 1014–27.

Berndt, Ernst R., Iain M. Cockburn, and Zvi Griliches. 1996. Pharmaceutical innovations and market dynamics: Tracking effects on price indexes for antidepressant drugs. *Brookings Papers on Economic Activity, Microeconomics,* 133–99.

Cardenas, Elaine M. 1996. Revision of the CPI hospital services component. *Monthly Labor Review* 119 (12): 40–48.

Castles, Ian. 1997. Review of the OECD-Eurostat PPP Programme. Presented at the meeting on the Eurostat-OECD Purchasing Power Parity Programme, Chateau de la Muette, Paris, 5–6 November.

Catron, Brian, and Bonnie Murphy. 1996. Hospital price inflation: What does the new PPI tell us? *Monthly Labor Review* 120 (7): 24–31.

Commission of the European Communities, International Monetary Fund, Organization for Economic Cooperation and Development, United Nations, and World Bank. 1993. *System of National Accounts 1993.* Office for Official Publications of the European Communities Catalogue number CA-81-93-002-EN-C, International Monetary Fund Publication Stock no. SNA-EA, Organization for Economic Cooperation and Development OECD Code 30 94 01 1, United Nations publication Sales no. E.94.XVII.4, World Bank Stock number 31512.

Conley, R., and M. Conwell. 1970. *The cost of mental illness, 1968.* Statistical Note no. 30. Rockville, Md.: National Institute of Mental Health, Survey Reports Section.

Cooper, Barbara S., and Dorothy P. Rice. 1976. The economic cost of mental illness revisited. *Social Security Bulletin* 39 (2): 21–36.

Cruze, A. M., H. J. Hanwood, P. C. Kristiansen, J. J. Collins, and D.C. Jones. 1981. *Economic costs to society of alcohol and drug abuse and mental illness, 1977.* Research Triangle Park, N.C.: Research Triangle Institute.

Cutler, David M., Mark McClellan, Joseph P. Newhouse, and Dahlia Remler. 1998. Are medical prices declining? Evidence from heart attack treatments. *Quarterly Journal of Economics* 113 (4): 991–1024.

DuPont, Robert L., Dorothy P. Rice, Leonard S. Miller, Sarah S. Shiraki, Clyton R. Rowland, and Henrick J. Harwood. 1996. Economic costs of anxiety disorders. *Anxiety* 2:167–72.

Ellison, Sara Fisher, and Judith K. Hellerstein. 1999. The economics of antibiotics. In *Measuring the prices of medical treatments,* ed. Jack E. Triplett, 118–43. Washington, D.C.: Brookings Institution.

Executive Office of the President. Office of Management and Budget. 1987. *Standard industrial classification manual.* Springfield, Va.: National Technical Information Service.

Fein, Rashi. 1958. *Economics of mental illness.* Monograph Series number 2. New York: Basic.

Feldstein, Martin S. 1969. Discussion of Some problems in the measurement of productivity in the medical care industry, by M. W. Reder. In *Production and productivity in the service industries,* ed. Victor Fuchs. NBER Studies in Income and Wealth, vol. 34. New York: Columbia University Press.

Fisher, Franklin M., and Karl Shell. 1972. *The economic theory of price indices: Two essays on the effects of taste, quality, and technological change.* New York: Academic.

Frank, Richard G., Ernst R. Berndt, and Susan Busch. 1999. Price indexes for the treatment of depression. In *Measuring the prices of medical treatments,* ed. Jack E. Triplett, 72–102. Washington, D.C.: Brookings Institution.

Frank, Richard G., and Mark S. Kamlet. 1985. Direct costs and expenditures for mental health care in the United States in 1980. *Hospital and Community Psychiatry* 36 (2): 165–68.

Freeland, Mark S., George S. Chulis, Aaron P. Brown, David Skellan, Brenda T. Maple, Naphtale Singer, Jeffrey Lemieux, and Ross H. Arnett, III. 1991. Measuring hospital input price increases: The rebased hospital market basket. *Health Care Financing Review* 12 (3): 1–14.

Garber, Alan M., and Charles E. Phelps. 1992. Economic foundations of cost-effective analysis. NBER Working Paper no. 4164. Cambridge, Mass.: National Bureau of Economic Research, September.

Gilbert, Milton. 1961. Quality changes and index numbers. *Economic Development and Cultural Change* 9 (3): 287–94.

Gold, Marthe R., Joanna E. Siegel, Louise B. Russell, and Milton C. Weinstein, eds. 1996. *Cost-effectiveness in health and medicine.* New York: Oxford University Press.

Griliches, Zvi. 1992. Introduction. In *Output measurement in the service sectors,* ed. Zvi Griliches, 1–22. NBER Studies in Income and Wealth, vol. 56. Chicago: University of Chicago Press.

Grossman, Michael. 1972. *The demand for health: A theoretical and empirical investigation.* NBER Occasional Paper no. 119. New York: Columbia University Press.

Harwood, Henrick J., Diane M. Napolitano, Patricia L. Kristiansen, and James J. Collins. 1984. *Economic costs to society of alcohol and drug abuse and mental illness, 1980.* Research Triangle Park, N.C.: Research Triangle Institute.

Hodgson, Thomas A. 1997. Medical care expenditures for major diseases, 1995. Unpublished paper, National Center for Health Statistics, Centers for Disease Control and Prevention.

Hodgson, Thomas A., and Alan J. Cohen. 1998. Medical care expenditures for major diseases, 1995. Unpublished paper, National Center for Health Statistics, Centers for Disease Control and Prevention.

Hodgson, Thomas A., and Andrea N. Kopstein. 1984. Health care expenditures for major diseases in 1980. *Health Care Financing Review* 5 (4): 1–12.

Keeler, Theodore E. 1996. Comments on Pharmaceutical innovations and market dynamics: Tracking effects on price indexes for antidepressant drugs, by Ernst R. Berndt, Iain M. Cockburn, and Zvi Griliches. *Brookings Papers on Economic Activity, Microeconomics,* 189–99.

Landefeld, J. Steven, and Robert P. Parker. 1997. BEA's chain indexes, time series, and measures of long-term economic growth. *Survey of Current Business* 77 (5): 58–68.

Lazenby, Helen C., Katherine R. Levit, Daniel R. Waldo, Gerald S. Adler, Suzanne W. Letsch, and Cathy A. Cowan. 1992. National health accounts: Lessons from the U.S. experience. *Health Care Financing Review* 13 (4): 89–103.

Levine, Daniel, and Dianne Levine. 1975. *The cost of mental illness, 1971.* DHEW Publication no. (ADM) 76–265. Rockville, Md.: National Institute of Mental Health.

Levine, D., and S. Willner. 1976. *Cost of mental illness, 1974.* Statistical Note no. 125. Rockville, Md.: National Institute of Mental Health.

Levit, Katherine R., and Cathy A. Cowan. 1991. Business, households, and governments: Health care costs, 1990. *Health Care Financing Review* 13 (2): 83–93.

Levit, Katherine R., Helen C. Lazenby, Bradley R. Braden, Cathy A. Cowan, Patricia A. McDonnell, Lekha Sivarajan, Jean M. Stiller, Darleen K. Won, Carolyn S. Donham, Anna M. Long, and Madie W. Stewart. 1996. National health expenditures, 1995. *Health Care Financing Review* 18 (1): 175–214.

Levit, Katherine R., Helen C. Lazenby, Bradley R. Braden, Cathy A. Cowan, Arthur L. Sensenig, Patricia A. McDonnell, Jean M. Stiller, Darleen K. Won, Anne B. Martin, Lekha Sivarajan, Carolyn S. Donham, Anna M. Long, and Madie W. Stewart. 1997. National health expenditures, 1996. *Health Care Financing Review* 19 (1): 161–200.

Levy, Frank, Anne Beamish, Richard Murnane, and David Autor. 1999. Computerization and skills: Examples from a car dealership. Paper presented to the Brookings Workshop on Measuring the Output of Business Services, Washington, D.C., 14 May. Available at http://www.brookings.org/es/research/projects/productivity/workshops/19990514.htm.

Lum, Sherlene K. S., and Robert E. Yuskavage. 1997. Gross product by industry, 1947–96. *Survey of Current Business* 77 (11): 20–34.

Manton, Kenneth G., and James W. Vaupel. 1995. Survival after the age of 80 in the United States, Sweden, France, England, and Japan. *New England Journal of Medicine* 333 (18): 1232–35.

Mark, Tami, David McKusick, Edward King, Henrick Harwood, and Jim Genuardi. 1998. *National expenditures for mental health, alcohol and other drug abuse treatment, 1996.* DHHS Publication no. SMA 98–3255. Rockville, Md.: U.S. Department of Health and Human Services.

Mathers, Colin, Ruth Penm, Rob Carter, and Chris Stevenson. 1998. *Health system costs of diseases and injury in Australia 1993–94: An analysis of costs, service use and mortality for major disease and injury groups.* Canberra: Australian Institute of Health and Welfare.

McGinnis, J. Michael. 1996. Preface. In *Cost-effectiveness in health and medicine,* ed. Marthe R. Gold, Joanna E. Siegel, Louise B. Russell, and Milton C. Weinstein. New York: Oxford University Press.

McGreevey, William. 1996. NHA at the World Bank, past and prospect. Paper presented at the Workshop on National Health Accounts: Developing Internationally Comparable Data on Health Care Expenditure and Financing. World Bank, Washington, D.C., 15 November.

McKeown, Thomas. 1976. *The role of medicine: Dream, mirage, or nemesis?* London: Nuffield Provincial Hospitals Trust.

McKusick, David, Tami L. Mark, Edward King, Rick Harwood, Jeffrey A. Buck, Joan Dilonardo, and James S. Genuardi. 1998. Spending for mental health and substance abuse treatment, 1996. *Health Affairs* 17 (5): 147–57.

Ministère du Travail et des Affaires Sociales. 1996. *Comptes nationaux de la santé 1993–1994–1995.* Paris: Ministère du Travail et des Affaires Sociales, Service des Statistiques, des Etudes et des Systèmes d'Information.

Mokyr, Joel. 1997. Valuation of new goods under perfect and imperfect competition. In *The economics of new goods,* ed. T. F. Bresnahan and R. J. Gordon. NBER Studies in Income and Wealth, vol. 58. Chicago: University of Chicago Press.

Moore, Rachel, Yang Mao, Jun Zhang, and Kathy Clarke. 1997. *Economic burden of illness in Canada, 1993.* Catalogue no. H21-136/1993E. Ottawa: Minister of Public Works and Government Services.

Moulton, Brent R. 1996. Constant elasticity cost-of-living index in share-relative form. Unpublished paper, Bureau of Labor Statistics.

Murray, Christopher J. L., and Alan D. Lopez, eds. 1996. *Global burden of disease: A comprehensive assessment of mortality and disability from diseases, injuries, and risk factors in 1990 and projected to 2020.* 2 vols. Cambridge, Mass.: Harvard University Press.

Newhouse, Joseph P. 1989. Measuring medical prices and understanding their effects—The Baxter Prize address. *Journal of Health Administration Education* 7 (1): 19–26.

Organization for Economic Cooperation and Development (OECD). 1997. *Principles of health accounting for international data collections: Working party on social policy ad hoc meeting of experts in health statistics.* Paris: Organization for Economic Cooperation and Development.

Paringer, L., and A. Berk. 1977. *Cost of illness and disease, fiscal year 1975.* Report no. B1. Washington, D.C.: Georgetown University, Public Services Laboratory.

Parsons, P. Ellen, Richard Lichtenstein, S. E. Berki, Hillary A. Murt, James M. Lepkowski, Sharon A. Stehouwer, and J. Richard Landis. 1986. *Costs of illness: United States, 1980.* National Medical Care Utilization and Expenditure Survey, Survey C, Analytical Report no. 3, DHHS Publication no. 86–20403. Washington, D.C.: National Center for Health Statistics, Public Health Service, April.

Pauly, Mark. 1999. Medical care costs, benefits, and effects: Conceptual issues for measuring price changes. In *Measuring the prices of medical treatments,* ed. Jack E. Triplett. Washington, D.C.: Brookings Institution.

Pommier, Philippe. 1981. Social expenditure: Socialization of expenditure? The French experiment with satellite accounts. *Review of Income and Wealth* 27 (4): 373–86.

Reder, M. W. 1969. Some problems in the measurement of productivity in the medical care industry. In *Production and productivity in the service industries,* ed. Victor R. Fuchs. NBER Studies in Income and Wealth, vol. 34. New York: Columbia University Press.

Rice, Dorothy P. 1966. *Estimating the cost of illness.* Health Economic Series no. 6, DHEW Publication no. (PHS) 947–6. Rockville, Md.: U.S. Department of Health, Education, and Welfare.

Rice, Dorothy P., Barbara S. Cooper, and R. Gibson. 1982. Accounting for health: An international survey. In *Le santé fait ses comptes,* ed. Emile Levy. Paris: Economica.

Rice, Dorothy, Sarah Dunmeyer, Sander Kelman, and Leonard S. Miller. 1990. *The economic costs of alcohol and drug abuse and mental illness: 1985.* DHHS Publication no. (ADM) 90-1694, San Francisco: University of California Institute for Health and Aging, Alcohol, Drug Abuse; Rockville, Md.: Mental Health Administration.

Rice, Dorothy P., Thomas A. Hodgson, and Andrea N. Kopstein. 1985. The economic cost of illness: A replication and update. *Health Care Financing Review* 7 (1): 61–80.

Rice, Dorothy P., Sander Kelman, and Leonard S. Miller. 1991. Estimates of economic costs of alcohol and drug abuse and mental illness, 1985 and 1988. *Public Health Reports* 106, no. 3 (May–June): 280–92.

Rice, Dorothy P., and Leonard S. Miller. 1998. Health economics and cost implications of anxiety and other mental disorders in the United States. *British Journal of Psychiatry* 173 (34): 4–9.

Scitovsky, Anne A. 1964. An index of the cost of medical care—A proposed new approach. In *The economics of health and medical care,* ed. Solomon J. Axelrod, 128–42. Ann Arbor: Bureau of Public Health Economics, University of Michigan.

———. 1967. Changes in the costs of treatment of selected illnesses, 1951–65. *American Economic Review* 57 (5): 1182–95.

Shapiro, Matthew P., and David W. Wilcox. 1996. Mismeasurement in the consumer price index: An evaluation. In *NBER Macroeconomics Annual,* vol. 11, ed. Ben S. Bernanke and Julio J. Rotemberg, 93–142. Cambridge, Mass.: MIT Press.

Sherwood, Mark K. 1999. Output of the property and casualty insurance industry. *Canadian Journal of Economics* 32 (2): 518–46.

Teillet, Pierre. 1988. A concept of satellite account in the revised SNA. *Review of Income and Wealth* 34 (4): 411–39.

Triplett, Jack E. 1983. Concepts of quality in input and output price measures: A resolution of the user-value resource-cost debate. In *The U.S. national income and product accounts: Selected topics,* ed. Murray F. Foss, 269–311. NBER Studies in Income and Wealth, vol. 47. Chicago: University of Chicago Press.

———. 1999. Accounting for health care: Integrating price index and cost-effectiveness research. In *Measuring the prices of medical treatments,* ed. Jack E. Triplett, 220–50. Washington, D.C.: Brookings Institution.

Triplett, Jack E., and Ernst Berndt. 1999. New developments in measuring medical care. In *Measuring the prices of medical treatments,* ed. Jack E. Triplett, 1–33. Washington, D.C.: Brookings Institution.

U.K. Department of Health. 1994. *Register of cost-effectiveness studies.* London: Department of Health, Economics and Operational Research Division.

U.K. Department of Health. National Health Service. 1996. *Burdens of disease.* Catalog number 96CC0036. London: Department of Health.

U.S. Congress. Joint Economic Committee. 1961. *Government price statistics: Hearings before the Joint Economic Committee, Congress of the United States.* 87th Cong., 1st sess., pursuant to Section 5(a) of Public Law 304 (709th Cong.), pt. 2, 1–5 May.

U.S. Department of Commerce. Bureau of Economic Analysis. 1989. *Government transactions.* Methodology Paper Series MP-6. Washington, D.C.: U.S. Government Printing Office.

U.S. Department of Health and Human Services. 1989. *The international classification of diseases, 9th revision, clinical modification: ICD-9-CM,* 3d ed., vols. 1–3. Washington, D.C.: U.S. Department of Health and Human Services, Public Health Service, Health Care Financing Administration.

U.S. Department of Labor. Bureau of Labor Statistics. 1992. *Handbook of methods.* Bulletin 2285. Washington, D.C.: U.S. Government Printing Office.

———. 1996. Changing the hospital and related services component of the consumer price index. *CPI Detailed Report* (June): 7–8.

———. 1999. Consumer price indexes—All urban consumers (current series), available at http://146.142.4.24/cgi-bin/dsrv?cu. Producer price index revision—Current series, available at http://146.142.4.24/cgi-bin/dsrv?pc.

Vanoli, A. 1975. *Comment structurer le système statistique d'un domaine et l'articuler avec les autres: L'exemple de la santé.* Warsaw: International Statistical Institute.

———. 1986. Sur la structure générale du SCN à partir de l'expérience du système élargi de comptabilité nationale française. *Review of Income and Wealth,* ser. 32, no. 2 (June): 155–99.

Vaupel, James W. 1998. Demographic analysis of aging and longevity. *American Economic Review* 88 (2): 242–47.

Waldo, Daniel R., Sally T. Sonnefeld, David R. McKusick, and Ross H. Arnett, III. 1989. Health expenditures by age group, 1977 and 1987. *Health Care Financing Review* 10 (4): 111–20.

Weisbrod, Burton A. 1999. Measuring health care prices. In *Measuring the prices of medical treatments,* ed. Jack E. Triplett, 251–55. Washington, D.C.: Brookings Institution.

World Health Organization (WHO). 1977. *Manual of the international classification of diseases, injuries and causes of death, 9th revision.* Geneva: World Health Organization.

Comment   Zvi Griliches

This is a masterful though incomplete discussion of concepts and data. I think that the analogy of health services to car repairs is very apt and illuminating, in more ways than Jack may be aware. Thinking about both tells one that the problem may not be as much in the measurement of health as it is a more general problem of concepts and uses of national income accounts and the interpretation that we give to such measurements.

First, I want to stress the parallels between health and car repair. In both cases more "output" does not necessarily mean more welfare. A flu epidemic or an ice storm both can create more health industry "output" and car repairs respectively without signaling an increase in welfare (relative to an earlier period), only an increase in resource use to cope with an adverse environmental shock.

Nor would we be doing much better in measuring health output if we were doing as well there as in the "easier understood" and "easier measured" car repair industry, as is implied by Jack. Look, for example, at the reported (by BLS) productivity growth numbers for the "easier" to measure industry, reported in table 1C.1.

Over the twenty year period 1973–93 there was no growth in car-repair productivity, but an actual and sizable decline, in spite of better diagnostic tools and increased specialization into muffler shops and so forth. Perhaps quality change in automobiles has reduced the need for repairs but left us with a larger standby industry?

The same facts stand out from an unpublished set of BLS multifactor productivity computations, shown in table 1C.2. Frankly, I do not believe the numbers for either industry. What they show is how far we have still to go in output measurement and that if we reach the great state of car-repair measurement, we should not rest there. We are still far from our destination. I agree with Jack that the main difference between these industries is in who is paying for the service (in other words, price = marginal utility = marginal cost) and in the relative ease of the junking decision.

The late Zvi Griliches was the Paul M. Warburg Professor of Economics at Harvard University and director of the Productivity and Technical Change Program at the National Bureau of Economic Research. He was past president of the Econometric Society and of the American Economic Association, and a member of the National Academy of Sciences.

Table 1C.1   **Productivity Growth in Auto Repair Shops**

Period	Output per Hour
1973–79	−0.7
1979–90	+0.2
1990–93	−1.0
1973–93	−0.3
1993–94	+7.6!!

Source: U.S. Department of Labor, Bureau of Labor Statistics, document no. 96-15.

Table 1C.2   **Estimated Multifactor Productivity Trends**

Industry	1963–77	1977–93
(75) Auto repair, services, and garages	−1.1	−1.5
(80) Health services	−1.2	−1.2

Source: Unpublished BLS computations.

I have a few more general comments suggested by Jack's exposition. I am not sure that there is that much contrast in the measurement of "health" as against the measurement of "health intervention." To measure H/m well, we may need to specify and estimate the whole H function. We may not have the luxury of observing pure intervention experiments. Moreover, while I also agree that the most promising empirical advances are likely to be made in the disease-by-disease approach, it is not obviously correct. There may be cross-effects between diseases and total output may not be just the sum of the partials. Moreover, this is not an obviously constant-returns-to-scale industry.

Finally, Jack distinguishes between national accounts, national health accounts, and cost-of-disease accounts. I would have liked to articulate an alternative view of health status and health transitions accounts, but time is too short for that. What I have in mind is a measurement of the functioning of individuals, by different levels of impairment, and the probabilities of their transitioning in and out of these various states. Here diseases explain, ex post, why one is in some state, and medical and other expenditures affect the probabilities of exiting the less desirable states. Quality improvements would be reflected in improved probabilities for a given level of expenditures, and so on. The data required for this are much more demanding, but some such more general-equilibrium view of life, health, and death as a series of random walks through the uncertainties of disease, accidents, and medical interventions may be required to make more complete sense of what is happening to us and how to measure these outcomes more appropriately.

Theoretical Foundations of Medical Cost-Effectiveness Analysis
Implications for the Measurement of Benefits and Costs of Medical Interventions

David Meltzer

2.1 Introduction

Increasingly, both private and public health care institutions in the United States are looking toward medical cost-effectiveness analysis as they consider complex resource allocation decisions concerning medical technologies. Though many of its key ideas originated in the United States, medical cost-effectiveness analysis has, until recently, been more widely accepted and used in a number of European countries, as well as in Canada, Australia, and New Zealand. These countries share with the United States a significant concern about the role of new technology in increasing health care costs, but also have national health systems that are well positioned with strong incentives to engage in formal technology assessment. The recent increase in interest in medical cost-effectiveness analysis in the United States differs from the experience with cost-effectiveness analysis in other countries in that the private sector has played a much larger role in the United States. In particular, the demand for cost-effectiveness analyses in the United States appears to have been significantly influenced by the desire of pharmaceutical companies to collect evidence concerning the cost-effectiveness of their products in order to encourage managed care organizations to include their products on formularies. This is evident in both the recent establishment of the Association for Pharmaceutical Outcomes Research with the heavy involvement of the pharmaceutical industry and the tremendous increase in interest in pharmacoeconomics in the

David Meltzer is assistant professor in the Section of General Internal Medicine, Department of Economics, and Harris Graduate School of Public Policy at the University of Chicago and a faculty research fellow of the National Bureau of Economic Research.

industry. This demand is also evident in the recent upsurge in interest in attempting to inform and even standardize methods for cost-effectiveness analysis in order to establish comparability among studies and minimize the chance for investigators with vested interests to use areas of methodological ambiguity to obtain desired results. This is most prominently evidenced by the report of the Panel on Cost-Effectiveness in Health and Medicine (Gold et al. 1996), but it is also shown by the work of Sloan (1995), the Task Force on Principles for Economic Analysis of Health Care Technology (1996), and others.

While attempting to enhance the comparability and validity of medical cost-effectiveness analyses, these recent efforts have also heightened the expectations for cost-effectiveness analyses and the scrutiny with which its methods are examined. This is perhaps particularly true of the report of the Panel on Cost-Effectiveness in Health and Medicine, which explicitly advocates that cost-effectiveness analyses adopt a "societal" perspective and asserts that the methods of cost-effectiveness analysis that adopt such a perspective have their roots in classical welfare economics.

This paper summarizes some recent and ongoing work in which I and others have been engaged that attempts to address the connection between the methods used in the most common form of medical cost-effectiveness analysis—that which utilizes quality-adjusted life years (QALYs)—and principles of welfare economics. While this paper is not intended to be a systematic review of this important topic, it aims to address two key issues concerning the connection between welfare economics and cost-effectiveness analysis: the measurement of benefits and the measurement of costs, especially future costs. In both of these cases, the application of basic principles of economic analysis provides unique insights into areas of ongoing controversy that are not apparent from other approaches. For example, by relying upon the economic principle of revealed preference, it is possible to learn about the validity of QALYs as a measure of patient preferences. Similarly, by defining a lifetime utility maximization model and deriving conditions for constrained maximization, formal models of utility maximization provide a framework for resolving methodological issues about the inclusion of costs in medical cost-effectiveness analysis. Though formal economic analysis could also be used to address other methodological issues in medical cost-effectiveness analysis, such as techniques for sensitivity analysis (Meltzer 1998) and challenges in incorporating distributional concerns into cost-effectiveness analyses (Wagstaff 1991), these will not be discussed in order to focus attention on the issues of the measurement of benefits and costs.

The paper proceeds as follows. Section 2.2 reviews the historical origins and development of cost-effectiveness analysis based on QALYs. Section 2.3 addresses the use of revealed preference measures to assess to what extent QALYs reflect patient preferences. Section 2.4 addresses the inclusion of future costs. Section 2.5 concludes.

2.2   Historical Origins and Development of Cost-Effectiveness Analysis Using QALYs

Though medical cost-effectiveness analysis using QALYs appears to have originated with the work of Fanshel and Bush (1970), its growth seems to have begun with the work of Milton Weinstein and William Stason (1976) on the cost-effectiveness of the treatment of hypertension. Published both as a substantial and detailed book (Weinstein and Stason 1976) and in abbreviated form as an article in the *New England Journal of Medicine* (Stason and Weinstein 1977), their work first brought into prominence the idea that the benefits of medical intervention be quantified in terms of life years weighted by quality adjustment factors between zero and one, in which zero is equivalent to death, and one to perfect health. Unlike analyses of the costs of achieving some fixed objective (often called cost-minimization analysis), this approach aimed to permit comparison of the value of expending resources to achieve alternative health-related objectives. The QALY framework was thus designed to serve as a general one under which the costs and benefits of interventions aimed at vastly different diseases might be compared. In the context of an increasing acceptance within medicine of the idea that health care should attempt not only to minimize mortality but also to minimize morbidity, the concept of quality adjustment was key to the attraction to the concept of quality-adjusted life expectancy.

Weinstein and Stason in turn refer to earlier work by Weinstein and Zeckhauser (1972) as providing the link between cost-effectiveness and welfare maximization. In essence, the argument is that the condition implied by utility maximization (that marginal utility be proportional to marginal cost for all goods purchased) implies that the ratio of marginal cost to marginal utility should be a constant. Interventions for which the ratio of costs to benefits exceeds that constant should be avoided, whereas interventions for which that ratio is smaller should be adopted. Coming out of utility maximization, decisions guided by these cost-effectiveness or cost-utility ratios are intended to direct resources toward efficient allocations generated by utility maximization under classical conditions. Findings such as these motivate the connection of cost-effectiveness analyses performed from a societal perspective to the realization of efficient allocations based on criteria of welfare economics (Weinstein 1995; Gold et al. 1996).

The methods of cost-effectiveness analysis and to what extent, if any, they provide a valid approach to resource allocation have long been subject to debate. Some of this debate relates to dissatisfaction with utilitarian models as a basis for resource allocation (e.g., La Puma and Lawlor 1990). A much larger portion of this literature, however, accepts these utilitarian underpinnings and asks whether the methods of cost-effectiveness analysis are up to the task of identifying utility-maximizing choices. While by no means intending to dismiss the concerns of this former group, the method-ological critiques of cost-effectiveness described later in this chapter fall into the latter group. As such, they may be viewed by some people as trying to fix a fundamentally flawed approach. This may be a valid criticism, but the importance of the issues addressed by cost-effectiveness analysis, its influence, and the lack of strong competitors to replace it suggest the need to probe into these issues even in the presence of concerns about whether the approach could ever be fully adequate to its task.

2.3   Measurement of Benefits

The attractiveness of quality-adjusted life years stems from its claim to be able to act as a global measure of preference for health-related deci-sions, allowing comparison of interventions that may have effects on length of life or quality of life for any intervention, regardless of the disease to which it is applied. This is essential if comparisons are to be made across interventions affecting disparate diseases, as is required for resource allo-cation decisions in practice.

However, the key concern about QALYs is their validity as measures of patient preferences. It is not an obvious proposition that people will prefer whichever lifestyle option that, when weighted between zero and one, will result in the highest number of quality-adjusted life years. Issues of risk aversion and the distribution of QALYs in a population are clearly crucial issues in this regard. Beyond this, however, there are more basic questions about the validity of QALYs even in the context of certainty. Are people truly indifferent between living two years with a quality of life weight equal to 0.5 or one year with a quality of life weight equal to 1? When quality weights are derived from linear analog ("Please rate health state X be-tween zero and one where zero is death and one is perfect health") or ratio scalings ("How much better/worse is health state X than health state Y?"), there is no reason to suspect that this restriction should hold. When qual-ity weights are derived from either standard gamble or time trade-off meth-ods, there is at least some theoretical structure that suggests that people who prefer the options described in the questions used to elicit quality of life weights should prefer options that maximize quality-adjusted life expec-tancy. For example, in the time trade-off method, people are asked whether they would prefer a longer life in less-than-perfect health or a shorter life in perfect health. Quality weights derived by this method could be consis-tent with utility maximization if utility is the product of quality factor Q

and time t and there is no discounting (i.e., $U = Q \times t$). In the standard gamble method, people are asked to choose between continuation of a less-than-perfect health state or a gamble in which they are returned to full health with probability p and die immediately with probability $(1 - p)$. If people maximize expected utility and there is no discounting, resource allocations based on quality of life estimates derived from this method may be consistent with utility maximization.

Under these conditions, the validity of QALYs as an outcome measure comes down to an empirical question concerning whether the assumptions required for the logical consistency of QALYs are an adequate reflection of people's preferences. The problem in determining this, however, has been the absence of a "gold standard" by which to measure people's actual preferences. In the absence of such a "gold standard," the most common approach in the psychometric literature has been to elicit quality of life weights using multiple methods such as linear analog, standard gamble, and time trade-off, and then determine to what extent these measures are correlated (e.g., Blumenschein and Johannesson 1998). Studies of this type have often (though not universally) found substantial correlation among these measures. Nevertheless, this may suggest more that these measures are quantifying the same or similar concepts than representing patients' actual preferences.

An alternative approach to assess the validity of QALYs, which I am using in some ongoing work, relies instead on the idea of revealed preference—that one can learn about people's preferences based on the choices they are observed to make. Though the term "revealed preference" is drawn from economics, the concept of revealed preference is indeed a—if not the—central tenet of the practice of medicine: that the best therapy for a patient is identified by informing the patient about her options and allowing her to choose. This naturally suggests an alternative approach to determine whether QALYs reflect patient preferences—to test whether the gain in QALYs from a medical intervention predicts whether patients choose that intervention.

We have been examining this question in the context of patient preferences for intensive therapy for type I diabetes mellitus (Meltzer, Polonsky, and Tobian 1998). From the Diabetes Control and Complications Trial (DCCT; DCCT Research Group 1993), it is now known that the frequent glucose checks and increased insulin dosing required under intensive therapy for diabetes can help prevent the early changes that may eventually result in the major complications of diabetes such as blindness, kidney failure, and neuropathy that can often result in amputation. On the other hand, the frequent glucose checks and insulin doses required for intensive therapy may be burdensome for many individuals and result in more frequent hypoglycemic symptoms. The decision to follow intensive therapy can be viewed as a trade-off involving quality and length of life now and quality and length of life in the future; thus, the choice between intensive and conventional therapy is a natural application of QALYs. Indeed, the DCCT investigators developed and published a cost-effectiveness analysis of intensive therapy based on the DCCT data. This suggests that intensive therapy is highly cost-effective, with an average cost of \$19,987/QALY (DCCT Research Group 1996). It is perhaps revealing about the ability of QALYs to reflect patient preferences that, despite this finding, many patients who are aware of the DCCT results, and even many who bear no out-of-pocket expenses for their care, have not elected to pursue intensive therapy.

In our work, my colleagues and I have surveyed approximately 130 patients with diabetes on either intensive or conventional therapy who are similar to the population examined in the DCCT to ask them all the questions necessary to calculate their quality-adjusted life expectancy with and without intensive therapy. The predicted gain in quality-adjusted life expectancy from intensive therapy is then compared to their actual choice of therapy to see if those people with the greatest gain in QALYs from intensive therapy are in fact those who choose intensive therapy. Because factors other than patient preferences, such as cost and the preferences of physicians, may also affect choice, we have also collected information on these factors, although our initial analyses do not suggest any substantial role for these factors in the choice of therapy in our study population.

While we have not yet completed our calculation of the gain in QALYs resulting from intensive or conventional treatment for each patient, preliminary analyses using logistic regression demonstrate that the elements used to calculate QALYs do predict choice. Specifically, we find that patients are more likely to report themselves as having chosen intensive therapy when they report the beliefs that (1) quality of life would be relatively lower with complications of diabetes, (2) quality of life is little affected by the demands of intensive therapy, (3) intensive therapy will reduce the likelihood of complications, and (4) the future is more important than the present (a positive rate of time preference). Combining these elements in a logistic regression, it is possible to plot a receiver operating characteristic (ROC) curve (figure 2.1), which has what to many may seem a surprisingly high area under the curve (0.84). This seems to suggest that the gain in QALYs has a substantial ability to predict a patient's reported choice of therapy. For example, an appropriately chosen cutoff for this regression would correctly classify about 80 percent of patients as preferring intensive or conventional therapy. This may surprise many in the economics community who have tended to view QALYs as having little connection to the actual preferences of patients, and who strongly preferred willingness-to-pay approaches. The ability of the predicted gain in QALYs based on the decision model (as opposed to the rather less restrictive logistic regression

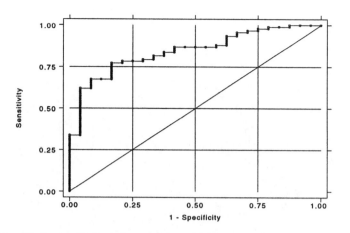

Fig. 2.1   ROC curve for logistic regression of QALY elements on reported therapy
Note: Area under ROC curve = 0.8442.

form) to predict choice may be somewhat less than this, but need not necessarily be.

Putting aside these issues of functional form, an important argument favoring the critics of the QALY approach is the possibility that any correspondence between choices and a gain in QALYs may reflect attempts of respondents to minimize cognitive dissonance. Cognitive dissonance is the idea that individuals experience an aversive state whenever their beliefs are inconsistent with their actions and may respond to minimize this discordance by changing either their actions or their beliefs (Festinger 1957). One piece of evidence supporting the potential importance of cognitive dissonance in determining how people respond to the questions used to calculate quality-adjusted life expectancy is a paper by Krumins, Fihn, and Kent (1988) that reports a very strong correspondence between patients' predicted gains in quality-adjusted life expectancy from surgery for benign prostatic hypertrophy and the incidence of patients' selecting surgery. The irreversible nature of prostate surgery is probably particularly likely to generate responses designed to minimize cognitive dissonance. Intensive therapy may be somewhat less affected by cognitive dissonance than prostate surgery. The reversible nature of the decision to follow intensive therapy presumably places an upper bound on the degree of cognitive dissonance, because people for whom that dissonance was sufficiently large would presumably alter their decision. Nevertheless, we find in our study that about one-third of patients who report themselves as following intensive therapy are actually on conventional therapy according to the strict definition of the DCCT, suggesting that patients may hold a belief that intensive therapy is the right thing to do and therefore report following

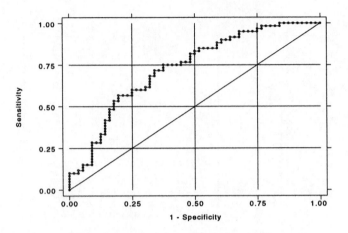

Fig. 2.2   ROC curve for logistic regression of QALY elements on actual therapy
Note: Area under ROC curve = 0.7318.

intensive therapy even when their therapy is not fully intensive. Interestingly, the area under the ROC curve for the regression of patients' answers to the QALY questions on actual choice of intensive therapy according to the DCCT definition is only 0.73 (fig. 2.2). This corresponds, for instance, to correctly classifying only two-thirds of patients as preferring intensive or conventional therapy. Thus the relationship between the psychometrically measured preferences used to calculate QALYs and stated therapeutic choices may be partially inflated by attempts to minimize cognitive dissonance. Validation of QALYs that would not be contaminated by cognitive dissonance would presumably require elicitation of preferences in a prospective setting before patients had even considered the choice they might face.

Given the diminution of the predictive power of QALYs for actual as opposed to reported therapeutic choice, it seems likely that a prospective analysis of the validity of QALYs that would presumably not be affected by attempts to minimize cognitive dissonance would suggest that QALYs are far less able to predict choice than is desirable. However, this has not yet been demonstrated, and even if it were shown to be the case, the revealed preference approach suggests that QALY measures might in time be improved by seeking methods to develop QALY measures that better predict choices. Thus, rigorous application of the principle of revealed preference offers the opportunity both to assess the validity of QALYs and potentially to improve their validity. Moreover, the principle of revealed preference could be used to compare the preference measures based on QALYs to the preference measure that most economists have favored: willingness to pay (Pauly 1995). If the prior beliefs of most economists are correct, the willingness-to-pay measure should outperform QALYs in predicting choice. Though willingness to pay has been shown to predict choice in some cases (Brookshire, Coursey, and Schulze 1987), many results of willingness-to-pay studies are clearly incompatible with observed choices (e.g., Fisher, Chestnut, and Violette 1989). A healthy competition between willingness-to-pay measures and QALY measures of health outcomes to predict behavior is likely to advance the quality of both measures. In the meantime, prudent investigators must be cautious in interpreting the results of any cost-effectiveness study that depends on the accurate measurement of the value of improvements in outcomes using any unitary scale of outcomes, whether QALYs or willingness to pay.

2.4 Measurement of Future Costs

Formal economic models of utility maximization also provide a valuable framework for considering the measurement of costs in medical cost-effectiveness analysis. Though it is not controversial, justification for the insistence of cost-effectiveness analysts on the measurement of marginal as opposed to average costs, for instance, comes directly out of the marginal conditions for utility maximization. Similar reasoning about marginal changes in expenditures can be applied to address the question of when marginal adjustments in other medical expenditures that take place when a medical intervention is undertaken need to be considered in a cost-effectiveness analysis (Meltzer 1997).

Unlike the question of whether to calculate average or marginal cost-effectiveness ratios, the question of whether to include future costs for "unrelated" illnesses and future nonmedical costs has been highly controversial. Nevertheless, it is equally amenable to analysis in a utility maximization model. Indeed, it is likely that one reason that the controversy about future costs has persisted so long is that the question has been subject to little formal analysis. For instance, while analysts have consistently argued the need to include future costs for related illnesses, analysts have come to dramatically divergent conclusions about whether future unrelated and future nonmedical costs should be included. For example, early work in cost-effectiveness analysis by Weinstein (1980) supported the inclusion of future costs for unrelated illnesses, arguing that "the cost of treating disease that would not otherwise have arisen must be considered" (p. 240). Though a few studies, such as the Office of Technology Assessment evaluation of influenza vaccination (U.S. Congress 1981), did at least consider this approach, the vast majority of studies have not included future costs for unrelated illnesses. Typical in justifying this approach is the argument of Louise Russell (1986) in "Is Prevention Better Than Cure?" where she argues, "Added years of life involve added expenditures for food, clothes, and housing as well as medical care. None of these is relevant for deciding whether the program is a good investment" (p. 36). Interestingly, Weinstein (1986) concurs about the exclusion of future nonmedical costs, but does so on the grounds that "the explicitly constrained resource is health care cost, and other costs are the price we all willingly pay to live" (p. 196). Thus there is a sense from the literature that it is reasonable to count certain costs while excluding others, though researchers disagree on which costs should fall into the two categories.

The persistence of the controversy concerning the measurement of future costs probably is related to the lack of formal analysis of the issue. However, two papers recently published in the *Journal of Health Economics,* one by Alan Garber and Charles Phelps (1997) and another by myself (Meltzer 1997), have applied formal economic analysis to this question. Unfortunately, the papers come to somewhat different conclusions. The Garber and Phelps paper concludes that under a rather restrictive set of assumptions, a set of rankings that excludes future costs will be the same as a set of rankings that includes future costs. My paper uses a more general model to show that, in the general case, a cost-effectiveness analysis should include all future costs, whether medical or nonmedical. Moreover, the set of restrictions under which the rankings would be preserved when future unrelated and nonmedical costs are excluded is shown to be far more restrictive than is recognized in the paper by Garber and Phelps. The restrictions turn out to make cost-effectiveness analyses that exclude future costs incompatible with important goals of cost-effectiveness analysis, such as comparing interventions at different ages and comparing interventions that have different effects on length of life and quality of life. Thus, the clear theoretical implication from a model of lifetime utility maximization is that cost-effectiveness analyses should include all future costs, whether medical or nonmedical. A corollary to this is that resource allocation decisions for medical spending cannot be made efficiently in isolation from the nonmedical cost implications of those decisions, as is implicit in the approach advocated by Weinstein (1986) that views health care spending as coming from a "health care budget."

A second critical result that comes out of the analysis in the Meltzer (1997) paper is that analyses that fail to include future costs will be biased in favor of interventions that extend life over interventions that improve the quality of life, especially among the elderly. These effects of future costs are most precisely described in the context of lifetime utility maximization models, such as those described in Meltzer (1997). However, the essence of the effects of including future costs in medical cost-effectiveness analysis can be described by breaking total costs into the sum of current costs and future costs and then assuming that future net resource use is equal to a constant amount C per life year multiplied by the number of life years saved (ΔLE). In that case, the cost-effectiveness ratio (cost per QALY) can be written

$$CE = \frac{\Delta cost}{\Delta QALY}$$

$$= \frac{\Delta present\ cost}{\Delta QALY} + \frac{\Delta future\ cost}{\Delta QALY}$$

$$= \frac{\Delta present\ cost}{\Delta QALY} + C \times \frac{\Delta LE}{\Delta QALY}.$$

The first term in this equation describes the cost-effectiveness ratio that only includes current costs. The second term in the equation describes the future costs that have traditionally been omitted from cost-effectiveness analyses. The equation implies that these costs will be largest when future costs per year of life lived (C) are large and when the ratio of the change in life expectancy to the change in quality-adjusted life expectancy is large.

Meltzer (1997) develops some rough but useful estimates of C based on population average data for consumption plus medical expenditures plus earnings by age the United States, suggesting that C varies from about $-\$10,000$ at age twenty to about $+\$20,000$ at age seventy and above. These numbers go gradually from negative to positive because young people on average produce more than they consume over their lifetime, whereas people who are older and have already passed through their working years on average consume more than they produce after that age. Table 2.1, reproduced from Meltzer (1997), uses these estimates and the approximation described above, based on the ratio of effects on length of life and quality of life, to estimate the effects of including future costs on the cost-effectiveness of a number of common medical interventions. The interventions are listed in the table in order of diminishing cost-effectiveness based on traditional estimates that exclude future costs for unrelated and nonmedical expenditures. The last column then reports the cost-effectiveness ratio that includes these future costs. The results clearly show that the relative rankings of interventions can change—rising or falling based on the effects on length of life and quality of life and on the age of the patient at the time of the intervention, which can imply positive or negative annual costs. Many of the changes in rankings appear at the top of the table and may be considered substantively important by some analysts, though perhaps not by others because even the ratios that include future costs suggest that the interventions remain relatively cost-effective by most standards (i.e., $<\$50,000 - \$100,000$/QALY; Goldman et al. 1991).

In contrast, some of the interventions at the bottom of the table imply larger changes that could alter whether an intervention is considered cost-effective. For example, the estimates that exclude future costs suggest that among sixty-year-old men, the treatment of hypertension and adjuvant chemotherapy for Duke's C colon cancer are both cost-effective compared to dialysis for end-stage renal disease that lies somewhat above the range

Table 2.1   Effect of Future "Unrelated" Costs on the Cost per Quality-Adjusted Life Year

Intervention	Change in Life Expectancy (LE)	Change in Quality-Adjusted Life Expectancy (QALE)	Change in LE/QALE	Annual Future Cost (C)	Bias Due to Future Cost	Reported Cost/QALY	Actual Cost/QALY
Adjuvant chemotherapy for Duke's C colon cancer age 55 (Smith et al. 1993)	2.4 yr	0.4 yr	6.00	3,000	18,000	16,700	34,700
Treatment of severe hypertension men age 40[a] (Stason and Weinstein 1977)	4 yr	3.9 yr	1.03	−5,000	−5,200	18,000	12,800
Adjuvant chemotherapy for node-negative breast cancer age 45 (Hillner and Smith 1991)	11 mo	5.1 mo	2.16	−4,000	−8,700	18,000	9,300
Adjuvant chemotherapy for node-negative breast cancer age 60 (Hillner and Smith 1991)	7.7 mo	4.0 mo	1.93	8,000	15,400	21,000	36,400
Treatment of severe hypertension, men age 50[a] (Stason and Weinstein 1977)	2.6 yr	2.5 yr	1.04	0	0	25,000	25,000
Coronary artery bypass 3-vessel disease, mild angina age 55 (Wong et al. 1990)	0.6 yr	0.7 yr	0.86	3,000	2,600	31,000	33,600
Coronary artery bypass 3-vessel disease, severe angina age 55 (Wong et al. 1990)	1.4 yr	1.4 yr	1.00	3,000	3,300	45,000	48,300

Adjuvant chemotherapy for node-negative breast cancer age 75 (Desch et al. 1993)	2.9 mo	1.8 mo	1.61	20,000	32,200	54,000	86,200
Hormone replacement therapy ages 55–65 (Tosteson and Weinstein 1991)	0.0458 yr	0.0387 yr	1.18	8,000	9,400	54,200	63,600
Treatment of severe hypertension, men age 60[a] (Stason and Weinstein 1977)	1.5 yr	1.4 yr	1.07	8,000	8,500	60,000	68,500
Adjuvant chemotherapy for Duke's C colon cancer age 60 (estimated based on Smith et al. 1993)[b]	1.8 yr	0.1 yr	18.00	8,000	144,000	67,000	211,000
Hemodialysis for end-stage renal disease (ESRD) men aged 30 (estimated based on Garner and Dardis 1987 and Hornberger, Redelmeier, and Peterson 1992)[c]	—	—	1.50	0	0	117,000	117,000
Hemodialysis for ESRD men aged 60 (estimated based on Garner and Dardis 1987 and Hornberger, Redelmeier, and Peterson 1992)[c]	—	—	1.50	8,000	12,000	117,000	129,000

Note: Costs converted to 1993 dollars using the medical CPI (U.S. Department of Labor 1994).

[a]Stason and Weinstein already include future unrelated medical costs, so the additional future costs here refer only to consumption net of earnings.

[b]Estimates made for sixty-year-old assuming life expectancy of sixteen years at age sixty as opposed to twenty years at age fifty-five used to calculate the cost-effectiveness at age fifty-five.

[c]Cost-effectiveness estimates based on Garner and Dardis (1987) using quality of life estimates from Hornberger, Redelmeier, and Peterson (1992).

that people often cite as cost-effective. In contrast, when future costs are included, the cost-effectiveness of adjuvant chemotherapy deteriorates markedly, rising to over $200,000/QALY. This large change in the cost-effectiveness ratio occurs because chemotherapy has large effects on length of life compared to quality of life. This illustrates the quantitative significance of the potential for excluding future costs to bias analyses to favor interventions that extend life over those that improve the quality of life.

Although these estimates of the effects of including future costs are based on the approximations described above, which may be inaccurate for a variety of reasons, other work that I have done with Magnus Johannesson and Richard O'Conor on the cost-effectiveness of treatment for hypertension suggests that the estimates based on this approximation correspond fairly well to estimates that directly incorporate future costs into the cost-effectiveness analysis (Johannesson, Meltzer, and O'Conor 1997). Other work I am involved in that directly incorporates future costs into a cost-effectiveness analysis of hip replacement among the elderly—which provides its benefit by improving quality of life—reinforces the finding that excluding future costs favors interventions that extend life over those that improve the quality of life (Meltzer et al. 1998). A contrasting example to the case of hip replacement is that of prostate cancer treatment, which may not offer any advantage in life expectancy—no less quality-adjusted life expectancy—because of the potentially substantial negative effects of treatment on quality of life. However, even if treatment does offer an advantage in life expectancy and quality-adjusted life expectancy, it is likely to have a small effect on quality-adjusted life expectancy compared to life expectancy. Indeed, the most optimistic cases considered by Fleming et al. (1993) concerning the value of radical prostatectomy for moderately differentiated prostate cancer in sixty-five-year-old men suggest an average gain in QALYs of 0.2 QALY compared to average gain in life expectancy of 0.7 life year. This suggests a ratio of $\Delta LE/\Delta QALY$ of 3.5, which, with a future cost C of $16,000 per year at age sixty-five, implies a cost-effectiveness ratio of $56,000 per year even if treatment of prostate cancer had no direct costs. Thus prostate cancer may be an excellent example of an intervention where the potential for negative effects on quality of life has important implications for cost-effectiveness.

2.5 Conclusion

This review has focused on two methodological areas in cost-effectiveness analysis—the validity of the measurement of benefits as quality-adjusted life years and the appropriate treatment of future costs—in which reliance on economic theory can provide valuable methodological insights. On the benefits side, the concept of revealed preference provides evidence consistent with the hypothesis that patients value gains in

QALYs, though the results may also be consistent with cognitive dissonance. Ultimately, the results suggest the need for further work using revealed preference to evaluate and improve quality of life measures, whether based on QALYs or willingness-to-pay measures, and suggest the need for caution in the interim whenever a study relies on such measures. On the cost side, models of lifetime utility maximization point out the need to include all future medical and nonmedical costs and also point out the bias in favor of interventions that extend life over the improvement in quality of life that often occurs when such future costs are excluded.

An important interaction between these two results relates to the dependence of the future-cost term on the ratio of changes in life expectancy to changes in quality-adjusted life expectancy. The presence of the change in QALYs in the denominator of this ratio implies a high degree of sensitivity of cost-effectiveness estimates to quality of life assessment. Thus the problems in accurately measuring quality of life can have immense effects on cost-effectiveness, especially once future costs are considered.

Though the application of insights from economic theory to the measurement of benefits and costs in medical cost-effectiveness analysis is important, there are other controversial issues in which economic theory may provide valuable insights into the methods needed to improve cost-effectiveness analysis as well. These include methods for sensitivity analysis based on utility maximization (Meltzer 1998) and techniques to address distributional concerns (Wagstaff 1991). Though neither question is provided an unambiguous response by the application of utility maximization, the discussion generated by such models provides a key framework for understanding these problems. If the influence of cost-effectiveness analysis is to continue to increase as it appears to be doing currently, and if it is to do more good than harm, it is crucial that its methods continue to undergo rigorous scrutiny.

References

Blumenschein, Karen, and Magnus Johannesson. 1998. Relationship between quality of life instruments, health state utilities and willingness to pay in patients with asthma. *Annals of Allergy, Asthma, and Immunology* 80:189–94.

Brookshire, David S., Don L. Coursey, and William D. Schulze. 1987. The external validity of experimental economics techniques: Analysis of demand behavior. *Economic Inquiry* 25 (2): 239–50.

Desch, Christopher, Bruce Hillner, Thomas Smith, and Sheldon Retchin. 1993. Should the elderly receive chemotherapy for node-negative breast cancer? A cost-effectiveness analysis examining total and active life-expectancy outcomes. *Journal of Clinical Oncology* 11 (4): 777–82.

Diabetes Control and Complications Trial Research Group. 1993. The effect of intensive treatment of diabetes on the development and progression of long-term complications in insulin-dependent diabetes mellitus. *New England Journal of Medicine* 329 (14): 977–86.

———. 1996. Lifetime benefits and costs of intensive therapy as practiced in the Diabetes Control and Complications Trial. *Journal of the American Medical Association* 276 (17): 1409–15.

Fanshel, Sol, and James W. Bush. 1970. A health-status index and its applications to health services outcomes. *Operations Research* 18 (6): 1021–66.

Festinger, Leon. 1957. *A theory of cognitive dissonance.* Stanford, Calif.: Stanford University Press.

Fisher, Anne, Lauraine Chestnut, and Daniel Violette. 1989. The value of reducing risks of death: A note on new evidence. *Journal of Policy Analysis and Management* 8 (1): 88–100.

Fleming, C., J. Wasson, P. Albertson, M. Barry, and J. Wennberg. 1993. A decision analysis of alternative treatment strategies for clinically localized prostate cancer. *Journal of the American Medical Association* 269 (20): 2650–58.

Garber, Alan, and Charles Phelps. 1997. Economic foundations of cost-effectiveness analysis. *Journal of Health Economics* 16 (1): 1–32.

Garner, Thesia, and Rachel Dardis. 1987. Cost-effectiveness analysis of end-stage renal disease treatments. *Medical Care* 25 (1): 25–34.

Gold, Marthe R., Joanna E. Siegel, Louise B. Russell, and Milton C. Weinstein. 1996. *Cost-effectiveness in health and medicine.* New York: Oxford University Press.

Goldman, Lee, Milton C. Weinstein, Paula A. Goldman, and Lawrence W. Williams. 1991. Cost-effectiveness of HMG-CoA reductase inhibition for primary and secondary prevention of coronary heart disease. *Journal of the American Medical Association* 265 (9): 1145–51.

Hillner, Bruce, and Thomas Smith. 1991. Efficacy and cost-effectiveness of adjuvant chemotherapy in women with node-negative breast cancer. *New England Journal of Medicine* 324 (3): 160–68.

Hornberger, J. C., D. A. Redelmeier, and J. Peterson. 1992. Variability among methods to assess patients' well-being and consequent effect on a cost-effectiveness analysis. *Journal of Clinical Epidemiology* 45 (5): 505–12.

Johannesson, Magnus, David Meltzer, and Richard O'Conor. 1997. Incorporating future costs in medical cost-effectiveness analysis: Implications for the cost-effectiveness of the treatment of hypertension. *Medical Decision Making* 17 (4): 382–89.

Krumins, P., S. Fihn, and D. Kent. 1988. Symptom severity and patients' values in the decision to perform a transurethral resection of the prostate. *Medical Decision Making* 8 (1): 1–8.

La Puma, J., and E. F. Lawlor. 1990. Quality-adjusted life years: Ethical implications for physicians and policy makers. *Journal of the American Medical Association* 263 (23): 2917–21.

Meltzer, David. 1997. Accounting for future costs in medical cost-effectiveness analysis. *Journal of Health Economics* 16 (1): 33–64.

———. 1998. Implications of utility maximization for methods for sensitivity analysis in medical cost-effectiveness analysis. Unpublished manuscript, University of Chicago.

Meltzer, David, Rowland Chang, Gordon Hazen, and Arthur Elstein. 1998. Effects of including future costs on the cost-effectiveness of hip replacement. Unpublished manuscript, University of Chicago.

Meltzer, David, Tamar Polonsky, and Janet Tobian. 1998. Do quality-adjusted life years predict patient preferences? Validation using revealed preference for treatment in IDDM. *Journal of General Internal Medicine* 13 (1): 33.

Pauly, Mark V. 1995. Valuing health care benefits in monetary terms. In *Valuing health care,* ed. Frank Sloan, 99–124. New York: Cambridge University Press.

Russell, L. B. 1986. *Is prevention better than cure?* Washington, D.C.: Brookings Institution.

Sloan, Frank. 1995. *Valuing health care.* New York: Cambridge University Press.

Smith, Richard, Jane Hall, Howard Gurney, and Paul Harnett. 1993. A cost-utility approach to the use of 5-fluorouracil and levamisole as adjuvant chemotherapy for Duke's C colonic carcinoma. *Medical Journal of Australia* 158 (5): 319–22.

Stason, William B., and Milton Weinstein. 1977. Allocation of resources to manage hypertension. *New England Journal of Medicine* 296 (13): 732–39.

Task Force on Principles for Economic Analysis of Health Care Technology. 1996. Economic analysis of health care technology: A report on principles. *Annals of Internal Medicine* 122:61–70.

Tosteson, A., and M. Weinstein. 1991. Cost-effectiveness of hormone replacement therapy after the menopause. *Balliere's Clinical Obstetrics and Gynaecology* 5 (4): 943–59.

U.S. Congress. Office of Technology Assessment. 1981. *Cost-effectiveness of influenza vaccinations.* Washington, D.C.: Office of Technology Assessment.

U.S. Department of Labor. Bureau of Labor Statistics. 1994. *Monthly labor review.* Washington, D.C.: U.S. Bureau of the Census.

Wagstaff, A. 1991. QALYs and the equity-efficiency tradeoff. *Journal of Health Economics* 10 (1): 21–41.

Weinstein, Milton. 1980. *Clinical decision analysis.* Philadelphia: Saunders.

———. 1986. Challenges for cost-effectiveness research. *Medical Decision Making* 6 (4): 194–98.

———. 1995. Theoretical basis of cost-effectiveness. In *Valuing health care,* ed. Frank Sloan. New York: Cambridge University Press.

Weinstein, Milton, and William B. Stason. 1976. *Hypertension: A policy perspective.* Cambridge, Mass.: Harvard University Press.

Weinstein, Milton, and Richard J. Zeckhauser. 1972. Critical ratios and efficient allocation. *Journal of Public Economics* 2 (2): 147–57.

Wong, John, Frank Sonnenberg, Deeb Salem, and Stephen Pauker. 1990. Myocardial revascularization for chronic stable angina. *Annals of Internal Medicine* 113 (1): 852–71.

Comment   Douglas L. Cocks

This paper provides an extremely useful contribution to the field of health economics as it is applied to the economic evaluation of pharmaceutical medical interventions. In recent years the quasi-application of economics to the evaluation of pharmaceuticals has come under the scrutiny of many diverse disciplines (medicine, pharmacy administration, sociology, psychology, business administration, anthropology, statistics, and others), which in turn derived the new discipline known as pharmacoeconomics.

Dr. Meltzer's discussion of the relationship between the concept of

Douglas L. Cocks is retired senior research scientist of health economics at Eli Lilly and Company.

quality-adjusted life years (QALYs) and the economic concept of revealed preference highlights the possible notion that the relationship between pharmacoeconomics and real health economic analysis is tenuous. The implication of the discussion is that the concept of QALYs confuses the basic microeconomic distinction between cardinal and ordinal utility. In essence, the QALY designation is founded as a cardinal representation of utility and therefore cannot be translated into the true concepts of classical welfare economics. As the paper points out, even the report of the Panel on Cost-Effectiveness in Health and Medicine "explicitly advocates that cost-effectiveness analyses adopt a 'social' perspective, and asserts that the methods of cost-effectiveness analysis that adopt such a perspective have their roots in classical welfare economics." This cardinal orientation renders the use of QALYs very limited, especially in making economic comparisons of drugs that are similar in therapeutic activity and chemical makeup.

The empirical data presented on the limitations of QALYs indicate that these measures are not necessarily a reliable measure of the *economic* significance of a particular medical intervention. The application of traditional microeconomic welfare economics to questions of the economic significance of medical interventions may be the best guide to both public and private policy issues concerning these interventions.

The second major part of the paper deals with the importance of dealing with future costs when analyzing the economic cost and benefits of medical interventions. This is an extremely important concept that is often misunderstood or forgotten in the field of pharmacoeconomics. This basic concept is related to an economic principle that is also misunderstood, the principle of the distinction between systems costs and component (sometimes known as line item) costs.[1] This distinction is important because much of the management of health care in the United States and in certain foreign health care systems relies on the use of component management, rather than addressing health care costs from a systems perspective. The major economic issue is centered around resource allocation decisions. Resource allocation decisions are grounded in production functions in classical economics, which require an answer to the question What allocation of inputs results in the greatest output at the lowest cost? The case for a systems approach, as opposed to a component/line item approach, has been analyzed empirically. Several studies have shown that focusing on one component of cost without considering interaction effects can cause the unintended effect of increasing total costs even as the cost of the single component is reduced.[2]

The concept of systems management can be framed analytically in a

---

1. This discussion is based on Cocks and Croghan (1996).
2. Soumerai et al. (1994); Sloan, Gordon, and Cocks (1993); Moore and Newman (1993); Dranove (1989); Horn et al. (1996).

methodology of economics known as economic growth accounting. This methodology, developed by Denison (1974), was first applied to health care by Klarman et al. (1970) followed by Virts (1977) and Virts and Wilson (1983, 1984).

The fundamental notion of economic growth accounting is that health care costs cannot be addressed until they have been broken down into their basic factors. From an economic perspective, these factors can be expressed in a simple identity,

$$\text{THE}_t = P_t \cdot U_t \cdot N_t,$$

where THE_t equals total health care expenditures in a given time period, t; P_t is the price per unit of health care goods and services in time period t; U_t is the utilization of health care goods and services—the number of units of health care goods and services consumed *per person* in time period t; and N_t is the number of persons consuming health care goods and services in time period t. Historically, identities have been used in economic analysis to convey fundamental economic concepts algebraically and graphically. The most recognized identity is the equation for the quantity theory of money (Glahe 1973).

The simple model of health care expenditures can be applied to the many institutional forms that make up the total health care system. At the aggregate level, total U.S. health care expenditures represent the summation of the many THE_t equations emanating from the myriad of health care delivery systems. Thus, the analytic or managerial problem is to determine how the level of total health care expenditures (THE_t) changes over time and the relative contribution of each major element (P_t, U_t, and N_t) to the growth in health care costs/expenditures.

In applying the basic model, a fundamental issue highlights the importance of a systems approach to health care management. Many interaction effects exist among the individual factors as those factors change both in magnitude and over time. For example, as the price of a good or service rises, the number of units purchased of that good or service usually falls. The price rise also results in increased consumption of an alternative or substitute good. These interaction effects are difficult to understand and even more difficult to account for numerically.

The relationship among the factors can be observed by examining the simple mathematics of change derived from the expenditure/cost equation, $\text{THE}_t = P_t \cdot U_t \cdot N_t$. Therefore, the changes in spending can be expressed as

$$\Delta\text{THE} = \Delta P + \Delta U + \Delta N + (\Delta P \cdot \Delta U) + (\Delta P \cdot \Delta N) + (\Delta N \cdot \Delta U).$$

In this relationship, the terms are defined as follows:

- $\Delta\text{THE} = \text{THE}_t - \text{THE}_0$—the change in total health care expenditures is the difference in total health care expenditures in the given year, t, and a beginning or base year, 0.

- $\Delta P = P_t - P_0$—the change in health care prices is the difference in the price level in the given year, t, and the base year, 0.
- $\Delta U = U_t - U_0$—the change in utilization is the difference in utilization in the given year, t, and the base year, 0.
- $\Delta N = N_t - N_0$—the change in the number of persons consuming health care goods and services is the difference in the number of persons in the given year, t, and the base year, 0.
- $(\Delta P \cdot \Delta U)$, $(\Delta P \cdot \Delta N)$, $(\Delta N \cdot \Delta U)$—represents the interaction effects that result from the individual factor changes that operate on each other.

This simple model as it is presented represents the aggregation of health care expenditures at a total level. Thus, the total health expenditures term, THE_t, represents the summation of expenditures for all the goods and services that constitute health care spending. In simple mathematical terms, this can be expressed accordingly:

$$THE_t = \Sigma SPE_{it},$$

where ΣSPE_{it} is the summation of spending on specific health care goods and services, i, for the time period, t. The term ΣSPE_{it} represents the crux of the problem of managing health care costs. The management problem this model exposes has four dimensions: (1) the complexity inherent in examining the number of items that make up health care spending, ΣSPE_{it}; (2) the need to determine the contribution of each component of individual spending (P_t, U_t, and N_t) to total expenditures, THE_t; (3) the need to specifically address the interaction effects among prices, utilization, and population $(\Delta P \cdot \Delta U)$, $(\Delta P \cdot \Delta N)$, and $(\Delta N \cdot \Delta U)$; and (4) the need to examine substitutions among health care goods and services that take place with the summation of expenditures, ΣSPE_{it}. In economic terms, the last dimension represents the need to address the elasticity of substitution among the various inputs that constitute total health care spending.

The purpose of the preceding discussion is to emphasize the importance of Dr. Meltzer's point on the significance of addressing the issue of future costs in cost-effectiveness studies. The economic implications of the introduction and use of innovative medical interventions have many dimensions that must be addressed when considering the allocation of health resources.

References

Cocks, D. L., and T. W. Croghan. 1996. The economic organization of health resource allocation: Decision making in the new environment. *American Journal of Managed Care* 2 (8): 1035–42.
Denison, E. F. 1974. *Accounting for United States economic growth 1929–1969.* Washington, D.C.: Brookings Institution.

Dranove, D. 1989. Medicaid drug formulary restrictions. *Journal of Law and Economics* 32:143–62.

Glahe, F. R. 1973. *Macroeconomics: Theory and policy.* Chicago: Harcourt Brace Jovanovich.

Horn, S. D., P. D. Sharkey, D. M. Tracy, et al. 1996. Intended and unintended consequences of HMO cost-containment strategies: Results from the Managed Care Outcomes Project. *American Journal of Managed Care* 2:253–64.

Klarman, H. E., D. P. Rice, B. S. Cooper, and H. L. Settler, III. 1970. Sources of increase in selected medical care expenditures. Staff Paper no. 4. Washington, D.C.: U.S. Department of Health and Welfare, Social Security Administration, Office of Research and Statistics.

Moore, W. J., and R. J. Newman. 1993. Drug formulary restrictions as a cost-containment policy in Medicaid programs. *Journal of Law and Economics* 36: 71–97.

Sloan, F. A., G. S. Gordon, and D. L. Cocks. 1993. Hospital drug formularies and the use of hospital services. *Medical Care* 31:851–67.

Soumerai, S. B., T. J. McLaughin, D. Ross-Degan, et al. 1994. Effects of limiting Medicaid drug-reimbursement on the use of psychotic agents and acute mental health services by patients with schizophrenia. *New England Journal of Medicine* 331:650–55.

Virts, J. R. 1977. U.S. health care spending: A macro analysis. *Business Economics* 12:26–37.

Virts, J. R., and G. W. Wilson. 1983. Inflation and sectoral prices. *Business Economics* 17:45–54.

———. 1984. Inflation and health care prices. *Health Affairs* 3:88–100.

Medical Care Output and Productivity in the Nonprofit Sector

Tomas Philipson and Darius Lakdawalla

3.1 Introduction

There is a growing concern about the productivity, or so-called cost-effectiveness, of the health care industry. Health care differs from many other industries in that most production takes place in the nonprofit sector.[1] Little is known about the economic forces which determine productivity in the nonprofit sector, especially compared to that which is known about the for-profit sector. There, productivity analysis is well developed, especially through recent work stressing the endogenous determination of technical change. This paper attempts to analyze the incentives which generate productivity differences between nonprofit and for-profit firms. We are particularly interested in interpreting some empirical differences between nonprofits and for-profits in mixed industries:[2]

Tomas Philipson is professor in the Irving B. Harris Graduate School of Public Policy, the Department of Economics, and the Law School at the University of Chicago and a research associate of the National Bureau of Economic Research. Darius Lakdawalla is an associate economist at the RAND Corporation, Santa Monica, California.

For their helpful comments, the authors are grateful to Charles Mullin, conference participants, and particularly their discussant, Richard Frank.

1. For a general discussion of the nonprofit sector see, e.g., Clotfelter (1992), Weisbrod (1977, 1987, 1988), Hansmann (1980), Powell (1987), Rose-Ackerman (1986, 1996) and the references contained therein. For discussions of nonprofit behavior in health care see Newhouse (1970), Pauly and Redisch (1973), Harris (1977), Becker and Sloan (1985), Dranove (1988), Gertler (1989), Gertler and Waldman (1992), and Sloan (2000).

2. See Sloan (2000) or Malani and Philipson (2000) for a review of the evidence. Further work on this subject may be found in Hansmann (1987), James and Rose-Ackerman (1986), Easly and O'Hara (1982), Philipson (2000), and Rudney (1987).

- Controlling for quality and quantity, the output of the nonprofit and for-profit sectors tend to be perfect substitutes in that they are identically priced.
- When both firm types coexist in a single industry, nonprofit firms tend to operate on a larger scale than for-profit firms.
- Nonprofit firms are often observed to use more inputs per unit of output, and have consequently larger average and marginal costs.
- Nonprofits often are more intensive in their investment in research and development (R&D) than for-profits.

These regularities raise some important questions. In the neoclassical analysis of competitive production, more efficient firms tend to be larger than less efficient firms, who tend to be driven out of business. It appears puzzling, therefore, that nonprofits tend to be larger and less efficient, yet they are able to coexist in, if not dominate, industries in which they are allowed to operate. It is particularly puzzling that the nonprofit form of production dominates industries like short-term health care in the United States. It is less puzzling for industries dominated by for-profits, like the U.S. long-term care industry. The prevalence of nonprofit R&D is also striking in the light of many "property rights" theories, which claim that for-profit firms have greater incentives to invest in productivity enhancements.

Our analysis aims at interpreting these regularities in an explicit and internally consistent framework. We discuss the implications for productivity yielded by the theory of nonprofit firms in Lakdawalla and Philipson (1997). The paper is organized as follows: Section 3.2 analyzes the productivity or cost-effectiveness of firms with "profit-deviating" preferences.[3] Building on this analysis, section 3.3 analyzes the productivity differences across the nonprofit and for-profit sectors when both firm types coexist in a mixed industry. We predict that, when both types coexist, nonprofits are larger and less efficient, but nevertheless become more numerous than for-profit firms under competitive conditions. In other words, nonprofits drive out for-profit firms through competition, although they exhibit higher marginal and average costs. This is not inefficient, because we argue that nonprofits can tolerate prices that are lower than marginal and average costs. We can observe direct evidence on such pricing, because in the U.S. nonprofit sector, sales by nonprofits do not cover total costs. For example, tuition revenue for most U.S. universities does not cover faculty salaries. Section 3.4 expands the analysis to consider the endogenous choice of R&D. We predict, contrary to property rights theory, that nonprofit firms invest more in cost-reducing R&D than for-profit firms, holding other factors, such as third-party insurance contracts, constant. Section 3.5 pro-

---

3. An early analysis of behavior by firms with profit-deviating preferences for the combination of inputs is Becker (1958).

vides some suggestive and aggregate evidence on the productivity differences between the two organizational forms in the short- and long-term care industries.

Both the theory and the evidence differ from the property rights theories of nonprofit firm behavior.[4] Such theories claim that the lack of residual claimants (i.e., the inability of nonprofit firms to retain profits) leads to inefficient behavior. We argue that such theories ignore the endogeneity of nonprofit status. Firms *choose* this status; it is not forced upon them. If nonprofit status is inefficient, it is hard to understand why it would be chosen. We argue that even though nonprofit firms lack residual claimants, their dependence on donations provides the same discipline as the dependence of for-profit firms on investors. We argue that donors are best interpreted as investors who require in-kind, rather than pecuniary, returns.[5] Just as investors have strong incentives to channel funds into firms that will maximize the investors' objectives, donors also have incentives to fund the firms that are most efficient at achieving their objectives, even if those objectives are not restricted to monetary reward. Fundamentally, the property rights theory of nonprofit firms is limited in two respects. First, it assumes that nonprofit status is imposed externally, rather than chosen by the firm. Second, it cannot explain why donors to nonprofit firms cannot discipline the firms as well as investors in for-profit firms.

3.2 Cost-Effectiveness and Profit Maximization

The standard theory of the firm generates the well-known result that a profit-maximizing firm also minimizes costs. This section analyzes the generalization of this implication to producers or donors who do not aim to maximize profits. The main result is that cost-minimization is not preserved when donors have preferences for inputs, although it is preserved when donors have preferences for output alone.[6]

In order to incorporate profit-deviating preferences, we view each firm as a single agent with access to a production technology, and preferences over output y, an $n \times 1$ vector of inputs x, and regular consumption z represented by $U(y, x, z)$. In a for-profit firm, the agent making the decisions is the firm's owner, while in a nonprofit firm, the decision maker is a charitable donor.[7] Let the output y be produced from inputs according to the production function $f(x)$. Each donor is endowed with a level of real con-

---

4. For a classic exposition of this argument, see Alchian and Demsetz (1972).

5. It is well known that private donations are a small share of capital in many health care industries in the United States, so this distinction applies mainly outside that sector.

6. The analysis also displays that profit-deviating firms may act as if they maximize profits, according to an analogy exploited in Philipson and Posner (2000).

7. We here make no distinction between ownership and control. In this way, our theory resembles the standard theory of the firm but differs from agency explanations for nonprofits (see, e.g., Hansmann 1980).

sumption z_0 and sells output at a unit price p, in terms of the numeraire of consumption. Formally, the firm solves the problem

$$\max_{y,x,z} U(y,x,z),$$

such that

$$y \leq f(x),$$

$$w \circ x + z \leq z_0 + py.$$

Because the constraints will hold with equality, the problem simplifies to

$$\max_{x} U[f(x),x,z_0 + \pi(x)],$$

where $\pi(x) = pf(x) - wz$ denotes profits. The first-order necessary conditions are, for $k = 1, \ldots, n;$

(1)
$$\left(\frac{U_y}{U_\pi} + p\right)f_k = w_k - \frac{U_k}{U_\pi}.$$

These first-order conditions can be seen as generalizing classic profit-maximization conditions if we recognize that profit deviators operate according to the "net price" of inputs and outputs, in which the net price includes both the pecuniary price and the nonpecuniary value of inputs and outputs. The nonpecuniary value of output in monetary terms is given by U_y/U_π, the marginal utility of output normalized by the marginal utility of the numeraire good of consumption. The net price of one unit of output is thus $p^* = U_y U_\pi + p$, the nonpecuniary value of one unit of output plus the pecuniary value. Similarly, the net input price will be given by the pecuniary price of an input minus its nonpecuniary value, U_k/U_π. The net price of input k is then $w_k^* = w_k - U_k/U_\pi$. From this point of view, it is apparent that equation (1) generalizes the usual profit-maximization condition for input use

$$p^*f_k = w_k^*.$$

It also generalizes the familiar first-order conditions of the cost-minimization problem, the equality between the ratio of marginal factor products and the ratio of factor prices:

(2)
$$\frac{f_k}{f_l} = \frac{w_k^*}{w_l^*}.$$

Firms that do not value inputs ($U_k = 0$ for all k) continue to minimize costs at the pecuniary factor prices w. Put differently, the net price of inputs simply equals the pecuniary price of inputs, so that the firm faces the same relative input prices as a profit maximizer. Then an output-preferring firm will have the same cost function $c(y)$ and conditional input demands $x(w, y)$ as a profit-maximizing firm. The optimal scale of such an output-preferring firm is given by

$$\max_{y} U[y, x(w, y), z_0 + py - c(y)].$$

Using the envelope theorem, the first-order condition for this problem is given by

$$p^* = p + \frac{U_y}{U_\pi} = c_y.$$

An output preferrer behaves exactly like a profit maximizer who faces prices p^*. Since $p^* > p$, an output preferrer produces more than a profit maximizer. This generates an important implication for long-run firm behavior: All firms will charge a long-run price p^* equal to minimum average cost, but output-preferring firms will charge a lower *pecuniary* price p than profit maximizers; therefore, free entry of such firms will drive the long-run pecuniary price *below* minimum average cost.

Alternatively, if the firm values inputs, cost minimization relative to the prices w need not result, because w^* may not be a scalar multiple of w. At a given level of output, an input-preferring firm may have incentives to use more of the inputs it prefers, relative to the cost-minimizing levels of input use. To illustrate, consider the case of linear preferences:

$$U(y, x, z) = \alpha_y y + \alpha \circ x + z.$$

The scalar α_y represents the constant marginal utility of output, and the vector α represents the marginal utilities of the various inputs. The firm behaves as if it faces the vector of input prices $w^* = w - \alpha$. If w^* is not a scalar multiple of w, the firm will act as if it faces different relative input prices and thus have a cost function c^* which differs from the minimum cost function c.

It is frequently argued that nonprofit firms do not behave efficiently, because they tend to operate at a larger scale and at greater input cost than for-profit firms. We have argued that such behavior is optimal when one recognizes that profit maximization is not the objective of the firm. Holding constant the output price, a firm which values outputs is of larger scale than one which does not. Moreover, holding output price and the level of output constant, a firm which values inputs uses more inputs. Therefore, the level of inputs per unit of output is higher for both input- and output-preferring firms.

3.3   Productivity Differences in Mixed Industries

In this section, we analyze the endogenous decision to enter for-profit and nonprofit status, in the context of a long-run competitive model, and the differences in productivity across profit status implied by this analysis. Since nonprofit status is chosen by profit-deviating firms, the predictions about the differences between such firms and profit maximizers will translate into predictions about the differences between nonprofit and for-profit firms. In the mixed industry equilibrium, the nonprofits are predicted to be larger, use more inputs per output, have larger average costs, but nevertheless drive the leaner for-profits out of business.

3.3.1   Scale Differences under Mixed Production

For simplicity, we will consider the case in which firms only have output preference, because the presence of input-preferring behavior will not substantially alter the predictions about scale differences. Suppose that we can index output preference by some parameter $\alpha_y \in [0, 1]$, where $\alpha_y = 0$ for a firm which does not value output. Denote by $U(y, \pi; \alpha_y)$ the utility firm α_y derives from output y and profits π. Let d indicate the regulatory choice of the firm, where $d = 1$ when a firm chooses to be for-profit and $d = 0$ when it decides to be nonprofit. We denote by $d(\alpha_y, p)$ the preferred status of a producer with preferences α_y when the price of output is p. The nonprofit sector is defined by a nondistribution constraint and lower input costs from tax breaks and donations of capital and labor. More precisely, under nonprofit status, the firm is constrained to have economic profits below a certain regulated level $\pi \leq \pi_R$ (we assume $\pi_R = 0$), but under for-profit status, profits are unconstrained. Cost functions differ across profit status: denoting by $c^d(y)$ the cost function in status d, suppose that $c^0(y) \leq c^1(y)$ and $c^0_y(y) \leq c^1_y(y)$; holding output fixed, both total and marginal costs are lower in the nonprofit sector. This difference in costs represents the tax breaks which favor nonprofit firms: For instance, nonprofits have lower corporate income, property, and benefit taxes. It also reflects the value of donated capital and labor in the nonprofit sector. If nonprofits were to have *higher* costs than for-profit firms, then in our setting no firm would choose to be nonprofit. In such a case, a firm could always do better with the lower costs and unconstrained profits of the for-profit sector. Therefore, mixed production reveals that nonprofit costs are lower.

In addition, mixed production reveals a scarcity of output-preferring firms, because an infinite supply of output-preferring firms would result in a strictly nonprofit industry. The following line of reasoning demonstrates this fact. In the long run, a firm will stay in an industry provided that at the prevailing price, it does at least as well as it would do outside the industry. For simplicity, suppose that a firm earns zero utility if it leaves the industry. When $\alpha_y = 0$, firms have no preference for output, and $U(y, \pi; \alpha_y) = \pi$, so that in the long run, profit maximizers will remain in an industry provided that the price weakly exceeds average costs. This leads to the familiar result that, given free entry, profit maximizers must produce at minimum average cost m in the long run. Profit maximizers remain in an industry provided that $p \geq m$, but competition ensures that $p \leq m$. However, when $p = m$, firms with $\alpha_y > 0$ earn positive utility in spite of their zero profits, because they also value output. Therefore, output-preferring firms will find it optimal to remain in an industry even if $p < m$. Given an infinite supply of such firms, output preferrers will enter until the price falls below m. At this point, all profit maximizers leave the industry, and all firms earn negative economic profits. Because profits are negative, the nonprofit constraint $\pi \leq 0$ fails to bind, and nonprofit status exacts no cost. As a result, all remaining firms become nonprofit.[8] As a result, we will consider the more relevant case in which output-preferring firms are scarce, and there exists an infinite supply of for-profit firms.

Suppose we have only the quantity A of firms with $\alpha_y > 0$, where the share of output-preferring firms with preference $\alpha \leq \alpha_y$ is given by the measure $\mu(\alpha_y)$. We know that any profit-maximizing firms in the industry will choose for-profit status. We can also show that output preferrers will always choose nonprofit status. Specifically, since $p \leq m$, any output preferrers will choose to earn strictly negative profits under for-profit status. If $p < m$, it is obvious that output preferrers must earn negative profits. To see this fact for the case in which $p = m$, observe that profit maximizers earn exactly zero profits in this case. Since output preferrers act as if they have lower cost than profit maximizers, they will produce more output, and thus earn less profit. As a result, they can do strictly better by switching to nonprofit status, because the cost reductions of nonprofit status will allow them to produce more output at a higher level of profit. However, even with scarce output preference, we need not have any profit maximizers, or for-profit firms, in the industry. For firms with strong output preference, the nonpecuniary portion of p^* is positive, so they can charge a pecuniary price below p^*. Therefore, output-preferring firms can survive at long-run prices strictly below m, the minimum average cost of a for-profit firm. Thus, if there are enough output-preferring firms to satisfy market demand at a price below m, no profit maximizers will enter the market. Formally, let $D(p)$ be the market demand function, and $y(p; \alpha_y)$ be the supply function of a firm with preferences α_y. If there exists a price $p' < m$ at which output preferrers can satisfy market demand, then the long-run price cannot rise above p', and profit-maximizers do not enter. No profit maximizers enter if there exists $p' < m$ such that

$$D(p') \leq A \int y(p; \alpha_y) d\mu(\alpha_y).$$

8. For a detailed analysis of optimal profit status choice, see Lakdawalla and Philipson (1997).

If this condition is satisfied, the industry will be strictly nonprofit, and all firms will be output preferrers. Suppose that this condition cannot be satisfied, and that we thus have a mixed industry. In such an industry, all for-profit firms will be strict profit maximizers, and all nonprofit firms will be output preferrers. The results of the previous section then imply that firm scale must be higher in the nonprofit sector, because output preferrers rationally choose to operate at a higher scale, holding the output price constant.[9] In addition, the output-preferring nonprofit firms will produce this output at higher marginal cost, because they face a higher net price p^*.

3.3.2   Cost Differences under Mixed Production

It is well known that in both the short-term care (hospital) industry and the long-term care (nursing home) industry, nonprofit firms use more inputs per unit of output and thus have larger unit costs than for-profit firms. For example, as is shown in the empirical analysis of this paper, the number of full-time equivalent employees per bed-day is larger for nonprofit firms in these industries. This section argues that these empirical patterns do not stem from inefficient behavior by nonprofit firms, but from the differences in preferences between nonprofit and for-profit firms. There are two major reasons for the observed differences in unit costs. We have already seen that output-preferring firms choose nonprofit status, while profit maximizers choose for-profit status. We show that the resulting differences in scale, when not accounted for, may induce larger unit costs among the output-preferring nonprofit firms. Second, we show that input-preferring firms choose nonprofit status over for-profit status, so nonprofit firms will tend to be more input-preferring than for-profit firms. This generates differences in unit costs across nonprofit and for-profit sectors, but these differences reflect efficient behavior by firms with different preferences.

First, we show how differences in scale can generate differences in unit cost across the nonprofit and for-profit sectors. Suppose that one defines the observed productive efficiency as simply the observed average or marginal *monetary* costs as is the norm in empirical studies on productivity differences. Scale differences across nonprofit and for-profit sectors may generate differences in average or marginal monetary costs which do not provide information about differences in productive efficiency. Therefore, comparing average monetary costs without considering scale may lead to misleading observations about productive efficiency. Recall from the previous section that for-profit firms will always be profit maximizers. The presence of profit maximizers implies in turn that the long-run output price must be equal to minimum average monetary cost m, because the for-profit firms needed to fill the residual demand (unmet by the scarce output

9. The larger scale of nonprofits is not naturally interpreted by theories of nonprofits as cooperatives (e.g., Pauly and Redisch 1973), because they predict smaller labor forces than profit maximizers given that labor shares the residual gain.

preferrers) will produce at price m, the price at which their average costs are minimized. Recall that the nonprofit firms are output-preferring firms. Such firms will produce strictly greater output than the for-profit firms. Specifically, they will set marginal cost equal to the net output price p^*. Because the output-preferring nonprofit firms face higher *net* output prices p^*, they will produce at higher marginal cost. Of course, the relation between average cost across sectors is technically ambiguous after tax, but before-tax cost differences should remain. However, the higher marginal cost of nonprofit firms will tend to drive up average costs as well. In any event, provided that the cost reductions are not very large in magnitude, average costs will also be higher in the nonprofit sector. This difference in costs follows as an implication of efficient behavior under output preference and does not provide evidence of differences in productive efficiency across the two sectors.

Second, the existence of input-preferring firms could also generate differences in average monetary costs which do not reflect inefficient behavior by nonprofit firms. Consider the case of two inputs x_1 and x_2, and a level of input preference over the input x_1 indexed by $\alpha \in [0, 1]$, where firms with $\alpha = 0$ have no preference for using x_1. Again suppose that we have an infinite supply of profit-maximizing entrants with $\alpha = 0$. We thus know that $p \leq m$. We also know that at any price p, the input-preferring firms will produce more than the profit maximizers. If $p = m$, the profit maximizers would earn zero profits. Since the input-preferring firms produce more than profit maximizers, at this price they must earn negative profits. Clearly, if $p < m$, the input preferrers must earn negative economic profits, because price lies below minimum average cost. Under these circumstances, all input-preferring firms will optimally choose nonprofit status, because they would earn negative profits under for-profit status anyway. All profit maximizers will optimally choose for-profit status, because they have nothing valuable to gain by accepting a constraint on profits. As a result, all nonprofit firms have stronger preferences for x_1 than all for-profit firms. We know that, holding the cost function constant, input preferences cause firms to use more inputs at a given level of output, because they face different relative net input prices. Therefore, provided that the cost reductions afforded by nonprofit status are not so large as to offset the force of input preferences, *nonprofit firms will have higher average costs, but not as a result of productive inefficiency.*

3.4   Research and Development by Nonprofit Firms

In the short-term care industry, a large amount of research and development is conducted by nonprofit teaching hospitals.[10] The property rights

10. We thank George Zanjani for providing us with a simpler derivation of the argument of this section than considered originally.

theory of nonprofit firm behavior seems inconsistent with the predominance of nonprofit firms in R&D, because it argues that nonprofit firms have weaker incentives to control costs. This section argues that profit-deviating firms often have stronger incentives to reduce the marginal cost of output through R&D than do profit maximizers.

We restrict our attention to R&D, which reduces the cost of producing extra quantity, although we discuss the straightforward application of our reasoning to a case in which R&D aims at increasing quality. Consider the case in which the firm maximizes a weighted sum of output and profits and has no input preferences:

$$U(y,\pi) = \alpha y + (1 - \alpha)\pi.$$

The extension to general preferences is straightforward, but algebraically tedious. Suppose that each firm may choose to attain a level of technology θ in its cost function $c(y, \theta)$ where θ reduces the marginal cost of output; $c_{y\theta} \leq 0$. Profits *gross* of investments in R&D are then defined as

$$\pi(y,\theta) \equiv py - c(y,\theta).$$

This implies that cost reduction raises gross profits more the larger the level of output; $\pi_{y\theta} > 0$. Attaining the level of technology θ requires a research budget of $r(\theta)$ units of real consumption. In this setting, the firm solves

$$\max_{y,\theta} \alpha y + (1 - \alpha)[\pi(y,\theta) - r(\theta)].$$

The first-order conditions are

$$\pi_y = -\frac{\alpha}{1 - \alpha},$$

$$\pi_\theta = r_\theta.$$

Absent output preference α, the first condition reduces to the standard profit-maximizing condition. The second condition equates the marginal increase in gross profits with the marginal cost of extra research. The second condition defines an implicit relationship between technology and output preference $\theta(\alpha)$ in which the benefit rises with output, because larger firms enjoy a larger reduction in costs for a given amount of R&D. Since output-preferring firms are larger than profit-maximizing ones, implicit differentiation yields the result that a larger output preference expands R&D:[11]

---

11. Define by D the determinant of the Hessian matrix. The second-order condition then implies that $D > 0$. Differentiating the first-order conditions yields $\partial\theta/\partial\alpha = [(1 - \pi_y)(1 - \alpha)\pi_{y\theta}]/D$. Since $\pi_y \leq 0$ at the optimal output choice, and $\pi_{y\theta} > 0$, the result follows.

$$\frac{d\theta}{d\alpha} \geq 0.$$

This effect depends entirely on the reduction of marginal costs. Because marginal costs represent the price of output relative to profits on the margin, reductions in this relative price are more valuable to firms with a stronger relative preference for output. Holding the cost function constant, output-preferring firms have a stronger incentive to invest in R&D because it reduces costs more. Thus, contrary to property rights arguments, nonprofit firms have a stronger incentive to invest in R&D than for-profit firms. Of course, nonprofit firms also have lower costs than for-profit firms if they are given tax breaks on inputs. This provides a competing incentive against R&D expenditure. Provided that the cost reductions of nonprofit status are not too large, nonprofit firms will undertake more R&D spending than for-profit firms.

Although we have not explicitly considered quality enhancements in this paper, investments in quality-enhancing R&D would operate similarly.[12] Firms with stronger relative preferences for quality over profits would tend to invest more in quality-enhancing R&D than other firms. Quality-preferring firms would have a stronger incentive to adopt nonprofit status, because their profits would be lower than those of profit maximizers (because they would forgo profits in the interest of raising quality), and because the cost reductions of nonprofit status may help them finance higher quality output.

3.5   Empirical Analysis of Productivity Differences in Long-Term Care

This section provides an illustrative discussion of some broad patterns on the productivity differences between nonprofits and for-profits in the U.S. long-term care industry. We will be concerned primarily with addressing the claim that nonprofit firms use more inputs per unit of output in their larger scaled production. We argued above that output preferrers will have higher unconditional input demands, while input preferrers will have higher conditional input demands. We consider differences in input demands between for-profit and nonprofit nursing homes. Using the nursing home–level data from the 1995 National Nursing Home Survey (NNHS), we estimate conditional input demand as a function of proxies for market price p, output level y, and relative wages w. Specifically, we estimate the following cross-sectional specification[13] of conditional input demand, for all facilities

---

12. For an early study on quality-preferring behavior by nonprofit firms, see Newhouse (1970).

13. Unfortunately, there exist no panel surveys of nursing homes. Such surveys would be useful if profit status were correlated with input use for other reasons that did not vary over

Table 3.1   Summary Statistics for Nursing Home Ownership and Input
                       Intensity (1995)

	Mean	Std Dev	Min	Max
FTE employees	128.81	109.49	1	1,049
FTE registered nurses	11.10	13.14	0	144
FTE nurses' aides	50.41	43.19	0	469
FTE doctors	0.65	2.95	0	82
Nursing home beds[a]	132.74	52.53	25	200
Medicaid per diem ($)	93.88	81.51	24	1,887
Services provided[b]	0.76	0.11	0.05	1
City[c]	0.69	0.46	0	1
For-profit[d]	0.66	0.48	0	1

Notes: Data are from 1995 National Nursing Home Survey (U.S. Department of Health and
Human Services 1995). FTE = full-time equivalent.
[a]NNHS categorizes homes into one of four bed size categories: 0–49 beds, 50–99 beds, 100–
199 beds, and 200+ beds. Beds variable constructed by assigning to each home the midpoint
value of its size category, or in the case of the 200+ category, the minimum value.
[b]Index of services, constructed by NNHS.
[c]Dummy variable equal to 1 if facility is located in a standard metropolitan statistical area.
[d]Dummy variable equal to 1 if facility is for-profit.

$$\ln(x_i) = \beta_1 + \beta_2 \ln(p_i) + \beta_3 \ln(w_i) + \beta_4 \ln(y_i) + \varepsilon_i.$$

The data used are summarized in table 3.1. We measure usage of four
inputs: full-time equivalent registered nurses (RNs), full-time equivalent
nurses' aides, all full-time equivalent employees, and full-time equivalent
doctors. To measure market price, we use the Medicaid per diem payment
received by the nursing home. To measure *quantity* of output, we use the
number of beds present in the nursing home;[14] and to measure *quality* of
output we use an index of services provided, which is constructed within
the NNHS. As a proxy for relative wages, we use a dummy for location
within a standard metropolitan statistical area. Due to urban amenities,
relative wages (relative to the urban price level) should be lower in cities,
that input usage should be higher.

Table 3.2 reports the type of finding discussed on the differences in conditional input demand functions between nonprofit and for-profit homes.
Controlling for output price, input price, and output level, nonprofit nursing homes use approximately 30 percent more RNs, 23 percent more

time. Indeed, we are not aware of any data sets on the effect of profit status conversion
on productivity.
    14. Although the NNHS does not directly report bed size for each facility, it does place
each facility into one of four size categories: 1–49 beds, 50–99 beds, 100–199 beds, and 200
beds or more. We construct a measure of bed size by assigning to each home in the first three
categories the number of beds equal to the midpoint of the category. For example, the homes
in the first category are assigned the value of 25 beds. To homes with more than 200 beds
we assign the value of 200.

Table 3.2   Effect of Nursing Home Ownership on Input Intensity (1995)

	Log FTE RNs		Log FTE Aides[a]		Log FTE Employees		Log FTE Doctors	
	Coefficient	t-Statistic	Coefficient	t-Statistic	Coefficient	t-Statistic	Coefficient	t-Statistic
Constant	−5.82[a]	−7.96	−1.77*	−5.53	−1.51*	−4.753	−1.81*	−1.684
Log nursing home beds	0.75*	17.35	0.94*	27.76	0.94*	31.482	0.20**	1.786
Log medicaid per diem	0.79*	4.55	0.24*	3.25	0.35*	5.031	0.38***	1.782
Services provided	0.98*	4.16	0.05	0.38	0.21**	1.844	−0.44	−0.617
City	0.24*	4.87	0.07*	2.19	0.11*	3.866	0.06	0.535
For-profit	−0.28*	−6.28	−0.23*	−7.48	−0.25*	−9.041	−0.10	−0.865
R^2	0.44		0.55		0.63		0.02	
No. of observations	1,195		1,180		1,202		152	

Note: All t-statistics are robust to heteroskedasticity.

[a]Aides are nurses' aides.

*Significantly different from zero with 95% confidence.

**Significantly different from zero with 90% confidence.

nurses' aides, and 25 percent more employees. All these coefficients are statistically significant at the 5 percent level. The coefficient for doctors is negative, but insignificant. The standard errors on all the coefficients rise dramatically in the regression for doctors, because we lose almost 90 percent of the sample. This relates to a finding reported by Borjas, Frech, and Ginsburg (1983), who did not find significant wage rate differences between nonprofit and for-profit nursing homes. This result is consistent with input preference among nonprofit nursing homes. Substantially similar results were obtained for the unconditional input demand equation, in which the output measures were excluded. This would also be consistent with output preference. Further simple analysis was consistent with output preference: Regression of total beds on profit status revealed that nonprofit homes have, on average, 6.5 more beds than for-profit homes,[15] and that this difference is statistically significant at the 5 percent level.

These findings relate to previous studies on the differential input use across the two regulatory forms. Table 3.3 shows the estimated specifications of Borjas, Frech, and Ginsburg (1983), which they use to advance the property rights theory of nursing homes. They advance the claim that nonprofit firms dissipate profits by paying abnormally high wages to workers. On the surface, the theory behind this regression is flawed. If workers in nonprofit nursing homes really received rents for identical labor, there would be long queues of people waiting to work in nonprofit nursing homes, and there could not be an equilibrium in the labor market. This theoretical objection aside, Borjas et al. do not even find evidence of a wage differential. Table 3.3 reports the results of regressing the wages of nurses on the individual characteristics of the nurses, a set of regional and geographical dummies, and the ownership status of the nursing home. Controlling for observable characteristics, there is found to be no statistically significant difference between the wages paid by secular nonprofit homes and those paid by for-profit homes. In fact, church-run nonprofit homes pay a *lower* wage than for-profit homes, perhaps due to the availability of workers who wish to serve the church for nonpecuniary reasons. The only evidence Borjas et al. point to comes from government-run nursing homes, which apparently do pay a wage which is about 6–7 percent higher than the for-profit wage. We will not dwell too long on this finding, because we have not attempted to model government-run homes, which would be subject to various political economic considerations. At any rate, it is possible that governments impose unobservable quality standards on employees and reward them accordingly. While wage rates for a homogeneous unit of labor cannot differ across firms in an equilibrium, firms may use inputs more or less intensively, depending on their preferences.

---

15. Since the average for-profit home has about 130 beds, this roughly translates into a 5 percent difference in output.

Table 3.3   **Effect of Nursing Home Ownership on Wage Rates for Nurses (1973–74)**

		Log Wage Rate	
	Mean[a]	Coefficient	t-Statistic
Constant	n.a.	−0.036	−0.40
Years of education	11.84	0.055*	7.46
Years of nursing education	1.71	0.174*	61.25
Experience	22.23	0.013*	11.77
Experience squared	669.04	0.000*	−8.55
Firm experience	2.08	0.007*	4.99
Nursing experience	0.78	0.005	1.59
Hospital experience	1.12	0.008*	5.23
Nondegree training[b]	0.47	0.077*	9.46
White male	0.07	0.414*	26.28
Black male	0.01	0.128*	3.21
Black female	0.14	−0.015	−1.23
Northeast region	0.28	0.073*	5.76
North central region	0.33	−0.022**	−1.79
Southern region	0.23	0.083*	−6.37
SMSA[c]	0.64	0.119*	14.02
Church-run nonprofit	0.07	−0.039*	−2.52
Nonchurch nonprofit	0.12	0.016	1.29
Government-owned	0.15	0.066*	5.68
R^2		0.44	
No. of observations		11,542	

Source: Borjas, Frech, and Ginsburg (1983), table 2.

Note: Data are from 1973–74 National Nursing Home Survey. n.a. = not applicable. *t*-Statistics are robust to heteroskedasticity.

[a]Refers to mean of independent variable.

[b]Received in the past year.

[c]Equal to 1 if nursing home located in a standard metropolitan statistical area.

*Significantly different from zero with 95% confidence.

**Significantly different from zero with 90% confidence.

In tables 3.4 and 3.5, we reproduce the results of other authors whose analyses of hospitals are broadly consistent with our findings for nursing homes. In table 3.4, we report the results of Sloan and Steinwald (1980), who study input intensity across nonprofit and for-profit hospitals. Sloan and Steinwald find that the number of full-time equivalent registered nurses per hospital bed is roughly 25 percent higher in nonprofit hospitals, while the number of full-time equivalent nonnursing employees is roughly 12 percent higher. No significant effect was found for licensed practical nurses, who might be viewed as cheaper substitutes for physicians. Since the dependent variable is normalized by the number of beds, they do not include output as a regressor and thus do not strictly estimate a conditional input demand function. However, they do control for the wage di-

Table 3.4   Effect of Hospital Ownership on Input Intensity (1969–75)

	Log FTE RNs per Bed		Log FTE LPNs per Bed[a]		Log Other FTEs per Bed	
	Coefficient	t-Statistic	Coefficient	t-Statistic	Coefficient	t-Statistic
Log wage[b]	−0.40**	−1.82	−0.72**	−1.80	0.31**	1.82
Medicaid eligibility[c]	0.04*	3.00	−0.04**	−1.74	0.01	1.37
Medicare eligibility[d]	−0.16*	−3.64	0.03	0.37	0.01	0.26
For-profit	−0.24*	−4.90	−0.03	−0.32	−0.12*	−3.33
Government-run	−0.06	−1.49	0.03	0.41	0.03	1.22
Medical school[e]	0.04	1.38	0.05	0.86	0.12*	5.00
Nursing school[f]	−0.01	−0.34	−0.13*	−2.20	−0.01	−0.44
R^2	0.18		0.12		0.18	
No. of observations	6,016		6,016		6,016	

Source: Sloan and Steinwald (1980), table 8.1.

Note: A variety of included regressors not of interest here are not reported. All regressions control for a hospital-specific fixed effect. t-Statistics are robust to heteroskedasticity.

[a]LPNs are licensed practical nurses.

[b]Wages for the class of employees in dependent variable.

[c]Statewide proportion of population eligible for Medicaid.

[d]Statewide proportion of population eligible for Medicare.

[e]Dummy variable indicating presence of medical school.

[f]Dummy variable indicating presence of nursing school.

*Significantly different from zero with 95% confidence.

**Significantly different from zero with 90% confidence.

rectly, and they control for market price using the proportion of people covered by Medicare or Medicaid. Therefore, their results also support the conclusion that holding output fixed, nonprofit hospitals use more RNs and more nonnursing staff.

In table 3.5, we reproduce the results of Gentry and Penrod (1998), who analyze the output of hospitals across profit status. Table 3.5 displays some aggregate patterns consistent with evidence that nonprofit hospitals have more beds and discharges, as well as longer durations of care than for-profit hospitals. In addition, they are more likely to have emergency rooms and delivery rooms. On this level of aggregation it appears that, for a variety of output measures, nonprofit hospitals produce more than for-profit hospitals. Since nonprofit hospitals also have more employees, it is clear that they have higher unconditional input demands than for-profit hospitals. Finally, we can see that nonprofits are more likely to have teaching programs than for-profits, programs which are strong indicators of R&D expenditure. This is consistent with our prediction that output-preferring nonprofit institutions are more likely to invest in R&D.

Table 3.5   Effect of Hospital Ownership on Output (1995)

	Nonprofit	For-Profit	Public
Median bed size[a]	170	138	70
Median discharges (yearly)[a]	4,975	3,609	1,233
Median length of stay (days)[a]	5.51	5.11	5.46
Median number of employees[a]	520	330	161
Percent with emergency room	97.8	93.2	99
Percent with delivery room	74.7	62.7	72.8
Percent with teaching program	29.2	12.7	9.1

Source: Gentry and Penrod (1998).

Note: Based on a sample of 4,996 general short-term hospitals from HCFA's public use file of 1995 Medicare Cost Reports.

[a]For these variables, the Kruskal-Wallis test of equivalent distribution across ownership types was rejected at a 0.01 level.

3.6   Conclusion

Although the nonprofit sector is responsible for a majority of the production of health care in many countries, little is known about the economic forces contributing to productivity differences between the nonprofit and for-profit sectors. In this paper we argued that some puzzling empirical regularities may be understood using the analysis of endogenous nonprofit status choice studied in Lakdawalla and Philipson (1997). We contrasted our arguments to the well-known claim that nonprofits are made inefficient by their lack of well-defined property rights. Most importantly, the property rights theory cannot explain why firms would voluntarily choose an inferior arrangement of property rights in the first place.

The analysis here suggests that one should be more cautious in interpreting differences in productivity, because the efficient behavior of a firm will depend on its objectives. We argued that firms which choose nonprofit status are as efficient as those which choose for-profit status even though they utilize more inputs per unit of output produced. Furthermore, we predicted that nonprofits would invest more in cost-reducing R&D than for-profits, contrary to the qualitative arguments of property rights theory. In addition, we argued that although these productivity differences lead them to have higher average costs, nonprofit firms will drive out for-profit firms in competitive markets. These predictions were consistent with the empirical finding reported from the long-term care industry showing that nonprofit nursing homes use 23 to 30 percent more labor inputs (full-time equivalents) than for-profit homes of the same size. It is also consistent with earlier empirical findings that in mixed industries, nonprofit firms tend to be larger and more R&D intensive but less efficient than for-profit firms, while at the same time they tend to be more numerous than their for-profit counterparts.

References

Alchian, A., and H. Demsetz. 1972. Production, information costs, and economic organization. *American Economic Review* 62:777–95.

Becker, E., and F. A. Sloan. 1985. Hospital ownership and preference. *Economic Inquiry* 23 (1): 21–36.

Becker, G. 1958. *The economics of discrimination.* Chicago: University of Chicago Press.

Borjas, George J., H. E. Frech III, and Paul Ginsburg. 1983. Property rights and wages: The case of nursing homes. *Journal of Human Resources* 17 (2): 231–46.

Clotfelter, Charles T., ed. 1992. *Who benefits from the nonprofit sector?* Chicago: University of Chicago Press.

Dranove, D. 1988. Pricing by non-profit institutions. *Journal of Health Economics* 7 (1): 47–57.

Easly, D., and M. O'Hara. 1982. The economic role of the nonprofit firm. *RAND Journal of Economics* 14:531–40.

Gentry, W. M., and J. R. Penrod. 1998. The tax benefits of not-for-profit hospitals. NBER Working Paper no. 6435. Cambridge, Mass.: National Bureau of Economic Research.

Gertler, P. 1989. Subsidies, quality, and the regulation of nursing homes. *Journal of Public Economics* 39:33–53.

Gertler, P., and D. Waldman. 1992. Quality-adjusted cost-functions and policy evaluation in the nursing home industry. *Journal of Political Economy* 100: 1232–56.

Hansmann, Henry B. 1980. The role of nonprofit enterprise. *Yale Law Review* 89: 835–901.

———. 1987. Economic theories of non-profit organizations. In *The non-profit sector,* ed. W. Powell. New Haven, Conn.: Yale University Press.

Harris, Jeffrey E. 1977. The internal organization of hospitals: Some economic implications. *Bell Journal of Economics* 8 (2): 467–82.

James, Estelle, and Susan Rose-Ackerman. 1986. *The nonprofit enterprise in market economics.* New York: Harwood.

Lakdawalla, D., and T. Philipson. 1997. The nonprofit sector and industry performance. NBER Working Paper no. 6377. Cambridge, Mass.: National Bureau of Economic Research.

Malani, A., and T. Philipson. 2000. Theories of nonprofit firm behavior: A synthesis and its empirical content. Chicago: University of Chicago Law School. Mimeo.

Newhouse, J. 1970. Towards a theory of non-profit institutions: An economic model of a hospital. *American Economic Review* 60 (1): 64–74.

Pauly, M., and M. Redisch. 1973. The non-profit hospital as a physician cooperative. *American Economic Review* 63:87–100.

Philipson, T. 2000. Asymmetric information in the not-for-profit sector: Does its output sell at a premium? In *The changing hospital industry,* ed. David M. Cutler. Chicago: University of Chicago Press.

Philipson, T., and R. Posner. 2000. Anti-trust and the nonprofit sector. Chicago: University of Chicago Law School. Mimeo.

Powell, W. 1987. *The non-profit sector.* New Haven, Conn.: Yale University Press.

Rose-Ackerman, S., ed. 1986. *The economics of non-profit institutions.* New York: Oxford University Press.

———. 1996. Altruism, non-profits, and economic theory. *Journal of Economic Literature* 34 (2): 701–29.

Rudney, G. 1987. The scope and dimensions of non-profit activity. In *The non-profit sector,* ed. W. Powell. New Haven, Conn.: Yale University Press.

Sloan, F. 2000. Not-for-profit ownership and hospital behavior. In *Handbook of health economics,* ed. J. Newhouse and A. Culyer. New York: Elsevier Science.

Sloan, Frank, and Bruce Steinwald. 1980. *Insurance regulation and hospital costs.* Lexington, Mass.: Lexington Books.

U.S. Department of Health and Human Services. National Center for Health Statistics. 1995. *National Nursing Home Survey.* Hyattsville, Md.: U.S. Department of Health and Human Services.

Weisbrod, B. 1977. *The voluntary non-profit sector: Economic theory and public policy.* Lexington, Mass.: Lexington Books.

———. 1987. Non profit organizations. In *The new Palgrave: A dictionary of economics,* ed. J. Eatwell, M. Milgate, and P. Newman. New York: Stockton.

———. 1988. *The non-profit economy.* Cambridge, Mass.: Harvard University Press.

Comment   Richard G. Frank

The paper by Tomas Philipson and Darius Lakdawalla extends a long line of research on the behavior of nonprofit organizations in the health care sector. This paper focuses on the objective function of nonprofit health care providers and their allocative and productive efficiency. These are concerns that have challenged and vexed economists for over thirty years (Frank and Salkever 1994). The paper also takes up two other topics: (1) cost and productivity differences among health care providers under mixed for-profit and nonprofit production; and (2) research and development by nonprofit firms. The empirical analysis focuses primarily on ownership, organizational preferences, and efficiency. I will briefly summarize the theoretical models proposed by Philipson and Lakdawalla, point out the main implication stemming from the models, and review the empirical strategy adopted for exploring behaviors of nonprofit nursing homes and hospitals.

The Basic Model

The point of departure for the theoretical analysis is a competitive model where free entry holds and firms are price takers. A general objective function for the health care provider is set out: $U = U(y, x, \pi)$. It consists of three arguments, output (y), inputs (x), and profit (π). The firms pursue their objectives subject to a production constraint and a break-even constraint. Because nonprofit organizations receive charitable donations, production costs can exceed revenues from sales.

Analysis of the model yields several implications:

- If the firm is not an "input preferrer" ($Ux = 0$), it pursues cost minimization. This is true of both profit-maximizing for-profit organizations ($Ux = Uy = 0$) and output-preferring nonprofits ($Uy > 0$).

Richard G. Frank is the Margaret T. Morris Professor of Health Economics at Harvard Medical School and a research associate of the National Bureau of Economic Research.

- If the firm "prefers inputs" ($Ux > 0$), it will not be allocatively efficient.
- Nonprofit firms of all types will use more inputs than for-profit firms. Only input preferrers will have higher conditional input demands than for-profits.
- Output preferring firms will have higher marginal costs and higher output than for-profit firms.
- The availability of donations and tax breaks will tend to drive out for-profit firms.

Philipson and Lakdawalla use this model as a guide for interpreting statistical analysis of the behavior of nursing homes and hospitals.

Evidence

The empirical analysis presented by Philipson and Lakdawalla focuses on the analysis of input demand functions. They present new results for a national sample of nursing homes and review the analyses of others for the hospital sector. There are two important refutable propositions that Philipson and Lakdawalla are seeking to test as a means of assessing the theory they have advanced. The first is that the estimated input demand functions are consistent with cost minimization: that is, the demand curves are downward-sloping. This would be inconsistent with the input-preferrer formulation. Second, holding constant quality and output quantity, nonprofit firms would use more inputs. This offers another test of the input-preferrer formulation.

Some previous research has provided evidence that nonprofit health care providers do not allocate inputs in a fashion consistent with cost minimization. Goldman and Grossman (1988) estimated production functions for community health centers and tested whether the ratio of marginal products was equal to the ratio of factor payments. They rejected the presence of that cost-minimizing equilibrium condition in that market. Frank and Taube (1987) took a similar approach to studying the behavior of ambulatory mental health care providers. They too rejected the proposition that those providers were hiring inputs in a manner consistent with cost minimization. This previous work argues against the profit-maximization and output-preferring nonprofit formulations.

Philipson and Lakdawalla's empirical work is aimed directly at the input demand function for nursing homes. In general the literature has tended to formulate input demand models in the health sector either as technical input demand functions which are derived by assuming cost minimization and no other behavior, or as a behavioral input demand function where profit maximization or some other objective is assumed. In the former case, for a two-input production process the Cobb-Douglas estimating equation might take the form

$$x = A w_1^\alpha w_2^\beta Q^\gamma,$$

where A is a constant incorporating Hicks-neutral technical change, w_1 and w_2 are input prices and Q is the quality-adjusted output. In the latter case the model might take the form

$$x = A w_1^\alpha w_2^\beta p,$$

where p is the output price for the profit-maximizing firm. Under these types of formulations ownership is specified in the context of the Hicks-neutral technical change term. Hence $A = a_0 + a_1 \text{Profit}$ (where Profit is an ownership dummy variable). The specification used by Philipson and Lakdawalla is something of a hybrid. They estimate a model of the form

$$x = A w^\alpha p^\beta Q^\theta.$$

They estimate models for four types of labor inputs of nursing homes: registered nurses, nurses' aides, all employees, and physicians. Separate equations are estimates for each input. On the right-hand side of the regression models are nursing home beds (as a proxy for quantity given nearly full occupancy), Medicaid per diem reimbursement (a measure of supply price), an index of the range of services provided by the nursing home (as an indicator of quality), a dummy variable indicating whether a nursing home is located in a city (as an indicator of relatively low wages for nursing home staff), and an ownership dummy variable.

The results reported show that holding constant beds, reimbursement, location, and the services index, for-profit nursing homes demand significantly lower quantities of all labor inputs except physicians. The magnitude of the response varies from about 24 percent for aides to 32 percent for registered nurses. These estimates are supportive of the input-preferrer hypothesis. Two factors cast some uncertainty on this result. First, there is evidence suggesting that nonprofit nursing homes tend to be of higher quality than their for-profit counterparts. Weisbrod and Schlesinger (1986) analyze complaint data from the state of Wisconsin and find evidence showing lower rates of complaints by customers of nonprofit homes. Gertler and Waldman (1991) also find evidence suggesting that nonprofit homes are of higher quality. If higher quality is correlated with levels of staffing, as one could plausibly conjecture, then the results obtained by Philipson and Lakdawalla may be sensitive to their ability to measure quality. This is not just a problem for Philipson and Lakdawalla, but one which plagues most empirical work on cost and production in health care. The services index is the sole measure of quality in the model. The construction of the variable is not well specified. While it is plausible that the range of services is correlated with quality, it is not directly linked to common notions of quality. Thus the degree to which the estimated coefficient for the ownership dummy reflects the structure of firm preferences versus differences in quality remains somewhat uncertain.

The second source of uncertainty is that if the input-preferrer formulation holds, then one would expect to reject cost minimization, which is weakly tested by assessing the shape of the input demand functions. The evidence for nursing homes is consistent with a downward-sloping demand curve if one accepts the proposition that city location offers amenities, which implies that "relative wages (relative to urban price level) should be lower in cities." There are other explanations for what a city location dummy might represent, and it may be premature to place such a strong interpretation on the positive coefficient estimate for that variable. The finding is further complicated when Philipson and Lakdawalla consider econometric results from hospital markets that provide evidence of downward-sloping input demand curves and higher levels of input demand by nonprofits (conditional on beds).

Concluding Comment

The paper by Philipson and Lakdawalla offers a theoretical discussion which provides some new ways to interpret differences in observed patterns of behavior by for-profit and nonprofit health care providers. It also suggests reasons why health care markets might so often have mixes of for-profit and nonprofit firms. The authors offer some refutable propositions and provide some evidence offering support for the input-preferrer structure of preferences among nonprofit nursing homes. Unfortunately, the empirical work offered by Philipson and Lakdawalla is plagued with difficulties in measuring quality, which have often frustrated empirical analyses of health care providers. The objective function of nonprofit nursing homes (and health care providers generally) remains uncertain and continues to pose a challenge to economists interested in the productivity of different institutional forms in the health sector.

References

Frank, R. G., and D. S. Salkever. 1994. Nonprofit organizations in the health sector. *Journal of Economic Perspectives* 8 (4): 129–44.
Frank, R. G., and C. A. Taube. 1987. Technical and allocative efficiency in production of outpatient mental health clinic services. *Social Science and Medicine* 24 (10): 843–50.
Gertler, P., and D. Waldman. 1991. Quality-adjusted cost-functions and policy evaluation in the nursing home industry. *Journal of Political Economy* 100: 1232–56.
Goldman, F., and M. Grossman. 1988. The impact of public health policy: The case of community health centers. *Eastern Economic Journal* 14 (1): 63–72.
Weisbrod, B. A., and M. Schlesinger. 1986. Public, private, nonprofit ownership and the response to asymmetric information: The case of nursing homes. In *The economics of nonprofit institutions: Studies in structure and policy,* ed. S. Rose-Ackerman, 133–51. Yale Studies on Nonprofit Organizations Series. New York: Oxford University Press.

4

Price Indexes for Medical Care Goods and Services
An Overview of Measurement Issues

Ernst R. Berndt, David M. Cutler, Richard G. Frank,
Zvi Griliches, Joseph P. Newhouse, and Jack E. Triplett

Statistics on medical prices should be improved; indexes of
medical productivity should be developed; and the search for
an understanding of the determinants of medical price and
cost behavior should be developed.
—U.S. Department of Health, Education, and Welfare (1967)

4.1 Introduction

The measurement of the output of the medical care system is necessary
to assess the productivity levels and growth of a country's economy and
of course of its medical care system. This is true in countries with universal
health care coverage or incomplete coverage, and regardless of the mix of
public and private provision of medical care.

Ernst R. Berndt is professor of applied economics at the Sloan School of Management of
the Massachusetts Institute of Technology and director of the NBER's Program on Technological Progress and Productivity Measurement. David M. Cutler is professor of economics
at Harvard University and a research associate of the National Bureau of Economic Research. Richard G. Frank is professor of health economics at Harvard Medical School and
a research associate of the National Bureau of Economic Research. The late Zvi Griliches
was the Paul M. Warburg Professor of Economics at Harvard University and director of the
Productivity and Technical Change Program at the National Bureau of Economic Research.
He was past president of the Econometric Society and of the American Economic Association and a member of the National Academy of Sciences. Joseph P. Newhouse is the
John D. MacArthur Professor of Health Policy and Management and is on the faculties
of the Kennedy School of Government, the Harvard Medical School, the Harvard School of
Public Health, and the Faculty of Arts and Sciences at Harvard University, and a research
associate of the National Bureau of Economic Research. Jack E. Triplett is a visiting fellow
at the Brookings Institution.

The authors gratefully acknowledge research support from the U.S. Bureau of Economic
Analysis (Berndt, Cutler, Griliches), the U.S. Bureau of Labor Statistics (Berndt, Cutler,
Griliches), Eli Lilly and Co. (Berndt, Frank, Griliches, Triplett), the National Institute of
Mental Health (Frank), the National Institute on Aging (Cutler), the National Science Foundation (Berndt, Griliches), Hans Sigrist Stiftung (Newhouse), and the Alfred P. Sloan Foundation (Cutler, Frank, Newhouse). The authors have benefited from conversations with numerous colleagues and friends, and in particular they thank Dennis Fixler of the Bureau of
Labor Statistics, Brent Moulton of the Bureau of Economic Analysis, and Richard Zeckhauser of Harvard's Kennedy School of Government for comments on earlier drafts. A substantial portion of this chapter also appears in Berndt et al. (2000), and is reprinted with
permission from Elsevier Science.

For most industries in most countries, real output measurement is accomplished by dividing data on revenues or sales by a price index to obtain a measure of real output. Reliable output measurement for an industry therefore requires correspondingly reliable revenue data and a price index. A number of conceptual difficulties and institutional characteristics of medical care markets, however, make reliable price measurement of medical goods and services particularly difficult and challenging.

For countries where medical care goods and services are provided by the government without direct charge, or with only nominal direct charges, data on revenue or receipts for medical care may not be available or may not be relevant. For these countries, the problem of measuring the output of medical care goes well beyond the inherent difficulty of measuring medical care prices. In such cases the difficult problem of measuring prices and output of medical care is combined with the equally formidable problem of measuring the output of the government sector.[1]

Medical price indexes have uses other than those involving output and productivity measurement. In the United States, both within the health sector and more generally, contracts occasionally contain provisions that depend on growth of the medical Consumer Price Index (CPI).[2] Medical CPIs and medical Producer Price Indexes (PPIs) are also employed in updating fee schedules for certain administered pricing schemes and payments to some health plans. Medical CPIs and PPIs are also employed by public policy analysts in projecting the impacts of changes in public policy.

Although medical CPIs and PPIs play prominent roles in private and public sector transactions and analyses, both the U.S. Bureau of Labor Statistics (BLS) and its critics have acknowledged that current BLS practices for tracking price changes in the medical care industries, industries that are characterized by dynamic technological and organizational changes, are likely to be inaccurate and in need of substantial improvement and overhaul.[3]

Several aspects of the medical care industry make the BLS's task of constructing accurate and readily interpretable medical CPIs and PPIs particularly difficult. Output measurement of the health care system is inherently difficult when mortality is but one possible outcome from treatment. Mortality is particularly inappropriate as an output measure for treatments of a variety of acute conditions that are not life threatening, and for many increasingly prevalent chronic illnesses. Additional attributes such

---

1. For a discussion of measurement issues in public sector output, see Kendrick (1991) and Griliches (1992, 18–19). Murray (1992) and the Swedish Ministry of Finance (1997) contain empirical analyses of publicly provided health sector output and productivity growth.

2. For general discussion of CPI use in escalation clauses, see Triplett (1983).

3. See, for example, U.S. Senate Finance Committee (1996); U.S. Department of Labor, Bureau of Labor Statistics (1997b); and Abraham, Greenlees, and Moulton (1998).

as morbidity, pain and suffering, functional and emotional impairment, and quality of life are each highly valued aspects of treatment response.

Another output measurement challenge that is rather unique to the medical care sector arises from the moral hazard, caused by health insurance, that causes marginal private and social costs to diverge. As emphasized by, among others, Newhouse and the Insurance Experiment Group (1993), the existence of demand-side moral hazard or administratively set prices makes it inappropriate to attribute the usual normative properties to medical CPIs that are commonly associated with other such price indexes. The provision of medical care services also involves a principal-agent relationship: In choosing treatment, patients typically rely considerably on the advice and counsel of their physician, whose incentives and financial interests may or may not align well with those of the patient. Any misalignment of interests may result in inefficient outcomes.

A third dimension of medical care that poses significant price measurement challenges relates to technological progress. While not unique to medical care, technological progress is nevertheless of great significance in this sector of the economy. New treatment technologies are continually emerging and being introduced into common clinical practice. This creates many of the problems of new goods, with which economists interested in index number and productivity measurement have struggled for many years.[4]

Finally, organizational changes have been dramatic in the medical care sector. The manner in which medical technologies are rationed, delivered, and even priced has evolved rapidly during the last decade. Managed care arrangements have resulted in changes in the locus of care, the organization of medical practice, contractual relations between buyers and sellers, and the manner in which inputs are combined to create treatment. Thus the way in which typical treatment for an illness such as depression is organized and provided has been remarkably altered in just a few years. Even given a known set of treatment technologies, important qualitative differences have emerged in the supply of treatment and in the way care is experienced by patients.

In this chapter we review in considerable detail the measurement issues that underlie construction of medical care price indexes; we describe procedures employed by the BLS in the construction of its medical CPIs and PPIs (including recent revisions and changes); we discuss alternative notions of medical care output that involve the price of an episode of treatment rather than the prices of fixed bundles of inputs; we outline salient features of a new medical care expenditure price index; and we suggest future research and measurement initiatives that are likely to be most fruitful. We begin with a description of the market environment underlying medical care CPIs and PPIs in the United States.

---

4. See, for example, the chapters and references in Bresnahan and Gordon (1997).

4.2   The Market Environment Underlying Medical Care CPIs and PPIs

Viewed by an economic statistician, the medical care sector is large and intimidating. As with an elephant, one can employ several approaches in cautiously observing, walking around, and measuring it. We begin by describing the principal actors, characteristics, and incentive structures that must be taken into account in providing a foundation for the measurement of medical care prices.

4.2.1   Distinguishing Features of the U.S. Medical Care Marketplace

Economists generally presume some form of consumer optimization and efficiency in the purchase of goods and services. As in other markets, consumers of medical services are envisaged as maximizing some notion of utility, buying goods and services that generate direct utility, and using some of these goods and services as intermediate goods to produce utility. In the medical care marketplace, however, this optimization and efficiency is exceedingly complex; it involves behavior based on the use of asymmetric information and personnel who act as imperfect agents for consumers, under rationing constraints that are not nearly as pervasive as in other consumer markets.

The medical care industry provides goods and services in a number of specific subsectors: hospitals (including hotel and cafeteria services), physician practices, laboratories, pharmaceuticals, clinics, medical devices, nursing homes, home health agencies, and so on. These services are provided to consumers, but consumers typically do not value these services per se. Rather, they value the health outcomes resulting from medical interventions provided by the medical care industry.[5] These impacts on health are conceptually the composite good that we want to price, but the nature of transactions in this industry is exceedingly complex.

As in any industry, market structure affects the industry's price level, and perhaps the rate of price growth, particularly if production efficiency is affected over time. Licensing, reputation, the regulatory environment, and intellectual property rights provide suppliers of medical services with varying amounts of market power, particularly because some medical service suppliers such as hospitals and physicians face limited competition outside rather narrow geographical market boundaries. In many cases fixed costs are high, to a great extent consumers arrive at random times, and price is greater than short-run marginal cost.

Buyers also have market power. Although the federal government has long been a major purchaser of medical services (providing funds for about 39 percent of personal health care expenditures in the United States in 1996),[6] within the last decade there has been much consolidation of

---

5. For further discussion, see Triplett (1999, chap. 1 in this volume).
6. Levit et al. (1998), exh. 3, p. 39 and exh. 4, p. 43.

buying power among health maintenance and managed care organizations. Thus on both the supply and demand sides of the medical care marketplace, market power is present. Moreover, since most medical care services are not resellable, price dispersion is not easily eliminated by arbitrage, price discrimination is prevalent, and thus the law of one price typically does not hold.

There are several other features of the market structure of the medical sector that, while present to some extent in other sectors, are particularly pervasive in medical goods and services. First, the vast majority of medical care payments are not made directly by consumers. Indeed, in the United States in 1996, out-of-pocket payments by consumers accounted for only about 19 percent of total personal health care service expenditures.[7] The remainder of medical care is largely paid for by insurers.[8] Insurance programs may be run publicly, as with Medicare, Medicaid, and other federal, state, and local funds, which together accounted for 53 percent of personal health care service expenditures in 1996; or the sources of funds may be private, which in 1996 made up 37 percent of personal health care service expenditures, primarily for the nonelderly. Ultimately, the insurance payments not paid directly by individuals are passed back to individuals, in the form of higher taxes or reductions in other forms of government spending when the insurance payments are by the public sector, or in the form of an adjusted employee compensation package when insurance is provided by employers.[9]

The predominance of the indirect nature of payments creates several difficulties for constructing and interpreting consumer price indexes. The most significant of these is moral hazard. If consumers pay for only, say, 20 percent of medical care at the margin, they will seek to consume medical care until its marginal value is only about twenty cents per dollar of spending. This is true even though people *on average* must pay for the full dollar of medical care. Individuals will therefore tend to overconsume medical resources—resources will be consumed that cost society $1 (less if there are rents) but are worth less than that at the margin.

The second important feature of the medical care market is that consumers do not always know what services they want. Patients tend to rely on physicians both to provide them services and to recommend the services they need. As a result, there is a principal-agent problem: Patients would like physicians to act in the patients' best interests, but physicians might not always have an interest in doing so.

In traditional U.S. health insurance arrangements, physicians and patients both had incentives for excessive medical care. Patients were well-insured at the margin and physicians were paid on a fee-for-service basis—

7. Ibid.
8. In the United States, however, about 4 percent derives from other philanthropic sources.
9. For a discussion of the incidence of employer-provided health insurance, see Gruber (1994, 2000) and Pauly (1997).

earning more when they did more because fees were generally above marginal cost. The result was an incentive structure on both the demand and supply side that induced excessive care. Today's environment in the United States is much changed, and increasingly involves more complicated rationing. Health plans now often operate under fixed budgets, whereas before they typically passed costs through to the employer or government. Thus they have begun to employ administrative mechanisms and financial incentives to control health care spending. The result is that, with increasing frequency, patient demand incentives are at odds with those of their health plans or physicians.

The implication of both of these pervasive features of the medical care industry is that revealed consumer purchases are *not* a reliable guide to the marginal value of medical care. This is in contrast to other markets, such as that for, say, compact discs, where consumers' marginal valuations are likely to be well reflected in prices and expenditures. Consumers may receive too much medical care, as they likely did under traditional insurance arrangements, or too little care, as some allege they do under managed care or capitated insurance (one price per patient per year, independent of the amount of services the patient actually receives). In many markets, it is eminently reasonable to relate relative prices to marginal rates of substitution in consumption, but in medical care this assumption is simply not tenable. As a practical matter, this inability to employ the assumptions underlying traditional revealed preference theory severely hampers the ability of economic statisticians to construct accurate and readily interpretable price indexes for medical care.

The extent to which medical care services differ from other services can be illustrated by considering a hypothetical transaction in a restaurant. Suppose an individual places an order for a particular set of items on the menu, and then leaves. Another person enters the restaurant, sits down at a table, eats the meal that was ordered, and then leaves. Finally, a third person comes in and pays for the meal. In medical care, these three persons are the physician, the patient, and the insurer. Whose valuation shall one measure?

As with many other services such as ATM banking services, the production function for medical care involves interdependent efforts of suppliers and consumers. This interdependent aspect of medical care production makes it more difficult to distinguish between producer and consumer price indexes. Moreover, for consumers, medical care, health, and utility are quite different. This occurs in part because the production function for health has a number of arguments, other than medical care. One formulation of the production function is as follows:

health =

$H($medical care, knowledge, time, lifestyle, environment, etc.$)$.

It is useful to consider these other inputs into the production of health.[10] Many of the inputs have been shown to contribute more to health than medical care (Fuchs 1974, 1983). Knowledge, for example, mediates between medical care and health. Medical treatments must not only be produced, but they must be used as well, and knowledge about how to use them changes over time. To the extent that knowledge is nonrivalrous in nature and has public good properties, its existence together with the interdependent nature of production makes it difficult to assess uniquely the impacts of changes in knowledge on prices for suppliers versus those facing consumers.

As an example of the importance of medical knowledge, suppose that medical research discovers that a particular pharmaceutical agent is just as effective when taken in half a dosage strength as when taken at full strength; something like this occurred for contraceptives several decades ago. Has the price of medical care changed? From the consumers' perspective, the answer is likely yes, for the cost of achieving a particular health state has fallen.[11] From the pharmaceutical manufacturers' perspective, however, the answer may be no, for the marginal cost of producing a milligram of the medication may not have changed. From the vantage of the family practitioner physician, whether the price has fallen depends in part on how one views physician services. The advice provided by the physician to the patient may still take the same amount of billable time, but if the physician is part of a staff model health maintenance organization with total pharmaceutical coverage, the price of providing family planning services may have fallen.

Knowledge, of course, is just one form of technological change. The reason we distinguish knowledge from other forms of technological progress is that knowledge is often envisaged as *disembodied* technological progress, while most new technologies are *embodied* in a particular service or product. Although the absorption of knowledge is not without cost, to some extent knowledge has public good properties and is nonrivalrous, quite unlike, say, a piece of medical diagnostic equipment.

These two types of technological change overlap, yet it is useful to distinguish between them. Significant quality changes are often embodied in new medical care–related goods and services, but use of the new good may require additional knowledge. For example, a new noninvasive operation is typically performed by physicians using novel inputs (endoscopic instru-

---

10. For a more complete discussion, see Grossman (1972a, 1972b).

11. Even here, matters are complex. For a number of brand name pharmaceuticals in the United States (but not in Europe), the price per tablet is the same regardless of strength. Moreover, in the example here it is implicitly assumed that the consumers' cost for a contraceptive medication is not fully covered by insurance. Until recently in the United States, unlike the case for most medications for which the patient makes a copayment, for contraceptives consumers have generally borne the entire direct cost of the prescription.

ments), and knowledge about such new treatments can be usefully employed by patients and clinicians alike. In any case, it is appropriate to envisage knowledge as an input into the production of health, distinct from medical treatments.[12]

Another input into the production of health is time. Producing better health requires time inputs from households as well as providers: Time is spent in seeking and receiving treatment, in recovery, and in assisting others. Some medical innovations (for example, new anesthetics) have shortened the recovery time for patients.[13] This too will reduce consumers' cost of better health, but may well leave producers' costs unchanged (say, if the new anesthetic cost the hospital as much as the old).

An individual's lifestyle is another input into the production of health. Eating habits, drinking patterns, exercise regimens, and the pursuit of risky behavior all affect an individual's health. In some cases greater use of medical care and unhealthy behavior occur simultaneously to maintain a given health state. For example, with the introduction of over-the-counter H_2-antagonists such as Pepcid AC, individuals can preemptively take a heartburn prevention medication and then eat a high-calorie, highly spiced meal.

The environment is yet one more input that affects health. Environmental changes may improve or retard health. For example, new diseases like AIDS may develop and be discovered while other diseases like smallpox may be eradicated. Changes in air and water pollution, in climate and weather, as well as in rates of criminal activity will also have important impacts on health. It is important that such environmental changes be envisaged as primarily affecting the quantity or quality of medical services provided, not their price.

The age distribution of the population might also be envisaged as an environmental input affecting health care spending of populations. As people age, typically more inputs of medical care are required to maintain health or to mitigate deterioration. Increased medical care expenditures, or increased health insurance premiums that reflect impacts of an aging population, are appropriately viewed as quantity rather than price increases; in such cases medical expenditures rise due to increased quantity consumption, not price changes.

Finally, it is important to emphasize that while the marginal utility of health is positive, health is not the only argument in an individual's utility function. Thus a utility function might be envisaged as follows:

utility $= U$(health, lifestyle, leisure time, other consumption goods

and services, environment, etc.).

---

12. For an exchange of views on this, see Gilbert (1961, 1962) and Griliches (1962).

13. Because the largest cost of receiving medical care is often the patient's time cost, there are substantial incentives to develop innovations that conserve on time, particularly when the cost of these innovations is covered by insurance.

Note that some factors such as lifestyle and environment not only have a direct impact on utility, but also have an indirect impact via health. One important implication of this, as has been emphasized elsewhere by Triplett (1999, chap. 1 in this volume), is that the output of the medical care industry is not something like the *average* health of the population, but rather is best viewed in *marginal* terms as the health implication of a medical intervention, conditional on lifestyle, environment, and other inputs affecting health.

The production function for health, as well as the utility function, has intertemporal aspects. Some current consumption goods affect future health states as well as current utility, while some medical interventions impact future consumption possibilities and patterns. Here we put these complications aside, but see Grossman (1972a, 1972b) and Meltzer (1997) for further discussion.

4.2.2 Pricing Medical Care Services

With this discussion of salient characteristics of the medical care marketplace as background, we now consider approaches to price measurement. A representative consumer can be envisaged as an individual who is making decisions before knowing what diseases he/she might eventually experience. Extensions to heterogeneous consumers complicate matters, but for our purposes it is sufficient initially to work here with the simpler representative consumer framework.[14] Let this representative consumer have a utility function that depends on consumption of goods and services (other than medical care) and health. For concreteness, assume there is only one disease, which everyone contracts; extending the analysis to multiple diseases and probabilities of having each disease is straightforward. Denote Y as exogenous income, H as the health state, M as the quantity of medical care and P_M its (normalized) price, I and P_I as the quantity and price (premium) of a constant-quality insurance policy, K as medical care knowledge, E as the state of the environment, L as leisure time, and T_M as time allocated to receiving medical treatments. For simplicity, M and P_M include both consumers' direct health expenditures and indirect medical services obtained through health insurance in a competitive, actuarially fair insurance market where changes in costs of medical services to insurers are passed on to consumers via insurance premium changes. In this context, I and P_I are associated only with pure insurance services. The utility function is then written as

$$(1) \qquad U = U[Y - P_M M - P_I I, H(M, K, E), L - T_M].$$

The first term is nonmedical care consumption (nonmedical expenditures divided by numeraire price), the second is health, and the third is

---

14. For an extension to heterogeneous consumers, see Pollak (1980, 1998) and Fisher and Griliches (1995).

nonmedical care time.[15] Although equation (1) embeds a multiyear framework, for simplicity we assume but one time period. Notice also that equation (1) makes no assumption about how medical treatment decisions are made, or how medical prices are set.[16]

Over time, medical care and its price may change, or there may be changes in knowledge, the environment, and time devoted to medical care. For concreteness, consider changes between periods 0 and 1. The question posed is, What is the correct price index for changes between periods 0 and 1, assuming that consumers optimize in each time period? We can define the *cost of living* in one of several natural ways—the change in the cost of living between periods 0 and 1 is the additional funds the individual needs in period 1 to be just as well off as he/she was in period 0. This amount may be positive, in which case the cost of living has increased, or it may be negative, in which case the cost of living has fallen.[17] This hypothetical is associated with the Laspeyres base period utility notion of cost of living. An alternative, associated with the Paasche notion, uses the current period utility as the point of reference, and asks, What is the change in funds the individual needs in period 0 to be just as well off as he or she is in period 1? We consider this distinction in further detail below. A third index, the Fisher ideal, is the geometric mean of the Laspeyres and the Paasche.

Consider the amount C of additional money the consumer requires in period 1 to make him/her indifferent between living in periods 0 and 1 (the Laspeyres notion):

$$(2) \quad U[Y - P_{M1}M_1 - P_{I1}I_1 + C, H(M_1, K_1, E_1), L - T_{M1}]$$
$$= U[Y - P_{M0}M_0 - P_{I0}I_0, H(M_0, K_0, E_0), L - T_{M0}].$$

C is the change in the cost of living—a positive C implies an increase in the cost of living, and a negative C a decrease.

To form a price index, one can scale C by the income required to produce utility in period 0, or Y. The cost-of-living index could therefore be

15. For simplicity, time at work is omitted.

16. The relationship between utility maximization and index numbers relies critically on a number of assumptions. In the present context, such assumptions might well be that the consumer chooses M, I, K, and T_M, given Y, P_M, P_I, P_K (which could be zero at the margin if knowledge is nonrivalrous), E, and L, so as to maximize U in each time period. As we point out at various times in this paper, these assumptions are likely to be particularly untenable in the medical care marketplace.

17. The issues under discussion here involving measurement of the cost of living are very different from those raised by the Boskin Commission, who recommended that the BLS move from a Laspeyres price index formula to a superlative index such as the trailing Törnqvist, the latter more closely approximating a much more narrow notion of a cost-of-living index. See U.S. Senate Finance Committee (1996); Boskin et al. (1998); Abraham, Greenlees, and Moulton (1998); and Persky (1998).

(3)   cost-of-living index $\equiv 1 + C/Y$.

Using a first-order difference approximation, we differentiate and rearrange equation (2), yielding

(4) $C \equiv \{d(P_M M + P_I I)/dt - (U_H/U_X)$

   $[H_M(dM/dt) + H(dK/dt) + H_E(dE/dt)] + (U_L/U_X)(dT_M/dt)\}$,

where U_H is the marginal utility of health; U_X is the marginal utility of nonmedical consumption ($X \equiv Y - P_M M - P_I I$); U_L is the marginal utility of leisure; and H_M, H_K, and H_E are partial derivatives of H with respect to M, K, and E.[18] Several comments are worth noting.

The first term on the right-hand side of equation (4), $d(P_M M + P_I I)/dt$, is additional spending on medical care and insurance services over time. A spending increase may be due to increased quantities of medical services provided (direct or via health insurance), increases in the prices paid for those medical services by consumers/insurers, increases in the carrying cost of insurance, or increases in the quantity of pure insurance services provided. Thus it is clear that an increase in the cost of medical services, ceteris paribus (in particular, health outcomes and environment assumed constant), increases the cost-of-living index. Notice that if the medical environment changes, such as if a new disease such as AIDS appears, medical expenditures will likely increase, but this is not properly viewed as a change in the cost of living, for the latter assumes an unchanged environment. As Griliches (1997) has pointed out, price index computations assume an average, unaging, unchanging individual living in a world in which nothing changes except prices. When a country's population becomes more aged, medical expenditure and the quantity of medical resources consumed increase, but as stated earlier, this is properly viewed as an expenditure and quantity increase, not a price increase. Similarly, because outcomes are being held fixed in the Laspeyres-type hypothetical, if bacteria develop drug resistance and low-priced antibiotics are replaced by more expensive drugs, the price index should increase, reflecting the reduced efficacy (quality deterioration) of the older antibiotic.

The second set of terms in the first line of equation (4), $-(U_H/U_X)$ $[H_M(dM/dt) + H_K(dK/dt) + H_E(dE/dt)]$, is the dollar value of change in health over time. Health may change because the quantities of M, K, and/ or E change, or because of, say, changed efficacy of a given medical treatment (change in H_M). The $-U_H/U_X$ term is the marginal rate of substitution between health and all other goods. Multiplying the health change by this amount expresses health in dollars. Note that an improvement in

---

18. We assume here that $dC/dt = U_X$, and that the marginal price of nonrivalrous additional knowledge is zero.

health through any of these three channels, ceteris paribus, reduces the cost-of-living index, or in other words, $C < 0$.

The final term in equation (4), $(U_L/U_X)(dT_M/dt)$, is the change in the time cost of receiving medical care. Hours are converted into dollars by multiplying hours by the marginal rate of substitution between leisure and goods (in most cases, equal to the after-tax wage). If more efficient delivery of medical care reduces patient travel and waiting time for medical care, or if recovery time from orthopedic surgery is reduced due to increased use of arthroscopic surgery, ceteris paribus, the cost of living falls.

Our discussion to this point on cost of living is that for a representative consumer. There are various ways in which group or aggregate cost-of-living measures and price indexes can be constructed, even when consumers' preferences are diverse and income (or total expenditure) has an unequal distribution. As discussed by, among others, Pollak (1980, 1998) and Fisher and Griliches (1995), a common aggregation procedure is to weight each person's utility in each of the two time periods by his/her dollar share in total expenditures; the share weights can be base period, current period, or some average of the two (the Törnqvist index). The aggregate cost-of-living indexes, analogous to equation (4), then include terms that represent share-weighted averages of various expenditures. Notice also that such aggregate cost-of-living indexes are conditional on the distribution of income and demographic composition of the population.[19]

Several other issues merit attention. First, it is useful to consider the $P_M M + P_I I$ term in equation (4) further. One possible price index to compute would involve asking what price the consumer would pay in two adjacent time periods for an actuarially fair medical care insurance policy to keep on the same expected level of utility, ceteris paribus? Note that this is not the same as a disability insurance policy, for with that the beneficiary only recovers lost income and medical care costs, and is not compensated, for example, for lost utility due to loss of vision. The consumer may have an expected life pattern in mind, with age-related probabilities of experiencing certain diseases. Thus the price index would be based on the price of contracting for a year of medical costs, given expected disease susceptibility, technology, efficacy, environmental factors, and so forth.

Realizations over the ensuing time period could well change the market price of such an insurance contract, for a variety of reasons, with differing implications for price and quantity. If the consumption of more medical related goods is induced by the expansion of technological opportunities (new artificial hips) or changes in the environment (increased sensitivity to allergens), the change is appropriately viewed as one of quantity or

---

19. Pollak (1980, 1998) therefore calls these aggregate price indexes "plutocratic," and contrasts them with ones he names "democratic."

quality, not price. The premium paid on repriced insurance policies might increase as a result, but that is because of the changed technology or environment, not because of a price change. Note also that because of moral hazard, when improvements in technology occur, they may be difficult to value properly within the medical marketplace.

Earlier we noted that a Laspeyres type of cost-of-living index uses the base period utility as reference, whereas the Paasche employs the current period utility as the reference point. Suppose that in the time interval between the base and current periods, the individual experiences a deterioration in health state so severe that it no longer is biologically feasible for the individual in period 1 to maintain the period 0 level of utility, for example, if the individual loses eyesight or develops an illness such as AIDS. In such a case, there may not be any feasible answer to the Laspeyres question, but one might still be able to answer the Paasche question.

A still deeper problem occurs when unexpected changes take place, such as those that result in the unanticipated lengthening of life expectancy. An individual might want to alter considerably his/her lifetime optimization plan given a change in information, yet he/she may lack the resources to modify consumption to a new path that has now become optimal. Hence it is possible for the cost of living *per year* to increase, for the cost of living *a lifetime* to increase, all as a result of this unanticipated *benefit* of increased life expectancy. This raises difficult issues, and mixes up changes in cost-of-living indexes with technological progress. Cost-of-living indexes typically refer to the cost of a flow of services over a relatively short time period. Converting from, say, a lifetime stock to an annual flow may be reasonable if the population is assumed to be ageless or has a fixed age composition, if there are no unexpected changes, and if ex ante decisions are still correct ex post. If these conditions are not met, paradoxes may well emerge.

4.2.3 Forming a Price Index

A fundamental issue is how one estimates the values of the variables in cost-of-living index equations such as those in equations (3) and (4). Suppose we focus attention just on how changes in the medical sector affect the cost-of-living index. Although current procedures used by the BLS in its medical care–related CPIs and PPIs are discussed in detail below, here we briefly consider several alternative procedures.

One approach used in other settings is hedonic price analysis. If one estimates a regression model where the price of a medical service is the dependent variable, and where attributes of the medical procedure, the patient, and the provider are explanatory variables, then one can decompose price changes over time into changes in the value of services to patients and pure changes in price. An example of this type of hedonic price measurement, for the treatment of acute phase depression, is in Berndt, Busch, and Frank (chap. 12 in this volume).[20]

There are a number of problems with using hedonic analysis in this market. At the level of individual diseases, hedonic prices are not necessarily equal to consumers' marginal valuations. Because consumers are insured, the price they pay for medical care at the margin is different from the cost of medical care to society. Further, providers have their own incentives in recommending treatment decisions, which may reinforce or contradict consumer preferences. Thus, both because of moral hazard and principal-agent issues, we would not necessarily expect treatment decisions to be made optimally. Estimated parameters in hedonic price equations could therefore be based on data points reflecting socially (and privately) inefficient actions by consumers, physicians, and/or insurers. This raises difficulties in placing any social welfare interpretations on movements in hedonic price indexes over time.

Alternatively, one might perform hedonic analysis at the level of the insurance plan, as was recommended by Reder (1969) and as has been implemented by Jensen and Morrisey (1990). One could estimate a hedonic model for the price of insurance, using the attributes of the insurance policy as regressors, and thus infer the residual price increase. The difficulties here are both theoretical and practical.

At the theoretical level, a theory about how consumers choose health insurance plans is required that incorporates consumers' self-selection, moral hazard (augmented by tax subsidies), and preferences for compensation. Because most private health insurance is provided through employment, this involves a link between workers and employers, and between different workers within a firm. Our knowledge about how insurance decisions are made in firms is very limited.[21] Hedonic analysis also presumes that consumers are fully aware of the attributes of the good they are buying. But with health insurance, there are often fundamental parts of the insurance contract that consumers do not know—indeed, cannot know—in advance.[22]

At the practical level, we probably are unable to control for many of the other factors that influence plan costs. For example, plan premiums will depend on the health status of people who are enrolled in the plan as well

20. For an introductory discussion to the hedonic method, see Griliches (1988), chaps. 7 and 8, and Berndt (1991), chap. 4. Other applications in the medical context include Trajtenberg (1990), Berndt, Cockburn, and Griliches (1996), and Cockburn and Anis (chap. 11 in this volume).

21. See Gruber (2000), Pauly (1997), and Summers (1989).

22. For example, most consumers do not know the details of who they are allowed to see for cancer care in advance of being diagnosed with cancer. Indeed, the specific benefits may depend on the severity of the cancer of the person and may change with new knowledge about cancer treatment.

as the benefits offered. But plan enrollment reflects adverse selection. When premiums change, we need to be able to decompose them into changes in the cost of a given set of benefits, and changes in the sickness of the people enrolled in the plan. Without knowing in detail who is enrolled in each plan and what their expected medical spending would be, we cannot adequately control for the many factors involved in premium variation. Moreover, data to control for these factors are typically unavailable.[23] As with observations on disease-specific treatment costs, the analysis of cross-sectional and/or time series insurance policy data might well be comparing various inefficient equilibria.[24] This is particularly likely with noncontractable aspects of health plan rationing under managed care.

Pauly (1999) has recently revived Reder's proposal to use medical insurance prices as the basis of a price index for medical care. Pauly contends that the development of willingness-to-pay techniques in economics has become sufficiently advanced that one could now ask respondents to put evaluations on an insurance policy that covered some new medical technique, or a bundle of new medical techniques, compared with an insurance policy that did not cover those techniques. One advantage of this form of pricing insurance policies would be that it would in theory capture behavior toward risk in a way that is typically neglected in studies that address only the ex post cost of treating an illness/condition. If one has a disease, the cost of treating the disease matters. If one does not have the disease, then insuring against the risk of a costly medical bill, if the disease is contracted, is important. Though this alternative approach may have advantages over attempting to construct price indexes for the treatment of specific diseases, pricing insurance policies also has significant disadvantages, as discussed earlier in this chapter and by Feldstein (1969) many years ago, and willingness-to-pay techniques remain subject to framing reference point and other issues. Moreover, empirical work to implement Pauly's suggestion is not yet available.

Yet another alternative to the hedonic and insurance policy approaches is to make specific assumptions about the way that medical treatment decisions are made. For example, one can assume that consumers have a specified known distribution of preferences for one prescription drug over another, as in Fisher and Griliches (1995) and Griliches and Cockburn (1994), or that consumers are making purchase decisions for goods with a high out-of-pocket share, such as for prescription drugs in Cockburn and Anis (chap. 11 in this volume). One can then combine this model with observed data on treatment and prices to form a component of the cost-

---

23. This data situation is gradually improving. See Cohen et al. (1996) for a discussion of the Medical Expenditure Panel Survey.
24. For further discussion, see Feldstein (1969) and Prescott (1997).

of-living index. While this approach is reasonable in some applications, it does not work well in markets where consumer information is poor and the share of out-of-pocket costs is low, as occurs in most medical care markets.

A third option involves more direct measurement. Suppose one focuses on a particular disease or condition and estimates empirically the changes in treatment costs and medical outcomes for that disease. If in addition one makes an assumption concerning the dollar value of health improvements, one can calculate the various individual factors in a cost-of-living index. This approach has recently been implemented by Cutler et al. (1998, chap. 8 in this volume). If such an approach were to be followed more generally, it would of course be necessary to undertake such analyses for a representative mix of illnesses, where outcomes could be reliably measured. We return to a discussion of this approach later in this paper.

With this discussion on the difficulties of conceptualizing and implementing price measurement of medical care services as background, we now turn to a review of price measurement procedures currently employed by the BLS in its medical care–related CPIs and PPIs. As we shall see, while changes have recently been implemented at the BLS in its medical care CPI and PPI programs, for the most part the BLS still treats medical care in the same way it treats other industry and consumer prices. The combination of inherent difficulties in measuring service industry prices, distinctive features of the medical care industry, and use of traditional index number procedures for measuring prices makes clear interpretation of the BLS's current medical care CPIs and PPIs very difficult.

4.3   Construction of Medical Care CPIs and PPIs at the BLS

The U.S. Bureau of Labor Statistics (BLS) constructs and publishes CPIs and PPIs for various components and aggregations of medical care goods and services. Hereafter we denote these medical care CPIs and PPIs by the acronyms of MCPIs and MPPIs, respectively. Although the essential structure and conceptual foundations of these price index measurement efforts have been in place for some time, the BLS has recently announced and undertaken a considerable number of changes in its MCPI and MPPI programs. Here we summarize both continuing and recently changing procedures. We begin with a more general overview of the CPI and the PPI, and then we consider issues particularly important to measuring prices and quantities of medical care goods and services in the MPPI and MCPI programs.

4.3.1   A Brief Summary of the CPI

According to the BLS, the CPI is "a measure of the average change in the prices paid by urban consumers for a fixed market basket of goods and services."[25] It is calculated monthly and is published about two weeks after the end of the month to which it refers.[26] From its first regular publication in 1921 until the end of World War II, the CPI was called a cost-of-living index. In March 1944 the chairman of the President's Committee on the Cost of Living appointed a group of technical experts (Wesley Mitchell, Simon Kuznets, and Margaret Reid) to examine whether the BLS's cost-of-living index was properly accounting for war-related quality deteriorations in goods and services, as well as for the effects of rationing and shortages. Controversy had emerged in part because in 1942 the "Little Steel Formula" had been adopted, which linked permissible wartime wage increases to the index, but representatives from organized labor argued that the cost-of-living index understated true price inflation.[27]

Along with a special committee of the American Statistical Association appointed in 1943, the technical experts concluded that "the index understated the wartime price rise to some extent because of a number of factors, of which incomplete account of quality deterioration was only one."[28] To avoid confusion with popular notions of cost of living, the president's committee, as well as the union critique of the index, also recommended that the name be changed to Consumers' Price Index, a change which was adopted in August 1945.[29]

Since 1945 many changes have occurred involving the BLS's construction of the CPI, but its underlying hierarchical structure has been relatively stable. The identity and number of items sampled, and the weights used in aggregating sampled items into increasingly comprehensive subindexes, constitute a hierarchical structure of market baskets that the BLS changes infrequently. Based on data from its Consumer Expenditure Surveys (CEX), the BLS identifies and defines a fixed "market basket" of goods, employing a classification system known as the item structure. The item structure has been updated approximately every ten years; the most recent update took place in January 1998.

For example, based on data from the 1993–95 CEX, the BLS identified

25. U.S. Department of Labor, Bureau of Labor Statistics (1992), 176.

26. Here we focus primarily on the CPI for All Urban Consumers (CPI-U), introduced in 1978 and representative of the buying habits of about 80 percent of the U.S. noninstitutional population. An alternative index, CPI-W (wage earners and clerical workers only), was introduced much earlier for use in wage negotiations, and represents only 32 percent of the U.S. population. The methodology for producing CPI-U is the same as that for CPI-W.

27. Hoover (1961), 1175. Union criticism of the index was written up in a "Meany Report," mentioned by Hoover. Also see Persky (1998).

28. Hoover (1961), 1175. Hoover reports that from January 1941 to September 1945, the estimated downward bias was 5 percentage points. Also see Weiss (1955).

29. Hoover (1961), 1175, n. 2; also see Weiss (1955), 23. Incidentally, the Meany report argued that "To most people, 'cost of living' means the amount of money a family spends. If it buys more food and finer clothes, or moves to a roomier home, its cost of living goes up. That interpretation is so widespread that we think the Bureau's index is misnamed" (quoted in Hoover 1961, 1175, n. 2).

eight major product groups of items for representation in the CPI beginning in January 1998: food and beverages, housing, apparel and upkeep, education and communication, transportation, medical care, entertainment, and other goods and services. In turn, these major groups are divided into seventy expenditures classes, which are disaggregated further into 211 item strata. Weights for the 211 item strata are fixed in between major revisions, as are those for the higher level of aggregations of strata into expenditure classes, intermediate aggregates, major groups, and all items indexes. The CPI calculations are done separately for thirty-eight geographic areas.[30]

CPI calculations are undertaken based on a modified Laspeyres price index. The Laspeyres price index is a weighted sum of price relatives, where the weights are revenue shares of each of the N item strata in the market basket. For month t, the Laspeyres price index is

$$(5) \qquad L_t \equiv \sum_{i=1}^{N} w_{ib}[p_{it}/p_{ib}], \quad w_{ib} \equiv \frac{p_{ib}q_{ib}}{\sum_{i=1}^{N} p_{ib}q_{ib}},$$

where p_{it} is the price of the ith item in time period t; $i = 1, \ldots, N$; p_{ib} are base period prices; q_{ib} are fixed base period quantities; and w_{ib} is the fixed base period expenditure weight. The term p_{it}/p_{ib} is often called the "price relative" of good i. An attractive feature of the Laspeyres index is that it is consistent in aggregation; in other words, one obtains the same composite Laspeyres index by aggregating over all items simultaneously, or first aggregating items into a set of subindexes, and then constructing a master aggregate from the weighted subindexes.

Because the CPI has 211 item strata, the terms p_{it}/p_{ib} in equation (5) are in fact price indexes, often called "basic components" or "elementary aggregates." There are thousands, perhaps millions, of items in a modern economy. Within each of the 211 item strata, BLS takes a probability sample of the detailed items (termed entry-level items, or ELIs) that are grouped together into each of the item strata. For example, in the medical care component, there are 13 item strata. Based on a nonlinear programming optimization algorithm, the BLS determines the optimal number of price quotes at the expenditure class level.[31] For some of the item strata (e.g., baby-sitting, carpooling), it is very difficult to obtain sample price data; thus for 27 of the 211 item strata, the BLS does not sample prices, but instead imputes prices from other goods and services in the same expenditure class. When a detailed item is selected for pricing in the CPI, a

---

30. Lane (1996), 22. Also see Ford and Ginsburg, (1998, chap. 5 in this volume). Several of these numbers have been revised since publication of these articles. We thank Dennis Fixler for providing final updates.

31. This optimization problem and its implementation are discussed in Leaver et al. (1997).

price for the exact same item is collected at regular intervals, usually monthly or bimonthly. These detailed prices are formed into the basic component price indexes, which are the lowest level for which price index information is published in the CPI.

To accommodate practical issues involving the fact that some products are discontinued and cannot be repriced, that consumers' point of purchasing items changes, and that the CEX provide data on expenditures rather than prices, current BLS practice incorporates a number of modifications. The related issues are discussed in further detail in U.S. Department of Labor, Bureau of Labor Statistics (1997b, 1998) and in Moulton and Stewart (1997).[32] Here it is worth emphasizing that while weights may change for elementary items within item strata (due in part to sample rotation), at the item strata level and above, the weights are fixed over time between major revisions, and thus for aggregate price indexes at the level of item strata and higher, use of equation (5) with its fixed weights is essentially what is done by the BLS.

In 1997 the BLS began issuing a monthly experimental measure constructed with use of the geometric mean formula for all index components at levels of aggregation underneath the item strata. The geometric mean index permits limited substitutability among products within the item strata. Provided that commodity substitution is the primary economic behavior that affects these lower level indexes, the difference between geometric and arithmetic mean item strata indexes can be interpreted as a measure of "lower level" substitution bias.[33] This experimental index using geometric means appears to lower the growth of the all-items CPI by approximately 0.25 percent per year.[34]

Recently the BLS announced that beginning in January 1999, the aggregating formula for constructing most of the elementary aggregates (comprising approximately 61 percent of total consumer spending) will be moved over to a geometric mean. Medical care CPI components are largely exceptions, however; all but prescription drugs, nonprescription drugs, and medical supplies will continue to be constructed by the traditional arithmetic mean calculation.[35] Note that for each of the more highly aggregated 211 item strata, fixed quantity weights will still be employed, reflecting the continuing assumption of zero substitutability *between* these strata.

With this overview of the CPI hierarchical structure, weights, and aggregation formulas as background, we now move on to a brief summary of the PPI.

32. Also see Moulton (1996) and Moulton and Moses (1997).
33. See Pollak (1998) for further discussion.
34. U.S. Department of Labor, Bureau of Labor Statistics (1997a).
35. U.S. Department of Labor, Bureau of Labor Statistics (1998), updated in Eldridge (1998).

4.3.2   A Brief Summary of the PPI

The Producer Price Index (PPI) "measures average changes in selling prices received by domestic producers for their output."[36] Before 1978 the BLS named this price series its Wholesale Price Index (WPI). The change in name to Producer Price Index emphasized that its conceptual foundations were based on prices received by producers from whomever makes the first purchase, rather than on prices paid to wholesalers by retailers or others further down in the distribution chain.[37] At the same time, the structure of the index was changed substantially. The old WPI corresponded, roughly, to the P in the well-known quantity theory of value expression, $MV \equiv PT$. In this view of an inflation index, all transactions mattered, so the WPI combined into one index the prices of, for example, iron ore, steel, and the automobile in which the steel was an input.[38] The resulting substantial double counting in the WPI was regarded as a serious problem.[39] In response, the BLS converted the old price index to the concept of an industry output price index.[40] As a result, the basic measurement unit for the PPI has become an industry—in the case of medical care, hospitals, physicians' offices and clinics, and nursing homes are each separate industries. The PPI publishes separate price indexes for the outputs of each of these industries.

The PPI is calculated monthly and is usually published in the second or third week following the reference month. The PPI involves pricing the output of domestic producers, while the BLS's International Price Program publishes price indexes for both imports and exports.

The PPI program at the BLS takes as its definition of an industry the one based on the Standard Industrial Classification (SIC) code.[41] Since its inception in 1902, the PPI has focused heavily on the goods-producing sectors of the U.S. economy, but ever since 1986, in recognition of the growing importance of services in the U.S. economy, the BLS has gradually begun to broaden the PPI's scope of coverage into the service sectors.

Currently the BLS does not calculate and publish an economy-wide aggregate goods and services PPI, although it plans to do so beginning in January 2002. Rather, PPIs are published by industry (based on the SIC four-digit industry code and higher levels of aggregation), by commodity

36. U.S. Department of Labor, Bureau of Labor Statistics (1992), 140.

37. Ibid., 141.

38. The WPI did not implement this theory completely, however, for it omitted nearly all service prices and also transactions in financial and secondhand assets.

39. See Council on Wage and Price Stability (the "Ruggles Report") (1977).

40. The implementation of an industry output price index was based on the theoretical model developed by Fisher and Shell (1972), and amplified by Archibald (1977) and Diewert (1983).

41. Issues concerning how industries are defined and aggregated, as well as economic issues underlying the SIC code system, are discussed in Triplett (1990).

classification (by similarity of end use or material composition, regardless of whether these products are classified as primary or secondary in their industry of origin, for fifteen major commodity groupings), and by stage of processing (according to the class of buyer and the amount of physical processing or assembling the products have undergone); separately for finished goods, intermediate materials, and crude materials; and both by commodity and industry classifications. In this chapter we focus primarily on PPIs by industry.

Within each industry, the BLS calculates aggregate PPIs using the Laspeyres price index formulas (see equation [5] above). At the most disaggregated level of PPI price measurement (called the cell index), the BLS defines a price as "the net revenue accruing to a specified producing establishment from a specified kind of buyer for a specified product shipped under specified transactions terms on a specified day of the month."[42] Prices are for output currently being provided or shipped, and not for order or futures prices.[43] Although in general the BLS seeks transactions rather than list prices for its price quotes, responses by firms are less cumbersome when list rather than transactions prices are reported.[44] Participation in the PPI by firms is on a voluntary basis. As of December 1992, the overall PPI "productive" response rate was 63 percent (Catron and Murphy 1996, table A.2).

The PPI is also based on a hierarchical system, though as noted above, unlike the case of the CPI, currently there is no economy-wide measure of the PPI. The BLS constructs and publishes aggregate PPIs for the total mining and total manufacturing industries, but apparently because of a lack of sufficient coverage, the BLS does not currently publish an aggregate PPI for total services; the BLS hopes to publish such an aggregate services industry PPI by January 2002.[45]

Price quotes from the most disaggregated cell indexes are aggregated via a Laspeyres weighting scheme, in which fixed weights are based on value of shipments data collected primarily by the Bureau of the Census; industry net output weights are employed to account for intraindustry sales. The net output weights therefore vary with the level of industry aggregation (e.g., four-digit to two-digit); the detailed industry flow data required to distinguish net from gross output are derived for the most part from use of input-output tables compiled by the Bureau of Economic Analysis. Beginning in January 1996, industry price indexes have been calculated pri-

---

42. U.S. Department of Labor, Bureau of Labor Statistics (1992), 141. Net revenue is net of any discounts as opposed to net of production costs.
43. Problems can emerge for industries in which a great proportion of currently shipped output is covered by long-term price contracts, but for which "spot" prices differ from contracted prices.
44. U.S. Department of Labor, Bureau of Labor Statistics (1992), 141–42.
45. U.S. Department of Labor, Bureau of Labor Statistics, 1996a, 1.

marily with net output weights based on 1987 input-output relationships. The 1992 input-output tables have just recently been released, and the BLS envisages using them by the end of 1998 or early 1999 (Lawson 1997).

With respect to the specific establishments and items sampled by the BLS in its PPI program, the BLS currently draws a sample of items for each industry on average every seven years or so, and then reprices this fixed set of items monthly until an entirely new sample is drawn. Since 1978, the BLS has attempted to employ a sampling procedure that makes the probability of selection proportional to a product's value of shipments. Because it recognized that in some technologically dynamic industries a seven-year time lag between samples could result in a sample of products and services much older and quite unrepresentative of market transactions, in 1996 the BLS announced that for certain industries, including pharmaceuticals and electronics, samples would be supplemented at one- or two-year intervals (Kanoza 1996).

Issues surrounding the reliability and possibility of biases in price index measurement have recently received much less attention for the PPI than for the CPI. Use of the Laspeyres weighting procedure, accounting for unmeasured quality changes, and discontinuation and exit of sampled goods and services raise issues which in many respects are similar for the CPI and PPI. On the other hand, a number of significant differences exist between the CPI and PPI medical care components.

First, the lowest level of aggregation is defined differently in the two indexes: The PPI is defined on four-digit SIC industries, and below that, the item detail is defined specifically to each of the diagnosis-related medical care industries (major groups for the hospital index, medical specialties for the physicians' index, and so forth). The item strata in the CPI are based on groups that, in principle, should correspond to consumer demand categories (Lane 1996).

Second, the frequency and nature of major revisions differ. The CPI has been revised every ten to twelve years, when new weights are assigned based on the consumer expenditure survey. The PPI is normally rebased every five years, with weights drawn from the economic censuses.[46]

For the medical price indexes, another major difference exists between CPI and PPI. In the case of the PPI, revenues and output prices collected from the sampled unit refer to revenues from all sources—government, industry, and final consumers. For the CPI, only consumers' out-of-pocket costs are included. Government expenditures made on behalf of consumers and financed by taxes and health expenditures by insurance companies

---

46. Another difference involves the length of time between collection of underlying sales revenue census/expenditure survey data and the introduction of new weights into the Laspeyres index. For the PPI, this is about one to two years, but for the CPI it has been about three to four years.

in which employers (but not consumers directly) pay the premiums are out of scope for the present definition of the CPI. We return to discuss this difference in scope in section 4.3.4 below.

With these overview discussions of the CPI and PPI as general background, we now move to consideration of issues of particular importance to medical care goods and services. We begin with the MPPI.

4.3.3 PPIs for Medical-Related Goods and Services

As noted above, the BLS does not construct and publish a PPI for an aggregate of services. Nor does the BLS publish a PPI for an aggregate consisting of medical-related goods and services. Indeed, it is only within the last decade that the BLS, as part of its increased effort to measure prices in the various service industries, has begun publishing price indexes for hospital and physician services.

Among the manufacturing industries associated with health care, the BLS has published PPIs for some time for industries such as pharmaceuticals; hospital beds; medical books; surgical, medical, and dental instruments and supplies; ophthalmic goods; and others. Among the service industries, separate PPIs for numerous health care–related industries are a rather recent development. A PPI for health services was introduced by the BLS effective December 1994, for offices and clinics of doctors of medicine in December 1994, for skilled and intermediate care facilities in December 1994, for hospitals in aggregate and by type in December 1992, and for medical laboratories in June 1994.

If the BLS is ever to construct an aggregate MPPI, as with other industry aggregates, it will need to distinguish net from gross output by industry, using some form of an input-output matrix to measure inter- and intraindustry flows. Given the major changes in the health care sectors over the last decade, including impacts from the growth of managed care, it will of course be necessary to employ input-output matrices that are based on much more recent data than the 1987 input-output matrix currently employed by the BLS for defining net output in other industries. While the BLS plans to begin using 1992 input-output data beginning in late 1998, these data will already be six years out of date, and much organizational and technological change has occurred in the health care industries since 1992.

Output Measurement in the MPPI

A central measurement issue in the construction of MPPIs involves the specification and implementation of a concept of industry output. Although the PPI program utilizes the four-digit SIC classification system to identify and define industries, this SIC structure does not provide information enabling the BLS to define what is the appropriate real output concept in medical care industries, or on how this output quantity and output price can best be measured.[47] As we shall see, important problems also emerge when medical treatments from distinct SIC industries are substituted for each other in treating an illness or condition.

In the United States, medical goods and services were traditionally paid for by fee-for-service arrangements. In a fee-for-service context, a reasonable business procedure involves identifying and separately billing for each particular component of medical care from, say, a physician, a hospital, and a pharmacy. The fee-for-service was essentially the price for the inputs to medical care.

In 1983 the Health Care Financing Administration (HCFA) introduced major changes in how general acute care hospitals treating Medicare patients were to be reimbursed. Specifically, beginning in 1983 HCFA implemented a prospective payment system for inpatient hospital care whereby general acute care hospitals received a fixed payment for almost every Medicare patient admission, regardless of the amount or duration of services actually provided to the patient. This prospective payment mechanism represented a sharp departure from the retrospective cost-based accounting framework used for many years.

Medicare prospective payment schedules are based on estimates of (average accounting) costs for the resources utilized in providing services for a typical patient in a given geographical area being treated for a particular medical case. As of 1995 payments were distinguished for treatments of twenty-four major diagnostic categories, which are broken down further into 495 medical and surgical groupings, known as diagnostic related groups (DRGs).[48] The DRG prospective payment schedules have been updated regularly by Congress utilizing recommendations from the Secretary of Health and Human Services and the Prospective Payment Assessment Commission (now the Medicare Payment Advisory Commission); updates include changes in "medical costs" and case-mix indexing to account in part for secular trends in upcoding, also known as "DRG creep."

DRGs provide one possible output concept, and while DRGs in theory are applicable to all populations, Medicare currently employs DRGs only to reimburse hospitals for inpatient hospital care; many outpatient commodities (e.g., home health care) and services for illnesses of the elderly, and particularly of the nonelderly, are not included in the DRG system.[49]

Classification schemes used for other services include version 4 of Cur-

---

47. For a discussion of the economic foundations underlying SIC definition, see Triplett (1990).

48. A number of these 495 DRGs are no longer valid. For a recent list, see Prospective Payment Assessment Commission (1995), app. E.

49. DRG weights have been calculated for nonelderly patients for Maryland, New Hampshire, and New York, but no DRG nonelderly weights exist based on national data. However, a limited number of private insurers use DRGs for nonelderly beneficiaries, as do several state Medicaid programs. Also see note 51.

rent Procedural Terminology (CPT4) codes, a list containing thousands of procedures for which physicians and hospitals can bill; these CPT4 codes can be envisaged as inputs into the treatment of an illness or condition.[50]

A systematic structure of diagnostic codes for illnesses and conditions is version 9 (now, version 10, but for most of this time period version 9; thus we refer to version 9) of the International Classification of Diseases (ICD-9).[51] Relationships among ICD-9, CPT4 and DRG codes are multi-faceted. A single DRG encompasses treatment of somewhat arbitrary ag-gregations of distinct ICD-9 diagnoses, alternative combinations of CPT4 codes can be used in the treatment of a particular ICD-9 diagnosis, and a given CPT4 procedure can be used in the treatment of various ICD-9 diagnoses. Other diagnostic-related systems used in setting risk-adjusted capitation rates include the Ambulatory Care Group algorithm (Weiner et al. 1996) and the Diagnostic Cost Group's Hierarchical Coexisting Condi-tions models (Ellis et al. 1996).

DRGs and their offspring represent the beginning of a structure which could facilitate defining, measuring, and pricing the output of medical care providers. In particular, the output of a particular DRG billing involves the treatments for an episode of hospitalization for a particular condition/ diagnosis. Instead of pricing each of the components of a hospitalization, with DRGs the composite bundle of hospital services is given a single ex ante price.[52]

Along with the development of CPT4 and ICD codes, the notion of an episode of illness or treatment has expanded far beyond the hospitalization realm, suggestive of yet alternative ways of measuring medical care out-put. Numerous professional medical associations, as well as the Agency for Health Care Research and Quality (AHRQ), an agency of the Public Health Service in the U.S. Department of Health and Human Services, have developed clinical practice guidelines and treatment protocols for various illnesses and conditions. These treatment guidelines, which change over time, define ex ante medically acceptable and often therapeutically similar bundles of treatment involving medical inputs such as laboratory tests, pharmaceuticals, minutes of service from physicians and other med-ical personnel, and various other inpatient and outpatient procedures. Health insurance plans, hospitals, and pharmaceutical companies have de-veloped programs and protocols for the management of certain diseases. These disease management programs implicitly, and sometimes explicitly, suggest outputs of the medical sector that facilitate the pricing of treat-

---

50. For a discussion of CPT4, see American Medical Association (1990).

51. ICD-9 codes are discussed and listed in U.S. Department of Health and Human Ser-vices (1980). The ICD-9 system with clinical modifications is called ICD-9-CM, and it has recently been updated to version 10.

52. The Medicare payment scheme reserves 5 percent of its payments for outlier or excep-tionally expensive cases. At the margin, these are reimbursed on a cost basis.

ment bundles and the accounting framework for assigning payments to providers.[53]

With this as background, we now turn to a discussion of how the BLS's PPI program has implemented medical care sector output price and quantity measurement, and how it has built on the notion of DRG treatment episodes as output measures in the health care sector. As noted earlier, within the last decade the BLS's PPI program has made major changes in health care related PPIs and introduced many new ones. We begin with a discussion of medical services—physicians and hospitals—and then we discuss selected medical goods, such as pharmaceuticals.

Physicians' Services in the MPPI. The PPI program has initiated procedures for constructing medical service PPIs at two rather aggregate levels, physicians' services and hospital services. Each of these two classes of services in turn encompasses a variety of more detailed physicians' and hospital service industries. In table 4.1 we list the entire set of detailed physician, hospital, and medical laboratory industries in SIC 80 for which the BLS is currently constructing health services subindex PPIs.

With respect to offices and clinics of doctors of medicine ("physicians' services"), the new BLS procedures distinguish Medicare from non-Medicare treatments. Within the non-Medicare treatments, multispecialty group practices are treated separately from one- and two-physician practices and single specialty group practices, with the latter in turn being broken down into nine specialties. For skilled and intermediate care facilities, public payers are distinguished from private.

The second principal subindex within health services is hospital services. As is seen in table 4.1, general medical and surgical hospitals are differentiated from psychiatric hospitals and other specialty hospitals aside from psychiatric. Both inpatient and outpatient treatments are separated into those involving Medicare patients, Medicaid patients, and all other patients; for the non-Medicare and non-Medicaid inpatients, hospital treatments are differentiated involving twenty-three distinct illnesses/diseases/conditions.

Development of the BLS's PPIs for physician services has benefited considerably from the prior implementation and common usage of the DRG, CPT4, and ICD classification systems by insurers, hospitals, physicians, and other providers.[54] Based on a sampling universe including all physician practices in the United States, the BLS employs probability sampling stratified by size and specialty. The size of a physician practice is based on the

---

53. See Triplett (1999) for further discussion.

54. It is interesting to note, however, that in 1996 the percentage of preferred provider organizations reimbursing hospitals by DRG-based methods was only 31.7 percent (80.2 percent used per diem methods), and that only 7.7 percent of hospitals were reimbursed by PPOs using DRG-based methods. See Hoechst Marion Roussel (1997), 86.

Table 4.1   **Subindexes of the Health Services Producer Price Index**

Industry	SIC Code
Health services	80
Offices and clinics of doctors of medicine	8011
Primary services	8011-P
Medicare treatments	8011-1
Non-Medicare treatments	8011-3
One- and two-physician practices and single specialty group practices	8011-31
General/family practice	8011-311
Internal medicine	8011-312
General surgery and other surgical specialties	8011-313
Pediatrics	8011-314
Obstetrics/gynecology	8011-315
Radiology	8011-316
Psychiatry	8011-317
Anesthesiology	8011-318
Other Specialty	8011-319
Multispecialty group practices	8011-331
Skilled and intermediate care facilities	8053
Primary services	8053-P
Public payers	8053-101
Private payers	8053-301
Other receipts	8053-SM
Hospitals	806
General medical and surgical hospitals	8062
Primary services	8062-P
Inpatient treatments	8062-1

(*continued*)

Table 4.1 (continued)

Industry	SIC Code
Medicare patients	8062-131
All medical diagnosis-related groups	8062-13101
All surgical diagnosis-related groups	8062-13103
Medicaid patients	8062-171
All other patients	8062-171
Diseases and disorders of the nervous system	8062-17101
Diseases and disorders of the eye	8062-17102
Diseases and disorders of the ear, nose, mouth, and throat	8062-17103
Diseases and disorders of the respiratory system	8062-17104
Diseases and disorders of the circulatory system	8062-17105
Diseases and disorders of the digestive system	8062-17106
Diseases and disorders of the hepatobiliary system and pancreas	8062-17107
Diseases of the musculoskeletal system and connective tissue	8062-1708
Diseases and disorders of the skin, subcutaneous tissue, and breast	8062-17109
Endocrine, nutritional, and metabolic diseases and disorders	8062-17111
Diseases and disorders of the kidney and urinary tract	8062-17112
Diseases and disorders of the male reproductive system	8062-17113
Diseases and disorders of the female reproductive system	8062-17114
Pregnancy, childbirth, and puerperium	8062-17115
Newborns and other neonates with conditions originating in the perinatal period	8062-17116
Diseases and disorders of the blood and blood-forming organs and immunological disorders	8062-17117
Myeloproliferative diseases and disorders, and poorly differentiated neoplasms	8062-17118
Infectious and parasitic diseases (systemic or unspecified sites)	8062-17119
Mental diseases and disorders	8062-17121
Alcohol/drug use and alcohol/drug-induced organic mental disorders	8062-17122
Injuries, poisonings, and toxic effect of drugs	8062-17123
Burns	8062-17124
Factors influencing health status and other contacts with health services	8062-17125

number of physicians in a given practice (not the number of employees, or revenues); the sample is stratified further into nine single specialty categories and one multispecialty category. Initially in 1993–94 it was expected that the total number of physician practices sampled would be about 400 and the number of quotes obtained would be about 1,150,[55] but by mid-1997 only 158 units remained in sample, yielding 845 quotes (Fixler and Ginsburg, chap. 6 in this volume).

Given the sampling unit, at the price quote initiation point in time, the BLS randomly chooses a bill that measures the net prices paid to a physician practice for the entire set of services or procedures provided during an office visit, distinguished by type of payer (cash, third party insurance, Medicaid, Medicare, etc.).[56] The physician's output from this visit is represented by the content of the patient's bill, including all the CPT codes associated with that visit. To ensure that the unique combinations of inputs listed on a bill associate with a particular medical condition or surgical procedure, an association which is critical for repricing, the BLS also employs the ICD system, a coding scheme with which physician offices have considerable familiarity.[57] It is worth noting that the net transactions price by payer type requested by the BLS represents the actual anticipated revenues, including discounts, and not billed charges based on, for example, a "chargemaster."

With this sample bill, the BLS contacts the sampled physician unit each month, and asks it to reprice what the current net transactions prices would be for that particular bundle/payer of services. Thus items on the sample bill remain fixed over time (between major revisions), but item prices could change. Because transaction prices may vary from private payer to private payer, this may present considerable difficulty in practice. Indeed, some payers pay the physician in part or in whole by capitation, thereby making the price for any specified mix of services arbitrary.

PPIs for physicians' services have been published since December 1993. Monthly repricing of physicians' bills presents the BLS with numerous practical difficulties. In some cases, bills are purged from the physicians' accounting systems, and therefore cannot be repriced; this has occurred for about thirty-five (4–5 percent of all) quotes each year. In other cases, the reporter at the sample unit has refused to provide line by line quotes; this has transpired for about twenty-five (3 percent of all) quotes each year (Fixler and Ginsburg, chap. 6 in this volume).

In addition to facing such repricing difficulties at physician practices that continue to cooperate with the PPI, the BLS is operating in an envi-

---

55. See U.S. Department of Labor, Bureau of Labor Statistics, n.d.-a, 2.

56. According to Fixler and Ginsburg (chap. 6 in this volume), in 1996 12 percent of physician revenues came from Medicaid, 43 percent from private insurance, 18 percent from consumers out-of-pocket, and 27 percent from Medicare.

57. How the pattern of comorbidities is allocated in such cases is not clear.

ronment in which the organization of physician practices has undergone dramatic changes in the last few years as practices have been consolidated and sold to larger provider groups. Thus it is not surprising that sample attrition for physicians' services has been considerable. The impact of this physician practice and bill repricing attrition on the representativeness of the current sample frame is currently unknown.

Finally, in terms of quality change, serious difficulties remain, even with the use of CPT codes. For example, if a new laboratory test becomes available that is more sensitive, reliable, and expensive, yet is used for diagnosis of the same condition and has the same CPT code as its predecessor, it will be considered a price change.[58] In such a case, quality improvements will not be incorporated. On the other hand, if the laboratory tests are read and examined by less experienced technicians having larger error rates but price is constant, quality declines would be overlooked. Currently the BLS makes no quality adjustments for the physician or laboratory services component of the MPPI.[59]

Hospital Services in the MPPI. We now turn to the PPI for hospital services, which the BLS has published since its December 1992 base period. The hospital services PPI measures anticipated net prices paid to hospitals for the entire bundle of services received during a hospital stay, given the type of payer. The hospital's output is represented by the content of a patient's bill, including all room charges, medical supplies, drugs, and ancillary services provided the patient during a single hospital stay; for an outpatient visit, the hospital output is the anticipated net revenues to be received for medical supplies, drugs, and ancillary charges accruing from a single hospital visit.

As with the PPI for physicians' services, the hospital service PPI attempts to be based on patients' bills that specify the purpose of the hospitalization, as recorded by ICD codes; such an association is important so that repricing is based on a unique combination of inputs listed on the bill with a particular medical condition or surgical procedure. This focus on hospitalization episode for a particular treatment is preferable to pricing based on bed-days, drugs, tests, and other factors irrespective of the patient's illness. To take into account the possibility that price per bed-day is increasing along with a reduction in average length of stay, when repricing the BLS's PPI program now explicitly asks whether there has been a change in average length of stay for the hypothetical price quote. If such a change has occurred, it is treated as a quality change, not simply a price change. As of 1998, the change in average length of stay is the only adjust-

58. If the CPT code changes, either a new bill will be constructed and repriced, or the new and old laboratory test will be linked in.
59. For further discussion of quality adjustments, see Moulton and Moses (1997) and Nordhaus (1998).

ment the hospital PPI makes for quality change (personal communication with Fixler).

In principle, net transactions prices incorporate effects of discounts, and therefore are not "list" or "chargemaster" prices. It is not known what proportion of transactions in hospitals *actually* involve only list prices, list prices less certain adjustments, or capitation, and how this has changed since, say, 1992. Although the BLS clearly seeks to obtain price quotes based on net transactions prices, in a recent General Accounting Office (GAO) report involving the MCPI it was noted that only about 15 percent of the hospital price quotes obtained by the BLS included discounts (U.S. General Accounting Office 1996, 58). In Catron and Murphy (1996), however, it is reported that with the MPPI, 43.4 percent of the sampled inpatient price quotes and 64.6 percent of its outpatient price quotes initially collected in 1992 were based on list prices. As with physicians' services, capitation for hospitals raises further issues, for it calls into question the whole basis of pricing, because it is based on health plan enrollment rather than use of hospital services by any given patient.

The sampling frame for the hospital services PPI is based on a universe compiled by the American Hospital Association, with the probability of a hospital being sampled being proportional to its revenues.[60] The sample is stratified on the basis of size (measured by number of beds), public versus private ownership, and type of medical specialty. When initially implemented in 1992, given an expected voluntary response rate of 63 percent (similar to that for other PPI industries), the expected sample size was 558, and the total number of expected monthly price quotes was 2,707. By mid-1997, however, the actual sample size was 42 percent smaller at 322,[61] and the number of quotes was 15 percent smaller at 2,302.[62]

Once a hospital is identified as a sample unit, at the time of sample initiation the BLS chooses a fixed subset of DRGs, and each hospital is then asked on a monthly basis to report on net transactions prices of a single representative patient bill (typically, the last patient bill on file for that DRG) for each of the randomly assigned DRGs. The DRGs are selected using selection probabilities proportional to expenditures in each DRG based on HCFA and other data from a number of payer sources. Since the identical treatment bundle is not always observed in subsequent

60. As noted by Catron and Murphy (1996), 25, federal hospitals, such as those associated with the military, Veterans Administration, and the National Institutes of Health are excluded from both the CPI and PPI hospital universe, because there are no measurable economic transactions between hospital and patient at these federal hospitals—many services are rendered free to the patient from a budget allocated to a federal entity.

61. Fixler and Ginsburg (chap. 6 in this volume). The breakdown of actual versus expected is 211 versus 358 for general hospitals, 39 versus 75 for psychiatric hospitals, and 72 versus 125 for specialty hospitals.

62. Ibid. The breakdown on actual versus expected quotes is 1,602 versus 1,889 for general hospitals, 209 versus 283 for psychiatric hospitals, and 72 versus 125 for other specialty hospitals.

months, BLS reporters construct subsequent hypothetical DRG bundle prices by repricing the identical inputs. BLS notes that when a particular hospital does not perform the targeted DRG service, the hospital can instead provide quotes for several alternative DRGs listed by the BLS on the quote assignment sheet.[63] Attrition in the BLS's hospital repricing program is likely to be affected by movement away from DRG billings by hospitals, particularly for non-Medicare patients, and is therefore an important issue worthy of close scrutiny in the very rapidly changing hospital marketplace.

It is also worth noting that in recent years, as hospital length of stay has fallen, the use of post–acute care services such as skilled nursing facilities and rehabilitation units has increased. Often these treatment centers are owned by and even physically located in the hospital. Pricing a hospital stay may present a substantially biased picture of the price of an episode of treatment.

Finally, as noted earlier, the PPI distinguishes as "industries" the "hospital industry" and the "physicians' office industry," largely because the mixes of production processes observed in these two types of establishments are, if not completely disjoint, at least demonstrably not the identical set of production processes. On its own terms, this is clearly reasonable. However, this industry distinction creates a substitution bias with respect to an index for the *purchasers* of health care. Specifically, the problem that arises is that from the purchasers' vantage, the same "product" or service might be "produced" by different industries or by different production processes. For example, with both the physicians' services and hospital services PPI, the nature of the fixed and itemized components for the price quotes requested by the BLS does not permit major input substitution for the treatment of a condition, such as changing the mix of psychotherapy and psychotherapeutic drugs used for the treatment of acute phase depression. When this occurs, even if the industry price indexes are in some sense measured correctly, the PPI measures will miss the purchasers' gain from shifting between different suppliers.

Medical Products in the MPPI: Pharmaceuticals. To this point we have discussed the services component of health care, rather than the goods or commodities components. Although numerous manufacturing products are related to the provision of health care, here we focus on one industry class that has received considerable treatment to date and is perhaps the most significant medical goods industry: prescription pharmaceuticals.[64]

Prescription pharmaceuticals is a relatively research intensive industry

---

63. U.S. Department of Labor, Bureau of Labor Statistics, n.d.-b.
64. Since sampling and disaggregation procedures for prescription pharmaceuticals are very similar to those in other PPI industries, we do not discuss construction of the pharmaceutical PPI in detail here. See Berndt, Griliches, and Rosett (1993), and the references cited therein, for further discussion.

characterized by a considerable number of new product introductions, and therefore it creates substantial challenges for accurate price measurement. Not surprisingly, the BLS's treatment of prescription pharmaceuticals has long been the subject of controversy. As Dorothy Rice and Loucele A. Horowitz noted thirty years ago (1967, 14) for many years the BLS sample tended to focus excessively on old products: "Until 1960, only three prescribed drugs—penicillin, a narcotic, and a non-narcotic—were included. In that year the list of prescripted drugs was increased to 16 items." Describing the Stigler Commission's Report of 1961, Rice and Horowitz noted (p. 15) that "The Subcommittee urged more prompt introductions of new products—a matter of particular importance in the case of drugs and prescriptions."[65]

More recently, a detailed audit of the BLS's PPI for prescription pharmaceuticals was conducted by Berndt, Griliches, and Rosett (1993), which was updated and extended by Berndt and Greenberg (1995). Although these studies examined transactions at a slightly different point in the distribution chain than does the PPI (transactions from wholesalers to retail drug stores, rather than from manufacturers to their initial customer, typically wholesalers), the Berndt studies raised a number of significant issues. In particular, three important findings from these studies were that (1) the BLS oversampled older goods and undersampled new and middle-aged pharmaceuticals, and (2) prices of older products increased more rapidly than those of products earlier on in their life cycle.[66] As a result, (3) the BLS overstated prescription drug price inflation, by perhaps as much as 3 percentage points a year over the 1986–91 time period. Corroborating evidence has since been reported by others, including the BLS.[67]

Partly in response to this research, the BLS implemented a new sampling method by which newer products are introduced more rapidly. Specifically, to compensate for the age bias in the BLS prescription pharmaceutical sample, in 1995 the BLS linked in a Supplement I sample of about 49 additional drugs newly approved by the FDA since 1992 (the original 1993 sample had 522 products from ninety-two manufacturers, but attrition to 1995 reduced the 571 to 544), and included these in their sample effective December 1995. As noted by Kelly (1997), the resulting PPI with supplemental sampling rose 2.1 percent in 1996. Had this supplement not been introduced, the PPI would have risen 2.7 percent (based on a BLS

65. The Stigler Commission report is found in U.S. Congress, Joint Economic Activity (1961). Also see U.S. Department of Health, Education, and Welfare (1967), 35.

66. These findings were essentially anticipated almost thirty years earlier by John Gardner, Secretary of Health, Education and Welfare. In his report to the president, Gardner stated "It is difficult to adjust the drug component of the CPI for the rapid changes in the character of the drugs prescribed. By the time a prescription item is incorporated into the index, its price may have fallen to a lower level than in previous years" (U.S. Department of Health, Education, and Welfare 1967, 35).

67. Kanoza (1996), Ristow (1996), and Kelly (1997).

research index); in three of the fourteen months since the introduction of the supplement, price changes in the published index exceeded that of the research index. One year later the BLS constructed and linked in a Supplement II sample, bringing the total number of observations to 561 (after additional attrition). As is noted by Kelly (1997, 17), "In the 14 months since January 1996, the published index has risen 3.3%. Had Supplements I and II not been introduced, the index would have risen 4.1%." Apparently the BLS now plans to add supplements to this industry on an annual basis.

Another area in which the BLS's MPPI has recently made substantial changes involves generic drugs. Until several years ago, the BLS's procedures for its pharmaceutical PPIs treated generic drugs as entirely unrelated to their patented antecedents. Griliches and Cockburn (1994) noted that generic drugs were a special case of the more general "new goods" problem facing statistical agencies such as the BLS. Since the U.S. Food and Drug Administration certifies generics as being therapeutically equivalent to brand name versions of the same chemical entity, conventional problems encountered when valuing new goods are much simpler with generic drugs. Griliches and Cockburn illustrated the empirical significance of linking generic drugs to their patented antecedents (based on an assumed uniform distribution of tastes between brands and generics), and contrasted their preferred price index construction procedure with that employed by the BLS at that time. Based on data for two antibiotic drugs, Griliches and Cockburn showed that with a Paasche approximation to the "true" index, using reservation prices based on the uniform distribution yielded a price index 25 percent lower after two years than a Törnqvist index that introduced generics as quickly as was feasible but treated them as new goods, and was 36 percent lower than an index that mimicked the procedures then employed by the BLS. Several years later, Berndt, Cockburn, and Griliches (1996) extended the Griliches and Cockburn research and showed that for the entire class of antidepressant drugs, the BLS's overstatement of price inflation due to the way it handled generic drugs was more than 4 percentage points per year from 1986 to 1996.[68]

The BLS has announced major changes in how it treats generic drugs in its PPI; these changes are summarized in Kanoza (1996) and Kelly (1997). In particular, effective January 1996, for drugs in the BLS sample losing patent protection and experiencing initial generic competition, the BLS split the fixed weight for that molecule into two parts—64.2 percent for the generic, and 35.8 percent for the brand. Thus the new BLS procedure treated the composite molecule price change as a pure price change.

---

68. In both the Griliches and Cockburn (1994) and Berndt, Cockburn, and Griliches (1996) studies, transactions were measured at the point of wholesaler to drugstore, and not at the initial point in the distribution chain, which is the focal point for the PPI.

The 64–36 percentages were arrived at as a result of a BLS literature review on typical generic penetrations following the expiration of patent protection. The percentage splits were the same for all molecules and were fixed over time. Beginning with the Supplement II sample introduced in late 1996, however, the BLS brand-generic split was based on actual brand-generic dollar sales, using data purchased by the BLS from IMS America.[69]

There is one other curiosum involving the prescription pharmaceutical PPI. As noted in Berndt, Cockburn, and Griliches (1996), for historical reasons involving preferential federal tax treatment, many U.S. pharmaceutical firms currently manufacture drugs in Puerto Rico; the Puerto Rican value of shipments for prescription pharmaceuticals is roughly 20–25 percent of that on the mainland, and is likely to be higher for newer molecules. For purposes of its PPI calculations, however, the BLS is mandated to treat Puerto Rico as outside the U.S., and thus the PPI excludes all Puerto Rican production.

It turns out that how one deals with Puerto Rican economic accounts differs across government statistical agencies, and even within the BLS. For example, the national income and product accounts of the Bureau of Economic Analysis exclude Puerto Rican production and that of other dependencies, but in the balance of payments accounts, Puerto Rico is treated as domestic. The Census Bureau defines the United States as the U.S. customs territory, which consists of the fifty states, the District of Columbia and Puerto Rico, plus U.S. foreign trade zones and the U.S. Virgin Islands. However, within the BLS's International Price Program (IPP), Puerto Rico is considered part of the United States, and thus currently no IPP price quotes are obtained for Puerto Rican pharmaceutical products shipped to the fifty United States.

The issue of how one treats Puerto Rican production is important to the reliability and interpretation of the prescription drug PPI. If Puerto Rico is to be excluded, as is now the case for the PPI, then to the extent public policy analysts and others seek to track the price growth emanating from U.S. producers (many of whom have chosen to produce significantly in Puerto Rico), it will be necessary to collect and publish "import" price series from Puerto Rico, and then to combine those data with the more narrowly defined "domestic" mainland price series.[70] Of total pharmaceu-

---

69. The relative growth rates of the published and research PPIs for the pharmaceutical industry, discussed in several earlier paragraphs, reflect the impacts of incorporating both new generics and new branded products into the sample.

70. One incentive for Puerto Rican production has been section 936 of the Internal Revenue Code, which has provided tax benefits to firms producing in Puerto Rico. It is worth noting that under the omnibus minimum wage bill enacted by the U.S. Congress in 1996, these tax incentives will be phased out over the next decade. Thus it is possible that the empirical significance of this out of scope Puerto Rican production will gradually decline. It is also worth noting that active ingredients of pharmaceuticals could be manufactured in

tical shipments "imported" into the United States from throughout the world, it appears that about 15 percent emanate from Puerto Rico.[71]

4.3.4   Medical Care Products and Services in the CPI and MCPI

Medical components of the CPI and PPI programs at the BLS have rather different heritages. It is only within the last decade that the BLS's PPI has extended coverage to a wide variety of service industries, such as medical care. Thus, construction and design of the recently introduced medical care–related PPIs, such as those for physicians' and hospital services, have had the opportunity of benefiting from recent thinking and developments on what in fact are the outputs of the service industries, and how one might measure prices in the context of rapidly changing market structure. By contrast, the medical CPI has been published for a very long period of time, regularly since 1935.[72]

A remarkable fact in the BLS's medical CPI is summarized in figure 4.1.[73] Since 1927, the first year for which MCPI data are available, and for each decade since then, measured medical inflation has generally been greater than that for all goods and services.[74] Over the entire 1927–96 period, the MCPI has risen at an average annual growth rate (AAGR) of 4.59 percent, almost half again as large as the 3.24 percent for the overall CPI.

Beginning with its January 1998 major revisions, the BLS has regularly published an aggregate medical care Consumer Price Index (MCPI), as well as price indexes for nine of the thirteen item strata in the MCPI. Separate MCPIs are also published for two expenditure groups (medical care commodities and medical care services). The four major subindexes of the MCPI, along with their 1993–95 percentage base period weights within the aggregate MCPI, are prescription drugs (14.9 percent); nonprescription drugs and medical supplies (7.6 percent); professional medical services (also called physicians' services, although dentists are included; 49.5 percent); hospital and related services (22.9 percent); and health insurance (5.0 percent).[75] Each of these price indexes is based on consumers' out-of-pocket (OOP) expenditures including employees' contributions to employment-based insurance, and thereby excludes all payments by gov-

---

Puerto Rico, shipped to the domestic United States, and then be encapsulated with inert materials into tablets and capsules in the United States. In such a case, the BLS's PPI program would consider it as within the scope of the PPI.

71. See table 2 in U.S. Trade with Puerto Rico and U.S. Possessions on the web site http://www.census.gov/prod/3/98pubs/ft895–97.pdf. We thank Dennis Fixler of the BLS for providing information on this matter.

72. For historical discussions, see Langford (1957) and Getzen (1992).

73. This table is taken from Berndt et al. (1998).

74. However, for several years within the 1927–46 period, year-to-year changes in the CPI were greater than for the MCPI. See Getzen (1992) for a discussion.

75. Taken from Ford and Ginsburg, chap. 5 in this volume, table 5.1. By December 1997, these relative importance weights were 14.6 percent, 7.2 percent, 50.0 percent, 23.8 percent, and 4.5 percent, respectively.

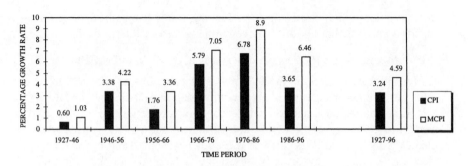

Fig. 4.1   Price inflation in the overall CPI and in the medical CPI, 1927–96
Source: Getzen (1992) and U.S. Bureau of Labor Statistics (http://stat.bls.gov/blshome.htm).

ernments and a portion of that from third party insurers. Any health insurance reimbursements for medical services received by a member of the sampled household are netted out to obtain a net out-of-pocket expenditure (Cardenas 1996a). Only that portion of third party insurance paid for out of pocket by consumers (and excluding employers' contributions to employee health insurance) is included within the scope of the MCPI.[76]

However, in constructing weights for the BLS's MCPI, the OOP payments for health insurance are in turn distributed into payments by insurers for medical services, medical commodities, and health insurers' retained earnings.[77] Analogous to equation (4) earlier, for each MCPI component, OOP expenditures plus the consumer-paid health insurance premium allocation yields a total component weight, which until recently was typically applied to list prices paid by cash-paying customers. Note that over the last decade, actual transaction prices were frequently considerably less than list prices, particularly as discounts to managed care organizations became more common.[78] To the extent that this occurred, over that time period it is likely that measured MCPIs overstated true price growth. However, particularly more recently, it is possible that discounts have become smaller and less frequent, in which case use of list prices could understate true price growth.

76. We defer additional discussion of OOP expenditure issues to later in this paper.
77. See Fixler (1996), Daugherty (1964), Ford and Sturm (1988), and Getzen (1992). In Ford (1995), for private insurance the allocation is 39.7 percent for hospital services, 28.4 percent for physician services, 5.7 percent for dental services, 0.3 percent for eyeglasses and eye care services, 6.2 percent for services by other medical professionals (including home health care), 6.2 percent for prescription drugs and medical supplies, and 0.6 percent for nursing home care. For Medicare Part B, there is only a four component breakdown: outpatient hospital services, 27.2 percent; physicians' services, 56.8 percent; services by other medical professionals, 9.2 percent; and supplies and durable medical equipment, 6.8 percent. The BLS's treatment of pure health insurance has been criticized by the U.S. Senate Finance Committee (1996).
78. On this see, for example, Dranove, Shanley, and White (1991).

The Item Structure of the MCPI

The basic unit of the hierarchical CPI involves definitions of the item strata. Identifying and defining item strata presents considerable difficulties, particularly when markets are undergoing dramatic change during times within the approximately once-each-decade major CPI revisions.

From January 1987 through January 1997, for example, the CPI hierarchical structure distinguished inpatient hospital services as an item stratum separate from outpatient hospital services. Over this same period of time, cost containment efforts by managed care and other health providers resulted in the transformation of many surgical procedures from inpatient to outpatient hospitalization. By shifting patients from inpatient to outpatient surgeries, hospitals and insurers were frequently able to cut down on total costs. Moreover, the average length of hospital stays declined over the 1987–97 period, as skilled nursing facility days and home health visits were substituted for hospital days.

One consequence of this change in place of service was that the case mix severity in both inpatient and outpatient settings increased, resulting in greater costs for the average case in both settings, even as total inpatient plus outpatient costs decreased. The mean inpatient severity likely increased, because the less complex and critical surgeries were shifted to the outpatient venue, leaving only the more critical and complex surgeries as inpatient. The mean outpatient severity also likely increased over this time, for outpatient surgeries were now being done on a much larger set of more complex patient cases. Total costs of treatment, taking into account the substitution from inpatient to outpatient, were lowered as a result.

It is illuminating to consider price index measurement implications of this cost containment approach employed by managed care. Because the BLS treated inpatient and outpatient hospitalizations as distinct item strata, and because the inpatient to outpatient substitution resulted in greater severity/complexity for both inpatient and outpatient services, price indexes for each item strata grew substantially, and given fixed weights for these item strata, the aggregate hospitalization price index also grew, even as total costs were likely to have decreased. Moreover, the CPI, though not the PPI, priced hospital days. There average severity also grew, due to shorter stays. Although empirical evidence is not available, we conjecture that over the January 1987–January 1998 period, the BLS's measured CPI inflation for hospitalization considerably overstated true hospital inflation, because it failed to account for substitution from inpatient to outpatient, and also failed to account for treatments involving greater severity of case mix in each component. This overstatement is consistent with the increased spread of the MCPI over the CPI between 1986 and 1996 (fig. 4.1) at a time when increased price competition should have decreased the spread.

The BLS has recognized the problem, and in January 1997, one year before its major CPI revisions introduced in January 1998, it began treating the aggregate of hospital inpatient and outpatient services as a single item stratum. It has also shifted to measuring hospital services by the stay rather than by the day, and it has classified inpatient and outpatient hospital services as substratum indexes (Ford and Ginsburg, chap. 5 in this volume) similar to the ELIs discussed in section 4.3.1. Information is not available, however, on how linking is implemented when, for example, a shift occurs from inpatient to outpatient surgery. Simple redefinition will not fully address the problem of inpatient-outpatient substitution unless a satisfactory linking procedure is developed and implemented as well.

A number of other important changes have recently been introduced into the CPI for hospital services, even before the 1997 and 1998 revisions. Until at least 1990, for example, in most cases procedures for the MCPI involved pricing specific input items at list prices, like chargemaster fees for x-rays, laboratory tests, and physicians' office visits rather than at the average actual charge for treatment of, say, a child's forearm fracture to a managed care organization obtaining a hospital discount.[79] According to Cardenas (1996b), since 1993, when redrawing outlet and item samples, the BLS has attempted to obtain quotes from hospitals for specific payers, thereby seeking to obtain transaction rather than list prices. Cardenas (1996a, 40) reports that "Employing the sample rotation construct as the vehicle for increasing the number of transaction prices in the CPI, however, has yielded slow progress to date." According to the 1996 GAO study cited earlier, only about 15 percent of the CPI hospital price quotes obtained by the BLS included discounts (U.S. General Accounting Office 1996, 58).

Obtaining transaction rather than list prices is not an easy task, particularly because with price discrimination and alternative pricing methods currently in the medical marketplace, there are frequently many transaction prices. Consider, for example, hospital services. Some insurers pay for medical care on a per diem basis—one price per day to cover all services provided. Other insurers pay on a DRG basis—one price per admission, differentiated only by the severity of the admission. Still other insurers pay on a capitated basis—one price per patient per year, independent of the amount of services the patient actually receives. Because the market has not settled on one basis of price, appropriate price indexes must be able to handle payments using all of these methods. Obtaining the transaction prices for all three methods will be difficult, particularly because transaction prices are frequently considered highly proprietary and confidential

---

79. For further discussion, see Armknecht and Ginsburg (1992); Cardenas (1996b); Daugherty (1964); Ford and Sturm (1988); and Ginsburg (1978).

by insurers. Moreover, because health plans have different degrees of bargaining power, the same provider may negotiate varying per diem rates with different health plans. These problems are not unique to the MCPI, but are relevant for the MPPI as well. Cooperation and joint efforts by the MCPI and MPPI programs in securing price quotes could be very fruitful.

Other recent changes implemented by the MCPI for hospitals involve item descriptions. At one extreme, one can assume zero substitutability among medical care goods and services for treatment of a condition, and simply take quotes of discrete hospital goods and services. An alternative, discussed above, is to employ DRGs. Although the BLS apparently employed non-Medicare DRG prices in three states beginning in 1990, two of those states have since terminated their state-regulated DRG programs. As of September 1992, approximately 6 percent of the CPI hospital quotes consisted of DRG descriptions (Cardenas 1996b). According to Cardenas (1996a, 40), use of DRGs is problematic, because "a DRG treatment path can be wide-ranging, contingent upon the treating physicians' approach"; for example, coefficients of variation range from 0.30 to over 1.5, thereby indicating considerable variation in the treatment strategies used to treat a case as defined by a DRG (Frank and Lave 1985). Currently the BLS is instead considering use of a "package" treatment, consisting of "highly standardized and tightly defined components and risk factors" for conditions such as appendectomies, tonsillectomies, and cataract surgery. Details on how such treatment packages would be defined and how representativeness would be ensured have not been released, nor have any data concerning the composition and nature of hospital quotes being obtained by the BLS's MCPI since the major revisions of January 1998.

Our MCPI discussion to this point has focused on hospital services. We have not seen comparable literature dealing with MCPIs for physicians' services, although informal conversations with BLS personnel suggest to us that issues of item description, list versus transaction prices, and lack of quality adjustment are similar for physicians' and hospital services.

Like the MPPI, the MCPI has a prescription drug component. Issues discussed earlier in the context of the MPPI concerning the linking of prices of newly entering generic drugs, just after branded drugs lose patent protection, to prices of their pioneer antecedents apply here as well. The MCPI program implemented changes involving generic drugs earlier than the MPPI. Effective January 1995, procedures involving the MCPI prescription drug treatment of generics changed considerably.[80] For branded drugs in the CPI sample losing patent protection, six months after patent expiration the BLS now follows a procedure whereby branded and generic

---

80. See Armknecht, Moulton, and Stewart (1994), and U.S. Department of Labor, Bureau of Labor Statistics, "Improvements to CPI Procedures: Prescription Drugs," n.d.-c.

versions of the molecule are randomly selected, in which the probability of selection is proportional to the sales of each version of the drug during the sixth month. If a generic substitute is selected, the entire price difference between the original drug and its generic substitute is treated as a price change. Obviously, if the branded version is selected, repricing will continue as before. Drugs entering the CPI sample after their patent has expired would of course not be affected by this new procedure, because during the CPI sample rotation process generic versions would also have had a chance of being selected. Note that use of a six-month window is somewhat problematic, for in many cases considerable additional diffusion of generics occurs beyond the six months immediately following patent expiration.[81]

Finally, regarding sample sizes for the MCPI and its components, as of February 1998 the total number of MCPI current price quotes was 7,676. This was broken down as follows: prescription drugs, 694; over-the-counter drugs, 423; nonprescription medical equipment and supplies, 252; physicians' services, 1,051; dental services, 927; eye care, 290; services by other medical professionals, 365; hospital services, 3,236; and nursing home services, 438 (Ford and Ginsburg, chap. 5 in this volume, table 5.4).

Weighting Issues in the CPI and MCPI

From January 1987 until January 1998, the item strata weights employed by the BLS in its CPI program were those based on the 1982–84 CEX; beginning in January 1998, the new weights are those based on the 1993–95 CEX. Thus weights used just before the most recent CPI revision were about fifteen years out of date, and the newly introduced "current" weights were already almost four years out of date at the time of unveiling. Up-to-date weights are particularly important in the case of medical care, where technological change may result in substantial shifts across weighting categories. For example, Cutler et al. (1998, chap. 8 in this volume) compare the old CPI medical methodology (pricing the hospital room rate and other hospital inputs with weights held fixed over a long time interval) with (1) a price index that priced the inputs but reweighted annually, and (2) a price index that was based on the cost of treating heart attacks. The quantitative impact on the price index from annual reweighting was greater than the impact of moving from pricing medical inputs to pricing the cost of treating heart attacks.

In some goods and services markets characterized by relative tranquillity and stability, it is possible that use of old weights in price index construction would not be problematic. In the health care goods and services

81. See, for example, Berndt, Cockburn, and Griliches (1996), table 2, 152.

markets, however, the last fifteen years—indeed, the entire post–World War II era—have been marked by dramatic changes in the number and quality of products offered and consumed, the identity of the payers (cash vs. third-party private or government payer), and in how and by whom the services are provided (e.g., from inpatient to outpatient hospitalization, and from fee-for-service to managed care). The pace of both institutional and technological change has been particularly rapid in the health care sector. Moreover, the role of health care expenditures in the overall consumer budget has changed considerably, in part because the BLS's measured MCPI has increased much more rapidly than that for the all-item CPI (6.46 percent for the MCPI 1986–96, 3.65 percent for the all-item CPI over the same time period).[82] We now examine some of the implications of these changes for CPI and MCPI measurement.

In the CPI hierarchical system used from January 1987 until January 1998, seven major product categories were represented, and in the 1998 revisions an eighth was added. In column (1) of table 4.2 we present 1982–84 CEX-based weights for the seven major product categories when they were originally introduced into the 1987 revision of the Consumer Price Index. As is seen there, when the 1987 basket was introduced, the Medical Care major product category received a weight of 4.80 percent. Because the BLS's measured price of medical care rose more rapidly than that of the overall CPI, the implicit budget share consistent with fixed 1982–84 base period quantity weights (inflating all base period quantities by CPI-measured price changes) increased over time; as is seen in column (2), by December 1995 the implicit relative importance of medical care increased to 7.36 percent. This raises a number of very important issues.

First, data from other government agencies, such as the Health Care Financing Administration, indicate that national health expenditures as a proportion of GDP are much higher than 7 percent; for example, Levit et al. (1998) report that in 1996, this proportion was 13.6 percent. Why is the CPI weight for medical care so low?

One important reason for this difference is that the MCPI weight reflects only a portion of total medical care outlays. Specifically, the MCPI weight incorporates only direct OOP cash outlays, plus direct household purchases of health insurance (including Medicare Part B), plus employee contributions to health insurance premiums purchased through work. Significantly, the MCPI excludes employer health insurance premium contributions, treating them as a business expense; MCPI also excludes Medicare Part A, 75 percent of Medicare Part B (the fraction paid from general government revenues), and Medicaid outlays. More generally, the MCPI excludes all medical services purchased by the government on behalf of

---

82. For a discussion of some of these changes, see Berndt et al. (1998).

Table 4.2   Major Product Groups of Items in the CPI: 1982–84 Weights, Implicit Relative Importance, and 1995 Actual Budget Shares

Product Group	1982–84 Weights in 1987 Revision (%) (1)	Implicit Relative Importance 1995:12 (%) (2)	1995 CEX Budget Share (%) (3)	Implicit Relative Importance 1997:12 (%) (4)
Food and beverages	17.84	17.33	15.57	16.31
Housing	42.64	41.35	44.37	39.56
Apparel and upkeep	6.52	5.52	5.57	4.94
Transportation	18.70	16.95	18.47	17.58
Medical care	4.80	7.36	5.21	5.61
Entertainment	4.38	4.37	4.78	n.a.
Recreation	n.a.	n.a.	n.a.	6.14
Education and communication	n.a.	n.a.	n.a.	5.53
Other goods and services	5.13	7.12	5.74	4.32
Total	100.01	100.01	100.00	99.99

Sources: (1) U.S. Department of Labor, Bureau of Labor Statistics (1987), fig. 1, all urban consumers; (2) U.S. Department of Labor, Bureau of Labor Statistics (1996b), all urban consumers; (3) U.S. Department of Labor, Bureau of Labor Statistics, *Consumer Expenditure Survey, 1995*, Table 1300; (4) U.S. Department of Labor, Bureau of Labor Statistics (1997c), table 1 (New Series), CPI-Urban.

Note: n.a. = not available.

its citizens/residents, and weights and prices only those components paid for out of pocket by consumers or from payroll deductions borne by employees.[83] Given this conceptual foundation of the MCPI, it is therefore not surprising that the MCPI weight is much smaller than the share of national health expenditures in GDP.[84]

Another issue is whether the implicit relative importance of the medical care component in the CPI (col. [2] of table 4.2) accurately portrayed actual average consumer budget shares in 1995. If the 1982–84 fixed quantity weights provide a poor approximation to actual quantity weights in, say, 1995, then these implicit relative importance percentages could be unreliable and inaccurate as well, thereby compromising the accuracy of the measured CPI and MCPI. Thus it is of interest to compare actual budget shares with implicit relative importance percentages based on fixed weights.

Actual average budget share data based on the 1995 CEX, in which budget shares are weighted averages over the various geographical areas making up the BLS sample, are presented in column (3) of table 4.2. As is seen there, the 1995 average budget share for medical care items is 5.21 percent, which is substantially smaller—2.15 percentage points, about 29 percent—than the implicit relative importance of medical care items (7.36 percent) based on the BLS's fixed 1982–84 quantity weights; alternatively, by 1995 BLS's use of the fixed weight index in its CPI resulted in the implicit relative importance of medical care being about 41 percent larger (7.36 percent vs. 5.21 percent) than was warranted.

The implicit relative importance of the eight major CPI components in the recently revised CPI, based on the 1993–95 CEX and updated to December 1997, are given in the final column of table 4.2. Interestingly, the new relative importance of medical care is 5.61 percent. An implication of this is that because updated data from the 1993–95 CEX replaced outdated data from the 1982–84 CEX, with the January 1998 revisions the weight given medical care fell 1.75 percentage points from 7.36 percent to 5.61 percent, a relative overstatement of 31 percent. This overstatement of the health care relative importance is greater in the 1998 major revision than it was for the major revision eleven years earlier in 1987. Then, as reported by Ford and Sturm (1988, table 1), the corresponding overstatement in December 1986 was 5.74 percent versus 4.66 percent, at 23 percent still substantial but considerably smaller than the 31 percent overstatement in 1998.

There are at least three reasons why the actual budget shares could di-

---

83. For further discussion, see Armknecht and Ginsburg (1992), particularly 124–42.

84. The appropriateness of this decomposition into employee out-of-pocket versus employers' contributions depends in part on the incidence of the income tax, and the extent to which employees are willing to substitute employers' health insurance contributions for other forms of wage and nonwage compensation. While very important, these issues are beyond the scope of this review. For a recent discussion, see Gruber (2000) and Pauly (1997).

verge so materially from implicit relative importance based on fixed quantity weights. First, the relative quantity weights could have changed over time, reflecting nonzero price substitutability inconsistent with the Laspeyres fixed weight assumption. For example, it is possible that efforts by managed health care organizations to contain medical expenditures have resulted in physicians' and hospitals' performing a smaller number of laboratory tests, scheduling fewer specialist physician visits, and shortening lengths of hospital stay. Hence it is possible that as a result of growth in managed care and other cost containment methods, the relative quantities of medical care items for which consumers made OOP expenditures has fallen since 1982–84.

Second, suppose that demand for health care had a zero price elasticity of demand. In such a case, the divergence would simply reflect overstated medical care price inflation, perhaps from failure to measure transaction prices accurately.

Third, if, however, the demand price elasticity for medical care were greater than unity (say, particularly for those components undergoing dramatic but not fully measured quality change), then the implicit relative importance of these items would be greater than the actual budget share, ceteris paribus.

Discovering which of these three reasons, or what weighted combination, contributed to the divergence between the actual 1995 budget shares and implicit relative importance requires additional empirical research. Econometric studies of demand for health care such as those based on the RAND Health Insurance Experiment report modest but price-inelastic demand; it is worth noting that the experimental design of that study in effect controlled for quality variations (Newhouse et al. 1993). Additional research that focused on price measures incorporating quality change, and then evaluated the responsiveness of demand to quality changes, would be useful.[85]

These discrepancies between actual budget shares and implicit relative importance values, resulting from the use of outdated CEX surveys, suggest that more frequent weighting could considerably strengthen the reliability of the MCPI. The frequency of such revisions does not necessarily need to be uniform across the entire CPI, but could involve more frequent updatings in some major product groups (such as medical care) than in others (such as housing). For the rapidly changing medical care sector, decennial updates of weights result in price indexes whose accuracy and reliability can legitimately be called into question.[86]

---

85. For discussion and references, see Ellison et al. (1997).

86. Suggestions for implementing alternative weighting schemes with time-varying weights have been proposed and evaluated by Shapiro and Wilcox (1997).

4.4   Related Research on Medical Care Price Indexes

The average consumer of medical care is not as interested in
the price of a visit or a hospital day as he is in the total cost
of an episode of illness.
—U.S. Department of Health, Education, and Welfare (1967)

For quite some time now, health economists and government statisticians have made recommendations concerning directions toward which
the pricing of medical care services should move, particularly concerning
the definition of the item or product that is to be priced. For example,
already in 1964 Anne Scitovsky proposed "an index which would show
changes, not in the costs of such items of medical care such as drugs,
physicians' visits, and hospital rooms, but in the average costs of the complete treatment of individual illnesses such as, for example, pneumonia,
appendicitis, or measles" (p. 133).[87] In Scitovsky (1967), this approach was
implemented on an illustrative basis for five medical conditions. Notably,
in the 1950s and 1960s the BLS price indexes appeared to have *understated*
medical price inflation, in large part because physicians' "customary"
pricing in an environment of extensive price discrimination began to
change as the proportion of patients covered by Medicare insurance increased.[88] Hence, the BLS's alleged upward bias in measuring medical
price inflation has not always been the indictment.

Shortcomings in the BLS's MCPI approach, and preference for the
treatment episode–outcomes-adjusted approach to price measurement,
have appeared steadily since 1967; see, for example, the chapter "Measuring Changes in the Price of Medical Care" in various editions of a well-
known health economics textbook by Paul Feldstein (1979, 1983, 1988) as
well as the Baxter Foundation Prize Address by Newhouse (1989).

More recently, price indexes for several specific medical treatments, taking outcomes changes into account, have been constructed, thereby demonstrating again the feasibility and importance of the Scitovsky approach.
Using one data set of hospital claims from a major teaching hospital and
another very large data set consisting of Medicare claims, Cutler et al.
(1998, chap. 8 in this volume) have contrasted input price indexes for the
cost of heart attack treatment that rise by 6.7 percent over 1983–94, with
an outcomes-adjusted index that takes into account changing treatment
regimens and a conservative valuation for the extension of life expectancy
attributable to new heart attack treatments; the latter price index increases
by only 2.3 percent per year (in real terms, an annual decrease of 1.1 percent), implying a net upward bias of 4.4 percent per year for an MCPI-
like index.

87. See Scitovsky (1964) and related discussions in Scitovsky (1967).
88. For further discussion, see Feldstein (1969, 1970).

Similarly, Shapiro and Wilcox (1996) have constructed a price index for cataract surgery, 1969–93, and find that a CPI-like fixed weight input-based price index increases by a factor of about nine; a preferred alternative price index incorporating realized reduced levels of hospital services (input changes), but ignoring any improvements in the quality of medical outcomes, increases by only a factor of three, implying an annual differential of 4.6 percent.

A number of other studies, based on retrospective medical claims data, provide additional evidence that implementation of disease or condition-specific measurement procedures that uses treatment episodes of care as a measure of output, is in fact feasible; see, for example, other papers presented at this conference by Berndt, Busch, and Frank (chap. 12 in this volume), Cockburn and Anis (chap. 11 in this volume), Cutler et al. (chap. 8 in this volume), and Shapiro, Shapiro, and Wilcox (chap. 10 in this volume).

4.5 A New Medical Care Expenditure Price Index Based on Episode Treatment Costs

One could envision an ideal medical care price index as providing accurate and reliable measures for use in at least five very important functions: (1) the measurement of quality of life, (2) the deflation of nominal industry output for the calculation of real output and productivity growth, (3) the indexing of health care benefits as a component of employee compensation, (4) the indexing of payments by health plans to providers of medical care, and (5) the indexing of payments in government transfer programs. Undoubtedly, additional purposes can be envisaged. Unfortunately, these various functions and purposes are very different, and there is no way a single index like the medical CPI (or PPI) can provide an accurate and reliable basis for such diverse needs. The search for a single price index that meets all these purposes is a futile one. But these diverse needs are real and important. We recommend that, rather than trying to change dramatically the conceptual foundations and measurement procedures of the MCPI and MPPI in an attempt to accommodate conflicting needs, the BLS consider constructing and publishing, on an experimental basis, a new price index that we tentatively call a *medical care expenditure price index.*

As we have discussed in considerable detail, the CPI and PPI medical price indexes are very different, they correspond to distinct index number concepts, and thus the appropriate uses to which they are applied must differ as well. The CPI is, in concept, a fixed weight approximation to a cost-of-living index, in which the cost-of-living index is defined as follows: What is the minimum change in expenditure necessary to purchase the set of market goods and services yielding the same standard of living as the set of market-purchased goods and services consumed in the base period?

The manner in which the BLS has implemented this cost-of-living definition in the case of the medical care CPI is to define the scope of the index to apply only to out-of-pocket expenditures. The reasoning is that employer-provided medical insurance is a nonwage part of compensation; BLS does not believe it to be appropriate to add consumption out of nonwage compensation into the consumer expenditures that are defined, implicitly, to be relevant to the wage part of compensation.[89]

Nevertheless, even if the CPI is continued to be defined to include only out-of-pocket expenditures, there are many important purposes for which one needs a price index covering all medical expenditures, no matter who (consumer, employer-provided health insurance, or government) is the nominal payer. This, for example, would be the concept of price change that one would want for most policy analytic purposes, such as containing medical care cost inflation, or examining the impact of new treatment technologies.

The PPI organizes and presents information by medical care *industry,* that is, hospitals, physicians' offices, nursing homes, pharmaceuticals, and so forth. The underlying PPI concept is an industry output price index. This index is useful for a number of purposes, such as comparing hospital price movements with the cost of hospital inputs (though one of the great weaknesses of the U.S. statistical system is its inadequacy of information on industry input quantities and input prices). Moreover, the PPI is a price index for *domestic* industries. It provides, for example, information about price movements for domestically produced pharmaceuticals at the manufacturer's level. But the PPI is not a price index for all pharmaceuticals consumed in the United States. It excludes, for example, imported pharmaceuticals and also, because of a definitional oddity in the U.S. national accounts, pharmaceutical production in Puerto Rico. Additionally, the PPI includes pharmaceuticals and medical devices that are produced in the United States and sold abroad.

Thus, just as the CPI does not provide a comprehensive price index for health care to U.S. purchasers, neither does the PPI provide this information. Even though the CPI and PPI measures are useful on their own terms (and we are not asserting that these measures are not useful or appropriate ones), there is a great gap in medical care price information. The missing part, regrettably, is probably the part that is most vital for medical care policy analysis; namely, the United States needs a comprehensive medical care price index for *expenditures* on medical care. Such a *medical care expenditure price index* would apply to all purchases of medical care, and it would take into account, as the present CPI and PPI do not, substitution by buyers or financiers of medical care across providers or industries that

89. For discussion of the incidence of these employer-subsidized health benefits, see Pauly (1997) and Gruber (2000).

produce medical care. In principle, separate medical care expenditure price indexes could be constructed for public and private sector expenditures, and for the elderly. The medical care expenditure price index would cover all consumption of medical care goods and services, be the providers/producers domestic or foreign. And it would, we believe, be profitably structured around determining the costs of treating an episode of a representative set of illnesses or conditions.

4.6   Where Do We Go from Here?

It is striking that a variety of researchers and government statisticians all agree that price measurement of medical care goods and services is particularly difficult, that current methods of measurement can be improved by measuring episode treatment costs and taking outcomes into account, and that research in this area should receive a high priority. For example, about six years ago BLS economists Paul Armknecht and Daniel Ginsburg (1992) stated, "Although it will be difficult to develop the methods for pricing total treatment, BLS is planning further research in this area" (pp. 141–42). Later, Armknecht (1996) added: "A new dimension needs to be included in the pricing of medical services that includes outcomes, so that if cancer treatment results in improved survival rates, this is reflected in the index. This area appears to have promise and is one that also needs to be pursued as part of the research agenda in quality adjustment" (p. 33). The Boskin Commission (Boskin et al. 1998) made similar recommendations, stating that "This new research . . . opens up the potential for major improvement in our understanding of the economics of medical care. This category should receive a substantial component of the CPI's future research investment, and we strongly endorse a move in the CPI away from the pricing of health care inputs to an attempt to price medical care outcomes. . . . This program should explore measuring the value of time saved by new medical procedures and communication devices, the value of life extended and its associated quality . . ." (pp. 60, 84).

The BLS's response to the Boskin Commission recommendations suggests considerable agreement concerning measurement problems in the medical care component of the CPI: "Although we acknowledge that there have been enormous improvements in medical technology over time, we also note the heterogeneity of the medical services category, which includes services as diverse as dentistry, eyeglasses and eye care, psychological counseling, podiatry, chiropractic, and physical therapy. . . . Some kinds of quality change are difficult to evaluate, involving changes in patient outcomes, such as improved mortality or reduction in pain. The BLS is continuing to support and encourage research on this topic. . . . The BLS recognizes the importance of the health insurance price movements to consumers as well as to policymakers and will continue to search for ways to overcome the obstacles to accurate adjustment for changes in policy characteristics."[90]

But where do we go from here? In the previous section we put forward a recommendation that the BLS consider constructing and publishing, on an experimental basis, a medical care expenditure price index. What new research, and what new related measurement initiatives, appear to offer the most promise if such a new price index is to be created?

A number of directions appear promising. First, although most of the public attention in recent years has focused on the CPI, as we have noted several times in this paper, many measurement issues involving medical care goods and services are common to the CPI and PPI. A medical care expenditure price index would have elements from both the CPI and PPI programs. An obvious implication is that the CPI and PPI programs should be encouraged to expand their joint efforts on designing research and measurement initiatives.

Second, as has been emphasized by, among others, Triplett (1999, chap. 1 in this volume), complementary research efforts on health care outcomes by medical researchers involving cost-effectiveness analyses, as well as the public availability of large retrospective health claims databases, now allow the BLS to build on others' research that defines and identifies episodes of treatment. This research would be particularly important were the BLS to initiate a medical care expenditure price index program. Note that in principle, outcomes research can help somewhat in overcoming the moral hazard problem underlying the failure of revealed preferences as measures of willingness to pay in medical care markets. Together with retrospective claims data, the outcomes studies provide a framework for identifying medical care outputs that incorporate quality change. What Anne Scitovsky proposed in 1962 and illustrated with a small sample of conditions in 1967, and what Health, Education, and Welfare Secretary John Gardner requested more generally in 1967 (U.S. Department of Health, Education, and Welfare 1967), is clearly possible on a much larger scale today.

Third, although the usual source of information for output measurement is based on actual market transactions, use of medical outcomes data to define measures of output implies an adjustment in thinking—to look outside of market transactions to consider what medical resources actually do for health.[91] A medical care expenditure price index program should, to as great an extent as is feasible, combine actual transactions data underlying treatment costs of an episode of an illness, with outcomes data from cost-effectiveness and related medical studies.

Fourth, it is likely that treatment episode price index measurement will

90. U.S. Department of Labor, Bureau of Labor Statistics (1997b), 18, 19, and 31.
91. For further discussion, see Triplett (1999, chap. 1 in this volume).

need to be done at a very disaggregated level of detail for a finite number of representative illnesses or conditions. The extent of medical care progress, as well as the underlying increases in medical scientific knowledge, have varied considerably across illnesses and disorders, with spectacular gains in treating conditions such as cataracts, retinal detachment, schizophrenia, and cystic fibrosis, but with apparently less progress for other conditions such as rheumatoid arthritis, Alzheimer's disease, and the common cold. While the Hicksian aggregation assumption of common proportional price changes over time across a variety of products may be a useful approximation within a number of other industries, for medical care it is not plausible. As suggested already in 1969 by Martin Feldstein, for the BLS to obtain useful measures of medical care output, it would appear to be most useful to obtain a sample of "a representative mix of illnesses" (p. 363). Research that helps identify an appropriate mix of illnesses and their treatments, ones for which outcomes measures and/or published treatment guidelines are available, and ones for which sample sizes in retrospective claims databases are sufficiently large, would seem to be particularly helpful.

Fifth, the pricing of health insurance remains a difficult issue. As noted above, empirical implementation needs theoretical foundations on how employers and employees choose health insurance, and on that issue there has not been much theoretical effort of late. This area seems particularly fruitful for economic theorists, since potentially complementary data are now becoming available. With funding from the AHRQ, the Census Bureau is now in the midst of collecting data for the Medical Expenditure Panel Survey (MEPS).[92] This is not a one-time survey, but instead involves a panel of 9,500 households, and links the households to the employers, the employers' set of health insurance plans, and the health care providers. If theoretical foundations can be established, it is possible that this database could provide the basis for ongoing hedonic price analyses of health insurance plans.[93]

However, in terms of measuring the price of health insurance, the growth of managed care makes measurement and the interpretation of hedonic price equations more problematic. In most nonmedical markets, if price increases, it is plausible to assume that those consumers rationed out of the market had a willingness to pay that was less than the now higher price. Although in some cases one might be able to argue that with fee-for-service medical care rationing was reflective of willingness to pay, with managed care consumers have no way by which to reveal their will-

92. Details on the MEPS are given in Cohen et al. (1996).
93. See Jensen and Morrisey (1990) for a hedonic price analysis of group health insurance plans.

ingness to pay at the time services are delivered. The rationing that occurs is instead based on clinical grounds. Thus the growth of managed care makes it difficult to derive economic welfare implications from the estimation of hedonic price equations.[94] This leads us to suggest that in the near future, research on the construction of a medical care expenditure price index might be fruitfully based on retrospective claims data, although research on the pricing of health insurance policies is also likely to be important.

References

Abraham, Katharine G., John S. Greenlees, and Brent R. Moulton. 1998. Working to improve the Consumer Price Index. *Journal of Economic Perspectives* 12 (1): 27–36.

American Medical Association. 1990. *Current procedural terminology (CPT)*. 4th ed. Chicago: American Medical Association.

Archibald, Robert B. 1977. On the theory of industrial price measurement: Output price indexes. *Annals of Economic and Social Measurement* 6 (1): 57–72.

Armknecht, Paul A. 1996. Improving the efficiency of the U.S. CPI in the future. Washington, D.C.: International Monetary Fund. Unpublished manuscript, March.

Armknecht, Paul A., and Daniel H. Ginsburg. 1992. Improvements in measuring price changes in consumer services: Past, present and future. In *Output measurement in the service sectors,* ed. Zvi Griliches, 109–56. NBER Studies in Income and Wealth, vol. 56. Chicago: University of Chicago Press.

Armknecht, Paul A., Brent R. Moulton, and Kenneth J. Stewart. 1994. Improvements to the food at home, shelter and prescription drug indexes in the U.S. Consumer Price Index. CPI Announcement—Version I, 20 October. Washington, D.C.: U.S. Department of Labor Bureau of Labor Statistics.

Berndt, Ernst R. 1991. *The practice of econometrics: Classic and contemporary.* Reading, Mass.: Addison-Wesley.

Berndt, Ernst R., Iain M. Cockburn, Douglas L. Cocks, Arnold Epstein, and Zvi Griliches. 1998. Is price inflation different for the elderly? An empirical analysis of prescription drugs. NBER Working Paper no. 6182. Cambridge, Mass.: National Bureau of Economic Research.

Berndt, Ernst R., Iain Cockburn, and Zvi Griliches. 1996. Pharmaceutical innovations and market dynamics: Tracking effects on price indexes for antidepressant drugs. *Brookings Papers on Economic Activity: Microeconomics,* 133–88.

Berndt, Ernst R., David M. Cutler, Richard G. Frank, Zvi Griliches, Joseph P. Newhouse, and Jack E. Triplett. 2000. Medical care prices and output. In *Handbook of health economics,* ed. Joseph P. Newhouse and Anthony J. Culyer. Amsterdam: Elsevier Science.

94. For an example of ambiguous welfare interpretations of increases in a medical CPI (the treatment of depression), see Berndt, Busch, and Frank (chap. 12 in this volume), who argue that increases in patient copayments might also reflect reduced moral hazard, and thus an indeterminate net effect on patient welfare.

Berndt, Ernst R., and Paul E. Greenberg. 1995. An updated and extended study of the price growth of prescription pharmaceutical preparations. In *Competitive strategies in the pharmaceutical industry,* ed. Robert B. Helms, 35–48. Washington, D.C.: American Enterprise Institute.

Berndt, Ernst R., Zvi Griliches, and Joshua G. Rosett. 1993. Auditing the Producer Price Index: Micro evidence from prescription pharmaceutical preparations. *Journal of Business and Economic Statistics* 11 (3): 251–64.

Boskin, Michael J., Ellen R. Dulberger, Robert J. Gordon, Zvi Griliches, and Dale W. Jorgenson. 1998. Consumer prices, the Consumer Price Index, and the cost of living. *Journal of Economic Perspectives* 12 (1): 3–26.

Bresnahan, Timothy F., and Robert J. Gordon. 1997. *The economics of new goods.* NBER Studies in Income and Wealth, vol. 58. Chicago: University of Chicago Press.

Cardenas, Elaine M. 1996a. The CPI for hospital services: Concepts and procedures. *Monthly Labor Review* 119 (7): 34–42.

———. 1996b. Revision of the CPI hospital services component. *Monthly Labor Review* 119 (12): 40–48.

Catron, Brian, and Bonnie Murphy. 1996. Hospital price inflation: What does the new PPI tell us? *Monthly Labor Review* 119 (7): 24–31.

Cohen, Joel W., Alan C. Monheit, Karen M. Beauregard, Steven B. Cohen, Doris C. Lefkowitz, D. E. B. Potter, John P. Sommers, Amy K. Taylor, and Ross H. Arnett III. 1996. The medical expenditure panel survey: A national health information resource. *Inquiry* 33 (winter): 373–89.

Council on Wage and Price Stability. 1977. *The Wholesale Price Index: Review and evaluation.* Washington, D.C.: U.S. Government Printing Office.

Cutler, David M., Mark B. McClellan, Joseph P. Newhouse, and Dahlia Remler. 1998. Are medical prices declining? *Quarterly Journal of Economics* 113:991–1024.

Daugherty, James C. 1964. Health insurance in the revised CPI. *Monthly Labor Review* 87 (11): 1299–1300.

Diewert, W. Erwin. 1983. The theory of output price index and the measurement of real output change. In *Price level measurement: Proceedings from a conference sponsored by Statistics Canada,* ed. W. Erwin Diewert and Claude Montmarquette, 1049–1113. Ottawa: Statistics Canada.

Dranove, David, Mark Shanley, and William D. White. 1991. Does the Consumer Price Index overstate hospital price inflation? *Medical Care* 29 (August): 690–96.

Eldridge, Lucy P. 1998. The role of prices in measuring productivity for the business sector of the U.S. economy. Washington, D.C.: U.S. Bureau of Labor Statistics, Office of Productivity and Technology. Draft manuscript, 29 July.

Ellis, Randall P., Gregory C. Pope, Lisa I. Iezzoni, John Z. Ayanian, David W. Bates, Helen Burstin, and Arlene S. Ash. 1996. Diagnosis-based risk adjustment for Medicare capitation payments. *Health Care Financing Review* 17 (3): 101–28.

Ellison, Sara Fisher, Iain Cockburn, Zvi Griliches, and Jerry Hausman. 1997. Price competition among pharmaceutical products: An examination of four cephalosporins. *RAND Journal of Economics* 28 (3): 426–46.

Feldstein, Martin S. 1969. Improving medical care price statistics. *1969 Proceedings of the Business and Economics Statistics Section,* 361–65. Washington, D.C.: American Statistical Association.

———. 1970. The rising price of physicians' services. *Review of Economics and Statistics* 52 (2): 121–33.

Feldstein, Paul J. 1979. *Health care economics.* New York: Wiley.

———. 1983. *Health care economics.* 2d ed. New York: Wiley.

———. 1988. *Health care economics.* 3d ed. New York: Wiley.

Fisher, Franklin M., and Zvi Griliches. 1995. Aggregate price indexes, new goods, and generics. *Quarterly Journal of Economics* 110 (1): 229–44.

Fisher, Franklin M., and Karl Shell. 1972. The pure theory of the national output deflator. In *The economic theory of price indexes,* ed. Franklin M. Fisher and Karl Shell, 49–113. New York: Academic.

Fixler, Dennis. 1996. The treatment of the price of health insurance in the CPI. Washington, D.C.: U.S. Department of Labor, Bureau of Labor Statistics. Unpublished manuscript.

Ford, Ina Kay. 1995. Memorandum to Mary Lynn Schmidt, 22 June. Washington, D.C.: U.S. Department of Labor, Bureau of Labor Statistics.

Ford, Ina Kay, and Philip Sturm. 1988. CPI revision provides more accuracy in the medical care services component. *Monthly Labor Review* 111 (4): 17–26.

Frank, Richard G., and Julie R. Lave. 1985. The psychiatric DRGs: Are they different? *Medical Care* 28 (11): 1145–55.

Fuchs, Victor. 1974. *Who shall live? Health, economics and social choice.* New York: Basic.

———. 1983. *How we live.* Cambridge, Mass.: Harvard University Press.

Getzen, Thomas E. 1992. Medical care price indexes: Theory, construction and empirical analysis of the U.S. Series 1927–1990. In *Advances in health economics and health services research,* 83–128. Greenwich, Conn.: JAI.

Gilbert, Milton. 1961. The problem of quality changes and index numbers. *Monthly Labor Review* 84 (9): 992–97.

———. 1962. Quality change and index numbers: The reply. *Monthly Labor Review* 85 (5): 544–45.

Ginsburg, Daniel H. 1978. Medical care services in the Consumer Price Index. *Monthly Labor Review* 101 (8): 35–39.

Griliches, Zvi. 1962. Quality change and index numbers: A critique. *Monthly Labor Review* 85 (5): 542–44.

———. 1988. *Technology, education, and productivity.* New York: Basil Blackwell.

———. 1992. Introduction to *Output measurement in the service sectors,* ed. Zvi Griliches. NBER Studies in Income and Wealth, vol. 56. Chicago: University of Chicago Press.

———. 1997. The commission report on the Consumer Price Index, *Federal Reserve Bank of St. Louis Review* 79 (3): 169–73.

Griliches, Zvi, and Iain Cockburn. 1994. Generics and new goods in pharmaceutical price indexes. *American Economic Review* 84 (5): 1213–32.

Grossman, Michael. 1972a. *The demand for health: A theoretical and empirical investigation.* New York: Columbia University Press.

———. 1972b. On the concept of health capital and the demand for health. *Journal of Political Economy* 80 (2): 223–55.

Gruber, Jonathan. 1994. The incidence of mandated maternity benefits. *American Economic Review* 84 (3): 622–41.

———. 2000. Health insurance and the labor market. In *Handbook of health economics,* ed. Joseph P. Newhouse and Anthony J. Culyer. Amsterdam: Elsevier Science.

Hoechst Marion Roussel. 1997. *Managed care digest series 1997.* Kansas City, Mo.: Hoechst Marion Roussel.

Hoover, Ethel D. 1961. The CPI and problems of quality change. *Monthly Labor Review* 84 (11): 1175–85.

Jensen, Gail A., and Michael A. Morrisey. 1990. Group health insurance: A hedonic price approach. *Review of Economics and Statistics* 72 (1): 38–44.

Kanoza, Douglas. 1996. Supplemental sampling in the PPI Pharmaceuticals Index. *Producer Price Indexes, Detailed Price Report* (January): 8–10.

Kelly, Gregory G. 1997. Improving the PPI samples for prescription pharmaceuticals. *Monthly Labor Review* 120 (10): 10–17.

Kendrick, John W. 1991. Appraising the U.S. output and productivity estimates for government: Where do we go from here? *Review of Income and Wealth* 37 (2): 149–58.

Lane, Walter. 1996. Changing the item structure of the Consumer Price Index. *Monthly Labor Review* 119 (12): 18–25.

Langford, Elizabeth A. 1957. Medical care in the CPI: 1935–1956. *Monthly Labor Review* 80 (9): 1053–58.

Lawson, Ann M. 1997. Benchmark input-output accounts for the U.S. economy, 1992: Make, use, and supplementary tables. *Survey of Current Business* 78 (11): 36–82.

Leaver, Sylvia G., William H. Johnson, Robert Baskin, Samuel Scarlett, and Robert Morse. 1997. Commodities and services sample redesign for the 1998 Consumer Price Index revision. Washington, D.C.: U.S. Bureau of Labor Statistics. Unpublished memo.

Levit, Katharine R., Helen C. Lazenby, Bradley R. Braden, and the National Health Accounts Team. 1998. National health spending trends in 1996. *Health Affairs* 17 (1): 35–51.

Meltzer, David. 1997. Accounting for future costs in medical care cost-effectiveness analysis. *Journal of Health Economics* 17 (4): 33–64.

Moulton, Brent R. 1996. Bias in the Consumer Price Index: What is the evidence? *Journal of Economic Perspectives* 10 (4): 159–77.

Moulton, Brent R., and Karin E. Moses. 1997. Addressing the quality change issue in the Consumer Price Index. *Brookings Papers on Economic Activity,* no. 1, 305–49.

Moulton, Brent R., and Kenneth J. Stewart. 1997. An overview of experimental U.S. Consumer Price Indexes. Washington, D.C.: U.S. Department of Labor, Bureau of Labor Statistics. Unpublished paper, March.

Murray, Richard. 1992. Measuring public-sector output: The Swedish report. In *Output measurement in the service sectors,* ed. Zvi Griliches, 517–42. NBER Studies in Income and Wealth, vol. 56. Chicago: University of Chicago Press.

Newhouse, Joseph P. 1989. Measuring medical prices and understanding their effects. *Journal of Health Administration Education* 7 (1): 19–26.

Newhouse, Joseph P., and the Insurance Experiment Group. 1993. *Free for all? Lessons from the RAND Health Insurance Experiment.* Cambridge, Mass.: Harvard University Press.

Nordhaus, William D. 1998. Quality change in price indexes. *Journal of Economic Perspectives* 12 (1): 59–68.

Pauly, Mark V. 1997. *Health benefits at work: An economic and political analysis of employment-based health insurance.* Ann Arbor: University of Michigan Press.

———. 1999. Costs, effects, outcomes, and utility: Concepts and usefulness of medical care price indexes. In *Measuring the prices of medical treatments,* ed. Jack E. Triplett. Washington, D.C.: Brookings Institution.

Persky, Joseph. 1998. Retrospectives: Price indexes and general exchange values. *Journal of Economic Perspectives* 12 (1): 197–206.

Pollak, Robert A. 1980. Group cost-of-living indexes. *American Economic Review* 70 (2): 273–78.

———. 1998. The Consumer Price Index: A research agenda and three proposals. *Journal of Economic Perspectives* 12 (1): 69–78.

Prescott, Edward C. 1997. On defining real consumption. *Federal Reserve Bank of St. Louis Review* 79 (3): 47–53.

Prospective Payment Assessment Commission. 1995. *Report and recommendations to the Congress.* Washington, D.C.: U.S. Government Printing Office.

Reder, Melvin W. 1969. Some problems in the measurement of productivity in the medical care industry. In *Production and productivity in the service industries,* ed. Victor Fuchs. New York: Columbia University Press.

Rice, Dorothy P., and Loucele A. Horowitz. 1967. Trends in medical care prices. *Social Security Bulletin* 30 (7): 13–28.

Ristow, William. 1996. IMS presentation to the BLS. Plymouth Meeting, PA: IMS America. Mimeo.

Scitovsky, Anne A. 1964. An index of the cost of medical care—A proposed new approach. In *The economics of health and medical care: Proceedings of the Conference on the Economics of Health and Medical Care, May 10–12, 1962.* Ann Arbor: University of Michigan.

———. 1967. Changes in the costs of treatment of selected illnesses, 1951–65. *American Economic Review* 57 (5): 1182–95.

Shapiro, Matthew D., and David W. Wilcox. 1996. Mismeasurement in the Consumer Price Index: An evaluation. In *NBER Macroeconomics Annual,* vol. 11, ed. Ben S. Bernanke and Julio J. Rotemberg. 93–142. Cambridge, Mass.: MIT Press.

———. 1997. Alternative strategies for aggregating prices in the CPI. *Federal Reserve Bank of St. Louis Review* 79 (3): 113–25.

Summers, Lawrence H. 1989. Some simple economics of mandated benefits. *American Economic Review* 79 (2): 177–83.

Swedish Ministry of Finance. Budget Department. 1997. *Public sector productivity in Sweden.* Papers on Public Sector Budgeting and Management in Sweden, vol. 3. Stockholm: Ministry of Finance.

Trajtenberg, Manuel. 1990. *Economic analysis of product innovation: The case of CT scanners.* Cambridge, Mass.: Harvard University Press.

Triplett, Jack E. 1983. Escalation measures: What is the answer? What is the question? In *Price level measurement: Proceedings from a conference sponsored by Statistics Canada,* ed. W. E. Diewert and C. M. Montmarquette, 457–87. Ottawa: Statistics Canada.

———. 1990. The theory of industrial and occupational classifications and related phenomena. In *Proceedings of the Bureau of the Census 1990 Annual Research Conference.* Washington, D.C.: U.S. Department of Commerce.

———. 1999. Accounting for health care: Integrating price index and cost-effectiveness research. In *Measuring the prices of medical treatments,* ed. Jack E. Triplett. Washington, D.C.: Brookings Institution.

U.S. Congress. Joint Economic Committee. 1961. *Government price statistics, hearings before the Subcommittee on Economic Statistics of the Joint Economic Committee, Congress of the United States.* 87th Cong., 1st sess., pursuant to Sec. 5(a) of P.L. 304 (79th Cong.), pt. 1, 24 January.

U.S. Department of Health, Education, and Welfare. 1967. *A report to the president on medical care prices.* Washington, D.C.: U.S. Government Printing Office, February.

U.S. Department of Health and Human Services. 1980. *International classification of diseases (ICD-9-CM),* 2d ed. (PHS)-80–1260. Washington, D.C.: U.S. Government Printing Office.

U.S. Department of Labor. Bureau of Labor Statistics. 1987. *The Consumer Price Index: 1987 revision.* Report 736. Washington, D.C.: U.S. Government Printing Office, January.

———. 1992. *Handbook of methods.* Bulletin 2414. Washington, D.C.: U.S. Government Printing Office, April.

———. 1995. *Consumer expenditure survey 1995.* Washington, D.C.: U.S. Government Printing Office.

———. 1996a. *Producer price index coverage expansion plan.* Washington, D.C.: U.S. Government Printing Office, December.

———. 1996b. *Relative importance of components in the Consumer Price Index 1995.* Bulletin 2476. Washington, D.C.: U.S. Government Printing Office, February.

———. 1997a. The experimental CPI using geometric means (CPI-U-XG). Washington, D.C.: U.S. Government Printing Office, 10 April.

———. 1997b. Measurement issues in the Consumer Price Index. BLS response to letter from Jim Saxton, chairman of the Joint Economic Committee, to Katharine Abraham, commissioner of the Bureau of Labor Statistics, June.

———. 1997c. *Relative importance of components in the Consumer Price Indexes: U.S. city average.* Washington, D.C.: U.S. Government Printing Office, December.

———. 1998. Planned changes in the Consumer Price Index formula. Washington, D.C.: U.S. Government Printing Office, 16 April.

———. N.d.-a. A description of the PPI physician services initiative. Washington, D.C.: U.S. Government Printing Office.

———. N.d.-b. A description of the PPI hospital services initiative. Washington, D.C.: U.S. Government Printing Office.

———. N.d.-c. Improvements to CPI procedures: Prescription drugs. Washington, D.C.: U.S. Government Printing Office.

U.S. General Accounting Office. 1996. *Consumer Price Index: Cost-of-living concepts and the housing and medical care components.* Report to the Ranking Minority Member, Committee on Banking and Financial Services, House of Representatives. GAOO/GGD-96-166, August. Washington, D.C.: U.S. Government Printing Office.

U.S. Senate Finance Committee. 1996. *Final report from the advisory commission to study the Consumer Price Index.* Washington, D.C.: U.S. Government Printing Office, 4 December.

Weiner, Jonathan P., Allen Dobson, Stephanie L. Maxwell, Kevin Coleman, Barbara Starfield, and Gerald Anderson. 1996. Risk-adjusted Medicare capitation rates using ambulatory and inpatient diagnoses. *Health Care Financing Review* 17 (3): 77–100.

Weiss, Samuel. 1955. The development of index numbers in the BLS. *Monthly Labor Review* 78 (1): 20–25.

Comment   Brent R. Moulton

Berndt, Cutler, Frank, Griliches, Newhouse, and Triplett have presented a comprehensive examination of the current state of knowledge on mea-

Brent R. Moulton is associate director for national income, expenditure, and wealth accounts at the Bureau of Economic Analysis, U.S. Department of Commerce.

The opinions expressed in this paper are those of the author and do not represent an official policy of the Bureau of Economic Analysis or the views of other BEA staff.

suring inflation in the medical care sector. They summarize the key market characteristics that make price and welfare measurement for this set of activities difficult. They then present a detailed and thorough discussion of the issues and problems associated with the consumer and producer price indexes for this sector. They briefly summarize the empirical studies that have attempted to design improved measures of price change for medical care. I note that these studies are very recent indeed; most have been written within the last three years. The authors conclude by making a series of recommendations for improving price measurement, most of which involve further cooperative efforts between the federal statistical agencies and the wider research community.

With respect to most of this paper, I found the presentation to be excellent and I have little to add. I would like to focus my remaining comments on the small section of the paper in which the measurement target, the conceptual cost-of-living index, is formulated.

Berndt et al. take a rather unusual approach to deriving a cost-of-living index. Usually, the cost-of-living index has been derived from the consumer's cost (or expenditure) function (Konüs 1939). Berndt et al., however, form the cost-of-living index from the direct utility function. The reasons for this choice are clear. The cost function is based on an assumption of consumer optimization, whereas Berndt et al. intend to allow for nonoptimal choices due to moral hazard and principal-agent problems, which are important features of medical care markets.

The resulting cost-of-living index, shown as their equations (3) and (4), has some unusual features. Although it measures the changes in the cost of living, it is not a price index; that is, it is a function of expenditures (specifically, "nonmedical expenditures divided by numeraire price"), rather than prices. Presumably, the numeraire price is the price index for nonmedical care expenditures.

The other thing I would point out is that the information requirements for this index are extremely high. These include, at a minimum, knowing (1) the marginal rate of substitution between health status and nonmedical care expenditures (which must be estimated without assuming that consumers are optimizing); (2) an index of health status that must be comprehensive enough to represent all of the medical conditions for which medical services are obtained; and (3) an index of the time allocated to medical treatments. In addition, a more comprehensive measure is suggested that would entail knowing the effects of changes in medical care knowledge and the environment on health status.

Contemplating the difficulties that would be associated with directly implementing this type of cost-of-living measure leads me to appreciate the relative simplicity of the traditional, Konüs-type approach. Berndt et al. should be complimented for comprehensively laying out the problems and suggesting some important improvements. They have also shown, however, that for those of us who would like to develop medical care price indexes that would be useful as a proxy for a well-established cost-of-living index, the task before us is daunting indeed.

Reference

Konüs, A. A. 1939. The problem of the true index of the cost of living. *Econometrica* 7:10–29.

II

Current State of Measurement

Medical Care in the Consumer Price Index

Ina Kay Ford and Daniel H. Ginsburg

5.1 Introduction

The medical care component of the Consumer Price Index (CPI) is evolving into a more comprehensive measure of household medical expense price movement in the economy. We discuss the CPI's use of medical care expenditures, measurement approaches, and other methodological issues to obtain weights and prices. Highlighting issues and our plans to address them, we emphasize the organization of the CPI medical care major group as of January 1998, when a revised CPI was introduced.

For both the CPI for all urban consumers (the CPI-U) and CPI for urban wage earners and clerical workers (the CPI-W), medical care is one of the CPI eight major groups. The medical care group contains thirteen item strata. The thirteen medical care strata form the basic framework within which the CPI defines and measures the change in medical care costs. The medical care item strata are

Prescription drugs and medical supplies
Internal and respiratory over-the-counter drugs
Nonprescription medical equipment and supplies
Physicians' services
Dental services
Eyeglasses and eye care
Services by other medical professionals

Ina Kay Ford is an economist in the Services Section in the Division of Consumer Prices and Price Indexes of the Bureau of Labor Statistics. Daniel H. Ginsburg is chief of the Services Section in the Division of Consumer Prices and Price Indexes of the Bureau of Labor Statistics.

Hospital services[1]
Nursing homes and adult daycare[2]
Commercial health insurance
Blue Cross/Blue Shield health insurance
Health maintenance plans
Medicare and other health insurance

5.2 Index Construction

Item strata within each of the thirty-eight CPI index areas[3] (the item/area strata) are the basic building blocks of the CPI. The Bureau of Labor Statistics (BLS) constructs a price index—called a basic index or elementary aggregate—for each item/area stratum. A basic index is computed from a sample of items belonging to the stratum in each index area. Every month or every other month (depending on the index area), BLS collects the prices of the items in the samples of each item/area stratum. The basic indexes are measures of the change in the prices for one item stratum in one index area. For example, there is a basic index for prescription drugs and medical supplies in the Boston metropolitan area. (It is an unpublished index because its sample size is too small to permit its publication, but it is a basic building block of higher-level published indexes.)

To construct higher-level indexes from the basic indexes for the item/area strata, the CPI needs a weight for each item/area stratum in addition to its basic index. Higher-level indexes, which BLS calls aggregate indexes, are weighted averages of the stratum-level basic indexes. For example, the CPI index for U.S. medical care is the weighted average of the thirteen medical care strata in the thirty-eight index areas. The weight of an item stratum in an index area is the average annualized expenditure that consumers living in the index area incurred to purchase items in the stratum during the CPI expenditure base period, which is 1993–95;[4] these weights come from the Consumer Expenditure Surveys (CEX) for those years.

5.3 Published Series

BLS publishes U.S. indexes for the first nine medical care strata (Grandits 1996). There are no published indexes for the health insurance strata because—as explained in detail below—BLS uses an indirect

---

1. Prior to January 1997, separate hospital and related services indexes existed for hospital rooms, other inpatient services (including nursing homes), and outpatient services. See Cardenas 1996.

2. See n. 1.

3. Prior to the January 1998 CPI, there were 44 index areas. See Williams 1996.

4. Prior to the January 1998 CPI, the expenditure base period was 1982–84. See Greenlees and Mason 1996.

method for pricing health insurance. BLS also publishes indexes for groups of strata; for example, the group for professional services combines the fourth through the seventh strata above. BLS publishes indexes for medical care in the four Census regions, thirteen region-size classes, and twenty-six metropolitan areas. BLS also produces U.S.-level substratum indexes, such as the indexes for inpatient and outpatient hospital services. Substratum indexes are byproduct indexes that are not building blocks of the CPI; we make them available for user convenience and to provide continuity with older series. The definitions of the CPI's published medical care series are in table 5.3, below.

5.4   Changes to the Medical Care Component of the CPI

Over the years BLS has made changes to the CPI medical care indexes and is considering future modifications. In addition, many outsiders have suggested changes. The proposals involve one or more of the following: changing the way we define the basic indexes of one or more of the strata; changing the way we define the weights for the strata; and changing the strata themselves. The change in January 1995 to the way BLS handled shifts from brand to generic prescription drugs is an example of the first type of change. Proposals to expand the realm of medical care beyond the CPI's traditional out-of-pocket coverage to include expenditures made by third parties, such as employers or governments, is an example of the second type of change. The January 1997 change, which reconstituted three hospital strata into two strata, is an example of the third type of change. These changes are discussed in detail below.

5.5   The Scope of the CPI for Medical Care

The CPI covers the prices of goods and services that people buy for day-to-day living. This means that the scope of most CPI components is limited to the costs that consumers incur out of pocket. Payments by other parties are out of scope. For example, the elementary and secondary education component of the CPI excludes the cost of public schools, which are funded through taxes rather than direct consumer expenditures.

The CPI has always treated medical expenses this way. Expenditure weights for the item strata in the medical care major group are what consumers directly paid for in the base period. They include insurance premiums paid by consumers, but do not include the expenditures of governments, employers, or charitable organizations made on behalf of consumers. Nor do they include the cost of medical care that is not paid for and that the industry absorbs. For this reason medical care's share of the CPI is smaller than its share in broader statistical measures such as those of the National Income and Product Accounts. Medical care's share of the CPI of other countries, where medical care is largely provided by the government, is usually very small; this can affect comparisons of inflation between countries.

The long-standing BLS practice of limiting the CPI to just the out-of-pocket cost of medical care is not without controversy. For example, the Report of the Advisory Commission to Study the Consumer Price Index,[5] which is commonly referred to as the Boskin Report, recommended that the medical care weights be expanded to include all medical care expenditures.

5.6   CPI and PCE Expenditure Comparison

The personal consumption expenditure (PCE) is the part of gross domestic product that approximately corresponds to the CPI.[6] The PCE for medical care covers expenditures of consumers, employers, and government, including expenditures on Medicare and Medicaid as well as employer payments for health insurance. Medical care accounts for 17.9 percent of total expenditures measured by the 1995 current dollars PCE, but only 7.362 percent of expenditures as measured in the December 1995 CPI-U. Since the expenditure weights used in the CPI are limited to consumer out-of-pocket spending, items eligible to be priced in the medical care component are also limited.

Federal and state governments fund the entire Medicaid program while the federal government, nonfederal employers, employees, and participants fund the Medicare program. This funding arrangement limits what services and prices are eligible for inclusion in the CPI. Medicaid prices are totally ineligible for the CPI because the program is funded completely by the government. Medicare is composed of two parts, Medicare Part A and Part B. Medicare Part A is an entitlement program funded by taxes that provides compulsory hospital insurance, and Medicare prices are not eligible within hospitals for the CPI. Medicare Part B, which covers physicians and other medical care providers, is voluntary supplementary medical insurance purchased by the participants as a form of health insurance; these prices and services are eligible to be priced in the CPI and the premium for Part B is included in the CPI weights.

In recent years, as the cost of providing health insurance has increased, there has been a trend toward employers paying less of their employees' insurance premiums. Because the CPI expenditure weight includes only the employee-paid share, such a trend would ultimately be reflected as an increase in the relative weight of medical care. It would not be treated, however, as an increase in price.

5. U.S. Senate Committee on Finance, December 1996.
6. For a complete decomposition of the CPI versus the PCE see Fixler and Jaditz 1997.

5.7   The 1998 CPI Revision: Expenditure Weights

Medical care strata are grouped into two aggregates: Medical care commodities comprise the first three strata; medical care services are the remaining strata. Weights for the medical care commodities item strata are calculated from the diary portion[7] of the CEX. The interview portion of the CEX is the source for the weights of the medical care services item strata. These expenditures reflect both out-of-pocket expenses not covered by health insurance and health insurance premiums by survey households. Effective with the CPI for January 1998, the CPI expenditure weights are based on CEX data for 1993–95; these replaced the weights based on expenditures for 1982–84, which were in use from January 1987 through December 1997.

Table 5.1 provides the shares of medical care components in total consumer spending reported in the CEX for 1982–84 and 1993–95. The percentages reflect spending by all urban consumers, the population base for the CPI-U. Table 5.1 also includes a column identifying the percentage each item stratum and aggregate comprises of total medical care for both time periods.

Many changes have taken place in how health care is purchased and paid for over the past decade. How consumers purchase and pay for health care contributes to small shifts in relative importance that many not be evident in other categories of the CPI. Consumers purchase health insurance directly or through their place of employment. If they purchase it through their place of employment, the employer may pay a portion of the cost of the health insurance, which is not included in the CPI weight. Changes in the portion of the cost of the health insurance the employers pay affects the out-of-pocket spending by the employee, and, in turn, the share of consumption spending recorded in the CPI. Changes in what type of health insurance the employee purchases—fee-for-service, health maintenance organizations (HMOs), or preferred provider organizations (PPOs)—also affect spending by consumers on health care and the CPI weights.

The shares of consumption spending shown in table 5.1 differ from relative importances (such as those given in section 5.6). Medical care's share of 1982–84 consumer spending, as shown in table 5.1, is much lower than its 1995 CPI relative importance in section 5.6. The difference reflects the CPI's Laspeyres formulation. Because medical care prices have been rising

---

7. The CEX is composed of two separate surveys—an interview survey and a diary survey—both conducted by the Census Bureau for BLS. The interview survey is used to collect data for expenditures that respondents can remember fairly accurately for periods of approximately three months. The diary survey is designed to obtain expenditure information for small frequently purchased items that consumers tend to forget. Approximately five thousand consumer units are contacted each year for each type of survey.

Table 5.1 **CPI Medical Care (MC) Components' Shares of Urban Consumers' All Items (AI) and the Medical Care Consumption Spending during the Two CPI Expenditure Base Periods from the Consumer Expenditure Surveys for Those Periods**

| | Expenditure Base Periods | | | |
| | 1982–84 | | 1993–95 | |
Item Strata and Aggregates	AI (%)	MC (%)	AI (%)	MC (%)
Medical care	4.796	100	5.434	100
Medical care commodities	0.946	19.7	1.225	22.5
Prescription drugs & medical supplies	0.583	12.2	0.810	14.9
Nonprescription drugs & medical supplies	0.363	7.6	0.415	7.6
Internal & respiratory over-the-counter drugs	0.232	4.8	0.279	5.1
Nonprescription medical equipment & supplies	0.131	2.7	0.136	2.5
Medical care services	3.850	80.3	4.209	77.5
Professional services	2.546	53.1	2.691	49.5
Physicians' services	1.313	27.4	1.392	25.6
Dental services	0.767	16.0	0.751	13.8
Eye care	0.320	6.7	0.285	5.2
Services by other medical professionals	0.147	3.1	0.264	4.9
Hospital and related services	1.178	24.6	1.246	22.9
Hospital services	n.a.		1.200	22.1
Nursing homes	n.a.		0.046	0.8
Unpriced items	0.003	0.1	n.a.	
Health insurance	0.125	2.6	0.272	5.0

Notes: 1982–84 was the CPI expenditure base period from January 1987 through December 1997. 1993–95 is the expenditure base period of the CPI effective January 1998. n.a. = not available. Hearing aid expenditures moved from nonprescription medical equipment and supplies to services by other medical professionals effective January 1998. Expenditures from the "unpriced" category under hospitals were moved to prescription drugs and medical supplies. The category represents expenditures for the rental and repair of hospital equipment. Health insurance reflects the retained earnings of health insurance providers—see section 5.12 in the text.

relatively rapidly, the fixed-quantity assumption underlying the CPI implies a growing relative importance of medical care in the CPI market basket. This, in turn, yields the somewhat surprising result that although consumers allocated a greater proportion of their total expenditure to medical care in 1993–95 than in 1982–84, the relative importance of medical care in the CPI fell in 1998 when the expenditure weights were updated. The relative importance of Medical care for the CPI-U as of December 1997 reflecting 1993–95 CEX data, updated for price change, is 5.614 percent.

The 1993–95 CEX data show that the medical care component increased its proportion of total consumption since 1982–84. The increase results primarily from changes in what consumers are purchasing and how they are paying for medical care. Looking at expenditure data for 1993–95 the medical care share increased by 13.3 percent (0.638 percentage points) from the 1982–84 period. An examination of the data at lower levels reveals that expenditures on prescription drugs, other medical professional services, and health insurance constitute a greater proportion of medical care based on the 1993–95 CEX versus the 1982–84 CEX. Other categories such as physicians' services, dental services, and eye care decreased as a proportion of medical care from the 1993–95 CEX.

One of the major observations is that spending on health insurance increased from 0.125 percent (2.6 percent of medical care) in 1982–84 to 0.272 percent (5.0 percent of medical care) in 1993–95. As the CPI reflects only consumers' own expenditures and employer- and government-provided benefits are not included, higher health insurance premium payments by households has contributed to this increase. According to the Employee Benefit Survey, in the eleven-year period between the two expenditure surveys, the average employee contribution for individual medical care coverage tripled from $10.13 to $31.55 per month (Foster 1996). Contributions for family coverage also tripled, from an average of $32.51 to $107.42 per month.

The changes taking place in the individual categories reflect changes that are taking place in the delivery of health care. A greater percentage of employed persons have switched their health insurance provider from fee-for-service to HMOs and PPOs. According to the Employee Benefit Survey, participation in health plans by type of provider for full time employees of medium and large private establishments for the period 1984–93 were as follows: Fee-for-service decreased from 95 percent to 50 percent; HMOs increased from 5 percent to 23 percent; and PPOs increased from 1 percent in 1986 to 23 percent in 1993 (Kane, Blostin, and Pfuntner 1996). HMOs and PPOs typically charge for health care based on all-inclusive fees rather than individual billing for each service provided as in fee-for-service plans. The shift to all-inclusive providers has led to more out-of-pocket spending on health insurance but less out-of-pocket spending on individual medical services. According to Gregory Acs and John Sabelhaus of the Urban Institute, "Consumers reacted to rising health care prices by purchasing more insurance, in the sense that the share of health spending attributable to co-payments and deductibles for hospitals and physicians actually fell from 30.1% to 20.9% between 1980 and 1992" (1995, 36). While medical care prices have risen at a rapid rate over the past decade, the average consumer's expenditures on medical care actually increased less rapidly due to changes in provider arrangements coupled with changes in the overall delivery of health care services.

5.8   Selection of Outlets for Pricing

The sample of retail outlets for most CPI basic indexes is drawn from the Point of Purchase Survey (POPS), which the Census Bureau conducts for BLS. To conduct the POPS, the Census Bureau surveys households in each of the CPI's pricing areas and identifies the name and location of the retail establishments where the surveyed household made purchases in each of the survey's categories of consumption. In addition, the survey collects how much the households spent at each establishment. BLS selects outlets within a CPI pricing area with probability proportional to expenditure. The outlets selected for medical care are selected from the POPS, with the exception of nursing homes.

The Census data collectors question consumers about expenditures they make for specific categories of goods and services; these categories correspond to one or more item strata. Each category has a specific recall period or length of time for the consumer to consider if they made a purchase. The recall periods are designed to allow a greater length of time for purchases that are not made frequently, such as hospital stays, and a shorter recall period for purchases that are made more frequently, such as prescription drugs. Table 5.2 provides the POPS categories and recall periods.

Table 5.2   Point of Purchase Survey (POPS)

Category	Recall Period
Physicians' services	1 year
Dental services	1 year
Eyeglasses and eye care	1 year
Services by other medical professionals	1 year
Hospital services	1 year
Adult day care	1 year
Nonprescription medical equipment, supplies, topicals, and dressings	1 month
Prescription drugs and medical supplies	2 weeks
Internal and respiratory over-the-counter drugs	2 weeks

The nursing home sample is selected from a secondary source of data, the 1991 National Health Provider Inventory: Nursing Homes and Board and Care Homes, which is conducted by the National Center for Health Statistics. The use of an alternate data source for the nursing home sample was necessitated due to insufficient outlets reported in the POPS. Nursing homes are an unusual consumer item in that only a small share of households incur expenses for them, but for those households they are often very large expenditures; this is a situation that is difficult for the POPS to cover accurately.

5.9   Sample Rotation

To ensure that the outlets where items are priced and the unique items selected for pricing at each outlet are current, samples are rotated each year using POPS data. Such rotation yields totally new outlet and unique item samples every five years. In the past, sample rotation took place in one-fifth of the CPI's area samples each year. Thus, over a five-year period, the entire CPI outlet sample and unique item sample were updated. Beginning in 1999 the CPI is changing to a new sample rotation methodology. The new sample rotation process rotates categories of commodities and services rather than a subset of the CPI pricing areas. The new methodology allows the updating of selected groups of item strata more frequently. The BLS will have more flexibility to update samples of items that need more frequent changes by moving to a rotation schedule based on category.[8]

5.10   Improvements to Procedures for Prescription Drugs

As of publication of the January 1995 CPI, BLS changed the way the CPI treats prescription drugs that lose patent protection (Knudsen 1994). Under the old procedure, the CPI did not allow for the opportunity to substitute to generic versions of the drug unless the selected retail outlet in which we were pricing stopped selling the brand name drug. (Sample rotation—the CPI process that keeps item samples up to date—brings new items such as generic drugs into the CPI samples, but the rotation process does not compare prices between the old and new versions of an item.) The new procedure gives generic versions of a drug a one-time chance to be substituted for the original brand name drug regardless of whether or not the store discontinues the brand name version. Six months after a drug in the sample loses patent protection, CPI field staff select among all therapeutically equivalent versions of the drug (including the original brand name version) sold in the store. The timing of the reselection allows the emerging generic drugs an opportunity to gain market

8. See Cage 1996 for further information on the new sample rotation process.

share, because the chance of selection is proportional to the number of prescriptions dispensed. When a therapeutically equivalent substitute is selected, the CPI treats the price difference between the original drug and its selected substitute as a price change that is reflected in the index.

The CPI is attempting to get more transaction prices in the index, and as CPI item and outlet samples rotate over time, outlets where prescription drugs are priced are now asked to provide transaction prices rather than cash or list prices. The transaction price is the documented amount the outlet actually is reimbursed for providing the prescription to the customer—the total payment received from all eligible sources, including the customer, the insurance provider, and any other party. Each part of the transaction price is incorporated into the reported price (the price the CPI uses). The pharmacist is usually able to identify any specific third-party payment plans, such as a specific commercial insurance PPO plan or an employer-based plan, and to determine if the customer must pay a portion of the price. The particular insurance provider payment arrangement for the identified drug is followed during subsequent visits to the outlet. This allows the index to reflect more actual transaction price changes.

Unfortunately, selecting a payer type at initiation has proved to be easier than obtaining the price associated with the payer during subsequent pricing. Too often the pharmacy's computer system does not allow access to the payer price for the prescription being priced, without actually filling a prescription. In such cases we must substitute to a cash price, unless the pharmacist has an alternative source for the selected payer's price.

The CPI excludes HMOs from outlet samples for prescription drugs. Because these outlets are owned and operated by insurance companies, purchases usually are based on only a copayment and not related to the real cost of the services. HMO third-party purchases are eligible in non-HMO-owned pharmacies where the total reported price is based on the HMO reimbursement and patient payment.

5.11   BLS Improvements to the Hospital CPI

Effective with the CPI for January 1997, BLS has restructured the CPI hospital index to make it better able to handle new items and changes in the way medical problems are treated within hospitals, and to allow for new ways of looking at the hospital sector of consumption. The previous structure of the CPI hospital index divided hospital room expenses, charges for other inpatient services, and the cost of outpatient services into three separate compartments, forcing the CPI to regard items that are actually inputs to medical treatment in hospitals as consumer items. There is a growing consensus that the correct view of medical services is treatment outcomes and that they, ideally, should be our consumer items. From this distinct vantage point, a day occupying a hospital room or the time spent in an operating room are not separate consumer services but part of an entire hospital visit that ultimately contributes to a treatment outcome for a patient. However, a strictly "outcomes" approach to pricing hospital services is still not possible.

For many diseases and injuries, the number of inpatient hospital days to achieve a given outcome is decreasing. Furthermore, other treatments that once required an inpatient hospital stay are now performed as outpatient procedures. In response to these prevailing conditions, BLS combined the current three CPI categories into one category called hospital services. Differentiation between inpatient and outpatient settings and among service types now will occur under the umbrella of this broad category. This restructuring allows for price comparisons not possible before, when procedures shift from inpatient to outpatient delivery settings.

In addition to the changes in classification structure, BLS introduced new procedures for hospital collection. The goal of the new process is to identify a payer, a diagnosis, and the payer's reimbursement arrangement. The item description is derived from a "live" hospital bill. Collecting information to describe a hospital visit from a real bill and recording the price based on the terms of the contract between the insurer and the hospital (the reimbursed amount) represent major improvements over the current use of the hospital chargemaster (the published list prices) as the reported price for the CPI. As always, BLS continues in its strong commitment to full confidentiality of all collected information.[9]

An additional benefit of the change to pricing hospitals was the creation of a separate index for nursing homes and adult daycare. Until late 1999, the index will reflect price movement for nursing homes only; subsequently, it will include prices for adult daycare as well. Out-of-pocket expenditures on adult daycare are included in the weight for the nursing home component.

As part of the 1998 CPI revision, BLS created two new indexes by separating hospital and related services into two major components, hospitals and nursing homes. BLS also calculates and publishes two substratum indexes (SRC), one for inpatient hospital services and one for outpatient hospital services. Substratum indexes are not used directly in the calculation of the overall CPI because the item samples are not designed to support them. Their weights are allowed to shift, and in the case of hospitals, medical treatments may move between them. These indexes are calculated using specification data. Additionally, as noted above, the nursing home stratum will be expanded to include adult daycare.

The only other significant change to the medical care component was to move expenditures for hearing aids from nonprescription medical

9. See Cardenas 1996 for further information on the 1997 change in the CPI hospital component.

equipment and supplies to services by other medical care professionals. In table 5.3, definitions of the indexes as they appear for the revision are given. Table 5.4 identifies the number of current quotes as of February 1998.

5.12   Health Insurance Pricing

The CPI has not been able to develop a feasible method to directly price medical insurance. To measure the change in the price of medical insurance appropriately, the CPI would need to exclude changes in both the quality of the insurance and in the quantity consumed. This means that for any medical insurance policy selected BLS would need to obtain values for any modifications of policy benefits from year to year (they are quality changes). In addition, BLS would need information on utilization, the increased or decreased use of medical insurance, or the health status of the insured group, because these are quantity changes in medical insurance. Because changes in benefits are changes to the quality of the insurance, and increased use is a higher quantity of medical insurance consumed, these are not changes in its price and the price index must isolate them from real price change.

Prior to the 1964 CPI revision, the CPI did price health insurance premiums directly. Since this was prior to the 1978 adoption of comprehensive probability sampling in the CPI, the CPI followed the prices of items that BLS staff judged to be representative of an item stratum. For health insurance before 1964, the CPI priced as a fixed amount of protection for the individual consumer the most widely held Blue Cross/Blue Shield family policy being sold to consumers. Using this method led to a number of problems involving quality and quantity changes over time. In pricing premiums directly, the BLS found it impossible to account for quality differences due to changes in both the benefits provided by policies and in utilization of the provided benefits. These problems led the BLS to switch to the current indirect method of pricing health insurance in the 1964 revision of the CPI (Fixler 1996). The feasibility of directly pricing health insurance policies was retested during 1984 and 1985 (Ford and Sturm 1988). The test results identified problems with obtaining data from insurers on quality changes and utilization changes in the benefit packages at that time. Further research on directly pricing health insurance is planned for 1998 and 1999.

The BLS does not publish indexes for health insurance premiums because the CPI employs an indirect method to measure price change for health insurance. This indirect approach decomposes medical insurance into three parts: changes in the prices of medical care items covered by health insurance policies; changes in the cost of administering the policies; and changes in the cost of maintaining reserves and, as appropriate, profits.

Table 5.3   **Definitions of Published Medical Care Indexes**

Item	Definition
Medical care	Medical care commodities and medical care services
Medical care commodities	Prescription drugs, nonprescription over-the-counter drugs, and other medical equipment and supplies
Prescription drugs	All drugs and medical supplies dispensed by prescription; mail order outlets included; prices reported represent transaction prices between the pharmacy, patient, and third party payer if applicable
Nonprescription drugs and medical supplies	All nonprescription medicines, vitamins, dressings, equipment, and supplies
Internal and respiratory over-the-counter drugs	Nonprescription medicines taken by swallowing, inhaling, as suppositories, or enemas, e.g., aspirin, cough medicine, or vitamins
Nonprescription medical equipment and supplies	Nonprescription medicines and dressings used externally, contraceptives, and general supportive and convalescent medical equipment, e.g., adhesive strips, heating pads, athletic supporters, or wheelchairs
Medical care services	Professional medical services, hospital services, nursing home services, and health insurance imputation
Professional medical services	Physicians, dentists, eye care providers, and other medical professionals
Physicians' services	Services by medical physicians in private practice, including osteopaths, that are billed by the physician; house, office, clinic, and hospital visits (excluding ophthalmologists—see eye care)
Dental services	Services performed by dentists, oral or maxillofacial surgeons, orthodontists, periodontists, or other dental specialists in group or individual practice; treatment may be provided in the office or hospital
Eye care	Services provided by opticians, optometrists, and ophthalmologists; eye exams, dispensing of eyeglasses and contact lenses, office visits, and surgical procedures in the office or hospital
Services by other medical professionals	Services performed by other professionals such as psychologists, chiropractors, physical therapists, podiatrists, social workers, and nurse practitioners in or out of the office
Hospital and related services	Services provided to inpatients and outpatients, emergency room visits, nursing home care, and adult day care; includes transaction and chargemaster prices
Hospital services	Services provided to patients during visits to hospitals or ambulatory surgical centers or other similar settings
Inpatient hospital services[a]	Services for inpatients, including a mixture of individual services, DRG-based services, per diems, packages, or other bundled services
Outpatient hospital services[a]	Services provided to patients classified as outpatients in hospitals, free standing facilities, ambulatory, and urgent care centers
Nursing home services and adult daycare	Includes charges for care at nursing homes, nursing home units of retirement homes, and convalescent or rest homes; adult daycare data will be included in this index in late 1999

[a]Substratum index.

Table 5.4	Number of Current Quotes as of February 1998	
Category		Quotes
Prescription drugs		694
Internal & respiratory over-the-counter drugs		423
Nonprescription medical equipment and supplies		252
Physicians' services		1,050
Dental services		927
Eye care		290
Services by other medical professionals		365
Hospital services		3,236
Nursing home services		438

Most of the expenditure for health insurance goes for the first item—the part that reflects the insurers' payments for medical treatment. The CPI allocates this part of health insurance spending to the indexes for those treatments. This means that most of the expenditures for health insurance reported on the CEX are assigned to the other medical care strata; the share assigned to each stratum is based on insurance industry information. The remaining weight, for the other two parts of insurance, is for the overhead of the insurers; this is all that remains in the unpublished health insurance index.

Price movement over time for the unpublished health insurance indexes in the CPI is determined by the movements of the other medical care strata, adjusted by changes in the retained earnings ratio. Movement in the unpublished medical insurance index reflects both changes in benefits paid and changes in the unit cost of administering these benefits. This process yields a measure of price change for insurance of constant coverage and utilization. That is, changes in benefit coverage and utilization levels will generally be offset by compensating premium charges and thus will not significantly affect retention rates. Implicit in the process is the assumption that the level of service from the individual carriers is strictly a function of the benefits paid. Other changes in the amount of service provided for policy holders, such as more convenient claims handling, will affect the movement of the index when—strictly speaking—they should be removed, but the effects are probably small.

The BLS obtains calendar year data for premium income, benefit payments, and retained earnings. Blue Cross/Blue Shield supplies their data directly to BLS. BLS gets data for commercial carriers from Bests Insurance. For each year, the ratio of retained earnings to benefit payments is calculated, yielding a retained earnings ratio. Next, the latest year's ratio is divided by the previous year's ratio, to obtain the relative of change in the ratios. Finally, this annual relative of change is converted to a monthly relative (by taking its twelfth root) so that the CPI can reflect the change month by month over the calendar year.[10] Because it is not feasible to obtain the monthly change in price caused by changing retention margins, spreading the annual change evenly over the year is preferable to reflecting the entire annual change in one month.

5.13 Alternative Approaches to the Measurement of Medical Care Price Change

Definition of what constitutes an item for pricing in the medical care component of the CPI has been a source of debate. Traditionally, items that were eligible for the CPI have been those that we could observe the consumer buying. In medical care these are items that today, at least, one might view as the inputs to medical care. Examples are a visit to a doctor, a purchase of a particular drug, a day in a hospital, an amount of time in an operating room, or a diagnostic test. This view of medical care is not concerned with what benefit, if any, the consumer receives from consuming medical care items; the presumption is that the consumer would not purchase them unless they wanted them.

This traditional way of viewing medical care items is sometimes called the *input* approach because the items eligible for the CPI are inputs to medical treatments. The input approach is inconsistent with the idea that the CPI should be a cost-of-living index. The cost-of-living index theory suggests that the items that should be included in the CPI should be those that directly yield consumer utility.

The *outcomes* approach is an idealized but as yet infeasible alternative to the inputs approach. It would price the cost of achieving a given degree of improvement for some medical condition. In theory this would allow new treatments for the medical condition, say a drug rather than surgery, to count as price change. The advantage of the outcomes approach is that it is patient-centered rather than inputs-centered. It is one path toward focusing on the consumer procurement of not just the inputs of health

10. A hypothetical example of the calculation of the change in retained earnings for commercial carriers:

Year	Income ($)	Benefits ($)	Retentions ($)	Retentions/Benefits Ratio
1	100,000	94,000	6,000	.063830
2	108,000	100,000	8,000	.080000

Year 2 adjustment for change in retentions: (a) (Year 2 ratio)/(Year 1 ratio) = .080000/.063830 = 1.253329 relative of change, or 25.33 percent, which is the annual increase in the retention to benefits ratio. (b) Spreading this annual change equally over twelve months is done as follows: $\sqrt[12]{1.253329} = 1.018995 = 1.9$ percent per month.

care but what they aim to achieve—improved health. Nevertheless, even an outcomes approach would not address every concern about measuring the change in price of medical care.[11]

Although with an outcomes approach it should be possible to follow the cost of recovering from an illness or injury, such as a heart attack or a broken leg, it would not be possible to account for reductions in the incidence of certain illnesses due to nonmedical reasons.[12] From the outcomes perspective, each medical condition would still have to be handled as an individual illness, rather than as a potential precursor to a more serious disease; and each condition's treatment would be seen only as corresponding to itself, rather than as a step toward prevention of a more serious condition. With respect to the CPI, implementing an outcomes approach would require radical modifications to the item structure, moving from strata composed of various health care inputs to strata consisting of various diseases or diagnoses.

Intermediate between the traditional and the ideal is what we call the *treatment* approach. BLS is attempting to move to this approach within the new hospital item stratum with the distinction that the treatment considered occurs within the confines of a discrete hospital visit defined by an individual patient bill. Under this approach, the CPI can replace old methods of delivering treatment for a given medical problem with new methods as long as they are in the hospital item stratum. For example, if a hospital in the CPI sample moves to an outpatient microsurgery treatment that replaces a more invasive inpatient surgery, we may be able to show the price difference as price change. In the future, we may extend this to other medical care strata, for example, allowing a new drug to replace an older, less effective drug.

References

Acs, Gregory, and John Sabelhaus. 1995. Trends in out-of-pocket spending on health care, 1980–92. *Monthly Labor Review* 118 (December): 35–45.

11. It should be emphasized that this issue is not confined to the medical care components of the CPI. Ideally, for example, one would price transportation outcomes, such as vacation travel or access to work, rather than inputs such as automobiles and gasoline. More broadly, health outcomes depend on both medical care and food inputs.

12. Factors external to the science of medicine that might serve to improve individual and public health are lifestyle changes such as reduced smoking, better nutrition, and increased physical activity; environmental improvements such as cleaner air, safer cars, and better roads; or enhancements in the quality and safety of the workplace. The outcomes approach would have to handle preventive medical care (such as treating high blood pressure and cholesterol) by viewing those conditions as illnesses, even though their treatment brings no immediate improvement to well-being. It would still miss the improvement to consumer welfare, such as the reduced incidence of major illness, that results from treating these conditions.

Cage, Robert. 1996. New methodology for selecting the CPI outlet samples. *Monthly Labor Review* 119 (December): 49–61.

Cardenas, Elaine. 1996. Revision of the CPI hospital services component. *Monthly Labor Review* 119 (December): 40–48.

Fixler, Dennis. 1996. The treatment of the price of health insurance in the CPI. Washington, D.C.: Bureau of Labor Statistics. Unpublished material, 30 August.

Fixler, Dennis, and Ted Jaditz. 1997. An explanation of the difference between the CPI and the PCE deflator. Washington, D.C.: Bureau of Labor Statistics. Draft, 29 December.

Ford, Ina Kay, and Philip Sturm. 1988. CPI revision provides more accuracy in the medical care services component. Appendix: Test of direct pricing of health insurance policies. *Monthly Labor Review* 111 (April): 25–26.

Foster, Ann C. 1996. Employee contributions for medical care coverage. *Compensations and Working Conditions* 1 (September): 51–53.

Grandits, Steve. 1996. Publication strategy for the 1998 revised Consumer Price Index. *Monthly Labor Review* 119 (December): 26–30.

Greenlees, John S., and Charles C. Mason. 1996. Overview of the 1998 revision of the Consumer Price Index. *Monthly Labor Review* 119 (December): 3–9.

Kane, John J., Allan P. Blostin, and Jordon Pfuntner. 1996. Changing survey strategies in the evolution of health care plans. *Compensations and Working Conditions* 1 (September): 3–8.

Knudsen, Dave. 1994. Improvements to CPI procedures: Prescription drugs. *CPI Detailed Report* (October): 4.

U.S. Senate Committee on Finance. 1996. Final report of the Advisory Commission to Study the Consumer Price Index. Washington, D.C.: U.S. Government Printing Office, December.

Williams, Janet. 1996. The redesign of the CPI geographic sample. *Monthly Labor Review* 119 (December): 10–17.

Comment   Joseph P. Newhouse

I thank the authors for providing an accessible but detailed description of the CPI. There are, of course, descriptions in Bureau of Labor Statistics publications and in the *Monthly Labor Review,* but this paper should reach a different audience. The paper indicates how BLS has been improving the index, despite severe budget constraints, and it is clear that it is a much improved index.

This paper stimulated two thoughts that had not been so well brought out before in my reading of the literature. First, the assumption of competitive markets is a problem with pricing managed care health insurance because there is no assurance that rationing is in accordance with willing-

Joseph P. Newhouse is the John D. MacArthur Professor of Health Policy and Management and is on the faculties of the Kennedy School of Government, the Harvard Medical School, the Harvard School of Public Health, and the Faculty of Arts and Sciences at Harvard University, and is a research associate of the National Bureau of Economic Research.

ness to pay. More specifically, the consumer/patient has no basis to express his or her willingness to pay at the point of service, and the contract is incomplete. Alas, we do not have a theory of rationing in this setting. Hence, one cannot use changes in a plan's retention as a measure of welfare.

Second, suppose the effect of managed care is to obtain discounts from providers, thereby transferring rents to insurers. Suppose further that the plan market is not competitive, so the retention/profits at managed care companies increase as the rents are transferred. As I understand the CPI, this would show up as an increase in the price of health insurance. But because the CPI is based on out-of-pocket price, there would probably be no corresponding fall in the price of hospital and physician services. Hence, this transfer of rents would show up as a spurious price increase.

An old but still important chestnut relates to the exclusion of government programs. This means any cost shifting from (or even to) government payers to private payers shows up as a price change. This is sensible from the point of view of the purpose of the overall CPI, but not sensible from the point of view of a medical care sector price deflator.

Also in my view the outcomes approach is more important with medical care than with transportation because of role of insurance and role of the physician as an agent.

I have two suggestions: The first is on collaboration among the groups constructing the various indexes. The CPI is obtaining the actual transaction price of prescription drugs, including the insurance payment, but it is not clear what it is doing with this. Could it give this information to the PPI, which should want the transaction price?

I applaud the movement of the CPI to pricing the hospital episode (end of paper), but as my second suggestion I recommend exploring the inclusion of post/acute care (e.g., for ninety days following discharge) to get at substitution for hospital days. One could do this easily for Medicare patients (who of course are not part of the CPI); it may not be as easy elsewhere.

Health Care Output and Prices in the Producer Price Index

Dennis Fixler and Mitchell Ginsburg

6.1   Introduction

In recent years considerable attention has been directed to the importance of the health care sector to the economy. As there is no formal definition of the sector, its definition is arbitrary. One naturally thinks of hospitals, physicians, and pharmaceuticals as part of the sector, but one could
also legitimately include the manufacturers of hospital equipment, ban-
dages, and so on. The sector, however, is generally defined to focus on the
treatment of ailments or the relief of pain and suffering, and this is the
perspective adopted by the Bureau of Labor Statistics (BLS). Within the
context of the Producer Price Index (PPI), the health care sector is viewed
as containing the following service and manufacturing industries (by Standard Industrial Classification [SIC]): hospital and related services (SIC
806), physicians (SIC 8011), medical labs (SIC 8071), nursing homes (SIC
8053), drugs (SIC 283), and home health care (SIC 8082).

The industrial classification of the relevant industries will change shortly
with the implementation of the North American Industrial Classification
System (NAICS) agreed to in 1996.[1] This system will allow the U.S. prod-

Dennis Fixler is research economist and chief of the Division of Price and Index Number
Research at the Bureau of Labor Statistics. Mitchell Ginsburg is an international economist
in the Applied Economics Division of the United States International Trade Commission.

The authors thank Greg Kelly, Teresa McKeivier, Bonnie Murphy, John Nelson, William
Page, and Roslyn Swick for their assistance. This paper represents the views of the authors
alone and does not represent either BLS or USITC policy or the views of other staff members. The paper was completed while Ginsburg was an economist in the Producer Price Index
Program in the Office of Prices and Living Conditions.

1. See Federal Register, 9 April 1997, for a description of NAICS.

uct codes to be mapped into a system that is similar to the ones used in other countries. Many of the changes are minor and concern small aspects of the above SIC categories; for example, transportation services supplied by ambulances are in the NAICS Health Care and Social Assistance sector (sector 62) but under the SIC system they were in the transportation sector.

To economize on the explanation of index number construction and the associated problems, the focus of this paper is on the PPI indexes for hospitals, physicians, and drugs. The indexes for medical labs, nursing homes, and home health care will also be briefly described. Before discussing the indexes, a brief description of the conceptual framework underlying the Producer Price Index is presented.

6.2 Conceptual Framework

The PPI conceptual framework relies on the theory of output price indexes as formulated by Archibald (1977), Diewert (1983), and Fisher and Shell (1972). In this framework firms are viewed as competitive price takers that choose output quantities to maximize revenue for given technology and inputs. The application of the framework to the health care sector is complicated by the prominence of nonprofit firms, especially hospitals, and the fact that the outputs are not standardized.[2] Each of these aspects is discussed below and we give a brief presentation of output price index number theory.

6.2.1 Aggregation across Firm Types

Given the variety of organizational types in the health care sector, an issue from the perspective of index number construction is whether it is legitimate to combine the prices collected from the various types of firms. To do so requires some assumptions: Output prices are exogenous, firms use the output prices to make their production decisions, and firms are efficient in the sense that they operate on their production and cost frontiers.

Price Exogeneity

Price exogeneity is usually not an issue of concern because of the presumption of a competitive industry. However, because of the prominence of nonprofit firms in the health sector, principally hospitals, it is necessary to consider whether such firms can be incorporated into the PPI framework. Considerable attention has been paid in the hospital literature to the behavioral differences between profit and nonprofit organizational types.[3] Nevertheless it is generally agreed that there is some form of competition

2. In the 1992 Census of Services there were about 3,800 general medical and surgical hospitals in SIC 8062. About 84 percent were exempt from federal income tax and therefore may be considered nonprofit.
3. See for example, Newhouse (1970), Weisbrod (1975), and Jacobs (1974).

between hospitals but that it may manifest itself more in terms of nonprice rather than price competition. Noether (1988) provides evidence that price competition plays an important role in the hospital industry.

Industry structure, however, is not the only factor affecting price exogeneity. One also has to consider the implications of the fact that most treatments are paid for by third parties, principally insurers (including government through Medicare and Medicaid). These payers negotiate with providers the price that they will pay for services, and recently they have begun to specify the content of treatments, as in the case of managed care.[4] One could argue that, given the increasing importance of these payers, especially Medicare, there is an increased focus on price competition. Further, because these negotiations cover all the treatments that a hospital may provide, one may view the price as being exogenous for a specific transaction between a hospital and a patient covered by a third-party payer.

Organization Decision Making

There are two dimensions to the impact of organizational type on output decisions. First, the difference in objective may cause nonprofit firms to produce output bundles that are systematically different from those produced by for-profit firms. Second, the output decisions of nonprofits may differ from those of for-profit firms because they may receive charitable contributions, which can reduce the need to pay for inputs through revenue generation, and because they face a zero corporate tax rate.

Evidence on the actual impact of these differences is slim. Needham (1978), for one, argues that these two organizational forms are more similar than different in their behavior. In fact, if one viewed nonprofit firms as using their charitable contributions and tax advantage to reduce input costs in a lump sum fashion and not to charge lower (or subsidized) output prices, then these influences would become unimportant. A related issue is that of efficiency of production. In order to compare the impact of relative price changes on the output decisions of the two firm types, one must assume that they are equally efficient. This assumption has empirical support in the sense that evidence suggests that the two firm types are equally inefficient.[5]

---

4. As will be discussed below, a change in the character of treatment is one of the main issues in accounting for change in quality.

5. Studies of hospital efficiency have found that on average both types of hospitals are inefficient; that is, they do not use the minimum quantity of inputs to produce a given level of output. See for example Register and Bruning (1987). A natural question arises about the implications for output quality of efforts to improve efficiency. One can envision degradation of output quality arising from such effort. For example, suppose that a hospital reduced the amount of time a nurse is to spend with a patient and thereby reduces the "attentiveness" aspect of care. The same level of output could be achieved with a smaller number of nurses and such a reduction may make the hospital more efficient. As will be explained later, the PPI looks at the nurse-to-patient ratio as one indicator of quality of service. Since that ratio declines in this example, the PPI would treat this change as a change in the quality of service.

In the context of the theory of the firm, the organizational type can be viewed as a parameter in the production function that affects the transformation of inputs into outputs. Changes in the organizational framework can thus be viewed as shifting the frontier or changing its slope at various points. Viewed this way the objective of either firm type would be to maximize revenue subject to the corresponding production frontier. These points are elaborated in section 6.2.4 after a discussion of the definition of price and outputs.

6.2.2   Output and Price

In theory, the output of the firm is an easily identifiable product/service whose price is well defined. The price should represent the transaction price. Also, to accurately gauge the movement of price over time, one should be able to identify changes in product quality and set the corresponding money value. Because achieving these measurement objectives is more difficult in the hospital and physician industries than in the drug industry, where at least the measurement of output is straightforward, our discussion focuses on hospitals and physicians.

Hospitals and physicians treat illness, and therefore the object of pricing for both is a treatment. Attaining this objective is far more difficult than it may appear on first examination. One reason is that for many treatments there is no obvious endpoint. For example, if an individual enters a hospital for chest pains, he may not only be treated for that particular episode but he may also be required to return for a series of follow-up examinations. The same problem exists for visits to a physician's office; it may take several consultations after a first visit for a problem before the treatment is completed. Varieties of physician skill and the uncertainty surrounding the probabilities of success for different treatments also determine the treatment package.

Another impediment arises from the fact that the PPI must define treatments within industry boundaries. Thus, if a treatment path requires a hospital stay and a series of visits to a physician, these will be treated separately. This constraint also affects the measurement of substitution among treatments; if pharmaceutical products were substituted for either physician or hospital services then the substitution would not be captured.[6]

To overcome some of the above complications, the PPI program defines a treatment within the context of a given bill for a single encounter between a patient and a hospital or a patient and a physician. The bill specifies the set of procedures supplied to a given patient, and it also allows the

---

6. See Frank, Berndt, and Busch (chap. 12 in this volume) for a demonstration of the importance of bundling physician services with pharmaceuticals in measuring the price change for the treatment of depression.

BLS to monitor the charges acceptable to different payers. But this solution is limited by the fact that patients are not homogeneous, so that a bill will vary by the severity of the condition in the patient.[7] In addition the reliance on a bill also implies that one must distinguish between billed charges and the actual reimbursement to the hospital, which would represent the transaction price.

6.2.3   New Goods and Change in Quality

The health care sector is one of the most dynamic sectors in the economy. There is a steady stream of new treatments, equipment, drugs, and so on. Indeed society pays an enormous amount of attention to innovations in the health field. For index number makers such dynamism presents major hurdles. First, for the continued pricing of specific goods, constancy of quality is necessary so that the measured price change is meaningful. Second, the introduction of new goods creates the problem of how to incorporate new products into the index in the best way. In the health care sector there is the additional problem of handling the substitution of one type of treatment for another. A new technique for a treatment may transform an inpatient hospital treatment into an outpatient treatment. Also, the introduction of a new drug may induce physicians to substitute drug therapy for hospital treatments—in the early 1990s the annual cost of drug therapy for ulcers amounted to $900 compared to the $28,000 for surgery (PhRMA 1997).

Because the methods used to adjust an index for new goods are different from those used for changes in the quality of existing goods, it is important to distinguish between the two. In principle, new goods could be designated as goods that did not exist previously or as major changes in an existing product's quality that render it no longer comparable to the previous version. Minor product changes would then be ones for which some adjustment can be made to the price of the new version that would still permit a valid comparison with the previous version. An example of the latter would be changes in the packaging of drug product, and an example of the former would be the replacement of surgery for kidney stones by lithrotripsy.[8]

The implementation of such adjustments, however, is often difficult because of the absence of information surrounding the efficacy and diffusion

---

7. An alternative scheme for the pricing of treatments would be to select a hospital and a payer and then sample among the bills for a treatment of an illness submitted to that payer. In this way one may capture the importance of patient characteristics and (perhaps more importantly) the fact there is a distribution of prices for a treatment within a hospital. Another scheme would be simply to take the average of all bills within a hospital for a given treatment, paid by a specific payer. Such a plan would impose substantial reporting requirements and complicate the measurement of price for a treatment in that there is not a specific bundle of attributes from which changes in quality could be ascertained.

8. Lithrotripsy is the use of ultrasound to crush stones, usually in the bladder or kidney.

of new techniques, equipment, and drugs. In the market for most goods and services the success of product and process innovations is determined relatively quickly by the interaction of supply and demand. In contrast, the success of innovations in the health care sector is determined by lengthy studies of efficacy. To illustrate some of the questions that arise, consider the introduction of new techniques and new products for hip replacement. At what point should these be incorporated into the price index—at introduction or when some threshold level of usage has been surpassed? If the changes in hip replacement techniques are relatively minor, should a change in the quality of hip replacements be automatically registered or should there be some evidence of efficacy? If a quality change is registered and at some future date a consensus deems the technique detrimental, should the past indexes be revised?

The handling of the types of product changes described above is most often accomplished by examining the characteristics of the product and ascertaining whether the new bundle of characteristics is a major or minor change from the product's existing product bundle. The identification of the set of relevant characteristics is not straightforward. For example in the case of measuring the quality of hospital treatments, it is not clear whether attention should be paid to process (hospital staff, facilities) or outcome (the efficacy of the treatment).[9] Nevertheless, in the theory outlined below there is a reliance on the incorporation of product characteristics and in the effectiveness of what is referred to as the hedonic approach.[10]

Perhaps one of the more complicating features of quality measurement is the fact that the payer also determines the treatment package and thereby can affect measured quality change. Consider two firms A and B and their coverage for the treatment of kidney stones. Suppose firm A pays x dollars for the surgical treatment of kidney stones while B pays y dollars for the use of lithrotripsy. Also suppose that at time t the PPI sampling procedure of hospitals selects the kidney stone treatment covered by A. In principle, the sampling procedure should select some lithrotripsy treatments at different hospitals. The sticky issue of quality change arises if at $t + n$ firm A decides to switch its coverage to lithrotripsy. More specifically the question is whether the switch is one for which an adjustment can be

9. There has been some discussion about the relative merits of focusing on process or outcomes in assessing the quality of medical care. See for example the 20 November 1996 exchange of letters in the *Journal of the American Medical Association* about assessing quality of care. How to measure medical outcomes has also received considerable attention. Aside from straightforward measures such as mortality, much research has been undertaken to develop the concept of quality-adjusted life years and its derivatives such as cost-effectiveness.

10. In the hedonic approach, typically the price of a product is regressed on product characteristics thought to affect price. The use of product characteristics in such a way is not without limitations. A discussion of the issues is presented in Pakes (1997).

made or one that is noncomparable and should be treated as a different treatment.

6.2.4   Theory of Output Price Indexes

Consider a firm that transforms the input vector v into the output vector x. The difference between the quantity-quality decisions of a for-profit and a nonprofit hospital can be viewed as affecting the way inputs are transformed into outputs. Let c denote the firm type characteristic. A firm's production relationship can be characterized as

$$F(v, c) = [x | (x, v, c) \in T],$$

for given v and c and where T is the technology set and denotes the v inputs that can produce x. $F(v,c)$ is thus the set of feasible outputs for a given quantity of inputs conditioned by the hospital type.

The conceptual output price index is based on a firm's revenue function. Define the revenue function for a hospital as

$$R(p, v, c) = \max_{x} [px | x \in F(v, c)].$$

The conceptual output price index between periods 0 and 1 is given by

$$(1) \qquad I(p^0, p^1, v^r, c^r) = \frac{R^r(p^1, v^r, c^r)}{R^r(p^0, v^r, c^r)},$$

where r denotes the reference period for the determination of the relevant technology set, input vector, and hospital characteristic. If r is equal to 0, then the index takes a Laspeyres perspective, and if r is equal to 1, then the index takes a Paasche perspective.[11] The index $I(\cdot)$ is for a specific hospital of type c. We can aggregate these indexes to obtain an industry index, conditioned on the various organizational forms. Because the above framework applies to the inclusion of any product characteristic, it forms the conceptual foundation for our hedonic approach to quality adjustment.[12]

Index number makers of course have to come up with a way of computing the index in equation (1). Most statistical agencies do so by setting r equal to $t - 1$, ignoring c (competitive firms are assumed), and using the Laspeyres index formula to obtain

$$(2) \quad I_L(p^t, p^{t-1}, v^{t-1}) = \frac{p^t \cdot x^{t-1}}{p^{t-1} \cdot x^{t-1}} = \sum_i \frac{p_i^t}{p_i^{t-1}} \times s_i^{t-1}; s_i^{t-1} = \frac{p_i^{t-1} x_i^{t-1}}{\sum_i p_i^{t-1} x_i^{t-1}}.$$

11. In a Laspeyres perspective, one answers the question "How much does a collection of goods selected in the past cost today?" In a Paasche perspective, one answers the question "How much would a collection of goods selected today cost in some past period?"

12. For an application of this framework to the construction of superlative index numbers see Fixler and Zieschang (1992).

The second equality in the second row shows the Laspeyres index as a revenue share weighted average of the price relative to the ratio of prices in each period. Observe that by definition the denominator in equation (2) is equal to the denominator in equation (1). The numerator in equation (2) is an unobservable lower bound estimate of the numerator in equation (1). It follows that the index in equation (2) is a lower bound to the index in equation (1) and therefore potentially understates the true level of inflation. This potential measurement error is a well-known property of the Laspeyres index number formula. Though there has been much work on the relative merits of various index number formulas, here the concern is with difficult measurement problems that would arise regardless of the index number formula selected. Consequently, the discussion will be in terms of the commonly used Laspeyres formula.

6.3   Hospital Price Indexes

6.3.1   Industry Definition

The hospital price index was first published in 1993 and the underlying development work began in the late 1980s. The current index is based on research launched and data collected in 1989 and will soon be updated as described below.[13]

In the 1987 SIC Manual, hospitals in SIC 806 are defined as those establishments primarily engaged in the provision of diagnostic services, extensive medical treatment including surgical services, continuous nursing services, and other health care related services. These establishments have an organized medical staff, inpatient beds, and equipment and facilities for providing complete health care. Hospitals are placed into categories: general medical and surgical (SIC 8062), psychiatric (SIC 8063), and specialty, excluding psychiatric (SIC 8069). Not included in this industry are veterinary services (SIC 074), convalescent homes with extended care (SIC 8051), and associations or groups which limit their services to the provisions of insurance coverage against hospitalization or medical costs (SIC major group 63). The SIC definitions do not distinguish between hospitals in terms of ownership and control.

General medical and surgical hospitals are defined as providers of general medical, surgical, and other hospital-related services. These establishments provide services that range from room, board, and nursing services to the provision of highly specialized diagnostic and therapeutic services. Outpatient departments operated by hospitals are also included. Psychiat-

---

13. Information provided in the following discussion of the hospital, physician, medical labs, nursing homes, and home health care indexes is from internal BLS documents if a source is not specifically cited.

ric hospitals are establishments that provide diagnostic medical services and inpatient treatment for the mentally ill. Establishments so classified include mental hospitals and psychiatric hospitals, including children's psychiatric hospitals. In general, all hospitals with a majority of revenues from psychiatric services are classified under SIC 8063. Hospitals or institutions for the mentally retarded are not included (SIC 8051). Specialty hospitals are defined as establishments providing diagnostic services, treatment, and other hospital services for patients with specified types of illnesses, except mental. Establishments included in this classification are children's hospitals; women's hospitals; orthopedic hospitals; rehabilitation hospitals; cancer hospitals; eye, ear, nose, and throat hospitals; tuberculosis and other respiratory illness hospitals; alcoholism and other chemical dependency hospitals, and other specialty hospitals, except psychiatric.

With the implementation of NAICS, minor changes will occur to the hospital industry definitions. Under NAICS, general medical and surgical hospitals (NAICS 62211) will also include children's hospitals, which under the SIC system are in the specialty hospital industry. Psychiatric and substance abuse hospitals will be combined under the NAICS classification code 62221.

6.3.2 Sample Unit Information

The sample frame (master list) used for the selection of hospitals was drawn from the 1989 American Hospital Association Guide to the Health Care Field (AHA Guide).[14] Federal hospitals such as military, Veterans Administration, and National Institutes of Health were eliminated because there is no measurable economic transaction between patient and hospital. Only hospitals with six or more beds could potentially be included in the index.

The sample frame was stratified into homogenous categories according to an urban-rural designation and the number of beds at the hospital. The stratification consisted of four categories: small rural (no more than 60 beds), large rural (greater than 60 beds), small urban (no more than 250 beds), and large urban (greater than 250 beds). This stratification was based on a study of the frequency distribution of treatments (Catron and Murphy 1996, 31).

The selection of a particular hospital was based on a probability proportionate to size sampling strategy. The size variable was the number of ad-

---

14. The AHA Guide was used as the frame instead of the Unemployment Insurance File (UI File), the typical PPI sampling universe, because the AHA Guide provided several potential size measures: employment, revenue, expenses, number of beds, and number of admissions. In addition, it provided details on each hospital's medical facilities, ownership, type of service rendered, and key contacts. The Unemployment File provided only establishment name, address, and employment.

missions, based on 1989 data.[15] In the cases where admission figures were not available from the American Hospital Association Annual Survey, the admissions figure was imputed using the number of annual admissions per bed and total number of beds.

For SIC 8062, 358 general hospitals were selected, which represents about 89 percent of all hospital revenue in 1989. According to the AHA Guide, over 83 percent of the 6,356 registered hospitals in 1989 (5,316) were general hospitals.[16] The number of beds and the hospital's urban/ rural designation determined the number of quotes assigned to the hospital.[17] The number of quotes assigned ranged from six to ten. Medicare inpatient price data is obtained directly by PPI because it is available from the Federal Register.

The AHA Guide also revealed that nearly 10 percent of the registered hospitals were psychiatric hospitals. For SIC 8063, 75 psychiatric hospitals were selected for inclusion in the index, representing 5.8 percent of 1989 hospital revenue. Fifty-five of the hospitals were private and the remaining twenty were state or county. Each sample unit was assigned six price quotes for collection. The Washington BLS office used AHA revenue data to determine the number of inpatient (Medicare and non-Medicare), outpatient, and miscellaneous quotes to be collected for each hospital. For the state/county hospitals, the last six transactions were selected. Four of the state/county hospitals were to provide price quotes for their last five treatments and one price quote for miscellaneous receipts.

According to the AHA Guide, approximately 7 percent of the registered hospitals were specialty hospitals. For SIC 8069, 125 specialty hospitals were selected for inclusion in the index, representing approximately 5 percent of hospital revenue. For the fifty-three selected children's and women's hospitals, between six and ten price quotes were assigned for collection. For the seventy-two other specialty hospitals, six quotes were assigned. The Washington BLS office randomly determined the number of inpatient, outpatient, and miscellaneous quotes to be collected for each hospital.

15. Prior to selecting admissions as the size measure, regression analysis was performed to determine which variable provided in the AHA Guide frame provided the best correlation to size. Other variables that were candidates for measures of size were total expenses, payroll expenses, full-time equivalent employees, average daily census, and number of beds.

16. The AHA Guide does not rely on the SIC definitions to categorize hospitals—the AHA count of hospitals is based on hospital registrations that meet ten requirements. Accordingly, the number of hospitals in the AHA Guide can be different from the number obtained using the SIC definition.

17. The PPI sampling procedure begins with the drawing of two independent samples (half samples). The number of quotes assigned to a sample unit depends on the number of half samples it was selected in. The numbers vary with industry but one of the common allocations is four, six, and eight. With this allocation a sample unit selected in one half sample is assigned four quotes, a sample unit selected in both half samples is assigned six quotes, and a sample unit that was certainty-selected is assigned eight quotes. Because the independent samples are proportionate to size, the larger the sample unit, the greater chance it will be certainty-selected or selected in both half samples and assigned a higher number of quotes.

The hospital sample size decreased as the index aged. As of July 1997, there were approximately 209 establishments with 1,602 quotes in the general hospital index, thirty-nine establishments with 209 quotes for the psychiatric hospital index, and seventy-two establishments with 491 quotes in the specialty hospital index. Two reasons can explain most of the erosion in the sample. First, many hospitals have changed billing systems and the older bills that were being used for repricing are no longer in the hospital billing system. When this occurs, the reporter cannot easily complete the repricing form.[18] Further, many reporters did not wish to provide new patients as substitutes and then canceled their participation. Second, reporters changed their minds about participating in the index. As reporters receive no compensation for their time and effort, it is not uncommon that they end their participation in the later years of an index. This phenomenon has affected the hospital index as well as the other health care indexes.

6.3.3   Output and Price Determination

Hospitals are viewed as providing treatments, each of which is a bundle consisting of medical procedures, room, medical supplies, drugs, and ancillary services. Though there are several schemes that could be used to bundle hospital services, the PPI uses the Diagnostic Related Groups (DRG) formulated by the Health Care Financing Administration (HCFA) to price services paid by Medicare. Each DRG consists of a bundle of diagnostic and procedural codes that are in turn based on the International Classification of Diseases, 9th revision (ICD-9). DRGs are also grouped into more general categories called major diagnostic categories (MDC). The various MDCs represent the different product categories for the hospital industry. Examples of MDCs are diseases and disorders of the nervous system; pregnancy, childbirth, and the puerperium; diseases and disorders of the eye; and diseases and disorders of the respiratory system. These product categories were used for the publication structure for general and surgical hospitals (SIC 8062); that is, the component service products of the index. The publication structure for specialty hospitals except psychiatric was based on the different specialty hospitals. For psychiatric hospitals, the publication structure was based on inpatient/outpatient status and whether the hospital was private or state/county. Appendix table 6A.1 provides the publication structure as well as recent index levels.

The process of data collection begins with the visit by a BLS field representative to the sample unit. Usually, at this visit the field representative determined, through a process called disaggregation, the item that will be priced. In the case of hospitals, however, the Washington BLS office selected the service to be priced in order to obtain a manageable number of

---

18. As explained later, the PPI program collects price information via a monthly repricing form mailed to reporters.

treatments. DRGs were randomly selected based on probability proportional to total expenditures from all payer sources in each DRG. To calculate these probabilities, the PPI analysts used the DRG frequency counts from the Hospital Cost and Utilization Project (HCUP), the average expenditure estimates from Medicare, and the DRG reimbursement rates published in the Federal Register. Due to the large number of DRGs, not all were used; 184 DRGs were chosen for the index based on revenue generation. DRGs were then randomly assigned to each hospital based on hospital characteristics provided in the sample frame.

In the cases where the hospital did not perform any services related to the assigned DRG, the field economist used a replacement DRG list to find a substitute DRG. The replacement DRG list was prepared specifically for each hospital and lists randomly selected alternative DRGs. The field economist started from the top of the list and worked down until a DRG was found that the hospital provided. In the case that a hospital provided the service, but refused to reprice the DRG, this was considered a refusal and no substitute was made for this DRG.

Once a DRG was assigned to a hospital, the price was obtained by the selection of a patient's bill, which serves as the measure of treatment and the basis for monthly repricing. A patient's bill lists the services provided during the entire length of stay and is conveniently presented in a standard format, uniform billing form UB-92 (formerly UB-82). This form is used by most hospitals and it lists a summary, usually by department, of the services provided. If physician fees and pharmacy charges are on the bill, they are included in the unit of measure. However, if these services are charged separately, then they belong to other SICs and are not part of the hospital unit of measure. Each hospital was asked to provide the *last* patient bill for each of the DRGs assigned to that hospital except in the case of the selection of a Medicare inpatient bill in SIC 8062. If a Medicare inpatient bill was selected for a SIC 8062 hospital, the hospital went to the next previous bill until a non-Medicare inpatient bill was selected for the assigned DRG.

Having selected a bill as the basis for price collection, the field economist next determined the expected reimbursement to the hospital. Because hospitals receive most payments for their services from third parties, they do not generally receive list prices as payments. Therefore, the price for hospital services is defined as the expected reimbursement from all payers for each patient bill.[19] Five types of prices were encountered during data collection: list prices, list price less adjustments, case rate, per diem, and capitation.

---

19. In some cases, the hospital may receive payments for a bill from more than one payer. This would be the case in which the patient has a primary insurance carrier and a secondary carrier that covers items not paid by the primary. The price in this case would be the sum of all the individual payers' reimbursements.

List prices were the net transaction price for hospital services for 45 percent of the initially collected data in 1992. This category includes those patients that pay the list price with or without any insurance compensation.[20]

Adjustments to list prices result from contract negotiations between hospitals and managed care organizations. Two common agreements for adjustments to list prices are discount from total charges and discount for prompt payment. Discounts from total charges typically range from 4 percent to 10 percent. The prompt payment discount is usually less and is given to insurance companies when payment is received within a specified time period, usually thirty days. Price movements for this price type can result from either changes in the line item price as documented on the patient bill or changes in the discount rates. Of the initially collected quotes in 1992, 19.4 percent were of this type.

Case rates are payments that are made for procedures (e.g., DRGs) or for illnesses remedied. This rate will normally cover all services required to treat the patient from admission to discharge. These rates are negotiated between the hospital and the payer on the premise that patients with similar diagnoses will receive similar services. Of the initially collected quotes, 20.7 percent were of this price type.

Some third-party payers prefer per diem rates. The per diem rate is the amount the hospital will be reimbursed per patient per day, regardless of the services provided by the hospital. This daily rate is multiplied by the length of the patient's stay to yield a total reimbursement. Under some contracts, the per diem rate is based on the type of room or bed patients occupy during their stay. The per diem rate is multiplied by the number of days at the hospital to obtain the price for the services. Of the initially collected quotes, 14.1 percent were of this price type.

Capitated reimbursement was the least common net transaction price encountered during the 1992 data collection. Capitation is a fixed, per capita amount paid to a hospital, regardless of the actual services provided or resources consumed by each patient. That is, the insurance company pays a hospital a fixed amount of money each month independent of whether policyholders enter it for treatment. This type of pricing shifts some of the risk from the insurance company to the hospital. Capitation accounted for 0.4 percent of the initially collected quotes. Capitation was deemed inconsistent with the index methodology for repricing because it is not a price per se—it is invariant to the service provided. Accordingly, these quotes were eventually removed from the sample.

---

20. Included in those without insurance coverage are patients who are ultimately designated as charity cases. This occurs because it is not known when a bill is generated whether a particular patient falls into such a category. The fact that a zero price is ultimately received does not create a problem qualitatively different from the general problem of having a difference between expected reimbursement and the amount the hospital actually receives.

Hospitals also receive revenues for services other than medical treatments. Approximately 2.8 percent of total hospital revenue is derived from cafeterias, gift shops, and parking. To reflect these additional revenue sources, quotes were collected on parking, gift shop items, and cafeteria items. One hundred seven quotes (3.6 percent of the total) were assigned to collect data on these miscellaneous receipts.

The weights for the hospital price index are based on 1987 industry revenue data from Census of Service Industries undertaken by the Bureau of the Census. For SIC 8062, such revenue data were not available for the individual cells, the MDCs. PPI analysts therefore calculated these weights by summing the revenues of each DRG comprising a MDC. DRG revenue was computed by multiplying DRG frequencies from the 1986 Hospital Cost Utilization Project and the mean DRG payment from the Federal Register. The weight for miscellaneous receipts is a weighted average from actual collected data. The weights for SIC 8062 were updated in 1995 using the same methodology and the 1992 revenue data for the Census Bureau.

For SIC 8063, the weight is the total revenue for the industry as reported in the Census of Service Industries. The weight for each publication cell is the percentage of revenues it generates multiplied by the total revenues of the cell one level above it. For example, the weight for the publication cell, private hospitals, is the percent of revenues generated in private hospitals for non-Medicare patients times the total revenues for non-Medicare patients. The weight for miscellaneous receipts is a weighted average from actual collected data. The weights for SIC 8063 were updated in 1995 using the 1992 Census of Service Industries. The weights for SIC 8069 were calculated in a similar manner.

6.3.4 Monthly Repricing of Output

Each month the hospital contact (reporter) receives a repricing schedule based on the earlier selected patient bill. This bill includes the entire ICD-9 and Current Procedural Terminology (CPT-4) sequence of treatments performed on the patient, the expected length of stay, the expected length of time spent in the operating room, and the nurse-to-patient ratio (according to hospital policy) in both the intensive care and general wards. Ideally, the reporter reviews this information when the repricing schedule is received and makes any appropriate changes. It is important to note that the BLS does not collect these characteristics every month; only changes in the levels first obtained are recorded. The reporter is not required to make any special calculations for repricing.[21]

Annually, the PPI industry analyst must calculate the Medicare Inpa-

---

21. Until January 1997 special repricing techniques were in place for many New York hospitals because they were paid at rates set by the state and these were changed only twice per year.

tient Treatments Index component of the General Hospital Price Index. The Medicare index shows fiscal year (October to September) changes in DRG payments to hospitals by Medicare, keeping the sample of hospitals and DRGs that were selected in 1992 constant. The analyst computes the total Medicare reimbursement amount for the PPI sampled hospitals under the prospective payment system for all inpatient treatments performed, keeping the total (national) number of discharges constant.

Substitutions, Changes in Quality, and New Services

Occasionally, substitutions of new bills for the bills initially selected must be made. If possible, the hospital selects another bill within the same DRG. If that is not possible, another DRG within the same MDC is selected. On average, there are three to four substitutions per month in this industry.

Substitutions occur for a variety of reasons. One reason is that a hospital is no longer able to price a specific bill because the bill has been purged from the computer system. Another reason is that a new person has been assigned to fill out the schedule and cannot understand the origins of the information on the initial bill. A substitution will also be made if a hospital contact refuses to review the bill line by line in determining the new price.[22]

In rare cases, hospitals may make substitutions when they no longer have a contract with the selected insurance company/payer. Because a comparison between two different payers cannot be made, a link to show no change is performed. A link to show no change is a method of quality adjustment in which the new price is not compared to previous prices; a new base price is calculated so that future prices can be compared from this point forward.

Two sources of change in service quality are technical change, both product and process improvements, and oversight by government and insurers. An example of the former is arthroscopic techniques (microsurgery through small incisions in the body) which are steadily being introduced in place of the customary invasive surgery. The new techniques often result in less pain for the patient and less damage to body tissues, thereby reducing lengths of stay. An example of the latter is the recent attempt by many insurance companies to limit hospital stays for childbirth to twenty-four hours; this attempt ended when the government mandated forty-eight hours of coverage. In addition, there can be changes in the notion of the standard treatment. For example, as mentioned earlier, lithrotripsy can replace the surgical treatment of kidney stones and does not require a

---

22. When some bills were originally selected, they contained prices for many line items. Many reporters have the habit of only looking at the DRG group or the insurance company's name and estimating the price for the service by using the overall chargemaster list instead of looking at each line item. When the reporter refuses to review each line item, a simpler bill is substituted for the original.

hospital admission. If the standard practice becomes lithrotripsy and the treatment being priced is the surgery, the price information received will not reflect current practice trends. All of these sources of change can detract from the usefulness of pricing a fixed basket of services whose quality is assumed to be constant over time. One of the ways that the PPI program generally tries to account for such changes in services is to resample an industry about every seven years.

Another approach is to identify indicators or characteristics of the service quality and adjust price changes for measured changes in quality. The determination of the relevant set of characteristics is a major concern of researchers; BLS is certainly not alone in trying to devise a method for quantifying the quality of hospital services. Many researchers have turned their attention to outcomes, specifically to mortality rates and to such measures as quality-adjusted life years. Regarding the potential use of mortality rates, Fixler and Jaditz (1997) showed that for a set of treatments where mortality is a likely outcome, the mortality rate provides an ambiguous signal of quality induced price change. As described above, the repricing form lists the following indicators of service quality: the expected length of stay, expected length of time in the operating room, and the nurse-to-patient ratio in both intensive care and general ward.

In the event of an identified change in quality, standard quality adjustment procedures of the PPI would be used. The following is an example of that procedure:

Suppose we have a hospital repricing a surgical treatment that originally was priced at $10,000 and took 100 minutes in the operating room (at a cost of $50 per minute). The procedure has been improved so that it only requires 90 minutes to complete the surgical treatment. The hospital reports that the price is still $10,000. In this situation, the producer's costs decline by $500 (10 minutes at $50 per minute). Using the explicit quality adjustment formula, the industry analyst calculates the new base price for this procedure:

$$\text{New Base Price} = \$10,000 \times \frac{\$10,000}{\$10,000 - (-500)} = \$9,523.80.$$

Though the price remained the same, due to the quality change, there is really a 5 percent increase in the price:

$$\text{Percent Change} = \frac{\$10,000 - \$9.523.80}{\$9,523.80} \times 100\% = 5\%.$$

Of course, the usefulness of the quality indicators on the PPI repricing form depends on the willingness of reporters to diligently review this information and update it as necessary. Even if the reporters were to update the indicators, the computation of a quality adjustment remains difficult.

Generally, to calculate a quality adjustment, the reporter would have to provide information on what the price would have been without any of the service changes so that a dollar value of the change could be estimated. Unfortunately, reporters rarely have access to this type of information. In most cases, when referring to a single service, the reporter does not know the specifics of price determination.

It is not surprising, therefore, that to date quality adjustments have rarely been performed. Through 1995, there have been approximately fifty changes to the length of stay, and no reported changes in nurse-to-patient ratio or time spent in the operating room. The instances in which the PPI has been successful in computing a quality adjustment are in the cases where a service has been split into two services, or two services have been combined into one. In these cases, the industry analyst attempts to determine the price as if the coding had remained the same.

6.3.5   Resampling and Future Plans

A new sample of hospitals and hospital treatments will be selected and information from this sample is currently scheduled for publication in January 2001. Research is currently underway to update the hospital pricing methodology to accommodate changes that have occurred in this industry since it was originally published in January 1993. One of these changes includes the addition of a methodology for pricing fairly new reimbursement methods used by both private insurers and public payers. Capitation is one such method that is an increasing share of payments from managed care organizations.[23]

Research into a new method of quality adjustment for hospital treatments has also begun. It is anticipated that some combination of frequency of treatment data from the MEDSTAT group, numerical values indicating health status (possibly using quality-adjusted life year data), along with accepted clinical treatment protocols for selected common ailments will be used to develop a quality adjustment model for this industry. This model will necessarily be limited to a few very common ailments where the industry has established treatment guidelines and frequency data for different treatment options are available.

A new publication structure is being developed for the new sample. Two new MDCs may be added to the publication structure: multiple significant trauma and human immunodeficiency virus infections. Inpatient and outpatient treatments will be combined into one cell. This merger potentially permits the capture of a price change that arises when there is a switch from inpatient care to outpatient care. Currently, in the event of such a

---

23. PPI is currently researching and testing a capitation methodology with physicians that might be implemented in the next hospital sample. Additionally in 2001, the MDC weights in 8062 will be constructed directly from MDC total charge data.

switch, the link to show no change method is used and this precludes any cost savings from affecting the index.

As mentioned previously, the industry analyst currently calculates the Medicare portion of the index. In the next sample, the industry analyst will no longer perform this computation because the Medicare portion will be sampled and repriced in the same manner as the rest of the index.

6.4   Physician Price Indexes

6.4.1   Industry Definition

The Physicians Services Price Index was first published in 1994 with a base period of December 1993. The current index is based on research conducted in the early 1990s, and is soon to be resampled as described below.

The PPI industry definition is a combination of the SIC Manual definition for offices and clinics of doctors of medicine (SIC 8011) and the American Medical Association (AMA) specialty classification system. The SIC definition includes establishments of licensed practitioners having the degree of M. D. and engaged in the practice of general or specialized medicine and surgery, and the AMA system includes physicians who are organized to provide medical care, consultation, diagnosis, and/or treatment for patients. The AMA's specialty classification system includes general/family practice, internal medicine, general surgery and other surgical specialties, pediatrics, obstetrics/gynecology, radiology, psychiatry, anesthesiology, and other specialties. Only those establishments with physicians practicing medicine are included in this industry. Practicing physicians include all physicians who are actively providing medical services, those for whom the plurality of their revenue comes from patient care and not administration or research. With the implementation of NAICS, minor changes will occur to the physician industry definitions. Under NAICS, health maintenance organization (HMO) medical centers (NAICS 621491), offices of physicians, mental health specialists (NAICS 621112), and surgical and emergency centers (NAICS 621493) will no longer be grouped in the physician industry, but in their own respective industries.

Establishments in the industry are organized in a variety of ways. Included organizational forms are solo and two-physician practices, single specialty group practices/clinics, multispecialty group practices/clinics, general medical and primary care clinics, outpatient care facilities, ambulatory surgical centers, freestanding emergency medical centers, and urgent care centers. A solo practice is one physician working independently to administer medical care, consultation, diagnosis, and/or treatment to patients. Though the solo practitioner commonly works alone, a physician may work in an office with other physicians and still be considered in a solo practice as long as there is no sharing of patients. A two-physician practice involves two physicians sharing the practice and patient base. The physicians need not be involved in the same specialty, but typically they practice the same or related specialties. As defined by the AMA, a group practice is the provision of health care services by three or more physicians who are formally organized as a legal entity in which business and clinical facilities, records, and personnel are shared. Income from medical services provided by the group is treated as receipts of the group and distributed according to some prearranged plan.

6.4.2   Sample Unit Information

The sample frame used for SIC 8011 was drawn from the AMA's Physician's Masterfile and the Group Practice File. These files were chosen because they are more comprehensive; they include the number of physicians in the practice, which is a better proxy for practice revenue than is total employment, the usual PPI measure of size. The Masterfile includes one record for every practicing office-based physician in the United States, including those in a group practice. Each record indicates the primary employment of the physician (e.g., solo practice, two-physician practice, or group practice). This file also includes the current specialty of the physician. Because the Masterfile does not provide any composition of a group practice, the Group Practice file was used as a supplement to the Masterfile for group practices. A sample unit is defined as a physician practice, not the individual physician. Although it is possible for a physician to belong to more than one practice, a sample unit always represents only one practice. However, the sample unit may encompass more than one physical location. For example, the physician may have an office located next to a hospital, where the doctor renders inpatient care, and one located in a neighboring town to see patients.

The Masterfile was used to select the solo and two-physician offices; these two practice types were treated as being the same. Selecting these practices from the Masterfile was hindered by the fact that this file contained a record for all physicians, regardless of type of practice, and the fact that a physician in a group practice may also have a solo practice. To separate the group practice physicians from the solo/two-physician practices, PPI analysts removed all physicians from the file for whom a zero was recorded for the number of hours in solo practice.

The Masterfile was then stratified into ten specialty strata: the nine AMA specialty classes and a "no specialty" category. A total of 220 sample units was selected from the Masterfile. Because each record represented one physician, the sample units were selected with equal probability within a given stratum. Physicians were placed in each stratum based on their declared area of specialization. In this industry, primary specialization is determined by the number of hours spent in the field and not by percentage of total revenues generated.

The Group Practice File was used to select group practices. This file

was stratified into twelve specialty strata: the nine AMA specialty categories, no primary specialty, multispecialty, and no specialty composition
listed. A total of 180 sample units was selected from the Group Practice
File. These sample units were drawn with probability proportional to the
number of physicians in each group practice, within each explicit stratum.
For records with the "number of physicians" field equal to zero or blank,
a one was substituted to provide for a chance of selection.

The number of price quotes assigned to each practice was based on
specialty and the number of physicians in the practice. Solo/two-physician
practices and single specialty practices with three to six physicians were
assigned four quotes each. Single specialty groups with seven to ten physicians and the specialties of radiology, psychiatry, and anesthesiology with
seven or more physicians were assigned six quotes. Single group practices
with more than ten physicians were assigned eight quotes. The exceptions
to these quote allocations were group practices in internal medicine and
surgery. For these specialties, groups with up to six physicians were assigned six quotes while groups with seven to ten physicians were assigned
eight quotes. Ten quotes were assigned to the groups with more than ten
physicians. For the multispecialty groups, six quotes were assigned to
practices of six or fewer physicians, eight quotes were assigned for groups
with seven to ten physicians, and ten quotes were assigned for groups with
more than ten physicians. As of July 1997, there were approximately 761
quotes in the physician index.

The physician price index used 1987 industry revenue data from the
Census of Service Industries to set the base period weights. Appendix
table 6A.1 presents the publication structure for the physician index.[24] The
four-digit cell weight was the total revenue as reported in the 1987 Census
of Services Industries. To calculate the weights for the five-digit cells, the
percent of revenue received from that payer type (Medicare or non-
Medicare) was multiplied by the total revenues for primary services.

To calculate the weights for the six-digit cells, it was first necessary to
determine the percentage of non-Medicare revenues in the cell. For each of
the nine specialty categories, total revenues were calculated using average
income (from AMA) multiplied by the number of physicians with that
specialty who are in either a solo, two-physician, or single specialty group
practice. The revenues for all specialty groups were summed together. This
procedure was repeated with the number of physicians in a multispecialty
group practice. The two revenue sums were then added together to calculate the percentage of revenue from solo and two-physician practices and
single specialty group practices. This percentage was multiplied by the

---

24. Though the publication structure for physicians is based on practice specialty, it is not
qualitatively different from the treatment-based structure in the hospital index because there
is a correspondence between MDC and physician specialty.

weight for non-Medicare treatments to arrive at the weight for solo and two-physician practices and single specialty group practices. The same procedure was used to calculate the weight for multispecialty groups.

The weights for the nine specialty seven-digit cells were calculated by taking the percentage of revenue generated by that specialty and multiplying it by the weight for solo and two-physician practices and single specialty practices. As with the hospital index, the 1992 industry revenue data from the Census of Services Industries were used to update the weights in 1995.

6.4.3   Output and Price Determination

BLS field economists visited the selected sample unit to determine the unique item that would be priced monthly. The item is selected according to a disaggregation process that depended on the practice characteristics and, at a minimum, the following variables were used: multiple-fee schedules, place of service of primary procedure, and type of payer. In a two-physician or group practice, the field economist was required to perform two disaggregations when the two physicians performed the same service but charged different rates. If a physician performed services at various locations and charged different rates, the field economist would be required to disaggregate between service locations. This circumstance may arise if the physician performed some procedures at his office and others at a clinic.

Accounting for payer type is important because physicians receive the majority of reimbursements for services from third-party payers, private and public, and because the type of payer affects the transaction price. The most common payer types include Medicare, Medicaid, private insurance (including managed health care), and out-of-pocket or self-pay.

In 1989, Medicare accounted for 23.4 percent of physician revenue.[25] At the same time, 44.1 percent of physicians were considered "participating" physicians; that is, they accepted Medicare and its fee assignment as payment in full.[26] In 1996, Medicare accounted for 27.4 percent of physician revenue.[27] HCFA directly reimburses participating physicians. Nonparticipating physicians can accept Medicare fee assignments but are reimbursed directly by the patient. As with the hospital price index, the prices for services covered by Medicare were computed by the Washington PPI office.

Medicaid is a program that is financed through a combination of state and federal funds and makes direct payments to enrolled physicians. Med-

---

25. 1989 data on payer type as percentage of physician revenues were obtained from the 1990 HCFA Symphony file which reports 1989 data.

26. In some cases, called outliers, Medicare acts as a fee-for-service insurance program reimbursing for costs. Such cases are truncated from the sample.

27. 1996 data on payer type as percentage of physician revenues were obtained from the American Medical Association *Physician Market Place 1996.*

icaid programs and rates vary by state, but physicians must accept Medicaid reimbursement as payment in full. Unlike Medicare, there are no co-payments or deductibles. In 1989, Medicaid accounted for 3.6 percent of physician revenue. By 1996, Medicaid accounted for 11.8 percent of physician revenue.

The reimbursements physicians receive from private health insurance depend on the type of insurance. HMOs, PPOs (preferred provider organizations), EPOs (exclusive provider organizations), and POS (point of service) providers usually provide reimbursement based on negotiated fee schedules. In most cases, these types of insurance require some copayment by the patient for services rendered. Another form of payment is provided by indemnity insurance, which is a fee-for-service type of reimbursement. Once the individual has covered the policy deductible, the private insurer will reimburse the doctor some percentage of the total billed amount and the patient is to cover the remaining portion of the bill. In 1989, private health insurance accounted for 47.6 percent of physician revenue. In 1996, private insurance had declined to 42.9 percent of physician revenue.

Out-of-pocket payments, or self-pay, accounted for 19 percent of total physician revenue in 1989. In 1996, out-of-pocket had decreased to 17.9 percent of physician revenue. In this situation, the patient is solely responsible for payment of the bill.[28]

The item selection process yielded a single patient bill, and a copy of it along with HCFA-1500 was requested from the reporter; these would be used for repricing.[29] A limitation of using a single patient bill to price physician services is that it generally does not represent a full treatment. Consider a patient visit to a doctor for the treatment of a sinus infection. The physician may request the patient to return two weeks later for a follow-up visit. If the first visit was billed separately, the unique item (services) would only reflect the treatment received at that single visit. Billing for the complete treatment (all office visits, supplies, etc.) is referred to as "global billing." In the surgical and obstetrics/gynecology specialties, global billing is a common practice.

All selected items for repricing were coded into different product categories for this industry. The product codes are based on the specialties used to stratify the physicians previously. Each specialty represents a product

28. Copayments are part of an insurer's coverage; that is, they are captured as part of the price of the treatment to the insurer and not considered "out-of-pocket." From the PPI perspective there is no reason to decompose such payments into an insured and insurer component. The phrase "out-of-pocket" is reserved for the uninsured and so the revenue share provided by out-of-pocket patients refers only to those who do not have insurance.

29. The HCFA-1500 form is the required health insurance claim form for Medicare reimbursement for physicians and has been adopted as the standard health insurance claim form by many other payers. In those circumstances where the field economist could not transcribe all the information from the patient bill and HCFA-1500 or acquire a copy of the actual bill, the quote was to be coded as a "refusal."

category. Each of these specialty categories also represented one of the publication goals for this index (see app. table 6A.1).

The transaction price for a physician service is defined as the expected reimbursement for one physician visit, except in the cases of global billing in which multiple visits are included. As in the case of hospitals, there can be a difference between the charge on the bill and the actual reimbursement. When a physician agrees to accept an insurer's negotiated fee as payment in full, then that is the net transaction price. Some physicians, however, will not enter into such agreements and will directly bill the patient the difference between the price charged for services rendered and the insurance coverage. This type of reimbursement practice is referred to as "balance billing." The net transaction price is then defined as the sum of the insurance payment and the patient payment.[30]

Managed care programs usually require that the patient make a copayment. Under most managed care agreements, the payer and physician negotiate a fee schedule as mentioned above. The net transaction price is the agreed-upon fee plus the patient copayment.

6.4.4   Monthly Repricing of Output

As part of the field economist's visit to the physician, a repricing plan is developed that enables the physician to price the identical service monthly. Each month, a repricing form is mailed to a physician practice. This schedule contains a shortened summary of the patient's actual bill that lists the diagnoses and procedures with the corresponding ICD-9 and CPT-4 codes, the medical services performed on the patient, and the supplies used. In addition, the schedule has a service identifier that indicates whether a hard copy of the bill is kept on hand in the office or is stored in a computer file. The reporter reviews this information and provides any changes. The reporter is not required to make any special calculations.

Annually, the industry analyst must calculate the Medicare portion of this index using data published by HCFA. This calculation shows the calendar year changes in physician payments by Medicare, keeping the services that were selected in 1992 constant.

Substitutions and Changes in Quality

Sometimes a substitution must be made for the item being repriced. Many of the reasons for substitutions are the same as those discussed under the hospital index. In addition to those reasons, substitutions have occurred in the physician index when the payer no longer reimburses for a specific ICD-9 or CPT-4. In this circumstance, a new ICD-9 or CPT-4

---

30. In some cases, a patient may have secondary insurance that may pay the copayment, the deductible, or the balance of the bill. In the example of the balance billing, the secondary insurance company would cover the share that the primary insurance company did not cover.

that provides similar services and will be reimbursed by the payer is substituted. There have been a few instances when a physician has discontinued providing a specific service, in which case a comparably priced substitute is selected. On average, there are three to four substitutions per month in this industry.

As was described in the case of hospitals, physicians respond to changes in techniques, to the introduction of new goods and equipment, and to the demands by government and insurers to contain medical care delivery costs. In addition there are changes in physician skills and the efficacy of various treatments. Because such changes in quality are extremely difficult to measure and price, it is not readily possible to adjust the observed service price change for such changes in quality.[31]

As in the case of hospitals, quality adjustments are rarely performed in this industry. Again, the major problem in calculating the quality adjustment is the lack of appropriate information; for example, reporters do not generally know what the price of the service would be without the quality change. Consequently, when a change in quality is encountered, the link to show no change method is usually employed.

There are other problems encountered in repricing physician services. Many reporters have complained that their prices do not change often and therefore object to undertaking the work involved in supplying monthly price reports. Some have complained that even a quarterly report was too frequent. In some cases, the industry analyst has agreed to contact the reporter to get price updates rather than having the repricing forms sent directly to the reporter each month or quarter. In addition, there is the ever-present problem of ensuring that the reported price is a transaction price and not a list price.

As with the hospital index, erosion of the sample is occurring as the index ages. The main reason for the decline in quotes is due to reporters' requesting removal from participation because they are tired of completing the forms. The retirement of physicians is another reason for sample erosion.

6.4.5 Resampling and Future Plans

A new sample of physicians and physician treatments was drawn in 1999 and information from this sample was published with the indexes for Janu-

---

31. Unlike the case of hospitals, it was not possible to identify indicators of quality change to place on the repricing form. The potential impact of unmeasured quality change on observed price change might be somewhat lessened by the facts that (1) most changes in service quality manifest themselves in the form of changes in the CPT code, (2) new equipment may be too expensive for small practices to acquire, and (3) major changes in treatments arising from new or improved drugs take a long time to be approved and accepted.

ary 2000. In addition, a new capitation reimbursement methodology was implemented for the January 2000 physician index.

The January 2000 indexes also for the first time incorporated changes from the offices of osteopaths and ambulatory and surgical centers. Other changes in the indexes include the elimination of the distinction between Medicare and non-Medicare payers, the combination of the anesthesiology and radiology cells into an "other specialty" cell, and the introduction of a different method of computation for the Medicare portion of the index. With respect to the last, the industry analyst no longer calculates that portion of the index. Instead, the Medicare portion is sampled and re-priced in the same manner as the rest of the index. One reason for this change is to allow the index to reflect the trend toward managed care in Medicare.

6.5 Drug Price Indexes

6.5.1 Industry Definition

The drug industry, SIC 283, consists of four components: medicinal chemicals and botanical products (SIC 2833), pharmaceutical preparations (SIC 2834), in vitro and in vivo diagnostic substances (SIC 2835), and biological products except diagnostic substances (SIC 2836). Generally, if a drug requires the approval of the Food and Drug Administration (FDA), it is placed in SIC 283. Other organic compounds are in SIC 2869; these substances do not require FDA approval. It should also be noted that pharmaceuticals manufactured in Puerto Rico, an important manufacturing center, are out of scope for the PPI.[32]

Under NAICS there will be some adjustment to the definition of the industry. SIC 2834 and part of 2835 will be combined into a NAICS category called diagnostic substances, except in vitro diagnostic. The remaining part of SIC 2835, in vitro diagnostic substances, makes up the entire NAICS category called in vitro diagnostic substance manufacturing. SIC 2834 is mapped into its own NAICS category.

---

32. In the case of drugs, like many other sophisticated products, the production process can spread across national boundaries. In the PPI, Puerto Rico is considered outside the United States, while for the official U.S. Import and Export Statistics and the Balance of Payments accounts, Puerto Rico is considered part of the United States. The BLS import price index for drugs, unfortunately, cannot be used to remedy this situation. First, both the import and export price indexes use the Balance of Payments definition of the United States and so there does not exist a direct measure of the importation of Puerto Rican goods into the United States. Indirect evidence, however, suggests that the volume of drug imports is relatively small, on the order of 8 percent of domestic drug production in 1996, though it appears that the number may be higher in 1997. Second, because the PPI drug index includes many more products than does the IPP import drug index, there is a small likelihood of matching products in the two indexes.

For the entire three-digit category, the following represents the allocation of sales in the late 1980s: manufacturing 14.5 percent, wholesale 45.7 percent, service 17.1 percent, and all others 22.7 percent. However, within the four-digit categories there is considerable difference in the pattern of sales; SIC 2833 has a larger percentage of sales to manufacturing than does SIC 2834 or 2835 and these last two SICs have a large percentage of sales to wholesalers. A large percentage of sales in SIC 2836 is to services.

6.5.2   Sample Unit, Output, and Price Determination

The sample frame of manufacturers is selected from a list compiled from various industry lists, the Census of Manufacturers, and the unemployment insurance (UI) file. The sample sizes are for medicinal chemicals, 78 sample units; for in vitro and in vivo diagnostic substances, 69 units; for biological products, 54 units; and for pharmaceutical preparations, 270 units. All sample units are stratified by size, which is approximated by employment. Unit size in turn determines the number of price quotes to be collected from a unit, except in the case of pharmaceutical preparations.

For SIC 2833, 2835, 2836, and the nonprescription portion of SIC 2834, an establishment-based sample is selected by probability proportionate to employment. Products are selected from the selected establishments according to the disaggregation process in which the BLS field representative uses the sales share of products sold and a random number table to select a unique product to price. The current number of price quotes in each SIC is as follows: SIC 2833, 84 quotes; SIC 2835, 306 quotes; SIC 2836, 121 quotes; and the nonprescription portion of SIC 2834, 228 quotes. For all of these price quotes, the BLS field representative takes note of the product details, form, strength, and presentation along with transaction characteristics. These characteristics will form the basis for substitutions and quality changes.

For the prescription portion of the pharmaceutical preparations industry (SIC 2834), the number of price quotes was determined for each therapeutic class; the number of quotes was roughly based on the value of shipments for that class but was modified as needed to ensure a sufficient number of quotes to meet publication requirements. (Appendix table 6A.2 provides a list of the therapeutic class price indexes along with recent index levels.) The current number of quotes for this industry is 593. Once the number of quotes was determined, a selection of drugs was made in each class according to probability proportional to prescription sales. All drugs in a class had a chance of selection.[33] Next, the form and strength of the selected drugs were in turn selected on the basis of national sales data.[34]

---

33. Accordingly, a multiproduct manufacturer had a chance that every drug it made would be selected—there was no limit imposed on the number of drugs selected from a manufacturer.

These two samples were drawn in the Washington office. Having selected drug products and their form and strength, the drug products were combined by manufacturer into a sample unit for data collection. The number of products assigned to companies varied from one to about sixty. The presentation variables (unit of measure, type of sale, type of buyer, adjustments to price, etc.) were selected when the field representative visited the sample unit.

Monthly Repricing of Output

Every month, the PPI program sends to reporters (manufacturers) a pricing schedule, which contains the description of the product to be priced. As for all industries, the PPI seeks to collect transaction prices. One complication to obtaining transaction prices derives from the Medicaid rules about "best" price that require manufacturers to provide rebates to Medicaid. In 1991 these rebates amounted to $553 million and in 1995 they amounted to $1,821 million (PhRMA 1997). The tremendous growth in third-party payers has also raised other complications because of the different purchasing schemes of the various insurers.

The PPI repricing strategy is based on the assumption that the exact same product will be available every month. This assumption is often difficult to maintain because of the steady stream of new drugs and generics. A complete resampling of the pharmaceutical preparations SIC is scheduled to begin in 1999 and the in vitro and in vivo diagnostic substances SIC is currently being resampled.[35]

6.5.3 New Drugs and Generics

The pharmaceutical industry is one that is notably dynamically competitive. Firms engage heavily in research and development with the intention of introducing new products to increase profits.[36] Because the patent protection for new drugs is finite, another dimension to the competitive nature of the industry is the introduction of generics. A common path for prices after the introduction of a generic is that the price of the pioneer goes up while the price of the generic falls over time.[37] These features create several difficulties for index number makers.

One issue in the handling of generics is the degree to which the generic is a substitute for the branded pioneer. Approval by FDA of a generic only

---

34. Two national sales data sets were used: one with product information and one with form and strength information.

35. The resampling of the remaining component industries has not yet been scheduled.

36. R&D expenditures by pharmaceutical companies increased by 11.5 percent over 1996 to reach a total of $18.9 billion. Companies have more than doubled their R&D expenditures since 1990. More than 84 percent of pharmaceutical R&D in the United States is geared toward new products. See PhRMA (1997).

37. See Berndt, Griliches and Rosett (1993). BLS researchers obtained similar findings; see Kelly (1997).

requires bioequivalency to the pioneer. In the test for bioequivalency blood samples are collected from sixteen to twenty healthy patients (none with the condition to be treated) and a comparison is made between the levels of the generic and the pioneer drug found in the blood. Bioequivalency is declared if the generic has a +25 percent or −20 percent variation in bioavailability (the rate at which the drug is absorbed) when compared to the pioneer. If the generic also has the same ingredients so that it is pharmaceutically equivalent, then the generic is labeled therapeutically equivalent. Because the generic is not exactly identical to the branded pioneer, it is not a perfect substitute for it, as demonstrated by the coexistence in the market of the branded pioneer and the generic, at least for some duration.[38]

Until January 1996, the PPI program resampled the industry approximately every seven years and treated generics as separate new goods.[39] However, this approach was criticized as being too slow in incorporating new goods, principally generics, and thereby caused the indexes to overstate price increases.[40] The PPI method was also faulted for having including too many old drugs—newer drugs seem to have smaller price increases than older drugs.[41]

In January 1996 a supplemental sampling protocol was introduced to capture new products and it is to be applied annually. The supplemental sample is to be drawn from the FDA list of approved drugs since the time of the drawing of the last sample. The focus of the selection is on generics introduced because of patent loss and on new products. Once the drug products are selected the next step in the protocol is to determine their market share. In the case of generics, the percentage market share is applied to the dollar value weight of the pioneer to determine the dollar value weight for the generic. Also, the base price for the generic is set to the price of the pioneer at the time the generic is introduced into the index. Thus the PPI program effectively treats generics as being identical to the pioneer, which given the earlier discussion is arguable. The 1996 supplement contained all drugs approved between December 1992 and April 1995. In that supplement the market penetration of the generic was estimated, as explained in Kanoza (1996). In the January 1997 supplement market penetration was measured as the actual percent of dollar sales as reported to IMS, a private firm that collects information on pharmaceutical sales. The January 1998 supplement covered drugs approved in the twelve months between June 1996 and May 1997. IMS data were again

---

38. The introduction of a generic can, however, greatly affect the sales of the pioneer. In a study of fourteen new chemical entities, Grabowski and Vernon (1994) found that the average percentage decline in sales in the first four years following patent expiration were 30 percent, 21 percent, 12 percent, and 12 percent, respectively.

39. Samples were introduced in July 1981, January 1987, and January 1994.

40. See Berndt, Griliches, and Rosett (1993) and Griliches and Cockburn (1995).

41. This is not to suggest that generics and new drugs follow the same price trend after introduction.

used to apportion the weight for generics having a branded predecessor in the index. The weight for new drugs was determined by value of shipment information collected from the manufacturer.[42]

It is important to note that the supplemental sampling focuses on specific drug products and not on therapeutic classes. The implication is that the addition of relatively more expensive drugs in a therapeutic class need not increase the measured movement of prices in that class. When the new drug is incorporated its price at the time becomes the base price and price movements are measured relative to that base. Thus only if the price change for the new drug was substantially greater than the other drugs in the class would the price of the therapeutic class increase. In short, it is the price change and not the price level that is the focus of attention.

Quality Adjustment

Accounting for the introduction of new drugs and generics is in a sense part of the issue concerning the measurement of changes in product quality. New drugs can be viewed as major changes in product quality while lesser changes in quality can include such features as changes in package size or dosage.[43] In general PPI analysts look to changes in production costs as the measure quality change. As described below, such a procedure is of limited usefulness in this industry and, correspondingly, quality adjustments are rare in this industry.

In many cases, certainly for new active ingredients, the major contributor to cost is not production cost but rather the underlying research and development (R&D) cost. Grabowski and Vernon (1994) show, however, that it is difficult to amortize R&D costs and to compute the cost of developing a new drug.[44] Accordingly, substantive changes in products, such as the inclusion of new active ingredients, are usually treated as new products. This is consistent with the fact that when drugs contain new active ingredients they are given a new National Drug Code (NDC) designation. As described above, the PPI program captures the introduction of these new products through its supplemental sampling procedure.

In the case of changes in presentation, inactive ingredients, or other such lesser changes in quality, the attendant changes in production cost are used when available. If they are unavailable, then other methods of quality adjustment are used, such as the overlap method or link to show no change.[45]

---

42. See Kelly (1997) for more discussion of the current supplemental sampling procedure.

43. Product line extensions are also common. Yet in such an event it is assumed that the original product is still available, in which case the price of the original product would be collected.

44. In addition, there are also the costs, in both time and money, associated with the clinical trials necessary for FDA approval. The current estimate of the average length of time required to develop a new drug is about fifteen years. See PhRMA (1997), chap. 2.

45. In the overlap method the new product's base price is computed as the base price of the old product multiplied by (new product price in $t - 1$/old product price in $t - 1$). Note that both the prices of the new product and old product have to be available in $t - 1$ for the

As mentioned at the outset the case of pharmaceutical products is somewhat different from the other health care indexes because they are manufactured and thereby avoid some of the measurement problems associated with services. In short, the focus is on the physical product and not on a treatment for a condition or illness. If the focus were to shift to treatments then one would also have to overcome the hurdle of the boundaries imposed by the SIC system now and NAICS in the near future. For example, there is no mechanism for incorporating changes in physician services that derive from changes in pharmaceutical products. Part of the problem is that the treatments associated with the sampled drugs may not correspond to the treatments in the sampled physician services. How to account for the interaction among different industries of changes in quality is an important issue because it bears on the measurement of treatment quality, an issue that is addressed by other papers in this volume.

6.6 Medical Laboratories

6.6.1 Industry Definition

PPI began the development of the medical lab index in the early 1990s and first published the index in July 1994 with a base period of June 1994. The 1987 Standard Industrial Classification Manual defines medical laboratories (SIC 8071) as establishments primarily engaged in providing professional analytic or diagnostic services to the medical profession or to the patient on prescription of a physician. For inclusion in this industry, BLS requires the laboratory to receive a plurality of its revenue from laboratory testing and the laboratory must be financially and operationally separate from the hospital or physician practice, with its own employment and recordkeeping. The revenue earned by laboratory testing in a physician practice is assigned to SIC 8071 only if testing is performed for patients from other practices.

Under NAICS there will be some adjustment to the definition of the industry. SIC 8071 medical laboratories will be split into two separate categories. Diagnostic imaging centers will form its own NAICS category called diagnostic imaging centers (NAICS 62151). Medical laboratories except diagnostic imaging centers will form the NAICS category called medical laboratories (NAICS 621511). In 1989, the Service Annual Survey estimated that SIC 8071 receipts were $8,396 million or 2.1 percent of the estimated $403,009 million in receipts for health services. They have remained approximately at that level.

---

overlap method to be used. If the price of the new product in $t - 1$ is unavailable then the link to show no change method is used; the ratio of prices becomes (new product price in t/old product price in $t - 1$).

6.6.2   Sample Unit, Output, and Price Determination

The sample of medical labs was selected from the UI file. The frame was stratified into radiology labs and all other labs. Twenty-seven sample units were allocated to the radiology stratum and ninety-three units to all other stratum. Four to six quotes were allocated to each sample unit except for certainty units, which were allocated eight quotes. A certainty unit is a firm that was automatically included in the sample due to its level of employment. The major tests included in the index are automated, multi-channel, urinalysis, chemistry, toxicology, therapeutic drug monitoring, hematology, immunology, microbiology, pathology, profiles and panels, and x-ray.

For all price quotes at the time of initiation (1992), the field economist recorded the test name, code, payer type, and any discounts. When panel tests were selected as the service for pricing, it was imperative that the field economist record all the tests included in the panel. This information would form the basis for substitutions and quality changes.

In this industry the two major price-determining factors are the services provided and the payer type. Services of medical laboratories are coded by CPT-4 code, which represent a wide range of laboratory and pathological services. Each CPT-4 code has a corresponding reimbursement rate. Types of payers include wholesale payers (physicians and hospitals) and retail payers (insurance companies, Medicare, Medicaid, and patients). Whole-sale payers tend to receive discounts from the labs in exchange for the large volume of services that could potentially be referred. In many cases, wholesale payers receive one bill a month for all lab work. Retail payers, on the other hand, usually pay higher prices for the same tests and are billed for each visit separately.

6.6.3   Substitution and Changes in Quality

In this industry there are two main reasons for substitution: The lab no longer provides a specific service or the lab's contract with a payer no longer exists. In both of these cases, new tests are substituted, and ideally the new tests belong to the same major service type as the original tests. A link to show no change is performed when making these substitutions. The few quality adjustments performed were to account for changes in the tests that comprise a panel or profile of tests. Due to the increase of managed care and the desire to reduce costs, occasionally a test will be removed from a profile or panel. In these rare cases, an explicit quality adjustment is calculated; in other words, the price is adjusted to reflect the removal of one or more of the tests from the profile or panel.

Erosion of the sample has occurred. Many of the establishments sampled have merged with others in the sample and the resulting consolidation accounts for a large percentage of the decrease in the sample size.

Additionally, as in the other health industries, reporters have tired of completing the forms; in this industry prices are relatively stable and so reporters view monthly repricing forms as unnecessary. As a result of the high level of sample erosion, PPI accelerated the collection of a new sample for this industry and published an index based on a new sample in January 1999.

6.7   Nursing Homes

6.7.1   Industry Definition

PPI began publication of the Nursing Home Index in January 1995 with a base period of December 1994. The development effort on this index began in the late 1980s and at that time nursing homes were classified either as skilled nursing facilities or as intermediate care facilities. On 1 October 1990, the regulatory distinctions between these two categories were eliminated. Responding to this change, BLS formed a new SIC, SIC 8053, entitled skilled and intermediate care facilities. This SIC is a combination of SIC 8051, skilled nursing care facilities, and SIC 8052, intermediate care facilities. For this SIC, nursing homes are defined as establishments primarily engaged in providing inpatient nursing and rehabilitative services to residents. The staff must include a licensed nurse on duty for eight consecutive hours per day, seven days per week. Facilities included in this industry are skilled nursing facilities, intermediate care facilities, convalescent homes with continuous nursing care, extended care facilities, and mental retardation hospitals not funded solely by state or federal money.

With the implementation of NAICS minor changes will occur in the nursing home industry definitions. NAICS 62311 will include skilled nursing care facilities except continuing care retirement communities, intermediate care facilities except mental retardation facilities and continuing care retirement communities, and other nursing and personal care facilities formerly included in SIC 8059.

6.7.2   Sample Unit Information

The UI file was used as the sample frame for nursing homes. The UI file was stratified by the former SIC codes 8051, skilled nursing facilities, and 8052, intermediate care facilities. As with the hospital sample, those facilities that are operated and funded solely by state or federal governments were truncated. One hundred twenty sample units were selected from former SIC 8051 and thirty sample units were selected from former SIC 8052. Four to six quotes were assigned to each sample unit based on the sample unit's employment size.

6.7.3   Output and Price Determination

Once the sample units were selected, the field economists conducted interviews with the staff at these units. The first step of selecting pricing items (disaggregation) was to choose between primary and miscellaneous services. For this industry, miscellaneous services include all pharmacy activity and any services or items provided by the establishment to nonresidents, where nonresidents include patients' guests and adult daycare or nightcare patients. Next, the field economist disaggregated by payer type. If the payer type selected was either out-of-pocket, Medicaid, or private insurance, further disaggregation by level of care (i.e., moderate supervision, intermediate care, or skilled care) was conducted. If Medicare was the selected payer, then the level of care selected had to be skilled care. Once the disaggregation process was completed, the latest bill that matched the results of the disaggregation process was selected. The bill selected could be for an entire stay or an interim bill, whichever was the shorter period. The services provided on this bill became the unique item for repricing.

In this industry, the standard price is expressed as a per diem rate. However, the services included in the per diem rate vary by facility. In many cases, an individual bill will include the per diem rate plus line items for additional services provided to the patient. As with hospitals and physicians, the definition of price is the expected reimbursement for a patient's bill, whether it is for the entire stay or an interim period.

As with the other health care services, the type of payer (Medicaid, Medicare, private insurance, and individual) affects nursing home prices. The case of Medicaid is straightforward because the reimbursement to the nursing home is set, though the level of reimbursement varies across states as each state may use its own payment methodology to determine reimbursements. Medicare also sets the reimbursement level. These reimbursements vary by geographic region. Medicare nursing home benefits, which fall under Medicare Part A, cover short-term coverage of certain skilled services required by patients recovering from a recent acute illness rather than long-term or custodial care.

In addition to these government sources of payment, there is also the relatively recent growth in private insurers offering long-term care insurance. These policies typically pay charges up to some limit, after which the patient assumes responsibility. The final major payer type is the individual who must pay the full per diem rate plus any additional charges out of pocket. For those who must remain in a nursing home for a long period, assets are usually depleted quickly and then they become eligible for Medicaid.

6.7.4   Substitutions and Changes in Quality

Substitutions are rare in this industry. When they have been performed, it was the result of the nursing home no longer having a contract with an insurance company. As with the other health services, a new patient bill is selected and a link to show no change is performed.

Quality adjustments are also rare for this industry. In principle, a quality adjustment would be made if there were an explicit change in the service bundle, such as the deletion or addition of a type of service. Usually, in such instances, the analyst performs a link to show no change because it is difficult to measure the associated change in cost. A quality adjustment would also be performed when the health status of patients change, even if there are no attending changes in the types of services included. The reason is that deterioration in a patient's health status, the usual occurrence, translates into a higher per diem rate. Medicare and Medicaid determine their per diem reimbursement rates based on the total cost reported by the facility, and so reimbursement rates would go up with a decrease in patient health because patients would require more of the services previously supplied. Thus it would be incorrect to record the increase in the per diem rate as a pure price change. Accordingly, when the health status of patients changes, the analyst performs the link to show no change adjustment procedure on the reported price.

6.8   Other Related Indexes

6.8.1   Home Health Care

The PPI program began publication of a home health care index in January 1997. In the SIC system home health care establishments are defined as those primarily engaged in providing skilled nursing or medical care in the home, under the supervision of a physician. Home health care services tend to be offered by home health care agencies. Agencies typically employ three or more staff members, offer at least two services and provide services in the patient's home.

The primary services associated with home health care usually fall into six categories as defined by Medicare: skilled nursing, physical therapy, occupational therapy, speech pathology, medical social service, and home health aide services. Accordingly, the unit of output for this index was set as the services provided during one visit, conditioned on the level of the provider (i.e., skilled nurse; RN; LPN; physical, occupational, or speech therapists; etc.), and the price was set as the per visit cost. Because services are priced on a per visit basis, the PPI approach captures all services performed within a visit as long as the services are included in the per visit cost.

For this industry, the two major price-determining characteristics are the type of payer and type of provider. Type of payer (Medicare, Medicaid, private insurance companies, HMOs, and self-paying patients) is the most important characteristic for price determination. As such, the index publication structure is based on payer type (Medicare and non-Medicare) and provider type (see app. table 6A.1). Because the home health care index is relatively new, there have been no issues relating to substitution of services or quality adjustment. One reason for the lack of substitution is that most are reporting expected reimbursements based on the provider type.

Minor erosion of the sample is occurring. The sample unit allocation was 225 establishments. In the past year, approximately 6 establishments have been deleted. Most requested removal because they were tired of completing forms given that prices rarely change.

6.8.2   Health Insurance

Research is currently being conducted on the development of a price index for the health insurance industry. Under the SIC classification, two industries, accident and health insurance (SIC 6321) and hospital and medical service plans (SIC 6324) provide what is generally called health insurance. These industries are contained in the insurance carriers group of the SIC system. The SIC Manual defines establishments providing accident and health insurance as those establishments which provide health insurance protection for disability income losses and medical expense coverage on an indemnity basis. The hospital and medical service plan industry is defined as those establishments primarily engaged in providing hospital, medical, and other health services to subscribers or members in accordance with prearranged agreements or service plans. With the implementation of NAICS, these two industries will be combined into the same industry classification code, NAICS 524114. The expected publication date has yet to be determined.

6.9   Summary

In this paper we have provided a relatively thorough description of the Producer Price Indexes for the main industries comprising the health care sector of the economy. Because the focus is on industry output prices, consumer or patient welfare is not a component of the underlying conceptual framework. The discussion of each index included a description of sampling issues, the determination of price and output, monthly repricing, adjustments for changes in quality, and new goods.

In the health care area there are clearly many difficult measurement issues that index number makers must address. The consequent "practical cuts" are almost by definition inferior to the procedures that the PPI program would ideally like to employ. By identifying these issues we hope that we will not only provide users a better understanding of the indexes but also stimulate research on how the indexes might be improved.

Nevertheless, the PPI indexes provide valuable information by enabling medical service expenditure movements to be decomposed into price and output movements. More specifically, the Bureau of Economic Analysis (Department of Commerce) uses the individual PPI health care indexes and the aggregate health services index (for those services classified in health services [SIC 80]—published since 1995) as a deflator in various components of the National Income and Product Accounts. Because the SIC system is the basis for the PPI indexes they are applicable to the medical services included in the National Health Accounts (NHA)—these accounts include medical services provided by establishments that fall into SIC 80 or are provided by government operations that mimic that classification. The NHA, like the PPI, tend to collect reimbursement amounts for services provided (not list prices) and include nonpatient revenues such as gift shops and parking. Thus the PPI is essential to the determination of real output of medical providers in the various SICs, and for the output measures in the NHA. By implication, the indexes are important to the construction of productivity measures for the health care sector. Finally, these health care price indexes are also used as measures of inflation. These indexes are used to escalate wage contracts as well as contracts for services, such as those between firms and health care providers.

Appendix

Table 6A.1   Publication Structure for Health Services Producer Price Indexes

Industry and Product	Industry Code	Product Code	Index, July 1998	Percent Change to July 1998 from	
				July 1997	June 1998
Health services	80		107.6	1.3	0.1
Offices and clinics of doctors of medicine	8011				
Primary services		8011-P	111.1	1.6	−0.2
Medicare treatments		8011-1	111.1	1.6	−0.2
Medicare treatments		8011-101	110.5	4.4	0
Non-Medicare treatments		8011-3	111.1	1.0	−0.2
One- and two-physician practices and single					
specialty group practices		8011-31	110.6	0.6	−0.2
General/family practice		8011-311	115.0	3.1	−0.1
Internal medicine		8011-312	111.7	0.4	0
General surgery and other surgical					
specialties		8011-313	105.2	−0.7	0
Pediatrics		8011-314	124.8	1.8	0
Obstetrics/gynecology		8011-315			
Radiology		8011-316	98.2	0	0
Psychiatry		8011-317	106.8	0	0
Other specialty		8011-319	108.0	−2.1	−1.9
Multispecialty group practices		8011-33			
Multispecialty group practices		8011-331	113.2	2.4	−0.1

(*continued*)

Table 6A.1   (continued)

Industry and Product	Industry Code	Product Code	Index, July 1998	Percent Change to July 1998 from	
				July 1997	June 1998
Skilled and intermediate care facilities	8053				
Primary services		8053-P	118.9	3.1	0.3
Public payers		8053-1	119.2	3.2	0.3
Public payers		8053-101	119.4	2.8	0.4
Private payers		8053-3			
Private payers		8053-301	119.0	3.7	0
Other receipts		8053-SM	108.6	1.5	0
Hospitals	806		114.4	0.8	0.2
General medical and surgical hospitals	8062		114.5	0.6	0.1
Primary services		8062-P	114.7	0.6	0.2
Inpatient treatments		8062-1	113.5	0.3	0.1
Medicare patients		8062-131	108.0	-1.0	0
All medical diagnosis related groups		8062-13101	107.0	-1.4	0
All surgical diagnosis related groups		8062-13103	109.1	-0.6	0
Medicaid patients		8062-151	109.8	-1.2	-1.2
All other patients		8062-171	117.8	1.4	0.5
Diseases and disorders of the nervous system		8062-17101	108.5	0.2	0
Diseases and disorders of the eye		8062-17102	112.0	2.2	0
Diseases and disorders of the ear, nose, mouth, and throat		8062-17103	116.0	1.0	0.4
Diseases and disorders of the respiratory system		8062-17104	120.3	1.0	0.4
Diseases and disorders of the circulatory system		8062-17105	118.9	-0.3	0.1

Diseases and disorders of the digestive system	8062-17106	119.2	2.1	0.8
Diseases and disorders of the hepatobiliary system and pancreas	8062-17107	128.6	2.7	0.2
Diseases and disorders of the musculoskeletal system and connective tissue	8062-17108	116.1	2.0	1.8
Diseases and disorders of the skin, subcutaneous tissue, and breast	8062-17109	115.5	2.0	1.3
Endocrine, nutritional, and metabolic diseases and disorders	8062-17111	124.7	4.5	0.5
Diseases and disorders of the kidney and urinary tract	8062-17112	121.3	3.8	−0.2
Diseases and disorders of the male reproductive system	8062-17113	110.0	2.3	0
Diseases and disorders of the female reproductive system	8062-17114	112.9	4.6	2.8
Pregnancy, childbirth, and puerperium	8062-17115	118.2	0.1	0.1
Newborns and other neonates with conditions originating in the perinatal period	8062-17116	119.5	0.8	0
Diseases and disorders of the blood and blood forming organs and immunological disorders	8062-17117	134.6	4.2	0.3
Myeloproliferative diseases and disorders, and poorly differentiated neoplasms	8062-17118	119.4	3.4	0.8
Infectious and parasitic diseases (systemic or unspecified sites)	8062-17119	111.1	0	0
Mental disorders and diseases	8062-17121	116.3	4.3	0
Alcohol/drug use and alcohol/drug induced organic mental disorders	8062-17122	123.4	4.0	0

(continued)

Table 6A.1 (continued)

Industry and Product	Industry Code	Product Code	Index, July 1998	Percent Change to July 1998 from July 1997	Percent Change to July 1998 from June 1998
Injuries, poisonings and toxic effects of drugs		8062-17123	110.4	1.4	0.3
Burns		8062-17124	106.9	−1.8	0.8
Factors influencing health status and other contacts with health services		8062-17125	112.7	−0.9	2.1
Outpatient treatments		8062-3	118.7	1.5	0.1
Medicare patients		8062-311	118.3	1.5	−0.1
Medicaid patients		8062-331	105.6	0.7	−0.1
All other patients		8062-351	120.0	1.5	0.2
Other receipts		8062-SM	108.7	2.1	0.1
Psychiatric hospitals	8063		108.3	0.6	0
Primary services		8063-P	108.3	0.6	0.1
Inpatient treatments		8063-1	107.2	0.7	0.1
Medicare patients		8063-101	121.2	1.8	0
Non-Medicare patients		8063-103	105.4	0.5	0
State and county hospitals		8063-10301	88.5	2.4	0.2
Private hospitals		8063-10303	111.1	0	0
Outpatient treatments		8063-2	122.2	0	0
Other receipts		8063-SM	109.7	0	0
Specialty hospitals, except psychiatric	8069		117.5	2.4	0.4
Primary services		8069-P	117.7	2.5	0.5
Inpatient treatments		8069-1	115.4	2.6	0.6
Rehabilitation hospitals		8069-101	108.2	0.4	0
Children's hospitals		8069-104	113.8	2.2	−0.1

Industry and type of service	Code	Item code	Index		
Alcoholism and other chemical dependency hospitals		8069-107	121.9	0.1	0
Other specialty hospitals, except psychiatric		8069-108	121.1	4.9	1.9
Outpatient treatments		8069-3	125.8	2.0	0
Other receipts		8069-SM	111.2	3.0	0
Medical laboratories	8071		106.4	0.2	-0.1
Primary services		8071-P	106.7	0.1	-0.2
Pathology and laboratory		8071-1	106.7	0.2	-0.1
Urinalysis		8071-102	127.8	0.3	0
Chemistry, toxicology, and therapeutic drug monitoring		8071-103	97.3	0.1	-0.4
Hematology		8071-104	127.8	0.7	-0.2
Pathology		8071-107	103.6	-1.1	0.1
Profiles and panels		8071-108	103.3	0.5	0
Radiological tests		8071-3	102.2	-2.0	0.1
Home health care services	8082		106.0	2.1	-0.1
Primary services		8082-P	102.9	1.9	-0.2
Medicare payers		8082-1	103.2	1.2	-0.5
Skilled nurse		8082-101	104.8	1.9	-0.5
Home health aide		8082-102	101.5	0.4	-0.4
Other provider		8082-103	101.7	0.6	-0.4
Non-Medicare payers		8082-2	102.8	2.4	0.1
Skilled nurse		8082-201	102.7	2.4	0.1
Home health aide		8082-202	104.7	3.7	0.4
Other provider		8082-203	99.3	-0.5	-0.7
Other receipts		8082-SM	163.9	4.5	0.1

Source: U.S. Department of Labor, Bureau of Labor Statistics, PPI detailed report for July 1998.

Note: The publication structure shown was the one in place at the time of the conference. As described in the text, some changes were made in January 2000.

Table 6A.2   Publication Structure for Drug Producer Price Indexes

Industry and Product	Industry Code	Product Code	Index, July 1998	Percent Change to July 1998 from	
				July 1997	June 1998
Drugs	283		207.3	12.3	1.3
Medicinal chemicals and botanical products (in bulk)	2833				
Primary products		2833-P	136.4	1.6	0
Synthetic organic medicinal chemicals		2833-1	134.0	1.4	0
Central stimulants and depressants		2833-131	133.6	1.4	0
All other synthetic organic medicinal chemicals		2833-1861	71.8	8.5	0
Other medicinals and botanicals		2833-3	110.3	0.8	0
All other organic medicinals		2833-398	131.8	1.4	0
Secondary products and miscellaneous receipts		2833-SM	133.6	2.1	0
Secondary products		2833-S	146.8	4.3	0
Other secondary products		2833-SSS	134.1	0.8	0
Pharmaceutical preparations	2834		298.2	15.2	1.6
Primary products		2834-P	321.5	17.5	1.4
Pharmaceutical preparations, prescription		2834-1	377.9	22.5	1.8
Analgesics		2834-102	451.7	9.2	4.4
Narcotic analgesics		2834-1021	423.2	13.2	5.5
Nonnarcotic analgesics		2834-1022	448.9	6.7	3.7
Synthetic, including acetaminophen and antimigraine		2834-10221	421.7	6.3	3.7
Antiarthritics		2834-105	191.5	-1.2	-2.6
Anticoagulants		2834-106	161.8	17.3	3.7
Anticonvulsants		2834-107	256.0	-33.5	9.6

Category	Code			
Systemic antihistamines	2834-109	481.3	3.1	0
Systemic anti-infectives	2834-111	241.5	6.5	-0.1
Broad and medium spectrum antibiotics	2834-1111	213.5	6.2	0
Cephalosporins	2834-11111	289.7	4.5	-0.1
Broad spectrum penicillins	2834-11112			
Other broad and medium spectrum antibiotics	2834-11119	103.3	1.6	0.2
Systemic penicillins	2834-11129	221.0	3.2	0
Antispasmodic/antisecretory	2834-116	388.6	3.8	0.2
Bronchial therapy	2834-118	510.0	11.5	6.3
Cancer therapy products	2834-119	548.9	8.4	-0.1
Cardiovascular therapy	2834-121	358.5	6.2	0.7
Antihypertensive drugs	2834-12119	371.2	8.9	0.2
Vasodilators	2834-12129	316.8	8.2	0.1
Other cardiovasculars	2834-12191	349.4	4.7	1.1
CNS stimulants/antiobesity preparations	2834-123	777.5	20.1	2.4
Cough and cold preparations	2834-125			
Oral cold preparations	2834-12511			
Other cough and cold preparations	2834-12519			
Dermatological preparations	2834-126	476.7	6.4	2.1
Acne preparations	2834-12611	264.5	12.5	0.9
Fungicides	2834-12619	399.0	9.9	1.3
Topical anti-infectives	2834-12631	107.8		0.7
Other dermatological preparations	2834-12691	505.1		2.8
Diabetes therapy	2834-127	262.3	17.8	0
Diuretics	2834-128	352.7	20.0	0
Hormones	2834-135	261.8	10.1	1.2
Hospital solutions	2834-136	84.5	2.8	
Muscle relaxants	2834-139	311.3	3.0	0
Nutrients and supplements	2834-141	376.5	5.8	3.8
Ophthalmic and otic preparations	2834-142	384.5	3.2	0.5

(*continued*)

Table 6A.2   (continued)

Industry and Product	Industry Code	Product Code	Index, July 1998	Percent Change to July 1998 from	
				July 1997	June 1998
Psychotherapeutics		2834-144	1776.6	243.4	5.7
Tranquilizers		2834-1441	1764.1	772.9	7.3
Major tranquilizers		2834-14411	383.0	148.2	151.1
Minor tranquilizers		2834-14412	3172.4	1180.2	0
Antidepressants		2834-1442	214.3	3.4	0
Sedatives		2834-145	835.5	10.9	0.8
Tuberculosis therapy		2834-147	319.8	0	0
Vitamins		2834-148	240.1	2.4	-0.2
B-complex		2834-14829	302.1	3.0	1.8
Other vitamins		2834-14839	164.4	2.0	-1.1
Miscellaneous prescription pharmaceutical preparations		2834-198	288.7	2.6	0
Pharmaceutical preparations, nonprescriptions		2834-2	197.9	0.4	0.1
Analgesics, internal (except antiarthritics)		2834-201	215.8	0.5	0
Aspirin/aspirin-salicylate compounds		2834-20101	295.9	0.8	0
Antacids		2834-202	195.3	0	0
Cough and cold preparations		2834-208	242.3	0.9	0.1
Cough syrups, elixirs, expectorants, drops, lozenges, gums, troches		2834-20819	194.4	1.0	0.5
Cold tablets, capsules (including antihistamine cold preparations)		2834-20831	292.8	1.0	0
Decongestants		2834-20849	283.9	0.4	0
Other cough and cold preparations, including decongestant and antihistamine mixtures		2834-20851	223.7	1.0	0
Dermatologicals		2834-209	198.6	3.1	0
Other dermatologicals		2834-20909	246.5	4.4	0

External analgesics and counterirritants		2834-211	119.4	0.7	0
Laxatives		2834-216	192.8	2.9	0
Nutrients and supplements		2834-217			
Ophthalmic preparations		2834-218	175.7	1.3	0
Vitamins		2834-221	155.6	-0.1	0
Adult multivitamins		2834-22101	146.0	0.8	
B-complex		2834-22102			
Other vitamins		2834-22109			
Miscellaneous nonprescription pharmaceutical preparations		2834-298	172.2	-3.1	0.3
Secondary products and miscellaneous receipts		2934-SM			
Miscellaneous receipts		2834-M	229.2	7.4	4.4
Resales		2834-Z89	230.7	7.9	4.7
Secondary products		2834-S	172.3	-1.4	0
Cosmetics and toiletries		2844-S	109.7	-2.6	0
In vivo and in vitro diagnostics	2835		178.3	7.3	0
Primary products		2835-P	118.7	3.5	0
In vitro diagnostic substances		2835-1	104.3	2.5	0.5
Clinical chemistry products		2935-1A	102.8	1.3	0.5
Reagents		2835-111	113.5	1.2	0.5
Standards and controls		2835-115	109.7	2.4	0
Blood bank products		2835-121	131.4	17.3	-0.2
Hematology products		2835-125	151.2	0.7	0
Microbiology, serology, histology, virology, and cytology products		2835-135	127.9	6.4	2.2
Culture media		2835-141	98.7	1.5	1.3
Other in vitro diagnostics, including coagulation products		2835-199	91.1	1.1	0
In vivo diagnostic substances		2835-2	110.6		-3.2
Contrast media (X-ray media)		2835-2A	112.1		-3.1
All other contrast media receipts		2835-215	125.8		-0.9

(*continued*)

Table 6A.2 (continued)

Industry and Product	Industry Code	Product Code	Index, July 1998	Percent Change to July 1998 from	
				July 1997	June 1998
Secondary products and miscellaneous receipts		2835-SM			
Miscellaneous receipts		2835-M	241.2	10.4	
Resales		2835-Z89	138.1	10.5	0
Secondary products		2835-S	228.4	20.7	
Biological products, except diagnostics	2836		114.9	1.4	0.9
Primary products		2836-P	113.5	1.5	1.0
Blood and blood derivatives, for human use		2836-1	135.0	6.4	3.1
Other blood and blood derivatives, except those used for passive immunization		2836-121	119.8	6.5	3.2
Other biologics for human use		2836-3	146.1	−0.9	0
Allergenic extracts for human use, excluding diagnostic allergens		2836-321	310.9	−0.9	0
Biologics for veterinary, industrial and other uses		2836-411	98.0	−1.3	−0.3
Veterinary vaccines		2836-411	120.5	−1.2	−0.6
Other biologics including antitoxins, immune serums, blood, and allergens, except diagnostics		2836-499			
Secondary products and miscellaneous receipts		2836-SM			
Secondary products		2836-S	121.6	−3.9	−0.2
Pharmaceutical preparations		2834-S	126.0	−4.2	
Secondary products except pharmaceutical preparations		2836-SSS	100	−2.8	0

Source: U.S. Department of Labor, Bureau of Labor Statistics, *PPI detailed report* for July 1998.

References

American Medical Association. 1996. *Physician market place 1996.* Chicago, Ill.: American Medical Association.

Archibald, R. 1977. On the theory of industrial price measurement: Output price indexes. *Annals of Economic and Social Measurement* 6 (1): 57–72.

Berndt, E., Z. Griliches, and J. Rosett. 1993. Auditing the Producer Price Index: Micro evidence from prescription pharmaceutical preparations. *Journal of Business and Economic Statistics,* 11:25–63.

Catron, B., and B. Murphy. 1996. Hospital price inflation: What does the new PPI tell us? *Monthly Labor Review,* 119 (7): 24–31.

Diewert, W. E. 1983. The theory of output price index and the measurement of real output change. In *Price level measurement,* ed. W. E. Diewert and C. Montmarquette, 1049–1113. Ottawa: Statistics Canada.

Fisher, F., and K. Shell. 1972. *The economic theory of price indexes.* New York: Academic.

Fixler, D., and T. Jaditz. 1997. Hedonic adjustment of hospital services price inflation: An application to Medicare prices. BLS Working Paper no. 299. Washington, D.C.: Bureau of Labor Statistics.

Fixler, D., and K. Zieschang. 1992. Incorporating ancillary measures of process and quality change into a superlative productivity index. *Journal of Productivity Analysis* 2: 245–67.

Grabowksi, H. G., and J. Vernon. 1994. Returns to R&D on new drug introductions in the 1980s. *Journal of Health Economics* 13: 383–406.

Griliches, Z., and I. Cockburn. 1995. Generics and the Producer Price Index for pharmaceuticals. In *Competitive strategies in the pharmaceutical industry* ed. R. B. Helms. Washington, D.C.: AEI Press.

Jacobs, P. 1974. A survey of the economic models of hospitals. *Inquiry* 11 (June) 83–87.

Kanoza, D. 1996. Supplemental sampling in the PPI pharmaceuticals index. *Producer Price Indexes,* January.

Kelly, G. 1997. Improving the PPI sample for prescription pharmaceuticals. *Monthly Labor Review* 120 (October): 10–17.

Levit, K. R., A. L. Sensenig, C. A. Cowan, H. C. Lazenby, P. A. McDonnell, D. K. Won, L. Sivarajan, J. M. Miller, C. S. Donham, and M. S. Stewart. 1994. National health expenditures, 1993. *Health Care Financing Review* 16 (1): 47.

Needham, D. 1978. *The economics of industrial structure conduct and performance.* New York: St. Martin's.

Newhouse, J. P. 1970. Toward a theory of nonprofit institutions: An economic model of a hospital. *American Economic Review* 60: 64–74.

Noether, M. 1988. Competition among hospitals. *Journal of Health Economics* 7: 259–84.

Pakes, A. 1997. New goods, characteristic based models, and the role of hedonics. Yale University Department of Economics, mimeo.

Pharmaceutical Research and Manufacturers of America (PhRMA). 1997. *Industry profile.* Washington, D.C.: PhRMA.

Register, C. A., and E. R. Bruning. 1987. Profit incentives and technical efficiency in the production of hospital care. *Southern Economic Journal* 53: 899–914.

Weisbrod, B. A. 1975. Toward a theory of the voluntary non-profit sector in a three sector economy. In *Altruism, morality and economic theory,* ed. Edmund Phelps. New York: Russell Sage Foundation.

Comment   Joseph P. Newhouse

I applaud these authors for providing an accessible but detailed description of the PPI.

The PPI is currently used in the GDP deflator. In addition, it is better suited to a health sector deflator than the CPI because it includes government programs and employer payments in both pricing and weights, thereby picking up any cost shifting.

Nonetheless, the PPI is still subject to large potential errors for the purpose of being a health sector deflator. These are mainly covered in the Berndt, Busch, and Frank paper (Chap. 12 in this volume), but I will talk about two here. First, in principle the PPI includes quality adjustments, and the hospital, physician, and drug sections of the paper acknowledge that such adjustments are important. Nonetheless, such adjustments in fact are rarely made because there is no accepted methodology that could easily be implemented to make them.

Although I am certainly sympathetic to the practical difficulties of adjusting for quality, it is important to get some sense of how large the bias might be from rarely adjusting. The results of the Cutler et al. heart attack paper (chap. 8 in this volume) suggest that the bias from the decrease in mortality alone could be on the order of 3–4 percentage points per year. But much of medical advance does not much affect mortality so we need a method to adjust for changes in quality of life; for example, better intraocular lenses for cataracts, drug rather than surgical treatment of ulcers, human growth hormone, noninvasive imaging, kidney transplants rather than dialysis, treatments for benign prostatic hypertrophy, better hearing aids, computerized drug entry to reduce adverse drug events, Rogaine, and even Viagra.

Second, it is hard to maintain the assumption of technical efficiency within hospital and physician sectors. Almost every study of care shows substantial amounts of off-frontier care, both in the United States and elsewhere in the world (Chassin et al. 1987, 1998; Brook 1993). This means potential moves toward the frontier, including not delivering services at all or delivering a much lower priced placebo (watchful waiting) are not valued in the index.

I have three nuts-and-bolts type comments. I would have liked more material on the adequacy of the sample. The paper gives numbers on attrition, but there is no effort to assess bias or variance. The paper notes that 21 percent of hospital quotes are of the DRG type, but Medicare alone accounts for 16 percent of discharges (33 percent of the dollars), and about

Joseph P. Newhouse is the John D. MacArthur Professor of Health Policy and Management and is on the faculties of the Kennedy School of Government, the Harvard Medical School, the Harvard School of Public Health, and the Faculty of Arts and Sciences at Harvard University, and is a research associate of the National Bureau of Economic Research.

half the state Medicaid programs use DRGs as do some private payers. So this value seems low. Second, the exclusion of Puerto Rico in the drug area may create a bias. I'm not clear about the arguments for not changing this policy, but it would be nice to have a sense of how large the bias could be. Finally, about 15 percent of the population is uninsured. These people generally receive some form of charity care. In principle, the actual price received by the hospital or physician is tracked, but I am unclear as to how often this happens. This would seem to be a particular problem with government hospitals that receive an appropriation to cover care.

References

Brook, Robert H. 1993. Maintaining hospital quality: The need for international cooperation. *Journal of the American Medical Association* 270 (8): 985–87.

Chassin, Mark, et al. 1987. Does inappropriate use explain geographic variations in the use of health care services? A study of three procedures. *Journal of the American Medical Association* 258 (18): 2533–37.

Chassin, Mark R., Robert W. Galvin, and the National Roundtable on Health Care Quality. 1998. The urgent need to improve health care quality. *Journal of the American Medical Association* 280 (11): 1000–5.

7

National Health Accounts/ National Income and Product Accounts Reconciliation
Hospital Care and Physician Services

Arthur Sensenig and Ernest Wilcox

7.1 The Reconciliation Project

· The Health Care Financing Administration (HCFA), an agency of the Department of Health and Human Services, in its National Health Accounts (NHA), and the Bureau of Economic Analysis (BEA), an agency of the Department of Commerce, in its National Income and Product Accounts (NIPA), each publish national data on expenditures for health care. These data are designed for different purposes and serve somewhat different audiences. The NHA show the interaction between health care services and funding sources and how these relationships change over time, and they also address policy issues that arise in the health care arena. The NIPA, summarized by GDP, provide an up-to-date, overall view of domestic and national production, its distribution, and its use as shown by the interrelated receipts and expenditures of producers, consumers, investors, government, and the foreign suppliers and customers of the United States. The health care estimates in the NIPA and in BEA's input-output accounts are consistent with national accounting conventions used to measure production.

In an effort to improve the consistency of these two sets of estimates, HCFA and BEA are engaged in a joint program to reconcile the health care estimates in the NHA and in the NIPA. The reconciliation project is important for several reasons. First, it will allow data users to understand the differences between the NHA and the NIPA estimates and do a rough

Arthur Sensenig is an economist in the Office of the Actuary, Health Care Financing Administration. Ernest Wilcox is an economist at the Bureau of Economic Analysis.

The views expressed are those of the authors alone and do not represent the positions of the Health Care Financing Administration or the Bureau of Economic Analysis.

Table 7.1   **1996 National Health Accounts, 1992–96 (billions of dollars)**

	1992	1993	1994	1995	1996
National health expenditures	836.6	895.1	945.7	991.4	1,035.1
Research	14.2	14.5	15.9	16.7	17.0
Construction	13.4	14.5	14.6	14.0	14.5
Health services and supplies	809.1	866.1	915.2	960.7	1,003.6
Administration and net cost of					
private health insurance	45.0	53.8	58.2	60.1	60.9
Public health activity	23.4	25.3	28.5	31.5	35.5
Personal health care	740.7	787.0	828.5	869.0	907.2
Hospital care	305.3	323.0	335.7	346.7	358.5
Physician services	175.9	183.6	190.4	196.4	202.1
Dental services	37.0	38.9	41.5	44.7	47.6
Other professional care	42.1	46.3	50.3	54.3	58.0
Home health care	19.6	22.9	25.6	28.4	30.2
Nondurable medical products	71.2	75.6	79.5	84.9	91.4
Durable medical equipment	11.9	12.3	12.5	13.1	13.3
Nursing home care	62.3	66.3	70.9	75.2	78.5
Other personal health care	15.4	18.0	21.9	25.3	27.6

Source: Levit et al. 1997, table 10.

crosswalk between the two series. In this way, data users will be able to use the series most appropriate to their needs. Second, the reconciliation project will allow HCFA and BEA to improve their estimates by reviewing and discussing their estimating methodologies. Finally, the reconciliation should result in greater consistency in the presentation of the two sets of estimates.

The estimates to be reconciled are shown in table 7.1 (NHA) and in table 7.2 (NIPA). For 1996, national health expenditures amounted to $1,035.1 billion in the NHA and selected health care expenditures amounted to $1,001.1 billion in the NIPA. The reconciliation will identify conceptual and definitional differences, as well as procedural and source data differences.

This paper is a preliminary report covering the reconciliation of hospital care (sec. 7.2) and physician services (sec. 7.3). In each section, there is a presentation of the published estimates, definitions, estimating procedures, and source data for both the NHA and NIPA estimates, and a summary of the differences.

7.2 Hospital Care

As part of the NHA, HCFA publishes annual estimates of total expenditures for hospital care and has underlying detail that provides separate estimates of private hospitals, state and local government hospitals, federal hospitals, hospitals of institutions (primarily university hospitals and state prison hospitals), and hospitals in the U.S. territories and Puerto Rico.

Table 7.2   **Selected NIPA Health Care Expenditures, 1992–96 (billions of dollars)**

	1992	1993	1994	1995	1996
Selected NIPA health care					
expenditures	811.6	866.4	909.5	955.2	1,001.1
Private structures (hospitals and					
institutions)	12.8	13.9	13.7	12.5	13.4
Personal consumption expenditures					
health care	733.2	785.5	826.1	871.6	912.8
Health insurance	42.7	53.6	55.0	53.6	56.3
Hospitals	268.8	285.8	298.1	310.6	325.1
Physicians	167.2	172.5	180.0	191.4	196.5
Dentists	38.5	40.8	43.9	47.6	50.9
Other professional services	78.2	87.6	95.7	104.4	110.2
Drug preparations and sundries	75.0	78.1	81.6	85.7	90.9
Ophthalmic and orthopedic					
products	11.6	11.8	12.9	13.1	13.9
Nursing homes	51.2	55.3	58.9	65.2	69.1
Direct government health care					
expenditures	65.6	67.0	69.7	71.1	74.9
Federal government consumption					
expenditures and gross					
investment	33.5	36.0	38.9	39.3	40.7
Health and hospitals	15.2	16.4	17.8	18.2	18.3
Medicare	2.9	3.1	3.2	3.1	3.3
Veterans hospital and medical	15.4	16.5	18.0	18.0	19.0
State and local government					
consumption expenditures					
and gross investment	32.1	31.0	30.8	31.8	34.2
Health	21.5	22.6	23.9	25.7	27.6
Hospitals	10.7	8.3	6.9	6.1	6.7

Notes: Except as noted below, these estimates represent those included in GDP. They are drawn from data published in two issues of the *Survey of Current Business:* NIPA tables 5.6 (structures) and 2.4 (personal consumption expenditures) in the August 1997 issue and NIPA tables 3.16 (federal government current expenditures and gross investment) and 3.17 (state and local government current expenditures and gross investment) in the October 1997 issue.

The following health care expenditures are included in GDP but are not included in selected NIPA health care expenditures in this table because separate estimates of this detail are not used in preparing GDP component estimates: purchases of producers' durable equipment, construction of medical care facilities other than hospitals, net exports of medical services, Department of Defense health care, student health care, medical research, and administrative and fundraising expenses of philanthropic organizations related to health care.

The NIPA expenditures data shown in this table are limited to those included in GDP. Consequently, they exclude transfer payments to persons by government such as Medicare and Medicaid, and intermediate expenditures by business, such as on-site health units.

As part of the NIPA, BEA's annual estimates of total expenditures for hospital care appear within two categories: personal consumption expenditures (PCE) and government consumption expenditures. The PCE estimates cover both private and government hospitals, to the extent the latter charge for their services. The government consumption expenditures estimates cover both federal and state and local government hospitals and are net of the receipts included in PCE. Separate detail is presented for state and local government hospitals. Detail on federal hospitals is not shown separately in the NIPA but is consolidated within other expenditure-type categories, such as military activities and veterans hospitals and medical care. For this paper, estimates have been prepared, beginning in 1993, for one unpublished category, that of federal hospitals operated by the Departments of Defense and Veterans Affairs, using the same U.S. budget data that are used to prepare the estimates of NIPA federal government consumption expenditures. Thus, a total NIPA hospital expenditures estimate is obtained by combining the published NIPA estimate of PCE for hospitals with the published and unpublished consumption expenditures for government hospitals.

7.2.1 Summary of Differences

Table 7.3 shows that overall, NHA hospital care is higher than the NIPA estimates for hospital expenditures by about $13 to $14 billion for 1993–95. The NHA estimates for private hospitals are $15 to $16 billion above the PCE estimates for private hospitals for 1993–95. The NHA estimates for state and local government hospitals are $6 to $7 billion below the corresponding NIPA estimates for 1993–95. The NHA estimates for federal hospitals are about $2 billion above the NIPA estimates for federal hospitals for 1993–95. It appears that the major sources of differences be-

Table 7.3   **NHA and NIPA Hospital Expenditures, 1992–96 (billions of dollars)**

	1992	1993	1994	1995	1996
NHA hospital care	305.3	323.0	335.7	346.7	358.5
Private hospitals	228.3	240.4	248.6	258.8	267.6e
State and local government hospitals	54.8	58.8	60.5	62.6	64.7e
Federal hospitals	20.7	22.0	22.7	23.2	24.1
Other[a]	1.6	1.7	1.9	2.1	2.1
NIPA hospitals	n.a.	309.8	321.3	333.6	350.0
Private hospitals	213.7	224.6	232.3	242.4	254.4
Proprietary hospitals	30.1	30.7	32.1	34.5	37.1
Nonprofit hospitals	183.6	193.9	200.2	207.9	217.3
State and local government hospitals	62.1	65.3	67.9	69.8	72.4
Federal hospitals[b]	n.a.	19.9	21.1	21.4	23.2
NHA less NIPA					
All hospitals	n.a.	13.2	14.5	13.1	8.5
Private hospitals	14.6	15.8	16.3	16.4	13.2
State and local government hospitals	−7.3	−6.4	−7.3	−7.3	−7.7
Federal hospitals	n.a.	2.1	1.6	1.9	0.9
Other	1.6	1.7	1.9	2.1	2.1

Note: e = estimate. n.a. = not available.

[a]Consists of hospitals of institutions and hospitals in U.S. territories and Puerto Rico.

[b]Consists only of hospitals operated by the Departments of Defense and Veterans Affairs.

tween NHA and NIPA estimates are the valuation of nonprofits and the treatment of nonoperating income, the treatment of secondary products, the timing of incorporation of newly available source data, and the differences in source data.

The first source of differences is conceptual, or definitional. In the NHA, the value of hospital care is a revenue measure for all types of hospitals, except those operated by the federal government, for which hospital care is measured by outlays or expenses. In the NIPA, the value of hospital care is measured by receipts for proprietary hospitals and by current operating expenditures, including consumption of fixed capital,[1] for private nonprofit and government hospitals. Furthermore, even for proprietary hospitals where both NHA and NIPA use revenue as the measure of the value of hospital care or expenditures, revenue is defined differently. NHA revenue includes nonoperating revenue (investment income, rents, gifts, contributions). Nonoperating revenue is excluded from all NIPA measures of expenditures because it is not considered to be related to the concept of current production that underlies gross domestic product.

For nonprofit and government hospitals, the NIPA use current expenditures because these hospitals are treated as nonmarket producers. As a group, they do not have enough receipts from the services they perform to cover operating expenses—in other words, they are supported, to varying degrees, by government taxes, private contributions, or investment income from endowments. To the extent that government appropriations, private contributions, or investment income, in addition to receipts, covered *only* expenses of producing hospital services, there would be no substantive difference between the NHA revenue measure and the NIPA expense measure.

The second source of differences is the coverage of services for each expenditure measure. NHA hospital expenditures consist of the revenue from hospital services, nursing home services, home health services, contract research, cafeteria sales, merchandise sales, and other services; NIPA hospital expenditures are almost entirely for the production of hospital services. Expenditures for nursing home and home health services produced in hospitals are recorded in their own categories in the NIPA.

The third source of differences is the use of different source data. The NHA uses the annual American Hospital Association (AHA) survey at the individual hospital level. The NIPA use the AHA survey at aggregate level for proprietary and nonprofit hospitals, but benchmark these data to the estimates from the quinquennial Census of Service Industries (CSI). The NIPA are currently benchmarked on the 1987 CSI; the effect of intro-

---

1. The services of fixed assets of nonprofit institutions are measured as the sum of consumption of fixed capital and an estimate of a net rate of return, assumed to equal the net interest paid by these institutions. For general government agencies, including government hospitals, the services of fixed assets are measured only by consumption of fixed capital.

ducing the 1992 CSI benchmark, which will be done in the next comprehensive GDP revision, is expected to increase the NIPA estimates by about $1 billion beginning with 1992. For state and local government hospitals, the NIPA estimates are from the annual Governmental Finance (GF) survey and the quinquennial Census of Governments (COG).

For federal hospitals, most of the difference is due to the exclusion from the NIPA estimates of separately identifiable estimates of consumption expenditures for hospitals operated by federal departments other than Defense and Veterans Affairs, such as the Department of the Interior, which operates the Indian Health Service hospitals. These amount to about $1 billion in the NHA estimates.

7.2.2   National Health Accounts

Since 1964, the U.S. Department of Health and Human Services has published an annual series of statistics presenting total national health expenditures during each year. The basic aim of these statistics, termed National Health Accounts (NHA), is to "identify all goods and services that can be characterized as relating to health care in the nation, and determine the amount of money used for the purchase of these goods and services . . ." (Rice, Cooper, and Gibson 1982).

The NHA constitute the framework within which estimates of spending for health care are constructed. The framework can be considered as a two-dimensional matrix; along one dimension are types of providers or services, and along the other dimension are sources of funds. The NHA recognize several types of spending. "Personal health care" comprises therapeutic goods or services rendered to treat or prevent a specific disease or condition in a specific person. "Government public health activity" involves spending to organize and deliver health services and to prevent or control health problems. "Program administration" covers spending for the cost of running various government health care programs, plus the net cost of private health insurance (the difference between premiums earned by insurers and the claims or losses for which insurers become liable). Finally, "research and construction" spending includes noncommercial biomedical research and the construction of health care facilities.

In addition to these types of expenditures, two layers of aggregation are shown. "Health services and supplies," which represents spending for care rendered during the year, is the sum of personal health care expenditures, government public health activity, and program administration. It is distinguished from research and construction expenditures, which represent an investment in the future health care system. The combined value of health services and supplies, research, and construction in the NHA is known as national health expenditures (NHE).

The NHA show how much is spent on the health of U.S. residents as measured through the revenue of health care providers, the net cost of health insurance, outlays for public health programs (such as the Centers for Disease Control [CDC] and state health departments), and spending for research and construction. Thus, estimates shown in this report cover the United States.[2] Medical services provided by the Department of Defense to military and civilian personnel overseas are included as well. However, no attempt has been made to increase expenditures by the value of health care "imports" (care rendered to U.S. citizens by providers in foreign countries) nor to reduce expenditures by the value of "exports" (care rendered to foreign citizens by U.S. providers). The scope of the NHA is determined by the type of good, or, in the case of services, the type of establishment providing the service. Goods are classified using the product codes used by the Bureau of the Census for the Census of Manufactures. Services are selected when they are provided through establishments that fall into Standard Industrial Classification (SIC) 80 or through government operations that mimic that classification (Lazenby et al. 1992).

Definitions

In the NHA, hospital care estimates reflect spending for all services provided by hospitals to patients. These services include room and board, ancillary services such as operating room facilities, services of resident physicians, inpatient pharmacy, hospital-based nursing home care, hospital-based home health care, and any other services billed by the hospital. Expenditures for services of physicians who bill independently for patients seen in hospitals are excluded.

Scope

All hospitals in the United States are included in the scope of the NHA. Expenditures are estimated separately for community hospitals and noncommunity hospitals. Community hospitals are nonfederal acute care hospitals that are open to the general public and have an average length of stay of less than thirty days. Noncommunity hospitals include long-term hospitals, hospital units of institutions, psychiatric hospitals, hospitals for tuberculosis and other respiratory diseases, chronic disease hospitals, institutions for the mentally retarded, and alcoholism and chemical dependency hospitals. Noncommunity hospitals are further subdivided into federal and nonfederal noncommunity hospitals for estimation in the NHA. Federal hospitals comprise hospitals operated by the Department of Veterans Affairs (DVA), the Department of Defense (DOD), the Indian Health Service (IHS), the National Institutes of Health (NIH) Clinical Center, federal prison hospitals, the Hansen's Disease hospital, and the Coast Guard Academy clinic/hospital.

---

2. For hospitals, these estimates also cover U.S. outlying territories (the Virgin Islands, Guam, American Samoa, and the Marshall Islands) and Puerto Rico.

Valuation

The value of nonfederal hospital output is measured by total net revenue. This includes gross patient revenues (billed charges) less contractual adjustments with insurers (indicating intended receipts, not charges), bad debts, and charity care. It also includes government tax appropriations, nonpatient operating revenue (gift shop and cafeteria revenue, parking lot receipts, and educational program revenue, for example), and nonoperating revenues, such as interest income, grants, and contributions. Revenues reflect an incurred rather than a receipt accounting method. Thus, although revenue is measured in accrued terms rather than cash terms, the value is expressed as what the hospital intends or expects to receive, rather than what the hospital charged. Nonpatient revenues are included in the value of national health expenditures because hospitals take anticipated levels of these revenues into account when setting patient revenue targets or charges. Nonpatient operating revenue includes revenue from nonpatient care services to patients and sales and activities to persons other than patients. The value of federal hospital output is measured by federal outlays for the operation of those facilities.

Data Sources

Except for federal hospitals, the basic data source used to prepare the hospital estimates is the AHA Annual Survey, which is on a fiscal year[3] rather than calendar year basis and is currently available through 1995. This survey elicits information from each hospital in the United States and its outlying territories and experiences a response rate of about 90 percent (American Hospital Association 1960–95). Data for nonresponding hospitals are imputed by AHA analysts, using data reported by similar hospitals. In some cases, the AHA survey also includes estimates for separate nursing home and home health care establishments owned by hospitals.

Methodology

Hospital national health expenditure is published at the nonfederal community, nonfederal noncommunity, and federal levels. Nonfederal hospital service estimates are estimated using fiscal year AHA annual survey expenses (table 7.4) for nonfederal community hospitals and noncommunity hospitals (which can be aggregated to private nonprofit, for-profit, and state and local government hospitals). Expenses are then converted to revenues based on revenue-to-expense ratios provided by the AHA.[4] The revenues are then converted to a calendar year basis using monthly data from the AHA National Hospital Panel Survey of participating hospitals.

The AHA data must be modified for the purposes of the NHA. These

3. Individual hospitals have different fiscal years.
4. Revenue is available in the AHA survey only for community hospitals.

Table 7.4   **AHA Annual Survey, Expenses (fiscal year) (billions of dollars)**

	1992	1993	1994	1995
Total	282.5	301.5	310.8	320.3
Federal	18.2	19.6	20.0	20.2
Nonfederal	264.3	281.9	290.8	300.0
Private	213.1	226.4	n.a.	n.a.
Nonprofit	186.4	199.6	n.a.	n.a.
For-profit	26.6	26.8	n.a.	n.a.
State and local government	51.3	55.5	n.a.	n.a.

Note: n.a. = not available.

modifications fall into four parts. First, the AHA Annual Survey is designed to be cross-sectional rather than longitudinal. Thus, these cross-sectional survey reports must be combined into one longitudinal file, creating one record for each hospital. During this process, a certain amount of editing is performed on classification codes to assure consistent reporting across time by individual hospitals. Second, revenues are imputed to each hospital on the basis of reported (or estimated) expenses. Expenses are inflated to revenues using aggregate revenue-to-expense ratios provided by the AHA. Community hospitals are differentiated by state and by broad type of control (nonprofit or other), and noncommunity hospitals are differentiated by type of service and by type of control. Third, individual hospitals' imputed accounting year revenues are apportioned among calendar years. For community hospitals, expenditure patterns from the AHA's National Hospital Panel Survey are used to make that split; noncommunity hospitals are assumed to spend one-twelfth of fiscal year revenues in each month of that year (American Hospital Association 1963–90). At this stage, imputations are made to account for missing periods or overlapping periods in a hospital's report stream. Overlapping periods arise primarily from mergers and sales of hospitals and the associated changes in reporting period. Fourth, aggregate community and noncommunity hospital data are extrapolated through 1996, using patterns of acceleration and deceleration observed in the AHA National Hospital Panel Survey data. The extrapolation is prepared by graphically analyzing annual survey revenues and panel survey revenues for total nonfederal hospitals and nonfederal community hospitals to estimate the most recent year's growth rate. Since 1987 the panel survey and the annual survey have been tracking very closely, so for more recent years the panel survey growth has been assumed to represent the annual survey growth. The estimates for federal hospitals are shown in table 7.5.

7.2.3   National Income and Product Accounts

The NIPA are a comprehensive set of accounts measuring the production and distribution of goods and services produced in the United States

Table 7.5   NHA Federal Hospitals (billions of dollars)

	1992	1993	1994	1995	1996
Federal hospitals	20.7	22.0	22.7	23.2	24.1
VA hospitals	10.8	11.6	12.4	12.7	13.5
DOD hospitals	8.9	9.3	9.1	9.3	9.2
Indian Health Service	0.6	0.7	0.7	0.8	0.8
Other hospitals[a]	0.4	0.4	0.4	0.4	0.5

[a]Data for the NIH Clinical Center and the Hansen's disease hospital are from budget documents. Data for federal prison hospitals are from the Department of Justice.

and the generation and distribution of income from this production. The geographic coverage of the United States is the fifty states plus the District of Columbia. Gross domestic product (GDP), which is the primary aggregate of these accounts, is the market value of the goods and services produced by labor and property located in the United States.

GDP is measured as the sum of final expenditures—consumer spending, private investment, net exports, and government consumption and investment. Consumer spending, or personal consumption expenditures (PCE), is the value of goods and services purchased by persons resident in the United States and includes goods and services produced by nonprofit institutions serving households, such as nonprofit hospitals. Private investment, or gross private domestic investment, is the value of fixed assets purchased by private businesses, including nonprofit institutions, and residential dwellings purchased by owner-occupants, and the change in inventories of private businesses. Net exports is exports minus imports. Government consumption expenditures and gross investment is the value of purchases of goods and services and structures from business and the rest of the world by general government agencies, including the compensation of employees and consumption of fixed capital, which represents the value of the current services of fixed assets of general government, less general government sales (primarily tuition payments and charges for medical care).

For hospitals, PCE includes expenditures by households at for-profit and government hospitals and current expenditures by nonprofit hospitals. Gross private domestic investment includes construction of new hospitals and purchases of hospital durable equipment. Government gross investment consists of expenditures for the same types of fixed assets by government hospitals. Government consumption expenditures consist of current expenditures by government hospitals reduced by receipts from the public by these hospitals, which are included in PCE. Thus, total GDP includes all receipts by private for-profit hospitals and consumption expenditures and investment by nonprofit and government hospitals. This section discusses only the PCE and government consumption expenditures estimates.

The reconciliation of investment in structures and equipment by private or government hospitals will not be covered in this paper.

NIPA Hospitals: Estimating Procedure, Data Sources, and Present Estimates

BEA's published estimates for hospitals, as well as for every other expenditure component of GDP, are benchmarked roughly every five years to the latest input-output table. Estimates between and beyond input-output estimates are interpolations and extrapolations, using various indicator series. In most cases, the input-output estimates are derived from data from the quinquennial economic censuses, conducted by the Bureau of the Census. The most recent benchmark input-output table incorporated into the NIPA is the 1987 table; some preliminary data from the 1992 Economic Censuses were also incorporated into the NIPA at the time of the comprehensive NIPA revision released in January 1996. The 1992 input-output table, which was published by BEA in November 1997, incorporates final and more comprehensive data from the 1992 Economic Censuses, which will be incorporated into the NIPA most likely in 1999.

Annual revisions, such as the one released in July 1997, incorporated source data for 1993 forward that had become available since the previous year's annual or comprehensive revision, as well as changes in methodology. BEA's usual procedure for an annual revision is to revise only the past three years and to incorporate new source data on a "best-change" basis beginning with the year subject to revision. For example, the July 1997 revisions were made to the period beginning with 1993. Thus, for any new source data available for prior years, BEA applied the new 1992–93 change to the published 1992 estimates to derive the revised estimates for 1993 forward. This approach provides estimates of changes, but not necessarily levels, that are based on the best available source data. At the time of the next comprehensive revision, the best level data for earlier periods will be fully incorporated.

Personal Consumption Expenditures for Hospitals

In NIPA table 2.4, BEA publishes an annual aggregate series of Personal Consumption Expenditures (PCE) for Hospitals (line 51) and three component series: Nonprofit Hospitals (line 52), Proprietary Hospitals (line 53), and Government Hospitals (line 54). (The estimates used in this paper appear in the August 1997 *Survey of Current Business.*)

Private Nonprofit Hospitals. Expenditures (PCE) for nonprofit private hospitals are measured as their current operating expenses, including consumption of fixed capital (depreciation) and excluding purchases of fixed assets. In addition, these expenses are net of receipts from sales of meals and beverages. Source data for annual estimates are total expenses for non-

Table 7.6   **Derivation of PCE for Nonprofit Hospitals (billions of dollars)**

	1992	1993	1994	1995	1996
AHA expenses, FY basis	186.9	199.9	206.8	212.0	220.5
Adjusted expenses, CY basis	190.6	202.2	208.7	214.6	223.3
Plus depreciation adjustment	2.7	2.8	2.8	2.9	2.9
Minus redefinitions	3.1	3.3	3.5	3.7	3.8
Minus purchases by government	3.2	3.1	3.1	3.2	3.2
Minus Medicaid donation	0.6	0.5	0.5	0.5	0.6
Equals extrapolator from 1987	186.5	198.0	204.4	210.2	218.7
Published NIPA PCE (best change from 1987)[a]	183.6	193.9	200.2	207.9	217.3

[a]Beginning with 1993, also includes small BEA adjustments for consistency with related source data.

government not-for-profit short-term and long-term hospitals from the annual AHA *Hospital Statistics* plus a BEA estimate for nonregistered (non-covered) hospitals. As shown in table 7.6, this total is adjusted by BEA to a calendar year basis using a ratio derived from the monthly AHA National Hospital Panel Survey. The calendar year total is then multiplied by a fixed ratio (1.0026) to agree with the corresponding benchmark total from the 1987 Census of Service Industries. This adjusted expense series is subject to several further adjustments. An estimate for the difference between current replacement cost[5] and the historical cost depreciation already included in the AHA expense data is added. Based on the 1987 input-output table, redefinitions, which cover nursing home services, home health care services, research, and medical equipment rental included in the 1987 CSI benchmark data, are subtracted, as are government purchases from private hospitals, which are based on estimates of the disposition of private hospital services from the 1987 input-output table. (The appendix discusses secondary products and redefinitions.) The AHA expense data include the net cost of the Medicaid donation, so a deduction is made for 1991–96 in deriving the PCE estimate.

Proprietary Hospitals. PCE for proprietary hospitals is measured as their current receipts. Primary source data for annual estimates are total expenses for investor-owned (for-profit) short-term and long-term hospitals from the annual AHA *Hospital Statistics.* Revenue is not available for all proprietary hospitals and it contains components not included in receipts, such as contributions, so it is not used. As shown in table 7.7, these ex-

5. This capital consumption adjustment is based on the nonprofit institution estimates of consumption of fixed capital from BEA's capital stock statistics.

Table 7.7   **Derivation of PCE for Proprietary Hospitals (billions of dollars)**

	1992	1993	1994	1995	1996
AHA expenses, FY basis	26.9	27.3	28.2	30.6	n.a.
Adjusted receipts, CY basis	30.7	31.3	32.8	35.2	36.6
Plus sales tax	0.1	0.1	0.1	0.1	0.1
Minus redefinitions	0.2	0.2	0.2	0.2	0.2
Minus purchases by government	0.5	0.5	0.6	0.6	0.6
Equals extrapolator from 1987	30.1	30.7	32.1	34.5	35.9
Published NIPA PCE	30.1	30.7	32.1	34.5	37.1

Note: n.a. = not available.

pense data are adjusted by a BEA estimate for nonregistered (noncovered) hospitals and converted to a calendar year basis using a ratio derived from the AHA National Hospital Panel Survey. Calendar year expenses are expanded to agree with expense data from the 1987 CSI and then adjusted to a receipts estimate using a ratio (1.1096) from the 1977 CSI. Estimates of sales tax are added and redefinitions and government purchases from private hospitals are deducted based on data from the 1987 input-output table. The most recent estimate from the annual AHA survey is for 1995; the 1996 estimate is based on a BEA projection, using monthly expense data from the AHA Panel Survey.

Government Hospitals. PCE for government hospitals (NIPA table 2.4, line 54) is measured as sales by all government hospitals to households. The series is calculated in two parts—sales by federal government hospitals and sales by state and local government hospitals. Federal government sales are derived from federal budget detail. State and local government sales are the sum of sales of state hospitals and sales of local government hospitals and include medical vendor payments (Medicaid) to hospitals and government payments for hospital services on behalf of indigents. Sales estimates for state and local government hospitals are derived from the Census of Governments (COG) Compendium of Government Finances or from the Annual Survey of Governmental Finance, and are adjusted from a fiscal year to a calendar year basis. Data for medical vendor payments collected in the COG do not include Medicaid expenditures to state and local government health facilities, so BEA makes a grossing adjustment; in other words, they adjust for the difference between total Medicaid expenditures from HCFA and the Census total for medical vendor payments. Unlike the PCE estimates for private hospitals, BEA does not presently make a redefinition adjustment (nursing home, home health, cafeteria) for state and local government hospitals, but will consider making such a change in methodology in the next comprehensive benchmark re-

Table 7.8   Components of PCE for Government Hospitals (billions of dollars)

	1992	1993	1994	1995	1996
Government hospitals	55.1	61.1	65.8	68.2	70.7
Federal hospital sales	0.4	0.6	1.2	1.0	1.3
S&L hospital sales	54.8	60.6	64.6	67.3	69.5
State hospital sales	19.9	22.2	23.5	24.1	24.4
Hospital charges	13.5	14.6	15.2	15.7	15.9
Medical vendor payment (Medicaid)	6.5	7.6	8.2	8.4	8.5
Local hospital sales	34.8	38.4	41.1	43.2	45.0
Hospital charges	26.2	28.2	29.9	31.4	32.8
Medical vendor payment (Medicaid)	8.6	10.2	11.2	11.7	12.2

vision. The components of PCE for government hospitals are shown in table 7.8.

Government Consumption Expenditures

In addition to sales of government hospital services that appear in PCE, transactions in government hospital services appear in the government sector of the NIPA in two forms, as parts of government consumption expenditures and gross investment in GDP, and as parts of government receipts and current expenditures, such as contributions for social insurance, transfer payments, and grants-in-aid to state and local governments. This paper will discuss only government consumption expenditures.

Government consumption expenditures are defined as expenditures by government agencies, except government enterprises, for the services of government employees, for goods and services purchased from private businesses and the rest of the world, and for consumption of government fixed capital. The expenditures are recorded net of sales (primarily to persons), which are included in PCE. Consequently, the output of government hospitals, as well as all other government agencies not classified as enterprises, is measured as current expenditures, the same definition used for the output of nonprofit institutions serving households. (No attempt is made to estimate the market value of the services provided by either type of institution.)

Table 7.9 shows the NIPA estimates for government hospital expenditures. The estimates for federal hospitals cover only DOD and VA hospitals and are derived from U.S. budget data. The estimates for state and local government hospitals combine the government consumption expenditures with sales from PCE to produce total expenditures for state and local government hospitals in GDP.

Federal Hospitals. Although government consumption expenditures for veterans hospitals, military hospitals, and other federal hospitals (Indian Health Service hospitals, NIH Clinical Center, federal prison hospitals,

Hansen's Disease hospital) are not broken out in NIPA calculations, underlying budget detail for veterans and military hospitals is available. Estimates of the consumption of fixed capital should be added to these figures. Expenditures for other federal hospitals appear to be about $1 billion, based on NHA estimates. In the NIPA, these expenditures are an integral part of the broader expenditure categories.

For veterans hospitals, the derivation of the estimate is shown in table 7.10. The NIPA estimate for VA hospitals is the "subtotal" line on a calendar year basis—it excludes nursing homes, contracts and grants, and education and training. The VA expenditures covered 172 VA hospitals and 128 VA nursing homes in 1993.

For military hospitals, the Defense Health Program covered 132 military hospitals/medical centers and 520 clinics in 1994. Consistent data for the Defense Health Program were not published in the U.S. budget prior to the fiscal year 1993 actual estimates. As shown in table 7.11, net outlays

Table 7.9   **NIPA Government Hospital Expenditures (billions of dollars)**

	1992	1993	1994	1995	1996
NIPA government hospitals	n.a.	82.2	89.0	91.2	95.6
Federal hospitals	n.a.	19.9	21.1	21.4	23.2
Defense health	n.a.	8.4	9.2	9.3	10.0
VA hospitals	10.8	11.5	11.9	12.0	13.2
State and local government hospitals	62.1	65.3	67.9	69.8	72.4

Note: n.a. = not available.

Table 7.10   **U.S. Budget, Department of Veterans Affairs, Veterans Health Administration, Medical Care (billions of dollars)**

	1992	1993	1994	1995	1996
FY (actual) basis					
Hospitals	6.6	6.9	7.2	6.8	7.1
Outpatient	3.3	3.6	3.9	4.2	5.2
Miscellaneous[a]	0.7	0.7	0.8	0.7	0.8
Subtotal	10.7	11.3	12.0	11.7	13.1
Education and training	0.8	0.8	0.8	0.9	0.0
Nursing homes	1.0	1.1	1.1	2.7	2.4
Contracts and grants	0.5	0.6	0.7	0.0	0.0
Investment	0.7	0.7	0.7	0.8	0.8
Total outlays	13.6	14.5	15.3	16.1	16.3
Net outlays, FY basis	13.6	14.3	15.1	15.9	16.0
VA hospitals, excluding nursing homes, research, investment, CY basis	10.8	11.5	11.9	12.0	13.2

Note: Net outlays are total outlays net of offsetting collections.
[a]Includes CHAMPVA.

Table 7.11   **U.S. Budget, Department of Defense-Military, Defense Health Program (billions of dollars)**

	1992	1993	1994	1995	1996
FY (actual) basis					
Operation and maintenance	n.a.	9.3	9.4	9.6	9.9
Procurement	n.a.	0.2	0.3	0.3	0.4
Total	n.a.	9.4	9.6	10.0	10.3
Net outlays	n.a.	8.2	9.2	9.2	9.9
Defense health, CY basis	n.a.	8.4	9.2	9.3	10.0

Note: n.a. = not available.

for the Defense Health Program rose from $8.4 billion in 1993 to $10 billion in 1996.

State and Local Government Hospitals. The primary source data for state and local government expenditures are the COG and the Annual Survey of Government Finances (GF), which provide estimates of expenses and receipts of state and local government hospitals, other than for compensation of employees; HCFA data on medical vendor payments, which are not included in the COG/GF sales data because they are treated as intragovernmental expenditures on behalf of indigents (Medicaid); tabulations of wages and salaries of state and local government employees covered by state unemployment insurance from the Bureau of Labor Statistics (BLS); BEA's estimates of consumption of fixed capital; and the Census Bureau's annual survey, *Public Employment.*

Consumption expenditures by state and local government hospitals are derived from COG/GF data on current expenditures less compensation of employees and transfer payments. State and local government hospital sales (charges) are calculated as receipts for hospital admissions from the COG/GF data on current charges and miscellaneous general revenue data plus medical vendor payments. Wages and salaries of state and local government hospital employees are estimated as an allocation of BLS data on wages and salaries, based on data on hospitals from *Public Employment.* The BLS data do not cover interns and student nurses employed by hospitals, so BEA makes an adjustment to cover them based on employment data from the annual Bureau of Census report *County Business Patterns.* The supplements component of compensation of employees is prepared in a similar way, using the same allocations as for wages and salaries. Lastly, the consumption of fixed capital is added. The estimates are shown in table 7.12. In the NIPA tables, consumption expenditures are published in NIPA table 3.17; sales for both hospitals and other health services are shown combined in NIPA table 3.9.

Table 7.12   **State and Local Government Hospitals—Total NIPA Consumption Expenditures (billions of dollars)**

	1992	1993	1994	1995	1996
Total NIPA consumption expenditures	62.1	65.3	67.9	69.8	72.4
Compensation	37.8	38.7	39.9	40.3	41.3
Consumption of fixed capital	2.4	2.5	2.5	2.6	2.7
Other consumption	21.9	24.1	25.5	26.9	28.4
Minus sales (PCE)	54.8	60.6	64.6	67.3	69.5
Equals consumption expenditures	7.3	4.7	3.3	2.6	3.0

Other NIPA-Related Hospital Care Estimates

GDP by Industry. Gross product, or gross product originating (GPO) by industry, is the contribution of each private industry and government to the nation's output, or GDP. An industry's GPO, often referred to as its "value added," is equal to its gross output minus its intermediate inputs. Estimates of GPO are published by BEA annually in the *Survey of Current Business,* most recently in the November 1997 issue. There is limited industry detail available in this series; separate industry detail is shown only for the health services industry (SIC 80) as a whole.

Benchmark Input-Output Accounts. These accounts are prepared every five years by BEA to coincide with the availability of the quinquennial economic censuses. The input-output accounts show the production of commodities by each industry, the commodity composition of GDP, and the industry distribution of value added. The benchmark input-output estimates of GDP and its commodity composition are incorporated into the NIPA estimates at the time of a comprehensive revision. The most recent benchmark input-output table, covering 1992, was published in the November and December 1997 issues of the *Survey of Current Business.*

7.2.4   Review of Primary Data Sources

In order to reconcile the NHA and NIPA estimates and to develop estimates for hospital production and hospital services, we identified differences in the four primary data sources: the AHA annual survey; the federal budget (for federal hospitals); the Census of Governments (for state and local government hospitals); and the Census of Service Industries.

The AHA Annual Survey

The AHA annual survey has about a 10 percent nonresponse rate (in terms of number of nonresponding hospitals). The AHA adjustment for unreported expenses is based primarily on reports of similar hospitals. The AHA annual survey also includes expenses for nursing homes (including institutions for the mentally retarded) and home health establishments owned by hospitals. If in the preparation of the NHA, the AHA hospital data are added to nursing home and home health data from the Census of Service Industries, which generally are based on separate reports for each establishment, the resulting totals will double-count data for these hospital-owned nursing home and home health establishments. Such an actual or potential double-count could be eliminated by benchmarking the NHA hospital estimates to the Census of Service Industries data.

U.S. Budget

As previously noted, the published NIPA estimates do not provide separate data on consumption expenditures by federal government hospitals. The U.S. budget includes data on outlays for the Defense Health Program (beginning with fiscal year 1993) and on veterans hospitals and nursing homes. For this paper, these data were used to separately identify for the NIPA estimates the current expenditures for these federal hospitals beginning with 1993. To prepare estimates for all federal hospitals and to extend the defense data back beyond 1993, additional work will be needed. Also, additional work is needed to provide improved estimates of the consumption of fixed capital for the fixed assets of these hospitals.

Census of Governments

The Census of Governments (COG) is a survey of the revenue and expenditures of government units: federal, state, local (county, municipal, township, special districts). The information is on a fiscal year basis, which varies from government unit to unit. Expenditures are organized by functional categories, including hospitals, which include expenditures for hospital facilities directly operated by state and local governments. For the NIPA, these hospitals should be compared to the coverage of privately owned hospitals in the Census of Service Industries to eliminate any duplication, particularly given conversions or acquisitions by for-profit hospitals.

Census of Service Industries

The Census of Service Industries (CSI) is an establishment survey that provides comprehensive data on hospitals, nursing homes, home health care, and other health care providers. The census collects data on receipts from nursing home and home health services within hospital establishments and data on other types of revenue (contract research, cafeteria, merchandise, government appropriations, contributions and gifts, investment income, rents). It also collects data on expenses for hospitals owned by nonprofit institutions and by governments. The extent of the data permits combination to measure hospital expenditures using different definitions. The Census of Service Industries receipts/revenues data and the sources of receipts/revenues data for 1992 are shown in table 7.13. Data from the CSI on private hospitals are used to benchmark the NIPA, but not the NHA; data from the CSI on government hospitals are not used in either the NIPA or the NHA. BEA has done an initial study of the CSI universe coverage for nonprofit private hospitals by comparing the CSI to publicly available lists and found several inconsistencies. BEA will pursue this further as part of the reconciliation project.

Table 7.14 shows a comparison of major types of hospital expenditures for three of the four primary data sources discussed above. (The U.S. budget is omitted because we have not yet obtained fiscal year 1992 figures from the underlying budget documents.) The comparison of the expenses data shows that the AHA survey data are low relative to the CSI expense data even though the AHA survey includes some nursing home, home health, and homes for the mentally retarded not included in the CSI hospital data. (The calendar year/fiscal year difference is about 1 percent based on the fiscal year/calendar year conversion for PCE nonprofit private hospital expenses, so this difference is not substantive.) This apparent inconsistency in the two data sources should be further explored by HCFA and BEA.

For state and local government hospitals, the COG and CSI estimates are within $1 billion. (Both sources exclude an estimate for depreciation, which was $2.4 billion for 1992.) However, the equivalent NIPA estimate is about $4 billion higher. This difference may in part reflect the NIPA procedure that allocates Medicaid payments between hospital and other health care. There are data from HCFA on these payments that might be used to evaluate the allocation.

7.2.5   Sources of Differences

As previously noted, NHA hospital care estimates are higher than the NIPA estimates for hospital expenditures by about $13–14 billion for 1993–95. The NHA estimates for private hospitals are higher, the NHA estimates for state and local government hospitals are lower, and the estimates for federal hospitals are about the same.

The NHA use the AHA annual survey as their data source for private and state and local government hospitals. The PCE estimate for private hospitals uses the AHA annual survey at aggregate level, but benchmarks the data on the CSI, although the current benchmark is for 1987. PCE will be benchmarked on the 1992 CSI in 1999, which should increase PCE for private hospitals by $1 billion for 1992–96.

The AHA annual survey has about a 10 percent nonresponse rate in terms of number of hospitals, and covers fewer hospitals than the CSI. The CSI has a smaller nonresponse rate and, unlike the AHA, has some up-to-date information on nonrespondents. However, although the CSI is based on a complete universe mailing list, it appears to have classification problems between private nonprofit and government hospitals. HCFA and

Table 7.13   1992 Census of Service Industries, Sources of Receipts or Revenues (billions of dollars)

	Proprietary	Nonprofit	Private	Government	Federal	S&L	Total
Expenses[a]	n.a.	194.4	n.a.	74.5	19.9	54.6	n.a.
Revenue[b]	n.a.	203.4	234.4	76.4	20.0	56.3	310.8
Receipts[c]	31.1	196.3	227.4	74.8	n.a.	n.a.	302.2
Hospital services	30.6	189.6	220.2	40.8			261.0
Nursing home services	0.1	1.0	1.1	0.8			1.9
Home health services	0.1	1.5	1.6	0.3			1.9
Contract research	0.0	0.4	0.4	0.0			0.4
Cafeteria	0.1	1.0	1.1	0.2			1.3
Merchandise	0.0	0.1	0.2	0.1			0.3
Other services	0.2	2.6	2.8	0.6			3.4
Other receipts	0.0	0.1	0.1	0.0			0.1
Government appropriations				32.0			32.0
Government contributions	n.a.	1.0	n.a.	0.5			1.5
Private contributions	n.a.	0.8	n.a.	0.1			0.9
Other tax-exempt revenue	n.a.	2.2	n.a.	0.5			2.7
Investment income	n.a.	2.7	n.a.	0.5			3.2
Rents	n.a.	0.3	n.a.	0.0			0.3
Total revenue/receipts	31.1	203.4	234.4	76.4			310.8

Source: 1992 Census of Service Industries, Subject Series 4 (Sources of receipts or revenues, tables 47–48) and Subject Series 5 (Miscellaneous subjects, tables 1a, 1b, and 21).

Note: n.a. = not available.

[a]Expenses include employee compensation, contracted or purchased services and supplies, interest, rent, and depreciation.

[b]Revenues of nonprofit and government hospitals are on an accrual basis and include interest, rent, dividends, grants and contributions; they exclude sales taxes.

[c]Receipts of proprietary hospitals are on an accrual basis and exclude sales taxes, interest, rent, dividends, grants, and contributions. The difference between revenues and receipts is that revenues include and receipts exclude interest, rent, dividends, grants, and contributions.

Table 7.14   Comparison of Primary Data Source Estimates for 1992 (billions of dollars)

	CSI CY Expenses	AHA FY Expenses	AHA/CSI (%)	CSI CY Receipts	CSI CY Revenue	COG FY Expenditure
Private		213.4		227.4		
For-profit		26.6		31.1		
Nonprofit	194.4	186.4	96	196.3	203.4	
Government	74.5	69.5		74.5	76.4	64.7
S&L government	54.6	51.3	94		56.3	55.7
Federal government	19.9	18.2	92		20.0	9.0
Total		282.5		302.2		

BEA should determine the nonresponse adjustments for each survey and compare the relative growth rates of the reporting and nonreporting components of the universe estimates. They should also work with the Census Bureau to improve the coverage of the CSI data.

The AHA annual survey includes some nursing home and home health facilities and "hospitals" for the mentally retarded. Relative to the NIPA estimates, this causes the AHA-based estimates to result in higher estimates of hospital expenses and revenues. It raises a double-counting issue in the NHA, which combine AHA hospital data with nursing home data from the CSI (i.e., the CSI conceptually covers the same nursing home and "hospitals" for the mentally retarded). We don't know how much this amounts to in the AHA data, but a comparison of the $3.7 billion of secondary production of nursing home and home health services from the CSI with the estimate of nursing home and home health in-hospital services in the 1996 NHA of $7.9 billion for 1992 suggests that the difference may not be minor. Some of this difference may be due to the broader definition of nursing home and home health services used by HCFA in creating NHA estimates. Rather than including only the value of the nursing home unit services, HCFA attempted to capture the value of all services provided to a nursing unit or nursing facility patient by including an estimate for ancillary services (e.g., physical, speech, and respiratory therapy) that would be supplied by other hospital cost centers.

The ratios of AHA fiscal year expenses for 1992 to CSI calendar year expenses for 1992 for nonprofit, state and local government, and federal government hospitals are 96 percent, 94 percent, and 92 percent, respectively. These comments should not be taken to imply that the AHA annual survey data are not useful. They provide useful and timely data on hospital expenses and revenues.

The NIPA estimate for state and local government hospitals is $62.1 billion for 1992. The COG fiscal year estimate is $55.7 billion for 1992 and the CSI estimate is $55.6 billion for expenses and $56.4 billion for revenue for 1992. The COG and CSI exclude a $2.4 billion adjustment for depreciation, but that still leaves us about $4 billion short. This shortfall may or may not be related to the NHA estimate being lower than the NIPA estimate for state and local government hospitals. It may be related to the BEA split in Medicaid expenditures going to state and local government hospitals. The difference between the BEA estimate and the source data is an unresolved issue.

The NHA include estimates for hospitals in U.S. territories and Puerto Rico and the NIPA do not. These amount to $1.6 billion in 1995.

Table 7.15   **NHA and NIPA Physician Expenditures, 1992–96 (billions of dollars)**

	1992	1993	1994	1995	1996
NHA Physician Services	175.9	183.6	190.4	196.4	202.1
NIPA Physician Services (PCE)	167.2	172.5	180.0	191.4	196.5
NHA less NIPA	8.7	11.1	10.4	5.0	5.6
Of which					
Osteopaths and laboratories	10.5	10.9	11.1	11.3	11.5
PCE coverage adjustment	−4.1	−4.2	−4.3	−4.6	−4.6

7.3 Physician Services

7.3.1 Summary

The NHA and NIPA estimates of PCE for physician services (table 7.15) differ in definition. The NHA include, and PCE exclude, osteopaths and medical laboratories that bill independently for their services in the estimates of expenditures for physician services. In the NHA, estimates of tax-exempt physician services (clinics) are valued by revenues; in the NIPA, these are valued by expenses. In addition, the PCE estimates include a coverage adjustment to the CSI data for misreporting in the tax-return data used by the Census Bureau for small firms; the NHA estimates do not include a similar adjustment. Most of the difference between the estimates is due to the inclusion of osteopaths and laboratories in the NHA estimates and the coverage adjustment in the PCE estimates. Government expenditures for physician services such as the public health services are not included in this paper.

7.3.2 NHA Physician Services

Definitions

In the NHA, physician services are expenditures for services rendered by a doctor of medicine (M.D.) or by a doctor of osteopathy (D.O.) in an office or clinic (including ambulatory surgical centers and freestanding emergency medical centers). The establishments are classified in SIC 801, offices and clinics of doctors of medicine; SIC 803, doctors of osteopathy; and a portion of SIC 8071, medical laboratories that directly bill patients for their services. Physician services also include services rendered by an M.D. or a D.O. in hospitals, if the physician bills independently for those services. Expenditures for services provided in staff-model and group-model HMO facilities are included in physician services.

Professional fees received by physicians from hospitals are subtracted from the NHA estimates of spending for physician services. Hospitals' professional fee arrangements with physicians include minimum guaranteed income, percentage of departmental billings, and bonuses. These fees are included in hospital expenditures because they are paid from revenues received by hospitals based on services performed at the facility. They are deducted from physician receipts to avoid double-counting.

The services of physicians working under salary for a hospital, nursing home, or some other type of health care establishment are included in the expenditures for the service offered by the establishment. The compensation of physicians serving in field facilities of the armed forces are included in "other personal health care" in the NHA. The compensation of physicians working for government agencies such as the Centers for Disease Control or a state health department are included in Government Public Health Activity in the NHA.

Scope

All physician services rendered in the United States are included in the scope of the NHA. Physician services rendered in outlying territories are not included in the scope of the NHA. The sole exception is that estimates of professional fees in the outlying territories, embedded in the source data for those estimates, are currently within the scope of the NHA. (This exception should be corrected in the next comprehensive benchmark of the NHA.)

Valuation

The value of physician services is measured by receipts for taxable establishments and by revenues for tax-exempt establishments.

Data Sources

Physician services are benchmarked on the quinquennial Census of Service Industries data on the receipts of taxable firms and on the revenues of tax exempt firms, and Services Annual Survey (SAS) data are used for the annual estimates. (In census years, SAS equals CSI.) Compensation of government physicians is from budget data.

The following data sources are used to verify the reasonableness of physician services expenditures estimates: data on employment, average weekly hours, and average hourly earnings in nongovernment health establishments from the Current Employment Statistics (Bureau of Labor Statistics 1972–96); estimates of price change provided by the Consumer Price Index (Bureau of Labor Statistics 1960–96); and indirect measures of professional services, such as hospital admissions, inpatient days, and so forth (American Hospital Association 1980–1996).

Methodology

The CSI and SAS data on receipts and revenues are modified by adding an estimate of the revenue of independently billing laboratories and subtracting an estimate of the professional fees paid by hospitals to physi-

Table 7.16   Derivation of NHA Physician Services (billions of dollars)

	1992	1993	1994	1995	1996
Physician taxable receipts[a]	151.8	156.3	161.1	164.6	168.8
Revenues of tax-exempt physician clinics	16.5	19.0	20.6	22.7	23.7
Osteopaths and laboratories	10.5	10.9	11.1	11.3	11.5
Less hospital professional fees	2.9	2.7	2.4	2.2	1.9
Equals NHA physician services	175.9	183.6	190.4	196.4	202.1

[a]HCFA estimated the breakouts of taxable and nontaxable receipts for 1993 and 1994 from aggregate data provided by the Census Bureau.

cians. The CSI and SAS data on receipts and revenues of taxable and nontaxable firms in SIC 801 and 803 do not capture the cost of services in medical laboratories that bill patients independently of these establishments. The adjustment for independently billing medical laboratories is constructed using Medicare program data and data on medical laboratories (SIC 8071) receipts from the SAS. HCFA has requested that Census include questions in the CSI and SAS for medical labs that would provide direct data for this adjustment.

The CSI and SAS data on the receipts and revenues of taxable and nontaxable firms in SIC 801 and 803 include professional fees paid by hospitals to physicians. The adjustment to remove professional fees is constructed using data on professional fees from the AHA's Annual Survey on hospital expenses (these data are not currently being collected, HCFA estimated 1995 and 1996) and American Medical Association data on financial arrangements with hospitals. HCFA's estimates include professional fees for hospitals in U.S. territories. These fees will be eliminated in the next benchmark revision to the National Health Accounts. The derivation of NHA physician services is summarized in table 7.16.

7.3.3   NIPA Physician Services

Personal Consumption Expenditures (PCE) for Physicians

In NIPA table 2.4, BEA publishes annual estimates of personal consumption expenditures (PCE) for physician services (line 47). The current PCE estimates are benchmarked to the 1987 input-output table estimates. The PCE physician services estimates are on a "best change" basis. PCE for physician services in taxable establishments is measured by their current receipts. In addition, taxable receipts are adjusted in the PCE estimates for coverage, using a ratio of 1.027, a measure of underreporting in the tax-return data for small firms. PCE for physician services in tax-exempt establishments is measured by current expenses. The sum of taxable receipts adjusted for coverage and tax-exempt expenses is adjusted by subtracting physicians' hospital professional fees (from the NHA physi-

Table 7.17   Derivation of PCE Physician Services (billions of dollars)

	1992	1993	1994	1995	1996
Physician taxable receipts	151.8	154.8	160.8	170.3	172.9
Coverage adjustment	4.1	4.2	4.3	4.6	4.6
Expenses of tax-exempt physician clinics	16.0	18.5	20.1	22.0	24.5
Physicians and clinics	171.9	177.5	185.2	196.9	202.1
Less hospital professional fees	4.0	4.2	4.4	4.6	4.8
Less government purchases	0.9	0.9	0.9	1.0	1.0
Equals PCE physician services	167.2	172.5	180.0	191.4	196.5

cian estimate). Adjustments for capital consumption, sales tax, and exports are made, but these are small. Finally, direct government purchases of physician services are excluded. The estimates of direct government purchases of physician services are based on the NHA physician services. The derivation of PCE physician services is summarized in table 7.17.

Government Expenditures for Physician Services

Governments are involved in two basic types of transactions with private sector physicians. First, governments transfer funds to households that are used to purchase the services of physicians. Second, governments purchase the services of private physicians directly. The first type of transaction, the transfer payment, is financing of purchases that appear in PCE. The second type, direct purchases, is included in the government consumption expenditures. Because PCE and government consumption are both components of GDP, an adjustment is made to PCE to exclude direct government purchases so as not to double-count the same purchases.

In addition, government employs physicians in work that is not part of another production component of GDP, such as physicians employed at CDC or in state public health departments. Expenditures for these activities are included in government consumption expenditures and are not estimated separately. More work will be needed to reconcile these government consumption expenditures. Finally, some expenditures are included in PCE for "other professional services" (NIPA table 2.4, line 49) for sales of government physician services to the public. This will be clarified at a later stage of the reconciliation project.

7.3.4   Reconciliation—NHA Physician Services/
         NIPA Physician Services

The differences shown in table 7.18 result from differences in definition between the NHA and the NIPA, from differences in adjustments made to source data, or from differences in the timing of the introduction of source data. The differences shown for the PCE coverage adjustment, expenses or revenues of tax-exempt clinics, government purchases, and os-

Table 7.18   **Reconciliation of Physician Services, NHA less NIPA PCE (billions of dollars)**

	1992	1993	1994	1995	1996
Physician receipts	0.0	1.5	0.3	−5.7	−4.2
PCA coverage adjustment	−4.1	−4.2	−4.3	−4.6	−4.6
Expenses of tax-exempt physician clinics	0.5	0.5	0.5	0.7	−0.8
Less hospital professional fees	1.0	1.5	2.0	2.4	2.8
Less government purchases	0.9	0.9	0.9	1.0	1.0
Osteopaths and laboratories	10.5	10.9	11.1	11.3	11.5
NHA less NIPA	8.7	11.1	10.4	5.0	5.6

teopaths and laboratories are differences of definition that will remain after the two series are benchmarked. Some of these differences in definition will be examined as the reconciliation project progresses. The NHA estimates of osteopaths and independently billing laboratories in physician services can be compared with the NIPA components of other professional services when the reconciliation of other professional services is prepared. The differences in taxable physicians receipts for 1995–96 result from the timing of revisions and should be substantially reduced after the regular annual NIPA revision in July 1998.

Other differences between the NHA and the NIPA also need to be investigated. The NIPA estimates of government expenditures for physician services need to be reconciled with the NHA estimates of government public health activity when that portion of the reconciliation is prepared. The differences due to the coverage adjustment in the NIPA should be examined to determine if a similar adjustment is appropriate in the NHA. Finally, any differences in source data should be examined to ensure consistency between the series after the next benchmark revisions.

Appendix
Treatment of Secondary Products

The section analyzing differences between the NIPA and NHA estimates of hospital services noted that one source of the difference was the definition of hospital services. In the NIPA, adjustments are made to the PCE estimates for private hospitals to exclude secondary production, or activities, by hospitals. The benchmark PCE estimates are from BEA's input-output (I-O) accounts and reflect the "redefinition" of secondary production in some industries to other industries. Redefinition results in the shift of outputs and their related inputs to the industries in which these activities are primary activities. In general, redefinitions are used only when the inputs related to the secondary activity are very different from those required for the industry's primary activity. For example, nursing home services would have a different mix of inputs (doctors, nurses, custodial staff, equipment) than hospital services.

For hospital services, the following secondary products are the major activities redefined, based on types of revenue/receipts data reported for private hospitals in the CSI: nursing home services, home health care services, meals and beverages (cafeterias), and merchandise sales and rentals. As shown in table 7A.1, redefinitions in 1992, based on the benchmark I-O tables and 1992 CSI, were about $4 billion. It should be noted that the redefinitions for nursing homes and home health care services affect only the commodity distribution of health expenditures in PCE, as the amounts redefined will be included in the NIPA data for nursing homes and so forth. For cafeterias, however, these receipts are included with the PCE category for food consumed away from home. (In the reconciliation project it was discovered that about $1 billion in similar receipts from sales of meals and beverages and other merchandise by government hospitals was not being redefined from receipts by hospitals to PCE for food consumed away from home.)

In the NHA, there are no redefinitions of secondary products reported in the AHA survey, and as noted earlier, this approach appears to account for a substantial part of the difference between the NHA and NIPA estimates of hospital services. For the 1996 accounts, the revenues for nursing home and home health services included in the estimates for hospital services were split out for the first time, as shown in table 7A.2.

Table 7A.1   **PCE Private Hospital Redefinitions by Type of Commodity, 1992 (billions of dollars)**

	Benchmark I-O Estimates
Total redefinitions	4.0
Nursing homes	1.1
Home health care	1.6
Cafeterias	1.2
Merchandise sales and rentals	0.1

Table 7A.2   **Expenditures for Nursing Home and Home Health Care Included in NHA Hospital Care (billions of dollars)**

	1992	1993	1994	1995	1996
Nursing homes	5.1	6.0	6.7	7.9	9.0
Home health	2.8	3.7	4.8	6.2	7.8
Total	7.9	9.7	11.6	14.1	16.8

The large differences between the PCE redefinitions and the NHA measures of hospital nursing home and home health services ($3.1 billion versus $7.9 billion in 1992) may reflect one or more of the following. The CSI hospital data may not have included the additional receipts because the hospitals filed separate nursing home or home health establishment reports in the Census. The NHA data are derived from Medicare expense reports and may reflect expenses not reported on the AHA reports, just as they might not have been included in the CSI reports. The differences may also reflect differences in the hospital establishments covered by the AHA data, the CSI data for hospitals, and the Medicare expense reports. Such coverage differences should be investigated and consistency between the reports improved.

Regardless of the explanation for the differences between the various estimates of secondary products noted above, HCFA should reexamine its classification concepts with regard to secondary production and whether receipts from sales of non-health-related goods and services should be included. BEA should reexamine the consistency of its use of redefinitions in both private and government hospitals. Both agencies also should look into related classification issues, such as emergency room services provided at freestanding treatment centers, which are now classified as physician services. Should they be redefined as hospital services? The classification of outpatient surgery at doctors' offices also should be examined.

References

American Hospital Association. Various years. *Hospital statistics.* Chicago: American Hospital Association.

Health Care Financing Administration. 1996. *NHE96.* Available at www.hcfa.gov.

Lazenby, H., K. Levit, D. Waldo, G. Adler, S. Letsch, and C. Cowan. 1992. National health accounts: Lessons from the U.S. experience. *Health Care Financing Review* 13 (4): 89–103.

Levit, K., H. C. Lazenby, B. R. Braden, C. A. Cowan, A. L. Sensenig, P. A. McDonnell, J. M. Stiller, D. K. Won, A. B. Martin, L. Sivarajan, C. S. Donham, A. M. Long, and M. W. Stewart. 1997. National health expenditures, 1996. *Health Care Financing Review,* 19 (1): 161–200.

Rice, D., B. Cooper, and R. Gibson. 1982. U.S. national health accounts: Historical perspectives, current issues, and future projections. In *La santé fait ses comptes (Accounting for Health),* ed. Emile Levy. Paris: Economica.

Seskin, E., and R. Parker. 1998. A guide to the NIPA's. *Survey of Current Business* 78 (3).

U.S. Department of Commerce. Bureau of Economic Analysis. 1988. *Government transactions.* BEA-MP-5, November. Washington, D.C.: U.S. Government Printing Office.

———. 1990. *Personal consumption expenditures.* BEA-MP-6, June. Washington, D.C.: U.S. Government Printing Office.

————. 1995. Preview of the comprehensive revision of the National Income and Product Accounts: Recognition of government investment and incorporation of a new methodology for calculating depreciation. *Survey of Current Business,* 75 (9).
————. 1997a. *Survey of Current Business,* table 2.4, 77 (8).
————. 1997b. *Survey of Current Business,* tables 3.16 and 3.17, 77 (10).
————. 1998. *National Income and Product Accounts of the United States, 1929–94.* Washington, D.C.: U.S. Government Printing Office.
U.S. Department of Labor. Bureau of Labor Statistics. 1997a. *Establishment data: Employment and earnings.* Washington, D.C.: U.S. Government Printing Office.
————. 1997b. Notes on current labor statistics: Price data. *Monthly Labor Review* 120 (1).

Comment   Haiden A. Huskamp

Estimates of health spending are used by health policy analysts, health economists, and health services researchers for a variety of purposes including tracking levels of health spending, identifying trends in spending over time, and estimating microsimulation models of the impact of policy changes on health expenditures. Analysts and researchers have easy access to estimates of health spending from both the National Health Accounts (NHA) and the National Income and Product Accounts (NIPA). Most policy analysts and researchers turn first to the NHA due to greater familiarity with the NHA estimates, although the NIPA estimates are sometimes available earlier and could be useful for answering some of their questions.

The methodology behind the NHA and NIPA estimates and the fine distinctions between the accounts are not clear to some of the analysts and researchers who use them. One set of estimates may be more appropriate for a particular question, so it is important for analysts and researchers to understand how the NHA and NIPA differ. This paper lays out the differences very clearly to help users of the accounts make better choices and to understand the implications of their choice for their analysis. In this paper, the authors take the two largest categories of health spending, physician and hospital spending, and describe in detail how the NHA and NIPA estimates for these spending categories were constructed. For each set of accounts, the authors describe the philosophy or approach of the accounts, how the accounts define expenditures for these two categories, the data used, and the adjustments made to the data.

A couple of years ago Joe Newhouse and I looked at the correlation between the annual NHA and NIPA estimates of total real per capita

Haiden A. Huskamp is assistant professor of health economics in the Department of Health Care Policy at Harvard Medical School.

spending for the period 1975–1993. We found the estimates to be quite similar: The correlation was 0.99. However, when one moves a level below total health spending and looks at components of health spending, such as hospital or physician expenditures, the differences between the NHA and NIPA estimates can be larger due to different estimation approaches for the two accounts. For example, for the period 1992–96, the difference between the NHA and NIPA estimates of annual physician spending was as high as 6 percent in a given year.

If one focuses on the estimates of hospital spending, the biggest difference between the NHA and the NIPA seems to be the treatment of nonprofit hospitals. The NHA use revenue of nonprofit hospitals as the measure of spending associated with these facilities and include as revenue all nonoperating income such as contributions, investment income, and contract research. The NHA also include as nonprofit hospital spending revenue from secondary products such as cafeteria products, merchandise sales and rentals, home health services, nursing home services, home health clubs, and wellness center services. On the other hand, the NIPA use a more narrow definition of hospital spending. The NIPA reclassify secondary services produced by hospitals into other nonhospital categories and use current operating expenditures as the measure of spending for nonprofit hospitals. The NIPA use this approach because the NIPA consider nonprofit hospitals to be nonmarket producers since receipts do not usually cover operating expenses and nonprofit hospitals rely to some extent on investment income from endowments, contributions, and other sources. As a result of these differences in definition and measurement used by the two sets of accounts, one would get a very different picture of nonprofit hospital spending if using the NHA versus the NIPA.

Changes in the behavior of nonprofit hospitals in recent years highlight the differences in methodology between the two accounts. In the past, charitable contributions and direct public appropriations were an important component of nonprofit hospital revenue. In recent years, there has been some evidence that nonprofit hospitals have begun behaving like for-profit hospitals in response to increasing competitive pressure in the market. Work by Frank and Salkever (2000) and by Sloan et al. (1990) has suggested that charitable contributions have declined as a proportion of revenue and that many nonprofit hospitals are looking beyond traditional inpatient services for other revenue producers. Many nonprofit hospitals are setting up for-profit subsidiaries and expanding into less traditional services like home health, wellness centers, health clubs, and other products. Also, a number of nonprofit hospitals are carrying large fund balances and earning a great deal of money by investing those balances.

How these changes in nonprofit hospital behavior would be reflected in the two sets of accounts has implications for which set of accounts an analyst would select to answer a particular question. For example, returns on fund balances, which are not something that one would normally consider hospital "output," would appear as revenue (and thus as hospital expenditure or output) in the NHA. As a result, the NIPA might be a better source if one wished to look at productivity or output. The NHA would capture most revenue for nontraditional product lines while the NIPA would not. Consequently, the NHA might be a better source if one were interested in revenue streams for nonprofit hospitals or a broader look at nonprofit hospital activity.

This example of the differences in the estimates of nonprofit hospital spending highlights the importance of thinking carefully about the question one needs to answer and which set of accounts is best structured to answer that question. To do this, one needs to be clear about the differences in methodologies used by the NHA and NIPA. This paper does an excellent job at explaining these differences.

This paper is part of a larger and very important effort by the Bureau of Economic Analysis (BEA) and the Health Care Financing Administration (HCFA) to reconcile and improve the NHA and the NIPA. I would encourage the BEA and the HCFA to think about how to disseminate this information to policy analysts and researchers to make the accounts more user-friendly. I would also encourage the publication of side-by-side annual reconciliations of these two accounts if possible.

References

Frank, R. G., and D. S. Salkever. 2000. Market forces, diversification of activity, and the mission of non-profit hospitals. In *The changing hospital industry: Comparing not-for-profit and for-profit institutions,* ed. D. Cutler. Chicago: University of Chicago Press.

Sloan, F. A., T. Hoerger, M. Morissey, and A. Hassan. 1990. The demise of hospital philanthropy. *Economic Inquiry* 28 (4): 725–43.

III

Recent Developments

8

Pricing Heart Attack Treatments

David M. Cutler, Mark McClellan,
Joseph P. Newhouse, and Dahlia Remler

Price index measurement, traditionally perceived as a relatively narrow and dry topic, has reached such a level of policy interest as to be mentioned regularly in *New York Times* articles and Federal Reserve Board Chairmen's speeches. Indeed, there was a special blue-ribbon commission devoted just to evaluating the Consumer Price Index (Advisory Commission on the Consumer Price Index 1996).

Price index measurement is central to appropriate public and private decision making. One common use of price indexes, for example, is to update payments for inflation. By law, Social Security benefits move in line with the overall Consumer Price Index, and cash wages in the private sector generally do informally. Price indexes are also a key item in setting monetary and fiscal policy. Finally, price indexes are used to make productivity estimates. For many goods, the most accurate measurement of real output is found by dividing increases in nominal output by increases in inflation.

For all of these reasons, it is important that price indexes be measured accurately. A substantial literature suggests that they frequently are not.

David M. Cutler is professor of economics at Harvard University and a research associate of the National Bureau of Economic Research. Mark McClellan is associate professor of economics and medicine at Stanford University and a research associate of the National Bureau of Economic Research. Joseph P. Newhouse is the John D. MacArthur Professor of Health Policy and Management and is on the faculties of the Kennedy School of Government, the Harvard Medical School, the Harvard School of Public Health, and the Faculty of Arts and Sciences at Harvard University, and a research associate of the National Bureau of Economic Research. Dahlia Remler is assistant professor in the Division of Health Policy and Management of the Joseph L. Mailman School of Public Health at Columbia University.

The authors are grateful to the Bureau of Economic Analysis, the Bureau of Labor Statistics, Eli Lilly and Company, the National Institute on Aging, and the Alfred P. Sloan Foundation for research support.

This is especially true about price indexes for services, and in particular, price indexes for medical care (Armknecht and Ginsburg 1992; Griliches 1992; Newhouse 1989; Ford and Sturm 1988). In its recent review of the Consumer Price Index (CPI), for example, the Advisory Commission to Study the Consumer Price Index concluded that "The medical care category may be the location of substantial quality change bias at a rate as rapid or more rapid than in [other goods]" (1996, 57) and suggested that the medical care price index could be overstated by 3 percentage points annually. In a response to the Advisory Commission Report, Brent Moulton and Karin Moses (1997) agreed that there are problems in measuring the medical care CPI: "Without necessarily endorsing the advisory commission's estimate of bias, we agree that BLS methods are not likely to capture fully the quality improvements that have occurred in medical services. Adjusting for quality change in this component is the most challenging in the index" (321).

In this chapter, we estimate price indexes for medical care, demonstrating the techniques that are currently used in medical care price index measurement and some alternatives that might be used. We begin by describing several conceptual issues related to medical care price indexes. We then treat formally two types of medical care price indexes, a service price index (SPI) and a cost-of-living (COL) index. A key practical problem in estimating both types of indexes is measurement: List prices ("charges") and harder-to-measure transaction prices have diverged increasingly, the development of new or modified medical treatments complicates the comparison of "like" goods over time, and determining the effects of medical treatment on important health outcomes is confounded by many intervening factors. We describe methods to address these obstacles.

Our presentation builds on our prior work on heart attacks (Cutler et al. 1998), which showed that carefully accounting for the development of new medical services substantially reduces an SPI, and that a COL index for heart attacks has increased more slowly than the economy-wide GDP deflator in recent years. However, the only health outcome examined in that study was mortality, and our study included inpatient expenditure data only through 1991. Mortality is an important outcome for heart attack care, and it is also relatively easy to measure. But much medical treatment, including that of heart attacks, is directed at the quality of life, rather than simply life itself. In this paper, we review the results for heart attack price indexes and extend them to include quality of life and more recent time periods.

8.1   Inflation Rates and Benefit Payment Updates

Before presenting estimates of price indexes, we remark on an important issue: As we noted, benefit payments are typically updated at the rate of inflation, but there is no reason why this need be the case. Indeed, the medical care context provides a particular example of why this might not be good policy.

Consider a relatively common medical care example: Suppose that as a result of technological advances in medical treatments, medical costs increase but survival increases even more. What happens to medical care inflation? Economics has a very specific view of inflation: The inflation rate is the increase in the amount of money consumers need to be just as well off as they were previously. Because people value living longer more than living less long, people may be better off than they used to be (assuming the increase in longevity is great enough), and thus inflation might fall.

But this does not imply that Social Security benefits should fall. After all, the elderly will live longer; don't they need more total resources? And aren't their out-of-pocket payments for medical care likely to rise? In this situation, one may want to index benefit programs at a rate separate from the overall inflation rate. If the elderly did not have a chance to save for the increased lifespan, perhaps society should insure them against unforeseen reductions in material resources (even if they involve overall increases in utility).

Indeed, politically sensitive distributional issues become central to this question. For example, many people think that medical care is a "right," not a "good," and therefore the government should make sure that people can afford the current "technological standard" at the same out-of-pocket cost over time. In this case, the medical care inflation rate will be irrelevant for updating Social Security benefits or the government contribution toward Medicare; rather, the update factor might be the actual rate of increase in private medical care spending adjusted for any age-specific items. Others (e.g., supporters of "voucher"-like programs for Medicare) think that the government contribution toward Medicare should rise at a relatively fixed rate. In this case, beneficiaries are not fully insured against increases in Medicare costs, on the argument that sharing some of the growth in costs as well as benefits of medical care will improve the efficiency of the health care system.

Thus, while we focus in this chapter on measuring medical care inflation, we are *not* answering the broader question about how social programs should be indexed to changes in medical costs.

8.2 Medical Care Price Indexes: Conceptual Issues

Constructing medical care price indexes poses several difficult challenges. The first problem is measuring the industry's product. The goods produced by medical providers are a complex array of personal interactions and diagnostic tests, which lead to insights about the nature of a patient's health problem and are typically followed by a range of treatments including drugs, procedures, devices, and counseling that may or may not affect the course of a particular individual's illness. These goods are not only difficult to measure precisely, they often differ from case to case. For example, physician time spent chatting with a mildly ill patient is different from time spent diagnosing problems in a more severely ill patient. Ideally, a price index should find some way to differentiate among these different goods.

The measurement of the industry's products is complicated by the fact that multiple bases of payment exist in the market. In traditional fee-for-service billing, prices exist for over seven thousand particular physician services, such as brief hospital visit or interpretation of an x-ray. But today transaction prices are frequently based on a more aggregated bundle of services, such as an all-inclusive payment for a bypass surgery operation, or even a single capitated payment for all treatments for all medical problems during a period of time.

Second, those services are not only difficult to measure, but they change rapidly over time as new goods appear and old goods change rapidly in quality and nature. For example, the features of a cardiac catheter, such as size and maneuverability, may change over time, so that catheter use in the base period and catheter use in the current period are different procedures.

Third, even when comparable goods can be found, their mix in a typical bundle changes rapidly. Consequently, price indexes are very sensitive to sampling frequency and reweighting, as in any market in which the goods consumed change rapidly.

Fourth, consumers rarely pay the entire cost of medical care out of pocket. Most of the payment is typically made by an insurer, public or private. Ultimately, however, consumers must bear the cost of medical care, through higher individually paid premiums, lower wages, higher product prices, or increased taxes. Therefore, while the official CPI only measures out-of-pocket expenses, we choose to allocate all of the costs of medical care to consumers in forming price indexes.[1]

The most fundamental measurement problem in constructing a medical care price index, however, is that to a first approximation consumers value the expected effect of medical care services on their health and not the medical care services themselves. Ideally, therefore, the output of medical care would be measured in units of expected health improvement. This is true for the consumption value of any product—consumers do not value an orange per se, but value the visual, taste, and nutritional consequences of its consumption. Medical care is a particularly difficult case, however, because the expected health output is difficult to measure and may change dramatically over time as medical technology advances, whereas the visual, taste, and nutritional aspects of an orange are reasonably stable.

We illustrate these issues through the development of two price indexes

---

1. Nordhaus (1996) discusses the need to consider indirect costs for nonmarket goods.

for medical care. The first index is a service price index, which prices the physical output of the medical sector. The current Consumer Price Index and Producer Price Index for medical care are conceptually most similar to the service price index, but the similarity is not exact. The second index is a cost-of-living index, which prices the health improvement that consumers receive from medical care. The cost-of-living index is a more radical departure from current medical care price indexes.

8.2.1   Service Price Indexes

Frequently, price indexes are not derived from a welfare-based concept, but rather come from calculating the amount of money required to purchase a particular bundle of goods at different points in time (Getzen 1992). In the medical care context this kind of index, which we term a *service price index* (SPI), is the price of a representative bundle of medical services (and/or goods) over time. We use the term service price index to reflect the focus on medical care services rather than patient welfare and use the term cost-of-living index to refer to the latter.

To form an SPI, we consider a vector of all possible medical treatments, denoted m. A typical set of treatments in period t_0 is denoted $m(t_0)$. The Laspeyres SPI is the relative cost of this fixed set of treatments over time:

$$(1) \qquad \text{SPI}_{t_0, t_1} \ = \ \frac{p(t_1) \cdot m(t_0)}{p(t_0) \cdot m(t_0)} \ = \ \alpha \cdot \frac{p(t_1)}{p(t_0)},$$

where $p(t)$ is the vector of prices for all the medical treatments in period t and α is the vector of the share of each service in total costs in the base period.

There are many potential SPIs, depending on the bundle of services chosen as the market basket (i.e., the specific values of $m(t_0)$) and the frequency with which the basket of goods is resampled (i.e., how frequently α is updated). In particular, the goods and services in the market basket that is priced may differ, and a given bundle of goods and services may be priced more or less frequently (e.g., annually, monthly).

A key question in forming a price index for medical care or anything else is the definition of the market basket being priced—what are the possible elements of $m(t_0)$? In most cases the unit in which the good is usually priced will dictate the degree of aggregation that is used in the different elements; for example, one would normally price one man's haircut.

As already noted, however, medical care presents numerous examples in which the same service has multiple bases of price. In the case of heart attack treatment, which we review extensively below, the pricing may be at a very disaggregated service level, for example, a charge for each day in the hospital, time in the operating room, and even each aspirin tablet. Or the price may be at a more aggregated level, for example, one price for the entire hospital stay.

Disaggregated Service Price Index

Traditionally the official medical care price indexes were highly disaggregated; they priced, for example, the daily cost of a semiprivate room and the cost of operating room time. Price indexes were formed in this way because this is how payment worked; essentially all payers paid on a fee-for-service (or discounted fee-for-service) basis. Although this had the appearance, at least, of a constant market basket, if there was a change in the methods of treating a given medical problem—for example, a substitution of home care for hospital days—the resulting price index could be misleading as an indicator of the cost of treating the illness.

Aggregated Service Price Index

The *aggregated* service price index is analogous to the disaggregated index except that the goods being priced, $m(t_0)$, are more aggregated. In the heart attack example, instead of pricing each day and each tablet of aspirin, the market basket consists of various treatment regimens, such as a bypass operation. We will describe these treatments in greater detail below. For now, we remark that the aggregate price index is more like pricing the automobile rather than the tires, brakes, headlights, engine, windshield, and so on.

8.2.2   Cost-of-Living Index

Although service price indexes are the method used by the official price indexes in the United States and elsewhere, they do not have an obvious utility interpretation. In particular, if the quality of a good increases—that is, if the same number of units of the good produces greater utility—the SPI will not make any adjustment for this.[2] We suggest a second index to account for this, which we term the cost-of-living index.

To derive the cost-of-living index, suppose that consumers may have a series of diseases, indexed by d (one disease can consist of not being sick). Having disease d results in the receipt of medical care $m_d(t)$, a vector of constant-quality treatments. If a new procedure is developed or the ability to perform a given procedure gets better over time, this would be represented as an addition to the set of m_d. For the moment, we want to ignore the issue of how the magnitude of the elements of m_d are determined; it may be through markets, through an administrative mechanism, through the beliefs of doctors, or a combination of all of these factors. We return to this below. The expected welfare of a representative consumer i in any period t is

---

2. Although, as we discuss in section 8.6.2, the Consumer Price Index and Producer Price Index do attempt to capture changes in quality.

$$(2) \quad U_i(t) = \sum_{d=1}^{D} \pi_d(t) \cdot U_i\{H_i[d, m_t(t)], Y_i - p_i(t) \cdot m_d(t) - T_i(t)\},$$

where $\pi_d(t)$ is the probability that the person has disease d at time t; U is the consumer's expected utility; H is the health of the person, which depends on the disease and the expected effects of medical care received; Y_t is income (assumed to be constant over time); $p_i(t)$ is the vector of effective prices to person i of medical care at time t; and $T_i(t)$ is lump-sum payments (insurance premiums or taxes) for medical services. The expression $p \cdot m + T$ denotes spending on medical care, so that the second argument of the utility function is just the consumption of nonhealth goods.

We assume that medical services do not have independent consumption value, beyond their effect on health, and therefore do not include them directly in the utility function. While this assumption neglects the consumption value of medical care for nonhealth reasons, such as hotel-like features of hospitals and the "caring" role of the medical care process (Newhouse 1977; Fuchs 1993), it captures the predominant value of medical care.

For simplicity, our specification does not capture some interactions between current medical services and future utility. For example, elderly people whose life is prolonged but who are left partially disabled may suffer increased risk of future uninsured nursing home expense. The utility cost of this risk should be counted as a cost of current medical care consumption, just as the longer life is a benefit. However, we do discount future health benefits and costs to current dollars.

We wish to focus on the effects of changing technology and prices over time and not on the effects of individuals' aging. Therefore, we abstract from the medical and economic effects of aging and implicitly analyze consumers with a constant age and income over time. Thus, we compare 65-year-olds in 1980 with 65-year-olds in 1990.

Consumer welfare may also change over time due to changes in disease incidence (Barzel 1968). Entirely new diseases such as AIDS may be added to the set of possible illnesses, and other diseases such as smallpox may be eliminated. Changes in lifestyles may change the incidence of a given set of diseases. For example, better diet, reduced smoking, and increased exercise have lowered the incidence of heart disease over time. We also abstract from these effects by estimating price indexes for a single disease. It is conceptually straightforward to apply similar methods to other diseases, and to reconstruct an aggregate price index from the specific illnesses. With a single disease, welfare is given by

$$(2') \qquad U(t) = U\{H[m(t)], Y - p(t) \cdot m(t) - T(t)\}.$$

With these assumptions, welfare changes are only a function of changes in medical treatments, their expected health effects, and payment over time. The question we pose is, How do these practice and payment changes affect the price of the medical services industry's product?

Following the literature on true cost of living indexes (Fisher and Shell 1972), we define the *cost-of-living index* as the amount consumers would be willing to pay (or would have to be compensated) to have today's medical care and today's prices, when the alternative is base period medical care and base period prices. The change in the COL index between t_0 and t_1, denoted C, is the amount of compensation required to equalize utility in those two states. It is implicitly defined from[3]

$$(3) \quad U\{H[m(t_1)], Y - p(t_1) \cdot m(t_1) - T(t_1) - C\}$$
$$= U\{H[m(t_0)], Y - p(t_0) \cdot m(t_0) - T(t_0)\}.$$

Taking a Taylor series expansion around t_0,[4] using x to represent consumption, and rearranging terms, we obtain

$$(4) \qquad\qquad C = \frac{U_H H_m}{U_x} dm - d(p \cdot m + T).$$

The first term on the right-hand side of equation (4) is the health benefit of changes in medical care, expressed in dollars, exactly the same concept as the benefit in a cost-benefit analysis. The second term is the change in the cost of medical care, the same concept as the cost in a cost-benefit analysis. If C is positive, the consumer is better off in period t_1 than he was in period t_0 and conversely.

The Laspeyres COL index between period t_0 and period t_1 is just the index of changes in C scaled by initial income[5]

3. Fisher and Shell (1972) define the cost-of-living index in terms of expenditure functions. The income required to reach utility U over time is $COL = e(U, p_1)/e(U, p_0)$. This formulation is based on optimizing behavior. As discussed, medical care may *not* be chosen at the optimal level; excessive resources may be devoted to medical care due to insurance and market failures. When the level of medical care is chosen optimally, $COL = 1 - [e(U, p_0) - e(U, p_1)/e(U, p_0) = 1 - C/Y_0$, and the two forms are equivalent. When the level of medical care is not chosen optimally, equation (3) still represents a valid definition for the COL index, although its interpretation is somewhat different. In this case, the COL index still represents the change in income needed to keep people equally well off but under the constraint that medical care is allocated in the manner that it is actually allocated. Intuitively, we cannot use the machinery of optimization, such as expenditure functions. However, we can measure the extent to which people are better or worse off.

4. This is a first-order expansion which neglects the higher-order terms. For major technological innovations involving major changes in health outcomes and medical care expenditures, higher-order terms could be important. Qualitatively, such higher-order terms depend on various curvatures of the utility function and the health production function. Nonetheless, the first-order terms capture the direct important welfare effects of medical care: the improvement in health and the loss of other goods.

5. The cost-of-living index can be formed using chain weights or other intertemporal aggregation methods.

(5)
$$COL_{t_0, t_1} = 1 - \frac{C}{Y_0}.$$

It is important to note that the cost portion of the COL index is the change in the *total cost* of care, not the change in an SPI (i.e., $p \cdot m + T$, not p). If consumers care only about health output, it is the total cost of treatment and its expected consequences for health that matter.

Because the COL index is a utility-based concept, the key question in implementing a COL index is what to assume about the relation between value and cost. In most markets, a reasonable assumption is that the marginal consumer's marginal valuation of the good equals its cost. Thus, we can link costs and value by observing how much consumers are willing to pay for the particular components in a bundled product. Indeed, this is the foundation of hedonic analysis (Griliches 1971). In medical care markets, however, this is not a tenable assumption. When medical care decisions are made by patients who are insured at the margin or by health care providers whose interests may not coincide with those of the patient, there is no presumption that the marginal value of care equals its social cost. Thus, we cannot a priori use hedonic analysis to measure changes in the COL index.

A second approach is to specify a model for how consumption decisions are made. Then, using the observed path of consumption and spending, one could infer the change in the COL index. Fisher and Griliches (1995) and Griliches and Cockburn (1994) take this approach for generic drugs. However, many complex medical treatment decisions may be involved even in the treatment of a single health problem, and there is no generally accepted model for how such decisions are made. Therefore, we do not pursue this approach.

A third approach is to use direct evidence on the expected value of medical care in improving health. Then the COL index can be calculated using the measured cost and value differences directly. This is the approach we pursue here.

8.3 Heart Attacks: Brief Medical Background

A heart attack (acute myocardial infarction or AMI) is a sudden death of the heart muscle, which impairs the heart's function in pumping blood through the body. The attack may be caused by lack of blood supply to the heart because of a blockage (occlusion) of the coronary arteries supplying blood to the heart. The location of the occlusion, as well as of other narrowings in the coronary arteries that create an elevated risk of further heart damage, can be determined by a diagnostic imaging procedure, cardiac catheterization. This procedure shows the degree of impairment of flow in the various coronary arteries supplying blood to the heart.

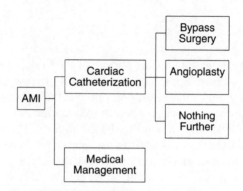

Fig. 8.1   Treatment of patients with a heart attack

If the catheterization shows that the blood supply is sufficiently impaired, and if the expected clinical benefits are high enough, one of two revascularization procedures may be performed to improve the blood supply to the heart and prevent further damage (i.e., subsequent AMIs): coronary artery bypass graft (CABG) or percutaneous transluminal coronary angioplasty (PTCA). A CABG splices a piece of vein or artery taken from some other part of the body around the portion of the artery that is blocked. An angioplasty threads a balloon-like material into the artery and expands it, thereby opening the artery for the flow of blood.

If revascularization is not performed, the patient will be managed with drugs, counseling, and further monitoring, which we term medical management. These options are diagrammed in figure 8.1. Although there are many other critical decisions in the treatment of AMI, we focus on the four treatment paths shown in figure 8.1: medical management and no catheterization, catheterization and no revascularization, a bypass operation, and angioplasty.

8.4   The Data

Data to analyze medical care prices are particularly difficult to acquire, because one cannot just ask patients what procedures they had and how much they cost. The prevalence of insurance means that patients often do not know this information. Thus, medical care price data must come from providers, insurers, or both, each of which has particular complications. Added to this is the reticence of many providers (and insurers) to indicate how much they are receiving (or paying) for particular types of care. Further, the cost-of-living index requires data on medical outcomes, which are also difficult to obtain.

We use two sources of data in our empirical work. The first is a complete set of billable services, list prices (charges), demographic information, and discharge abstracts for all heart attack patients admitted to a major teaching hospital (MTH) between 1983 and 1994. The hospital that provided the data asked not to be named explicitly. The second data source is national data on everyone in the Medicare population with a heart attack between 1984 and 1994.[6] Because Medicare covers essentially all of the elderly, and since two-thirds of heart attacks occur in the elderly, Medicare data can provide a relatively comprehensive picture of the cost and outcomes of heart attacks in the elderly population.

Each of the data sets has advantages and disadvantages. The advantage of the MTH data is that we have the complete records from the hospital admissions; we know all the particular items that were given to the patient (often numbering in the hundreds). Because Medicare does not pay on a fee-for-service basis, the details of many services provided are not recorded by Medicare. All that is known reliably is the major treatments provided (catheterization, bypass surgery, and angioplasty). The advantages of the Medicare data are that the samples are larger, and they contain reimbursement information. For confidentiality reasons, MTH would not give us data on transactions prices for each patient—only list prices. In addition, the Medicare data can be linked to Social Security death records, which we have done, allowing us to record this important outcome for the Medicare population. We do not have information on out-of-hospital outcomes for patients at MTH.

We created the sample of all patients with a new heart attack by identifying all claims with a primary diagnosis of heart attack (ICD-9 code 410), other than rule-out codes.[7] Heart attacks are a severe diagnosis, and essentially everyone with a heart attack who survives the immediate attack and thus receives any treatment will be admitted to a hospital; it is thus natural to start with the initial hospitalization. We also exclude readmissions for a previous heart attack in each data set. In the MTH data, we restrict the sample to those patients for whom the observed heart attack was their first treated at this hospital. In the Medicare sample, we choose patients who had not been hospitalized with a heart attack in the year preceding the admission of interest.

Treatments for a heart attack may extend over several weeks or months. For example, physicians may delay a cardiac catheterization or revascularization procedure to see if the patient's heart muscle improves without these interventions. Indeed, there have been changes in the timing of these

---

6. In our earlier paper, we were only able to extend the data through 1991. This paper thus offers substantially more evidence on the price of heart attack care.

7. Some patients are admitted to a hospital to rule out a heart attack. Generally, these patients do not have a diagnosis of acute myocardial infarction (instead, unstable angina is the typical diagnosis). However, we also excluded patients admitted with a diagnosis of AMI for less than three days, counting transfers, who were discharged alive, as such short lengths of stay would be extraordinary for a true elderly AMI patient.

procedures over time in the United States, with more of them being performed sooner after the heart attack occurs. To adjust for this, we define the "heart attack treatment episode" as all medical care provided in the ninety days beginning with the initial heart attack admission. We choose a ninety-day window because past analyses have suggested that this time period is adequate to capture essentially all of the initial treatments without including a large share of treatments for heart attack complications (McClellan, McNeil, and Newhouse 1994).

The Medicare data are available for the fee-for-service program only. Managed care organizations participating in Medicare have generally not submitted reliable utilization information to the government, and thus we exclude these people. For most of our time period, managed care enrollment was a small part of Medicare (less than 10 percent), so this omission is unlikely to have important effects on our results. In future years, however, this problem could become increasingly important if steps are not taken to improve data reporting by managed care plans.[8]

Table 8.1 shows the sample sizes for the two data sets. The MTH data have about 300 heart attacks annually.[9] The Medicare data have about 225,000 heart attacks annually. This number is relatively stable, even with the nearly 2 percent growth in Medicare enrollees annually, implying that heart attack incidence rates are falling.

The next columns of the table show the age and sex mix of people with a heart attack. The heart attack population is increasingly older over time. In 1984, 49 percent of heart attacks were in people aged 65–74; by 1994, this was down to 45 percent. The increased age of heart attack sufferers reflects both the increased age of Medicare enrollees in general and the fact that younger people are taking better care of themselves over time (better diet and exercise) so that heart attack rates are falling in the younger elderly. Slightly over half the heart attack population is male.

Medicare records indicate the amount of money Medicare paid the hospital for the care. We add up reimbursement in the year after the heart attack to form transactions prices. We use a one-year period to capture any related heart attack spending not picked up in the ninety-day period.

Measuring prices in the MTH data is more difficult. To facilitate exposition, a discussion of hospital accounting may be helpful. All hospitals have list prices or "charges" for very disaggregated services, such as minutes of operating room time or specific drugs. Until recently, the official price indexes for medical care, including hospital care, were based entirely on

8. The Balanced Budget Act requires Medicare managed care plans to submit complete encounter data in future years. However, it is not yet clear how soon this requirement will be implemented effectively.

9. We do not know if the patient had an earlier heart attack elsewhere. However, we do know if they were transferred to MTH from another hospital. We have experimented with restricting the sample to nontransfers, without important effect on the results.

Table 8.1   **Characteristics of the Medicare Population with Heart Attacks**

Year	MTH Data (1983–94) Number of Heart Attacks	Medicare Data (1984–94) Number of Heart Attacks	Age Distribution (%) 65–74	75–84	85+	Percent Male
1983	156	—	—	—	—	—
1984	209	233,284	49	39	12	51
1985	205	233,886	48	39	13	51
1986	222	223,573	48	39	14	51
1987	242	227,894	47	39	14	50
1988	214	223,178	46	39	14	50
1989	206	218,052	46	40	15	50
1990	309	220,643	46	40	15	50
1991	365	235,827	46	39	15	51
1992	471	240,573	46	39	15	51
1993	566	175,985	46	39	15	52
1994	477	238,480	45	39	16	51

Source: Data are from MTH and the Medicare program.

these charges. At MTH, these are the data we were provided, and we use them to mimic the historical Bureau of Labor Statistics (BLS) methods.[10] But increasingly many payers do not pay list price. For example, Medicare and Medicaid pay hospitals an administered price; many Blue Cross plans receive discounts off charges, and managed care organizations often negotiate prices for broader groups of care, such as an all-inclusive per diem amount or an amount per admission. To approximate actual transactions prices, we use more accounting information. Profits for most hospitals—particularly not-for-profit major teaching hospitals, of which MTH is one—are close to zero (Prospective Payment Assessment Commission 1996). Thus, average accounting costs will roughly equal average reimbursement. We therefore form a measure of average treatment "costs" for heart attack patients, which we use as a proxy for average transactions prices. Average treatment costs are formed by multiplying charges by the hospital- and department-specific "cost-to-charge" ratios. These ratios, provided to Medicare by the hospital, are used for certain Medicare billing purposes and are believed to be accurate.[11]

10. Transaction prices are not available for private payers for privacy reasons. Partly for this reason the BLS historically used list prices in the actual CPI.
11. For ancillary departments such as laboratory or pharmacy the method multiplies charges that arise from that department (such as blood chemistry) by an overall department cost-to-charge ratio. Costs of room and board services (mainly nurses' salaries) are computed directly and converted to an average daily rate. Overhead costs are allocated in a prescribed fashion for each department. Our method of deflating charges is fairly common in the literature (Newhouse, Cretin, and Witsberger 1989).

Throughout the paper all medical care inflation figures are the excess over general inflation. To measure general inflation we chose the GDP deflator, rather than the personal consumption expenditure deflator, in order to reflect opportunity cost in the overall economy. Use of another general inflation measure would, however, not substantively affect our results. All dollar figures are in 1991 dollars.

8.5   Changes in the Treatment of AMI

We begin with some basic descriptive information on changes in the treatment of AMI over time. Figure 8.2 shows the real cost of treating an AMI between 1984 and 1994. Treatment costs are based on the Medicare data. The cost of a heart attack increased from $11,500 in 1984 to over $18,000 in 1994, a 4.6 percent annual increase. Cost increases have been particularly rapid since 1990.

Table 8.2 shows more detail about the price of particular treatment regimens. We group all heart attack patients into four treatment regimens: people whose heart attack was medically managed; people who received cardiac catheterization but no revascularization procedure; people who received bypass surgery; and people who received angioplasty. The first rows of the table show the average cost of each treatment regimen in the Medicare data (the first columns) and the MTH data (the second columns).

Price changes within treatment regimens are relatively minor. In the

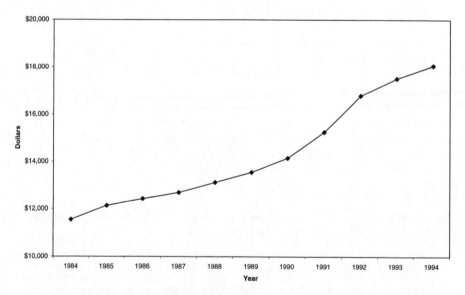

Fig. 8.2   **Real cost of AMI treatment**

Table 8.2   Share of Patients and Expenditures for Treatment Regimens

Treatment Regimen	Medicare Sample			MTH Sample		
	1984 ($)	1994 ($)	Change[a] (%)	1983–85 ($)	1992–94 ($)	Change[a] (%)
	Average cost of treatment regimen					
Medical management	10,155	13,190	2.6	13,900	11,769	−1.8
Catheterization only	15,887	15,673	−0.1	15,290	15,105	−0.1
Angioplasty	26,661	19,309	−3.2	16,124	18,441	1.5
Bypass surgery	29,176	36,564	2.3	37,437	50,874	3.4
	Share of patients receiving treatment regimen (%)					
Medical management	89	53	−3.6	65	23	−4.7
Catheterization only	6	16	1.0	20	21	0.1
Angioplasty	1	17	1.6	3	30	3.0
Bypass surgery	5	15	1.0	11	27	1.8

Note: Costs are in 1991 dollars, adjusted using the GDP deflator.

[a]Change is annual percentage points for treatment shares and annual percent for costs.

Medicare data, prices for medical management and bypass surgery rose in real terms, but the annual increases are small. The price of catheterization and angioplasty fell substantially—by 0.2 to 3.6 percent, respectively. In each case, the reduction in reimbursement was by design. In 1984, angioplasty was new and was perceived to be expensive. It was thus placed in a relatively highly reimbursed category. As the procedure spread and Medicare officials learned that it was less expensive than previously thought, angioplasty was moved to a less expensive reimbursement category. Payments for cardiac catheterization only fell as more catheterizations were done in the initial hospital visit or on the same admission as more expensive revascularization procedures. In the MTH data, costs of medical management and cardiac catheterization fell in real terms, while angioplasty and bypass surgery rose. Only the bypass surgery increase was large, however, and we suspect that some of this reflects changing patient demographics into and out of MTH over time. It is clear from both the Medicare and MTH data, however, that price increases do not explain the growth of heart attack spending.

The next rows show the change in the utilization of these procedures over time. AMI treatment changed markedly during the period of our study. In both samples, the use of the two invasive procedures rose substantially. In the mid-1980s only about 10 percent of elderly heart attack patients received at least one of the three major procedures (35 percent at MTH, including nonelderly). By the mid-1990s, nearly half of elderly heart attack patients received one (75 percent at MTH). MTH is more intensive than the average hospital (as expected), but the trends at MTH are similar to those for the nation as a whole.

As an accounting matter, the increase in treatment intensity is the predominant factor in explaining the growth of medical spending. We make this formal with an accounting identity. The average cost of treating a heart attack is the sum over treatment regimens of the share of patients receiving each treatment times the average cost of that treatment, or

(6) $$AC = \sum_t q_t p_t.$$

To a first approximation, then, the change in treatment costs[12] is given by

(7) $$\Delta(AC) = \sum_t \Delta q_t p_0 + q_0 \Delta p_t.$$

Table 8.3 shows the amount of the increase in treatment costs that can be explained by price changes and quantity changes. The table shows that a large share of the increase in spending is a result of changes in the type of treatments patients are receiving; a much smaller share is a result of

12. This is an approximation because it ignores the covariance term.

Table 8.3   **Decomposition of the Growth of Heart Attack Spending**

Measure	Medicare	MTH
Increase in average cost ($)	6,515	8,452
Increase resulting from price changes ($)	2,977	125
	[46%]	[2%]
Increase resulting from quantity changes ($)	5,109	4,658
	[78%]	[55%]

Note: Based on table 8.2. Numbers in brackets are the share of the total increase that can be explained by that factor. Percents do not add to 100 percent because of covariance term.

increases in the cost of a given treatment regimen. In the Medicare data, for example, 78 percent of cost increases result from increasing intensity of treatments. The price component is relatively large as well (46 percent), but this is somewhat deceptive; angioplasty, which was essentially nonexistent in 1984, fell in price substantially over this period while bypass surgery, which was much more common, rose in price. If we use 1991 quantity weights instead of 1984 quantity weights, the component of cost increases resulting from price increases would be less than half as large.

The MTH data suggest that only 2 percent of spending increases result from cost increases. Increases in the intensity of treatment, in contrast, explain over half of the increased cost of heart attack care.

These results presage our later result that if conventional price indexes used the treatment regimen approach they would not find a substantial increase in medical spending over time. This finding also highlights the importance of quality adjustment. Doctors are providing these additional high-tech services at least in part because they believe them to be valuable—they increase survival or reduce morbidity. To form an accurate price index, we need to value these changes in quality.

8.6 Service Price Indexes

8.6.1 Disaggregated Service Price Indexes

Prior to 1997, the official CPI for medical care was based on disaggregated service prices (Cardenas 1996).[13] The goods priced and the hospitals in the sample were kept constant, if possible, for five years, at which time both hospitals and goods were resampled. Figure 8.3 shows the real medical care CPI from 1983 to 1994 (when this method was followed), and table 8.4 shows mean growth rates. Over this time period the real medical care CPI rose 3.4 percent annually. The real hospital component of the CPI increased even more rapidly, 6.2 percent annually.

13. The PPI for medical care used aggregated service prices beginning in 1993.

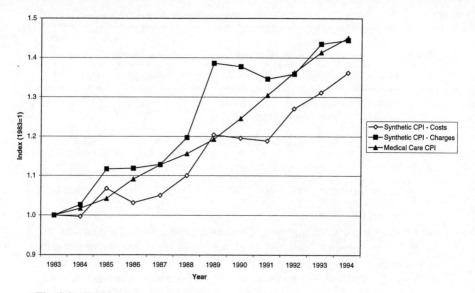

Fig. 8.3   Real consumer price indexes

Table 8.4   Summary of Price Indexes

Index	Real Annual Change (%)
Service price indexes	
Disaggregated service price indexes	
Official medical care CPI	3.4
Hospital component	6.2
Room	6.0
Other inpatient services	5.7
Synthetic CPI for MTH—charges	3.3
Synthetic CPI for MTH—costs	2.4
Heart attack episode—disaggregated price index	
Fixed basket index	2.8
Five-year chain index	2.1
Annual chain index	0.7
Aggregated service price indexes (Medicare/MTH)	
Fixed basket index	2.3/−1.3
Annual chain index	1.7/0.4
Cost of living index	
Years of life	−1.5
	[−0.2, −13.7]
Quality of life	−1.7
	[−0.3, −16.8]

Notes: Service price indexes for the 1983–94 period, with the exception of other inpatient services, which begins in 1986. Aggregated SPIs for Medicare data and cost-of-living index are for 1984–94. The values in brackets for the cost-of-living index are based on higher and lower estimates of the net value of a life year. Real changes are estimated using the GDP deflator.

Although the CPI resamples goods every five years, it traditionally did not price the goods used by an average patient. For example, it always priced a one-day stay, independent of trends in actual length of stay. When actual care changed (for example, shorter stays), no adjustment was made to the index. An alternative methodology is to choose the average patient in each year and price the services used by that average patient over time. If we resample patients frequently enough, changes in the care provided would be incorporated in the index (Scitovsky 1967).

The difficulty with sampling patient bills over time is that the set of goods provided changes; some goods disappear and others newly appear. The detailed MTH data permit the extent of market basket change to be quantified. In consecutive years, we can match services for 98 percent of charges. But over five years, we match only 42 percent of charges, and over 11 years (the maximum span of our data), we match only 27 percent of charges. Many of the changes are straightforward (e.g., a different code for an additional intensive care unit); when we allow for this, our ability to match charges increases substantially. Over the eleven-year period 78 percent rather than 27 percent of expenditures can be matched.[14]

Truly new goods pose a more difficult problem. For example, intra-aortic balloon pumps—small pumps inserted near the heart that can temporarily help the heart pump blood—did not exist in 1987 but had grown to almost 1 percent of heart attack spending by 1994. Like the BLS we link such new goods as we are able, but make no adjustment for potential quality change (U.S. Department of Labor 1992).[15]

The upper line in figure 8.4 and the next row of table 8.4 show the disaggregated SPI calculated using the market basket for the average patient in the initial year. This index increases 2.8 percent annually in real terms, close to the increase in the cost-based synthetic CPI, as we would expect. The next rows of the table examine the effects of resampling patients more frequently. Using a Laspeyres index that resamples patients every five years the annual increase in real prices is only 2.1 percent, and a chain-weighted Laspeyres index (annual resampling) increases only 0.7 percent. The bias from fixed weights is thus substantial. The difference in these indexes results almost entirely from the weight placed on room

14. Over five years the figure is 85 percent; the one-year figure remains 98 percent.

15. The BLS treats new and obsolete goods using three possible methods. In some cases, a new good is considered to be a direct and fully equivalent replacement for an old good (termed direct comparability). In other cases, quality adjustments are made for the shift from an old to a new good (termed direct quality adjustment), although this method is rarely used in practice due to the difficulties in quantifying quality improvements. Other new goods are linked into the old index, which is equivalent to assuming that the quality-adjusted price change in the substitution period is exactly equal to the price change of the other goods in the category. For our longer indexes, linking underweights the kinds of goods that appear and disappear frequently, such as pharmaceuticals, and overweights the kinds of goods that exist over long periods, such as intensive care unit rooms. The BLS is trying to integrate quality changes into the new PPI, as we discuss in the conclusion.

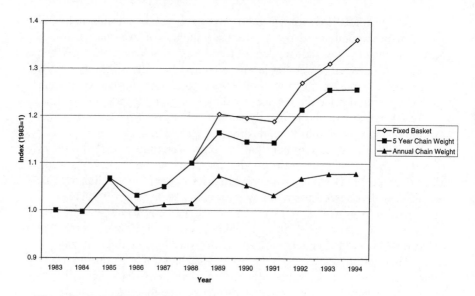

Fig. 8.4   Real disaggregated service price indexes

charges. Between 1983 and 1994, the price of a hospital room rose 60 percent, while the average length of stay for AMI patients fell 36 percent.

8.6.2   Aggregated Service Price Indexes

We next explore changes in the definition of the good being priced. As noted above, health care providers are frequently paid on the basis of more aggregated bundles of services than our disaggregated indexes price. For example, hospitals receive a fixed amount from Medicare for the entire admission of every patient in a given Diagnostic Related Group (DRG)— for example a patient with bypass surgery—regardless of the actual services used by the particular patient.[16] Managed care insurers typically pay on a DRG basis or an inclusive per diem rate. In such a situation, it is more appropriate to price an aggregated set of services than the disaggregated services.[17]

To construct an aggregated SPI, we use the same methodology as for the disaggregated service price index, but we choose as our goods the four treatment regimens discussed above. The aggregated SPIs are noisier than the disaggregated SPIs, since the aggregated SPI is based on actual average treatment costs, which vary substantially with patient severity. This is par-

16. This is a bit simplified. More is paid for particularly costly patients than for average patients. But this description is approximately correct.
17. Even when payment is based on a more disaggregated level of service than the DRG, an aggregated SPI may be more informative if the aggregated service is a better proxy for a constant-quality medical care good.

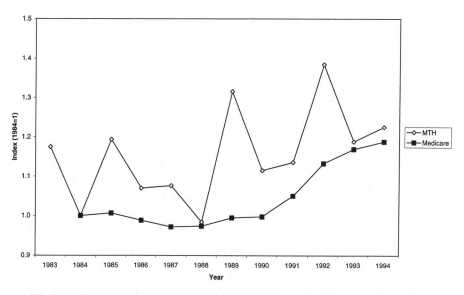

Fig. 8.5   Real aggregated service price indexes

ticularly true for the MTH data, where the sample sizes are smaller.[18] We thus focus predominantly on the aggregated SPIs for Medicare.

Using both fixed basket and annual chain-weighted Laspeyres price indexes, aggregated SPIs grow less rapidly than most of the disaggregated SPIs (fig. 8.5 and table 8.4). The fixed basket index increased 2.3 percent per year in the Medicare data, and the annual chain-weighted index increased 1.7 percent per year. The changes at MTH are smaller. Our preferred estimate of real price increases using an aggregated SPI is therefore about 1.5 percent annually. This is approximately 1.0 to 2.0 percentage points below a price index reflecting historical BLS methods.

The increase in the aggregated SPI for Medicare in the 1984–94 period is greater than the increase in the 1984–91 period reported in our earlier paper (Cutler et al. 1998). In that paper, we reported a growth of the aggregate SPI using Medicare data of 1.1 percent (the fixed weighted index) and 0.6 percent (the chain-weighted index). The higher inflation rates reported here reflect the much more rapid growth of Medicare spending after 1991 than prior to 1991. Figure 8.5 shows the growth of the aggregated price index over time. In 1992, the inflation rate with the Medicare data was nearly 8 percent, followed by 3 percent in 1993 and 2 percent in 1994. As

18. The MTH index is particularly variable because annual fluctuations in the average severity of admissions affect the average cost in each category and therefore this index. To eliminate some of these fluctuations, we formed an alternative price index using a three-year moving average of costs for each treatment regimen and the share of patients receiving each treatment regimen. The resulting chain-weighted index fell 0.1 percent annually.

with any series, cumulative inflation rates will be more variable over shorter time periods than over longer time periods.

8.7 Cost-of-Living Index

Forming a cost-of-living index is more complicated than forming an SPI because one must price improvements in health rather than just specific medical services. Thus, we have to measure and price health improvements after a heart attack. Since outcome data are most readily available for the Medicare sample, we use only the Medicare data to form the cost-of-living index.

As noted above, the demographics of the heart attack population are changing somewhat over time. To account for this, we adjust all of our estimates for changes in the age and sex mix of the population. We group the population into five age groups (65–69, 70–74, 75–79, 80–84, and 85+) and two sex groups, for a total of ten demographic cells. The data are adjusted to the average demographic mix of the heart attack population over the eleven-year period.[19] We would like to adjust for clinical characteristics of the heart attack as well (the extent of blood flow, other complications and/or comorbidities), but such data are either not present on the discharge abstract (e.g., the extent of blood flow) or are not coded reliably (e.g., complications may be recorded less often for patients who die during the hospitalization). We thus adjust for demographics only. Other clinical reviews (e.g., McGovern et al. 1996) suggest that the severity of heart attack patients has not changed much since the mid-1980s.

8.7.1 Length of Life

We begin with data on the length of life after a heart attack. Figure 8.6 shows survival rates over time (adjusted for demographics), based on the year of the heart attack. We show cumulative mortality rates on the day of the heart attack, by ninety days, one year, two years, three years, four years, and five years after the heart attack. We show survival for people with heart attacks in 1984, 1987, 1991, and 1994. Because the Social Security data are only available through 1995, we cannot compute some of the mortality rates; for example, five-year mortality rates for people with a heart attack in 1994 would require death records through 1999, which did not yet exist when we carried out this work. Still, we can assemble a time series of long-term changes in mortality for many years.

Mortality rates after a heart attack have declined substantially over time. In the first day after the heart attack, for example, mortality rates

19. In our earlier paper (Cutler et al. 1998), the data were adjusted to the demographic mix between 1984 and 1991. Thus, the data are not strictly comparable in the two analyses, although all of the trends are exactly the same.

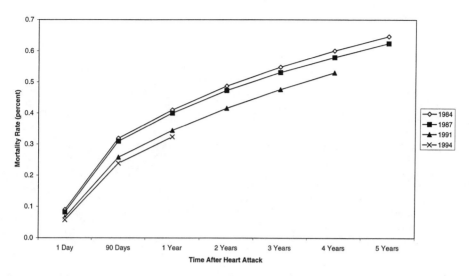

Fig. 8.6   Cumulative mortality rates after a heart attack

were 9.0 percent in 1984, 8.2 percent in 1987, 6.6 percent in 1991, and 5.7 percent in 1994. Mortality rates at one year after the heart attack have fallen by 9 percentage points. As figure 8.6 shows, the decline was particularly pronounced in the mid-1980s, but mortality rates fell in all years.

Determinants of Mortality Improvement

The central question about the improvement in the length of life is whether it results from improved medical care or other factors. Heidenreich and McClellan (chap. 9 in this volume) look at this issue in some detail. They find considerable evidence that medical innovations are an important contributor to improved survival, and in particular that they explain the bulk of survival during the acute treatment period. We summarize their results briefly.

Heidenreich and McClellan first document the reduction in AMI mortality over time. Between 1975 and 1995, acute heart attack mortality (in the first thirty days after the AMI) fell from 27.0 percent to 17.4 percent, a decline of nearly 2 percent per year. To analyze why heart attack mortality fell so rapidly, Heidenreich and McClellan review the (literally) hundreds of published studies and meta-analyses of heart attack treatments and their effectiveness.

Table 8.5 summarizes the evidence on the effect of acute treatments on AMI mortality. The first column reports the mortality odds ratio of the technologies, using results from clinical trials and meta-analyses. Many of the technologies have quite substantial health impacts (values below 1) although some of the technologies are now believed to be harmful, such

Table 8.5   **Estimated Acute Mortality Benefits of Changes in Acute Treatment of AMI**

Therapy	Odds Ratio	Change in Use, 1995–75 (%)	Share of Total Improvement[a] (%)
Pharmaceuticals			
Beta blockers[b]	0.88	29.0	6.1
Aspirin[b]	0.77	60.0	27.5
Nitrates	0.94	30.0	−5.5
Heparin/anticoagulants	0.78	4.0	−0.5
Calcium-channel blockers	1.12	31.0	−7.3
Lidocaine	1.38	−15.0	10.7
Magnesium	1.02	8.5	−0.3
ACE inhibitors[b]	0.94	24.0	2.7
Thrombolytics[b]	0.75	31.0	16.1
Procedures			
Primary PTCA[b]	0.50	9.1	9.8
CABG	0.94	6.7	0.6
Total—Major treatments only			62
All treatments			60

Note: Based on data analysis in Heidenreich and McClellan (chap. 9 in this volume).

[a]Percentage of 1995–75 decrease in AMI case fatality rates explained by changes in use of each treatment.

[b]Major treatment.

as calcium-channel blockers and lidocaine. Heidenreich and McClellan define as "major technologies" those treatments where the clinical trial evidence is particularly advanced—beta blockers, aspirin, ACE inhibitors, thrombolytics, and primary PTCA.

The second column shows the change in the share of patients receiving these treatments over time. Treatment changes have been substantial. Thrombolytics, for example, were not used in heart attack care in 1980, but were used in almost one-third of heart attacks by 1995. The use of aspirin, beta blockers, and heparin also increased. Calcium-channel blocker use increased rapidly in the early 1980s and then fell, following the publication of studies documenting potentially harmful effects of their use in acute management. Use of lidocaine and other antiarrhythmic agents also fell over the time period, in conjunction with new information on their potential harmfulness for typical AMI patients. And as noted above, both PTCA and bypass surgery increased in use by a substantial amount.

The third column shows the share of the total mortality change between 1975 and 1995 attributable to these treatments. Two summary estimates are presented in the last rows of the table. The first estimate uses evidence on the major treatments only. By this estimate, 62 percent of the reduction in AMI mortality in the past twenty years is attributed to changes in acute treatments. The second estimate uses all of the technologies; the attributable share is very similar, 60 percent.

Three drug therapies in particular account for the largest improvements in heart attack mortality—aspirin, thrombolytics, and beta blockers. Indeed, beta blocker use alone accounts for over one-quarter of the mortality decline and use of thrombolytics accounts for an additional 15 percent. The development and spread of PTCA explains nearly 10 percent of the mortality decline.[20]

Heidenreich and McClellan also review the more limited evidence on other sources of improvement in acute mortality over time. Though changes in monitoring methods were important sources of mortality improvements in the 1960s and early 1970s (Goldman and Cook 1984), they have been less important recently. Coronary care units, for example, had largely diffused by the mid-1970s, and right-heart (pulmonary artery) catheterization for functional assessment, which has spread rapidly, does not result in clear survival improvements.

Changes in prehospital care may be more important. Emergency 911 systems and (recently) enhanced 911 systems have become more widely available, and the content of ACLS procedures has evolved. Several studies have failed to document improvements in mortality following activation or enhancement of 911 systems, however. Similarly, time between hospital arrival and the delivery of key AMI treatments (thrombolytics, primary angioplasty) appears to have declined, although again the evidence on how important this is in increasing survival is limited. It is likely that improvements in prehospital care and reductions in time to treatment have led to a modest improvement in AMI mortality, perhaps 5–10 percent, but this conclusion is speculative.

Changes in the type of AMIs admitted to hospitals might also explain about 10 to 20 percent of improved survival over this period, particularly between 1975 and 1985. The average age of AMI patients in the Minnesota and Worcester registries, and the proportions of male and female patients were essentially constant. Data on specific measures of heart attack severity (such as anterior MIs, non-Q-wave infarcts, and high blood pressure at admission) suggest a modest improvement in severity of heart attacks.

Altogether, changes in acute treatment, prehospital care, and patient characteristics may explain as much as 80 percent of the total improvement in acute mortality for heart attacks. The remaining 20 percent likely

---

20. The finding that pharmaceutical use explains a larger share of mortality declines than intensive surgical procedures may understate the role of these technologies in contributing to mortality reductions, since it does not account for learning by doing, which will be more important in surgical procedures than in pharmaceuticals. On the other hand, much of the improvement in learning by doing involves reducing the risk of complications from the procedure—so that patients expected to have relatively modest benefits become better candidates as experience improves.

results from other technologies that we have not studied in detail, improvements in physician acumen in applying technologies, differential diffusion in subgroups of heart attack patients (with differential effects), and miscellaneous other factors.

Long-term survival rates are also influenced by postacute care. As figure 8.6 shows, postacute mortality for heart attack patients is substantial. Many innovations have occurred in postacute treatment of heart attack patients, including expanded cardiac rehabilitation programs as well as drug therapies such as ACE inhibitors and anticoagulation therapy. However, few studies exist that quantify the effects of long-term therapies for heart failure patients. The best evidence exists for ACE inhibitors, but limited quantitative data on the changes in heart failure prevalence after heart attacks makes it difficult to quantify these important effects. The same is true about secondary prevention of AMI through diagnostic procedures for risk stratification, risk factor counseling, pharmacologic therapies, and invasive procedures. Once again, studies show that many of these techniques result in significant reductions in long-term mortality after heart attacks, but data on changes in utilization or efficacy of these therapies are lacking.

Taken together, the factors discussed here suggest that innovations in each of primary prevention, acute and postacute management, and secondary prevention have led to substantial reductions in acute and long-term AMI mortality. We cannot quantify each of the components of improved long-term health, but medical interventions appear to be particularly important.

In light of this evidence, we assume that the mortality improvements shown in figure 8.6 are the outcome of medical treatments. This assumption is essentially correct for mortality improvements since 1985, and is largely correct over the entire 1975–95 period. As we show in other work (Cutler et al. 1998), assuming that only a relatively small share of the mortality improvement results from medical interventions does not appreciably affect our results about cost of living indexes.

Cost-of-Living Price Indexes

To estimate the price index for heart attack care, we need to turn these mortality improvements into changes in the value of remaining life. We start with some notation. Denote the share of people who die in period s after a heart attack occurring in year t as $d_s(t)$. The values of s correspond to our intervals above: one day after a heart attack, ninety days after a heart attack, and so on. We assume that people who died in each interval died exactly halfway through that interval. Thus, people who died between one day and ninety days after a heart attack lived exactly 1.5 months, people who died between ninety days and 365 days after a heart attack died after 7.5 months, and so on. Denote the length of life for people who died in each interval as l_s and the value of a year of life as V. For the moment, we assume that V is constant over time and across people; we discuss this assumption in more detail below.

The present value of remaining life is given by

$$(8) \qquad PV[\text{life}] = \sum_s \frac{V d_s l_s}{(1 + r)^s},$$

where r is the real discount rate. In our analysis, we assume a real discount rate of 3 percent; the results are not particularly sensitive to this assumption.

To estimate equation (8) empirically, we need to determine the share of people dying in each interval after a heart attack. Our data give us much of this information. If the cumulative mortality rate after a heart attack is $CM_s(t)$, the share of people dying in interval s is just $CM_s(t) - CM_{s-1}(t)$. But we do not know the cumulative mortality rate for every interval s in every year—for example, five years after a heart attack that occurred in 1994. To estimate these cumulative mortality rates, we begin by forming the annual mortality hazard. For example, the hazard rate between years 2 and 3 is the share of people alive at the end of year 2 who die in year 3. We form the mortality hazard rate for as long a time as we are able. For example, in 1994, we are able to form the mortality hazard rate between ninety days and one year for every calendar year, the mortality hazard rate between one year and two years for each calendar year through 1993, the mortality hazard rate between two years and three years for each calendar year through 1992, and so on.

Consistent with the reduction in cumulative mortality rates, the mortality hazard rates are declining over time. For example, the hazard rate between one year and two years after an AMI was 13.1 percent in 1984 and 10.7 percent in 1993. We need to forecast this hazard rate through 1994. To be conservative, we assume that the mortality hazard rate in 1993 (10.7 percent) continued through 1994. Since the mortality hazard rate was falling up through 1993, and mortality hazard rates at durations shorter than two years were falling between 1993 and 1994 as well, this assumption almost surely understates the reductions in mortality hazard rates in 1994. By understating the reduction in the mortality hazard rate, we understate life expectancy in later years of the sample and thus overstate the change in the cost-of-living index. We use the constant mortality hazard rate assumption to forecast all of the unknown mortality hazard rates through five years after a heart attack.

We then need to determine life expectancy for a person surviving five years after a heart attack. Our data provide no evidence on this. We again make a conservative assumption. We start with national data on survival in 1984, matched by age and sex to the demographic mix of the heart attack population. For this population, we first find the mortality hazard rate between four and five years after the age at which they match the heart attack population. This mortality rate is 8.6 percent. We then compare this to the mortality hazard rate between four and five years after the heart attack for people with a heart attack in 1984. This mortality rate is 10.4 percent, or 21.5 percent above the mortality hazard rate for the population as a whole. We assume that for every subsequent year after a heart attack, people who have had a heart attack have a 21.5 percent greater mortality hazard rate than people who have not had a heart attack. We can then simulate future survival rates for people who have survived five years after a heart attack. These calculations suggest that people who have lived five years after a heart attack can expect to live another seven years on average.

We assume that this seven-year additional survival is the same for a person with a heart attack in every year. This is a conservative assumption, since mortality hazard rates up to five years are declining over time, and there is no reason to think that mortality reductions would cease after five years. By making this assumption, we likely understate gains in survival over time and thus likely overstate the cost-of-living index.

The first column of table 8.6 shows life expectancy after a heart attack. Life expectancy rose from five years in 1984 to six years in 1994. The increase in life expectancy was particularly concentrated in the 1987–1990 period. In those three years, life expectancy rose by six months, compared to two months before and four months after.

To determine the value of this life extension, we need to know the worth of a year of life. This is a venerable question in the health economics literature (Viscusi 1993; Tolley, Kenkel, and Fabian 1994). There are three approaches that have been used to estimate the value of life. The first ap-

Table 8.6   **Cost-of-Living Index for Heart Attacks, 1984–94**

Year	Life Expectancy	Value of Additional Life for Dollar Value of a Life Year of:			Medicare Spending ($)	
		$10,000	$25,000	$100,000	Cost	Change
1984	5 yrs 0 mnths	—	—	—	11,483	
1985	5 yrs 0 mnths	625	1,564	6,254	12,066	583
1986	5 yrs 1 mnth	978	2,445	9,780	12,395	912
1987	5 yrs 2 mnths	1,939	4,847	19,390	12,673	1,190
1988	5 yrs 4 mnths	3,200	8,001	32,003	13,123	1,640
1989	5 yrs 6 mnths	4,751	11,877	47,510	13,588	2,105
1990	5 yrs 8 mnths	5,690	14,226	56,903	14,186	2,703
1991	5 yrs 9 mnths	6,847	17,116	68,465	15,293	3,810
1992	5 yrs 10 mnths	7,650	19,124	76,495	16,867	5,385
1993	6 yrs 0 mnths	8,648	21,620	86,482	17,581	6,098
1994	6 yrs 0 mnths	8,639	21,597	86,388	18,165	6,682

Source: Data are from the Medicare population.

proach is contingent valuation—asking people the value they are willing to pay for increased length of life. This approach suffers from the usual drawbacks of surveys, however, including the fact that people have frequently not thought about the question in advance. The second approach is the compensating differentials approach. In many situations, people have to make job choices where risk of injury or death varies across jobs. On average, people get paid more to work in riskier jobs than in safer jobs. The risk premium that people need to be compensated to work in riskier jobs is an estimate of the value of life. The third approach is to use data on individual purchases of safety devices (for example, airbags in cars). By knowing the probability that an airbag will save one's life, researchers can back out the implicit value people place on their life.

A rough consensus from this literature (Tolley, Kenkel, and Fabian 1994) is that life for a prime-age person is worth about $3 million to $7 million, or about $75,000 to $150,000 per year. Cutler and Richardson (1997, 1998) suggest a value for the population as a whole of $100,000 per year of life.

It is not immediately apparent whether we should use this estimate in our research. We are evaluating life years for the elderly, while most studies look at life years for prime-age people as well as the elderly. One might value a life year more when one has young children, for example, than when one does not. Indeed, surveys conducted by Murray and Lopez (1996) show that people value years of life for middle-aged people the most, relative to years of life for the young or the old. Similarly, the life years that we are evaluating are after a heart attack, and their quality might be lower than years of life without a heart attack (a topic we return to below). For these reasons, we make a benchmark assumption that a year of additional life is worth $25,000. To evaluate the sensitivity of these results, we alternately assume a year of life is worth $10,000 and $100,000.

The next three columns of table 8.6 show the implied change in the value of life. Under our benchmark assumption, the additional years of life added between 1984 and 1994 are worth over $20,000. This varies between $9,000 when we assume a life year is worth $10,000 and $86,000 when we assume a life year is worth $100,000.

Cost-Benefit Analysis and the Cost-of-Living Index

To form the cost-of-living index, we need to compare this additional value of life with the cost of producing those additional years. To determine these costs, we use the data on Medicare spending in the year after a heart attack. The next column of table 8.6 shows average Medicare costs of treating a heart attack, in 1991 dollars.[21] Medicare spending on heart

---

21. Costs should be put in the same dollars as the value of a life. It is not clear what year's dollars the $25,000 assumption applies to. Since 1991 is about the middle of our data (and is the year we used in our previous research), we assume the $25,000 is the value of a life in 1991 dollars.

attacks is substantial—nearly $20,000 by 1994. And as noted above, spending has increased over time, by $6,682 between 1984 and 1994. The increase in Medicare spending is shown in the last column of the table.

Comparing the increase in the value of life with the increase in Medicare spending yields a clear conclusion: The value of increased longevity is greater than the increase in spending required to produce that additional life. Using our benchmark estimates, the net value of additional life between 1984 and 1994 is $14,915 ($21,597 − $6,682). Under the low and high assumptions for the value of a life year, the net gains are $1,957 and $79,706, respectively.

The fact that the estimated value of improvements in heart attack mortality is greater than the total increased expenditures has a direct implication for price index measurement: it implies that the cost of living for heart attacks is falling. To turn these estimates into a price index, we need to scale them by the cost of reaching the baseline level of utility in 1984. On net, the elderly consume roughly $25,000 per person per year (including medical care expenses). Thus, we assume that baseline resources involved in providing for the elderly is $25,000 per year, times the five years of expected survival for an elderly person with a heart attack, or $107,000 in present value.

Figure 8.7 shows the implied cost-of-living index. Under our benchmark assumption, the cost-of-living index falls by 1.5 percent per year. Using the conservative estimate of the value of a year of life, the decline is 0.2 percent, and using the higher value yields a decline of 13.7 percent. Thus,

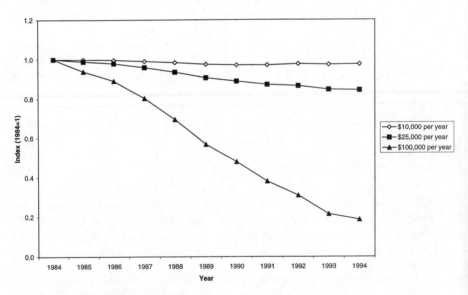

Fig. 8.7   Cost-of-living index

in each case the cost-of-living index is falling. This is in marked contrast to conventional medical care price indexes, which have been rising rapidly in real terms over this period.

8.7.2   Quality of Life

In addition to the length of life, people also care about its quality. Quality of life was mentioned implicitly in the previous section; in this section, we discuss it explicitly. There are several dimensions to quality of life. Physical health is one of them—can the individual ambulate independently? Can they manage tasks of daily living? Do they need specialized nursing care? Mental health is also important: Depression is a commonly reported complication after heart attack, and a few recent studies have even found an association between antidepressant treatment and heart attack survival.

To make sense of these differing components to quality of life, we think of quality of life on a 0 to 1 scale, where 0 is death and 1 is living in perfect health. If we can estimate quality of life after a heart attack, we can then form the expected number of quality-adjusted life years for a person, rather than just the expected number of years remaining.[22]

To do this, we need to be more precise in our definitions. We denote the quality of life in any year as Q, which ranges from 0 to 1. For data reasons (discussed below), we assume Q is the same in each year after a heart attack. We define V as the value of a year in perfect health. Then, the present value of remaining quality-adjusted life years is

$$(9) \qquad PV[\text{quality-adjusted life years}] = \sum_{s} \frac{VQd_s l_s}{(1 + r)^s}.$$

To measure quality of life for heart attack patients, and quantify how it has changed over time, we examine a number of different measures. One aspect of quality of life is the need for additional medical care. Heart attack patients who fare poorly may need to be readmitted to the hospital for one of several reasons. The person may have a subsequent AMI or develop serious ischemic heart disease (IHD) symptoms (including severe chest pains, palpitations, and other symptoms that resemble those of a heart attack) or they may develop congestive heart failure (insufficient pumping function by the heart, causing a reduced exercise tolerance and even severe difficulty breathing if fluid "backs up" into the lungs).

Table 8.7 and figures 8.8 to 8.11 show trends in readmission for these

---

22. Other approaches also exist for assessing the value of survival years in less than perfect health. For example, Murray and Lopez (1996) favor the use of disability-adjusted life years (DALYs), and other cost-effectiveness experts have favored healthy-year equivalents (HYEs). For purposes of the expected utility calculations underlying the COL index, however, quality-adjusted life years are the most natural index.

Table 8.7   Readmission Rates within One Year after a Heart Attack, 1984–94

	Readmission Diagnosis (%)			
Year	AMI	CHF	IHD	Other
1984	6.5	8.4	11.3	25.1
1985	6.2	8.1	11.4	24.1
1986	6.0	8.3	11.7	23.7
1987	5.8	8.6	11.9	24.0
1988	5.6	8.7	11.5	24.0
1989	5.5	9.1	11.6	24.6
1990	5.6	9.4	11.4	25.1
1991	5.7	9.5	11.0	25.4
1992	5.5	9.5	11.0	25.1
1993	5.8	9.8	11.1	26.4
1994	5.8	9.7	11.1	26.6

Source: Data are from the Medicare population.

reasons over time.[23] The trends differ by complication. The incidence of subsequent heart attacks (fig. 8.8) has been declining over time. In 1984, 6.5 percent of people had a subsequent heart attack in the year after their first heart attack; by 1994 the share was 5.8 percent. But at the same time, admissions for congestive heart failure (fig. 8.9) have increased. In 1984, 8.4 percent of heart attack patients were readmitted for congestive heart failure in the year after their heart attack, and this rose to 9.7 percent in 1994. Readmissions for ischemic heart disease and other diagnoses were essentially unchanged over the time period (fig. 8.10 and 8.11, respectively).

In addition to the absence of needing future medical care, one can also look at the direct measures of health status. We examine these measures using data from the National Health Interview Surveys (NHIS). The NHIS has been conducted annually for many decades. Microdata are available in public form beginning in 1969. While the NHIS does not ask if the person has suffered a heart attack, it does ask whether the person has been hospitalized for ischemic heart disease (ICD-9 codes 410–414), which includes heart attacks. We thus examine the trend over time in the health of people who have had ischemic heart disease. Consistent with the reduction in AMI mortality, the prevalence of IHD in the population has been increasing over time; we suspect that some of this is increased survival for people with severe IHD, suggesting that, in the absence of any true quality improvement, reported quality of life should be falling. In all

23. We include only readmissions occurring at least thirty days after the initial heart attack. Early readmissions are probably the result of complications from the heart attack itself, or of further treatment for it. Later readmissions are much more likely to reflect true impairments in quality of life.

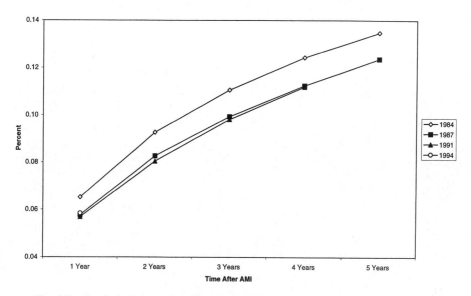

Fig. 8.8   Readmission rate for subsequent AMI

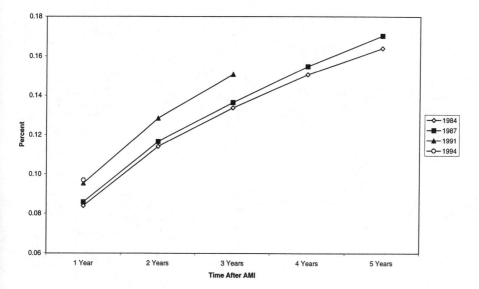

Fig. 8.9   Readmission rate for subsequent CHF

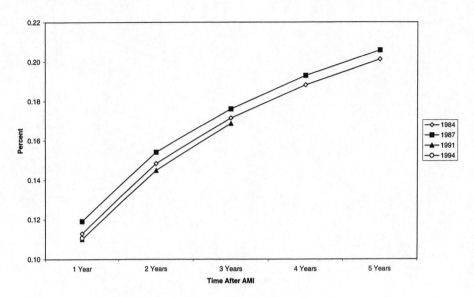

Fig. 8.10   Readmission rate for subsequent IHD

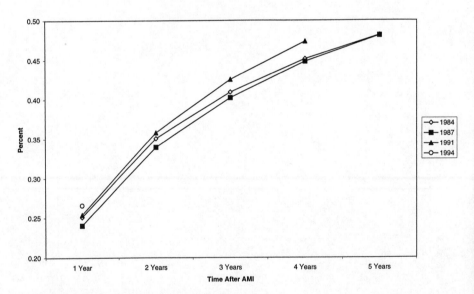

Fig. 8.11   Readmission rate for other diagnoses

Table 8.8   **Characteristics of the Population with Ischemic Heart Disease, 1972–94 (%)**

Limitation	1972	1981	1982	1994
Activity limitation[a]				
Can't perform usual activity	17.4	15.8	15.1	7.2
Can perform usual activity, but limited in amount/kind	28.4	21.2	12.3	8.6
Can perform usual activity, but limited in outside	6.7	5.1	8.4	6.7
Not limited	47.5	57.9	64.3	77.5
Work limitation[b]				
Unable to work			18.0	8.6
Limited in kind/amount of work			13.0	9.2
Limited in other activities			6.1	12.4
Not limited			62.9	69.7
Frequency of bother				
All the time	22.6	15.5		
Often/once in a while	53.5	49.6		
Never	23.1	29.0		
Don't know	1.9	6.5		

Source: Data are from the National Health Interview Survey.

[a]In 1982, this was changed to "Unable to perform major activity," "Limited in kind/amount of major activity," "Limited in other activities," "Not limited."

[b]Data are for 1984 instead of 1982.

cases, we adjust the data to the demographic mix of the population with ischemic heart disease in 1982.

Table 8.8 shows measures of functional status for people with IHD. The first rows indicate the share of people reporting activity limitations. Between 1972 and 1981, there was a marked reduction in the extent of activity limitations. Forty-six percent of people in 1972 could not perform their usual activities or were limited in the kind or amount of usual activities they could undertake. By 1981, that share fell by 9 percentage points, to 37 percent. Although the question changed in 1982 (to ask about major activities rather than usual activities), the trend in responses is similar. Twenty-seven percent of people reported being substantially limited in their major activities in 1982, compared to 16 percent in 1994.

The next rows report questions about work limitations. The share of population that was unable to work or limited in the kind and amount of work they could undertake fell from 31 percent in 1984 to 18 percent in 1994. And as the last rows show, the frequency with which people are bothered by IHD fell over the 1970s.

Table 8.9 shows data on a related, but broader, measure of health status. We tabulate answers to an NHIS question asking people to self-report their health: excellent, very good, good, fair, or poor (very good was added

Table 8.9   Self-Reported Health Status of the Elderly with and without IHD, 1972–94 (%)

Self-Reported Health Status	1972	1981	1982	1994
People with IHD				
Excellent	9.5	12.9	4.5	5.6
Very good			12.2	13.6
Good	32.8	32.6	26.5	33.6
Fair	36.3	28.9	28.2	26.0
Poor	20.9	24.8	28.0	21.1
Overall elderly population				
Excellent	30.1	28.6	14.9	15.8
Very good			19.1	23.0
Good	38.1	40.7	30.4	33.1
Fair	22.4	21.5	22.8	18.1
Poor	8.5	8.6	11.7	9.4

Source: Data are from the National Health Interview Survey.

in 1982). The upper part of the table shows the tabulation for people with IHD; the lower part shows the tabulation for the elderly population as a whole.

Self-reported health for people with IHD has improved over time. In the 1980s, the share of people with IHD reporting their health to be fair or poor fell from 57 to 53 percent; in the 1980s the decline was even more dramatic—from 56 to 41 percent. Some of this trend is mirrored in the elderly population as a whole, but to a lesser extent. In the 1970s, self-reported health status of the elderly was largely unchanged. Self-reported health status improved in the 1980s but by a smaller amount.

Self-reported health status can be used to construct an overall quality of life for people with IHD (see Cutler and Richardson 1997 and 1998 for details). Suppose we assume that quality of life can be scaled on a 0 to 1 basis. We denote a person's underlying health status as h^*. We assume that health status is related to the person's demographics and their underlying medical conditions as

$$(10) \qquad\qquad h^* = X\beta + \varepsilon,$$

where demographics are proxied by age and sex and we include as many medical conditions as the NHIS asks about. We do not have good information on when the person was admitted with IHD, however, so we assume that quality of life is the same for everyone alive, independent of when the heart attack was suffered. Quality of life can change over time, however.

If people respond to questions about self-reported health with an estimate of h^*, we can estimate the coefficients β by relating self-reported health to people's demographic characteristics and the set of diseases they report. In particular, if ε is normally distributed, equation (10) can be estimated as an ordered probit model for self-reported health.

Estimates of the effect of having been in a hospital for IHD on self-reported health show that IHD has a negative and statistically significant effect on self-reported health status. The magnitude of this health effect falls over time, however, indicating that it is less bad to have had IHD now than it was in the past. The implication is that the quality of life for people with IHD is rising. Indeed, when we evaluate the quality of life disutility for IHD (see Cutler and Richardson 1997 and 1998 for details), the disutility is .36 in 1980 and .29 in 1990, on the scale where 1 is death compared to perfect health.

We can use these quality of life weights to form a more accurate cost-of-living index for heart attacks. Table 8.10 shows the calculations. The first column reports expected longevity, as above. The second column is the quality of life weight. We assume that in the absence of IHD, the person would have a quality of life of 1. The values reported subtract from 1 the imputed disutility from IHD in each year. The product of the length of life and the quality of life is the number of quality-adjusted life years remaining in expectation.

We now need to know the value of a year in perfect health. This should be greater than the average value of a year of life people report in surveys, since people answering the surveys are not in perfect health. Available evidence has not attempted to distinguish between the value of a year of life and the quality of those years, however. For simplicity, and for comparison with our earlier results, we assume that $25,000 is actually the value of a year in perfect health.

The next three columns show the increase in the value of quality-adjusted life over time. In our benchmark case, we find a greater increase in the value of additional life after we account for changes in morbidity.

Table 8.10   **Cost-of-Living Index for Heart Attacks, Including Quality of Life, 1984–94**

Year	Life Expectancy	Quality of Life	Value of Additional Life in Dollars for Dollar Value of a Year in Perfect Health of:			Medicare Spending in Dollars	
			$10,000	$25,000	$100,000	Cost	Change
1984	5 yrs 0 mnths	.67	—	—	—	11,483	
1985	5 yrs 0 mnths	.68	722	1,805	7,219	12,066	$583
1986	5 yrs 1 mnth	.68	1,266	3,166	12,664	12,395	912
1987	5 yrs 2 mnths	.69	2,235	5,588	22,352	12,673	1,190
1988	5 yrs 4 mnths	.70	3,426	8,566	34,263	13,123	1,640
1989	5 yrs 6 mnths	.70	4,839	12,096	48,386	13,588	2,105
1990	5 yrs 8 mnths	.71	5,839	14,596	58,385	14,186	2,703
1991	5 yrs 9 mnths	.72	7,007	17,518	70,070	15,293	3,810
1992	5 yrs 10 mnths	.72	7,936	19,840	79,360	16,867	5,385
1993	6 yrs 0 mnths	.73	9,019	22,548	90,193	17,581	6,098
1994	6 yrs 0 mnths	.74	9,373	23,431	93,727	18,165	6,682

Source: Data are from the Medicare population.

Using our benchmark estimate of $25,000 for the value of a year of life, the increase in the value of life is $21,597 accounting for only mortality, and $23,431 accounting for morbidity as well.

Relative to the change in costs, the change in the net value of life again suggests reductions in the cost of living over time. Indeed, the magnitudes are about the same: a 1.7 percent decline in the cost of living in the benchmark case, with a range from 0.3 percent to 16.7 percent using the lower and higher value of an additional year of life in perfect health.

Thus, we find substantial reductions in the cost of living for people with a heart attack. While the specific calculations relied on one measure of quality of life, a broad range of quality of life indexes suggest that quality of life after heart attack has improved, or at worst remained the same. We therefore suspect that our qualitative conclusion—that the quality-adjusted cost-of-living index has declined—is robust. This finding about cost-of-living indexes is in marked contrast to service price indexes, which increase from 1.5 to 3.5 percent annually, depending on the particular index employed.

8.8   Implications

Our detailed illustrations of medical price indexes suggest, at least for the case of heart attacks, that medical prices are not rising very much and may well be declining. These results have several implications, which we draw out in this section.

8.8.1   A "Nonmedical Consumption" Index

At first look, our results may seem counterintuitive to the general public. Substantial real increases in the "price" of their medical care have, with only a few recent exceptions, been an accepted fact of life for the past forty years. Why is the public so wrong about this? There are two components to the answer. First, the public is using data about *spending* to proxy for data about *prices*. As we have shown, however, spending increases are mostly driven by changes in the quantity and type of services provided, not changes in the price of a given service. Thus, consumers are implicitly drawing implications from the wrong variable. Our analysis of the consequences of these changes in quality suggests that, with reasonable valuations of health outcomes, the increase in AMI costs may well have been worthwhile.

The distinction between our results and conventional wisdom relates to our earlier discussion about what rate should be used to index benefit payments over time. We have presented an inflation rate for AMI treatment; that is different from presenting an optimal rate by which to increase Social Security payments or Medicare payments.

Indeed, in deciding on the appropriate update factor for public programs, policymakers may want to answer the question, As medical care changes, how much of an increase in total income would be required to hold nonmedical consumption constant? That is, the desired update may not be the one that leaves Medicare beneficiaries just as well off in terms of total utility but one which insures the elderly against the cost of unforeseen technological advances, allowing them to share in medical progress without compromising their purchasing power of other goods and services.

Of course, if medical expenditures rise more quickly than per capita income or people on average live longer but work the same amount, it is not possible to have such updates for everyone. This discussion highlights the important redistributional features of price indexes. Given the magnitude of health care spending, especially for the elderly, choosing the technical method for construction of a medical care price index is a politically sensitive topic.

8.8.2   The Value of Increased Life

Some have made the argument that prolonging life is not of value because people still have to buy groceries (Tobin 1997). Thus, the calculated inflation rate suggests the elderly need less income as they live longer, but in reality they might need more.

There are two issues in this argument. The first is the marginal rate of substitution between health and consumption—V in our analysis—which presumably depends on the ratio of health to other goods consumption. As people live longer but have less and less income, we expect V to fall— the marginal value of additional health in terms of consumption goods will decline. Thus, it would not be appropriate to use our results, nor the results of the economic literature on valuing life more generally, to extrapolate to the value of large changes in the length of life.

In addition, there is an issue about potential changes in lifetime wealth. One potential response to people knowing they will live longer is to work longer, so they can have more consumption and money for medical care when they are elderly. Indeed, the nation is undergoing a gradual increase in the normal retirement age for Social Security (to sixty-seven years of age), and there is a notable fall in disability among the elderly (Manton, Corder, and Stallard 1997). With an increased number of healthy years, there is reason to think lifetime income will not be constant. Just as families appear to adapt to decreased infant mortality by decreasing fertility, one might suppose that individuals will react to increasing healthy years of life with increased work over the life cycle. We thus continue to maintain the commonsense notion that increased life expectancy has a positive value.

8.8.3   Unresolved Issues in the Construction of Medical Price Indexes

We chose to illustrate our points about the problems with current medical price indexes using heart attacks. We focused on heart attacks because the detailed analysis of medical treatments and outcomes is much more straightforward at the level of a particular disease. Heart attacks provide a particularly useful illustration because of the relative ease of measuring relevant outcomes and the substantial previous research on this condition. Nonetheless, one can ask where future work on heart attacks should go, and even more importantly how representative the findings for heart attacks are.

One issue is that one person's heart attack is different from another's and thus treatments of different individuals' heart attacks are effectively different goods. If we are only interested in pricing an "average" heart attack and the mix was constant, this would not be a problem. However, the mix does vary. For example, if people get better at preventing heart attacks, the heart attacks actually suffered may become different in nature—on average a somewhat different disease. In principle, to account for changes in the mix, one could construct a "market basket" of different types of heart attacks, apply the methods presented above, and obtain an overall heart attack price index by using an appropriate set of index weights for the different types of heart attacks. But this would require even more clinically detailed analysis, and the evidence that the nature of heart attacks has not changed much in recent years suggests that such adjustments would not affect our conclusions very much.

A more difficult question is the extent to which our results for heart attacks are representative of price indexes for a broader range of illnesses. The representativeness of the heart attack example can be asked at two levels. One is whether the conclusion that the price increase is less than the general price index in recent years holds for other diseases. Work on the treatment of depression in the 1990s arrived at a similar conclusion (Berndt, Busch, and Frank, chap. 12 in this volume), but at present such evidence exists for few diseases.

Will it be as easy to make progress with other diseases as it was with heart attacks? There are several factors that make heart attacks a relatively easy case to study. First, they are an acute event, so that initiation of care can be dated, and a reasonable approximation to termination is also possible. Second, the major procedures performed will be documented in administrative databases. Finally, mortality is a relevant outcome, though of course not the only relevant outcome.

Indeed, it is with the valuation of outcomes that the most difficult problems probably lie. For example, Berndt, Busch, and Frank (chap. 12 in this volume), in estimating a price index for treating depression, considered those treatments that were therapeutically equivalent in a clinical trial to be on the same isoquant. But a substantial portion of actual treatment was off the frontier. The off-the-frontier treatment may have had no value or may have even had negative value. A full assessment of outcomes would pick up the effects of these treatments, but without studies specifically designed to do that, we are not likely to have reliable answers. Such studies would have to begin with a sample of patients with the disease and knowledge of relevant outcomes. The various dimensions of outcomes would have to be valued.

Even if heart attacks are not representative of medical care in general, forming price indexes for heart attacks highlights two issues that will be common to *any* medical care price index. First, our results suggest that a price index should price the treatment of a *medical condition,* not a *particular medical procedure.* The medical procedures that are used—the number of hospital days, tests, and so on—vary over time quite dramatically. The way to integrate these changes is to look at them in the context of treating particular conditions.

Second, our results highlight the fundamental role of measuring quality in forming medical care price indexes. Incorporating quality change into the AMI price index has a dramatic effect on our results. Because medical technology is changing so rapidly in so many areas, we suspect that measuring quality change in the treatment of other conditions is equally important.

The Bureau of Labor Statistics has recently been improving its measurement of quality in medical care prices. Recently revised BLS methods attempt to include a quality adjustment by asking hospitals to report when major changes occurred in the treatment for the indicated condition, but we think there is a better method.[24] Both the rapidity of advance in health care and the spread of managed care argue for trying to value outcomes explicitly and develop COL indexes, as we have done here. While many types of uncertainty surround outcome-based indexes, they can still provide useful guidance for policy.

References

Advisory Commission to Study the Consumer Price Index. 1996. Toward a more accurate measure of the cost of living: Final report to the Senate Finance Committee. Available at www.ssa.gov/history/reports/boskinrpt.html.

Armknecht, Paul A., and Daniel H. Ginsburg. 1992. Improvements in measuring price changes in consumer services: Past, present, and future. In *Output measurement in the service sectors,* ed. Zvi Griliches. Chicago: University of Chicago Press.

---

24. Hospitals are asked to report to the BLS when treatment for the patient has materially changed, so that quality adjustments can be made. In practice, however, few hospitals do so. This may be because treatment changes are less obvious when they occur gradually as opposed to all at once. In the case of AMI, for example, large changes in treatment over a five- or ten-year period are the cumulative effect of many modest changes in treatment; it is not obvious that hospitals could easily identify these changes as "material" and report them in any given year.

Barzel, Yoram. 1968. Cost of medical treatment: Comment. *American Economic Review* 58 (September): 937–38.

Cardenas, Elaine M. 1996. Revision of the CPI hospital services component. *Monthly Labor Review* 209 (December): 40–48.

Cutler, David M., Mark McClellan, Joseph P. Newhouse, and Dahlia K. Remler. 1998. Are medical prices declining? Evidence from heart attack treatments. *Quarterly Journal of Economics* 113 (November): 991–1024.

Cutler, David M., and Elizabeth Richardson. 1997. Measuring the health of the United States population. *Brookings Papers on Economic Activity, Microeconomics,* 217–70.

———. 1998. The value of health: 1970–1990. *American Economic Review* 88 (2): 97–100.

Fisher, Franklin M., and Zvi Griliches. 1995. Aggregate price indices, new goods, and generics. *Quarterly Journal of Economics* 110 (February): 229–44.

Fisher, Franklin M., and Karl Shell. 1972. *The economic theory of price indices.* New York: Academic Press.

Ford, Ina Kay, and Philip Sturm. 1988. CPI revision provides more accuracy in the medical care services component. *Monthly Labor Review* 111 (4): 17–26.

Fuchs, Victor. 1993. *The future of health policy.* Cambridge, Mass.: Harvard University Press.

Getzen, Thomas E. 1992. Medical care price indexes: Theory, construction, and empirical analysis of the U.S. series, 1927–1990. In *Advances in health economics and health services research,* ed. R. M. Scheffler and L. F. Rossiter. Greenwich, Conn.: JAI Press.

Goldman, L., and E. F. Cook. 1984. The decline in ischemic heart disease mortality rates: An analysis of the comparative effects of medical interventions and changes in lifestyle. *Annals of Internal Medicine* 101 (6): 825–36.

Griliches, Zvi, ed. 1971. *Price indexes and quality change.* Cambridge, Mass.: Harvard University Press.

———, ed. 1992. *Output measurement in the service sectors.* Chicago: University of Chicago Press.

Griliches, Zvi, and Iain Cockburn. 1994. Generics and new goods in pharmaceutical price indexes. *American Economic Review* 84 (December): 1213–32.

Manton, Kenneth G., Larry Corder, and Eric Stallard. 1997. Chronic disability trends in the elderly United States populations: 1982–1994. *Proceedings of the National Academy of Sciences* 94 (6): 2593–98.

McClellan, Mark, Barbara J. McNeil, and Joseph P. Newhouse. 1994. Does more intensive treatment of acute myocardial infarction reduce mortality? *Journal of the American Medical Association* 272 (September): 859–66.

McGovern, P. G., J. S. Pankow, E. Shahar, K. M. Doliszny, A. R. Folsom, H. Blackburn, and R. V. Luepker. 1991. Recent trends in acute coronary heart disease—Mortality, morbidity, medical care, and risk factors: The Minnesota Heart Survey Investigators. *New England Journal of Medicine* 334 (14): 844–90.

Moulton, Brent R., and Karin E. Moses. 1997. Addressing the quality change issue in the Consumer Price Index. *Brookings Papers on Economic Activity,* no. 1, 305–49.

Murray, Christopher J. L., and Alan D. Lopez, eds. 1996. *The global burden of disease: A comprehensive assessment of mortality and disability from diseases, injuries, and risk factors in 1990 and projected to 2020.* Cambridge, Mass.: Harvard University Press.

Newhouse, Joseph P. 1977. Medical care expenditures: A cross national survey. *Journal of Human Resources* 12 (winter): 115–25.

———. 1989. Measuring medical prices and understanding their effects—the Baxter Prize address. *Journal of Health Administration Education* 7 (winter): 19–26.

Newhouse, Joseph P., Shan Cretin, and Christina J. Witsberger. 1989. Predicting hospital accounting costs. *Health Care Financing Review* 11 (fall): 25–33.

Nordhaus, William D. 1996. Beyond the CPI: An augmented cost of living index. Yale University, manuscript.

Prospective Payment Assessment Commission. 1996. *Medicare and the American health care system: Report to the Congress.* Washington, D.C.: The Commission.

Scitovsky, Anne A. 1967. Changes in the costs of treatment of selected illness, 1951–67. *American Economic Review* 57:1182.

Tobin, James. 1997. Thoughts on indexing the elderly. *Public Interest Report* (Federation of American Scientists) 50 (2): 13–20. Available at www.fas.org/faspir/pir9607.html.

Tolley, George, Donald Kenkel, and Robert Fabian, eds. 1994. *Valuing health for policy: An economic approach.* Chicago: University of Chicago Press.

U.S. Department of Labor. Bureau of Labor Statistics. 1992. The Consumer Price Index. In *BLS handbook of methods,* chap. 19. Bulletin no. 2414. Washington, D.C.: Government Printing Office.

Viscusi, W. Kip. 1993. The value of risks to life and health. *Journal of Economic Literature* 31:1912–46.

Comment   Frank C. Wykoff

Ever since Congress passed Medicaid and Medicare in 1965, many economists and commentators have held the view that the medical treatment sector of the economy has acted like an economic version of a physics black hole.[1] The health care sector, broadly defined, seems to suck in more and more resources over time without yielding increases in output; in other words, despite huge and sustained increases in expenditures on health care over the last thirty-some years, societal indicators of health have not been improving—infant death rates, male life expectancy, proportion of citizens who have no health insurance, and the like have shown little or no improvement. That the medical care industry is a black hole has, I believe, become conventional wisdom.

I too hold roughly this view. In fact, when asked to speak to medical groups or to the press, I have been telling them that the real crisis in American health care is a financial problem, not a coverage problem—the problem is how to prevent this sector from consuming ever larger shares of GDP without hampering the sector's performance.[2] The U.S. economy has

Frank C. Wykoff is the Eldon Smith Professor of Economics at Pomona College.

1. The black hole analogy comes from Milton Friedman (1992). Friedman freely acknowledges difficulties in output measurement, but at the time, only one of the usual social indicators showed measurable improvement—the life expectancy of women had increased.

2. The need for federal health care reform was recognized of course in the first year of the Clinton administration. Thus President Clinton's first term was consumed by an attempt to radically reform the financing, delivery, and provision of medical care. Unfortunately, an error in diagnosis by the Clinton team doomed their reform effort from the start. They

grown at remarkable rates during the last fifty years—the 1948 U.S. economy was the largest in the world in both absolute terms and in terms of the income at the median. That 1948 economy has since been multiplied about sixfold. This has not been rapid enough, though, to support growth at a constant GDP share of the medical treatment industry. The share of GDP has grown from around 7 percent to about 14 percent of GDP.[3]

No matter how you slice and dice the data, medical care has been a long-range fiscal disaster. Nothing else Americans spend money on—food, defense, Social Security—has grown as much as medical care.[4] This problem is not unique to the United States, because while financial problems are most acute in the United States, they also characterize other industrial societies' medical treatment systems, from Japan to Canada to Germany.[5] All suffer the same problem—growth of medical care threatens to outstrip growth in sources of funding.

For federal government budget policy, health care is an even bigger problem. Practically nonexistent in the 1950s (less than $0.5 billion in 1955), less than a decade after Medicare passed, in 1975 total federal health care spending reached $32 billion per year. By 1995 total federal outlays for medical and health care had reached $280 billion, larger than defense, interest on the debt, and income security, an amount exceeded only by Social Security. Projections by the Congressional Budget Office based on current law, standard growth projections, and demographic trends are even scarier. By 2005, the federal government expects to spend $876 billion on health and medical care. By 2010 Medicare and Medicaid

---

thought the key problem was inadequate coverage of health care insurance, especially for the poor and children, when the real problem was fiscal—health care financing by the federal government was threatening to destroy the long-range federal budget equilibrium. Instead of trying to solve this fiscal problem, the Clinton reformers tried to opt for universal coverage with the same level of treatment for all recipients. This not only would have failed to solve the fiscal problem, but might have made it worse. The Clinton reform also would have required radical surgery of the entire health care sector. This was a radical surgery that those in the sector fought to avoid.

Finance was the key problem, not universal coverage, because the only incremental aspect of the system was its prospective financial insolvency as a result of actuarially impossible legislative intentions written into current law, given demographic trends and the technological, diffusion, and growth dynamics of the industry. America has never had universal medical care. In fact, throughout human history, very few people have even had modern medical care, so the absence of universal care or insurance could not have been a crisis.

3. U.S. National Institutes of Health, *Health Affairs,* fall 1994. Most of the data on federal budgets and health care spending as a portion of GDP come from the Congressional Budget Office on-line web site.

4. There is nothing inherently wrong with the medical care share of a growing GDP growing, but it certainly suggests we should be getting a good deal of social gains from this sector, and the question we are raising is, Do the increases in social welfare from health care spending reflect this rapid growth in medical care expenditures? Or would society be better off were we to reallocate resources away from medical care toward something else, say, child care, criminal deterrence, housing, education, or another area?

5. *Health Affairs,* fall 1994 contains growth rates by country that suggest all of the industrial societies are struggling to get a grip on medical (especially government financed) spending.

will have surpassed Social Security in the budget. From 4 percent of GDP in 1995, *federal* health care spending will rise to 10 percent of GDP in 2035. Bluntly put, these medical cost growth rates, expected to run up at twice the rate of GDP, will not be sustained.

The immediate reasons, if not underlying causes, of this explosive growth of medical care expenditures are well known—an aging population; more health care per person; new, more costly technologies; and especially rapid diffusion of these new technologies into standard practice. My view is that a major cause of growth in medical costs has to do with government insurance and tax policy distortions since 1967. The argument frequently given, that technological change is a cause of rising costs, is odd.[6] Most industries adopt new technologies only if they raise demand or lower costs. If it is true that technology is raising costs without better products and that this, in turn, is causing medical expenditures to rise, then this signals an unhealthy industry—seriously noncompetitive and possibly a black hole.

In short, I thought the medical care industry was fiscally sick and out of control. Now along come Cutler, McClellan, Newhouse, and Remler (Cutler et al.) to tell us that the prices of heart attack treatments have not been rising but falling, that the quantity of treatments has increased and that the quality of these treatments has improved. Similar results are announced for cataract surgeries and for depression treatments in other papers. The theme of this conference volume seems to be that, with exceptions like rheumatoid arthritis, medical treatments are getting much better—faster, less invasive, safer, and with better outcomes, in terms of longer life expectancy and especially in terms of improvements in posttreatment quality of life. It looks like public perceptions, or at least mine, have been wrong.

Instead of sucking up resources and releasing no improvements, medical care has gotten so much better that, once properly measured, output and quality can be seen to have been rising and prices falling. Instead of carping about increased costs, budget problems, and black holes, it turns out we should be thanking the medical profession for making us so much better off. How can we (me, the public, and the statistical agencies) have been so wrong yet again?

Economists, myself included, used to worry about the productivity growth slowdown with the consequent wage stagnation grinding the economy down since the early seventies. Then along came the Boskin Commission to tell us that statistical agencies had chronically overstated price increases, consequently understating output and productivity growth. Rather than lamenting the productivity growth slowdown, we should have been patting our leaders on the back while basking in the glory of the

---

6. I wish to thank Thomas Hazlett who suggested to me the possibly noneconomic impact of technology on health care efficiency.

highest living standards in history. We were not falling behind the rest of the world (i.e., Japan). We were kicking some serious economic butt. Also, I was thin until a new National Institute of Health study told me I was fat. The question all these new research announcements raise is, Are the new experts right? How does one explain this evident disconnection between common perceptions buttressed by previous research and official statistical indicators on the one hand and evident reality revealed by new research on the other?

Summary of the Paper

Basically, Cutler et al. argue that the traditional BLS producer and consumer price indexes misinterpret quantity of service increases and quality of service improvements as price increases. Thus, the official medical price indexes are biased upward. As a critique of the traditional approach, the story Cutler et al. tell is credible. Based on heart attack treatment episode cost data compiled from a (not to be identified) major teaching hospital, the authors give two reasons why medical PPI and CPI indexes are biased upward. Traditional medical price indexes indicate, as cost increases, shifts toward more expensive treatments (such as bypass surgery) and away from less expensive treatments (such as medical management). This measurement error is classic substitution bias resulting from fixed-weight index procedures. Correctly measured, these shifts represent increases in the quantity of treatments, thus the official indexes incorrectly partition heart attack expenditures biasing prices upward and quantities downward.

The second reason official statistics overstate increases is that insufficient allowance is made for quality improvements in treatments. New treatments are better—the quality of health care has improved—because both procedures (such as angioplasty and bypass surgeries) and outcomes are better for patients. Procedures are better because downtime during treatment is less, procedures are more reliable, and pain and suffering is lower. Outcomes are better because patients live longer, and the quality of these incremental years is better because people are more ambulatory, more active, and more satisfied with the quality of their lives.

As Cutler et al. show, when proper allowance is made for shifts to better procedures, the price of heart attack treatments has been falling, not rising. They conclude, "Our detailed illustrations of medical price indexes suggests, at least for the case of heart attacks, medical prices are not rising very much and may well be declining." They aptly note that their results seem counterintuitive and ask, "Why is the public so wrong about this?" They attribute the public misperception to the above measurement error.

Critique of the Paper

As discussant, my job is to ask a different question: "Are the authors right?" And, in addition, I ask, "Even if they're right, does this research imply that the public is wrong?" My short answers are yes and no. The research is a sound and important contribution, but I do not think it follows that public perceptions (and my own) are completely off as a result.

First, I would like to stress that this is a good paper. Fixed-weight design in construction of medical PPIs and CPIs produces serious substitution bias. The authors show that the measurement bias for heart attack treatments is so serious that the *signs* of price and quantity changes may be wrong. Statistical agency focus on medical care inputs (hospitals, doctors, drugs, etc.) rather than outputs (heart attack treatment results) can generate seriously misleading indexes. The authors succeed in moving us a good deal closer to understanding the social consequences of medical care. In measuring the costs and benefits of heart attack treatments, the authors do an excellent job. They make sensible inferences and imputations when necessary and derive viable and reasonable results. They convinced me that the price of a heart attack treatment has fallen over the sample period and that improvements in quality and length of life have increased. They have persuasive evidence supporting the conclusion that measured price increases in official medical care indexes contain measurement error and actually reflect increases in the quantities of expensive treatments and improvements in the quality of these treatments.

I would like to raise two concerns I have. I am a little concerned about the authors' index number model's connection to economic theory, and I still think the medical care industry is growing like topsy and needs to be slowed down and probably restructured rather radically.

At the heart of my concern with the paper is a problem suggested by Berndt, Cutler, Frank, Griliches, Newhouse, and Triplett (chap. 4 in this volume). A consumer's decisions reflect only marginal costs to the consumer; in other words, all relevant costs are in the future. If market arrangements cause the marginal cost of a medical treatment to the consumer to be 20 percent of the price, then the consumer will consume medical care until the marginal utility falls to 20 percent of the price too.[7]

The prevalence of insurance-induced moral hazard implies that individuals will value the medical treatment itself well below its total costs. Berndt et al. argue that, mainly because of the prevalence of insurance-induced moral hazard, standard revealed preference theory may not apply to medical care index number construction.[8] This argument is extremely troubling, because if it is correct, the failure of revealed preference theory removes the key intellectual tool underpinning virtually all useful implications of

7. "If consumers pay for only, say, 20 percent of medical care at the margin, they will seek to consume medical care until its marginal value is only about twenty cents per dollar of spending. This is true even though people *on average* must pay for the full dollar of medical care" (Berndt et al., chap. 4 in this volume, p. 145).

8. "As a practical matter, this inability to employ the assumptions underlying traditional revealed preference theory severely hampers the ability of economic statisticians to construct accurate and readily interpretable price indexes for medical care" (Berndt et al., chap. 4 in this volume, p. 146).

consumer price indexes. This in turn vitiates all price and quantity partitions of expenditure flows related to medical care which, in turn, diminishes their policy effectiveness.

Unless revealed preference theory can be employed or at least the problems its absence presents finessed in some way, the economic statistician, as Berndt et al. point out, has no firm theoretical basis for contributing to the social implications of medical care. After all, without revealed preference theory, economists have very little to contribute to meaningfully measuring output and productivity in this sector. This charge, then, of the failure of revealed preference theory, is very damaging and needs to be addressed directly.

Cutler et al. are certainly aware of the difficulties of applying standard revealed preference theory to medical care. They argue that one cannot simply place medical services in the consumer utility function and then optimize this function subject to a budget constraint and derive price indexes in the usual way—that is, in their own and in Berndt et al.'s terms, they spurn revealed preference theory. I was so dismayed on being told that statistics could not be built on standard consumer optimization methods that I felt economists had to abandon the field. The authors, however, moved forward and produced index numbers evidently without having to rely on consumer utility maximization (as they criticize hedonic and other approaches for doing).

How do Cutler et al. finesse the problem of constructing an index without any underlying utility optimization in which medical treatments appear in the utility function? Well, it turns out they do this very cleverly. The problem is, I don't think their procedure is entirely on the up-and-up.[9] They do build their model of treatment cost differences over time from a utility model, but the role of health care in the model is unusual and perhaps not quite kosher.

Equation (2) of Berndt et al. and equation (3) of Cutler et al. both express differences in utility between the base period without treatment and the period with treatment for the same type of utility function and for the same type of change. In particular, paring away irrelevancies, utility is derived from health which in turn depends on a medical treatment and from total expenditures on "everything else" in the consumer budget. Equating utility without treatment to utility with treatment and with less income for everything else, the authors are, in fact, imposing a first difference version of a standard utility maximization exercise. Health care expenses and insurance costs enter the function indirectly through their effect on the ability of consumers to obtain utility from everything else.

---

9. My critique of the theoretical model is based on the discussion in Berndt et al. as well as on Cutler et al. From the point of view of my critique, they use the same model, even though there are some differences in details.

The problem is that "everything else" enters the function as a value term, not a quantity, so that strictly speaking this is not a utility function, but a function in which it is already implicitly assumed that the consumer has obtained the quantity of "everything else" versus medical care treatment that optimizes utility. All those partial derivatives reflect someone's margin. They do not just appear. The authors invoke Fisher and Shell (1972), but Fisher and Shell's index number theorizing is based on consumer optimization. Unless the change in cost of living between utility with and without treatment, is optimal, it has no utility interpretation and is arbitrary measurement without theory. I do not see how utility or welfare conclusions can be derived from this model without an optimization going on somewhere. Thus, I am not entirely convinced that the authors, or anyone else for that matter, can draw welfare implications from models in which no one is making rational decisions. Perhaps the economic statisticians abandon standard "revealed preference theory" at their peril.

Implications of Marginal Analysis

Actually, standard revealed preference theory[10] can be used to analyze medical care and to partition expenditures into price and quantity components, so that one can draw social implications from price indexes, output measures, and productivity indicators. However, revealed preference theory does need to be applied correctly, and that is tricky for all the reasons Berndt et al. indicate. One thought for a solution is to recognize that relevant costs from a consumer choice, and thus a social welfare, point of view reflect only the future costs—that is, marginal costs only, not total costs incurred at the decisive moment.

Berndt et al. make this point themselves when they note that, within their model, consumption of medical care services will be valued, at the margin, by the consumer, by the marginal cost of the product. Consider the implications of this point in the following example. Utility depends on three goods, x, y, and z. The first two, x and y, are medical care treatments (cataract surgery and angioplasty) and good z is bananas. Because there

---

10. The authors use the phrase "standard revealed preference theory." In my lexicon they mean standard consumer utility theory, of which revealed preference theory is one example. In equations (1) and (2) in this comment, I use marginal utility analysis. It is easy to extrapolate from this to marginal rates of substitution by computing ratios of marginal utilities, i.e., $U_x/U_y = MRS_{xy}$. To me, the phrase "revealed preference theory" refers to a small piece of consumer utility theory developed by Paul Samuelson in his *Foundations of Economic Analysis* (1963). Samuelson showed by successive experiments in which a representative consumer is faced with income-compensated alternative budget constraints that his behavior reveals his preference ordering. This is an econometric model of consumer theory. The discussions in the papers here are questioning the use of consumer theory itself, not simply Samuelson's revealed preference version.

Despite my view that "revealed preference theory" is not "consumer utility theory," I adopt the authors' use of the term in this comment.

is nothing about medical care treatments which says consumers will not do what they see as being in their own best interests, they will, if allowed, consume these three products until the following optimizing condition is met:

$$(1) \qquad\qquad U_x/P_x \ = \ U_y/P_y \ = \ U_z/P_z.$$

The marginal utility of a dollar spent on each good must be equal. This theory is not wrong; however, it is a tool that, like all tools, needs to be applied properly.

An important question is, What are the relevant P_x, P_y, and P_z? These have to be the incremental costs incurred by the consumer when the decision is made to consume the services. In the cases of x and y, P_x and P_y are the future costs to the consumer when he/she decides to have the procedure. To be accurate these costs need to include copayments, opportunity costs of time in treatment, pain and suffering, transportation costs, recovery time, risks of failure, and the like. All other costs associated with medical care treatment—the hospital building, the machines, the doctors' training, the acquisition of anesthetics, and so forth are irrelevant to the consumer's marginal decision. These costs are irrelevant to the consumer's decision, and marginal utility, for two possible reasons—either someone else incurs them, or they are sunk costs. But these are details. Suppose the nonpecuniary and nonmedical marginal costs are the same proportion of each good, x, y, and z.

Let the total medical cost of each treatment, x and y, be C_x and C_y, respectively, and let C_z be the cost of z, the banana. Then, if the copayment on x is 20 percent of C_x and on y is 5 percent of C_y, and if the full marginal cost to the consumer of the banana is 100 percent of C_z, then consumer choice calculus tells that the marginal condition is

$$(2) \qquad\qquad U_x/.2C_x \ = \ U_y/.05C_y \ = \ U_z/C_z.$$

Equation (2) is quite a bit different from equation (1), because equation (2) implies that the increment to utility from different medical treatments will differ depending on the financing method.[11] If one incurs, at the margin, only 5 percent of the costs of treatment y, then y is worth, at the margin, 5 percent of the medical cost of that treatment to the consumer versus 20 percent of x. Even more importantly, if $C_z = C_x = C_y$, then

11. This model roughly underlies the Berndt, Busch, and Frank (chap. 12 in this volume) construction of their CPI-like index for major depression treatments. They measure the portion of total treatment cost borne directly by the patient as the consumer price which they distinguish from the producer price. Even here, though, they do not measure only direct incremental costs to the consumer and commingle fixed and marginal costs. They note, with some consternation, that changes in insurance plan design have a serious impact on their consumer price indexes.

consumers value some medical treatments at 5 percent and some medical treatments at 20 percent of a banana! Suppose further that the total costs of these three items, x, y, and z reflect social costs, then this analysis suggests that very large social costs, in the form of valuable resources, are being used up by the medical treatment sector for which consumers are getting back very little utility.[12] This sure sounds like an economic version of a black hole to me!

An Enigma Suggests a New Perspective

There remains an enigma with marginal analysis of the industry which suggests that something is missing. If consumers only value medical care at the margin equal to the copayment, then how does society justify all these fixed costs associated with the treatment? The utility, at least in some sense, of medical care must exceed the marginal cost of the treatment. Otherwise, society chronically spends way too much on medical care. Put another way, if the only social welfare from medical care is based on the marginal utility to the patient from the treatments, then why does society persist in spending so much more for medical care than can be justified by these 10 percent or 30 percent copayments? Is such a major nonmarket (government or nonprofit sector) failure likely? Should we cut medical care sector spending back to 10 to 30 percent of its current size? Would refinancing techniques, like medical IRAs, designed to shift more costs incurred by the patient to the future, cause a radical decline in the social costs of medical care? In short, do we need to neutralize this black hole before it sucks us financially dry?

Maybe, but maybe not. Obviously, this policy issue has something to do with insurance and its resultant moral hazard and principal agent problems noted by Berndt et al. and with the role of the government and nonprofit organizations. Is this a case of poor policy design based on poor policy analysis of the nonprofit and public sectors, which has ignored modern public choice theory, and in so doing has allowed this industry to grow like topsy? All of this may be true, but is it?

One possible out can be found in Philipson and Lakdawalla (chap. 3 in this volume) on nonprofit sector conduct. The Philipson and Lakdawalla model suggests that utility from medical care services is enjoyed by economic agents other than the patient. The authors argue that donors to nonprofits obtain utility from both medical care output and from medical care input. If so, then society, in some large sense, may be providing welfare from medical care beyond that enjoyed by the patient. This model is suggestive, but, according to Richard Frank's critique, still has some way to go before we can accept it as viable.

---

12. All of this analysis can be done with marginal rates of substitution or with Samuelson's revealed preference model, but the above approach makes the points more clearly.

I would like to suggest a different way of looking at the problem. I suggest a model which regrounds medical price indexes on standard economic theory, partially reconciles this evident social failure, and suggests some different directions for new research. Let us take a tip from Jack Triplett's notion that human bodies, like cars or other machines, require maintenance and repair, and that there are many parallels between the two industries. Like Triplett, I am not so crass as to suggest humans are machines, but, also like Triplett, I believe one can gain insight into medical care by looking at how economic statisticians price automobile repair.[13]

I shall build on Triplett by beginning with Zvi Griliches's critique of the Triplett paper, in which Griliches points out that economic statisticians evidently do not construct very good indexes of car repair either.[14] Productivity growth figures for the automobile repair industry, compiled by Griliches from official statistics, imply negative average annual productivity growth. Negative productivity growth, in Griliches's judgment, is not credible. It fails what Chuck Hulten (1990) calls the "interocular test"—the error is so large that it hits you right between the eyes. While Griliches's point that car repair indexes are seriously flawed is persuasive, rather than answering a question it begs one—Why do we construct such poor automobile repair indexes? Just as we might learn about medical care by seeing what we do right elsewhere, perhaps errors we make in measuring car repair index design can tip us off to what is wrong with health care measurement.

I think we need to apply capital theory carefully to both car repair and to health care. One way to do this in the health care case is to reinterpret insurance policies as acquisition of capital assets by the insured. The capital asset purchased can be viewed as an ownership right in a medical-care-industry (mc) asset. This mc asset is capable of generating various services, treatments, diagnostic tests, service inspections, tune-ups, and so forth. In other words, suppose consumers view an insurance contract as purchasing ownership rights to an asset with known properties. These known properties consist of reasonable access in the future to medical care (under the terms of the insurance contract).

While, from an insurance company's point of view, an insurance contract may be a *contingent* contract for a service that may or may not be

---

13. Triplett points out, in chapter 1 of this volume, that many of the problems analysts normally think are unique to medical care are also encountered in the automobile repair industry. Asymmetric information, stochastic demands, principal agent problems, and moral hazard under insurance all occur in the automobile industry as well. The only real difference seems to be that one can trade in old cars for new models, but the old body has to last until death. With organ transplants and genetic engineering, even this distinction may soon disappear.

14. Griliches, in his comment to chapter 1 in this volume, shows that the productivity growth figures for medical care and for automobile repair have both been negative in recent years. Do we really think that with all the new diagnostic methods available in both areas efficiency and economic performance have declined?

needed at some future time, with the resultant moral hazard problem of overconsumption, this view may not represent the consumer's perspective, and after all we certainly ought to take the consumer's perspective in designing a consumer price index. Building on capital theory, assume that the consumer views his insurance premiums as buying ownership rights to an mc asset. This mc asset can be thought of as ownership in a "firm" that produces a flow of medical services available to the owner when he or she chooses to use them.[15] The service flow that derives from the asset is analogous to the service flow from any other asset or, if you will, machine (or, à la Triplett, car).

From Jorgenson's model of capital theory,[16] competitive equilibrium implies that the acquisition price of a new asset in period t, $q(0, t)$, equals the present discounted value of the future flow of user costs of capital on the asset over the life of the asset, so that

$$(3) \qquad q(0,t) = \sum_{s=0}^{s=L} \frac{c(s, t + s)}{(1 + r)^s},$$

where s indexes time and where L is the life of the asset.[17] Note that the cost of using the asset in period $t + s$ is $c(s, t + s)$, the cost of the period $t + s$ flow of services, not $q(0, t)$ nor $q(0, t + s)$. At acquisition, given either perfect foresight or rational expectations, the asset price paid for the insurance, the present discounted value of the premium stream, must equal $q(0, t)$ and therefore this asset price represents the marginal utility to the consumer of buying that asset in period t.

Now one may argue that because health care is financed through work, the market is noncompetitive. This may be partly so. Certainly, we all know that the tax system biases these prices. One may also argue, as Philipson and Lakdawalla do, that since the industry is nonprofit, normal competitive conditions do not explain production. But beyond these distortions, the assumption that competitive forces work on health insurance packages available to and acquired by workers seems pretty good. After all, workers can change jobs; they can change health plans; they do have periodic choices. Thus, I, for one, am comfortable with the assumption that after allowing for tax policy distortions, the cost of insurance represents the utility the payer associates with the present value of *access* to the future flow of medical care services.[18]

---

15. The owner here is a producer who uses the asset to produce health; or, more precisely, uses the flow of services from the mc asset to maintain his human capital asset producing at some optimal level. This producer is, of course, the same person as the consumer/worker/human/insured.

16. See, for example, Jorgenson (1973), Hulten (1990), and Wykoff (1998).

17. Strictly speaking s indexes age and $t + s$ date, because with machines age of the asset matters. We discuss the meaning of s in the case of an mc asset below.

18. The utility and welfare implications of Medicare insurance and other government programs are different. One may want to build a model directly on a societal welfare function rather than from a consumer utility model. I ignore this issue in this comment.

Leaving aside copayments for the moment, suppose the entire cost of medical care is covered by insurance companies (from premiums) with whom the members of the HMO (or health plan) are insured. If we compute the asset price $q(0, t)$ of the insurance contracts, then the marginal utility to the representative health care consumer of period $t + s$ health care, in equilibrium, must equal the user cost of capital $c(s, t + s)$ from equation (3).[19] If this were not so, then the consumer/worker would change assets; in other words, he would sell this contract and buy another one.

Put another way, optimizing economic agents, on the buyer's side of the medical care industry, purchase assets at prices that reflect the marginal utility they associate with the assets. This means that the "marginal utility" of medical care, when the insurance is purchased, is the product of the price of the insurance asset times the number of consumers who purchase these assets. The sum over the patient population of these expenditures covers the cost of producing medical care, including the cost of financing it. Thus, the relevant price index, from the consumer's point of view, for any one period, is simply that period's user cost of the mc asset.

All that remains to be done is compute the user cost. That is, one needs to spread the acquisition cost of the asset over its life into period-by-period components. This has been done with machines and human capital by Jorgenson and Associates (see, e.g., Lau 2000) by defining the efficiency function, $\phi(s)$, which indicates the in-use productive efficiency of an asset age s relative to the efficiency of a new asset. The meaning of age-based efficiency for an ownership right in a medical care asset is different from efficiency by age of machines. In general, though, the ϕ function can take many possible forms anyway. It need not even be a function, but can be a sequence. One can normalize $\phi(s)$ on a new asset, so that $\phi(0) = 1$. For machines, which depreciate, ϕ is then a nonincreasing function like

$$s = 1 \quad 2 \quad 3 \quad 4 \quad \ldots$$

$$\phi(s) = 1 \quad .9 \quad .8 \quad .6 \quad \ldots.$$

The efficiency function of an mc asset need not be nonincreasing. In fact, with health care, it is important to note that efficiency will change with technological change, and this suggests an important research topic for the future. In the absence of technological change, though, perhaps the mc asset $\phi(s)$ is the same for all s. Such a machine is called a one-horse-shay asset in the capital theory literature.

---

19. I am assuming away here problems associated with coercion in forcing workers to choose from a limited list of possible health care plans, so that the market for choice is thick enough that the representative health care consumer can buy what he or she wants. In fact, this model suggests why disputes occur over the packages offered by various employers—these disputes may simply reflect consumer demands to include their optimal asset package in their set of options.

Using the concept of an efficiency function here for this medical care asset, and, assuming competitiveness in the asset market, we can simplify equation (3):

$$(4) \qquad\qquad q(0,t) = \sum_{s=0}^{s=L} \frac{\phi(s)c(0,t)}{(1 + r)^s}.$$

Now allocating insurance costs over the life of the plan member or patient boils down to determining acquisition cost of the insurance contract and the form of the efficiency function. As a first approximation, this approach will produce a more accurate measure of the price/quantity partition of medical costs than either pricing hospitals, which is current official practice, or treatments, which is suggested by the paper under review as well as by others in this volume.

A natural objection to this asset approach is that it does not account for the stochastic use of the health care asset or what is the same thing for differences in use patterns over the life of the asset. However, that is exactly the point of this exercise. Measuring the cost of specific treatment events or the cost of hospitals and medical personnel both miss the main point of the medical care product from the consumer's point of view. This becomes clear when one considers the machine analogue. Suppose a consumer buys a telephone, and economic statisticians want to know the utility derived from the phone by the consumer. Economic statisticians usually do one of two things. They price phones and construct indexes on phone production. Or they allocate this asset acquisition price over the life of the phone and build an index on the user cost. The latter approach is clearly more accurate for measuring consumption of phone services per period than the former, and this point is the essence of the Jorgenson user-cost contribution to production theory and measurement.[20]

But neither approach tries to dig into the issue of when exactly owners are *using* the phone. Do you only use your phone when you talk on it? Do you only use it when you get a call? No. That asset is providing you a flow of services, just like your desk, chair, and car, all the time. It makes little sense to only place utility on your phone or chair when you are talking or sitting. In fact, ownership of assets generally provides two types of service flows: a "passive flow" by being there when and if needed—to receive calls, to be sat in, to be ready for workers to employ—and an "active flow"—driving it, drilling with it, sitting on it.[21]

This is not to say that the question of when you actually consume or

---

20. Copayments may be integrated into the model, but will require distinguishing between those one expects to incur and those that come as surprises. This distinction is discussed below.

21. The idea that service flows from assets may consist of more than active use comes from Charles R. Hulten (1990), though he bears no fault for my use of the idea here.

produce "active services" with an asset, whether it be health care or cars or phones, is uninteresting. It is to say that this is not the only use one gets from the asset. Furthermore, this suggests to me that approaching the problem of measuring social valuations of health care by trying to measure these "active services" or treatment costs alone is going to give the wrong answer.[22] The economic statistician will accurately value the phone only if utility from the phone derives solely from actual calls.

This capital theory focus suggests a line of research that needs to be developed both for understanding asset use and for understanding issues like maintenance and repair of cars and provision of health care. How do we disentangle the value of the asset and its future flow of user costs for the entire asset including the "passive services" from the "active services" measures, such as treatment costs and their marginal valuations? This will not be easy to do, which is probably why it has not yet been done.

To begin thinking about what it means to use an asset, and to maintain and repair it, requires, I think, modeling expected and unexpected uses of the active service. No one buys a machine or car expecting it to be an infinitely lived one-horse-shay and no one expects an infinite life span with perfect health. (We may pray for this, but we do not expect it.) Owners of both machines and humans (ourselves) expect these assets to incur downtimes, to require maintenance and repair, and to have finite lives. The lengths of these lives also are uncertain in both cases.

This approach suggests that rational economic agents fully expect a stochastic stream of care in order to maintain the output service flow from capital assets, whether human or not. In each case, then, one can acquire an a priori contract to provide, under predictable cost conditions, the necessary maintenance and repairs. Owners in both cases also can (usually) decide they would rather not pay to acquire the contracts or insurance policies to cover future stochastic maintenance and repair events, and simply pay as they go.[23] From an indexing point of view, of course, the latter financing option is easy for the economic statistician to deal with. The former is what is giving us fits. But the former is easier if one simply views the contract insurance policy to cover the utility to the consumer of access to the medical care asset when needed, knowing that it will be needed, but not exactly when. In other words, the full price of the contract for the patient groups under private insurance covers the entire *expected* future flow of medical care services. Only unexpected events need to be accounted for in addition.

Measurement problems occur when reality diverges from expectations, even if both are stochastic. In general, though, I would argue that most

---

22. See Berndt and Fuss (1986) for an interesting perspective on capital utilization.
23. Under perfect foresight or rational expectations, copayments as well as premiums can be integrated into $q(0, t)$ by appropriately discounting these expenses to time t.

insurance costs cover expected treatment flows. Two kinds of unanticipatable deviations present problems. These would be events that are so rare that economic agents cannot be expected to form probabilities of their occurrence.[24] One type of unexpected change is environmental shocks and surprising changes in the demographic composition of the patient group—climate warming and depletion of the ozone layer or hard-to-predict increases in life spans and changes in conduct while living can all radically alter health care costs.[25] Earthquakes, hurricanes, tornadoes, and the like can be expected to occur with some probability, so they are covered. Normal population growth, though not war-related baby booms, can be expected. Normal day-to-day activities and accidents can be expected. It is only inexplicable deviations from normal that cannot easily be subsumed under some probabilistic contractual basis.

The other true surprises are unexpected jumps in technology which alter the relationship between the present value of premiums and the present value of the costs of supplying the medical care asset. As in the cases of environment and demographics, some stream of technological change can be expected, but not sudden large jumps—such a sudden jump might be the discovery of Viagra, a unexpected new impotence treatment that is naturally very much in demand.[26] More typical, in recent years, is that new expensive treatments become available and are rapidly diffused into popular use. HMO insurance contracts tend to promise "standard practice" treatment. As a practical matter, standard practice changes over the course of the insurance contract.[27] Does the promise of standard practice care mean that HMOs and patients are willing to accommodate any and all technological shocks? No.

In recent years, the notion of standard practice treatment may have gotten both buyers and sellers into trouble, because very expensive treatments are rapidly diffused into becoming standard practice, even though both sides of the market may want to avoid new costly procedures.[28] Thus, insurance contracts are being regularly renegotiated to reflect the very rapidly changing technology. This recontracting and rapid technological change issues can be integrated into the capital theory approach, but that is another subject for future research.

24. Keynes (1935) draws this distinction in his analysis of liquidity preference.
25. Food supplement advertisements targeted at aged populations suggest that older people take up scuba diving and other risky activities. If older people undertake risky activities, then the accident rate and incidence of active service flow from the medical care asset could rise.
26. Kaiser Permanente, a major HMO, announced in June 1998, as this is being written, that if it were to cover Viagra, it would become insolvent.
27. HMOs will provide new treatments to avoid litigation and negative press. They do not want to deny care, because they fear adverse reputation effects which lower the value of the firm.
28. This problem is especially acute when new discoveries result in very expensive treatments that are then used for patients whose conditions are not medically suitable.

I want to repeat that the paper by Cutler et al. is a very exciting piece of research into a problem of major social concern. The authors have taken on a difficult task and succeeded in stimulating a good deal of thinking about this very important issue.

References

Berndt, Ernst R., and Melvyn A. Fuss. 1986. Productivity measurement with adjustments for variations in capacity utilization, and other forms of temporary equilibrium. *Journal of Econometrics* 33:7–29.

Fisher, Franklin M., and Karl Shell. 1972. *The economic theory of price indexes.* New York: Academic.

Friedman, Milton. 1992. *Input and output in medical care.* Stanford, Calif.: Hoover Institution, Stanford University.

Hulten, Charles R. 1990. The measurement of capital. In *Fifty years of economic measurement: The jubilee of the Conference on Research in Income and Wealth,* ed. Ernst R. Berndt and Jack E. Triplett. NBER Studies in Income and Wealth, vol. 54. Chicago: University of Chicago Press.

Jorgenson, Dale W. 1973. The economic theory of replacement and depreciation. In *Econometrics and economic theory: Essays in honor of W. Sellykraerts.* New York: Macmillan.

Keynes, John Maynard. 1935. *The general theory of employment, interest, and money.* New York: Harcourt, Brace and World.

Lau, Lawrence J., ed. 2000. *Econometrics and the cost of capital: Essays in honor of Dale W. Jorgenson.* Econometrics, vol. 2. Cambridge, Mass.: MIT Press.

Samuelson, Paul A. 1963. *Foundations of economic analysis.* Cambridge, Mass.: Harvard University Press.

U.S. National Institutes of Health. 1994. *Health Affairs,* fall.

Wykoff, Frank C. 1998. Comment on Barbara Fraumeni, "Expanding economic accounts for productivity analysis: A nonmarket and human capital perspective." Paper presented at NBER CRIW conference on New Directions in Productivity Research, Silver Spring, Md., April.

Trends in Heart Attack Treatment and Outcomes, 1975–1995
Literature Review and Synthesis

Paul Heidenreich and Mark McClellan

9.1 Introduction

Age-adjusted mortality rates for ischemic heart disease have fallen for the last three decades (Goldman and Cook 1984). The reasons for the decline—which include primary prevention of coronary events, secondary prevention, improved outcomes of the events themselves, and changes in event severity—have been the subject of considerable debate. Much of the debate centers on the relative importance of medical technology versus lifestyle changes or other sources of reductions in risk factors. The debate has important implications for priorities in health care research and policymaking: If medical interventions have been relatively unimportant, then the direction of more resources to research and education on preventive care may be worthwhile. But resolving the debate is very difficult due to the complexity of health care interventions and disease processes.

Several well-known studies have assessed the contribution of broad categories of explanatory factors by synthesizing evidence from clinical trials, changes in medical practices, and changes in population risk characteristics. Risk factor reduction leading to primary and secondary prevention of fatal coronary events, including acute myocardial infarction (AMI) and ischemia-induced ventricular arrhythmias, appears to have been respon-

Paul Heidenreich, a practicing cardiologist, is assistant professor of medicine at Stanford University. Mark McClellan is associate professor of economics and medicine at Stanford University and a research associate of the National Bureau of Economic Research.

The authors thank David Cutler, Alan Garber, and Jack Triplett for helpful discussions and comments, and the National Institute on Aging and the Veterans Administration for financial support. All errors are the authors'.

sible for most of this decline up to the early 1980s. Goldman et al. (1982) estimated that changes in lifestyle leading to disease prevention accounted for 54 percent of the decline in ischemic heart disease mortality between 1968 and 1976. Medical interventions accounted for 40 percent; among these interventions, 13.5 percent of the decline was attributed to coronary care unit treatments, 7.5 percent to treatment of hypertension, 4 percent to prehospital resuscitation, 3.5 percent to coronary artery bypass surgery, and 10 percent to other medical treatments of ischemic heart disease (IHD), particularly chronic beta-blockade therapy.

Weinstein and colleagues (1987) have developed the Coronary Heart Disease model, a state-transition computer model of outcome from ischemic heart disease for patients in the United States, to address this question more comprehensively. The first study using the model concluded, like Goldman et al., that the bulk of mortality improvement prior to 1980 was the result of lifestyle-related changes in risk factors. However, recent results indicated that lifestyle improvements could explain less than 20 percent of the total reduction in heart disease mortality between 1980 and 1990. Moreover, primary and secondary prevention through risk factor reduction may be increasingly associated with treatment changes as well, such as increased use of lipid-lowering and antihypertensive agents with better side-effect and compliance profiles. Thus, medical interventions seem to be growing increasingly important in explaining IHD mortality improvements.

Despite the apparent increasing importance of changes in medical technology, few studies have sought to identify the contributions of specific treatment changes. For example, Goldman et al. considered only five major medical interventions in their analysis (and some of these, like coronary care unit adoption, actually consisted of a bundle of new medical treatments); and the recent Coronary Heart Disease model report (Hunink et al. 1997) attributed approximately half the IHD mortality reductions to unspecified "treatment changes." One reason for this lack of evidence on the contributions of particular interventions is the difficulty of separating out the contribution of each. Even less evidence exists on the cost implications of these different interventions.

Yet identifying the contribution of specific treatments to the observed improvements in outcomes is important for several reasons. First, it is only at the level of specific treatments that the contribution of medical care to the overall outcome improvements can be determined explicitly. Second, examining specific factors may provide insights about which types of medical treatments have made the greatest contributions to both outcome improvements and cost increases. For example, "high-tech" treatment use has changed in substantially different ways in different hospitals (Cutler and McClellan 1998) and around the world (McClellan et al., in press). Do such differences have any important consequences for health outcomes?

Moreover, this analysis might identify the most cost-effective opportunities for future changes in heart disease outcomes, and help forecast future improvements in heart disease outcomes.

In this study, we provide a first step toward synthesizing evidence from the clinical literature and a range of empirical databases to try to identify the contributions of particular changes in medical treatment in acute myocardial infarction (AMI) over the last twenty years. Deaths classified as due to AMI make up a relatively small share, perhaps 10 percent, of total IHD mortality. Even though its apparent share is small, there are several important reasons to study this condition carefully. IHD treatments and mortality are closely related to AMI, even though deaths are generally classified as caused by AMI if the death occurs during or soon after the AMI hospitalization. Many more IHD deaths reflect longer-term consequences of AMI; for example, arrhythmias resulting from unstable conduction pathways, in turn the result of permanent heart damage from a prior AMI. Another reason is that the available clinical trial and medical practice evidence on the outcomes of "AMI episodes" is far more extensive than that available for more chronic forms of IHD treated on an outpatient basis. Finally, previous studies of long-term outcome trends for AMI patients show that most of the improvement in outcomes for AMI patients, and all of the improvement attributable to hospital care, arises within the first week after an AMI (McClellan and Noguchi 1988; McClellan and Staiger 1998). After we present our detailed analysis of trends in AMI outcomes, we consider the implications of our results for IHD and other illnesses.

In this review, we estimate the reduction in age-adjusted thirty-day mortality rates for hospitalized AMI patients, place this improvement in the context of overall improvements in population AMI mortality, and summarize the impact on AMI mortality trends of the most notable specific changes in AMI treatment, from 1975 to 1995. Thrombolytic therapy, primary angioplasty, aspirin, early beta blockade, and ACE-inhibition, among other treatments, have been shown to reduce mortality in AMI patients (Lau et al. 1992; ISIS-4 Collaborative Group 1995). How much of the reduction in thirty-day mortality rates is explained by changes in medical and surgical therapies during the AMI episode? What other factors are likely to have contributed to the observed improvements? Changes in prehospital or posthospital care? Changes in the characteristics of AMI patients? We find that identifiable changes in these factors, especially in acute treatment, can explain the bulk of the observed improvements in AMI mortality for hospitalized patients. Published evidence is insufficient to reach exact conclusions on the contributions of these improvements to overall IHD mortality trends, and on improvements in the long-term quality of life of AMI survivors. We review qualitative evidence on these issues, which also suggests that the changes in medical treatments reviewed here have been among the principal factors responsible for improvements in these outcomes as well.

9.2 Methods

9.2.1 Trends in Incidence, Treatments, and Thirty-Day Mortality

We performed searches of the MEDLINE database and reviewed the bibliographies of review articles to identify studies describing treatment for AMI. We used population-based studies with at least a ten-year range whenever possible to determine changes in incidence, thirty-day mortality rates, and intervention rates during this period. We reviewed studies describing trends in prehospital, in-hospital, and posthospital treatments of acute myocardial infarction. Published results from randomized controlled trials were used to estimate the probable average benefit from changes in these various interventions. These estimates of benefit were considered an upper limit for effectiveness, given that the patients enrolled in the trials and the trial settings themselves are often not representative of the general population. Data were also obtained from large databases of Medicare patients, including the Cooperative Cardiovascular Project (CCP) and Medicare claims files.

We obtained estimates of AMI incidence and case fatality rates (CFRs)[1] from the National Hospital Discharge Survey (NHDS). NHDS trends may not accurately reflect true trends in AMI case fatality for two reasons. First, length of stay increased in the late 1970s, but has decreased somewhat since the early 1980s. Other things equal, patients remaining in the hospital longer are more likely to die in the hospital, so that some of the apparent CFR decline may be the result of reduced length of stay. Second, transfers have also increased over time, and until recent years (after 1990) transfer AMI patients were not reliably distinguishable from new AMI patients based on diagnosis codes. Thus, trends in the apparent number and mortality of AMI cases from the NHDS may be misleading. We identified AMI discharges that met the NHDS definition from 1982 onward, which includes all patients with primary diagnosis of AMI or secondary diagnoses of AMI if the reported primary diagnosis was a circulatory disease.[2] To improve the comparability of results across time periods that differed in average length of hospitalization and transfer rates, and thus in

---

1. Here we follow the convention of most of the literature and use the term *case-fatality rate* to describe the mortality rate during the initial AMI hospitalization (possibly including transfers).

2. This coding convention reflects the fact that, even if the non-AMI circulatory diagnosis was a principal reason for admission to the hospital, it was probably a consequence of the AMI. For example, diagnoses of ischemic heart disease complications or heart failure probably resulted from the accompanying AMI, even if these diagnoses were regarded as the principal reason for admission.

their apparent CFRs, we converted case-fatality rates based on all AMI admissions to standardized thirty-day mortality rates (MRs) that account for trends in transfers and readmissions. That is, we developed a conversion factor $F(N)$ based on the average length of stay in the study:

$$F(N) = \text{[Estimated true MR at 30 days]/[Observed CFR at } N \text{ days]}.$$

To form this conversion factor, we used longitudinal data including transfers for Medicare patients in 1984 and subsequent years, which provides complete information on mortality at one, seven, and thirty days after AMI (McClellan and Noguchi 1988). Because it fit the data well, we assumed a logarithmic relationship between the number of days following AMI and AMI CFRs after day one to approximate the relationship between the expected thirty-day CFR and a reported CFR for average length of stay N. That is,

$$F(N) = \text{[Medicare FR at 30 days]/[Estimated Medicare CFR at } N \text{ days]},$$

where estimated Medicare CFR at N days is given by

[Medicare CFR(1)]

$$+ \;[\ln(N - 1)/\ln(29)][\text{Medicare MR}(30) - \text{Medicare MR}(1)].$$

Thus standardized thirty-day CFR for a study with average length of stay N was calculated as

$$\text{Standardized 30-day mortality} = (\text{Reported CFR}) \times F(N).$$

Such CFRs were constructed using NHDS data for 1975, 1980, 1985, 1990, and 1995.

9.2.2 Contributions of Treatments to Changes in Case-Fatality Rates

The contribution of each technology to the reduction in case-fatality rate was estimated from the absolute mortality benefit reported for each technology (primarily obtained from meta-analyses of published studies), accounting for important interactions with other technologies, and from the estimated change in use of each technology over time. Because AMI treatments have been evaluated separately and at different times, the reported benefit of the therapies evaluated earlier (beta blockade) may not be equal to their benefit when used with therapies that have been applied more recently, such as thrombolysis and aspirin.

To estimate the contribution of each treatment, we first calculated the adjusted odds ratio $\text{AOR}_j(t)$ for each therapy j in each year t. If the published odds ratio $\text{POR}_j(Y)$ from meta-analyses of trials performed around year Y was less than 1 (i.e., the therapy was beneficial), then

$$\text{AOR}_j(t) = 1 - [1 - \text{POR}_j(Y)] \times (\text{Interaction effect})_{jt},$$

where

$$(\text{Interaction effect})_{jt} = \Pi_i\{1 - [\text{Use}_{ij}(t) - \text{Use}_{ij}(Y)] \times \text{Factor}_{ij}\},$$

and $\text{Use}_{ij}(t)$ is the joint usage of drug i with drug j in year t, $\text{Use}_{ij}(Y)$ is the joint usage in the (approximate) trial period Y, and Factor_{ij} is the relative decrease in effectiveness of drug j when used with drug i. In other words, we model the impact of changes in other treatments since the treatment of interest was studied as a relative reduction in the benefit compared to the time of the study; joint effects are generally somewhat less than their individual effects. Where possible, we used published evidence on interactions of treatment effects to guide our assumptions about the magnitudes of the interaction effects.[3] Where empirical evidence was lacking but clinical considerations suggested that interactions were probably nontrivial, we assumed that the effect of a second treatment on the treatment of interest was proportional to the published benefit of the second therapy, using the following formula: $\text{Factor}_{ij} = 0.2 \times |1 - \text{POR}_i|$. We conducted a sensitivity analysis by reducing the assumed interaction to 0. Our "base case" interaction assumptions resulted in noticeable but modest reductions in the effectiveness of individual treatments over time. For example, in our analysis, the use of aspirin with beta blockade decreases the effectiveness of beta blockade by 5 percent (in relative terms) and the effectiveness of aspirin by 2 percent.

If the published odds ratio was greater than 1.0 and the interaction effect was greater than 1, then

$$\text{AOR}_j(Y) = (\text{POR}_j)/(\text{Interaction effect})_{jt},$$

and if the published odds ratio was greater than 1.0 and the interaction effect was less than 1, then

$$\text{AOR}_j(Y) = 1 - [(1 - \text{POR}_{(j)}) \times (\text{Interaction effect})_{jt}].$$

Evidence on the joint usage of medications over time is also scant; virtually all studies report only univariate trends in treatment rates. Conse-

---

3. For example, the majority of studies of beta blockade were performed prior to the use of thrombolysis. The TIMI-2 trial (McClellan and Staiger 1999), which evaluated beta blockade in conjunction with thrombolysis, found a decrease in recurrent myocardial infarction but not in mortality (overall hospital mortality in the substudy was only 2 percent). Similarly, nitrate therapy was found to have a positive mortality benefit in studies prior to the use of thrombolysis (Van de Werf et al. 1993). In the postthrombolysis era, ISIS-4 (McClellan et al., in press) found a minimal benefit which is consistent with a lack of independence between the effects of nitrates and more recently used agents (thrombolysis and aspirin). We assumed that the absolute benefit for thrombolysis and aspirin was reduced by 2 percent when the two drugs were given together based on the ISIS-2 trial. There were no data describing the interactions between other medications. We assumed the reduction in published benefit would be proportional to the published benefit of the added drug.

quently, we also conducted sensitivity analyses on our assumptions about the frequency with which drugs are used together. In our base case, we assumed that use was independent; that is, $\text{Use}_{ij}(t) = \text{Use}_i(t) \times \text{Use}_j(t)$. For sensitivity analysis, we alternatively assumed that use was as correlated as possible; that is, $\text{Use}_{ij}(t) = \min[\text{Use}_i(t), \text{Use}_j(t)]$.

The absolute benefits from interventions were then calculated from the AORs for 1975, 1985, and 1995, using the mortality rate from 1975 and the AMI hospitalization rate in the comparison year. For example, we calculated the absolute change in thirty-day AMI deaths attributable to treatment j as follows. The relative outcome change attributable to the change in use of treatment j between 1995 and 1975 is given by

$$AOR_j(95) \times \text{Use}_j(95) - AOR_j(75) \times \text{Use}_j(75).$$

Multiplying this relative outcome change (which accounts for changes in the use of other treatments) by the standardized thirty-day mortality rate for 1975 gives the absolute thirty-day mortality benefit attributable to the change in use of the intervention. Multiplying this estimated absolute mortality benefit times the number of patients hospitalized with AMI in 1995 gives the total number of 1995 AMI deaths averted because of the change in treatment.

9.2.3   Cost-Effectiveness Calculations

To estimate the overall cost-effectiveness of all AMI treatments combined, we determined the total cost of care and the expected quality-adjusted life years gained for patients following myocardial infarction. Medicare data were used to determine changes in acute (thirty-day) cost of care from 1984 to 1994. All costs were adjusted to 1995 dollars using the gross domestic product deflator. Rates of change in acute care costs over this period were used to extrapolate costs to 1975 and 1995. We estimated long term expenditures ($2,000 per year) for survivors of myocardial infarction based on Medicare data. We estimated the acute survival by using the difference in thirty-day mortality rate from 1975 to 1995 as described above. Long-term survival was determined using several different expected survival periods following MI (five years to fifteen years). We adjusted years of life gained for quality of life using the time-trade-off utility of 0.88 (Tsevat et al. 1993). All future costs and benefits were discounted using a rate of 3 percent. We assumed that changes in MI treatments were responsible for all increases in cost per case, but that they provided only a fraction of the total benefit as calculated above. All costs were adjusted to 1995 dollars using the GDP deflator.

9.3   Results

9.3.1   Trends in the Incidence and Mortality of AMI

Trends in AMI Hospitalizations

The decline in the incidence of new AMI *hospitalizations* has been more modest. The total number of hospitalized admissions for AMI, as reported in the NHDS, actually increased over the 1975–95 time period, especially between 1975 and 1985 (table 9.1, line 1). As we described in section 9.2, we used the ratio of new AMIs to all AMI discharges from Medicare for individuals aged sixty-five to sixty-nine in 1984–94 (table 9.1, line 2) to estimate the share of reported AMI admissions that represented new patients, rather than transfers or readmissions.[4] The increase in transfers and readmissions over time accounts for much of the apparent increase in AMIs in NHDS, though this adjustment does not completely account for an anomalous bulge in AMI hospitalization rates in the early- to mid-1980s (table 9.1, line 3). This change may be due in part to idiosyncrasies in the reporting of AMI discharges around the introduction of Medicare's Prospective Payment System in 1983, as well as improved diagnostic techniques for detecting AMI (we analyze this hypothesis in more detail below). To compute AMI incidence rates over time, we accounted for growth in the at-risk population aged thirty-five and over (summarized in table 9.1, line 4). The resulting estimated trend in AMI incidence, based on the population distribution in either 1995 (table 9.1, line 5) or 1975 (table 9.1, line 6), suggests that the incidence of new AMI hospitalizations in the U.S. population has declined substantially, from 613 per 100,000 population aged thirty-five and over in 1975 to 437 per 100,000 in 1995 (1995 population). Because of population aging and population growth, the total number of new hospitalizations with true AMIs in the United States has remained relatively constant, around 540,000 per year, and our benchmark analyses are based on this figure.[5]

Trends in Mortality for Hospitalized AMI Patients

In 1975 the case fatality rate (CFR) per AMI admission (not counting transfers) according to NHDS was 19 percent (table 9.1, line 7, and fig. 9.1). To develop a measure more comparable to the clinical literature, which typically considers transfers in case fatality rates, we adjust for the share of admissions not transferred (table 9.1, line 8) and for population trends. The result is an estimate of a true, age- and sex-adjusted case fatal-

4. Our results were not sensitive to alternative reasonable assumptions about transfer rates and readmission rates within thirty days, for example by using a readmission correction based on all Medicare beneficiaries rather than sixty-five-to sixty-nine-year-old beneficiaries.

5. This estimated number of AMIs is smaller than the estimated number of "coronary events" leading to hospitalization that are reported by the American Heart Association; these estimates may include many unstable angina patients as well.

Table 9.1   Calculations of CFR, Incidence Including Age Breakdown

	1975	1980	1985	1990	1995	Source
1. AMI hospital discharges (thousands, unadjusted)[a]	577	572	710	652	679	Calculated from NHDS
2. Fraction due to new patients[b]	0.94	0.91	0.88	0.83	0.80	Calculated from Medicare
3. New AMI hospital discharges (thousand unadjusted)[c]	542	521	625	545	540	Line 1 × Line 2
4. Adult U.S. population age 35+ (millions)	90	94	102	111	124	Statistical Abstract of the United States
5. New AMI discharge rate (age/gender adjusted to 1995)	613	527	591	481	437	Lines 3, 4
6. New AMI discharge rate (age/gender adjusted to 1975)	603	527	583	472	431	Lines 3, 4
7. Case fatality rate (%) (no age/gender adjustment)	19.2	20.4	17.0	14.1	11.9	Calculated from NHDS
8. Fraction of MI admissions not transferred[b]	1.0	0.99	0.95	0.90	0.85	Calculated from Medicare
9. Case fatality rate (%) (adjusted for transfers, age/gender adjusted to 1995)	23	32.4	19.3	16.3	14	Lines 3, 4, 8; NHDS
10. Estimated 30-day fatality rate (%) (age/gender adjusted to 1995)[c]	27.0	27.9	24.1	20.4	17.4	Line 9, adjusted for dying in 30 days
11. Total AMI deaths	325	299	274	239	218	NCHS
12. Inpatient AMI deaths in thousands (no age/gender adjustment)	111	109	111	84	77	Lines 3, 4, 9
13. Estimated deaths in 30 days among hospitalized AMI patients in thousands, no age/gender adjustment (% of all AMI deaths)	158 (49)	130 (44)	146 (53)	117 (49)	112 (52)	Line 12, adjusted for dying within 30 days

[a] Adjusted for coding changes, discharged alive with length of stay less than three days and age < thirty-five excluded.
[b] Age group sixty-five to sixty-nine; data for 1975 and 1980 are extrapolated from the 1985–94 trends.
[c] Based on an exponential decline in daily mortality from day seven to day thirty (see text).

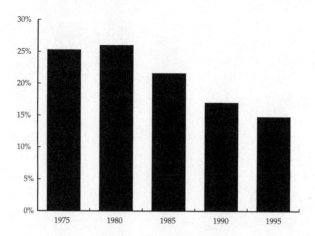

Fig. 9.1   Change in thirty-day acute MI mortality rate over the last twenty years

ity rate per new (nontransfer) AMI admission (table 9.1, line 9). Using the extrapolations described above based on Medicare data, this CFR corresponds to a thirty-day mortality rate of 27 percent (table 9.1, line 10). By 1995 the admission CFR had declined 12 percent, corresponding to a new-case CFR of 14 percent and a thirty-day mortality rate of 17 percent. Because length of stay decreased during the last twenty years, the reduction in CFR (40 percent) is greater than the reduction in thirty-day mortality rate (36 percent). This absolute drop in thirty-day mortality of 9.6 percentage points corresponds to approximately 52,000 more patients per year surviving to thirty days. Much of our subsequent analysis focuses on the factors explaining this substantial mortality trend since 1980.

Overall (In-Hospital and Out-of-Hospital) AMI Incidence and Mortality

We were unable to identify any published studies that permitted us to quantify long-term trends in the number of out-of-hospital AMIs and of AMI deaths in patients who were not hospitalized for AMI directly. However, using estimates of total AMI deaths and our results for hospitalized AMI patients, we were able to estimate these trends indirectly.

The remainder of table 9.1 places the mortality trend for hospitalized AMI patients in the context of overall AMI mortality trends, including deaths in patients who do not survive to hospitalization. According to the National Death Index, the total number of AMI deaths among Americans thirty-five and over was approximately 325,000 in 1975 and 218,000 in 1995 (table 9.1, line 11). To explore the contribution of the mortality decline among hospitalized AMI patients to this overall mortality decline, we calculated the total deaths among hospitalized patients implied by our analysis, which was based on data independent of the death index. In 1975, our estimate of in-hospital case fatalities (before discharge, but possibly after transfer) was 111,000, and the corresponding number for 1995 was 77,000 (table 9.1, line 12). Because death index records should generally classify AMI patients who die acutely (within thirty days) as AMI deaths, an increasing number of patients who die after discharge or readmission will be missed using the case-based approach. Consequently, the final line of table 9.1 (line 13) reports our estimate of the total number of deaths within thirty days after AMI, based on our estimated trends in thirty-day fatalities. These deaths declined from 158,000 in 1975 to 112,000 in 1995.

Because total AMI deaths consist of prehospital deaths and of deaths in hospitalized patients, our findings provide an indirect approach for quantifying trends in prehospital deaths.[6] Our estimates of trends in death for hospitalized AMI patients imply that approximately 214,000 AMI patients died before hospitalization in 1975 and 106,000 did so in 1995, and that hospitalized AMI patients accounted for 49 percent of the total AMI deaths in 1975 and 52 percent in 1995. These findings on the relative importance of prehospitalization and posthospitalization deaths are consistent with estimates from earlier years (Goldman et al. 1982) that 50 to 60 percent of acute MI deaths occurred outside the hospital.

They are also consistent with previously published studies on the decline in out-of-hospital deaths from ischemic heart disease. Because of these difficulties in quantifying out-of-hospital AMI deaths separately,[7] most published studies consider trends in out-of-hospital IHD deaths generally, including deaths from cardiac arrest as well as AMI. The number of such deaths has declined impressively over the last twenty years. The incidence of out-of-hospital IHD deaths in the Minneapolis area was approximately 150 per 100,000 in 1990, a reduction of more than 50 percent compared to the 1970 rate of 330 per 100,000 (McGovern et al. 1996; Gillum et al. 1983). This community study concludes that the reduction in out-of-hospital deaths, which include a substantial number of AMI deaths, accounts for the bulk of the observed improvements in overall IHD mortality rates. Our results imply a similar conclusion for AMI: The improvements in mortality for hospitalized AMI patients, impressive as they were, accounted for only around 30 percent[8] of the total decline in AMI deaths between 1975 and 1995—though they were relatively more important in

6. Note that this cannot be done directly from death records, even though they report whether a death occurred in or out of the hospital. The out-of-hospital group includes those dying of AMI prior to hospitalization, as well as the increasing number of patients dying after their initial hospitalization.

7. We emphasize that it is difficult to quantify reliably the number of deaths from AMI without hospitalization. Especially if autopsy of an individual "found down" is not performed, it may be difficult to determine whether patients with IHD died from a new AMI or from a ventricular arrhythmia. As a result, most out-of-hospital deaths in the setting of IHD are classified with a nonspecific IHD diagnosis (McClellan and Staiger 1999). One reason that reported AMI mortality rates are so low relative to IHD mortality rates is that such nonspecific out-of-hospital deaths are relatively common.

8. Total deaths among hospitalized patients declined by 46,000, while total prehospital deaths declined by 108,000.

1985–95 than in the previous decade. Part of this decline resulted from an increasing share of AMI patients being hospitalized—according to our estimates, 72 percent in 1975 compared to 84 percent in 1995. But this increasing rate of hospitalization accounts for only a small fraction of the more than 100 percent decline in prehospital deaths.

Our estimates imply a decline in the number of AMI events resulting in either prehospital deaths or hospitalization from 757,000 in 1975 to 646,000 in 1995. With the growth and aging of the population during this period, this trend implies a decline in the rate of serious AMI events of more than 40 percent over the twenty-year period. The true decline in both the rate and number of serious AMI events may be even larger. Trends in the number of individuals who have a mild AMI but do not seek treatment cannot be estimated from any reported health statistics. With public education campaigns about the importance of responding to classic AMI symptoms, it is possible that patients are increasingly seeking out medical care, but the magnitude of this trend toward patient-initiated hospitalization for AMI is unclear. More clear, as we describe below, is the effect of changes in technology for diagnosing AMI on the detection, and probably the hospitalization, of patients with mild AMIs. In any case, as we turn to our detailed analysis of changes in treatment and outcomes given the occurrence of AMI, it is worth noting that a decline in the rate of serious AMI events was the most important contributing factor to the reduction in AMI mortality over the past twenty years.

9.3.2   Mortality Consequences of Changes in Acute In-Hospital Treatment

Thrombolysis

By 1995 thrombolytic use was 31 percent, according to data from the National Registry of Myocardial Infarction (NRMI) (Rogers et al. 1996) (table 9.2). The use of thrombolytic therapy in 1975 was effectively 0 percent. After adjustment for concomitant use of other drugs, we estimated that the absolute mortality reduction due to thrombolytics in 1995 was 4.6 percent. This would explain 16 percent of the reduction in the AMI thirty-day mortality rate from 1975 to 1995.

Time from symptom onset to treatment is a major determinant of successful thrombolysis. If thrombolysis can be initiated within one hour then the relative risk reduction is near 50 percent, which would lead to an absolute mortality reduction of as much as 9.5 percent. If we assume that in 1995 such rapid treatment was actually achieved, then thrombolysis could explain 35 percent of the overall reduction in thirty-day mortality. However, this estimate is likely to be much too high. Data from Worcester in 1985 (median time to hospitalization 2.0 hours) (Yarzebski et al. 1994a), NRMI (2.8 hours to treatment in 1990 and 2.7 hours in 1993) (Rogers et

Table 9.2   Use of Interventions for Acute Myocardial Infarction

	1973–77	1978–82	1983–87	1988–92	1993–96	Source/Comment
Medications						
Beta blockers	20.6	41.5	47.5	47.3	49.8	Goldberg et al. (1987b); Gurwitz et al. (1994); McLaughlin et al. (1996)
ASA	15	14.1	20.1	62	75	Rogers et al. (1994); Goldberg et al. (1987b); Burns et al. (1997)
Nitrates	55.8	83.1	93.2	93	93	Goldberg et al. (1987b). 1990–1995 values are assumed equal to 1985.
IV nitroglycerin	29.1[a]	40.9	76.4	75	59	Rogers et al. (1994); McGovern, Burke, et al. (1992)
Heparin/anticoagulants			53	75	70	McGovern et al. (1996); Rogers et al. (1994)
Calcium antagonists	0	0	63.9	59	31	Rogers et al. (1996); McGovern, Burke, et al. (1992); Gurwitz et al. (1994); Pashos et al. (1994)
Lidocaine	30	48.2	46.5		16.2	Goldberg et al. (1987b); Chandra et al. (1996)
Other antiarrhythmics	30.7	22.5	21.9			Goldberg et al. (1987b)
Magnesium					8.5	Ziegelstein et al. (1996)
ACE inhibitors	0	0	0		24	Cooperative Cardiovascular Project
Thrombolytics	0	0	9.3	24.5	30.6	Rogers et al. (1996); Chandra et al. (1997)
Procedures						
Cardiac catheterization	3	5	10	35	42	Gore et al. (1987); Paul et al. (1996); Tu et al. (1997)
Primary PTCA	0	0	0		9.1	Rogers et al. (1996)
Any PTCA	0	0	6	21	15	McGovern et al. (1996); Paul et al. (1996)
CABG	3[a]	6	8	10	14	McGovern et al. (1996); McGovern, Folsom et al. (1992); Medicare

Note: In-hospital or thirty-day use.
[a] Average of 1970 and 1979 values.

al. 1994), and GUSTO (median time to treatment 2.7 hours) (GUSTO III Investigators 1997) suggest that there has been little improvement in time from symptom onset to thrombolysis up to 1995. Largely anecdotal results since 1995 suggest that time to thrombolytics may be declining, perhaps accounting for very recent mortality improvements.

Beta Blockade

In 1985 and 1990, beta blockade use was stable at 47 to 48 percent of MI cases (table 9.2). Data from Minnesota in 1992–93 indicate a slight increase to 53 percent use. This is more than double the 1975 value of 21 percent. The published odds ratio demonstrating a survival benefit with beta blockade is 0.88. However, the majority of data regarding the benefit of beta blockade was collected prior to the use of thrombolysis and primary pecutaneous transluminal coronary angioplasty (PTCA). Thus, the benefit may not be as great in conjunction with other current treatments (Becker 1994; Van de Werf et al. 1993). After adjustment for interactions with other therapies, we estimate that increased use of beta blockers accounts for an absolute mortality reduction of 2.0 percent, or 6 percent of the reduction in the thirty-day mortality rate.

Aspirin

Aspirin use in 1995 was estimated to be 75 percent, in contrast to 15 percent use in 1975 (table 9.2). If we assume that the absolute survival benefit from aspirin after adjustment for use of thrombolysis is 4.0 percent (ISIS-2 Collaborative Group 1988), then aspirin use would explain 28 percent of the reduction in thirty-day mortality rates. These results suggest that the increase in aspirin use had a far greater impact on the acute MI thirty-day mortality rate than thrombolysis or beta blockade. A major reason for aspirin's estimated importance is the magnitude of its increase in use, perhaps because of less physician concern about complications compared to thrombolytics or beta blockers.

Calcium Channel Blockers

It is unclear whether calcium channel blockers provide any benefit in AMI. Meta-analyses by Lau et al. (1992) and Teo, Yusuf, and Furberg (1993) have demonstrated a harmful nonsignificant trend with the use of these drugs (table 9.3). We assumed that 1995 use was similar to 1993 use of 31 percent based on data from NRMI (Rogers et al. 1994)—it may in fact be somewhat lower. Use in 1975 was zero, as these drugs had not yet been developed. Based on Lau et al.'s summary odds ratios, greater calcium channel antagonist use would account for a 7 percent absolute increase in mortality, leading to 4,700 more deaths (assuming 540,000 myocardial infarctions in 1995). However, newer calcium channel blockers have not been evaluated in these meta-analyses. Their effect on AMI mortality is unclear, and possibly favorable.

Table 9.3   Effects of Interventions for Acute Myocardial Infarction

	Published Odds Ratio		Calculated Odds Ratio			Source
	Estimate	Upper, Lower	No Other Treatments	1975	1995	
Medications						
Beta blockers	0.88	0.80, 0.98	0.88	0.88	0.91	Lau et al. (1992)
ASA	0.77	0.70, 0.89	0.74	0.75	0.78	Lau et al. (1992)
Nitrates	0.94	0.90, 0.99	0.91	0.92	0.94	ISIS-4 Collaborative Group (1995); Hennekens et al. (1996)
Heparin/anticoagulants	0.78	0.65, 0.92	0.77	0.78	0.83	Lau et al. (1992)
Calcium antagonists	1.12	0.92, 1.39	1.14	1.13	1.10	Lau et al. (1992)
Lidocaine	1.38	0.98, 1.95	1.40	1.38	1.29	Teo, Yusuf, and Furberg (1993)
Magnesium	1.02	0.44, 1.08	1.03	1.03	1.02	ISIS-4 Collaborative Group (1995); Hennekens et al. (1996)
ACE inhibitors	0.94	0.89, 0.98	0.91	0.92	0.94	ISIS-4 Collaborative Group (1995); Hennekens et al. (1996)
Thrombolytics	0.75	0.71, 0.79	0.71	0.73	0.77	Lau et al. (1992)
Procedures						
Primary PTCA[a]	0.5	0.35, 0.71	0.46	0.48	0.50	Weaver et al. (1997)
CABG[b]	0.94	0.71, 1.26	0.93	0.93	0.95	Koshal et al. (1988)

[a] Calculated assuming an odds ratio of 0.75 for thrombolytics and an odds ratio with benefit of PTCA vs. thrombolysis of 0.66.

[b] Absolute benefit assumed equal to nitrate therapy and ACE inhibition. Upper absolute benefit estimate assumed equal to thrombolysis. Lower absolute estimate = base estimate (0.01) − upper estimate (0.052) = −0.42.

Nitrates

It is also unclear if nitrates still provide any survival benefit in acute MI. A meta-analysis reported with the results from ISIS-4 demonstrated a small survival benefit with oral nitrates (ISIS-4 Collaborative Group 1995). A metanalysis of IV nitroglycerin in acute MI in the prethrombolytic era found a more substantial mortality reduction of 20 percent (Yusuf et al. 1988). An explanation for these seemingly contradictory findings is that the nitrate effect is not independent of the effect of thrombolysis and aspirin. Another possible explanation is that the intravenous route is more beneficial than the oral route. We used the more conservative ISIS-4 value for our analysis (odds ratio 0.94), which reflected interaction effects with other treatments that were less prominent in earlier years. Because the increase in use of more potent therapies that interacted with nitrate effects was large, the incremental contribution of nitrates to AMI survival in 1995 was slightly less than in 1975.

Heparin

In studies performed before widespread use of thrombolytics, heparin and other anticoagulants have been shown to reduce mortality (summary odds ratio 0.78, equivalent to a 3.9 percent absolute benefit with 1975 overall mortality) (Lau et al. 1992). In 1993 NRMI, 70 percent of patients receive heparin. Because heparin is now often considered part of "thrombolytic therapy" we assumed that all patients receiving thrombolytics would receive heparin and that heparin provided no substantial additional benefit in these patients. Of the 69 percent that did not receive thrombolytics in 1995, 57 percent were estimated to have received heparin, that is, $(69 - 31)/(100 - 31)$. No data were available on heparin use in 1975; data from 1985 (Minnesota) showed that 53 percent of patients received heparin (McGovern et al. 1996). Summary data from the Worcester cohort from 1975 through 1988 found that 65 percent of patients received anticoagulants (Goldberg et al. 1991), suggesting that heparin use did not increase markedly from 1975 to 1985. If the increase in use over the last twenty years was only 4 percent (53 percent to 57 percent) then less than 1 percent of the improvement in MI thirty-day mortality rates is explained by heparin use. However, if heparin use was in fact much lower in 1975, then it would explain more of the mortality improvement: If 1975 use were 20 percent, then the increased use would explain 15 percent of the 1975–95 mortality reduction.

Lidocaine

It is now known that prophylactic lidocaine is not beneficial and is probably harmful in the setting of AMI (Teo, Yusuf, and Furberg 1993). Lidocaine use was 31 percent in 1975 (Goldberg et al. 1987b), increased in the early 1980s, and subsequently dropped to 16.2 percent in 1995 according to NRMI (Chandra et al. 1996). Data from Minnesota (which did not include patients of age seventy-five years or older) suggested an even greater use of lidocaine (43 percent in 1970 and 67 percent in 1979) (McGovern, Folsom, et al. 1992). If we assume that nonprophylactic, potentially beneficial use remained constant from 1975 to 1995, then the absolute decrease in prophylactic use is approximately 15 percent (31 − 16, according to Worcester data). Meta-analyses have suggested that the lidocaine increases mortality by an absolute 6 percent, assuming a 22.6 percent overall mortality (Teo, Yusuf, and Furberg 1993). Thus the substantial decline in the use of prophylactic lidocaine since 1975 would have explained 11 percent of the reduction in thirty-day mortality rates.

Magnesium

Early studies of intravenous magnesium suggested an absolute survival benefit for patients with AMI (Teo et al. 1991). However, a large recent trial (ISIS-4 Collaborative Group 1995) found no benefit and a slight harmful trend. Because there is no evidence that the recent finding reflects an interaction of newer therapies with the magnesium benefit, we used the estimated effect from ISIS-4. Magnesium use was 8.5 percent in 1995 according to NRMI data, and we assumed it to be 0 percent in 1975. Thus in any case, because so little magnesium is used, the effect on overall mortality is very small (<1 percent). If an absolute harm of 0.3 percent is assumed, then magnesium use would have led 180 extra deaths within thirty days following MI in 1995.

Primary PTCA

Primary PTCA use in 1995 was estimated to be 10 percent based on data from NRMI (Rogers et al. 1996) and 0 percent in 1975. Using a 3.8 percent absolute benefit of primary PTCA (assumed equal to thrombolysis [Every et al. 1996], table 9.3) the increased use would explain 4.6 percent of the reduction in thirty-day mortality rates. A meta-analysis by Weaver et al. (1997) suggests that PTCA has an absolute survival benefit over thrombolysis. If this is true (absolute benefit 9.9 percent) then 9.8 percent of the reduction in the acute MI mortality rate is attributable to primary PTCA.

Immediate or Urgent Coronary Artery Bypass Graft (CABG)

One small randomized trial suggested no benefit to urgent CABG versus waiting (Koshal et al. 1988). Data from NRMI suggest that use of CABG during acute MI has not increased markedly (5.7 percent in 1995) compared to an estimate of 2.3 percent for 1975 (average based on Minnesota data from 1970 and McGovern et al. 1996; McGovern, Folsom, et al. 1992). If we assume that urgent CABG has a modest net absolute benefit (1 percent) in the additional patients who received it, then the increased use of CABG would explain 0.6 percent of observed decline in the thirty-day mortality rate. Even if we assume a comparable benefit to early PTCA, the small increase in CABG use explains only a small share of the mortality improvement.

Acute Revascularization

Use of catheterization and revascularization, particularly angioplasty, within thirty days of AMI has increased markedly in use since 1975. The mortality benefits of these changes in treatment are not clear. Several recent studies have documented no survival benefit (and possible harm) from routine catheterization and revascularization soon after AMI in cases without recurrent chest pain or other ischemic symptoms (Boden et al. 1998). Thus, for most AMI patients, thirty-day mortality benefits of early revascularization are probably zero. However, a subset of AMI patients who experience recurrent ischemic symptoms soon after infarct are generally viewed as appropriate candidates for revascularization (Ryan et al. 1996). Unfortunately, no trial results are available regarding urgent revascularization for patients presenting with MI. Both PTCA and CABG may have longer-term mortality benefits that are greater than their acute benefits; we return to this issue below.

Few patients hospitalized for AMI underwent CABG or angioplasty within thirty days in 1975. According to Medicare data, 5.8 percent underwent revascularization in 1985; assuming that the relative odds of procedure use were constant, this corresponds to a rate of 7.3 percent of nonelderly patients. In 1994 the elderly rate was 14.8 percent, compared with 18.6 percent among the nonelderly in California. If we assume an average absolute thirty-day mortality benefit of 1 to 2 percent in these patients—which probably consists of a more substantial benefit for a small share of patients, and little benefit for others—then increased revascularization explains 0.6 to 1.2 percent of the reduction in acute mortality.

Pulmonary Artery Catheterization

Use of pulmonary artery catheterization increased from 1975 to 1984, then declined thereafter among all patients with AMI studied. Among high-risk patients with AMI complicated by heart failure or hypotension, use of pulmonary artery catheterization increased until 1988, then declined in use from 1990. For the combined study periods, 14.7 percent of all patients with AMI studied and 25.4 percent of those with complicated AMI underwent pulmonary artery catheterization (Yarzebski et al. 1994b; Gore et al. 1987). To date there is no evidence that pulmonary artery catheterization improves mortality in patients with myocardial infarction (Zion et al. 1990). In fact, there is concern that these procedures may increase mortality, possibly by causing infection or by direct cardiac injury (Connors et al. 1996; Dalen and Bone 1996). For our analysis, we assumed no mortality effect from pulmonary artery catheterization.

Coronary Care Units

The diffusion of coronary care units was largely complete by the late 1970s. Although we cannot rule out a subsequent mortality benefit from improvements in arrhythmia detection and complex AMI management, other changes in CCU technology are unlikely to have made a substantial contribution in themselves to the drop in thirty-day mortality rates from 1975 to 1995. We discuss the harder-to-measure benefits of increasing skill and experience in CCU and other decisions below.

Overall Effect of Changes in Acute Inpatient Treatments

The contribution of each of these treatments to the overall reduction in mortality rates during the last twenty years is summarized in table 9.4 and figure 9.2. This analysis compares benefit and use in 1995 with benefit and use in 1975. An alternative analysis is displayed in table 9.5, which examines the impact of increasing treatment use from 1975 to 1995 levels holding all other drug use constant at 1995 levels. Table 9.4 shows that increased use of beta blockers, aspirin, thrombolysis, primary PTCA, and ACE inhibitors can explain 62 percent of the reduction in thirty-day mortality from 1975 to 1995. Including the treatment changes in lidocaine, calcium channel blockers, nitrates, magnesium, and revascularization increases the share of the reduction explained to 60 percent, or approximately 6 percentage points lower mortality.

Our findings are mildly sensitive to the assumed joint effects and uses of therapies. If no interaction between therapies is assumed, then 79 percent of the reduction would be explained. Our base-case analysis also assumes that therapies are used independently. If we instead assume that drugs are always given together (patients receive many therapies, or almost no therapies), then the consequences of interactions between treatments will be larger. If this assumption is true, then the five major therapies would explain only 59 percent of the decline in mortality, and all of the therapies would explain about 56 percent.

To explore whether the treatments we identified made different contributions over different time periods, we examined the time periods from 1975 to 1985 and 1985 to 1995 separately (table 9.4). From 1975 to 1985, increased use of the five major MI therapies explained 42 percent of the reduction in mortality during this period. The moderate increase in therapies mirrored the moderate drop in mortality during this decade. Increased use of beta blockers accounted for 20 percent of the drop in mortality, followed by thrombolysis (16 percent) and aspirin (6 percent). Nitrate therapy may have had a greater impact on mortality during this period when little thrombolysis or aspirin were used. If the survival benefit for nitrate therapy is as estimated by Yusuf et al. (1988) (odds ratio 0.79 for oral nitrates), then the increased use of nitrates from 1975 to 1985 would

Table 9.4 Calculation of Benefit from Acute Myocardial Infarction Therapies

	Odds Ratio			Increase in Use (%), 1995–75	Reduction in Mortality Explained[a] (%)				
	Published	1975	1995		Major Therapies, 1975–95	Major Therapies, 1975–85	Major Therapies, 1985–95	All Therapies, 1975–95	All Therapies, No Interaction, 1975–95
Medications									
Beta blockers	0.88	0.88	0.89	29	6.1	20	-0.7	6.1	7.3
ASA	0.77	0.76	0.77	60	27.5	5.8	33.3	27.5	30.2
Nitrates	0.94	0.87	0.92	30				-5.5	4.7
Heparin/anticoagulants	0.78	0.78	0.79	4				-0.5	1.9
Calcium antagonists	1.12	1.12	1.12	31				-7.3	-7.4
Lidocaine	1.38	1.38	1.38	-15				10.7	10.6
Magnesium	1.02	1.02	1.02	8.5				-0.3	-0.3
ACE inhibitors	0.94	0.87	0.92	24	2.7	0	3.6	2.7	3.0
Thrombolytics	0.75	0.74	0.76	31	16.1	16.1	14.5	16.1	17.1
Procedures									
Primary PTCA	0.5	0.48	0.50	9.1	9.8	0.0	12.8	9.8	10.8
CABG	0.94	0.92	0.94	6.7				0.6	0.8
Total					62	42	64	60	79

[a] Percent of 1995–75 decrease in acute MI thirty-day mortality rates explained by each intervention. "No Interaction" assumes no interaction between drugs.

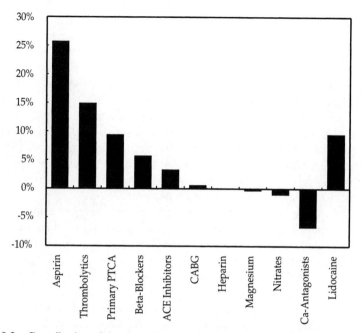

Fig. 9.2 Contribution of the change in usage of individual therapies to the reduction in case-fatality rate from 1975 to 1995

Note: The total percent explained is 61 percent. This analysis assumes that point estimates of effect size from the meta-analysis are correct. The contribution of lidocaine was due to a reduction in use.

Table 9.5   **Reduction in Mortality Explained Due to Increasing Drug Use from 1975 to 1995 Levels (%)**

	Direct Effect	Indirect Effect (Interactions)	Total Effect
Medications			
Beta blockers	6.6	−0.75	5.9
Aspirin	27.5	−1.83	26.5
Nitrates	4.2	−0.49	3.7
Heparin/anticoagulants	1.8	−0.17	1.6
Calcium antagonists	−7.3	0.08	−7.2
Lidocaine	10.5	−0.09	10.4
Magnesium	−0.3	0.01	−0.3
ACE inhibitors	2.7	−0.33	2.4
Thrombolytics	16.1	−0.83	15.3
Procedures			
Primary PTCA	9.8	−0.83	8.9
CABG	0.7	−0.09	0.6

Note: Percent of 1995–75 decrease in acute MI thirty-day mortality rates explained by increasing an individual drug usage from 1975 to 1995 levels. All other drugs are assumed to be used at 1995 levels. Indirect effects are opposite to direct effects because of negative interactions with other drugs.

have explained a much larger share (22 percent) of the decline in thirty-day mortality rate during this period.

From 1985 to 1995, a more substantial drop in thirty-day mortality occurred compared to the 1975–85 period (approximately 6.7 versus 3.7 percentage points, table 9.1). This greater improvement was associated with a large increase in the use of the major therapies shown to be effective in AMI care (tables 9.1 and 9.2). The relative contribution of different treatments to the drop in mortality also changed substantially. Beta blockers, the use of which increased only modestly during this time period, were unimportant. Aspirin explained 33 percent of the decline, the increased use of thrombolysis explained 15 percent, primary PTCA explained 13 percent, and ACE inhibition explained 4 percent.

In contrast to our base case, if we assume the average harm from calcium channel blockade is as reported in the meta-analyses, then the impact of changes in interventions on the overall mortality rate during these two time periods differs markedly. Because there was a large increase in calcium blockade from 1975 to 1985, the benefit from proven therapies is largely offset by the harm from rapid diffusion of calcium channel blockers.[9] Conversely, because calcium channel blockers (and to a lesser extent lidocaine) were used less frequently by 1995, the overall contribution of effective treatments to the reduction in mortality from 1985 to 1995 increases to 84 percent. We find these average effects for potentially harmful treatments to be implausible. In any case, all of our estimates suggest that medical treatments for acute MI were much more important in reducing AMI mortality during the ten years following 1985 compared to the prior ten years.

The major changes in inpatient AMI treatment we evaluated do not include all of the changes in the acute hospital management of AMI that have occurred in the past two decades. Other treatment changes that may have contributed to the reduction in AMI mortality include improved supportive care for heart failure and shock, improved arrhythmia monitoring and defibrillation, stenting and other treatments to improve vessel patency after angioplasty, and miscellaneous other therapies. The importance of these additional changes in the mortality trends is unclear, because of the absence of published information on effects from randomized controlled trials or other studies on effectiveness, and on trends in treatment use over time. Even though none of these treatments are used on a large share of AMI patients, they may nonetheless account for part of the residual unexplained mortality trends. However, the following sections describe explanations for the remaining mortality improvement other than these additional changes in hospital care.

9. Lidocaine also accounts for a less substantial adverse change in outcomes from 1975 to 1985, but the effect is smaller since its change in use was smaller.

Changes in Appropriateness of Care

In the preceding subsections, we have focused on changes in treatment *rates* in AMI patients. Even if treatment rates and AMI patient characteristics remain unchanged, outcomes may nonetheless improve if treatments are allocated to patients more effectively. Treatment allocation may improve as clinical knowledge improves (e.g., with the publication of new studies on large benefits or adverse effects of treatment) or as clinical experience increases (e.g., as cardiologists become more familiar with the types of patients likely to benefit from intensive procedures).

Unfortunately, obtaining longitudinal information on appropriateness of treatment is very difficult. Though many studies report information on the clinical characteristics of enrolled patients, they generally do not report statistics on treatment rates in particular clinical subgroups of patients at the level of detail required for appropriateness judgments. Even if they did, the sample sizes involved would likely be too small to reach definitive conclusions about changes in appropriateness over time. Finally, studies designed to examine appropriateness of care at a point in time often classify a large share of patients into a "possibly appropriate" category, where benefits of treatment are uncertain, and judgments about appropriateness may differ (Ayanian et al. 1998). For all of these reasons, the clinical-trial literature and our analysis necessarily focus on average effects of treatment across broad groups of patients. Though we must treat it as a residual, we suspect that improvement in appropriateness of care also contributed to the observed improvements in outcomes.

9.3.3   Prehospital Treatment Changes

As we noted above, much of the decline in out-of-hospital deaths from AMI (and IHD-associated ventricular arrhythmias) appears to be the result of a decline in the total incidence of AMI and cardiac-arrest events. In this section, we review evidence on the prehospital treatment of AMI and AMI- and IHD-related cardiac arrest. If more AMI patients survive to hospitalization as a result of improved prehospital treatment, then the share of AMI hospitalizations among total AMIs will increase. The substantial decline in out-of-hospital IHD death rates relative to the AMI hospitalization rate suggests that this is indeed the case. To the extent that these additional hospitalized patients have more or less severe AMIs than average, these changes may have implications for apparent survival rates after hospitalization for AMI.

Advanced Cardiovascular Life Support (ACLS) Availability

Goldman and Cook (1984) estimated that ACLS accounted for 8.4 percent of the reduction in IHD mortality between 1968 and 1976. They estimated that if ACLS had been widely available, 36,000 deaths per year during this period could have been prevented. However, only 600 lives per year were actually saved, because most people had access to basic life support only. The availability of ACLS may have increased over the last twenty years due to increased use of ambulances by the public and the diffusion of the 911 system. It is now estimated that over 90 percent of the U.S. population has emergency medical services available within ten minutes (Cummins 1993), and that most have access to basic 911 services (Hunt et al. 1989).

Although improved access to defibrillation has probably improved outcomes of cardiac arrest victims, it is unclear if the improved access to care has had an effect on mortality from AMI for patients without a cardiac arrest (tables 9.6 and 9.7). There is little evidence that rates of ambulance use by AMI patients have increased. According to a review by Ho et al. (1989), 30 to 50 percent of MI patients used an ambulance in 1975, compared with 42 percent for the Minneapolis metropolitan area in 1990. Even though ACLS availability has increased substantially, its actual emergent use for AMI patients has probably increased only modestly. Thus, the share of mortality improvement for hospitalized AMI patients explained by changes in ACLS availability up to 1995 is probably small.

Cardiac Arrest Treatments

Several studies have documented improvement in survival from out-of-hospital cardiac arrest following implementation of systems using paramedics or defibrillation-trained emergency medical technicians (EMTs) (Vukov, White, and Bachman 1988; Weaver et al. 1986). In Seattle, the percent of patients discharged alive increased from 10 percent in 1971 to 25 percent in 1973 following the establishment of a comprehensive program to improve access to advanced cardiac life support including defibrillation (Weaver et al. 1986). Little improvement occurred during the subsequent ten years (26 percent survival to discharge in 1983) despite implementation of new treatments such as automated defibrillators (Cummins et al. 1987), and dispatcher-assisted cardiopulmonary resuscitation (CPR) (Eisenberg et al. 1985). A similar improvement in survival (2.5 percent to 12 percent) for cardiac arrest patients with ventricular fibrillation was observed following the use of defibrillators by EMTs (Vukov, White, and Bachman 1988). The focus of cardiac arrest treatment has been on defibrillation because 50 to 80 percent (Eisenberg et al. 1990; American Heart Association 1992) of patients are found in this rhythm (Cummins 1993).

A few additional treatments have been noted to improve survival in cardiac arrest. Bystander CPR, when performed correctly, has been associated with an increased probability of the patient's being in ventricular fibrillation when emergency personnel arrive, and with an improved outcome (4.6 percent survival with effective CPR versus 1.4 percent with ineffective

Table 9.6   Trends in Prehospital Treatment for Myocardial Infarction

	1973–77	1978–82	1983–87	1988–92	1993–95	Source
Patient-Related						
Time to call 911 (hours)			2–2.6	2.1	> 6 in 40%	Ho et al. (1989); Sharkey et al. (1989)
Use of ambulance (%)	33–50		50	44	42	Ho et al. (1989); Sharkey et al. (1989); Kereiakes et al. (1990)
Time to hospitalization (hours) mean (median)	> 4 in 40–50%		4.1 (2.0)	4.6 (2.0)	(2.7)	Yarzebski et al. (1994a); GUSTO III Investigators (1997); Ho et al. (1989); Maynard et al. (1995)
Hospital						
Arrival-lytics (minutes) mean (median)			90		99 (57)	Sharkey et al. (1989)
Arrival-lytics CCU (minutes)			102	73		Sharkey et al. (1989); Maynard et al. (1995)
Arrival-lytics ER (minutes)			67	47		Sharkey et al. (1989); Maynard et al. (1995)

Table 9.7   **Effects of Different Prehospital Technologies for Acute Myocardial Infarction and Cardiac Arrest**

Effects	Estimate: Absolute Benefit	Source/Comment
Use of paramedics or EMT-D[a] (%)	15	Survival increased from 10% to 25% (Weaver et al. 1986)
Effective bystander CPR (5)	3.2	4.6% survival with effective CPR vs. 1.4% with ineffective CPR (Gallagher, Lombardi, and Gennis 199)
Media campaign to increase use of EMS[b] (%)	0	No effect on time delay or use of ambulance (Ho et al. 1989; Blohm et al. 1996)
Prehospital thrombolysis (%)	2.2	(Weaver 1995)
Prehospital ECG (%)	4.3	Decreased time to lytics by 40 mins (Barbash et al. 1990; Canto et al. 1996)
Lytics in 1 hour (%)	6.9	(Boersma et al. 1996)
Lytics in 6 hours (%)	2.6	(Boersma et al. 1996)
Paramedics vs. EMT (%)	8	24% paramedics vs. 16% EMTs (all benefit in hypotensive patients) (Pressley et al. 1988)

[a] EMT-D: emergency medical technicians with defibrillation training.
[b] EMS: emergency medical services.

CPR) (Gallagher, Lombardi, and Gennis 1995). In contrast, other treatments such as the use of high-dose epinephrine (Callaham et al. 1992), transcutaneous pacing (Cummins et al. 1993), and active compression-decompression CPR (Schwab et al. 1995) have not been shown to improve survival to hospital discharge.

It is unclear if the 911 system has an effect on acute MI mortality apart from improved access to defibrillation. A study of trauma patients in North Carolina found no improvement in trauma death rates following institution of the system (Patsey et al. 1992). A comparison with counties that lacked 911 also did not show a benefit. Although similar data for AMI patients are lacking, the time from symptoms to hospitalization, an important determinant for benefit from thrombolysis, has not changed dramatically (table 9.6). Taken together, these improvements in prehospital care for AMI and arrest appear to account for a small part of the overall IHD and AMI mortality reduction.

Overall Changes in Survival to Hospitalization of AMI Patients

The changes in out-of-hospital treatment probably had a relatively modest effect on the higher rates of survival to hospitalization of AMI patients. In this section, we compare this evidence on prehospital treatment changes to the overall changes in survival of out-of-hospital arrests and severe AMI events.

Different studies have reported widely divergent survival rates for out-of-hospital events, and Becker, Smith, and Rhodes (1993) demonstrated a striking inverse relationship between reported incidence and survival. Studies with an incidence of 120 per 100,000 had survival rates of 2 to 3 percent. Other studies with higher survival rates (5 to 18 percent) had much lower incidence rates (40 per 100,000) (Cummins et al. 1985). Although these differences may be related to differences in patient populations, the threefold variation in reported incidence among studies strongly suggests that different inclusion criteria were used to identify the population receiving prehospital care. After adjustment for differences in incidence rates, there was no clear trend in survival rates over time from the data reported between 1970 and 1990. This observation is limited by publication bias: Areas with advanced prehospital care programs may be more likely to report data. If we assume that lower incidence rates in some areas result from more patients receiving no prehospital care before death, we can assume that the rate of out-of-hospital events is approximately 150 cases of arrest and AMI-related cardiogenic shock per 100,000. The survival rate for out-of-hospital events (using an incidence of 150 arrests per 100,000) is 1 to 5 percent. As our review of changes in prehospital technologies suggested, the actual improvements in prehospital treatment appear to account for only a modest increase in the number of AMI patients reaching the hospital alive.

Though they may have modestly improved population AMI survival rates, these prehospital treatment changes did not necessarily improve the thirty-day survival rate for hospitalized AMI patients. The "marginal" patients saved in the field may be relatively ill when reaching the hospital. In support of this hypothesis are data from Minnesota, which demonstrate an increase in the death rate from ischemic heart disease in the emergency room from 1970 to 1978 (Gillum et al. 1983). Partly for this reason, we examine trends in the characteristics of hospitalized AMI patients to assess their contribution to the apparent trends in AMI survival rates.

9.3.4   Changes in Characteristics and Reporting of AMI Hospitalizations

Outcomes of hospitalized AMI patients will change over time in the absence of changes in effective treatment if the characteristics of the AMI populations change. Changes in survival to hospitalization are one source of changes in patient characteristics, but changes in the health risks of patients hospitalized with AMI, diagnostic accuracy, and other factors may also have contributed. In this section, we review the evidence on whether changes in the nature or severity of hospitalized AMIs have affected outcome trends.

Presenting Characteristics

Data on all hospitalized AMI patients from NHDS show some changes in AMI patient demographics (table 9.8).[10] The average age of the acute MI patient has increased from sixty-four to sixty-nine years. The proportion of MI patients that are female has increased from 33 percent in 1975 to over 40 percent in the 1990s (Goldberg et al. 1986; Chandra et al. 1997). Data from Minnesota demonstrate some reduction in the risk-factor profile (cigarette smoking, hypercholesterolemia, systolic blood pressure) from 1985 to 1990, which might lead to better outcomes. The precise extent to which these modest changes in risk factors have affected thirty-day AMI mortality is unclear, but the impact has probably not been substantial.

Infarct Type, Location, and Severity

According to data from the Worcester Heart Attack Study, between 1975 and 1981 the rate of non-Q-wave MI increased relative to the Q-wave MI rate (Goldberg et al. 1986). A likely reason for this increase is the improved detection of MI with creatine kinase (CK) cardiac enzymes. In 1975 medium serum creatine kinase (CK-MB) fractions and other chemistry tests for AMI confirmation were used in 5 percent of infarcts, compared to 58 percent in 1981 (Goldberg et al. 1986) and in over 90 percent of cases by the late 1980s. This increased use of cardiac enzymes may in part explain the observed increase in acute MI discharges at a time when overall mortality from MI was decreasing. In addition, improved initial detection and treatment of AMI may decrease the myocardial damage, resulting in a greater share of non-Q-wave infarcts. Non-Q-wave infarctions have better short-term mortality than Q-wave infarcts, although this difference does not appear to persist for long-term outcomes (Goldberg et al. 1987a; Behar et al. 1996). If we assume that two-thirds of the decline in Q-wave MI is due to improved treatment, then the remaining decline due to improved detection would explain 27 percent of the overall decline in thirty-day mortality.

Anterior location of the infarct appears to have dropped, perhaps also because of increased diagnosis of nonanterior infarcts, from 58 percent in 1975 to 43 percent in the early 1990s (Goldberg et al. 1986; Chandra et al. 1997). However, recent data from the GUSTO trials (GUSTO III Investigators 1997) suggest that the proportion of patients with anterior infarcts may have increased somewhat since 1993 (40.9 percent to 47.5 percent in 1996). Past studies have shown that mortality from an anterior MI is 50

10. Because we have used age-specific incidence rates to calculate the overall death rate, the impact of changing distributions of ages does not account for the unexplained reduction in our reported case-fatality rates. However, these demographic changes may be associated with other changes in case characteristics.

Table 9.8   **Trends in Patient Characteristics**

	1973–77	1978–82	1983–87	1988–92	1993–95	Source
Age (years)	64.1	65.5	67.5	68.4	69.1	NHDS
Female gender (%)	33	37	40	40	40	NHDS
Anterior or lateral location	58	58		44	46	GUSTO III Investigators (1997); Goldberg et al. (1986); Chandra et al. (1997); Mickelson, Blum, and Geraci (1997)
Q-wave MI	72	57		48	32	Goldberg et al. (1986); Mickelson, Blum, and Geraci (1997); McGovern et al. (1997)
Shock	7.6	7.3	7.6	9.1	2.9	Goldberg et al. (1991); Goldberg et al. (1986); Canto et al. (1996)

Note: The presence of Q-waves is a function of both patient characteristics and treatment.

Table 9.9   Infarct Characteristics and Mortality

	Effect Size	Odds Ratio
	Age	1.05
	Male	n.s.
	Anterior location	1.52
	Q-wave MI	2.32
	Shock (Killip IV)	7.89

Source: Canto et al. (1996).
Note: All $p < 0.001$; n.s. = not significant.

percent greater regardless of Q-wave or non Q-wave type, and anterior MIs have higher mortality than inferior infarcts even after adjusting for size of infarction (table 9.9) (Behar et al. 1993, 1996; Haim et al. 1997; Kornowski et al. 1997). If we assume that the relative death rates for anterior and inferior infarcts did not change, then the change in distribution of MI (more inferior) would explain 12 percent of the decrease in case-fatality rates.

A final source of evidence on changes in severity of infarcts is the share of patients who experience symptoms of cardiogenic shock. There is some evidence that average AMI severity given distribution increased through the late 1980s. According to the Worcester series, the incidence of shock increased slightly, from 7.6 percent in 1975 to 9.1 percent in 1988 (Goldberg et al. 1991). However, data from NRMI suggest that the prevalence of shock in more recent years is less than 5 percent, and shows no clear trend. If the NRMI data are correct, then decreasing MI severity over the entire time period can explain up to 30 percent of the reduction in AMI mortality.

Available data on patient characteristics and infarct severity do not permit definitive conclusions, but the bulk of the evidence suggests that the changes in the nature of AMIs in hospitalized patients accounts for a significant part of the observed improvements in outcomes, especially between 1975 and 1985. Taken together, the changes in infarct type, severity, and location would plausibly explain around one-third of the thirty-day mortality improvement for AMI between 1975 and 1995.

Changes in Reporting

Changes in coding practices and consequent increases in noncardiovascular death rates may explain some of the decline in IHD death rates (Pankow et al. 1994). A mathematical model of the decline in ischemic heart disease mortality estimated that 5 to 10 percent of the decline in mortality from 1970 to 1989 is due to definitional changes in the cause of death (Gilbertson et al. 1992). However, this model applied to all AMI deaths, including the predominant out-of-hospital deaths that are difficult to classify precisely. Studies based on clinical audits of Medicare discharge records suggest that the discharge diagnosis of AMI has a positive predictive value of 95 percent or higher for true AMIs (Green and Wintfeld 1993). This high level of accuracy for AMI does not appear to have changed much over time. Thus, it appears unlikely that changes in reporting practices have had a substantial impact on observed AMI trends.

9.3.5 Changes in Postacute Care and Long-Term Outcomes

Our results suggest that most of the substantial improvement in thirty-day AMI mortality over the past twenty years can reasonably be attributed to changes in medical treatments. An important question is the extent to which the thirty-day mortality improvements translate into long-term reductions in mortality for AMI patients. Medicare beneficiaries hospitalized with AMI between 1984 and 1994 had larger mortality reductions up to three to five years after AMI than they did at thirty days (McClellan and Noguchi 1988). However, variations in hospital treatment explained a significantly smaller share of one-year than thirty-day mortality variations for these patients (McClellan and Staiger 1999), suggesting that the long-term mortality improvements required the interaction of changes in hospital treatment with changes in subsequent treatment and behavior that led to secondary prevention. Unfortunately, less quantitative evidence exists on the effectiveness of postacute treatments, and especially on trends in their use in post-AMI patients. We review the available evidence here, which permits only qualitative estimates of the sources of improvements in long-term outcomes after AMI.

Reductions in mortality with beta blockers (odds ratio 0.81, 95 percent confidence interval [CI] 0.73–0.89), antiplatelet agents (0.90, 0.82–1.0), cholesterol lowering agents (0.86, 0.79–0.94), anticoagulants (0.78, 0.67–0.90) and rehabilitation programs (0.80, 0.65–0.95) have been demonstrated by multiple randomized trials. The benefit of calcium channel blockers is unclear (odds ratio 1.01, 95 percent CI 0.90–1.12), while class 1 antiarrhythmic agents appear to be harmful (1.28, 1.02–1.61) (see Lau et al. 1992 for a summary of these trials).

Changes in the use of these and other postacute treatments are less clear than the evidence on their likely effectiveness. A survey of internists by Hlatky et al. (1988) found increased long-term beta blockade, from 35 percent in 1979 to 82 percent in 1987, for a patient with an uncomplicated MI. Actual use is likely to be considerably lower because many patients have complicating factors that make them less than ideal candidates, and because of compliance problems. Data from outside the United States show an increase in postdischarge beta blockade use from 30 to 40 percent in the early 1980s to over 60 percent in the 1990s (Myers 1985, Thompson et al. 1992). Our analysis of data from the Cooperative Cardiovascular Project (CCP) has found that although beta blockers were given during admission to 46 percent of Medicare patients, only 27 percent received them at discharge.

A substantial increase in long-term aspirin use was also reported in Hlatky et al.'s (1988) physician survey, from 35 percent in 1979 to 82 percent in 1987. Data from Medicare beneficiaries in 1992–93 found that 76 percent of patients without a contraindication received aspirin (Krumholz et al. 1996). Non-U.S. data also suggest that postdischarge aspirin use has increased significantly worldwide, from 33 percent in 1985 to over 80 percent in the early 1990s (Thompson et al. 1992; Smith and Channer 1995). The increase in long-term aspirin use may be an important contributor to long-term outcome improvements.

Data from Medicare (CCP) in 1994 reveal that 26 percent of patients received calcium channel blockers, 24 percent received ACE inhibitors, and 11 percent received warfarin at discharge. NRMI results also show that use of ACE inhibitors at discharge appears to be increasing slowly but steadily in the United States, to around one-fourth of AMI patients by 1995 (McClellan et al., in press). International data document increasing use of calcium channel blockers from their first use in the early 1980s to a peak in the mid- to late 1980s of 40 to 50 percent, followed by a subsequent decline (Smith and Channer 1995; Zuanetti et al. 1996; Heller et al. 1992). Long-term use of nitrates and anticoagulants show no dramatic trends following AMI, at least over the past decade (Myers 1985; Thompson et al. 1992; Smith and Channer 1995; Heller et al. 1992).

In 1990 an estimated 10 to 15 percent of MI survivors participated in a supervised outpatient cardiac rehabilitation program (Wittels, Hay, and Gotto 1990; American College of Physicians 1988). This is less than the fraction of MI survivors (38 percent) in the GUSTO trial who were enrolled in cardiac rehabilitation programs (Mark et al. 1994). However, the GUSTO patients were a select group whose use of rehabilitation services may differ from that of the general population. The use of rehabilitation appears to be increasing over time, but little quantitative data exist on the magnitude of these trends.

Post-AMI catheterization and revascularization procedures, particularly angioplasty, became much more widespread between 1975 and 1995. Clinical trials have only documented a clear long-term mortality benefit from revascularization for a small fraction of IHD patients (Yusuf et al. 1994), and even in these cases the mortality differences were not evident until six months following surgery. Several recent trials have found no mortality benefit and possibly increased mortality risk with routine catheterization after AMI (Boden et al. 1998). Thus the limited available clinical trial evidence suggests that the additional procedures have had a modest impact on overall mortality trends. International comparisons of trends in long-term outcomes for AMI patients find results consistent with this conclusion: Countries like Canada that have had far less rapid growth in procedure use have had near-identical trends in mortality improvements (McClellan et al., in press). Some observational evidence suggests that more intensive procedure use may lead to improved quality of life (Rouleau et al. 1993). But few studies have evaluated trends in quality of life for AMI patients, so that conclusions about the contribution of more intensive procedures to long-term quality of life would be highly speculative.

Risk factors have also improved over the last several years for the general population, and improvements are likely to be similar if not greater for patients following MI. Smoking rates have dropped steadily between 1975 and 1995. Cholesterol levels dropped between 1960 and the mid-1980s, largely due to changes in diet (Goldman and Cook 1984), and they have dropped more substantially since the late 1980s, probably as a result of increased use of cholesterol lowering agents (statins). Data from the National Health and Nutrition Examination Survey (NHANES) indicate a yearly drop in total and LDL (low-density lipoprotein) cholesterol of 0.25 to 0.6 percent. Hypertension is also better controlled, particularly systolic hypertension in the elderly, again probably as a result of both behavioral changes (especially before 1980) and new drug treatments. Diastolic blood pressure has also decreased approximately 0.15 to 0.2 percent per year according to data from Minnesota (McGovern, Burke, et al. 1992). Obesity rates, in contrast, have increased from the mid-1980s onward. Data from NHANES suggest a 0.25 to 0.4 percent increase in body mass index per year. Taken together, these reductions in risk factors may be important contributors to the long-term sustainability of the short-term outcome improvements that we have described in detail. Both behavioral changes, especially in the early period of our study, and more effective drug therapy in more recent years have mediated these effects.

These results on long-term outcome improvements after AMI yield several qualitative conclusions. First, the substantial improvements in short-term mortality appear to translate into long-term mortality improvements. Second, changes in both postacute treatment—increased use of drugs including aspirin, beta blockers, statins, and antihypertensive drugs, and (perhaps to a lesser extent) increased use of revascularization procedures—as well as changes in risky behaviors have contributed to these improvements. Though quantitative conclusions are not possible using published data on effectiveness and treatment trends, it is likely that behavioral changes were relatively important up to the early 1980s, and that changes in medical treatments have accounted for the bulk of the improvements since. These qualitative conclusions about long-term mortality are generally consistent with our findings on the sources of acute mortality improvements, as well as with the conclusions of more general studies of IHD mortality trends (Goldman and Cook 1984; Weinstein et al. 1987; Hunink et al. 1997).

9.3.6   Cost-Effectiveness of Technological Change for AMI Care

Our results indicate that changes in medical technology have accounted for the bulk of improvements in acute AMI mortality, and probably of long-term AMI mortality, over the past two decades. With the cost of AMI treatment increasing substantially over the same period (McClellan and Noguchi 1988; Cutler et al. 1998), an important policy question is whether these changes have been cost-effective. A comprehensive approach to this question would require a detailed analysis of the cost of each of the technologies that we have studied, including their downstream impact on other expenditures. Such an analysis is beyond the scope of this paper. Here, we review some of the overall changes in thirty-day and longer-term expenditures on AMI patients, and discuss their implications for cost-effectiveness.

Resource Use, Costs, and Expenditures

The length of stay for patients hospitalized with myocardial infarction has declined consistently since 1975 (table 9.10). Data from discharge surveys and GUSTO I-III (GUSTO III Investigators 1997) show a drop from fifteen days in 1976 to seven or fewer in 1995. Medicare data on total length of stay for the thirty days and year after AMI show a similar, though slightly less dramatic, decline in total hospital days over the past decade. The decline is slightly less dramatic due to the increasing use of readmissions and transfers documented in table 9.1.

Despite the reduction in use of hospital days, total resource use in AMI care has increased substantially over the past two decades. Because of increasing use of intensive cardiac procedures, thrombolytics, other drugs, and intensive procedures during the initial AMI episode of care, the cost of each hospital day has grown more than enough to offset the reduced length of stay. Hospital list charges for AMI care have increased enormously: $4,752 in 1975 in Boston (Cretin 1977), $15,900 in San Francisco in 1982 (Sawitz et al. 1988), and $30,000 in Midwestern community hospitals (Leimbach et al. 1988) to $39,000 in Ann Arbor (Chapekis, Burek, and Topol 1989) in 1987. List charges are increasingly misleading measures of resource use, particularly since the late 1980s, because of managed-care contracting and government price regulation. However, studies based on estimated resource costs and actual reimbursements for medical services have qualitatively similar results. Studies from Boston hospitals using detailed cost per charge ratios to estimate costs have found an increase in mean costs from $10,638 in 1986 (Tosteson et al. 1996) to $15,073 in 1992 (Di et al. 1996). These trends are reflected in provider payments for AMI care: The thirty-day DRG payments for the Medicare population have increased steadily since 1985, and their growth may have accelerated since 1992 (McClellan and Noguchi 1988).

Table 9.10   Trends in Resource Utilization and Cost

	1973–77	1978–82	1983–87	1988–92	1993–95	Source
Length of stay (days)	16.5	14.0	10.5	8.3	7.1	HCIA Inc.
ICU length of stay (days)			5.8	4	3.5	Leimbach et al. 1988; Mark et al. 1995; Reeder et al. 1994
Hospital charges 1 year (1995$)	4,740	15,900	38,800			Cretin 1977; Sawitz et al. 1988; Chapekis, Burek, and Topol 1989
Hospital costs 1 year (using cost-charge ratio) (1995$)			12,100	15,000		Tosteson et al. 1996; Paul et al. 1995
Hospital costs 30-day (using Medicare reimbursements) (1995$)			8,100	9,500	12,300	Medicare data from 1985, 1990, 1994
Hospital costs 1 year (using Medicare reimbursements) (1995$)			12,100	14,200	18,200	Medicare data from 1985, 1990, 1994

Cost-Effectiveness

Using Medicare data on thirty-day expenditures for treatment, we estimated the aggregate cost-effectiveness of interventions for MI by determining the total cost of care and the expected quality-adjusted life years gained from all acute MI treatments. If we extend the 5.0 percent yearly real increase in total thirty-day medical expenditures observed between 1985 and 1995 (McClellan et al. in press) back to 1975, we would have observed a total increase in medical expenditures of $8,500 over the last twenty years. Because a greater percentage of patients are surviving their AMI, their long-term medical and nonmedical costs also rise. If we assume that the quality-of-life adjustment for surviving post-AMI has remained constant at 0.88 (Tsevat et al. 1993), then the discounted (3 percent per year) quality-adjusted life years (QALYs) over five years are forty QALYs per 100 patients treated (table 9.11). If quality of life of AMI survivors has actually improved over time, for example through better symptomatic relief from medications and revascularization, the QALY gains would be even larger.

Our estimates indicate that changes in AMI technology accounted for over 60 percent of the increase in QALYs. If we further assume that the changes in technology were responsible for all of the expenditure growth (Cutler and McClellan 1998), then the marginal cost-effectiveness for all

Table 9.11   Cost-Effectiveness Calculations

	5-Year Survival	10-Year Survival	15-Year Survival
Increase in MI cost (1995–75) per 100 patients ($)	8,500	8,500	8,500
Increase in MI survivors (1995–75) per 100 patients	8.3	8.3	8.3
Quality adjustment for living post-MI	0.88	0.88	0.88
Increase in long-term health costs due to MI survivors per 100 patients (assumes $4,000/year/survivor) ($)	181,000	337,000	472,000
Increase in total costs per 100 patients ($)	1,029,000	1,185,000	1,319,000
Increase in quality-adjusted life years (QALYs) per 100 patients	40	77	108
· costs/· QALYs ($)	26,000	15,000	12,000
QALYs due to interventions (QALYs × 0.62) per 100 patients[a]	25	48	67
Adjusted · costs/· QALYs ($)	42,000	25,000	20,000
Adjusted · costs/· Life years ($)	35,000	20,000	15,000

Note: All long-term costs and utilities are discounted at 3 percent per year (1995 dollars).

[a] Uses estimate of reduction in mortality from medical technologies from table 9.4.

treatments combined is $42,000 per QALY if patients survive five years post-MI, and $25,000 per QALY if patients survive ten years. Assuming a fifteen-year life expectancy following AMI (Mark et al. 1995), the cost per QALY gained is $20,000 and the cost per year of life gained is $16,000. These values cluster toward the low end of commonly accepted thresholds for cost-effectiveness of $25,000 to $100,000 per year of life saved (Laupacis et al. 1993).

The favorable results on the average value of all the changes in medical technology for AMI care do not imply that all of the many particular changes in AMI treatment have been cost-effective. For example, greater use of catheterization and revascularization can explain almost all of the growth in hospital payments for Medicare beneficiaries with AMI over the past decade (Cutler and McClellan 1998). But the evidence reviewed here suggests that these procedures account for only a small part of the short- and long-term mortality improvements, and these particular treatments may not have favorable cost-effectiveness ratios in themselves. In contrast, the cost-effectiveness of aspirin is extremely favorable.

9.4 Discussion

The treatment of AMI has changed enormously during the past twenty years. The use of interventions that have been shown to be effective in randomized clinical trials (aspirin, beta blockers, primary PTCA, thrombolytics) have increased, while the use of possibly harmful technologies (lidocaine, calcium channel blockers) has declined. Many other technologies with uncertain effectiveness have also become more widely used.

Recently, Hunink et al. (1997) reported the results of a Markov model of coronary heart disease to evaluate the importance of such changes in care for understanding the decline in IHD deaths from 1980 to 1990 (see also Weinstein et al. 1987). The study estimated that improvements in the thirty-day mortality rate for acute MI explained 15 percent (19,000 deaths) of the drop during this period. The coronary heart disease policy model did not incorporate individual treatment for acute myocardial infarction such as thrombolytic therapy or primary angioplasty, thus, the particular contributions of these interventions could not be determined.

Our goal was to understand the extent to which specific changes in AMI treatment and other factors could explain outcome trends for AMI patients. We developed quantitative estimates of changes in overall AMI mortality, including both hospitalized patients and those who die before hospitalization. Though we explored the likely consequences of changes in prehospital treatment and postacute AMI care, published studies were adequate to provide quantitative estimates only of the consequences of changes in acute mortality for hospitalized AMI patients. For this important group of AMI patients, we quantified the likely effects of all of the significant medical and nonmedical factors that might explain the decline. We found that changes in medical technology explain around two-thirds of the decline in thirty-day mortality rates. A small part of the residual decline in thirty-day mortality rates may be due to other treatments for which quantitative evidence on effectiveness and use was not available. But changes in AMI patient characteristics are probably responsible for the bulk of the residual one-third reduction. Among the nontreatment factors, improvements in diagnosis appear to have led to improved case-fatality rates as more patients with small, mild infarcts are being identified. However, improved early diagnosis, leading to more rapid use of effective technologies and thus more "incomplete" non-Q-wave AMIs, may also have contributed to this effect.

Technologies differed substantially in their impact on the reduction in thirty-day mortality rates. The use of beta blockade and anticoagulants increased only slightly and minimally contributed to the decline in case-fatality rates. Thrombolysis and primary PTCA have also become much more widespread since 1985, contributing significantly to the mortality improvement over the past decade. The greatest contributor to the decline in case-fatality rates was the diffusion of aspirin. Clinical trials have documented a substantial effect of aspirin on mortality, even in the postthrombolytic era. More importantly, aspirin use increased enormously, from around 15 percent in 1975 to 75 percent in the early 1990s. The use of aspirin for secondary prevention of MI has also increased in the United States. Thus aspirin appears to be the most important factor in explaining the cost-effectiveness of technological change in AMI care for both short- and long-term mortality improvements. Other changes in technology have probably been less cost-effective, and may not have been worth their additional resource costs.

To our knowledge, this is the most detailed quantitative analysis of the contribution of specific changes in medical technology to changes in population outcomes. Our findings suggest that the medical treatment changes can explain over 60 percent of the observed improvements in mortality for hospitalized AMI patients, and have been particularly important since 1985. The remainder of the mortality improvement can probably be attributed to reductions in the average severity of hospitalized AMI patients, in association with improvements in techniques for diagnosing mild non-Q-wave MIs. Important as the changes in acute treatment collectively appeared to be, we found that they accounted for only a minority—less than one-fourth—of the overall decline in population AMI mortality rates during the 1975–95 period. Most of the observed reduction in AMI mortality was associated with a large decline in the number of serious AMI events resulting in either prehospital deaths or hospitalization. Further studies could extend our detailed decomposition techniques to explaining "primary prevention" trends, building on the general descriptive work of Hunink et al. and others. Fewer quantitative clinical studies have examined the use of preventive medical treatments and their individual effects on outcomes, so a quantitative analysis of the contribution of particular preventive treatments to the reductions in AMI event rates that we estimate may be difficult. The same problem applies to understanding the specific factors responsible for improvements in long-term AMI outcomes. Nonetheless, a careful review of the changes in treatments and outcomes for primary and secondary prevention could provide important insights into why these outcomes have changed and the cost-effectiveness of these changes, as well as identifying key areas of uncertainty for future clinical studies.

Our results demonstrate that changes in medical treatment are becoming more important, and changes in behavior are becoming relatively less important, in accounting for the substantial improvements that have occurred in acute and long-term AMI outcomes. Steady growth in the use of particular technologies suggests that the use of beneficial acute therapies may become even more widespread over the next several years. To explore the consequences of increased use of beneficial therapies, we determined the improvement in thirty-day mortality rate that would occur if (1) aspirin use increased to 90 percent, (2) beta blockade increased to 80 percent, and (3) thrombolysis or primary PTCA increased to 50 percent. These changes in treatment, which may occur over the next five to ten years if current trends continue, would reduce thirty-day mortality to 15 percent (14 percent relative decrease, 2.5 percent absolute decrease relative to 1995 mortality). Because these therapies are relatively underused in the elderly, who still have relatively high mortality rates, even larger reductions might be possible.

Changes in prehospital care also remain a potential source of outcome improvements. Treatment of cardiac arrest with early defibrillation has become more readily available. However, few studies have suggested that other aspects of prehospital treatments for AMI have changed substantially between 1975 and 1995. For example, studies of 1975 and 1990 AMI patients found similar rates of ambulance use, and several studies have failed to document improvements in death rates for urgent conditions following activation or enhancement of 911 systems. Improving these emergency responses and reducing time to effective therapy remains a policy priority through initiatives such as the National Heart Attack Alert Program and the Cooperative Cardiovascular Project. Perhaps these initiatives are beginning to pay off: In the last few years, evidence from particular hospitals suggests that time between hospital arrival and the delivery of key AMI treatments (thrombolytics, primary angioplasty) is declining. Even though they do not appear to have played a large role in the improvements between 1975 and 1995, it is possible that changes in prehospital care and reductions in time to treatment will also lead to further improvements in AMI mortality.

Many unanswered questions about technological change in AMI care remain. The lack of quantitative evidence on postacute care for AMI patients complicates forecasts of future changes in AMI patient outcomes. The enormous apparent variation in the cost-effectiveness of the various changes in AMI treatment that have occurred suggests there is considerable room for further improvements in the "productivity" of AMI care. Have any changes in AMI treatment been clearly cost-ineffective, and why did they occur? Which economic incentives encourage the most rapid adoption of cost-effective innovations in treatment? Have changes in appropriateness of treatment choices and the expertise of providers been important contributors to outcome trends? Our results suggest that further integration of studies on treatment effectiveness with descriptive studies on trends in actual patient characteristics, treatments, and outcomes holds considerable promise for addressing these questions.

References

American College of Physicians. Health and Public Policy Committee. 1988. Cardiac rehabilitation services. *Annals of Internal Medicine* 109 (8): 671–73.

American Heart Association. Emergency Cardiac Care Committee and Subcommittees. 1992. Guidelines for cardiopulmonary resuscitation and emergency cardiac care. Part II, Adult basic life support. *Journal of the American Medical Association* 268 (16): 2184–98.

Ayanian, J. Z., M. B. Landrum, S. L. Normand, E. Guadagnoli, and B. J. McNeil. 1998. Rating the appropriateness of coronary angiography: Do practicing physicians agree with an expert panel and with each other? *New England Journal of Medicine* 338 (26): 1896–1904.

Barbash, G. I., A. Roth, H. Hod, H. I. Miller, M. Modan, S. Rath, et al. 1990. Improved survival but not left ventricular function with early and prehospital treatment with tissue plasminogen activator in acute myocardial infarction. *American Journal of Cardiology* 66 (3): 261–66.

Becker, L. B., D. W. Smith, and K. V. Rhodes. 1993. Incidence of cardiac arrest: A neglected factor in evaluating survival rates. *Annals of Emergency Medicine* 22 (1): 86–91.

Becker, R. C. 1994. Beta-adrenergic blockade following thrombolytic therapy: Is it helpful or harmful? *Clinical Cardiology* 17 (4): 171–74.

Behar, S., M. Haim, H. Hod, R. Kornowski, H. Reicher-Reiss, M. Zion, et al. 1996. Long-term prognosis of patients after a Q wave compared with a non-Q wave first acute myocardial infarction. Data from the SPRINT Registry. *European Heart Journal* 17 (10): 1532–37.

Behar, S., B. Rabinowitz, M. Zion, H. Reicher-Reiss, E. Kaplinsky, E. Abinader, et al. 1993. Immediate and long-term prognostic significance of a first anterior versus first inferior wall Q-wave acute myocardial infarction. Secondary Prevention Reinfarction Israeli Nifedipine Trial (SPRINT) Study Group. *American Journal of Cardiology* 72 (18): 1366–70.

Blohm, M. B., M. Hartford, B. W. Karlson, R. V. Luepker, and J. Herlitz. 1996. An evaluation of the results of media and educational campaigns designed to shorten the time taken by patients with acute myocardial infarction to decide to go to hospital. *Heart* 76 (5): 430–34.

Boden, W. E., R. A. O'Rourke, M. H. Crawford, A. S. Blaustein, P. C. Deedwania, R. G. Zoble, et al. 1998. Outcomes in patients with acute non-Q-wave myocardial infarction randomly assigned to an invasive as compared with a conservative management strategy. Veterans Affairs Non-Q-Wave Infarction Strategies in Hospital (VANQWISH) Trial Investigators. *New England Journal of Medicine* 338 (25): 1785–92.

Boersma, E., A. C. Maas, J. W. Deckers, and M. L. Simoons. 1996. Early thrombolytic treatment in acute myocardial infarction: Reappraisal of the golden hour. *Lancet* 348 (9030): 771–75.

Burns, M., R. Becker, J. Gore, C. Lambrew, W. French, and W. Rogers. 1997. Early and predischarge aspirin administration among patients with acute myocardial infarction: The second National Registry of Myocardial Infarction (NRMI 2). *Journal of the American College of Cardiology* 29 (2): Abstract 738–1.

Callaham, M., C. D. Madsen, C. W. Barton, C. E. Saunders, and J. Pointer. 1992. A randomized clinical trial of high-dose epinephrine and norepinephrine vs standard-dose epinephrine in prehospital cardiac arrest. *Journal of the American Medical Association* 268 (19): 2667–72.

Canto, J., W. Rogers, L. Bowlby, W. French, and D. Pearce. 1996. Pre-hospital electrocardiogram in the Second National Registry of Myocardial Infarction (NRMI-2). *Journal of the American College of Cardiology* 27 (2): Abstract 1030–52.

Chandra, H., J. Yarzebski, R. J. Goldberg, J. Savageau, C. Singleton, J. H. Gurwitz, et al. 1997. Age-related trends (1986–1993) in the use of thrombolytic agents in patients with acute myocardial infarction. The Worcester Heart Attack Study. *Archives of Internal Medicine* 157 (7): 741–46.

Chandra, N., R. Ziegelstein, J. Hilbe, W. French, L. Sanathanan, and N. Investigators. 1996. Lidocaine use in acute MI: A marker for increased mortality. Observations from the National Registry of Myocardial Infarction-2 (NRMI-2). *Circulation* 94 (8): Abstract 2083.

Chapekis, A. T., K. Burek, and E. J. Topol. 1989. The cost:benefit ratio of acute intervention for myocardial infarction: Results of a prospective, matched pair analysis. *American Heart Journal* 118 (5, pt 1): 878–82.

Connors, A. J., T. Speroff, N. V. Dawson, C. Thomas, F. J. Harrell, D. Wagner, et al. 1996. The effectiveness of right heart catheterization in the initial care of critically ill patients. SUPPORT Investigators. *Journal of the American Medical Association* 276 (11): 889–97.

Cretin, S. 1977. Cost/benefit analysis of treatment and prevention of myocardial infarction. *Health Services Research* 12 (2): 174–89.

Cummins, R. O. 1993. Emergency medical services and sudden cardiac arrest: The "chain of survival" concept. *Annual Review of Public Health* 14:313–33.

Cummins, R. O., M. S. Eisenberg, A. P. Hallstrom, and P. E. Litwin. 1985. Survival of out-of-hospital cardiac arrest with early initiation of cardiopulmonary resuscitation. *American Journal of Emergency Medicine* 3 (2): 114–19.

Cummins, R. O., M. S. Eisenberg, P. E. Litwin, J. R. Graves, T. R. Hearne, and A. P. Hallstrom. 1987. Automatic external defibrillators used by emergency medical technicians. A controlled clinical trial. *Journal of the American Medical Association* 257 (12): 1605–10.

Cummins, R. O., J. R. Graves, M. P. Larsen, A. P. Hallstrom, T. R. Hearne, J. Ciliberti, et al. 1993. Out-of-hospital transcutaneous pacing by emergency medical technicians in patients with asystolic cardiac arrest. *New England Journal of Medicine* 328 (19): 1377–82.

Cutler, D., and M. McClellan. 1998. Technological change in Medicare. In *Frontiers in the economics of aging,* ed. David A. Wise. Chicago: University of Chicago Press.

Cutler, D., M. McClellan, J. Newhouse, and D. Remler. 1998. Are medical prices declining? Evidence from heart attack treatments. *Quarterly Journal of Economics* 113:991–1024.

Dalen, J. E., and R. C. Bone. 1996. Is it time to pull the pulmonary artery catheter? *Journal of the American Medical Association* 276 (11): 916–18.

Di, S. T., S. D. Paul, J. D. Lloyd, A. J. Smith, L. G. Villarreal, V. Bamezai, et al. 1996. Care of acute myocardial infarction by noninvasive and invasive cardiologists: Procedure use, cost and outcome. *Journal of the American College of Cardiology* 27 (2): 262–69.

Eisenberg, M. S., A. P. Hallstrom, W. B. Carter, R. O. Cummins, L. Bergner, and J. Pierce. 1985. Emergency CPR instruction via telephone. *American Journal of Public Health* 75 (1): 47–50.

Eisenberg, M. S., B. T. Horwood, R. O. Cummins, R. Reynolds-Haertle, and T. R. Hearne. 1990. Cardiac arrest and resuscitation: A tale of 29 cities. *Annals of Emergency Medicine* 19 (2): 179–86.

Every, N. R., L. S. Parsons, M. Hlatky, J. S. Martin, and W. D. Weaver. 1996. A comparison of thrombolytic therapy with primary coronary angioplasty for acute myocardial infarction. Myocardial Infarction Triage and Intervention Investigators. *New England Journal of Medicine* 335 (17): 1253–60.

Gallagher, E. J., G. Lombardi, and P. Gennis. 1995. Effectiveness of bystander cardiopulmonary resuscitation and survival following out-of-hospital cardiac arrest. *Journal of the American Medical Association* 274 (24): 1922–25.

Gilbertson, D., P. McGovern, D. Jacobs, L. Gatewood, and H. Blackburn. 1992. A mathematical modeling approach toward explaining the decline in coronary heart disease mortality. Abstract. *Circulation* 86 (suppl.): I597.

Gillum, R. F., A. Folsom, R. V. Luepker, D. R. Jacobs Jr., T. E. Kottke, O. Gomez-Marin, et al. 1983. Sudden death and acute myocardial infarction in a metropolitan area, 1970–1980. The Minnesota Heart Survey. *New England Journal of Medicine* 309 (22): 1353–58.

Goldberg, R. J., J. M. Gore, J. S. Alpert, and J. E. Dalen. 1986. Recent changes in attack and survival rates of acute myocardial infarction (1975 through 1981). The Worcester Heart Attack Study. *Journal of the American Medical Association* 255 (20): 2774–79.

———. 1987a. Non-Q wave myocardial infarction: Recent changes in occurrence and prognosis—a community-wide perspective. *American Heart Journal* 113 (2, pt 1): 273–79.

———. 1987b. Therapeutic trends in the management of patients with acute myocardial infarction (1975–1984): The Worcester Heart Attack Study. *Clinical Cardiology* 10 (1): 3–8.

Goldberg, R. J., J. M. Gore, J. S. Alpert, V. Osganian, J. de Groot, J. Bade, et al. 1991. Cardiogenic shock after acute myocardial infarction: Incidence and mortality from a community-wide perspective, 1975 to 1988. *New England Journal of Medicine* 325 (16): 1117–22.

Goldman, L., and E. F. Cook. 1984. The decline in ischemic heart disease mortality rates: An analysis of the comparative effects of medical interventions and changes in lifestyle. *Annals of Internal Medicine* 101 (6): 825–36.

Goldman, L., F. Cook, B. Hashimotso, P. Stone, J. Muller, and A. Loscalzo. 1982. Evidence that hospital care for acute myocardial infarction has not contributed to the decline in coronary mortality between 1973–1974 and 1978–1979. *Circulation* 65 (5): 936–42.

Gore, J. M., R. J. Goldberg, D. H. Spodick, J. S. Alpert, and J. E. Dalen. 1987. A community-wide assessment of the use of pulmonary artery catheters in patients with acute myocardial infarction. *Chest* 92 (4): 721–27.

Green, J., and N. Wintfeld. 1993. How accurate are hospital discharge data for evaluating effectiveness of care? *Medical Care* 31 (8): 719–31.

Gurwitz, J. H., R. J. Goldberg, Z. Chen, J. M. Gore, and J. S. Alpert. 1994. Recent trends in hospital mortality of acute myocardial infarction—the Worcester Heart Attack Study: Have improvements been realized for all age groups? *Archives of Internal Medicine* 154 (19): 2202–8.

GUSTO III Investigators. 1997. A comparison of Reteplase with Alteplase for acute myocardial infarction. *New England Journal of Medicine* 337:1118–23.

Haim, M., H. Hod, L. Reisin, R. Kornowski, H. Reicher-Reiss, U. Goldbourt, et al. 1997. Comparison of short- and long-term prognosis in patients with anterior wall versus inferior or lateral wall non-Q-wave acute myocardial infarction. Secondary Prevention Reinfarction Israeli Nifedipine Trial (SPRINT) Study Group. *American Journal of Cardiology* 79 (6): 717–21.

Heller, R. F., A. J. Dobson, H. M. Alexander, P. L. Steele, and J. A. Malcolm. 1992. Changes in drug treatment and case fatality of patients with acute myocardial infarction: Observations from the Newcastle MONICA Project, 1984/1985 to 1988/1990. *Medical Journal of Australia* 157 (2): 83–86.

Hennekens, C. H., C. M. Albert, S. L. Godfried, J. M. Gaziano, and J. E. Buring. 1996. Adjunctive drug therapy of acute myocardial infarction—evidence from clinical trials. *New England Journal of Medicine* 335 (22): 1660–67.

Hlatky, M. A., H. E. Cotugno, D. B. Mark, C. O'Connor, R. M. Califf, and D. B. Pryor. 1988. Trends in physician management of uncomplicated acute myocardial infarction, 1970 to 1987. *American Journal of Cardiology* 61 (8): 515–18.

Ho, M. T., M. S. Eisenberg, P. E. Litwin, S. M. Schaeffer, and S. K. Damon. 1989. Delay between onset of chest pain and seeking medical care: The effect of public education. *Annals of Emergency Medicine* 18 (7): 727–31.

Hunink, M. G., L. Goldman, A. N. Tosteson, M. A. Mittleman, P. A. Goldman, L. W. Williams, et al. 1997. The recent decline in mortality from coronary heart disease, 1980–1990: The effect of secular trends in risk factors and treatment. *Journal of the American Medical Association* 277 (7): 535–42.

Hunt, R. C., J. B. McCabe, G. C. Hamilton, and J. R. Krohmer. 1989. Influence of emergency medical services systems and prehospital defibrillation on survival of sudden cardiac death victims. *American Journal of Emergency Medicine* 7 (1): 68–82.

ISIS-2 (Second International Study of Infarct Survival) Collaborative Group. 1988. Randomised trial of intravenous streptokinase, oral aspirin, both, or neither among 17,187 cases of suspected acute myocardial infarction: ISIS-2. *Lancet* 2 (8607): 349–60.

ISIS-4 (Fourth International Study of Infarct Survival) Collaborative Group. 1995. ISIS-4: A randomised factorial trial assessing early oral captopril, oral mononitrate, and intravenous magnesium sulphate in 58,050 patients with suspected acute myocardial infarction. *Lancet* 345 (8951): 669–85.

Kereiakes, D. J., W. D. Weaver, J. L. Anderson, T. Feldman, B. Gibler, T. Aufderheide, et al. 1990. Time delays in the diagnosis and treatment of acute myocardial infarction: A tale of eight cities. Report from the Pre-hospital Study Group and the Cincinnati Heart Project. *American Heart Journal* 120 (4): 773–80.

Kornowski, R., U. Goldbourt, H. Reicher-Reiss, L. Reisin, M. Haim, Y. Moshkovitz, et al. 1997. Prognostic significance of infarction location in patients with recurrent myocardial infarction. SPRINT Study Group. Secondary Prevention Reinfarction Israel Nifedipine Trial. *Cardiology* 88 (5): 441–45.

Koshal, A., D. S. Beanlands, R. A. Davies, R. C. Nair, and W. J. Keon. 1988. Urgent surgical reperfusion in acute evolving myocardial infarction: A randomized controlled study. *Circulation* 78 (3, pt 2): I171–78.

Krumholz, H. M., M. J. Radford, E. F. Ellerbeck, J. Hennen, T. P. Meehan, M. Petrillo, et al. 1996. Aspirin for secondary prevention after acute myocardial infarction in the elderly: Prescribed use and outcomes. *Annals of Internal Medicine* 124 (3): 292–98.

Lau, J., E. M. Antman, S. J. Jimenez, B. Kupelnick, F. Mosteller, and T. C. Chalmers. 1992. Cumulative meta-analysis of therapeutic trials for myocardial infarction. *New England Journal of Medicine* 327 (4): 248–54.

Laupacis, A., D. Feeny, A. S. Detsky, and P. X. Tugwell. 1993. Tentative guidelines for using clinical and economic evaluations revisited. *Canadian Medical Association Journal* 148 (6): 927–29.

Leimbach, W., Jr., A. D. Hagan, H. L. Vaughan, R. C. Sonnenschein, J. D. McCoy, and L. L. Basta. 1988. Cost and efficacy of intravenous streptokinase plus PTCA for acute myocardial infarction when therapy is initiated in community hospitals. *Clinical Cardiology* 11 (11): 731–38.

Mark, D. B., M. A. Hlatky, R. M. Califf, C. D. Naylor, K. L. Lee, P. W. Armstrong, et al. 1995. Cost effectiveness of thrombolytic therapy with tissue plasminogen activator as compared with streptokinase for acute myocardial infarction. *New England Journal of Medicine* 332 (21): 1418–24.

Mark, D. B., C. D. Naylor, M. A. Hlatky, R. M. Califf, E. J. Topol, C. B. Granger, et al. 1994. Use of medical resources and quality of life after acute myocardial infarction in Canada and the United States. *New England Journal of Medicine* 331 (17): 1130–35.

Maynard, C., W. D. Weaver, C. Lambrew, L. J. Bowlby, W. J. Rogers, and R. M. Rubison. 1995. Factors influencing the time to administration of thrombolytic therapy with recombinant tissue plasminogen activator (data from the National Registry of Myocardial Infarction). Participants in the National Registry of Myocardial Infarction. *American Journal of Cardiology* 76 (8): 548–52.

McClellan, M., N. Every, A. Garber, P. Heidenreich, M. Hlatky, D. Kessler, et al. In press. Technological change in heart attack care in the United States. In *Technological change in health care: A global analysis of heart attacks,* ed. M. McClellan and D. Kessler. Ann Arbor: University of Michigan Press.

McClellan, M., and H. Noguchi. 1988. Technological change in heart-disease treatment: Does high tech mean low value? *American Economic Review* 88 (2): 90–96.

McClellan, M., and D. Staiger. 1999. The quality of health care providers. NBER Working Paper no. 7327. Cambridge, Mass.: National Bureau of Economic Research.

McGovern, P. G., G. L. Burke, J. M. Sprafka, S. Xue, A. R. Folsom, and H. Blackburn. 1992. Trends in mortality, morbidity, and risk factor levels for stroke from 1960 through 1990. The Minnesota Heart Survey. *Journal of the American Medical Association* 268 (6): 753–59.

McGovern, P. G., A. R. Folsom, J. M. Sprafka, G. L. Burke, K. M. Doliszny, J. Demirovic, et al. 1992. Trends in survival of hospitalized myocardial infarction patients between 1970 and 1985. The Minnesota Heart Survey. *Circulation* 85 (1): 172–79.

McGovern, P. G., J. Herlitz, J. S. Pankow, T. Karlsson, M. Dellborg, E. Shahar, et al. 1997. Comparison of medical care and one- and 12-month mortality of hospitalized patients with acute myocardial infarction in Minneapolis–St. Paul, Minnesota, United States of America and Goteborg, Sweden. *American Journal of Cardiology* 80 (5): 557–62.

McGovern, P. G., J. S. Pankow, E. Shahar, K. M. Doliszny, A. R. Folsom, H. Blackburn, et al. 1996. Recent trends in acute coronary heart disease—mortality, morbidity, medical care, and risk factors. The Minnesota Heart Survey Investigators. *New England Journal of Medicine* 334 (14): 884–90.

McLaughlin, T. J., S. B. Soumerai, D. J. Willison, J. H. Gurwitz, C. Borbas, E. Guadagnoli, et al. 1996. Adherence to national guidelines for drug treatment of suspected acute myocardial infarction: Evidence for undertreatment in women and the elderly. *Archives of Internal Medicine* 156 (7): 799–805.

Mickelson, J. K., C. M. Blum, and J. M. Geraci. 1997. Acute myocardial infarction: Clinical characteristics, management and outcome in a metropolitan Veterans Affairs Medical Center teaching hospital. *Journal of the American College of Cardiology* 29 (5): 915–25.

Myers, M. G. 1985. Changing patterns in drug therapy for ischemic heart disease. *Canadian Medical Association Journal* 132 (6): 644–48.

Pankow, J. S., P. G. McGovern, J. M. Sprafka, D. J. Jacobs, and H. Blackburn. 1994. Trends in coded causes of death following definite myocardial infarction and the role of competing risks: The Minnesota Heart Survey (MHS). *Journal of Clinical Epidemiology* 47 (9): 1051–60.

Pashos, C. L., S. L. Normand, J. B. Garfinkle, J. P. Newhouse, A. M. Epstein, and B. J. McNeil. 1994. Trends in the use of drug therapies in patients with acute myocardial infarction: 1988 to 1992. *Journal of the American College of Cardiology* 23 (5): 1023–30.

Patsey, T., J. Messick, R. Rutledge, A. Meyer, J. M. Butts, and C. Baker. 1992. A population-based, multivariate analysis of the association between 911 access and per-capita county trauma death rates. *Annals of Emergency Medicine* 21 (10): 1173–78.

Paul, S., C. Lambrew, W. Rogers, and M. Fifer. 1996. A study of 118,276 patients with acute myocardial infarction in the United States in 1995: Less aggressive care, worse prognosis, and longer hospital length of stay for diabetics. *Circulation* 94 (8): Abstract 3576.

Paul, S. D., K. A. Eagle, U. Guidry, T. G. DiSalvo, L. G. Villarreal, A. J. Smith, et al. 1995. Do gender-based differences in presentation and management influence predictors of hospitalization costs and length of stay after an acute myocardial infarction? *American Journal of Cardiology* 76 (16): 1122–25.

Pressley, J. C., H. J. Severance, M. P. Raney, R. A. McKinnis, M. W. Smith, M. C. Hindman, et al. 1988. A comparison of paramedic versus basic emergency medical care of patients at high and low risk during acute myocardial infarction. *Journal of the American College of Cardiology* 12 (6): 1555–61.

Reeder, G. S., K. R. Bailey, B. J. Gersh, D. J. Holmes, J. Christianson, and R. J. Gibbons. 1994. Cost comparison of immediate angioplasty versus thrombolysis followed by conservative therapy for acute myocardial infarction: A randomized prospective trial. Mayo Coronary Care Unit and Catheterization Laboratory Groups. *Mayo Clinic Proceedings* 69 (1): 5–12.

Rogers, W., N. Chandra, W. French, J. Gore, C. Lambrew, and A. Tiefenbrunn. 1996. Trends in the use of reperfusion therapy: Experience from the second National Registry of Myocardial Infarction (NRMI 2). *Circulation* 194 (8): Abstract 1138.

Rogers, W. J., L. J. Bowlby, N. C. Chandra, W. J. French, J. M. Gore, C. T. Lambrew, et al. 1994. Treatment of myocardial infarction in the United States (1990 to 1993): Observations from the National Registry of Myocardial Infarction. *Circulation* 90 (4): 2103–14.

Rouleau, J. L., L. A. Moye, M. A. Pfeffer, J. M. Arnold, V. Bernstein, T. E. Cuddy, et al. 1993. A comparison of management patterns after acute myocardial infarction in Canada and the United States. The SAVE investigators. *New England Journal of Medicine* 328 (11): 779–84.

Ryan, T. J., J. L. Anderson, E. M. Antman, B. A. Braniff, N. H. Brooks, R. M. Califf, et al. 1996. ACC/AHA guidelines for the management of patients with acute myocardial infarction. A report of the American College of Cardiology/ American Heart Association Task Force on Practice Guidelines (Committee on Management of Acute Myocardial Infarction). *Journal of the American College of Cardiology* 28 (5): 1328–1428.

Sawitz, E., J. A. Showstack, J. Chow, and S. A. Schroeder. 1988. The use of in-hospital physician services for acute myocardial infarction: Changes in volume and complexity over time. *Journal of the American Medical Association* 259 (16): 2419–22.

Schwab, T. M., M. L. Callaham, C. D. Madsen, and T. A. Utecht. 1995. A randomized clinical trial of active compression-decompression CPR vs standard CPR in out-of-hospital cardiac arrest in two cities. *Journal of the American Medical Association* 273 (16): 1261–68.

Sharkey, S. W., D. D. Bruneete, E. Ruiz, W. T. Hession, D. G. Wysham, I. F. Goldenberg, et al. 1989. An analysis of time delays preceding thrombolysis for acute myocardial infarction. *Journal of the American Medical Association* 262 (22): 3171–74.

Smith, J., and K. S. Channer. 1995. Increasing prescription of drugs for secondary prevention after myocardial infarction. *BMJ* 311 (7010): 917–18.

Teo, K. K., S. Yusuf, R. Collins, P. H. Held, R. Peto. 1991. Effects of intravenous magnesium in suspected acute myocardial infarction: Overview of randomised trials. *BMJ* 303 (6816): 1499–1503.

Teo, K. K., S. Yusuf, and C. D. Furberg. 1993. Effects of prophylactic antiarrhythmic drug therapy in acute myocardial infarction: An overview of results from randomized controlled trials. *Journal of the American Medical Association* 270 (13): 1589–95.

Thompson, P. L., R. W. Parsons, K. Jamrozik, R. L. Hockey, M. S. Hobbs, and R. J. Broadhurst. 1992. Changing patterns of medical treatment in acute myocardial infarction: Observations from the Perth MONICA Project 1984–1990. *Medical Journal of Australia* 157 (2): 87–92.

Tosteson, A. N., L. Goldman, I. S. Udvarhelyi, and T. H. Lee. 1996. Cost-effectiveness of a coronary care unit versus an intermediate care unit for emergency department patients with chest pain. *Circulation* 94 (2): 143–50.

Tsevat, J., L. Goldman, J. R. Soukup, G. A. Lamas, K. F. Connors, C. C. Chapin, et al. 1993. Stability of time-tradeoff utilities in survivors of myocardial infarction. *Medical Decision Making* 13 (2): 161–65.

Tu, J. V., C. L. Pashos, C. D. Naylor, E. Chen, S. L. Normand, J. P. Newhouse, et al. 1997. Use of cardiac procedures and outcomes in elderly patients with myocardial infarction in the United States and Canada. *New England Journal of Medicine* 336 (21): 1500–1505.

Van de Werf, F., L. Janssens, T. Brzostek, et al. 1993. Short-term effects of early intravenous treatment with a beta-adrenergic blocking agent or a specific brady-cardiac agent in patients with acute myocardial infarction receiving thrombolytic therapy. *Journal of the American College of Cardiology* 22 (2): 407–16.

Vukov, L. F., R. D. White, J. W. Bachman, P. C. O'Brien. 1988. New perspectives on rural EMT defibrillation. *Annals of Emergency Medicine* 17 (4): 318–21.

Weaver, W. D. 1995. Time to thrombolytic treatment: Factors affecting delay and their influence on outcome. *Journal of the American College of Cardiology* 25 (7, suppl.): 3S–9S.

Weaver, W. D., L. A. Cobb, A. P. Hallstrom, M. K. Copass, R. Ray, M. Emery, et al. 1986. Considerations for improving survival from out-of-hospital cardiac arrest. *Annals of Emergency Medicine* 15 (10): 1181–86.

Weaver, W. D., R. J. Simes, A. Betriu, C. L. Grines, F. Zijlstra, E. Garcia, et al. 1997. Comparison of primary coronary angioplasty and intravenous thrombolytic therapy for acute myocardial infarction: A quantitative review. *Journal of the American Medical Association* 278 (23): 2093–98.

Weinstein, M. C., P. G. Coxson, L. W. Williams, T. M. Pass, W. B. Stason, and L. Goldman. 1987. Forecasting coronary heart disease incidence, mortality, and cost: The Coronary Heart Disease Policy Model. *American Journal of Public Health* 77 (11): 1417–26.

Wittels, E. H., J. W. Hay, and A. M. Gotto Jr. 1990. Medical costs of coronary artery disease in the United States. *American Journal of Cardiology* 65 (7): 432–40.

Yarzebski, J., R. J. Goldberg, J. M. Gore, and J. S. Alpert. 1994a. Temporal trends and factors associated with extent of delay to hospital arrival in patients with acute myocardial infarction: The Worcester Heart Attack Study. *American Heart Journal* 128 (2): 255–63.

———. 1994b. Temporal trends and factors associated with pulmonary artery catheterization in patients with acute myocardial infarction. *Chest* 105 (4): 1003–8.

Yusuf, S., R. Collins, S. MacMahon, and R. Peto. 1988. Effect of intravenous nitrates on mortality in acute myocardial infarction: An overview of the randomised trials. *Lancet* 1 (8594): 1088–92.

Yusuf, S., D. Zucker, P. Peduzzi, L. D. Fisher, T. Takaro, J. W. Kennedy, et al. 1994. Effect of coronary artery bypass graft surgery on survival: Overview of 10-year results from randomised trials by the Coronary Artery Bypass Graft Surgery Trialists Collaboration. *Lancet* 344 (8922): 563–70.

Ziegelstein, R., J. Hilbe, W. French, L. Sanathanan, N. Chandra, and N. Investigators. 1996. Magnesium use in the treatment of acute MI: Is a little still too much? Observations from the National Registry of Myocardial Infarction-2 (NRMI 2). *Circulation* 94 (8): Abstract 1541.

Zion, M. M., J. Balkin, D. Rosenmann, U. Goldbourt, H. Reicher-Reiss, E. Kaplinsky, et al. 1990. Use of pulmonary artery catheters in patients with acute myocardial infarction: Analysis of experience in 5,841 patients in the SPRINT Registry. SPRINT Study Group. *Chest* 98 (6): 1331–35.

Zuanetti, G., R. Latini, F. Avanzini, M. G. Franzosi, A. P. Maggioni, F. Colombo, et al. 1996. Trends and determinants of calcium antagonist usage after acute myocardial infarction (the GISSI experience). *American Journal of Cardiology* 78 (2): 153–57.

Measuring the Value of Cataract Surgery

Irving Shapiro, Matthew D. Shapiro,
and David W. Wilcox

10.1 Health Care and the Cost of Living

The standard analytic framework for constructing a cost-of-living index compares the change in expenditure between a base and a reference period needed to deliver a fixed level of utility.[1] This framework, which relies on a stable, well-defined function relating per period expenditure to prices and utility, has serious limitations for measuring how health-care expenditures affect the cost of living.

- Health expenditure on life-extending therapies can not only increase current-period utility, but have durable effects on utility. Durability per se is not special to health care. The purchase of a refrigerator or car also provides for a flow of utility into the future. This aspect of durability can be handled in a cost-of-living index by taking a service-flow approach.[2] By making the number of periods of life endogenous,

Irving Shapiro is medical director at the Phillips Eye Institute, Minneapolis, and clinical professor of ophthalmology at the University of Minnesota. Matthew D. Shapiro is professor of economics and senior research scientist at the Survey Research Center at the University of Michigan, and a research associate of the National Bureau of Economic Research. David W. Wilcox is assistant secretary for economic policy at the U.S. Department of the Treasury.

The authors are grateful to Praveen Kache and Laura Marburger for research assistance. Matthew Shapiro gratefully acknowledges the financial support of the National Institute on Aging through the Michigan Exploratory Center on the Demography of Aging and program project 2-P01 AG 10170. The authors gratefully acknowledge the very helpful discussions with and comments of Andrew Abel, Zvi Griliches, Richard Suzman, and participants in the NBER Summer Institute. The views expressed in this paper are not necessarily those of the U.S. Department of the Treasury.

1. See Pollak (1989) or Diewert (1987).

2. For the U.S. Consumer Price Index, housing purchases, but not purchases of other durables, are accounted for on a service-flow basis. Hence, while the data requirements and

health care expenditures can cause interesting, and even perverse, implications for cost-of-living measurement. Specifically, a life-saving expenditure can substantially increase the annuity value of expenditure needed to maintain a fixed level of per-period utility over a longer lifetime.[3] Traditional cost-of-living measurement, which takes a per-period rather than a lifetime perspective, does not account for this effect.

- Most health care expenditure is driven by adverse shocks to health. Again, standard cost-of-living analysis, which compares a stable utility function across time, does not account for this aspect of health expenditure. These shocks will have direct effects on the demand for health care expenditures. They will also have cross-effects on demand for other expenditures even after compensation for the wealth effects of the health shock.

- Many medical treatment decisions are binary, with little scope for varying either the quantity of treatment or its quality. Especially in the United States, only treatments at or close to the state of the art are offered.[4] Hence, health expenditures appear to be lumpy and exogenous, especially given the importance of third-party payment. Consequently, health care is not easily modeled in the marginalist framework that underlies the theory of cost-of-living indexes.

These points about health care—their potential life-and-death nature, their state-contingency, and their exogeneity—might drive one to the conclusion that economic analysis of the choice to undertake treatment is inappropriate. In this paper we argue, however, that economic decision making by patients is important for understanding the demand for certain medical procedures. Shocks to health need not require acute treatment. Many conditions are chronic and progressive. The patient may face a slow, variable, and unpredictable progression of disease. In such cases, the timing and nature of the treatment might be highly uncertain and variable across patients. Moreover, over time as treatment regimes change, the medical intervention may take place at a different point in the course of the

---

other conceptual problems for measuring health remain highly problematic, durability in itself is not a unique complication.

3. We are grateful to Zvi Griliches for emphasizing this point to us.

Indeed, for a person with fixed lifetime resources, this life-extending intervention could lead to an impoverishment of nonhealth expenditures as fixed resources are more thinly spread to maintain consumption over a longer lifespan. The annuity features of Social Security and Medicare, however, provide some insurance against these consequences of health expenditure.

4. The state of the art does diffuse slowly, so there may be variation by the setting where the health care is delivered, by region, and so on. Moreover, patients with different access to health care (owing to insurance coverage, locale, education, or income) may receive different treatment. Yet, for a particular patient, there is typically little economic trade-off in the choice of treatment.

disease. Even if the medical intervention once it is indicated is exogenously determined by the state of the art, with little or no scope for varying the quantity or quality of the intervention, the timing of the intervention may be highly endogenous.

Some medical procedures have declining costs over time, possibility in pecuniary terms, but especially when quality of outcomes and reduced morbidity are taken into account. This declining cost has important consequences for the demand for the procedure to the extent that it relaxes the medical criteria for receiving treatment. Heterogeneity in the course of the disease makes it important to distinguish between these two margins of adjustment. For some patients, relaxed criteria for receiving a medical intervention will affect the timing of treatment, with treatment being received earlier in the course of the disease as criteria become more relaxed; for others with less serious disease, or with disease that is slower to progress, they might never become candidates for a treatment under tighter criteria, but will receive it under relaxed criteria, perhaps quite early in the course of the disease.

The demand for the procedure will increase as the effective price falls and the equilibrium moves down the demand curve. The movement down the demand curve means that the marginal valuation of the procedure is lower. Hedonic regression or survey assessments of the quality of outcomes from medical procedures will reveal declining marginal benefit over time. It would be incorrect, however, to mechanically apply such results in a cost-of-living analysis. In particular, to the extent that patients receive the intervention earlier in the course of the disease, the main benefits of the procedure might come many periods after the procedure. While the benefits of having the new procedure might be quite small in the period the procedure is carried out, substantial benefit accrues in subsequent periods where the patient avoids suffering the progressively worsening symptoms and disability while waiting to become a candidate for the former procedure. A cost-of-living index that takes into account only the benefit in the period the procedure is carried out will have a potentially large upward bias.

This paper will present a case study of cataract surgery. Dramatic changes in the technology for cataract surgery make it an excellent illustration of the importance of accounting for the timing of procedure in the course of a disease. We will argue in the conclusion, however, that similar considerations apply to the treatment of various medical conditions.

The organization of the remainder of the paper is as follows. Section 10.2 outlines developments in the techniques of cataract surgery since midcentury. It then discusses how these improvements in technique have reduced the degree of visual impairment of patients receiving cataract surgery, thereby dramatically increasing the rate of surgery. Section 10.3 discusses how the benefits of surgery should be valued across time given the changing visual function at time of surgery. Section 10.4 discusses the resource and monetary costs of cataract surgery. It presents a cost index for cataract surgery and contrasts the results with the current Bureau of Labor Statistics (BLS) procedures for measuring health cost. Section 10.5 makes recommendations for measuring prices in the health care sector based on the findings about cataract surgery. Section 10.6 offers conclusions.

10.2   Treatment of Cataract

Section 10.2.1 gives the chronology of treatment for cataract since World War II. Section 10.2.2 describes how changes in the techniques for cataract surgery and for postoperative optical correction changed the criteria for cataract surgery over time. Section 10.2.3 describes how these improvements have led to relaxed criteria for extraction of cataracts and dramatically increased rates of cataract extraction.

10.2.1   Techniques of Cataract Surgery: A Chronology

The lens focuses light coming into the eye onto the retina. A cataract is a cloudy lens, which can impair vision. Cataracts are removed surgically. Up to the late 1970s, no other lens was inserted into the eye, so anyone whose cataracts had been removed required thick glasses or contact lenses to provide focus. In the late 1970s, however, surgeons in the United States started inserting an intraocular lens (IOL) as a replacement for the cloudy, natural lens. IOLs eliminate the need for thick glasses or contact lenses. They leave the patient with much better postoperative vision than they could have obtained with the cataract glasses and eliminate the need for inserting, removing, and caring for contact lenses.

There have been dramatic changes in the technique of cataract surgery—how the incision is made, how the cataract is extracted, and how the incision is closed. In the immediate post–World War II period, extracapsular extraction was the standard technique. This technique did not necessarily remove all the cataract. In the early 1950s, the technique switched to intracapsular extraction, in which the entire cataract and its enclosing envelope (capsule) were removed by suction or freezing. Because these techniques required a large incision, standard postoperative care included hospitalization often as long as a week. Through the 1960s, techniques of extraction and suturing gradually improved. These improvements were facilitated by the routine use of an operating microscope. Hospital stays were reduced to a typical stay of three days.

The modern era of extracapsular extraction opened in the early 1970s. This technique was pioneered with phacoemulsification, a technique where the cataract was broken into tiny pieces and removed from the eye by controlled suction. The smaller incisions allowed by phacoemulsification made outpatient treatment increasingly prevalent. Yet, the typical extractions remained intracapsular. Improvements in sutures and suture technique, giving more secure wound closure, allowed hospital stays with intra-capsular extraction to fall to a single night. At the end of the 1970s, there was an increasing trend toward the use of phacoemulsification with its smaller incision. The 1980s saw an increased use of phacoemulsification because of its small incision, complete removal of the cataract, and the re-duced postoperative complications allowed by leaving the posterior capsule intact. Leaving the posterior capsule intact reduced postoperative com-plications.[5]

By 1990, phacoemulsification was common for extraction of the cata-ract. Improvements in techniques in the 1990s included further reduction in the size of the incision. Smaller incisions can be closed with fewer su-tures, resulting in better and faster healing of the wound. IOLs were de-signed to fit through the small incision. Indeed, it is now possible to make incisions that heal without suturing. With reduced or no time needed for suturing, the operation can be completed quickly, sometimes in less than ten minutes. This improvement in surgical technique has allowed for inno-vations in the delivery of anesthesia. The standard technique has been to inject the anesthetic agents beside the eye and behind it. With a fast and highly controlled operation, anesthesia can now be in the form of topical drops on the eye and anesthetic agent in the irrigating solutions within the eye. New developments in IOLs are improving postoperative vision. Standard IOLs are focused at a fixed distance. Multifocal lenses, which are recently becoming common, allow focus at several distances.

See table 10.1 for a summary of the evolution of cataract treatment, and an estimate of the number of days in hospital each treatment required for a typical patient with no other complications.[6] The outpatient surgery includes both surgery done in a hospital and surgery done in outpatient clinics, which tends to cost less.

10.2.2   Interaction of Improvement in Surgical Techniques and the Threshold for Surgery

Throughout the period being studied, the criteria for surgery have been based on the extent to which the cataract impairs activities of daily life, such as work, reading, driving, and leisure activities. There are objective tests of visual acuity (e.g., Snellen visual acuity),[7] which are indicative of whether a patient is a candidate for surgery, but there are no hard and fast rules for assessing whether a patient is a candidate for surgery based on these measurements alone. The physician must assess other underlying medical conditions—both of the eye and generally. Moreover, patients

---

5. The YAG laser could treat a clouded posterior capsule without invasive surgery.
6. There has also been a drop in the number of postoperative office visits required for follow-up of the surgery and the length of time patients are routinely followed after surgery. Moreover, currently follow-up visits are included in the surgeon's fee, while previously they were billed separately.
7. The Snellen index is the familiar 20/20 scale.

Table 10.1   Typical Cataract Treatment: A Brief Chronology

Year	Procedure	Typical Length of Hospital Stay (Nights)	Comments
1947	Extracapsular extraction	7	Cataract removed by irrigation
1952	Intracapsular extraction	7	Cataract removed by freezing and/or suction
1969	Intracapsular extraction	3	Improved methods of extraction and suturing; routine use of operating microscope
1972	Controlled extracapsular extraction	1	Modern extracapsular extraction pioneered with phacoemulsification; typical extraction remains intracapsular
1979	Intracapsular and extracapsular	1 or outpatient	IOLs in increasing use
1985	Extracapsular extraction with IOL	Outpatient	Techniques to lessen complications; improved incisions and placement of IOL
1990	Extracapsular extraction with IOL	Outpatient	Phacoemulsification now common for extraction; IOLs developed for small incision
1995	Extracapsular extraction with IOL	Outpatient	New incisions
1998	Extracapsular extraction with IOL	Outpatient	Quicker operations allow reduced anesthesia; anesthesia infused; multifocal IOL becoming more common

with similar visual impairment and medical conditions might have differing demands for treatment depending on how much they rely on good vision for work and daily life.

Refractive Correction of Operated Eye

Whether a cataract is operated depends largely on the visual acuity in the other eye. If the other eye has good vision, it is possible for a patient to function well using the vision principally from that eye. Hence, in the era when cataracts were relatively costly and burdensome for the patient, it was not uncommon to leave a cataract unoperated when the other eye provided acceptable function. How an operated eye would interact with the unoperated eye had significant implications on the decision to operate. Prior to the widespread adoption of intraocular lenses, either spectacles or contact lenses supplied the refraction in place of the extracted, natural lens. Spectacles had the drawback of magnifying the image in the operated eye. Consequently, an operated eye corrected with spectacles could not be used in conjunction with another eye with good vision. This fact often led to a delay of surgery until the better eye deteriorated—often because of a second cataract that would be subsequently operated.

Table 10.2   **Postoperative Optical Correction**

Optical Correction	Ease of Use	Magnification
Spectacles	Fair to good	Yes
Contact lens	Fair to poor	Minimal
Intraocular lens	Excellent	No

Note: Magnification of corrected vision in operated eye impairs use of unoperated eye.

A contact lens could be used as an alternative to spectacles. Contact lenses did not magnify the visual image nearly as much, so the operated eye could be used in conjunction with the other eye. Contact lenses had other drawbacks. In particular, they were relatively difficult to insert, remove, and maintain. Especially for the relatively elderly population of cataract patients, contact lenses were an unattractive or sometimes infeasible alternative to spectacles. (See table 10.2 for a summary of characteristics of alternative refractive corrections.)

The advent of the IOL radically altered the postoperative refractive correction. A modern IOL, apart from its fixed focus, provides essentially the same vision as a natural lens. It solved the problem of magnification by spectacles without the cumbersomeness of contact lenses.[8] Hence, the advent of the IOL made it reasonable to operate a cataract of a substantially broadened population of patients, particularly those who had good vision in the unoperated eye. This technical change made a substantial contribution to the growth in the incidence of cataract surgery discussed in section 10.2.3.

Recovery and Complication

The advent of the IOL was not alone responsible for the reduced thresholds of visual impairment for cataract surgery. The changes in techniques discussed in section 10.2.1 substantially reduced the cost of cataract surgery from the point of view of the patient by providing for much faster recovery and substantially reduced risk of complications.

Ambulation. Currently, cataract surgery is performed almost exclusively on an outpatient basis. The surgery itself takes less than half an hour; the whole process takes only several hours. The patient is immediately

8. The IOL currently costs between $100 and $200. Spectacles and especially contact lenses probably cost more, when fitting and replacement are taken into account. The insertion of the IOL is included in the surgeon's fee for the cataract. (See Drummond 1988 for a discussion of the relative costs of IOL and pre-IOL treatment in the United Kingdom.)

Even with an IOL, the patient commonly needs to wear normal spectacles or contact lenses to correct the other eye and for focuses other than that provided by the IOL. The patient has the option of choosing an IOL that is in focus at reading or distance level. What focus is chosen depends on the vision in the other eye and the preferences of the patient. Multifocal IOLs are now becoming available. These reduce or eliminate the need for spectacles over a range of distances.

ambulatory. In contrast, early cataract extraction required a hospital stay of a week, with the patient in bed to assure healing of the wound. During the 1960s and 1970s, the length and arduousness of the hospital stay decreased as improved surgical techniques made for faster healing (see table 10.1).

Complications. Rates of complication have also declined substantially over the years. In earlier years, infection and problems with the incision were significant risks. Glaucoma was also a possible complication. The improvements in the operation reduced these complications progressively. The transition to intraocular lens implantation was not without its own complications. As with any new procedure, there is a learning curve. Moreover, the IOL implantation sometimes led to a clouding of the posterior capsule, which needed to be treated subsequently by laser.

10.2.3   Changing Rates of and Thresholds for Cataract Surgery

Rates of Cataract Extraction

Rates of cataract surgery have increased dramatically. A number of factors could account for the increase, such as improved access to care, higher rates of insurance coverage, improved general health among older patients, or increased incidence of the underlying disease. While we have not located studies that control for such factors, the consensus in the literature appears to be that the improvements in cataract surgery and reduced burden of surgery on the patient largely account for the increase in rates of surgery. For example, among residents of Olmsted County, Minnesota, where the population was presumably stable and insurance coverage for individuals over age sixty-five nearly universal, the rate of cataract extraction for individuals over sixty-five increased by a factor of nearly four from 1980 to 1994. As figure 10.1 shows, most of the increase occurred in the 1980s, although the rate was still increasing in the 1990s (Baratz et al. 1997). Other countries have also experienced substantial increases in rates of cataract extraction since approximately 1980. In earlier years, the rate of cataract surgery increased steadily, but at a much slower rate (Nadler and Schwartz 1980).

Preoperative Visual Acuity

The time series of the distribution of visual acuity for patients having cataract operations confirms that cataracts are being extracted in patients with progressively better vision.[9] Increased willingness to operate a cata-

---

9. Visual acuity is far from a sufficient statistic for whether a patient is a good candidate for cataract surgery. Bass et al. (1997) show that patients' desire to have surgery is more closely related to their survey responses about vision-related problems with daily life than to visual acuity. The differences in patients' function and preferences account for the heterogeneity in acuity before surgery.

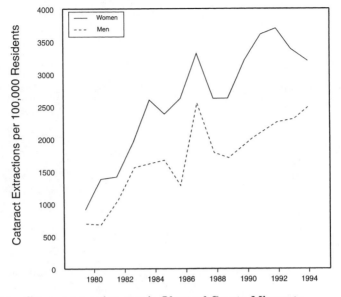

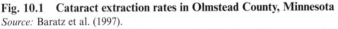

Fig. 10.1   Cataract extraction rates in Olmstead County, Minnesota
Source: Baratz et al. (1997).
Note: The rates are for individuals at least sixty-five years old.

ract when the other eye is providing good vision indicates falling patient burden and improved results of the procedure.

Table 10.3 shows the visual acuity in the better eye (almost always the unoperated eye) for patients undergoing cataract surgery. Some care should be taken in comparing the results across location and across time. While the authors of the studies are aiming for consistency across time in the patient mix (e.g., by excluding young patients or those with glaucoma, by sampling from the same practice over time), the controls in these retrospective studies are not perfect. More important, across location, there are substantial differences in design of the studies (the first eye of bilateral cataract in the first two Danish studies, monocular cataract in the second Danish study, a sample of all cataracts extracted in the U.S. study). Nonetheless, taking into account these fixed effects, a clear pattern emerges over time. In the years immediately after World War II, cataracts were seldom extracted when the better eye had good visual acuity (15 percent of cataract patients in Copenhagen in 1947–50 had acuity better than 20/60 in the better eye). Thirty percent of these patients were legally blind in the better eye (20/200 or worse). By 1969–70, while it was still uncommon to operate when the better eye had good acuity, acuity in the better eye was substantially less likely to suffer extreme impairment. In 1947–50, acuity is uniformly distributed within the middle range. By 1969–70, it is skewed toward the better acuities. From 1970 to 1980 (Aarhus), there was only

Table 10.3   Indications for Cataract Surgery: Visual Acuity in Better Eye

Location	Years	Percent of Patients by Visual Acuity			Operated Eye	Source
		>20/60	20/60– 20/100	≤20/200[a]		
Copenhagen	1947–50	15	55	30	Bilateral;	A
	1969–70	15	68	17	first eye	
Aarhus	1970	28	64	9	Bilateral;	B
	1980	33	59	8	first eye	
Aarhus	1980	27	62	11	Monocular	C
	1992	56	42	1		
Baltimore;	1974	48	30	16	First eye	D
hospital	1982	67	20	14		
practice	1988	68	21	10		
Baltimore;	1974	54	33	12	First eye	D
community	1982	46	37	17		
practice	1988	60	33	6		
Baltimore;	1974	59	14	27	Second eye	D
hospital	1982	80	9	11		
practice	1988	84	5	11		
Baltimore;	1974	83	10	7	Second eye	D
community	1982	92	3	5		
practice	1988	93	7	0		

Sources: A: Braendstrup (1977). Patients admitted for operation of first cataract of bilateral cataract at the Municipal Hospital of Copenhagen. Patients at least forty years old.

B: Bernth-Petersen (1981). Patients at Aarhus Kommunehospital. Monocular. Bilateral also reported (not tabulated). Patients with glaucoma excluded.

C: Nørregaard, Bernth-Petersen, and Andersen (1996). Patients at Aarhus University Hospital (from B) and from national sample of public health service hospitals. First eyes only. Patients with glaucoma and dementia excluded.

D: Moorman et al. (1990). Randomly selected cataract operations from hospital- and community-based physicians. Mix of first and second eyes.

Note: For the Danish studies, visual acuities are converted from metric units.

[a] For source B, the 20/100 acuity is excluded from the second column and included in the third.

a slight improvement. This study does, however, document an increased tendency to operate the second eye during this period.

A dramatic change occurred during the transition from modern extra-capsular extraction to intracapsular extraction with IOL implant. This transition is documented in the 1980/1992 data from Aarhus and the 1974/1982/1988 data for Baltimore. At the beginning of these periods, modern extracapsular extraction was almost universal. By the end, intracapsular extraction with IOL was almost universal. In Aarhus, the transition to IOLs led to an increase from one-quarter to one-half the fraction of cata-ract patients with acuity of better than 20/60 in the better eye. The increase in Baltimore was smaller owing to the more aggressive treatment there at the beginning of the period. Nonetheless, for both the hospital-based

Table 10.4   **Indications for Cataract Surgery: Visual Acuity in Operated Eye**

		Percent of Patients by Visual Acuity				
Location	Year	>20/60	20/60–20/100	≤20/200	Operated Eye	Source
Aarhus	1980	0	31	69	Monocular	C
	1992	13	59	28		
Baltimore;	1974	12	21	67	First or	D
hospital	1982	19	30	51	second	
practice	1988	24	36	40		
Baltimore;	1974	11	34	55	First or	D
community	1982	5	30	65	second	
practice	1988	8	70	22		

Note: See notes to table 10.3.

and community-based practices in Baltimore, there is a substantial shift toward better acuity in the better eye for first cataract surgery. There is also a pronounced increase in the acuity of the better eye for second cataract surgery, especially in the hospital-based practice, after the transition to IOLs.[10]

Table 10.4 shows how the transition to IOL also led to better acuity in the operated eye at the time of cataract extraction. Cataracts are now typically extracted well before patients meet the threshold of legal blindness and occasionally in eyes with quite good acuity. Also, the IOL period brought a lengthening of the interval between first and second cataract extractions, which indicates that the first cataract is being operated earlier in the course of the disease (Moorman et al. 1990, 765).

Age

Cataract is primarily a disease of older individuals. Moreover, some but not all of cataracts are slowly progressive. Hence, reduced thresholds for treatment might lead to the average age of those getting cataract to fall over time. Other factors work in the opposite direction. Lengthening lifespans and improved health of the elderly increases the number of candidates for the operation. Moreover, the reduced burden of the operation on the patient makes it possible for a larger group of patients to receive it. Looking across studies, the average age of patients appears to be increasing.[11]

10. In 1974, the fellow eye of the second operated eye would not have an IOL. In 1982, about half had IOLs. By 1988, almost all did.

11. In Nørregaard, Bernth-Petersen, and Andersen (1996), it increased from 72.7 to 73.2 years from 1980 to 1992. It also increased in Moorman et al. (1990). Miglior et al. (1992) report that average age of cataract patients at a clinic in Milan, Italy, increased from 67.5

10.3   Valuing Cataract Extraction over Time

How does one value having a cataract extracted? The good is not the operation per se, but an improvement in vision. There is a literature on methods for valuing the improvement in vision from having a cataract extracted.[12] This literature takes a lifetime perspective in evaluating the benefits of the procedure. Hence, it accounts for the durability of the operation, which is critical for appropriately accounting for the procedure in a cost-of-living index. The literature, like almost all the medical literature, does not compare the value of procedures over time. The medical literature is typically forward-looking. It asks, should a new procedure replace a current procedure, or is a procedure worth doing at all? It is typically not concerned with how today's standard of care compares with the standard of care from years ago. Yet, this comparison is what is required for construction of price and cost-of-living indexes. It is possible to string together a series of valuations of the standard of care at different points in time to construct a time-series of valuations.[13] The message of the last section is, however, that changes in the standard of care change the mix of patients receiving the care. A contribution of this paper is to provide a framework for taking into account how the mix of patients varies endogenously with the changes in the cost of the procedure.

10.3.1   Equilibrium Decision to Be Operated for Different Patients under Different Treatment Regimes

Figure 10.2 gives a stylized presentation of how changing criteria for surgery affect the timing of and benefit from getting a treatment. For each of the panels, the medical condition is shown on the vertical axis. In the case of cataract, this is visual function. As discussed above, visual function is related to, but not identical to, visual acuity. The vertical axis should be thought of as a scale that physician and patient use to determine whether or not to extract a cataract. Perfect vision is at the top of the scale; blindness is at the bottom. The horizontal axis is age. Tracking the disease as the patient ages has two purposes. First, it makes concrete the durable benefit of the procedure. (Drummond 1988 has a similar diagram.) Second, it shows how the timing of the operation changes for different progressions of the disease when the criteria for surgery change.

The solid line in figure 10.2 shows the progression of the disease in terms of visual function. The two left-hand panels show the progression for a

---

years in 1956 to 71.5 years in 1987. Again, changes in mix of patients and the fact that in the case of the Baltimore study they are drawn from the potentially aging practices of particular physicians make interpretation difficult.

12. See Drummond (1990) and especially Ferguson, Buxton, and Drummond (1990) for an overview of different methods.

13. For procedures far back in time, the valuations would need to be done retrospectively.

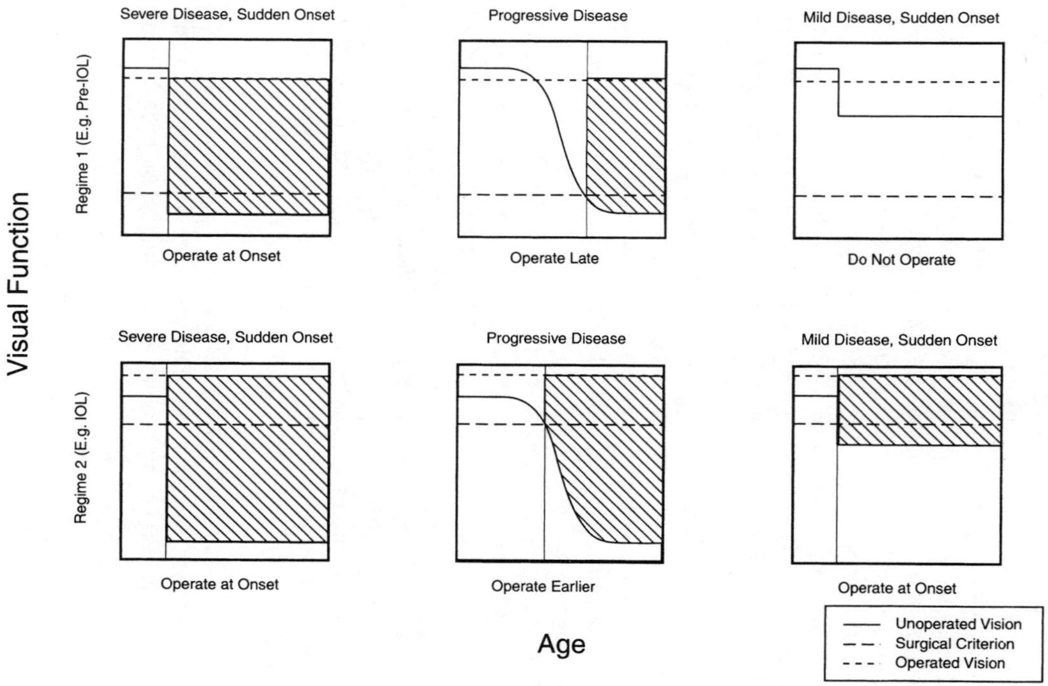

Fig. 10.2 **Timing of surgery under changing treatment regimes for patients with different courses of disease (benefits shaded)**

sudden onset of a severely debilitating cataract. The two middle panels show a pattern of gradual worsening. Vision deteriorates slowly, perhaps over a period of several years. The two right-hand panels show the sudden onset of a mild disease.[14] The large-dashed horizontal line shows the criterion for surgery. When visual function intersects this line, the operation is carried out. In the top panels, the criterion is at a low level of visual function, for example, corresponding to the relatively low levels of visual acuity for the typical cataract surgery patient in the pre-IOL era. In the bottom row of panels, the threshold for surgery is at a substantially better level of visual function, corresponding to current practice.[15]

The short-dashed line at the top of the figures is the postoperative visual function. In the bottom row, it is somewhat higher than in the top row, reflecting the better postoperative results in the regime with relaxed surgical thresholds (i.e., IOLs give better results than spectacles or contact lenses). How it stands in relationship to the pre-onset function is an empirical matter. Figure 10.2 is drawn under the assumption that in the strict regime, the function does not recover to the pre-onset level. In the relaxed regime, visual function is actually better after the procedure than before the onset. This parameterization reflects the possibility that IOLs provide better refractive correction than did the patients' spectacles immediately before the onset of cataracts.

The shaded area is the benefit of having the operation, that is, the difference between the postoperative function and the function without the operation. Care should be taken in interpreting these figures. The criterion is not independent of the postoperative outcome. It is an equilibrium outcome based on a calculation that weighs the benefits of the operation cumulated over time—reflected in the shaded area—against the costs. These costs include the monetary cost discussed in the next section and the patient burden in terms of recovery and complications discussed above. For many procedures, the relaxation of the threshold will be mainly determined by the improved outcome. In others, the postprocedure outcome is identical; the only change in criterion arises from reduced cost and patient burden.[16] In cataract, the improved outcome plays an important role, but the reduced cost is also an important factor. Nonetheless, even though the

14. Many other courses of the disease are possible. There are different rates of progression, different timings of onset, and different levels of severity. The patterns shown in figure 10.2 are, however, sufficiently general to capture the main interactions of criteria for treatment and the course of the disease.

15. Visual function depends on both eyes. Thus, the thresholds shown in figure 10.2 do reflect how changes in technique changed the role of vision in the unoperated eye in determining whether to do cataract surgery. A more complete analysis would, however, treat first and second cataract surgeries separately.

16. Chernew, Fendrick, and Hirth (1997) suggest that the increase in removal of gall bladder with the advent of much less invasive surgical techniques falls into this category.

intersection of the solid line and the dashed line represent an equilibrium outcome, not a decision rule, the shaded area in figure 10.2 does represent the equilibrium benefit of having the procedure.

With sudden onset of severe disease, the patient gets the operation under either the strict or relaxed surgical procedure. The patient benefits from the improved outcome in the regime depicted in the bottom row of figure 10.2. With mild disease (right-hand panels of fig. 10.2), there is a dramatic difference in the treatment of disease. Under the criterion appropriate for the treatment regime depicted in the top row, the patient does not get the operation even though postoperative visual function would be improved. These benefits do not outweigh the cost, which may be monetary or in the form of burden on the patient of the operation (pain, recovery period, risk of complications). Under the regime depicted in the bottom row of figure 10.2, this same patient with mild disease would get the operation, getting substantial gain in visual function.

The middle panels of figure 10.2 depict a patient with progressive disease. With the strict criterion, the operation is delayed. During this period, the patient suffers progressively worsening disease, but not serious enough disability to get the operation. Under the relaxed criteria, the patient gets the operation earlier, avoiding the potentially long period of worsening function while he or she would have been waiting to become a candidate under the former regime. Expectations about the course of the disease will be important in determining when the operation occurs. Early on, the patient with the progressive disease might not be distinguishable from the patient with mild disease. Because the course of cataract is difficult to predict, under the regime depicted in the top row, the operation would have been delayed. Under the second regime, both the mild and progressive cases would be operated relatively early. The benefit of the procedure to the patient who would have been progressive is much greater, though this patient will not be easy to distinguish ex post; yet it would be a serious mistake to value the procedure the same for such a patient.

10.3.2 Valuing the Benefits of the Operation

To construct a price or cost-of-living index, the benefits depicted in figure 10.2 need to be translated into units of value. In doing so, there are both conceptual difficulties and difficulties with lack of information. Two issues need to be addressed: What is the metric for translating benefit into value? What is the population distribution of the course of disease?

Metric for Valuing Benefits

There is substantial literature on assessing the visual outcomes of cataract surgery. It is difficult to compare the studies across time because they typically report differing and somewhat vague subjective responses to questions about visual function (ability to read newspapers, ability to drive, etc.). With some effort, an expert probably could, however, translate these survey responses into a standardized index of visual function. More recent studies use standardized survey instruments which yield standard indexes of visual function, which will facilitate comparison across time and locale (Steinberg et al. 1994).

One leading approach to assessing benefits of a medical procedure is the increment to quality-adjusted life years (QALYs). Drummond (1988) uses Torrance, Boyle, and Horwood's (1982) utility-based model of health states to assign a QALY to blindness and then discussed how that would be capitalized to take into account the multiyear benefit of cataract surgery. He also discusses a QALY calculation concerning the relative value of contact lenses versus IOLs for refractive correction after cataract surgery. The aim of this literature is to compare the cost-effectiveness of different treatments at a point in time (e.g., cataract extract versus hip replacement) rather than comparing the standard of care for a single disease over time. However, it could be adapted to that purpose.[17]

To use QALYs as units in a cost-of-living index, they need to be translated into units of value. An approach to doing so would be to measure willingness to pay. Studies assessing the willingness to pay for a QALY could be used to convert the disease-specific assessment of QALYs into monetary values. Alternatively, the use of the QALY could be dispensed with if direct measures of willingness to pay were available. Such measures of willingness to pay could be obtained either by survey techniques or by observing patient choices when paying for the surgery is required or is an option to get faster or better care.[18] Anderson et al. (1997) report the result of a survey of patients waiting for cataract surgery at public clinics in Barcelona, Denmark, and Manitoba. They find that between one-sixth and one-fourth of patients who expected to wait over seven months for the operation were willing to pay an amount averaging $1,000 (roughly the actual cost of getting the operation privately) to get it immediately. Smaller, but nonzero, factions were willing to pay to eliminate shorter waiting times.[19] Willingness to pay increased with severity of the visual deficit and decreased with the amount to be paid.

Anderson et al. also present some confounding evidence on actual willingness to pay. In all three locales, private clinics are available as an alternative to the public clinics. Only 2 percent of the survey respondents switched to private clinics after being put on the waiting list at the public clinic. However, a substantial fraction of cataracts are done at these clinics (40 percent in Barcelona, 15 percent in Denmark, and not known in Mani-

17. For further discussion, see Shapiro, Shapiro, and Wilcox (1999).
18. Such behavioral estimates would need to be done with great care owing to selection on income and seriousness of disease.
19. For Barcelona, willingness to pay decreased with waiting time.

toba).[20] Hence, a sizable fraction of the population is willing to bear a substantial cost to gain a relatively short period of incremental benefit. This valuation could be used to value a per-period slice of the benefits depicted in figure 10.2. The Anderson et al. survey also has the advantage of containing information about visual function, so the differing incremental benefits could be quantified.

Assessing the Heterogeneity of the Course of Disease

Figure 10.2 presents paths of visual function for different types of patients. While the paths are typical of the various possibilities of the course of development of a cataract, they are highly stylized. There is little empirical basis for quantifying these paths precisely, or establishing the distribution of courses of disease in the population. There are several problems with the base of knowledge. First, the medical literature tends to report visual function immediately before the operation. To distinguish among cases of sudden and progressive onset, it would be necessary to know visual function for several periods—possibly spanning years—before the operation. We know of no such study, although it could be done retrospectively by studying patient charts. Second, as noted above, the data on visual function are truncated at the point of the operation. Moreover, the point of truncation has varied endogenously over time. Therefore, even were the problem of valuing benefits solved, there is not enough information now in hand to calculate the population distribution of the benefits at different points in time.

10.4   A Prototypical Cost Index for Cataract Surgery

The previous sections discuss how the techniques of cataract surgery have changed and how the reduced cost (mainly in terms of patient burden) and improved outcomes have increased the demand for the procedure. In this section, we focus on the monetary cost of cataract extraction. We do so by comparing the procedure the BLS would use in the Consumer Price Index (CPI) to price a cataract with an alternative procedure that more accurately reflects the actual cost.[21] Our cost index—like the CPI—is based on the cost of inputs. In section 10.5, we discuss an alternative methodology based on unit values for delivering care. Moreover, the calculations in this section do not reflect any adjustment for the quality of the outcome or the value of having the procedure earlier. We return to that issue in section 10.5.

---

20. A serious limitation of the study is that it excludes patients who were treated initially at private clinics, that is, who never entered the public system. Private patients were paying to avoid getting on waiting lists and for potentially better care.

21. This section gives a more detailed discussion and update of the procedure introduced in Shapiro and Wilcox (1996).

The CPI does not price treatment for cataracts per se, but instead prices hospital services and physician services, among other items. The BLS constructs an index of medical prices by first determining the relative importance weights in the base period (currently 1982–84) of the various inputs it is going to track, and then applying these weights to price indexes for the individual inputs. The BLS will reweight the basket of medical inputs in 1998 according to expenditure shares in 1993–95, and will then compute changes in the index from 1998 forward as weighted averages of the changes in the prices of the inputs.

This approach has a startling implication: Technological change that increases the efficiency of inputs in producing a good or service affects only the rate of change of the index of medical prices, but not in the first instance the level of the index. Indeed, the rate of change is only affected to the extent that the component price indexes grow at different rates. In the case of a procedure like cataracts, which has undergone revolutionary technological change, the change in the composition of the market basket (reflecting the sharp decline in the average length of hospital stay) will only be relevant for the subsequent growth of the index; the decline in the quantity of hospital services consumed will never be reflected in the level of the index.

To illustrate this problem, we have constructed a hypothetical CPI for cataracts. Our hypothetical CPI for cataract treatment is based on the information in table 10.1 and on the CPI components for physician and hospital services. We construct the hypothetical index by first estimating relative importance weights in hypothetical benchmark years for the physician services and hospital services required to treat a standard cataract patient. We then use these relative importance weights to aggregate the CPI components for physician and hospital prices. Specifically, we assume the quantities of services supplied are as in table 10.5. The units of table 10.5 are normalized to equal one night in the hospital. Somewhat arbitrarily, but not totally unrealistically, we have set the surgeon fee equal to the cost of 1 night in the hospital in the middle of the time period. There is no attempt to account for the cost of the refractive correction (spectacle or contacts in the early periods, IOLs in the later periods).[22] The first column repeats the information on hospital nights from table 10.1. In 1979, we assume that half the patients are treated in hospital and that half are treated on an outpatient basis. We calibrate the cost of the operating room in a hospital to equal the charge for 4 inpatient nights. For outpatient surgery, we calibrate it to equal 1.5 nights. In 1998, we reduce this to 1.3 owing to reduced costs of anesthesia. The fourth column of table 10.5 is thus the amount of hospital or outpatient clinic resources consumed by a

---

22. The table also subsumes the cost of the anesthesiologist into the hospital charge. It is often billed separately.

Table 10.5   **Inputs for Cataract Surgery**

Year	Hospital Nights	Hospital Operating Room	Outpatient Operation Room	Total Hospital/ Outpatient	Surgeon
1969	3	4	0	7	1
1972	1	4	0	5	1
1979[a]	.5 × 1	.5 × 4	.5 × 1.5	3.25	1
1985	0	0	1.5	1.5	0.8
1994	0	0	1.5	1.5	0.7
1998	0	0	1.3	1.3	0.5

Note: Units: 1 = one night in hospital.
[a]In 1979, one-half inpatient and one-half outpatient.

Table 10.6   **Expenditure Weights for Cataract Surgery**

Year	Hospital/Outpatient	Surgeon
1969	0.808	0.192
1972	0.776	0.224
1979	0.736	0.264
1985	0.656	0.344
1994	0.725	0.275

cataract operation. It falls dramatically owing to the decline in inpatient nights and the lower cost of outpatient surgery. The surgeon time remained relatively constant through the earlier period. With the improvements in technique in the IOL period, it has fallen. Currently, cataracts can be extracted with substantially less time than at the end of the modern extracapsular regime in the mid-1970s owing mainly to changes in techniques for incisions and suturing.[23]

Table 10.6 shows the expenditure weights calculated by scaling the quantities in table 10.5 by the level of the CPI components for hospital (CPI series SE56) and physician (CPI series SE5701) services and calculating expenditure shares.[24] The CPI component for hospital services grew somewhat faster than that for physician services (see table 10.7), so the decrease in the quantity of hospital services is somewhat offset by the increase in price in calculating its share. At the beginning of the period, about one-fifth of the expenditure was on the surgeon. The share increased to about one-third in 1985, when it began to decline.

To calculate the hypothetical CPI, we weight the increases in the component indexes by the shares in hypothetical benchmark years of 1969 and

23. Also, with faster healing, follow-up office visits have been reduced substantially.
24. In this version of the paper, the calculations in tables 10.6 and 10.7 end with data in 1994.

Table 10.7   **Rates of Price Change (percent per year)**

| | Cataract Surgery | | CPI | | |
| | Prototypical | Hypothetical | Hospital | Physician | |
Year	Index	CPI	Room	Services	Total
		Nominal			
1969–72	0.2	9.6	10.5	5.5	4.5
1972–79	5.5	10.8	11.4	8.0	8.2
1979–85	−0.1	10.9	11.5	8.4	6.8
1985–94	7.1	7.9	8.3	6.0	3.6
1969–94	4.1	9.6	10.2	7.1	5.7
		Relative to Total CPI			
1969–72	−4.3	5.2	6.1	1.1	
1972–79	−2.7	2.6	3.2	−0.2	
1979–85	−6.9	4.1	4.7	1.6	
1985–94	3.5	4.3	4.7	2.4	
1969–94	−1.7	3.9	4.4	1.3	

1979. As noted above, this procedure—which mimics that of the official CPI—never accounts for the fall in the level of hospital services. The level of the hypothetical CPI is shown as the white bars in figure 10.3; its growth rate is shown in the second column of table 10.7. In contrast, we construct a prototypical unit value index by taking ratios of total expenditure, that is,

$$\frac{\sum_i q_{it} p_{it}}{\sum_i q_{ib} p_{ib}},$$

where q_{it} is the quantity of component i at time t (table 10.5), p_{it} is the corresponding CPI component, and b is the base year. In contrast to the CPI, this index does take into account the change in the level of the services. It does inherit any problems with the CPI component price indexes. For example, the CPI for physician services might not fully account for the discounts of actual from posted fees, which have increased substantially for cataract. On the other hand, surgeons' fees for cataract extraction have not declined in correspondence to the decline in inputs given in the last column of table 10.5. Hence, the CPI for physician services times the input quantity may be biased up or down as an estimate of the per operation expenditure for surgeons' services.

The level of prototypical cost index is shown as the black bars in figure 10.3; the growth rate is shown in the first column of table 10.7. The prototypical index taking into account the decline in the level of inputs grows dramatically more slowly than the hypothetical CPI. For the 1969–94 period as a whole, the hypothetical CPI grew 9.2 percent per year, or 3.5 percent per year relative to the total CPI. The prototypical index grew 4.1

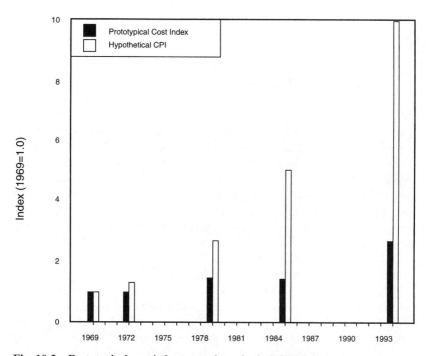

Fig. 10.3   Prototypical cost index versus hypothetical CPI for cataract surgery
Source: Authors' calculations. See text for details.

percent per year. It actually fell relative to the total CPI over the whole period, and for all but one of the subperiods.

Hence, *even without taking quality improvement into account,* the prototypical index shows that the cost of cataracts fell relative to the published general price level.[25] Admittedly, we selected cataract as an example because we knew it had dramatic changes that the CPI would miss. Nonetheless, it has features that are widely shared with other medical procedures, and indeed other goods.

10.5   Lessons for Constructing Cost-of-Living Indexes

This section outlines specific recommendations for constructing price indexes for health care based on what we have learned about the cost and value of cataract surgery in the preceding sections. It will fall short of

25. The comparison with the published general price level is somewhat misleading because the total CPI is subject to an upward bias, estimated to be about 1 percentage point per year. See Shapiro and Wilcox (1996). Part of this bias arises because the CPI misses the decline in many levels of prices, not just in medical care. For example, when a discount store enters a market, none of the decline in the level of its prices is recorded in the CPI unless they are matched by outlets already sampled by the CPI.

offering a quality-adjusted price index owing to the data limitations discussed in section 10.3.

10.5.1   Measure Cost with Unit Values for Treating a Medical Condition

Recommendation on Unit Values

We recommend that unit values for treating a medical condition be used to measure the cost of health care. This recommendation has two components. First, the good should be defined as relief of a specific medical condition, not the receipt of a specific set of inputs. In the case of cataract, the good is the restoration of visual function following the clouding of the lens of the eye. Second, instead of pricing a basket of inputs, the statistical agencies should measure the cost of getting whatever current inputs are used to treat the diagnosis.

In the case of cataract surgery, the bundle of goods has changed substantially—notably the shift from multiday hospitalization to outpatient surgery. By pricing the care for the cataract rather than a fixed bundle of inputs, more subtle changes in treatment could also be measured. For example, before IOLs, the cost of prescribing, fitting, and purchasing spectacles or contact lenses would be included. With IOLs, those charges would disappear, but charges for prescribing the IOL in advance of surgery and for the IOL itself would appear. Additionally, changes in the cost of how anesthesia is administered as operative techniques have improved could be taken into account. Finally, a unit value approach would capture fee reductions and discounts specific to the particular procedure. For example, Medicare has substantially reduced reimbursement for cataract relative to other procedures, so the BLS component index will overstate the increase in physician cost as it applies to cataract.

Cataract is perhaps a more circumscribed or easier-to-define diagnosis than average. Nonetheless, this approach should be feasible for other diseases. For example, for kidney stones, what should be priced is the removal of the stones, whether by surgery or lithotripsy. More open-ended treatments, such as for management of chronic hypertension, might be harder to define. Nonetheless, experts could specify treatment regimes for such diseases that could be changed as medical practice warrants.

At least for the period for which Medicare data are available, it might be possible to construct a unit value series for cataract along the lines Cutler et al. (chap. 8 in this volume) have done for heart attacks. We have not attempted to do so, however, for this paper.[26]

---

26. Using Medicare records to study cataract is complicated, however, by the change from hospital (covered by part A) to outpatient (covered by part B).

BLS Procedures

As discussed above, the BLS pricing of medical care has been based on the pricing of inputs. Recently, the BLS has made substantial progress away from pricing inputs toward the pricing of medical treatments.[27] In much of the PPI for hospital services and to a more limited extent in the CPI, the BLS prices hospital bills. Its procedure is to sample a non-Medicare bill for a predetermined procedure. It then returns to the hospital on a monthly basis and reprices the items that appear on the bill. By pricing a bill over time, the BLS has made a major step toward pricing the treatment of the disease per se rather than a fixed bundle of inputs. It does have an important limitation in that it does not automatically capture changes in the treatment for a diagnosis. For example, a bill for a cataract extraction might have an entry for the suture. Increasingly, cataract operations are sutureless. The BLS procedure would continue to price the suture even if the item were dropped from the bill, absent an adjustment.[28] Such changes in treatment of a fixed bundle are very common. They can either increase or decrease cost.

The BLS does recognize the issue of changing treatment. There are procedures for making adjustments in the bills to be priced to take them into account. Yet, as of this writing, such adjustments have not been made. Moreover, making such adjustments requires substantial medical knowledge. For substantial changes in treatment, it would probably be necessary to have the linkage of bills to be priced monitored by medical experts (see Shapiro, Shapiro, and Wilcox 1999 for such a suggestion).

An alternative procedure could address the problem of changing techniques of treatment. Instead of sampling a fixed bill and attempting to reprice it, the BLS could price hospital admissions or physician care for a fixed diagnosis. That is, it should price a bill for a routine cataract extraction, a heart attack without other medical problems, the setting of a broken bone, the removal of kidney stones or gall bladder, and so on. If the treatment modalities change over time, at increased or decreased cost, those changes should be reflected in the unit value. Presumably, such a procedure would require some oversight by medical experts, for example, to alert the BLS to the shift from spectacles to IOLs. This oversight need not be month-to-month, but it would have to be much more frequent than the ten-year periods that typically elapse between benchmark revisions.

---

27. For a description of health care in the PPI, see Fixler and Ginsburg (chap. 6 in this volume); for the CPI, see Ford and Ginsburg (chap. 5 in this volume).

28. Saving the cost of the suture is not the main reason for moving to sutureless surgery. Sutureless surgery can result in superior postoperative results and increased rates of recovery.

10.5.2   Durability and Quality Adjustment

Medical procedures such as cataract extraction provide a service flow often extending far beyond the period the treatment is received. The failure to appropriately account for durability arises for many goods, not just health care. Indeed, only for housing is there a systematic attempt in the CPI and the National Accounts to account for the service flow rather than the purchase of the durable good.

Health care could be handled analogously to housing by imputing a service flow to the stock of health procedures. In the case of cataract extraction, this procedure would keep track of all those alive who had the operation. It would impute a flow value of having had the operation to this stock. While conceptually feasible, this approach would require substantial data and the ability to impute value. Unlike housing, where there is a rental market that can be used to impute value,[29] the value of medical procedures would have to be imputed indirectly.

Even if the rental-equivalence approach were not taken, the durability of a medical procedure needs to be taken into account when considering its purchase price. As discussed in section 10.3, the capitalized benefit of medical procedures includes the avoidance of worsening symptoms as the disease progresses in the future. To appropriately quality-adjust the purchase of a medical procedure, this future value must be taken into account. Hence, measuring the quality-adjusted purchase price does not avoid the problems of imputing the value of the stock of health care procedures that appears in the rental-equivalence approach. It merely changes what stock gets valued. For the rental-equivalence approach, the stock of procedures across individuals at a point in time must be valued. For the purchase-price approach, the discounted value of the procedure for the cross-section of individuals currently receiving the procedure must be valued.

10.5.3   Heterogeneity of Valuations

The reduced cost and increased benefit of cataract surgery have substantially increased the demand for the procedure. As section 10.3 makes clear, the valuations of different patients getting the surgery are quite different. When the underlying disease progresses at different rates, patients who look identical at the time of surgery might have very different lifetime valuations. Hence, even a careful study of the improvement in visual status arising directly from the operation will not capture all of the differences in valuation. As the cost falls and the aggregate demand for the procedure increases, at the time of surgery, a patient with progressive disease will move from being pooled with those with severe disease to being pooled with those who have mild disease. Absent a dynamic model

29. The service flow of cars could similarly be imputed using lease payments.

of the underlying disease, the benefits of the procedure might be substantially understated.

10.6   Conclusions

In this paper, we presented evidence about the costs and value of cataract surgery. We find that the monetary cost of cataract—in contrast to standard price indexes for health care—has not been increasing faster than the general price level. Moreover, we discuss how improvements in the technique for cataract extraction and the transition from spectacles or contact lenses to intraocular lenses have improved the quality of the outcomes. As techniques have changed, patients have much faster ambulation, face lower rates of complications, and have better postoperative visual outcomes. These reductions in the total cost of the procedure from the point of view of the patient have led to substantial increases in the rate of cataract extraction. Patients with less severe disease are having the operation, and patients are getting the operation earlier in the course of the disease. While there is not a sufficient knowledge base to quantify the gains in lifetime utility arising from the greater frequency of cataract operations, it is clear that a quality adjustment would—on top of the essentially flat relative price of cataract extraction in monetary terms—lead to a substantial decline in the real price of cataract extraction.

The analysis of cataract extraction leads us to make some specific recommendations that have broader applicability to measuring the price of health care. First, the cost of procedures should be measured in terms of unit values for treating particular diagnoses. Second, the durability of the benefits accruing from medical procedures needs to be taken into account in measuring their value. Third, changes in the cost of medical procedures changes the mix of patients getting the treatment, in terms of both the severity of the disease and the timing of the procedure within the course of the disease. Consequently, patients with progressive disease will be treated when their symptoms are severe when costs are high and when their symptoms are less severe when costs are lower. How the population of patients receiving treatment changes endogenously in response to changes in cost needs to be taken into account appropriately.

The lessons from cataract should have wide applicability. In particular, for many diseases, treatment has moved earlier in the course of the disease as the treatment regime has improved. Potentially important examples include increasing rates of heart bypass operations, especially for pain and function; more frequent joint replacements; and cochlear implants for less severe nerve deafness. While the monetary cost of these procedures might not have the favorable dynamics of those for cataracts, they share with cataracts that much of their benefits occur as patients, by getting the procedures earlier, avoid a substantial period of worsening symptoms and declining quality of life. Therefore, the lessons of cataract surgery should have wide application to measuring health care prices.

References

Anderson, Gerald, Charlyn Black, Elaine Dunn, Jordi Alonso, Jens Christian Nørregaard, Tavs Folmer-Anderson, and Peter Bernth-Petersen. 1997. Willingness to pay to shorten waiting time for cataract surgery. *Health Affairs* 16: 181–90.
Baratz, Keith H., Darryl T. Gray, David O. Hodge, Linda C. Butterfield, and Duane M. Ilstrup. 1997. Cataract extraction rates in Olmsted County, 1980 through 1994. *Archives of Ophthalmology* 115:1441–46.
Bass, Eric B., Stacey Wills, Ingrid U. Scott, Jonathan C. Javitt, James M. Tielsch, Olivier D. Schein, and Earl P. Steinberg. 1997. Preference values for visual states in patients planning to undergo cataract surgery. *Medical Decision Making* 17: 324–30.
Bernth-Petersen, Peter. 1981. A change in indications for cataract surgery? A 10 year comparative epidemiologic study. *Acta Ophthalmologica* 59:206–10.
Braendstrup, P. 1977. Senile cataract: Account of cataract extractions performed in an urbanized population during the third quarter of the present century. *Acta Ophthalmologica* 55:337–47.
Chernew, Michael, A. Mark Fendrick, and Richard A. Hirth. 1997. Managed care and medical technology. *Health Affairs* 16:196–206.
Diewert, W. Erwin 1987. Index numbers. *The new palgrave.* London: Macmillan.
Drummond, Michael F. 1988. Economic aspects of cataract. *Ophthalmology* 95: 1147–53.
———, ed. 1990. *Measuring the quality of life of people with visual impairment.* NIH Publication no. 90–3078. Bethesda, Md.: National Institutes of Health.
Ferguson, B. A., M. J. Buxton, and M. F. Drummond. 1990. Measuring and valuing health states relating to visual impairment: A review of the literature, concepts, and methods. In *Measuring the quality of life of people with visual impairment,* ed. M. F. Drummond, app. A. Bethesda, Md.: National Institutes of Health.
Miglior, Stefano, Alfredo Nicolosi, Paolo E. Mariaghi, Luca Migliavacca, Cristina Balestreri, Pasquale Troiona, Mario Miglior, and Nicola Orzalesi. 1992. Trends in cataract surgery in Milan (Italy) from 1956 to 1987. *Acta Ophthalmologica* 70:395–401.
Moorman, Consuela, Alfred Sommer, Walter Stark, Cheryl Enger, John Payne, and A. Edward Maumenee. 1990. Changing indications for cataract surgery: 1974 to 1988. *Ophthalmic Surgery* 21:761–66.
Nadler, Daniel J., and Bernard Schwartz. 1980. Cataract surgery in the United States, 1968–1976: A descriptive epidemiologic study. *Ophthalmology* 87:10–17.
Nørregaard, Jens Christian, Peter Bernth-Petersen, and Tavs Folmer Andersen. 1996. Changing threshold for cataract surgery in Denmark between 1980 to 1992. *Acta Ophthalmologica Scandinavica* 74:604–8.
Pollak, Robert A. 1989. *The theory of the cost-of-living index.* New York: Oxford University Press.
Shapiro, Irving, Matthew D. Shapiro, and David W. Wilcox. 1999. Quality im-

provements in health care: A framework for price and output measurement. *American Economic Review Papers and Proceedings* 89 (2): 333–37.

Shapiro, Matthew D., and David W. Wilcox. 1996. Mismeasurement in the Consumer Price Index: An evaluation. In *NBER Macroeconomics Annual,* ed. Ben S. Bernanke and Julio Rotemberg. Cambridge, Mass.: MIT Press. 93–142.

Steinberg, Earl P., James M. Tielsch, Olivier D. Schein, Jonathan C. Javitt, Phoebe Sharkey, Sandra D. Cassard, Marcia W. Legro, Marie Diener-West, Eric C. Bass, Anne M. Damiano, Donald M. Steinwachs, and Alfred Sommer. 1994. The VF-14: An index of functional impairment in patients with cataract. *Archives of Ophthalmology* 112:630–38.

Torrance, George W., Michael W. Boyle, and Sargent H. Horwood. 1982. Application of multi-attribute utility theory to measure social preferences for health states. *Operations Research* 30:1043–69.

11

Hedonic Analysis of Arthritis Drugs

Iain M. Cockburn and Aslam H. Anis

11.1 Introduction

This study examines the market for a group of drugs used to treat rheumatoid arthritis (RA) during the period 1980–92. Rheumatoid arthritis is a painful, debilitating, and progressive disease which affects millions of people worldwide, with very substantial effects on health and the economy. Regrettably, in contrast to some other major health problems such as heart disease, depression, ulcers, and bacterial infections, this is an area where therapeutic innovations have thus far had comparatively little impact on physicians' ability to reverse the disease. RA currently has no "cure" and the effectiveness of available treatments is limited. Compared to other drug classes the rate of new product introductions has been slow, and, at the time of writing, there have been no breakthroughs of the same order of significance as the discovery and development of SSRIs for treatment of depression, H_2 antagonists for ulcers, or ACE inhibitors for hypertension.

Nonetheless, the market for RA drugs is far from static. There have been significant changes over the past fifteen years in the market shares of competing products. Interestingly, relative prices have changed relatively

Iain M. Cockburn is professor of finance and economics at Boston University and a research associate of the National Bureau of Economic Research. Aslam H. Anis is associate professor of health economics in the Department of Health Care and Epidemiology, University of British Columbia, and team leader of health economics at the Center for Health Evaluation and Outcome Sciences, St. Paul's Hospital, Vancouver.

The authors thank Ernst Berndt, Zvi Griliches, John Esdaile, and NBER seminar participants for helpful comments, and Jennifer Anderson and David Felson for access to their databases on safety/efficacy profiles. The authors are grateful to BC Pharmacare for access to claims data; BEA, NBER, and Eli Lilly for financial support; and Merck for access to library records. Sophia Wang provided invaluable and very competent research assistance. The authors take full responsibility for any remaining errors.

little, and these market dynamics appear to be driven primarily by other factors. Here we focus on the role played by publication of clinical research findings. In contrast to traditional hedonic analysis where product characteristics are fixed but new products incorporating different quality levels appear over time, here the set of products is fixed while their measured quality changes over time. New information about the relative efficacy and toxicity of existing drugs accumulates through the publication of clinical trial results, and this information appears to have had a significant impact on the pattern of drug use.

A number of clinical aspects of rheumatoid arthritis are important structural features of the market for drugs used to treat the disease. We therefore begin with a brief review of the nature of RA and its treatment. We then discuss issues related to the measurement of the relative efficacy and toxicity of drug treatments for RA. Next, we present economic data on the market for a specific set of drugs used in the treatment of severe RA and consider them in the context of models of demand for differentiated products. We then report the results of estimating price and market share equations. In the concluding section, we suggest alternative approaches that may provide some additional insight, in particular analysis of the role of advertising and promotional expenditures.

11.2   Rheumatoid Arthritis

RA is one of the most prevalent diseases affecting joints and connective tissue. RA is an autoimmune disease: For reasons that are still poorly understood, the body's immune system begins to malfunction, attacking healthy tissue. Like related conditions such as lupus erythematosus, psoriatic arthritis, and scleroderma, the disease is *systemic* and *chronic*. Tissues are affected throughout the body, and although some patients experience prolonged periods of remission, most are affected for a lifetime.[1]

RA is characterized by inflammation of the synovium (a membrane which lines the joints) resulting in stiffness, pain, warmth, and swelling in joints. As the disease progresses, inflamed cells release an enzyme which erodes surrounding bone and cartilage, resulting in increased pain, loss of movement, and eventually destruction of the joint.[2] Patients experience greater and greater pain and loss of mobility. Fatigue often accompanies the "classical" joint symptoms. In late stages of the disease, skin and vascular problems (such as leg ulcers) may develop, along with damage to eyes and nerves and inflammation of lymph nodes, heart, and lungs.

---

1. Brewerton (1994) gives a comprehensive and readable overview of arthritis and its treatment. See also Cash and Klippel (1994), Wolfe (1990) and Steinman (1993).

2. Establishing a conclusive diagnosis of RA can be difficult, especially in its early stages, since it shares many symptoms with other autoimmune diseases. Note that RA should not be confused with osteoarthritis, an even more prevalent disease, which has a distinct clinical profile and disease process.

Research into the fundamental causes of the disease has inconclusively investigated many factors ranging from endocrine disorders to nutrition, geography, psychological conditions, and occupational hazards. Current thinking suggests that some infectious agent may trigger the damaging autoimmune response in persons who have a genetic predisposition. However, while a specific genetic marker (HLA-DR4) has been found to be present in a large fraction of RA patients, not all patients have the marker, and only a small fraction of people who have the marker go on to develop RA. Neither has the proposed infectious agent (possibly an unknown virus) been identified, though various other arthritic and rheumatic conditions have been associated with infection by a number of organisms such as *borellia* (the Lyme disease spirochete) and some streptococcal bacteria.

RA affects between 1 and 2 percent of the population of OECD countries. Women are two to three times more likely than men to develop disease. In adults the onset of the disease is typically between ages forty and sixty, though significant numbers of people experience severe symptoms in their thirties and forties, and the disease can occur at any age. In some patients deterioration is rapid, while in others the disease progresses very slowly. Once affected, the outlook for most patients is poor. In many cases patients experience temporary relief of symptoms, but only very few have a complete remission of the disease. Chronic severe pain and restricted mobility have a very significant impact on the quality of life of RA patients. Even with aggressive drug therapy, 7 percent of RA patients are significantly disabled within five years, and 50 percent are too disabled to work ten years after the onset of the disease. In addition to the morbidity effects of RA, Pincus and Callahan (1993) estimate that life expectancy is reduced among patients with RA by at least ten years.

By any measure the total burden of the disease is substantial. Quality-adjusted life years (QALYs) lost may be as many as seven million per year in the United States.[3] The combination of severe health impact, widespread incidence, and relatively early onset mean that very substantial economic losses are attributable to RA. For example, in 1997 the Arthritis Foundation reported that musculoskeletal conditions such as RA cost the U.S. economy approximately $65 billion per year in direct expenses and lost output.

11.2.1 Treatment Options for Rheumatoid Arthritis

Over the course of the disease, medical treatment of RA patients consists of physical intervention and drug therapy. Counseling or other psy-

---

3. In Canada, RA occurs in approximately 1 percent of the population, or about 270,000 people. It has been estimated that the average Canadian has significant pain and/or disability from arthritis resulting in an average of 2.5 quality-adjusted life years (QALYs) lost. See Torrance and Feeny (1989) and Reynolds et al. (1993). Since RA tends to be more frequently disabling than osteoarthritis, a conservative estimate of the total disability among Canadians from RA would hence be 675,000 QALYs lost.

chotherapeutic intervention may also play an important role in helping patients cope with the impact of the disease, and many patients also turn to "alternative" medicine. Physical intervention takes the form of physical therapy directed toward preservation of joint function and surgical procedures to address severe pathologies of specific joints (e.g., hip replacement). Drug treatment, the focus of this study, is given to almost all patients who consult a physician: Of the approximately 5.1 million patient visits per year in the United States where RA is a primary diagnosis, more than 90 percent involved one or more drugs' being prescribed.

Two principal classes of drugs are used to treat RA: nonsteroidal antiinflammatory drugs (NSAIDs) and disease-modifying antirheumatic drugs (DMARDs). These two classes account for more than 65 percent of all prescriptions to RA patients, with corticosteroids accounting for a further 19 percent. It is important to note that drug therapy for RA normally follows a treatment hierarchy: Drug treatment begins with NSAIDs and moves on to DMARDs as the disease progresses.

NSAIDs are the most frequently prescribed drugs for RA. Large numbers of drugs fall into the NSAID class; among the most commonly used are aspirin, ibuprofen (Motrin), naproxen (Naprosyn), diclofenac (Voltaren), and piroxicam (Feldene). NSAIDs reduce inflammation and have an analgesic effect but do not affect progression of the disease. NSAIDs act quickly and are well tolerated by many patients but can cause a number of dangerous side effects, particularly when used in the high dosages indicated for RA. Gastrointestinal bleeding is the most frequently encountered severe side effect.[4] While NSAIDs are the first line of defense, they offer only palliative treatment of symptoms, and as the disease progresses patients will typically be given one of the DMARDs. This does not usually imply discontinuation of NSAID therapy, and in fact between 80 and 90 percent of patients are prescribed drugs from both classes.

The second-line DMARDs can suppress symptoms and slow the progress of the disease, though they cannot halt it. DMARDs are slow acting, taking weeks or months before any significant improvement is noticed by the patient, and are often poorly tolerated. Different drugs are used with varying degrees of success in different patients. Furthermore, many patients are forced to discontinue the drug because of serious side effects. Minor, though uncomfortable, side effects such as dermatitis, nausea, and mouth ulcers are quite frequently experienced. The incidence of serious side effects such as retinal damage, renal failure, liver damage, and reduction in blood cell counts, while uncommon, nonetheless requires close medical supervision and frequent diagnostic testing.

---

4. COX-2 inhibitors, a new class of NSAIDs with a more selective mechanism of action and lower incidence of side effects, have recently been introduced into the U.S. market. These drugs include celecoxib (Celebrex) and rofecoxib (Vioxx).

Table 11.1   **DMARD Drugs**

Drug	Brand Name(s)	U.S. Market Intro	Other Indications	Manufacturer
Auranofin	Ridaura	1985		SKB
Azathioprine	Imuran	1968	Immune suppression for transplants	Glaxo Wellcome
Gold sodium thiomalate	Myochrysine	<1980		Merck
Aurothioglucose	Solganal	1989?		Schering
Hydroxychloroquine	Plaquenil	1956	Malaria	Winthrop
methotrexate	Rheumatrex	1955	Leukemia, psoriasis	Lederle, generics
D-penicillamine	Cuprimine	1963	Chelation	Merck, Wallace
Sulfasalazine	Azulfidine	1952	Ulcerative colitis, Crohn's disease	Kabi, generics

The DMARDs approved for treatment of RA during the period of this study are listed in table 11.1. One point to note from this table is that many of these drugs are quite old, having been first introduced to the market many years ago. Auranofin (Ridaura) was the only strictly new molecule approved for RA in the period covered by this study. Other products such as methotrexate are new to the market in the sense that they have recently gained regulatory approval for treatment of RA, though they may have been approved for other indications for many years or may have been used informally or in research settings for treatment of RA. (Lederle introduced Rheumatrex, a formulation of methotrexate specifically targeted at the RA market, in 1986.) Sulfasalazine, methotrexate, and the antimalarials are off-patent, but generic production is significant only for methotrexate. It is also important to note that the original or primary indication of most of the drugs was not RA. With the exception of the gold compounds, the activity of the DMARDs against RA was discovered subsequent to their first introduction to the market. Methotrexate was an early treatment for cancer, while hydroxychloroquine was developed as an antimalarial. The precise mechanism of action of most of these drugs is not well understood, though most have their therapeutic effect through suppressing the immune response. The anti-inflammatory activity of gold compounds appears to be specific to arthritic conditions, while the immunosuppressant activity of azathioprine and methotrexate is much more general.

In addition to DMARDs, physicians may also prescribe corticosteroids. This occurs in about 20 percent of patient visits in the United States. While these drugs can often produce dramatic short-term improvement in symptoms, their long-term use is limited by serious side effects, principally osteoporosis and increased susceptibility to infections. As a last resort, patients may also be prescribed highly toxic third-line immunosuppressant drugs such as cyclophosphamide, cyclosporine, or chlorambucil. Without a new therapy which induces a lasting remission, physicians face difficult decisions and trade-offs in drug therapy for RA.[5]

The timing of moving a patient from well-tolerated NSAIDs to the more toxic DMARDs is controversial, with some physicians arguing for early and aggressive second-line therapy to preempt irreversible joint damage, despite serious side effects. Even within the DMARD class it is far from clear which drug to prescribe. Only a fraction of patients obtain significant benefit from any one agent and even then the effect is often short-lived, typically lasting for only a few months or years. Over the twenty- to thirty-year course of the disease, a patient will typically cycle through a series of therapeutic alternatives as their physician attempts to arrest, or often merely to minimize, the cumulative destruction wrought by the disease. Furthermore, professional opinion has changed over time regarding which drugs to use, and when. The information base on the relative efficacy and toxicity of these agents continues to evolve as new scientific evidence from clinical trials is published and physicians individually and collectively accumulate more experience. The efficacy/toxicity trade-off lies at the heart of the prescribing decision, and changing perceptions of where drugs are located in this space drives our analysis of demand for these drugs.

11.3   Measuring the "Quality" of Drug Treatments for RA

We attempt to measure the characteristics of different DMARD drugs in two general dimensions: efficacy and toxicity. Unlike some previous work on hedonics of pharmaceutical products we pay little attention to differences in the dosage regimen. Though characteristics such as the number of times a day the patient must take the drug appear to be an important determinant of the relative value of different ulcer drugs and antidepressants (see Suslow 1992, 1996 and Berndt, Cockburn, and Griliches 1997), we believe them to be much less important here. The very close involvement of the physician and the severe nature of the disease suggest to us that the impact of dosing regimens on patient compliance is unlikely to be an important factor.[6]

5. Leflunomide (Arava), approved by the FDA in September 1998, is a new DMARD with a novel mechanism of action and potentially less severe side effects. A number of experimental drugs, largely from the biotech sector of the industry, hold some promise for significant progress in treating arthritis and other autoimmune inflammatory disorders. Infliximab (Enbrel), a genetically engineered protein, was approved by the FDA for treatment of RA in late 1998, but of most of these "large molecule" drugs are still in the early stages of testing. See *Wall Street Journal,* 17 July 1997, B1.

6. As a practical matter, dosage regimens for these drugs vary widely, are difficult to compare directly, and often involve complicated "ramp-up" schedules paced over many weeks. For example, the maintenance dose of methotrexate is 7.5 mg spread over a week, while

Our primary measures of efficacy and toxicity are computed from the reported results of published clinical trials. We assume that the best available information about the relative efficacy and toxicity of substitute drugs comes from published reports of clinical trials that appear in peer-reviewed scientific journals. These reports constitute a longitudinal data set which tracks the evolution of information on each drug over time.

Based on Felson, Anderson, and Meenan (1990), we begin with the universe of 216 published trials published between 1966 and 1995 listed in the MEDLINE database. Protocols and methodology vary widely across trials, and to establish a basis for comparison of results across trials (and to maintain a minimal level of methodological quality) papers were excluded if they did not meet the following criteria:

Patient profile: adults eighteen and older, meeting American Rheumatism Association diagnostic criteria for RA
Random assignment to treatment groups
Blinded trial (at a minimum single-blinded)
Appropriate minimum dosage levels
At least eight weeks' duration

Imposing these criteria resulted in all but 66 of the original set of published trials being excluded.

11.3.1 Efficacy Measures

Efficacy of drugs in these trials is established by compiling measurements of a number of standard physiologic markers and outcome measures for patients in the different treatment groups at the beginning and end of each trial. These were

Erythrocyte sedimentation rate (ESR), which is a physiologic marker of the level of overall systemic inflammation, derived from testing blood samples drawn from trial participants at predefined intervals during the trial
Tender joint count (TJC), which is a measure of the extent and severity of the disease in terms of the number of affected joints, compiled according to a standard protocol by a physician or nurse who assesses the patient and measured as difference (or percentage difference) over baseline
Grip strength (GS), which is another measure of the extent and severity of the disease, performed by measuring the pressure the patient is able to exert on a standard mechanical device, captured as either mean percent-

---

sulfasalazine must be taken in relatively large amounts several times per day, and most of the gold compounds are injectable. Quantifying dosage regimens with variables measuring route of administration, dosage frequency, and so on is tantamount econometrrically to simply using drug dummies.

age improvement over baseline or the mean improvement standardized by baseline standard deviation

Apart from these measurements, efficacy can also be measured by the reported rate at which patients dropped out of each trial due to "lack of efficacy."

11.3.2   Toxicity Measures

Toxicity is much harder to measure consistently. We have not been able to assemble consistent data on the actual incidence of side effects in each trial. Following previous work we have experimented with variables constructed by counting the number of side effects listed under categories such as "severe" or "frequent" in standard reference sources, or constructing dummy variables reflecting the locus of specific side effects (kidney damage, central nervous system, retina, etc.) but these perform poorly in experimental regressions.[7] Our preferred measure of toxicity is the reported rate at which patients dropped out of clinical trials due to "toxicity." Summary statistics for these variables are given in table 11.2.

11.3.3   Changes in Quality over Time

Because new trials are conducted periodically, information accumulates steadily over time, and variables constructed from reported trial results form a longitudinal data set. We combine data from different trials in a variety of ways intended to capture the evolution over time of the scientific information available to prescribing physicians.

One possibility is to simply assign a value to each variable in each year based on the most recently published study. Thus we "ratchet" the level of each variable up or down in each year that a new trial came out, and carry forward the previous value otherwise. (In tables below we refer to these measures as "latest.")

A second approach is to do a "rolling" cumulative meta-analysis which pools treatment groups over time and across drugs. As new trials are published results for each group of patients are added to the previous total, resulting in a continuously expanding sample. Mean treatment effects are the weighted sum of treatment effects in all trials to date.

Third, we modify the cumulative meta-analysis by imposing various schemes of declining weights over time to capture "depreciation" of knowledge. We expect the results of trials conducted many years in the past to weigh less heavily upon current prescribing practice than more recent evidence. The simplest such weighting scheme is a three- or five-year moving average. Alternatives such as a perpetual inventory deprecia-

---

7. Clinicians may be most strongly influenced by the relative incidence of severe adverse reactions. We have not yet compiled data on these effects. But note that since these events are very rare, their probability of occurrence is difficult to measure precisely.

Table 11.2   **Summary Statistics and Characteristics of DMARDs**

	Sample Means				
	Efficacy			Toxicity	
Drug Name and Daily Dose	TJC	GS	ESR	Dropout	Price[a]
Auranofin, 6mg	8.44	26.98	10.79	0.16	1.91
Azathioprine, 100mg	9.78	33.11	13.73	0.27	1.67
Gold salts, 7mg	9.15	38.20	10.79	0.40	1.07
Antimalarials, 400mg	9.21	39.89	11.41	0.04	1.42
Methotrexate, 12.5mg	13.23	33.11	13.49	0.16	1.31
D-penicillamine, 600mg	8.78	37.26	22.65	0.33	1.70
Sulfasalazine, 2.5g	12.28	28.53	20.64	0.37	0.84
Placebo, n.a.	4.80	9.74	1.26	0.07	n.a.

Note: n.a. = not available.
[a] 1992 U.S. dollars per daily maintenance dose.

tion scheme or fixed declining weights do not yield materially different results.

11.4   Model

The theoretical literature provides little guidance on the appropriate functional form for estimating quality-adjusted prices. Following many previous hedonic pricing studies (for pharmaceutical products, see Suslow's analysis of ulcer drugs [1996] or Berndt, Cockburn, and Griliches's work on antidepressants [1997]) we use a semilog reduced form:

$$(1) \qquad \ln(p_{jt}) = x_{jt}\beta + Z\gamma + \varepsilon_{jt},$$

where x_{jt} represents the measured quality (i.e., toxicity and efficacy) characteristics of drug $j; j = 1, \ldots, J$ at time t; Z_t is a set of time dummies; and p_{jt} denotes the time series of prices for drug j.

For the market share equation, we follow Berry (1994) and Berry, Levinsohn, and Pakes (1995) in specifying a logit type discrete choice model of demand for differentiated products to analyze the DMARD market. See King (1996) for a successful application of a modification of this approach to the anti-ulcer market. Following Berry we postulate that the utility of consumer i for product j is given by the function $U(x_j, \xi_j, p_j, \Theta_d, v_i)$, where $x_j, \xi_j, p_j, \Theta_d$ are observed product characteristics, unobserved product characteristics, and price and demand parameters, respectively. The term v_i is unobserved by the econometrician and represents a consumer-specific component of utility. To implement the model, one has to make specific parametric assumptions about the consumer-specific variables, analogous to the choice of functional form for a homogenous good demand equation. The utility derived by consumer i for product j can be written as

(2) $$u_{ij} = x_{ij}\beta_i - \alpha p_j + \xi_{ij} + \varepsilon_{ij}.$$

Averaging over consumers (we assume that the physicians who exercise control over the drug consumption decision act as perfect agents for their patients) and introducing time subscripts to reflect the fact that the perceived safety and efficacy characteristics of drugs change over time, we obtain a mean consumer utility level from choosing drug j at time t as

(3) $$\delta_{jt} = x_{jt}\beta - \alpha p_j + \xi_{jt},$$

where ξ_{jt} may be interpreted as the mean of consumers'/physicians' valuations of an unobserved product characteristic that is not captured by x_{jt} and we use the assumption that $E[\varepsilon_{ij}] = 0.$[8]

In addition to the competing DMARDs, $j = 1, \ldots, J$, we also assume the existence of an outside good j_0 with price p_0. In this context, consumption of the outside good can be thought of as the quantities of NSAIDs and all other non-DMARDs consumed by RA patients. (Empirically, almost all RA patients' visits to doctors result in their being prescribed either an NSAID or a DMARD or both. Only a tiny number of patients receive no drug therapy.) Letting q_j and q_j and q_0 denote the quantities of drug j and the outside good, respectively, market shares for drug j are just $s_{jt} = q_{jt}/(q_{jt} + q_{-jt} + q_{0t})$.

In this model it is assumed that all aspects of market demand are completely determined by the mean utility level δ_{jt} and, without going into the specifics of supply side dynamics and alternative characterizations of market equilibrium, we adopt the special case of the logit model to solve for mean utility levels as a function of observed market shares. Given the utility function in equation (2), if $\beta_i = \beta$ for all consumers i, and ε_{ij} is an iid variable which follows the type I extreme value distribution, then market share of drug j is given by the logit formula

(4) $$s_{jt}(\delta_{jt}) = \exp(\delta_{jt})/\exp(\delta_{0t} + \Sigma\delta_{jt}).$$

By substitution and by normalizing the mean utility of the outside good to equal zero, we get the following linear model for market shares:

(5) $$\ln(s_{jt}) - \ln(s_{0t}) = \delta_{jt} = x_{jt}\beta - \alpha p_j + \xi_{jt},$$

where s_{jt} and p_{jt} are the quantity share and price of the jth DMARD at time t. The unobserved characteristics of the drug, ξ_{jt}, becomes the error term.

In our implementation of this basic estimating equation we deflate prices by the BLS producer price index for pharmaceuticals to remove the general trend of inflation. (This is equivalent to a slightly different

8. See Berry (1994) for more on possible ways of decomposing β_i and on the assumptions that yield invariant α and β across individuals.

specification of equation [2] with a normalization of the utility level of the outside good which leaves the price of the outside good in the estimating equation.) As argued below, we believe prices to be largely exogenous to this market and are therefore unconcerned about endogeneity of this variable. Given the panel structure of the data, we can address the issue of potential correlation between ξ_{jt} and the other explanatory variables by including a fixed drug effect, so that $\xi_{jt} = \mu_j + \eta_{jt}$ with η_{jt} assumed to have the usual desirable properties.

11.5 Price and Quantity Data

Econometric analysis of the market for DMARDs requires basic data on prices and quantities of these drugs sold, and careful attention to the definition of the RA market. Our primary data on prices and quantities for the DMARDs are drawn from reports of wholesale transactions in the United States published by IMS America Inc., a market research company. IMS collects information on revenues and quantities of individual drug products by wholesale distributors at a very fine level of detail; for example, 100-mg tablets, 100-count bottle. (We have also collected data on retail transactions in British Columbia which were reimbursed under the province's Pharmacare program. The Pharmacare program is universal and covers all residents with varying levels of coverage depending on sociodemographic status. Trends in these data match the U.S. wholesale market very closely.)

A major difficulty with these kinds of data, however, is that they are collected by drug product, not by disease indication. As pointed out above, many of the DMARDs have multiple uses, and in fact their primary use may be for quite different medical problems. Analyzing demand for these drugs for treatment of RA requires that we distinguish between these uses. This may not be important for measuring prices: Lacking some means to discriminate among consumers through packaging or reformulation it is not unreasonable to assume that one price holds for all sales of a particular formulation of a drug regardless of the intended use. This is likely to be particularly true for the wholesale market. By contrast, in measuring quantities it is vitally important to distinguish between markets in the sense of different medical conditions. Large (and varying) amounts of these drugs are used for treatment of other diseases.

Figure 11.1 presents series on U.S. wholesale prices for DMARDs for the period 1980–92. Prices are measured in dollars per daily dose unit. Daily doses are the "typical maintenance dose" taken from a number of standard reference publications such as the *Physician's Desk Reference*. It should be noted that the dosage given to any particular patient may vary substantially from the amounts we use here: Treatment of most patients may involve considerable experimentation with dosages. Some of the drugs

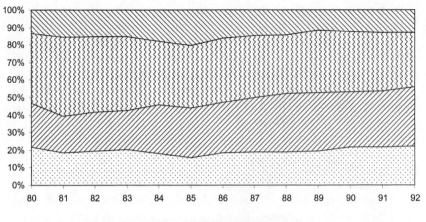

□ cortisone ☑ DMARDs ☒ NSAIDs ☒ other

Fig. 11.1   Drug class shares of NDTI mentions for RA

also have a fairly complicated "ramp-up" dosage regime lasting many weeks before the maintenance dose is treated. Relative prices based on the cost of initiating drug therapy and maintaining it for a total of three months are very similar to the daily dose prices presented here.

Perhaps the most striking feature of figure 11.1 is that prices are so similar across the major products and move so closely together. Over time prices rise steadily with general inflation, with few significant changes relative to one another. The major exception is sulfasalazine, whose roughly constant nominal price corresponds to a sustained decline—in real terms, a steady fall. Methotrexate's price rises relatively steeply during the mid-1980s, driven largely by the introduction of Lederle's branded Rheumatrex product, while the rate of increase in the price of the injectable gold products moderates somewhat toward the end of the period.

To address the market definition problem, we need information on the fraction of each drug's consumption which is specifically for the treatment of RA. For this we turn to another IMS publication, the *National Drug and Therapeutic Index* (NDTI). The NDTI reports results from surveying a sample of physicians. Each physician is asked to supply various pieces of information about patient visits; for our purposes the most useful data are the reports on primary diagnosis and which drugs (if any) were prescribed. In these reports a "drug mention" is equivalent to one prescription. IMS imputes figures for the total U.S. population from the survey sample and provides tabulations by drug and by diagnosis. Thus for each drug we can compute a breakdown of prescriptions by diagnosis, and for the diagnosis of RA, a breakdown of prescriptions by drug. These data provide valuable insight into market dynamics.

Table 11.3 summarizes information on consumption of DMARDs by diagnosis, reporting the percentage of prescriptions of each drug for which RA was the primary diagnosis. This fraction is high and stable for some drugs such as injectable gold salts and auranofin, indicating that their principal market is indeed RA. For other DMARDs, such as sulfasalazine and azathioprine, the "outside" uses are very substantial, averaging more than 75 percent of prescriptions. Furthermore, there are significant changes in these fractions over time. The fraction of d-penicillamine used for RA falls from 91 percent in 1980 to 72 percent in 1992, while the same statistic for azathioprine rises from zero in 1980 to more than 50 percent in the mid-1980s before declining to 12 percent by 1992.

Table 11.4 summarizes prescriptions for each drug for which the primary diagnosis was RA. The total number of mentions is greater than the number of visits because patients may be given more than one drug per visit (this occurs in approximately 80 percent of visits). Since these data are compiled from simple counts of mentions and thus do not reflect differences in the size of prescriptions, these are approximations at best. The share of gold salts, for example, may well be overstated because patients

Table 11.3   **NDTI Drug Mentions by Diagnosis: Fraction of RA by Drug**

Drug	1980 (%)	Mean (1980–92 %)	1992 (%)	Major Other Use (Mean 1980–92, %)
Auranofin[a]	92	87	84	
Azathioprine	0	26	12	Transplant, 56
Gold salts	92	91	91	
Antimalarials	79	64	56	Circulatory disorders, 9
Methotrexate, injectable	3	21	22	Cancer, 59
Methotrexate, oral	0	65	69	Skin disease, 17
D-penicillamine	91	81	72	
Sulfasalazine	0	8	11	Digestive disorders, 83

[a]Introduced in 1985.

Table 11.4   **Share of NDTI Drug Mentions for RA (Mean 1980–94)**

Drug Category	Share of Mentions (%)
Cortisone	19.8
Other	14.6
NSAIDs	36.2
DMARDs	29.4
Auranofin	4.7
Azathioprine	4.5
Gold salts	37.3
Antimalarials	17.4
Methotrexate	23.7
D-penicillamine	9.4
Sulfasalazine	2.6

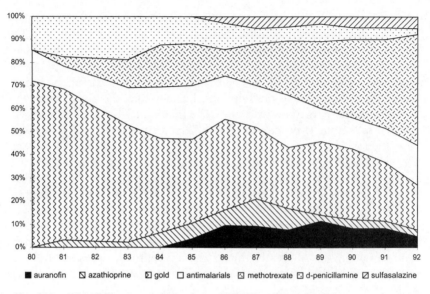

■ auranofin   ◫ azathioprine   ◫ gold   □ antimalarials   ◫ methotrexate   ◫ d-penicillamine   ◫ sulfasalazine

Fig. 11.2   DMARDs: share within class of NDTI mentions for RA

make weekly visits to their physician for an injection. On the other hand, methotrexate may be prescribed in a more traditional manner with the patient visiting the physician (and obtaining a new or refill prescription) much less frequently. Nonetheless these fractions are our best estimate of each drug's share of the RA market.[9]

Figure 11.2 summarizes quantity shares within the DMARD market graphically. The total size of the DMARD market (as measured by the number of mentions of these drugs in the NDTI grew somewhat over time from about 1.9 million mentions per year in the early 1980s to around 2.4 million in the early 1990s. Much of this growth was driven, however, by increases in the numbers of patients diagnosed with RA, which reflect changes in the demographics of the U.S. population. DMARDs as a class were a somewhat larger share of the total RA market at the end of our sample period (around 28 percent in 1992 compared to 21 percent in 1980) which may reflect some market-expanding effect of improved quality and new product introductions, but these changes are dominated by movements within the DMARD market. The most striking feature of figure 11.2 is the substantial fall in the share of injectable gold and the rise in the share of methotrexate. D-penicillamine's share falls steadily over time while the other drugs' shares are relatively small and stable. These patterns

9. As an alternative to using NDTI data we have explored a small data set constructed from the B. C. Pharmacare database where we include only prescriptions written by rheumatologists. The shares of different DMARDs in these data are very similar to those in the NDTI, but the data cover a somewhat shorter time period.

reflect the general impression to be gained from reading the clinical literature: An increasing tendency to use methotrexate instead of gold, with
mixed opinions about the therapeutic value of the other agents. Auranofin,
the only new chemical entity to enter this market in the sample period,
was launched in the mid-1980s as an orally administered alternative to the
injectable gold compounds, but achieved only a modest 10 percent share.

To examine the relationship of prices and quantities to measured quality
more carefully, we turn next to our estimation results.

11.6   Results

11.6.1   Price Equation

Table 11.5 reports results from estimating the reduced form hedonic
price equation (1) using data on U.S. wholesale prices. To the extent that
we expect relative prices to respond to changes in measured characteristics, the results are disappointing. In models 1 and 2 we regress the log

Table 11.5   **OLS Results: U.S. Wholesale Prices, 1980–92**

	Model 1	Model 2	Model 3	Model 4	Model 5
Constant	4.84 (0.94)	−0.14 (0.14)	−1.10 (0.14)	−0.12 (0.79)	−0.77 (0.17)
Efficacy[a]	−5.68 (1.03)			−1.11 (0.81)	
Toxicity[b]	1.15 (0.38)	0.82 (0.41)		0.55 (0.26)	0.83 (0.22)
Improvement in GS		−0.44 (0.42)			−1.37 (0.22)
Improvement in TJC		−1.22 (0.40)			0.22 (0.29)
Improvement in ESR		0.39 (0.38)			−0.36 (0.23)
Dummy 1981			0.11	0.10	0.04
Dummy 1982			0.30	0.26	0.09
Dummy 1983			0.51	0.44	0.23
Dummy 1984			0.66	0.59	0.41
Dummy 1985			0.83	0.77	0.72
Dummy 1986			0.95	0.88	0.82
Dummy 1987			1.03	0.96	0.89
Dummy 1988			1.17	1.10	0.78
Dummy 1989			1.23	1.14	1.12
Dummy 1990			1.34	1.22	1.24
Dummy 1991			1.44	1.32	1.34
Dummy 1992			1.48	1.36	1.38
R^2	0.29	0.24	0.72	0.74	0.84

Note: Standard errors in parentheses; $N = 78$. Dependent variable: Current U.S. dollars per daily dose.
[a]Efficacy = (1 − dropout rate for lack of efficacy).
[b]Toxicity = dropout rate for toxicity.

of daily dose price on to characteristics variables alone. The estimated parameters are contrary to our prior beliefs: Efficacy (whether measured by the fraction of patients who do not drop out of trials because of lack of efficacy, or by changes in the physiological measurements GS, TJC, and ESR) is negatively associated with price, while toxicity is positively associated. These results do not change when we add a set of year dummies to the list of explanatory variables, though the fit of the equation improves markedly. Coefficients on the time dummies imply a steady upward movement in prices, which is very similar whether or not we attempt to control for quality change.

Why the characteristics variables should perform so poorly is puzzling. Considerable experimentation with alternative ways of computing these quality measures from the clinical trials data did not improve these results. Regardless of whether efficacy and toxicity are measured relative to placebo or as unadjusted changes, or which of the alternative weighting and updating schemes discussed above is used, we still obtain the "wrong" signs on the estimated coefficients. One reason may be that measurement error is biasing the coefficient estimates.[10] This possibility should be taken seriously as the clinical trials literature is not unambiguous, and prescribing physicians may be unaware or skeptical of the results reported in the studies we use here.

We prefer, however, to interpret these findings as evidence of an alternative hypothesis about the nature of this market. Given the serious medical situation of most patients who are given DMARDs, and their lack of alternatives, it seems likely that demand is quite inelastic. With many of these drugs having their primary use elsewhere, it is plausible that their prices are essentially exogenous to the RA market. Casual inspection of the raw data suggests that the level of prices for these drugs bears little relationship to measured characteristics, with some of the most toxic and least efficacious drugs having the highest prices. Furthermore, looking at changes over time, we see that prices for most of the drugs move steadily upward with general inflation, with little change in relative prices. Where movements in prices conform to our priors, any correlation with changes in measured quality appears to be swamped by the rest of the data. Seen in this light, the results obtained in the price equation may simply be spurious, with the coefficients on the characteristics variables reflecting confounding with other factors determining prices.

Experience with other pharmaceutical price data as well as informal evidence gathered in discussion with industry executives and other experts suggests also that relative prices for these products are very sticky. There is some evidence for sensitivity of pharmaceutical prices to exogenous

---

10. Recall that with more than one variable potentially mismeasured, the resulting bias on estimated coefficients is hard to predict and need not always be toward zero.

shocks such as regulatory changes; see Anis and Wen (1998) and Scott Morton (1997). On the other hand, other studies have found prices of branded products to be remarkably insensitive to patent expiration and large-scale entry by generics (see Griliches and Cockburn 1995). It may not therefore be a gross mischaracterization of historical industry pricing practice to summarize it as setting prices once (in real terms) at the time of product launch, with subsequent revisions limited largely to adjustments for general inflation applied across a producer's entire product line. Any price premium related to improved quality will therefore be difficult to see except in markets with substantial numbers of new products entering over time, which is not the case here. In this light, it is worth pointing out that poor results were also reported in Berndt and Finkelstein's (1992) study of hedonic pricing of anti-hypertensives, another drug class with a low rate of substantively new chemical entities reaching the market.

With prices set exogenously to this market, and given that relative prices are likely far down the list of patients' and physicians' concerns when choosing which drug to use, it is likely that the impact of changes in quality manifest themselves in the market largely in changes in quantities, which is where we turn next.

11.6.2   Market Share Equations

Table 11.6 presents estimates of the parameters of equation (5), with and without fixed drug effects. In models 6 and 8 the toxicity and efficacy

Table 11.6   **OLS Results: Quantity Share Regression, 1980–92**

	Model 6 (latest)	Model 7 (MA)	Model 8 (latest)	Model 9 (MA)
Constant	−18.81 (3.47)	−15.73 (3.58)	−8.63 (2.15)	−8.50 (2.13)
Efficacy[a]	8.94 (3.73)	4.87 (4.04)	−0.94 (2.12)	−1.70 (2.27)
Toxicity[b]	−0.15 (0.91)	−0.53 (0.92)	−4.48 (1.59)	−4.11 (1.55)
Improvement in GS	1.59 (0.85)	2.48 (1.25)	0.38 (0.47)	0.00 (0.67)
Improvement in ESR	0.92 (0.72)	2.53 (0.99)	−0.41 (0.49)	1.23 (0.94)
Price	−0.43 (0.61)	0.09 (0.68)	0.30 (0.48)	0.36 (0.48)
Dummy auranofin			−0.48 (0.46)	−0.33 (0.46)
Dummy azathioprine			−0.52 (0.33)	−0.15 (0.39)
Dummy gold salts			2.36 (0.28)	2.34 (0.27)
Dummy antimalarials			−0.09 (0.51)	0.14 (0.50)
Dummy methotrexate			1.41 (0.31)	1.63 (0.34)
Dummy d-penicillamine			0.71 (0.31)	0.58 (0.30)
R^2	0.26	0.29	0.79	0.80

Note: Standard errors in parentheses; $N = 78$. Dependent variable: Current U.S. dollars per daily dose.
[a] Efficacy = (1 − dropout rate for lack of efficacy).
[b] Toxicity = dropout rate for toxicity.

variables are based only on the most recently published trial in each year, while in models 7 and 9 they are computed as a three-year moving average of published trial results. In both cases the drug effect is calculated relative to placebo, but very similar results are obtained using just the change relative to the baseline values.

Results in models 6 and 7 are encouraging. The signs of the coefficients on the characteristics variables conform to our priors, with increased toxicity negatively associated with market share, and increased efficacy positively associated. Though the coefficient on price is insignificant, and corresponds to a very small elasticity, it is at least negative in model 6. A very small price effect is also consistent with our interpretation of results from estimating the price equation.

Models 8 and 9 include fixed drug effects in the estimation to control for drug-specific problems in measuring market share or characteristics. Several of these dummies are highly significant, and they markedly improve the fit of the model, suggesting that we do indeed have systematic problems in measuring market shares. Furthermore the estimated coefficients on the other variables change substantially when we include fixed drug effects, indicating that the equations omit significant variables driving quantities consumed, either quality characteristics of drugs or other drug-specific factors which determine demand.

11.7 Conclusion

Economic considerations appear to play a relatively minor role in the market for DMARDs. Information from published clinical trials relating to key quality characteristics of these drugs (efficacy and toxicity) is statistically associated with changes in their quantity shares in this market, but has no consistent impact on relative prices. Given the nature of RA, these results may not be too surprising. They do, however, point to some interesting economic issues which we have not attempted to address in this study.

First, there is the question of using prices to measure the impact of technical change on consumer welfare in markets such as this one. Most prior work on innovation, quality change, and pricing has examined the prices of new goods which embody technological change in the form of improvements to tangible aspects of quality. Here the technical change takes a rather unusual form: R&D generates revisions to the intangible information set possessed by physicians and patients, affecting perceived quality rather than physical characteristics such as speed, durability, weight, and so on. R&D surely improves welfare in this context, but the fact that relative prices in this market change very little (and are most likely determined exogenously) and that demand appears to be quite price inelastic means that its impact is very difficult to see in price space. Rather, the most visible direct effect of changes in quality is seen in movements in quantities, which has significant implications for how we should interpret movements in, for example, a fixed-weight price index.

Second, these results hint at an interesting variety of nonprice competition. Rents to producers in this market are determined initially by the level of prices (which to a rough approximation they set once in real terms, often based upon conditions prevailing in unrelated markets) and then by the evolution of quantities as consumers and/or their agents respond to exogenous changes in perceived quality. In such circumstances the role played by marketing and promotional activity may well be very important. Our analysis here is based on the generation of new information about product quality in the form of publication of research results in peer reviewed journals by (hopefully) impartial authors. The question of how this information reaches practicing physicians and their patients has not been examined here. In future work we hope to extend our analysis of this market to include marketing and promotional activity by producers of these drugs, which may shed light on the interesting question of the relative importance of objective versus persuasive information in drug choices.

References

Anis, A. H., and Q. Wen. 1998. Price regulation of pharmaceuticals in Canada. *Journal of Health Economics* 17 (1): 21–38.

Berndt, E. R., I. M. Cockburn, and Z. Griliches. 1997. Pharmaceutical innovations and market dynamics: Tracking effects on price indexes for antidepressant drugs. *Brookings Papers on Economic Activity, Microeconomics,* 133–88.

Berndt, E. R., and S. N. Finkelstein. 1992. Price indexes for anti-hypertensive drugs that incorporate quality change: A progress report on a feasibility study. MIT Program on the Pharmaceutical Industry, Working Paper no. 6-92.

Berry, S. B. 1994. Estimating discrete-choice models of product differentiation. *RAND Journal of Economics* 25:242–62.

Berry, S. B., J. Levinsohn, and A. Pakes. 1995. Automobile prices in market equilibrium. *Econometrica* 63:841–90.

Brewerton, D. 1994. *All about arthritis.* Cambridge, Mass.: Harvard University Press.

Cash, J. M., and J. H. Klippel. 1994. Second-line drug therapy for rheumatoid arthritis. *New England Journal of Medicine* 330:1368–75.

Felson, D. T., J. J. Anderson, and R. F. Meenan. 1990. The comparative efficacy and toxicity of second-line drugs in rheumatoid arthritis: Results of two meta-analyses. *Arthritis and Rheumatism* 33:1449–59.

Griliches, A., and I. M. Cockburn. 1995. Generics and new goods in pharmaceutical price indexes. *American Economic Review* 84:1213–32.

IMS America Inc. 1980–94. *National drug and therapeutic index—Drugs.* Plymouth Meeting, Pa.: IMS America.

———. 1980–94. *National drug and therapeutic index—Diagnosis.* Plymouth Meeting, Pa.: IMS America.

King, C. 1996. Marketing, product differentiation, and competition in the pharmaceutical industry. MIT Program on the Pharmaceutical Industry, Working Paper no. 39–96.

Medical Sciences Bulletin. 1994. *Focus on rheumatoid arthritis.* Levittown, Pa.: Pharmaceutical Information Associates.

Pincus, T., and L. F. Callahan. 1993. The "side-effects" of rheumatoid arthritis: Joint destruction, disability and early mortality. *British Journal of Rheumatology* 32 (suppl.): 28–37.

Reynolds, D. L., et al. 1993. Modelling the population health impact of musculoskeletal diseases. *Journal of Rheumatology* 20 (6): 1037–47.

Scott Morton, F. 1997. The strategic response by pharmaceutical firms to the Medicaid most-favored-customer rules. *RAND Journal of Economics* 28: 269–90.

Steinman, L. 1993. Autoimmune disease. *Scientific American* 269 (3): 106–14.

Suslow, V. 1992. Are there better ways to spell relief? An hedonic pricing analysis of ulcer drugs. School of Business Administration, University of Michigan Working Paper no. 696.

———. 1996. Measuring quality change in the market for anti-ulcer drugs. In *Competitive strategies in the pharmaceutical industry,* ed. R. Helms. Washington D.C.: American Enterprise Institute.

Torrance, G. W., and D. Feeny. 1989. Utilities and quality-adjusted life years. *International Journal of Technology Assessment in Health Care* 5:559–75.

Wolfe, F. 1990. 50 Years of Antirheumatic Therapy: The Prognosis of RA. *Journal of Rheumatology.* 22 (suppl.): 24–32.

Comment   J. Steven Landefeld

First, let me begin by saying that this is a good piece of research. It deals with an important problem in an interesting manner. As the authors point out, arthritis has a large economic impact, imposing a cost in the United States, for example, of over $65 billion in medical treatment costs and lost wages and salaries associated with morbidity. The disease also has an important "quality" dimension aside from its impact on mortality in that its main effect is a reduction in quality of life for patients who experience significant pain and suffering.

The study represents an original application of hedonic analyses: Instead of examining a set of new goods or services with new or different characteristics, as most hedonic studies of quality change have (new generations of computers, new types of telecommunications equipment, new treatments for heart attacks), it looks at a mainly fixed set of drugs whose "perceived" characteristics change. Most of the drugs examined in this study have been in use for a long time; what has changed is the medical profession's assessment of their efficacy and toxicity.

The results of the study are also interesting. While quality (as measured

J. Steven Landefeld is director of the Bureau of Economic Analysis, U.S. Department of Commerce.

by efficacy and toxicity) appears to affect the share of the market accounted for by the various drugs, there does not appear to be any discernible impact of quality differences on their prices relative to one another. Indeed, quality and price appear to be inversely correlated—in that higher prices are associated with lower efficacy and higher toxicity. In explaining this result, the authors point to the importance of other factors in determining prices, including the use of these same drugs to treat other diseases; inelastic demand by patients with rheumatoid arthritis (RA); institutional stickiness in prices; and other price-determining factors such as promotional expenditures.

As the representative of a U.S. statistical agency, I was particularly interested in what we at statistical agencies, along with other researchers, could learn from this study. The first lesson that I take away from this study is that hedonics may not always work. Hedonic regressions are an attempt to use observable differences in the qualities and characteristics of goods to see what consumers are willing to pay for those differences. Where those differences are hard to measure or where there are imperfections in markets that make prices insufficiently reflective of consumer preferences, hedonics may not work or may produce implausible results. Alternatively, perhaps we should interpret the results of this study as an example where the measured price increase for the product understates the real (quality-adjusted) price increase. That is, drug prices went up, but quality declined. However, in this case, the issue would appear to be mainly related to problems in measuring quality change and imperfections in the market for these drugs.

In addition to these general conclusions, there are a number of more specific lessons to be learned from this study. First, in setting up a study, one should avoid cases where prices are exogenously determined. As the authors point out, most of the drugs used in treating RA were developed for treating other diseases and a very large share of total demand for these drugs is for other diseases. As a result, changes in the perceived quality of the drugs in treating RA may have little impact on the price of the drug. It is difficult to assess the significance of this problem because of difficulties in interpreting drug mentions in the *National Drug and Therapeutic Index* (NDTI) and changes in the share of mentions over time. However, for a number of the drugs, other diseases accounted for the majority of the therapeutic drug mentions.

Second, one should be aware of the degree to which the price of the good or service in question is competitively determined and thus reflective of consumer preferences. It is only in competitive markets free of externalaties that we can presume that price is equated with marginal utility, which in turn is equated with marginal cost. If these conditions are not likely to be fulfilled, it is difficult to justify the use of hedonics to measure the value of changes in product quality. As economists and statisticians, we have no special expertise in estimating value and would rather observe through hedonics what consumers are willing to pay; however, if other factors have a large impact on market prices there is little justification for the use of the results from hedonic regressions.

In the case of drugs, there are significant problems fulfilling the competitive requirements for hedonic analysis. The demand for the product is in great part determined by the physician rather than the consumer. Long-lived patents, advertising, distribution networks, and physician incentives have frequently been cited as sources of market power in the determination of drug prices. In addition, the third-party payment system means that the price faced by the consumer is often below the market price. In 1995, for example, third-party payments covered about 40 percent of overall drug expenditures and the proportion for prescription drugs such as those studied in this paper are probably higher.

The third thing that we learn from this study is the importance of having a good measure of quality (or of measuring a product whose quality actually changes). Most of the drugs used to treat RA have been in use for a long period of time and it seems unlikely that the quality of these drugs (as measured by efficacy or toxicity) changed over time. However, the measure of quality used in the study—perceived quality by physicians as a result of successive results from clinical trials—did change. The results from the study may simply reflect the fact that from the patient's viewpoint there were no changes in underlying quality and thus there was no little or no impact on price.

Indeed, the results of the study may fit expectations—with both market share and prices increasing with quality improvements—for the two drugs that are considered new. The first of these is Rheumatrex, which is not really a new drug, but was originally developed (under the name methotrexate) for use in the treatment of cancer. As the authors point out, Lederle gained regulatory approval for a formulation of methotrexate specifically targeted to the RA market and introduced it under the brand name Rheumatrex in 1986. Rheumatrex's price has increased more quickly than those of other drugs in the period following its introduction. During the study period, 1980–92, Rheumatrex's share of the market for RA drugs rose from 0 to 50 percent and appears to have accounted for the decline in the share of other drugs. The only other drug whose share has risen was auranofin, another new drug. Although the paper does not present separate quality-adjusted results for these drugs, the existing results suggest that one should concentrate on new products where characteristics are changing. If the characteristics of the other, older drugs really didn't change, the results—that the coefficients with respect to the effect of quality on price were mainly negative and insignificant—should not be surprising. And the apparent relationship between quality and market shares for the broad group of drugs may be a spurious correlation driven by the rising share accounted for by Rheumatrex.

Given this list of things to watch out for in future studies, what advice can we offer the authors and other researchers? The authors of this study might profitably concentrate on methotrexate and auronafin. They might also develop an expanded joint product model for these two drugs that examines their other uses and the effect of promotional efforts on their prices and market shares.

With respect to other researchers about to embark on hedonic analyses, they might profit when deciding on a subject for study by examining the list of factors listed above (exogenously determined prices, serious imperfection in markets, and inadequacies in measure of quality change). Researchers may also want to examine the data a bit, including quick reviews of simple correlations, before they commit to a particular project.

If a number of these problems are present, the researcher faces the choice of moving on to another research project or seeing what useful information can be extracted from the study. Researchers should be careful not to move on to another project too quickly. Moving on not only risks ignoring an important issue (either in terms of economic importance or in terms of social policy), but may bias the results by ignoring those cases where quality has gone down. Thus, work on important issues should not be too quickly discarded even with the presence of the problems discussed above, but should be considered and where feasible work should proceed sequentially with each step having varying degrees of immediate application.

One could, for example, begin by using the IMS and NDTI data in this study to develop a drug services price index that would measure the changing cost of drug therapy for treating a case of rheumatoid arthritis. Given the importance of this disease, such an index would be most useful even if a hedonic quality-adjusted price index were not available. One could probably also use the annual price information and market share information to create an annual-weighted Fisher index to avoid the bias that would be introduced into a fixed-weighted price index by the increasing market share of Rheumatrex. Finally, as suggested above, by focusing on the new drugs Rheumatrex and auranofin, and enriching the model to consider other factors influencing price and market share, one might develop a hedonic quality-adjusted index.

Treatment Price Indexes for Acute Phase Major Depression

Ernst R. Berndt, Susan H. Busch,
and Richard G. Frank

It is not well to sneer at political economy in its relation to the
insane poor. Whether we think it right or not, the question of
cost has determined and will continue to determine their fate
for weal or woe.
—Asylum Superintendent George Cook, 1866

12.1 Introduction

Much has been written in the last decade on broad trends in medical
care spending in the United States. Although the most recent evidence is
somewhat ambiguous, the apparent slowdown in the rate of increase in
aggregate health expenditures over the last five years has been welcomed
by many governments, employers, patients, and insurers. Relatively little
attention, however, has focused on components of the change in expenditures. Is the trend change in medical care expenditures due to changes in
price, quantity, quality, or a combination of all three? What has been the
role of organizational change, such as the growth of managed care, relative
to technological/pharmaceutical innovation, such as new medications, on
expenditure trends?

A standard procedure for economists analyzing changing expenditures
over time is to employ official government price indexes, divide nominal
expenditures by such a price index, and thereby decompose expenditures

Ernst R. Berndt is professor of applied economics at the Sloan School of Management of
the Massachusetts Institute of Technology and director of the NBER's Program on Technological Progress and Productivity Measurement. Susan H. Busch is assistant professor in the
Division of Health Policy and Administration of Yale Medical School. Richard G. Frank is
professor of health economics at Harvard Medical School and a research associate of the
National Bureau of Economic Research.

The authors gratefully acknowledge research support from Eli Lilly and Company, the
U.S. Bureau of Economic Analysis, National Science Foundation grant SBR-9511550, and
National Institute of Mental Health grant MH43703. The authors are also grateful to Douglas Cocks, Thomas Croghan, David Cutler, Dennis Fixler, Mark McClellan, Will Manning,
Thomas McGuire, Joseph Newhouse, Charles Phelps, Jack Triplett, and seminar participants
at the Carnegie Mellon–University of Pittsburgh Applied Micro Workshop for helpful comments on earlier drafts.

into price and quantity components. Further analysis might then focus on factors affecting real quantity growth, such as productivity gains.

In fact, the Bureau of Labor Statistics (BLS) medical consumer price index (CPI) is often used by analysts interested in undertaking such expenditure decompositions. It is well known that such a practice is frequently inappropriate and misleading, for the medical CPI deals only with consumers' direct out-of-pocket payments and does not include payments from employers to insurers.

A deeper issue, however, involves the conceptual foundations underlying the medical CPI and producer price indexes (PPIs). Although some revisions are gradually being implemented, the BLS price indexes are based largely on the repricing over time of a fixed bundle of inputs. For decades, health economists have argued that a more appropriate price index is one based on the entire episodic treatment of selected illnesses and conditions, incorporating technological and institutional innovations that change the mix of inputs used to treat the condition, and including any effects on changed medical outcomes.

Developing a price index in health care can be viewed in terms of the unique characteristics of the health services in question. Consider creating a price index for a good that displays the following features:

- Consumers pay only a portion of the gross price due to insurance. The insurance is associated with moral hazard resulting in "too much" use of the good.
- There have been dramatic technical change and great advances in the benefits offered by the good, yet the full range of benefits is difficult to measure.
- There is great variety in the forms that the good takes and consumers value those forms differently.
- The supply side of the market for the good has experienced fundamental changes in its organization.
- The good is viewed as so important in some cases that the government compels people to use it.

The treatment of major depression, one of the most prevalent and disabling mental disorders, exhibits all of the features listed above. In this paper we report on the first three years of a research program aimed at measuring prices and output for the treatment of this important disease. The approach taken in this program of research builds on several recent efforts to construct price indexes for medical care. That recent research includes work by Cutler et al. (1998) that contrasts input price indexes for the treatment of heart attacks that rose by 6.7 percent per year over 1983–94, with an outcomes-adjusted index that takes into account a conservative valuation for the extension of life expectancy attributable to new heart attack treatments and increases by only 2.3 percent per year, implying a net bias of 4.4 percent annually. Focusing on a price index for cataract surgery, Shapiro, Shapiro, and Wilcox (chap. 10 in this volume) find that a CPI-like fixed-weight input-based index increases by a factor of about nine between 1969 and 1993, whereas their preferred alternative index incorporating realized reductions in hospital lengths of stay, but ignoring any improvements in the quality of medical outcomes, increases by only a factor of three, implying an annual differential of 4.6 percent.

Because depression is a chronic recurring illness and mortality is not an endpoint, we must rely on indirect methods of incorporating information on clinical effectiveness and outcomes. In our research we have made use of results from the published clinical literature, and from official treatment guideline standards, to identify therapeutically similar treatment bundles that can then be linked and weighted to construct price indexes for treatment of specific forms of major depression. Preliminary results from this research have been published in Frank, Berndt, and Busch (1999) and Frank, Busch, and Berndt (1998).

In this paper we consolidate our findings and extend our analysis considerably. Specifically, we refine our definition of eligible treatment episodes, develop new imputations for missing data, expand the set of treatment bundles from five to seven, and estimate hedonic price regressions.

We begin the paper with an overview of current BLS procedures for constructing medical care price indexes, and then provide a background on the nature of and alternative treatments for acute phase major depression. We outline features of the retrospective medical claims database from MEDSTAT, and then discuss our implementation of treatment episode definition and identification. We then report on quantities and prices of the treatment bundles from 1991 to 1995, we construct and interpret CPI-like and PPI-like aggregate price indexes, and we comment on an initial analysis involving hedonic price procedures. We end the paper with a discussion section, followed by concluding remarks.

12.2   Current Procedures for Measuring Medical Care Price Indexes

In the U.S. context, it is useful to distinguish "supply" and "demand" prices for medical care. By supply prices we mean the total payments received by health care providers for a particular medical treatment, consisting of the sum of payments from health insurance plans (both private and public) plus that from patients' direct out-of-pocket payments (OOPPs). At this level of generality, our supply price concept relates to components of the Producer Price Index (PPI) published by the BLS.

The demand price notion we employ here is the consumers' direct OOPPs, consisting of copayments and deductible cash payments made by the patient/consumer to providers for a particular medical treatment. Thus, in our price index changes in supply price are indicative of changes in the cost of treatment, while changes in the demand price can be traced both to changes in the cost of treatment and changes in benefit design. Our demand price concept relates to the medical care component of the BLS Consumer Price Index (CPI). As we discuss below, the presence of insurance clouds the interpretation of the demand price index for depression as a CPI. We also discuss important differences concerning the treatment of indirect consumer payments via, for example employees' contributions to employment-related health insurance.

To associate the notion of a price index for treatment episodes of care with official price indexes published by the BLS, we now describe index number procedures currently employed by the BLS, beginning with its PPI.[1]

12.2.1   BLS Procedures for Medical Care Related PPIs

The PPI "measures average changes in selling prices received by domestic producers for their output," separately by industry.[2] The PPI takes as its definition of an industry that based on the Standard Industrial Classification (SIC) code, using four-digit SIC industries and their aggregates.[3] Since its inception in 1902, the PPI has focused rather heavily on the goods-producing sectors of the U.S. economy. In 1986, in recognition of the growing importance of services, the BLS gradually began to broaden the PPI's scope of coverage in the services sectors, including medical care.

Within each industry, the BLS calculates aggregate PPIs using a modified fixed-weight Laspeyres price index formula over individual price quotes, where fixed weights are based on value of shipments data. The primary price quote at the "cell index" level of disaggregation is "the net revenue accruing to a specified producing establishment from a specified kind of buyer for a specified product shipped under specified transactions terms on a specified day of the month."[4] Although the BLS seeks transaction rather than list prices for its price quotes, the agency is well aware that compliance by firms is easier with list than with actual transaction prices. Participation by firms in the PPI is voluntary, with a "productive" compliance rate being about 63 percent in 1992 (Catron and Murphy 1996, 131, table A-2).

The BLS currently draws a sample of items for each industry on average about every seven years, and then reprices this fixed set of items monthly until an entirely new sample is drawn. In 1995 the BLS announced that for certain industries, particularly technologically dynamic ones such as pharmaceuticals and electronics in which seven-year time lags could yield a sample of products and services much older and quite unrepresentative

---

1. A more detailed discussion of the medical CPI and PPI data construction procedures is given in Berndt et al. (chap. 4 in this volume).

2. U.S. Department of Labor, Bureau of Labor Statistics (1992), 140.

3. See Triplett (1990) for economic issues involved in defining and aggregating industries within the SIC system.

4. U.S. Department of Labor, Bureau of Labor Statistics (1992), 141.

of market transactions, samples would be supplemented at one- or two-year intervals.

For quite some time, the BLS has published PPIs for certain medical-related manufacturing industries, such as pharmaceuticals and diagnostic equipment. It is only recently, however, that the BLS has begun publishing PPIs for medical service industries such as hospital services and physician services. The BLS initiated a PPI for an aggregate of health services in December 1994, for offices and clinics of doctors of medicine in December 1993, and for hospitals in aggregate and by type in December 1992.

A central measurement issue in the construction of medical price indexes involves the specification and implementation of a concept of industry output. For obvious reasons, the SIC structure is not well equipped to provide guidance to the BLS on what is the appropriate real output concept in medical care industries, nor on how this output quantity and output price can best be measured.

An alternative source for guidance on implementation of a medical care output concept is provided by the Health Care Financing Administration (HCFA). In 1983 HCFA implemented a prospective payment schedule for inpatient hospital care whereby hospitals received a fixed payment for each Medicare patient admission, regardless of the amount or duration of services actually provided the patient. These Medicare prospective payment schedules distinguish treatments by twenty-four major diagnostic categories, which are broken down further into 495 groupings of medical diagnoses and surgical procedures, known as diagnostic related groups (DRGs).[5]

DRGs provide one possible output concept, but currently DRGs only measure output for inpatient hospital care; many outpatient commodities (e.g., prescription pharmaceuticals) and services are not included in the DRG system. Classification schemes used by health care payers include version 4 of Current Procedural Terminology (CPT4) codes, a list containing thousands of procedures for which physicians and hospitals can bill; these CPT4 codes can be envisaged as inputs into the treatment of an illness or condition.[6] A systematic structure of diagnostic codes for illnesses and conditions is version 9 of the International Classification of Diseases (ICD-9).[7] Relationships among ICD-9, CPT4, and DRG codes are multifaceted; a single DRG encompasses treatment of somewhat arbitrary aggregations of distinct ICD-9 diagnoses, alternative combinations of CPT4 codes can be used in the treatment of a particular ICD-9 diagnosis, and a given CPT4 procedure can be used in the treatment of various ICD-9 diagnoses. The DRG system makes use of both ICD-9 and CPT4 coding

5. For a recent list of DRGs, see Prospective Payment Assessment Commission (1995), appendix E. Note also that some private insurers and Medicaid programs make use of DRGs for purposes of hospital payment.

6. For a discussion of CPT4, see American Medical Association (1990).

7. ICD-9 codes are discussed and listed in U.S. Department of Health and Human Services (1980). The ICD-9 has recently been updated to version 10.

systems. Other diagnostic-related systems used in setting risk-adjusted capitation rates include the Ambulatory Care Group algorithm (Weiner et al. 1996) and the Hierarchical Coexisting Conditions model (Ellis et al. 1996).

The BLS PPI program has initiated procedures for construction of medical service PPIs at two rather aggregate levels, physician services and hospital services. In turn these encompass a variety of more detailed industries, such as physician services from psychiatrists, general/family practitioners, internists, and hospital services from general medical and surgical hospitals, psychiatric hospitals, and specialty nonpsychiatric hospitals.

With respect to physician services, based on a sampling universe of all physician practices in the United States, the BLS constructs a sample frame of physician practice units. From this sample unit, the BLS randomly chooses a bill that measures the net price paid to the practice for the entire set of services and procedures provided during an office visit, distinguished by payer type. The physician's output from this visit is represented by the content of the patient's bill, including CPT codes associated with that visit, and is related to a particular ICD-9 diagnosis. Given this sample bill, the BLS contacts the physician practice unit each month and asks it to reprice what the current net transaction prices would be for that particular fixed bundle/payer of services. Since the organization of physician practices has undergone considerable upheaval and consolidation in the last few years, however, sample attrition in the BLS physician services PPI has been considerable, and maintaining a sufficiently large response rate for repricing has proven to be difficult.[8]

The hospital services PPI measures net prices paid to hospitals for the entire bundle of services received during a hospital stay associated with a particular ICD-9 diagnosis, given the payer type. Hospital output is represented by the content of a patient's bill, including all charges for room, medical supplies, drugs, and ancillary services provided the patient during a single hospital stay.

The sampling universe for the hospital services PPI is taken from the American Hospital Association, stratified by hospital size, public versus private ownership, and type of medical specialty. Once a hospital is identified as a sample unit, the BLS chooses a fixed subset of DRGs, and each hospital is then asked on a monthly basis to report on net transaction prices of a single representative patient bill (typically the last patient bill on file for that DRG). Because the identical treatment bundle is not always observed in subsequent months, BLS reporters construct subsequent fictitious DRG bundle prices by repricing the identical inputs.[9]

---

8. For further discussion, see Fixler and Ginsburg (1997).
9. For further details, see Catron and Murphy (1996), Fixler and Ginsburg (1997), and U.S. Department of Labor, Bureau of Labor Statistics (n.d.).

It is worth noting that with both the physician services and hospital services PPIs, BLS use of fixed itemized components for obtaining price quotes does not capture major input substitution of treatment for a condition, such as the changing mix of psychotherapy and psychotherapeutic drugs used for the treatment of acute phase depression. Such a zero-substitutability definition of physician and hospital output leads to the existence of a substitution bias, but that bias is of course not confined to medical PPIs, for it pervades the entire fixed-weight Laspeyres price index computational procedures.

Finally, for our purposes it is also useful to note that the BLS publishes a PPI for prescription pharmaceuticals. Although pricing the output of prescription pharmaceuticals presents some particularly interesting issues involving treatment of generic drugs and of quality improvements in new products, those issues are beyond the scope of this paper.[10]

12.2.2   BLS Procedures for Medical Care Related CPIs

According to the BLS, the CPI is "a measure of the average change in the prices paid by urban consumers for a fixed market basket of goods and services."[11] Based on data from its Consumer Expenditure Surveys (CEX), the BLS identifies and defines a fixed "market basket" of goods, employing a classification system known as the item structure, which is updated approximately every ten years. In January 1998 the BLS introduced its most recent major item structure and fixed weight revisions, based on the 1993–95 CEX; from January 1987 until January 1998, fixed weights had been based on the 1982–84 CEX.

In contrast to the BLS's recently initiated medical PPI program, the medical CPI has been published regularly since 1935.[12] Currently the BLS publishes a monthly aggregate medical care CPI (MCPI), subindexes for medical care commodities and medical care services, as well as for prescription drugs and medical supplies, nonprescription drugs and medical supplies, physician services, hospital and related services, and health insurance. Each of these medical related CPIs is based on consumers' OOPPs, and thereby excludes all medical payments by governments, as well as employers' contributions to employee health insurance; only medical OOPPs plus that portion of third-party insurance paid for out-of-pocket by employees is included within the scope of the MCPI. Thus, although national health spending in 1996 constituted 13.6 percent of GDP, the total weight given medical care items in the CPI in 1997 is only 5.4 percent.[13]

10. For further discussion, see Berndt, Cockburn, and Griliches (1996), Griliches and Cockburn (1994), Kanoza (1996), and Kelly (1997).
11. U.S. Department of Labor, Bureau of Labor Statistics (1992), 176.
12. For historical discussions, see Langford (1957) and Getzen (1992).
13. Levit et al. (1998); Ford and Ginsburg (1997).

Recently the medical CPI has introduced a number of changes, some of which are similar to those implemented several years earlier in the PPI. Until at least 1990, in most cases the MCPI priced specific input items at list prices (e.g., "chargemaster" fees for x-rays, laboratory tests, and physicians' office visits) rather than at the average actual transaction price for treatment of, say, a child's forearm fracture to a managed care organization obtaining a hospital discount.[14] Since 1993 the BLS has attempted to obtain hospital transaction rather than list prices, but through 1996, efforts "yielded slow progress to date" (Cardenas 1996b, 40). Beginning with the January 1998 major revisions, more aggressive efforts have been made to obtain actual hospital prices by payer, but information is not yet available on the composition and nature of hospital quotes now being obtained. While DRG hospital quotes have been considered for use in the MCPI, the BLS is instead contemplating pricing "package" treatments, consisting of "highly standardized and tightly defined components and risk factors" for conditions such as appendectomies, tonsillectomies, and cataract surgery (Cardenas 1996b, 40). Details on how such treatment packages would be defined have not been released. Finally, while revisions involving hospital service components of the MCPI have been announced, the BLS has not yet published comparable information on revisions to the physician service components of the MCPI.[15]

12.2.3   BLS Procedures for Pricing Medical Treatments: Comments

For some time now, health economists and government statisticians have pointed to directions toward which the pricing of medical care services should move. Here we briefly summarize several of the directions suggested by this literature. First, as early as 1962 Anne Scitovsky proposed "an index which would show changes, not in the costs of such items of medical care such as drugs, physicians' visits, and hospital rooms, but in the average costs of the complete treatment of individual illnesses such as, for example, pneumonia, appendictis, or measles."[16] In Scitovsky (1967), this treatment episode approach was implemented on an illustrative basis for five medical conditions. Discussions of shortcomings and biases inherent in the BLS MCPI approach, and of the preference for the treatment episode approach to medical price measurement, have appeared steadily since 1967; see, for example, the chapter "Measuring Changes in the Price of Medical Care" in various editions of the well-known health economics textbook by Paul Feldstein (1979, 1983, 1988) and the Baxter Foundation Prize address by Joseph Newhouse (1989).

Second, experts agree, the measurement of changes in the price of medi-

14. See, for example, Armknecht and Ginsburg (1992) and Cardenas (1996a, 1996b).
15. For a discussion of the pricing of prescription pharmaceuticals in the MCPI, and treatment of generic drugs, see Armknecht, Moulton, and Stewart (1994), and U.S. Department of Labor, Bureau of Labor Statistics (1995).
16. Scitovsky (1964); also see Scitovsky (1967).

cal services should incorporate major quality changes, such as those involving adjustments for improvements in health care outcomes. In 1996, for example, Paul Armknecht noted that "A new dimension needs to be included in the pricing of medical services that includes outcomes, so that if cancer treatment results in improved survival rates, this is reflected in the index" (33). The Boskin Commission final report went further, asserting that "we strongly endorse a move in the CPI away from the pricing of health care inputs to an attempt to price medical care outcomes" (U.S. Senate Finance Committee 1996, 60). Although incorporation of quality and outcomes changes into medical price indexes presents some significant conceptual challenges[17] and implementation difficulties, it is clear that failing to address these aspects is likely to result in price measures that are unreliable and inaccurate.

Third, use of fixed weights over extended periods such as ten to twelve years in constructing sub- and aggregate price indexes is particularly inappropriate in the medical care sector, where both institutional and technological changes are rapidly occurring. Note that the frequency with which fixed weights are updated is distinct from the issue of which index number formula (e.g., Laspeyres, Paasche, or Törnqvist approximation to the Divisia) is preferable. For the rapidly changing medical care sector, decennial updates of fixed weights with old weights being fifteen years out of date before the new revision occurs (i.e., use of 1982–84 CEX weights through December 1997) results in price indexes whose accuracy and reliability can legitimately be called into question.

In the research reported here, we extend previous research aimed at constructing CPI- and PPI-like medical price indexes that deal with prices of treatment episodes rather than prices of discrete inputs, that are based on transaction rather than list prices, that take quality changes and expected outcomes into account, and that employ more current expenditure weights in the aggregation computations. Before describing the components of this research, however, we digress to discuss the illness whose treatment price we measure, namely, acute phase major depression.

12.3 The Nature and Prevalence of Major Depression

Depression is commonly characterized by melancholy, diminished interest or pleasure in all or most activities, sleep disorders, and feelings of worthlessness. In order for a patient's condition to be considered an episode of major depression, a clinician must determine that a very specific set of clinical criteria have been met. According to the fourth edition of the *Diagnostic and Statistical Manual* (DSM-IV) of the American Psychiatric Association (APA), major depression is diagnosed when the following is observed:

17. See, for example, the discussion between Gilbert (1961, 1962) and Griliches (1962).

The presence of one of the first two symptoms, as well as at least five of nine total symptoms. The symptoms must be present most of the day almost every day, for at least two weeks. The symptoms include:
1) depressed mood most of the day nearly every day;
2) markedly diminished interest or pleasure in almost all activities most of the day;
3) significant weight loss/gain;
4) insomnia/hypersomnia;
5) psychomotor agitation/retardation;
6) feelings of worthlessness (guilt);
7) fatigue;
8) impaired concentration (indecisiveness); and
9) recurrent thoughts of death or suicide. (APA 1994, 161)

Two dimensions of depression involve its persistence. A single episode of the illness is self-explanatory given the above diagnostic criteria. A recurrent depression is defined by two or more major depressive episodes each separated by at least eight weeks of return to usual functioning (APA 1993). Episodes of illness come and go, last from several weeks to several months, and are followed by periods of relatively normal mood and behavior. Untreated, the average depressive episode lasts from four to six months. Although the vast majority of individuals who experience an episode of major depression return to their original level of functioning, between 20 and 35 percent experience persistent symptoms; when these persistent symptoms last for twenty-four months or longer, these cases are referred to as chronic depression.[18] Approximately 50 percent of all people having a depressive episode can be expected to have a recurrence, usually within two or three years. Once an individual has a second episode, additional recurrence is 70 percent likely (APA 1993). The lifetime average for depressive episodes is five to seven, but as many as forty episodes have been reported (Papolos and Papolos 1992, 7).

A number of studies have shown that depression has similar or greater functional impairments than those attributed to other episodic and chronic medical illnesses.[19] Episodes of depression can be classified according to severity: mild, moderate, or severe. Mild depression typically involves the minimum number of symptoms required to meet clinical criteria and minor functional impairment. Moderately severe episodes are characterized by an excess in symptoms above the minimum to meet clinical criteria and by greater degrees of functional impairment. Severe major depression involves a number of excess symptoms above the minimum and significant degrees of functional impairment including the ability to work or conduct usual activities.

Epidemiological research indicates that in the early 1990s, 10.3 percent

18. See Keller et al. (1984), and Keller, Lavori, Rice, et al. (1986).
19. See, for example, Broadbent et al. (1990); Wells et al. (1989); Hays et al. (1995).

of the U.S. population met the criteria for major depression at some time during a twelve-month period (Kessler et al. 1994). Depression is often accompanied by other forms of ill health, such as anxiety, eating disorders, substance abuse, or other medical conditions (Kendler et al. 1995). Although the reasons are still not well understood, women—particularly women under age twenty-five—are much more likely to suffer from depression than are men; the relative lifetime female/male prevalence rate is about 1.7. Rates of recurrence and chronicity for major depression appear to be no different for women and men (Kessler et al. 1993).

12.4 Alternative Treatments for Acute Phase Major Depression

The acute phase of major depression is typically defined as the stabilization of most acute symptoms. In practice, standards of care typically identify the acute phase as occurring over a twelve-week period. In this research we allow protocol levels of acute phase treatment to occur over a six-month period to recognize that actual practice departs from the controlled environment of efficacy research. In clinical practice, continuation therapy frequently follows on acute phase treatment in hopes of preventing relapse. If a recurrent episode of major depression occurs, maintenance treatments are often initiated to prevent further recurrences (Kupfer 1991).

Given the information available in claims data, distinguishing between acute and continuation phase treatment is difficult. We employ acute phase standards of care to establish expected outcomes, but in our empirical implementation we undoubtedly will mix acute and other phases of care. Clinical research on the continuation phase of treatment is less developed, and definitive protocols have not been as widely adopted in many clinical settings.

12.4.1 Recent Developments in Psychotherapy
and Antidepressant Medication

Treatments for acute phase major depression have advanced considerably during the last two decades. In the area of psychotherapy, a variety of new techniques has expanded treatment options well beyond traditional psychodynamic or psychoanalytic approaches. Interpersonal therapy (IPT), behavior therapy (BT), family therapy, and cognitive behavior therapy (CBT) are all relatively new. Evidence from controlled clinical trials suggests that when applied as the single mode of treatment for less severe forms of acute phase major depression, each of these therapies reduces depressive symptoms. Moreover, relative to antidepressant medication as the sole treatment, each has generally been shown to perform at comparable levels of efficacy and to have similar outcomes.[20]

---

20. See Beck et al. (1979), Elkin et al. (1989), Frank et al. (1990), Kupfer et al. (1992), and Beach, Sandeen, and O'Leary (1990).

Extraordinary advances have been achieved in the last two decades in the area of antidepressant medication. Although very recent developments expand the therapy set even further, over the 1991–95 period examined here three general classes of antidepressant medications were employed. These are (1) cyclic antidepressants that include the widely used tricyclic antidepressants (TCAs) and a number of lesser-known drugs such as trazodone; (2) selective serotonin-reuptake inhibitors (SSRIs), which include brand name drugs such as Prozac, Zoloft, Paxil, and Luvox;[21] and (3) monoamine oxidase (MAO) inhibitors which, due to considerable side effects and dangerous interactions, are generally used only for patients resistant to other forms of treatment.

Newer SSRIs offer some distinct advantages over older TCAs, although in randomized controlled trials clinical efficacy rates are similar. SSRIs are associated with lower risk of overdose, and reduced levels and numbers of side effects. Important side effects frequently associated with TCAs include drowsiness, dry mouth, impaired ability to concentrate, seizures, and weight gain.[22] The side effects most prominently associated with use of SSRIs relate to sexual dysfunction (particularly for males) and anxiety. The advantages of SSRIs come at a significantly higher pecuniary cost than most TCAs.

Psychotherapeutic interventions have frequently been combined with antidepressant medication as a combination strategy for treating major depression. The specific interventions that have been most intensively studied are the use of TCAs in combination with either IPT, BT, or a general unspecified form of short-term psychotherapy. To date, no clinical studies have been reported in the literature which systematically assess the combination of the newer SSRIs and psychotherapy.[23] It is generally presumed, however, that such combinations will be at least as efficacious as the combination of TCAs and psychotherapy.

Finally, electroconvulsive therapy (ECT) is an effective treatment, but ECT is typically limited to rather special circumstances when the patient's depression is severe and is complicated by a number of other psychiatric symptoms including psychosis, catatonic stupor, or high risk of suicide.

In the analysis reported below, we focus on outpatient treatments for major depression; these constitute the vast majority of treatment episodes (75 to 80 percent). We do this for several reasons. First, inpatient claims data typically do not contain information on the drugs prescribed for treat-

21. Recent variations slightly distinct from the SSRIs include the brand name drugs Effexor, Serzone, and Remeron.

22. Considerable variation exists in side effects among the TCAs; see Berndt, Cockburn, and Griliches (1996, 142–43, table 1) for details.

23. Using MEDSTAT retrospective claims data, Croghan et al. (1999) provide evidence suggesting that the combination of SSRIs and psychotherapy is more effective than psychotherapy alone in patients receiving continuous treatment. For a discussion of related SSRI-psychotherapy research, see Wilde and Benfield (1998).

ment; thus characterizations of inpatient care are inherently incomplete.[24] Second, because of other incomplete information regarding illness severity and comorbid conditions, it is difficult to use administrative claims data to characterize fully an illness diagnosis, and therefore to make judgments about the appropriate use of hospital services for treating major depression. Third, few clinical trials specifically address inpatient treatment for major depression, making it difficult to assign outcomes to treatments. Finally, because there was considerable evidence of overuse of hospital services in the aggregate during the late 1980s and early 1990s, the inclusion of hospital services in our 1991 base year could make interpretation of price changes troublesome.[25] This strategy of limiting severity of cases by excluding individuals hospitalized for treatment of depression is likely to be only partly successful. During the 1990s there were a substantial reduction in inpatient psychiatric admissions and in the length of stay for hospitalized cases. The implication of this is that the population of people treated only on an outpatient basis may be getting sicker over time.

In our analysis, we therefore focus on the use of various antidepressant medications alone, several forms of psychotherapy alone, and several drug-psychotherapy combination treatments. Because of very small sample sizes, we do not incorporate treatment involving ECT or the MAO inhibitors.

12.4.2   Results from Comparative Efficacy Studies

We now provide a brief summary of research results comparing the efficacy of alternative treatments for depression of varying severity. We divide depression severity into two classes: severe and less severe (hereafter, mild). We have reviewed approximately thirty major clinical trials and meta-analyses from the clinical literature on comparative efficacy of acute phase treatments (Busch, Frank, and Berndt 1996). This literature points to several key conclusions.

First, psychotherapies of all kinds have been shown to result in superior outcomes compared to no treatment. When compared amongst themselves, the different forms of psychotherapy appear to have no significant differences in outcomes.[26]

Second, for less severe forms of depression, psychotherapies alone, TCAs with medical management, and SSRIs with medical management appear to produce comparable outcomes. Each of these therapies produced significantly better outcomes than placebo treatments. Versions of these results have been reported in numerous large treatment trials and by

---

24. A significant portion of inpatient episodes have unspecified outpatient follow-up, thereby limiting that avenue for identifying treatments.

25. For a discussion, see Mechanic (1989) and McGuire (1989).

26. The AHCPR Depression Guidelines Panel (U.S. Department of Health and Human Services 1993) provides a summary and interpretation of the evidence on this point.

meta-analyses of smaller clinical trials. Combination treatments with these as components also generate equivalent levels of efficacy for less severe forms of depression.

Third, for more severe forms of depression, the bulk of the evidence suggests that TCAs alone, SSRIs alone, and combinations of drugs and psychotherapy have comparable levels of efficacy, and each results in superior outcomes compared to psychotherapy alone. Recently some evidence has emerged showing some extra improvement from the combination treatments relative to medication alone (APA 1993). We believe it is premature to conclude that combination treatments offer significantly higher levels of efficacy than do antidepressant medications alone (or with medical management, as is typically the case).

Based on these observations from the literature, we view all the major treatment technologies as offering comparable expected outcomes for the average care of less severe acute phase depression. For severe depression, we view TCAs and SSRIs alone as comparable to each other and to combinations of TCAs and SSRIs with psychotherapy.

12.5   Identifying Comparable Treatment Bundles from Claims Data

The results from our review of the clinical trials literature enable us to develop a set of treatment "bundles" that group together therapeutically similar treatments of a specific form of major depression. This identification of treatment bundles that result in similar expected health outcomes is a crucial step in the construction of medical treatment price indexes that take expected outcomes into account. The implicit assumption we adopt here is that obtaining therapeutically similar outcomes from alternative treatments provides a useful approximation to achieving similar expected utility levels.[27]

12.5.1   The MEDSTAT Data

To identify empirically comparable treatment bundles for acute phase major depression, we employ a data set consisting of retrospective insurance claims from four large self-insured employers that offered twenty-five health plans to 428,168 employees and their dependents for the years 1991 through 1995. The data were obtained from MEDSTAT, Inc., and contain information on prescription drug claims, inpatient hospital treatment, outpatient visits, ICD-9 diagnoses, CPT4 procedures, and the demographic characteristics of all covered individuals. The health benefits offered to

---

27. We recognize this is only an approximation. This is particularly the case for depression, where the constellation of side effects across treatment can vary significantly and can lead to differential patient compliance and patient preferences between the SSRIs and TCAs. See Crown et al. (1996) and Wilde and Benfield (1998) for evidence on differential TCA-SSRI compliance among patients.

enrollees in this database are quite generous relative to the general market for private health insurance in the United States.

During the five years we observed, important changes occurred in the terms of insurance coverage for mental health care. While the vast majority of plans represent so-called managed indemnity plans (90 percent–94 percent), the management of mental health care benefits changed for a substantial number of enrollees between 1991 and 1995. Beginning on 1 January 1994, about 8 percent of enrollees had their mental health coverage "carved out" to a specialty mental health managed care company.[28] In January 1995 an additional 35 percent of enrollees had their mental health benefits carved out.

It is reasonable to expect that these carve-out arrangements affected both the input prices and the quantities of specific delivered services, such as visits.[29] Changes in the extent of carve-out arrangements might also have affected the general clinical strategies used in treating major depression. Recent analyses by Wells et al. (1996) and by Berndt, Frank, and McGuire (1997) show clear differences in treatment patterns between carve-out managed care plans and treatment of mental health care financed by general health insurers, with carve-out arrangements being associated with a higher likelihood of using prescription drug treatments.

Each outpatient and prescription drug claim can accommodate two ICD-9 diagnostic codes. In identifying cases of major depression, we used ICD-9 codes 296.2 (major depressive disorder, single episode) and 296.3 (major depressive disorder, recurrent episode) to define patients diagnosed with major depression. We do this for three reasons. First, the clinical trials literature has for the most part employed these definitions in their entry criteria. Second, chart reviews have indicated that the specificity of these two diagnoses is high (i.e., the proportion of true positives and false negatives is high, while the proportion of false positives is very low). Third, clinicians could employ a more ambiguous diagnosis such as "depression not elsewhere classified" or "neurotic depression." That clinicians designated their diagnosis as either 296.2 or 296.3 indicates a conscious act of volition.[30]

Using the diagnostic information and dates contained in the claims, we construct episodes of treatment. Because we do not directly observe symptoms in retrospective claims data, we cannot make our claims-based definition of an episode of treatment correspond directly to an episode of

---

28. Specialty carve-out management occurs when a portion of the health risk is managed separately from the rest of health care. See Frank, McGuire, and Newhouse (1995) for further discussion.

29. For discussion, see Goldman, McCulloch, and Sturm (1998), and Ma and McGuire (1998).

30. Thus we exclude other 296 ICD-9 diagnoses, depression not elsewhere classified, as well as some other broad depression-related conditions such as neurotic depression.

the illness.[31] When claims data indicate that psychotherapeutic drugs were prescribed, we consider the number of days of treatment provided by the prescription as the time period over which an individual received care. We follow American Psychiatric Association (1993) guidelines in defining an episode of depression as new if a diagnosis is preceded by a period of at least eight weeks of not meeting clinical criteria for depression.[32] Thus we use an eight-week period without treatment to define new treatment episodes. In preliminary analyses, we experimented with alternative definitions, such as those involving six- or twelve-week intervals; results were essentially unaffected. For treatments lasting longer than six months we count quantities of visits and drugs meeting guideline standards for acute care occurring with the first six months of care (e.g., fifteen psychotherapy visits even if year totals were twenty-five visits). To ensure that we consider the full set of claims associated with the acute phase of treatment, we exclude episodes beginning in the last six months of 1995, the last year in our sample.

When these criteria were applied to the MEDSTAT data set, we defined 18,920 episodes of acute phase outpatient care over the 1991–95 period. Because we cannot fully observe the treatment received for censored cases, we confine our attention to the 15,750 uncensored episodes in which we observe at least eight weeks without treatment before the beginning of an episode; as noted above, 1,548 episodes beginning in the last six months of 1995 were also excluded. In order to limit the sample to less severe forms of depression, we eliminated individuals with episodes involving inpatient hospital treatment for a mental illness any time during the five years. This reduced the number of episodes to 10,067.

Using information on procedures (e.g., type of visit, whether drug prescribed) as given by the CPT4 codes, we can describe the composition of treatment that occurred within a treatment episode. Drug treatment is based on the national drug codes (NDC) reported on the claim. The NDC classification of antidepressant medications revealed use of seven TCAs, three SSRIs, two other serotonin-related drugs,[33] three MAO inhibitors, four anxiolytics, and four heterocyclics for treatment of depression. In terms of composition, 54 percent of the drug claims involved SSRIs, 19 percent TCAs, 19 percent anxiolytics, and 7 percent heterocyclics.[34]

In previous research, we have reported that in the MEDSTAT claims

31. For discussion of defining episodes of care, see Keeler et al. (1986) and Wingert et al. (1995).

32. We count days without treatment only after the number of days of supply in a drug prescription has been exhausted, thereby assuming full compliance with the daily recommended dosage.

33. These were brand name drugs Effexor and Serzone.

34. These compositional figures are consistent with IMS aggregate national sales data for antidepressant medication over this time period, as reported by Berndt, Cockburn, and Griliches (1996).

database, the share of treatment accounted for by treatment involving psychotherapy claims appeared to increase significantly in 1995, after having fallen steadily from 1991 to 1994.[35] Subsequent research has indicated to us that while procedure codes are missing for many outpatient claims—a common problem with claims data, the extent of missing claims in the MEDSTAT data set is particularly large in 1991–94. Thus, the apparent sudden increase in psychotherapy claims in 1995 could simply reflect considerable missing claims from 1991 through 1994. Hereafter we call the data underlying this previous research our "old" data set.

To identify missing psychotherapy claims not explicitly delineated by CPT4 codes, for our "new" data set we have developed an algorithm in which a psychotherapy procedure code is assigned to claims with missing CPT4 codes if two visits are within fourteen days of each other, if they have the same charge, and if a previously psychotherapy-identified claim in the episode has the same charge.[36] Use of this algorithm contributed to an increase in the number of identified episodes.

Our primary analysis of the claims data considers only "pure" or "strict guideline" treatments. That is, initially we will only consider episodes of care that adhere strictly with treatment definitions as tested in the clinical trials literature. In this way we can directly link the "price" of an episode of a well-defined treatment to the price of other therapeutically similar treatments. However, we will also report results based on findings derived from episode treatment definitions that relax this stringent guideline restriction, in which we include treatments slightly below guideline criteria and those involving some continuation phase treatment.

In our strict guideline analyses we identify seven major classes of treatments that have been proven effective in the treatment of depression: (1) psychotherapy alone, six to fifteen visits "PT alone"; (2) short-term TCA treatment alone or with medical management—"TCA alone"; (3) short-term SSRI treatment alone or with medical management, 31–180 days—"SSRI alone"; (4) short-term TCA treatment (31–180 days) with some psychotherapy—"TCA+PT"; (5) short-term SSRI treatment (31–180 days) with some psychotherapy—"SSRI+PT"; (6) short-term combined TCA/SSRI treatment (31–180 days) with some psychotherapy—"TCA/SSRI+PT." With the exception of psychotherapy alone, episodes with anxiolytics also being prescribed are combined into the appropriate class defined above. Use of seven major classes of treatments in this new data set represents an expansion from the five used in our previously published research. Another significant change in the new data was to include epi-

---

35. See Frank, Berndt, and Busch (1999) and Frank, Busch, and Berndt (1998).

36. Additional checks were done to ensure that these newly identified psychotherapy visits were not in fact instead a sequence of medical management visits. Robustness checks revealed that only a small number of claims were reclassified when cost thresholds of about $50 were used to mark medical management from psychotherapy.

sodes that involved long-term treatments or those extending beyond twenty visits or six months. For those episodes we included the components of care consistent with the acute phase bundles specified above and excluded spending on the remainder of the "episode." Using this expanded definition of an episode, we are more likely to include continuation treatment in the analysis. This may be especially true in the later years as new recommendations about continuation treatment diffused into practice. Thus, the new data set may be "pricing" acute plus early continuation phase care in the later years. This would tend to bias an index upward. Evidence for this is reflected by an upward trend in the average duration of SSRI treatment during the five years (from 87 days in 1991 to 126 in 1995). This change contributed to a substantial increase in the number of cases used in the analyses.

The new data set also improved the definition of censoring. In the "old" data set, to limit our analysis to episodes for which we had information on the entire episode, all cases which included treatments in the last eight weeks of 1995 were eliminated. This means that more episodes were eliminated from 1995 than from any other year. More severe episodes in need of longer term treatment may therefore have been disproportionately dropped from previous analyses. This may have biased the price index downward. We have now corrected that "late '95" censoring problem by limiting our analysis to the first six months of treatment. As mentioned previously, to ensure we consider all treatments in the first six months of the episode, we do not consider episodes begun in the last half of 1995.

Finally, the new data set allows drug switching if it is consistent with standards of care in clinical trials. Again, the change would tend to increase the severity and complexity of the treated population. Drug switching has been increasing over time as new pharmaceutical agents have become available (SSRIs and serotonin-norepinephrine reuptake inhibitors [SNRIs]).

It is informative to compare episodes defined in our new data set with those in the old. As seen in table 12.1, the most obvious change is that the number and proportion of episodes receiving guideline-compatible treatments increase very substantially, from 2,348 to 5,039, or from 23 percent to 50 percent. There are 2,980 guideline-compatible episodes in the new data set that were not in the old, and 289 in the old that do not appear in the new.

There is also some evidence suggesting that in the new data set, a greater number of episodes are associated with other mental health comorbidities. While new-old differences are relatively small in terms of substance abuse comorbidities in guideline-compatible episodes (2.5 versus 2.8 percent), 17.9 percent of acute phase depression episodes in the new data set simultaneously involve treatment of schizophrenia or bipolar depression, while in the old data set this proportion was a smaller 15.8 percent. For the various panic and anxiety comorbidities, the new-old proportions are 3.3

Table 12.1   **Comparison of Data Sets Based on New and Old Episode Definitions**

	New Data	Old Data	In New but Not in Old Data	In Old but Not in New Data
Total episodes	10,067	10,368		
Episodes guideline compatible	5,039	2,348	2,980	289
Mental health comorbidities (%)[a]				
Substance abuse	2.5	2.8	2.6	4.2
Schizophrenia/bipolar	17.9	15.8	20.1	23.2
Anxiety/panic	3.3	2.9	3.9	6.2
Sum of other medical comorbidities (%)[b]				
0	48.2	48.3	47.5	41.5
1	37.9	36.2	39.3	38.8
≥2	13.9	15.6	13.2	19.7

[a]Panic/anxiety diagnoses are ICD-9 300, 300.1–300.4; schizophrenia/bipolar are all 295s, 296.0–296.1, 296.4–296.8; other includes obsessive/compulsive disorders (300.3), bulimia (783.6), depression not otherwise specified (311), and dysthymia (300.4).

[b]Other medical comorbidities are sense organs, circulatory system, cerebrovascular, digestive system, kidneys, prostate, pregnancy, and nervous system.

versus 2.9 percent. The literature, as well as our own discussions with clinicians, suggests that (1) major depression and bipolar illness are often mistaken for one another, and (2) treatment of depression with comorbid psychoses and substance abuse is both common and difficult. We interpret differences between the new and old data sets as therefore moving us away from the more pristine world of clinical trials to a more realistic and more complicated treatment environment in which mental illness comorbidities are more prevalent.

It is worth noting that differences between the new and old data sets in terms of other, nonmental health comorbidities are rather minor. As seen in the bottom panel of table 12.1, for example, the proportion having no such comorbidities is 48.2 percent in the new data set, and 48.3 percent in the old; relative to the old data set, the proportion having one other medical comorbidity is slightly higher (37.9 percent versus 36.2 percent), but is slightly lower for two or more comorbidities (13.9 versus 15.6 percent).

12.5.2   On Guideline Compatibility

Earlier we noted that of the 10,067 episodes identified in the new data set from 1991 through 1995, 5,039 (50 percent) were guideline compatible. It is interesting to note that in our new data set the proportion of episodes receiving guideline-compatible treatment rose from 35 percent in 1991 to 42 percent in 1992, then increased sharply in 1993 to 56 percent, and remained at 56 percent in 1994 and 1995.

The interpretation of guideline-incompatible treatments is difficult with claims data. For example, 1,308 episodes (33 percent of the 3,965) treated with psychotherapy alone consisted of a single visit. In addition, 1,672 or 16 percent of all episodes received neither psychotherapy nor an anti-depressant drug. Such single visits might have taken place for the purpose of "ruling out" major depression as the relevant condition to be treated in favor of a somatic condition or another mental disorder. In such cases, the visit should not be viewed as "inappropriate treatment" but rather as an appropriate assessment, consistent with the Depression Guideline Panel statement (1993, 36): "Effective treatment rests on accurate diagnosis. The practitioner must first determine whether the patient has a clinical depres-sion or is simply suffering normal sadness or distress. . . . For patients who have very mild cases of major depression or whose diagnosis is unclear and who are not in immediate danger or are not suffering significant functional impairment, the practitioner may want to schedule one or two additional weekly evaluation visits to determine whether symptoms will abate with-out formal treatment. . . ." The implication of this is that with retrospective claims data, distinguishing treatment and assessment is quite uncertain. Hence we are somewhat unclear as to whether only 50 to 60 percent of care lies on the production frontier, or whether another 10 to 20 percent of treatments were dealt with properly but did not require treatment of the type studied here. It is important to note here that our use of guideline standards of care imposes a rather unrealistic shape on the production function for treatment of depression. It takes on a step function form. For example, if one were to receive six psychotherapy visits for treatment of depression, our analysis would treat the case as "effective," whereas four or five visits would be viewed as "ineffective." This is unlikely to be an accurate representation of clinical reality. Nevertheless, there is little sys-tematic analysis upon which to make alternative assumptions. Thus, we use the step function production model as a point of departure.

With these difficulties in appropriate interpretation as a caveat, we now examine in greater detail the extent of guideline compatibility in the vari-ous treatment bundles of the new data set.

Of the 10,067 episodes, 3,765 were treated with psychotherapy alone, and 376 with psychotherapy and anxiolytics. Within the claims data, no distinction was made between different types of psychotherapy. Consider-ing the 3,044 treatments involving fifty-minute psychotherapy sessions, we find that 1,658 received four or fewer visits, and 800 only a single visit. Of the 921 episodes involving twenty-minute psychotherapy alone, 508 in-volved just one brief visit, while 178 episodes were treated with between two and five brief sessions. An additional twenty episodes involved some form of group therapy treatment, with only 25 percent of those having more than three visits.

While clinical trials data indicate that individuals show partial response to psychotherapy with six weeks of treatment (with weekly sessions) and remission in twelve weeks, published guidelines for the treatment of acute phase depression do not indicate any demonstrated effectiveness for fewer than six visits. The benefits of short psychotherapy visits, in the absence of antidepressant medication, have not been studied and therefore cannot be considered either effective or ineffective treatment. Although clinical trials and published treatment guidelines indicate psychotherapeutic treatment alone is an effective treatment, in our data, of the 3,044 episodes given this treatment, only 1,386 episodes (46 percent) can be considered to have completed a psychotherapy regimen that is consistent with guideline treatments.[37]

Turning attention now to treatments involving antidepressant medications, we begin by noting that claims data do not include information on how many days medication was actually taken; as a proxy, we use the number of days of treatment for which a prescription was filled.

Of the 10,067 episodes considered, 231 were treated with TCA either alone (176) or in combination with anxiolytic medication (55). Of these 231 episodes, 55 (24 percent) were treated with fewer than thirty days of medication and 29 were treated with ten or fewer days. Generally, the clinical literature (and the APA guidelines) indicates that while patients may show some improvement from antidepressant medication by the end of the first week, full response to acute phase depression may take four to six weeks.

An additional 741 episodes were treated with SSRIs either alone (604) or in combination with anxiolytic medication (137); 77 (10 percent) of these episodes were treated with fewer than thirty days of medication. Because individuals have differing reactions to drugs, some individuals are appropriately treated with one class of antidepressants, and then switched to another class. In our sample, 95 episodes were treated with both TCAs and SSRIs, but 20 of these episodes had less than thirty days of both drugs.

Several episodes were treated with medications other than SSRIs and TCAs. In our sample 10 episodes were treated with MAO inhibitors, while 164 were treated with heterocyclics. An additional 124 episodes were treated with antianxiety medication alone, a protocol which has not been approved by the FDA for the treatment of major depression. The use of antianxiety medication in the treatment of depression remains controversial. The use of alprazolam may be appropriate, if other medication is contraindicated. There is no clinical trial evidence for the efficacious use of other anxiolytic medications.[38]

Finally, in terms of combination treatments, the share of episodes treated with psychotherapy and antidepressant medication grew over time. Over the entire five-year period, 552 treatment episodes involved both

37. For a related discussion, see Katon et al. (1992).
38. See Wells et al. (1994, 1996) for further discussion.

some TCA and some psychotherapy, while 2,169 included both SSRI and some psychotherapy. A large share (36 percent) of the episodes treated with combination treatments had three or fewer psychotherapy visits, and an additional 382 episodes were treated with some TCA, some SSRI, and some psychotherapy.

12.5.3 Comparison with Results from Other Studies

The patterns of care observed in this data set raise issues related to the likely effectiveness of treatment, given the substantial proportion of episodes involving guideline-incompatible treatments. One potential criticism of the patterns of treatment bundle data presented above is that they are based on retrospective claims data. Claims data are useful in that the retrospective medical treatment of many individuals can be analyzed efficiently and at minimal expense. In addition, such observational data reveal the "real world" practice of medicine, not the pristine clinical trial environment. Claims data are also used for quality assessment by organizations constructing "report cards" on health care organizations. Yet claims data have been fairly criticized for several reasons. The accuracy of diagnoses and recorded data are sometimes questioned, and omissions in records are common. For example, depression has been shown to be underdiagnosed by primary care physicians and overdiagnosed by psychiatric clinicians (Schulberg et al. 1985).

Other studies have found treatment patterns for depression that are generally consistent with the patterns we observe here. The Medical Outcomes Study (MOS) consisted of 635 individuals diagnosed with depression or with current depressive symptoms for whom data were collected by self-administered questionnaires, patient diaries, phone interviews, and health examinations. The MOS found that only 23 percent of depressed patients had used an antidepressant medication in the prior month or used it daily for a month or more in the prior six months. Of those patients using an antidepressant medication, 39 percent used an inappropriately low dose (Wells et al. 1994).

The MOS did not report number of psychotherapy visits. Instead it reported "counseling," defining it as three or more minutes of counseling during the screening interview. This makes comparison with published standards of care difficult. Although 90 percent of patients of mental health specialists were counseled, among general medical practitioners where most study participants were treated, only 20 percent of managed care and 40 percent of fee-for-service patients were counseled.

Another study of eighty-eight outpatients enrolled in the Clinical Research Collaborative Program on the Psychobiology of Depression of the National Institute of Mental Health (NIMH) found that prior to entry into the study, only 19 percent of patients received an adequate dose and duration of antidepressant medication, while 24 percent received some antianxiety medication. Regarding psychotherapy visits, 44 percent were seen for at least one hour weekly (Keller, Lavori, Klerman et al. 1986).

Thus, the substantial proportion of patients in the MOS and NIMH studies apparently not obtaining efficacious treatments, while perhaps surprising, is consistent with the treatment patterns found in the claims data we observe here.

For our purposes of constructing price indexes for the treatment of acute phase major depression, we must decide whether to utilize the data suggestive of treatment not consistent with Food and Drug Administration (FDA) approvals and Agency for Health Care Policy and Research (AHCPR) guidelines. Since the interpretation of such treatments is problematic, in our "strict guideline" analysis we confine our attention to episodes of treatment defined as being consistent with AHCPR guidelines; however, in a separate analysis we also include treatment bundles that are "close" to guideline standards. Additional research on guideline-incompatible care and the shape of the production function for treatment of depression is currently under way.

12.6   Quantities and Prices of Alternative Treatment Bundles

We begin our empirical analysis by characterizing quantities and prices of the seven treatment bundles. In table 12.2 we report guideline-compatible treatment quantities by year. Censoring at the beginning and end of our time span implies that in 1991 and in 1995, about 1,500 episodes are identified, whereas in 1992–94 the number is considerably larger at about 2,400 per year. The two most common treatment bundles are SSRI+PT and PT alone. Because of varying sample size by year, quantity trends are more easily discerned by examining quantity proportions rather than absolute levels; guideline-compatible treatment bundle quantity proportions are reported in table 12.3.

A number of notable trends appear in table 12.3. First, there has been

Table 12.2   **Guideline-Compatible Treatment Bundle Quantities, by Year**

Treatment	1991	1992	1993	1994	1995	Total
PT alone	214	311	321	311	229	1,386
TCA alone	32	45	43	37	19	176
SSRI alone	52	113	188	205	110	668
TCA+PT	63	111	129	73	33	409
SSRI+PT	125	292	528	644	400	1,989
TCA/SSRI	9	14	23	23	6	75
TCA/SSRI+PT	27	53	121	98	37	336
Sum	522	939	1,353	1,391	834	5,039
Total episodes	1,479	2,211	2,426	2,468	1,483	10,067
Percent guideline-compatible	35.3	42.5	55.8	56.4	56.4	50.1

Table 12.3   Guideline-Compatible Treatment Bundle Quantity Proportions, by Year

Treatment	1991	1992	1993	1994	1995	Total
PT alone	0.409	0.331	0.237	0.224	0.275	0.275
TCA alone	0.061	0.048	0.032	0.027	0.023	0.035
SSRI alone	0.100	0.120	0.139	0.147	0.132	0.133
TCA+PT	0.121	0.118	0.095	0.052	0.040	0.081
SSRI+PT	0.239	0.311	0.390	0.463	0.480	0.395
TCA/SSRI	0.017	0.015	0.017	0.017	0.001	0.015
TCA/SSRI+PT	0.052	0.056	0.089	0.070	0.044	0.067

a very substantial decline in PT alone treatments, from 41 percent in 1991 to 22 percent in 1994, and then up slightly to nearly 28 percent in 1995. Second, for the medication only treatments, SSRI alone has grown from 10 to 13 percent, even as TCA alone declined from 6 to 2 percent; the sum of the two medication only treatments has remained relatively constant at 15 to 16 percent. Third, most of the compositional change among treatment bundles has involved the medication-psychotherapy combination treatments. While the TCA+PT combination fell from 12 to 4 percent between 1991 and 1995, the SSRI+PT treatment share doubled, from 24 to 48 percent of all treatments. By 1995, the SSRI+PT combination had become the modal treatment bundle.

In table 12.4 we report the average supply price for each treatment bundle, by year; recall that this supply price captures the sum of payments from insurers and patients/consumers to providers. As is seen there, annual price movements represent a mix of increases and decreases. Between 1993 and 1994, for example, the price of one bundle increases and that of all other six bundles decreases, while for 1994–95. price movements are reversed—six up, and one down. Of particular interest is the extent to which compositional changes in quantities of treatment bundles appear to be negatively related to changes in relative prices. When entries in tables 12.3 and 12.4 are considered together, it becomes clear that compositional quantity changes do not follow simple conceptions of downward-sloping demand curves where quantity and "price" changes are clearly negatively related. From 1991 to 1992, for example, even as the supply price of SSRI alone more than doubled from $52 to $113, the SSRI alone share increased from 4 to 6 percent; similarly, the cost of the SSRI+PT combination bundle increased by about 150 percent from $125 to $292 between 1991 and 1992, yet the quantity share grew from 24 percent to 31 percent. It is important to note that the quality of treatment bundles may vary (e.g., side effects). Also, insurance coverage drives a wedge between the supply and demand prices. Both of these factors may help explain observed patterns and they are discussed below.

This positive relationship between changes in supply price and quantity share is observed in other years as well. From 1992 to 1993, for example, the supply price of TCA+PT fell by about 18 percent from $882 to $745, but its quantity share also dropped from 12 percent to 10 percent. Between 1993 and 1994, while the cost of PT alone fell about 5 percent from $866 to $818, the PT quantity share fell from 26 percent to 23 percent. Similarly, for both TCA alone and TCA+PT, between 1993 and 1994 both prices and quantity shares fell.

What these quantity and supply price data suggest, therefore, is that factors other than supply price are likely to have induced compositional changes among treatment bundles for acute phase major depression. Prominent among these, we conjecture, is the increased knowledge and experience gained by physicians on the efficacy and effectiveness of the SSRI medications, particularly in combination with a limited amount of psychotherapy and changing insurance arrangements.

Although compositional changes among treatment bundles may reflect a host of price and nonprice influences, it is clear that the dollar expenditure shares among the seven treatment bundles have been greatly affected between 1991 and 1995. These dramatic changes are evident in table 12.5. While the expenditure share going to PT alone fell from 45 percent to

Table 12.4   **Average Supply Price of Treatment Bundle, in Dollars, by Year**

Treatment	1991	1992	1993	1994	1995	Average[a]
PT alone	876	853	866	818	819	846
TCA alone	236	310	318	204	226[b]	267
SSRI alone	311	387	309	308	344	328
TCA+PT	932	882	745	706	941	820
SSRI+PT	941	983	949	958	972	961
TCA/SSRI	649[b]	361[b]	449	423	328[b]	439
TCA/SSRI+PT	1,002	1,021	1,062	953	977	1,010
Average[a]	805	817	802	788	825	

[a]Denotes a weighted average.
[b]Denotes a cell with less than twenty observations.

Table 12.5   **Total Expenditure Shares by Treatment Bundle, by Year**

Treatment	1991	1992	1993	1994	1995	Average
PT alone	0.446	0.346	0.256	0.232	0.273	0.310
TCA alone	0.018	0.018	0.013	0.007	0.006[a]	0.012
SSRI alone	0.038	0.057	0.054	0.058	0.055	0.052
TCA+PT	0.140	0.128	0.089	0.047	0.045	0.090
SSRI+PT	0.280	0.374	0.461	0.563	0.565	0.449
TCA/SSRI	0.014[a]	0.007[a]	0.010	0.009	0.003[a]	0.008
TCA/SSRI+PT	0.064	0.071	0.118	0.085	0.053	0.078

[a]Denotes a cell with less than twenty observations.

27 percent between 1991 and 1995, by 1995 the SSRI+PT bundle was responsible for more than half (56 percent) of all dollar expenditures, up from 28 percent in 1991. In 1991 the three single bundles of PT alone, TCA alone, and SSRI alone accounted for 50 percent of all treatment dollars in 1991, but by 1995 they only captured 33 percent of expenditures.

Together, the patterns observed in tables 12.2 through 12.5 suggest to us that rather than PT and the SSRIs being viewed as simple single substitutes in the production of treatments for acute phase depression, they are more accurately envisaged as being complementary in the sense that the PT+SSRI combination has now become the modal treatment.

To this point, our discussion of treatment bundle price has focused on the supply price—the sum of payments received from insurers and patients/consumers. The demand price notion reflects the fact that patients receiving treatment for acute phase depression provide direct payments in the form of copayments and deductibles. In table 12.6 we report average demand prices for each of the seven treatment bundles, annually. Trends in the demand price differ quite markedly from those of the supply price.

Recall from table 12.4 that the average supply price across all bundles fell slightly from $805 in 1991 to $788 in 1994, and then increased to $825 in 1995. In contrast, as seen in table 12.6, from 1991 to 1994 the average demand price increased from $100 to $105, and then it increased very sharply to $128 in 1995. This sharp increase of 22 percent between 1994 and 1995 in the average demand price across all treatment bundles reflects corresponding jumps in the PT alone (26 percent), SSRI alone (19 percent), SSRI+PT (17 percent), and TCA/SSRI+PT (21 percent) bundles.

Two main factors may account for changes in demand prices that differ so starkly from supply price changes. First are the changes in cost-sharing provisions. These are documented in the MEDSTAT data set. The MEDSTAT data indicated to us that in 1995, for a number of insurance plans, benefit changes were introduced that substantially increased the copayments and deductibles required of plan enrollees.[39] Second is the tendency to use out-of-network providers in the context of managed care. Coverage of care provided by nonnetwork providers typically carries higher copayments than does care received from a network clinician. During the time period observed, networks were becoming more restrictive and behavioral health carve-outs were introduced, which may have increased the share of care provided by nonnetwork providers. The impact of these benefit design changes can be seen by computing the portion of the total treatment cost

39. Data from Marion Merrell Dow's *Managed Care Digest* (1993–1994, 1996) indicate that over all HMOs surveyed, average copayment per prescription rose from $6.78 in 1993 to $7.43 in 1995 for brand name drugs, and from $4.75 to $5.22 for generics. While the MEDSTAT increases appear to be larger, they also include deductibles for psychotherapy visits, not just copayments for drugs.

Table 12.6   **Average Demand Price of Treatment Bundle, in Dollars, by Year**

Treatment	1991	1992	1993	1994	1995	Average[a]
PT alone	121	122	122	123	155	128
TCA alone	39	46	46	48	51	46
SSRI alone	23	30	24	27	32	27
TCA+PT	128	124	116	113	117	120
SSRI+PT	102	105	115	121	142	120
TCA/SSRI	43[b]	47[b]	46	51	21[b]	45
TCA/SSRI+PT	102	121	131	135	163	132
Average[a]	100	101	102	105	128	

[a]Denotes a weighted average.
[b]Denotes a cell with less than twenty observations.

borne directly by the patient, that is, computing the ratio of the demand price in table 12.6 to the corresponding supply price in table 12.4; we call this the OOPPs ratio.

For the SSRI alone bundle, the OOPPs ratio increased only marginally, from 7 percent in 1991 to 9 percent in 1995. For the very low total cost TCA alone bundle, the OOPPs ratio increased more markedly, from 16 percent in 1991 to 23 percent in 1995; in absolute terms, this additional burden borne by the patient was only $12 (from $39 to $51). For the combination treatments involving PT and the SSRIs, however, the increase was much more substantial, both in terms of OOPPs ratio and absolute dollar burden. In the SSRI+PT bundle, for example, the OOPPs ratio rose from 11 percent to 15 percent between 1991 and 1995, with the demand price increasing $40 from $102 to $142; even more dramatically, for the TCA/SSRI+PT bundle the OOPPs ratio rose from 10 percent to 17 percent, while the demand price jumped $61 from $102 in 1991 to $163 in 1995. The changes resulted from increased cost sharing for psychotherapy.

One important implication of these findings is that when considering construction of price indexes for the treatment of a medical condition such as depression, it is imperative that demand prices be distinguished from supply prices, for changes in insurance plan design benefits over time can introduce sharp differences into their time trends.

12.7   Aggregate Price Indexes for the Treatment of Depression

With the prices and quantities of the seven treatment bundles as elementary building blocks, we now move on to the construction of aggregate supply and aggregate demand price indexes. A variety of price indexes can be computed, each having implicit assumptions on the extent of ex ante substitutability among the seven bundles. Since we have discussed these alternative index number formulas and underlying assumptions else-where,[40] and since they are well known in the literature on index numbers,[41] we provide only a very brief discussion here.

Fixed quantity weight indexes such as Laspeyres and the Paasche in-dexes reflect an assumption of zero ex ante substitutability among the seven treatment bundles; the Laspeyres employs a base-period fixed weight, the Paasche the final-period fixed weight. The Cobb-Douglas em-ploys a fixed expenditure weight (here, equal to the mean expenditure share for each bundle over time), and assumes that the elasticity of substi-tution among treatment bundles equals unity for all pairs of bundles. When demand curves are downward sloping and bundle prices are all in-creasing, between any two adjacent time periods the Laspeyres price index is greater than the Paasche.

In general the chained, or sequentially updated, price indexes are viewed as being preferable to the fixed-weight indexes. The Törnqvist discrete ap-proximation to the Divisia, and the Fisher ideal, make no a priori assump-tions on the extent of substitutability among treatment bundles. The Törn-qvist weights percentage changes in each of the treatment bundles by the arithmetic mean of the expenditure share in the two time periods, whereas the Fisher ideal is the geometric mean of the corresponding Laspeyres and Paasche indexes. A commonly observed empirical pattern is that the Törnqvist and Fisher ideal price indexes are very close to one another, and both tend to be in between the Laspeyres and Paasche price indexes.

With this as background, we now report results of various aggregate price index calculations, first in table 12.7 as viewed from the supply price (i.e., PPI) vantage, and then in table 12.8 from the demand side (i.e., CPI).

The most striking result that immediately emerges from table 12.7 is that, regardless of which index number procedure is employed, over the 1991–95 period the treatment price index for acute phase major depression has hardly changed, remaining at 1.00 or falling slightly to around 0.97. Each of the price indexes reveals an increase from 1991 to 1992, they all fall in 1993, all fall again in 1994 (to between 0.95 and 0.97), and then all increase in 1995. Given some of the data problems in 1995, this last finding should be viewed with caution. Differences among the various fixed and chained indexes are relatively minor.

By comparison, in the bottom panel of table 12.7 we report various PPIs published by the BLS. Over the 1991–95 period, the aggregate PPI for all finished goods increased about 5 percent, and that for antidepressant prescription drugs increased by about 20 percent. From 1992 to 1995, the PPI for psychiatric hospital services increased by about 10 percent, while between 1994 and 1995 the overall health services PPI increased 2.4 per-

---

40. See Frank, Berndt, and Busch (1999) and Frank, Busch, and Berndt (1998).
41. See, for example, Diewert (1976, 1981).

Table 12.7   **Alternative Aggregate Producer ("Supply") Price Indexes for the Treatment of Acute Phase Major Depression**

Price Index	1991	1992	1993	1994	1995
Fixed weights					
Laspeyres	1.000	1.003	0.975	0.931	0.976
Paasche	1.000	1.027	0.996	0.974	1.000
Cobb-Douglas	1.000	1.018	0.985	0.953	0.992
Chained weights					
Laspeyres	1.000	1.003	0.969	0.938	0.968
Paasche	1.000	1.011	0.976	0.952	0.978
Fisher ideal	1.000	1.007	0.97	0.945	0.973
Törnqvist	1.000	1.007	0.972	0.945	0.972
BLS PPIs[a]					
Aggregate PPI	1.000	1.012	1.025	1.031	1.051
Health services				1.000	1.024
Antidepressants	1.000	1.076	1.134	1.162	1.204
Psychiatric hospitals		1.000	1.024	1.060	109.9

[a]BLS indexes are normalized to appropriate base year.

Table 12.8   **Alternative Aggregate Consumer ("Demand") Price Indexes for the Treatment of Acute Phase Major Depression**

Price Index	1991	1992	1993	1994	1995
Fixed weights					
Laspeyres	1.000	1.028	1.041	1.063	1.266
Paasche	1.000	1.037	1.080	1.118	1.334
Cobb-Douglas	1.000	1.037	1.069	1.110	1.300
Chained weights					
Laspeyres	1.000	1.028	1.048	1.081	1.281
Paasche	1.000	1.032	1.065	1.104	1.317
Fisher ideal	1.000	1.030	1.056	1.092	1.299
Törnqvist	1.000	1.030	1.057	1.093	1.298
BLS CPIs[a]					
All Items	1.000	1.030	1.061	1.088	1.119
Medical Care	1.000	1.075	1.146	1.205	1.266
Prescription drugs	1.000	1.075	1.117	1.155	1.177

[a]BLS indexes are normalized to 1991 base year.

cent. Thus, while our various supply price indexes for the treatment of acute phase depression are either flat or very slightly falling, they all grow considerably less than the various official PPIs. The "real," all-items CPI inflation-adjusted price index for the treatment of acute phase depression has fallen over the 1991–95 time span.

Index number afficionados might notice, however, that the typically observed inequality relationships among the Laspeyres and Paasche price indexes are not present here. For example, for both fixed- and chained-weight versions, the Paasche price index is larger than the Laspeyres. The reason this occurs is that, as noted in section 12.6 above, in a number of cases changes in treatment bundle supply prices and quantity shares are positively rather than negatively correlated. Because the price index calculations do not take into account factors affecting demand other than price, and because consumers do not face supply prices, there is the appearance of a positive relation between quantity and supply price. We discuss other price-related issues in section 12.8 below, where we deal with hedonic price indexes. Finally, note that as is usually the case, the Fisher ideal and Törnqvist indexes are always in between the chained Paasche and Laspeyres indexes.

We now turn to a discussion of aggregate price indexes viewed from the demand side, or the patients' consumers' OOPPs. As seen in table 12.8, the demand aggregate price indexes have very different time trends than do the supply aggregate price indexes. Each of the price indexes exhibits an increase between each pair of adjacent years, with the 1994–95 price increase being particularly dramatic. By 1995, the fixed-weight price indexes (normalized to 1.000 in 1991) ranged between 1.27 and 1.33, while the chained indexes had a slightly smaller variation, between 1.28 and 1.32. Between 1991 and 1994, the price indexes increased by only about 10 percent, but in 1995 the increase was much larger, averaging around 20 percent. As discussed in section 12.6, we attribute this sharp increase to benefit design changes in 1995 that increased patient copayments and deductibles.

The discrepancy between the PPI and CPI results highlights several important points in interpretation of the data. First is that if the elasticity with respect to the demand price is less than unity (in absolute value), spending must increase. Because cost sharing increased notably and demand estimates suggest an elasticity of less than unity, it is not surprising that the CPI increases over time. Second, and more important, is the welfare interpretation of these changes. It is well known that low levels of demand side cost sharing in medical insurance are associated with welfare losses due to moral hazard (Newhouse et al. 1993). Thus, changes in the CPI for depression may reflect reduced moral hazard in addition to higher prices per unit of "effective care." Research by Manning and Marquis (1989) suggests that 50 percent cost sharing for mental health care was optimal in a fee-for-service context. Because observed rates in our data are quite a bit lower, gains from reduced moral hazard may be significant. Since interpretation of the CPI is unclear, we focus more attention on the PPI.

12.8   Hedonic Price Indexes

An enduring issue in price index measurement is how one should make adjustments for quality change. Quality adjustments could be significant here, for it is reasonable to expect that the characteristics and attributes of the acute phase of treatment for depression have changed over time, and that changes in the underlying patient population might also have occurred.

Although its use to date in the medical marketplace has been limited, the hedonic price approach has been used in many other contexts to adjust price movements for (not fully priced) quality changes.[42] We now briefly outline our implementation of hedonic price measurement for the treatment of acute phase depression.

We expect that treatment costs for depression are affected by patient characteristics, various attributes of antidepressant medications, the type of treatment given the patient, and the year in which the treatment episode began. Patient characteristics for which we have data include the patient's gender, age, general medical condition (measured by the number of comorbid general medical conditions, as noted on the bottom of table 12.1), the industry in which the plan enrollee is employed (transportation, communication, and utilities; services; or government), and information on the patient's mental health comorbidities. With respect to these mental health comorbidities, we construct dummy variables for whether the patient is also diagnosed with a substance abuse disorder, a panic/anxiety disorder, schizophrenia or bipolar depression, depression not otherwise specified, and whether the current episode involves a recurrence of major depression. For attributes of the various antidepressant medications, we employ data on the half-life of the medication and on the number of side effects that frequently accompany use of the medication.[43] Regarding treatments, we create dummy variables for each of the seven guideline-compatible treatment bundles described earlier. We also create a dummy variable indicating whether at the start of the episode the individual was enrolled in a behavioral health carve-out. Finally, we create dummy variables indicating the year in which the treatment episode began.

The dependent variables in the hedonic regressions are the natural logarithm of the supply price and of the demand price. The explanatory variables are the patient, medication, treatment, and time variables discussed above. The set of omitted dummy variables, and thus the reference case, is that for a female; where the enrollee is employed in the transportation, communication, or utilities industries; has none of the mental health comorbidities noted above; is not being treated for a recurrent episode of acute phase depression; treatment consists of PT alone; and the treatment episode began in 1991. Parameter estimates for the supply price equation

---

42. For an introductory discussion to the hedonic method, see Griliches (1988), chapters 7 and 8, and Berndt (1991), chapter 4. Applications in the medical context include Trajtenberg (1990) and Berndt, Cockburn, and Griliches (1996).

43. The side effect data are discussed in detail in Berndt, Cockburn, and Griliches (1996). We sum up the 0 (rare) to 4 (common) ratings across the various side effects. Here we also assume that psychotherapy has no side effects.

are in the left-hand panel of table 12.9, while estimates for demand price equation are in the right-hand panel. A number of results are worth mentioning in detail. We begin with the supply price.

First, characteristics of the patient and his or her illness have a statistically significant impact on treatment costs. While age does not appear to affect the supply price, mental health comorbidities such as anxiety/panic, schizophrenia/bipolar depression, and depression not otherwise specified all have a positive and significant impact. Somewhat surprisingly, comorbid substance abuse has a negative coefficient estimate, although not significant. The sum of the patient's other general medical comorbidities is also negative, but not significant. Finally, treatment costs for patients in which the enrollee is employed in the services or government sectors are considerably lower than if the industry involves transportation, communications, or utilities.

Second, attributes of the antidepressant medications also affect supply prices of treatment, even when one controls for type of treatment. Specifically, within the various bundles involving prescription drugs, greater side effects are associated with lower supply prices (lower side effects with higher supply prices), and increased half-life of the drug (mitigating the negative impacts of occasionally forgetting to take the medication) also raises the supply price. Relative to PT alone, treatment with TCA alone or SSRI alone reduces the supply price significantly, while use of SSRI + PT or TCA/SSRI + PT increases supply price.

Somewhat surprisingly, we find that whether at the beginning of the treatment episode the patient was enrolled in a mental health carve-out has no significant impact on supply price. To check whether the carve-out impact was diluted because of differential treatment bundles used by the carve-out, we also estimated a supply price equation in which the treatment bundle dummy variables were deleted; results are given in the second column of parameter estimates in table 12.9. Although the goodness of fit was reduced considerably when the treatment bundle variables were deleted, the carve-out parameter estimate remained insignificant. This may be due in part to the fact that the comparison conditions involved managed indemnity arrangements which tend to negotiate price discounts and shift care patterns.

Of particular interest are the parameter estimates on the 1992–95 yearly dummy variables. In the context of the hedonic price equation, these parameter estimates indicate how the supply price changed relative to 1991, holding constant the various patient characteristics, medication attributes, and the treatment bundle composition. Each of the four parameter estimates is small and insignificantly different from zero; hedonic price indexes computed as antilogarithms of these coefficients are 1.049, 1.004, 0.980, and 1.027 for 1992 through 1995, respectively (1991 = 1.000). These quality-adjusted hedonic price indexes are consistent with traditional aggregate supply price indexes reported in table 12.7 above. Adjusting for

Table 12.9   **Parameter Estimates from Hedonic Price Regressions**

Variable	Supply Price ("PPI") Equations		Demand Price ("CPI") Equations	
Constant	6.528	6.587	4.614	4.658
	(112.60)	(98.91)	(51.88)	(47.39)
Male	−0.016	−0.005	−0.090	−0.056
	(0.75)	(0.18)	(2.26)	(1.29)
Age	0.003	0.000	0.011	0.008
	(3.38)	(0.09)	(6.71)	(4.19)
Anxiety/panic	0.258	0.350	0.126	0.266
	(5.68)	(7.06)	(0.89)	(1.84)
Schizophrenia/bipolar	0.235	0.393	0.233	0.458
	(9.94)	(14.62)	(5.86)	(10.56)
Other depression	0.128	0.183	0.070	0.125
	(5.32)	(6.16)	(1.75)	(2.61)
Substance abuse	−0.136	−0.093	−0.529	−0.478
	(1.38)	(0.87)	(2.71)	(2.36)
Recurrent	0.080	0.124	0.050	0.132
	(4.04)	(5.32)	(1.44)	(3.42)
Sum medical	−0.025	−0.024	−0.029	−0.031
comorbidities	(2.04)	(1.58)	(1.29)	(1.24)
Government	−0.121	−0.172	−0.858	−0.936
	(3.07)	(3.74)	(17.21)	(16.10)
Services	−0.184	−0.225	−0.991	−1.053
	(4.62)	(4.92)	(21.59)	(19.53)
Sum side effects	−0.084	−0.129	0.025	−0.104
	(3.33)	(10.45)	(0.78)	(6.26)
Halflife	0.001	0.001	0.000	−0.001
	(4.01)	(4.47)	(1.31)	(3.53)
TCA alone	−1.170	n.a.	−1.483	n.a.
	(10.15)		(8.77)	
SSRI alone	−0.892	n.a.	−1.847	n.a.
	(13.50)		(19.18)	
TCA+PT	0.137	n.a.	−0.116	n.a.
	(1.38)		(0.89)	
SSRI+PT	0.195	n.a.	−0.122	n.a.
	(3.21)		(1.41)	
TCA/SSRI	−0.654	n.a.	−1.320	n.a.
	(5.71)		(8.32)	
TCA/SSRI+PT	0.301	n.a.	0.007	n.a.
	(4.15)		(0.07)	
Carve-out	−0.047	0.025	−0.028	0.092
	(0.90)	(0.43)	(0.44)	(1.24)
Start 1992	0.048	0.072	0.108	0.099
	(1.23)	(1.60)	(1.62)	(1.35)
Start 1993	0.004	0.054	0.114	0.094
	(0.11)	(1.21)	(1.71)	(1.30)
Start 1994	−0.021	0.025	0.145	0.097
	(0.54)	(0.58)	(2.09)	(1.31)
Start 1995	0.026	0.059	0.366	0.296
	(0.59)	(1.14)	(4.92)	(3.53)
R^2	0.328	0.088	0.277	0.083
RMSE	0.689	0.802	1.168	1.315
N	5,034	5,034	5,034	5,034

Notes: Absolute value of *t*-statistic in parentheses, from robust standard error. n.a. = not applicable.

various patient, medication, and treatment changes over time does not appear to affect the central finding that from 1991 to 1995 there was very little change in the supply price for treating acute phase major depression.

We now turn to the demand price hedonic equations, whose parameter estimates appear in the last two columns of table 12.9. In general, the pattern of results from the hedonic demand price equations involving quality attributes is not as strong and dramatic as is that of the hedonic supply price equation. For example, while parameter estimates on the patient's mental health comorbidities are of the same sign, in the demand price equation several of them are no longer statistically significant; attributes of the antidepressant medication are not significant as well. As with the supply equation, the mental health carve-out coefficient is insignificant.

However, in contrast to the supply price equation, for the demand hedonic price equation the parameter estimates on the 1992–95 year dummy variables are positive, and by 1994 and 1995 they become statistically significant. Relative to 1991 = 1.000, holding constant patient characteristics, medication attributes, and treatment composition, the hedonic price indexes for 1992–95 (computed as antilogs of the estimated parameters) are 1.114, 1.121, 1.155, and 1.443. Compared to the traditional aggregate demand price indexes reported in table 12.8, the time trends in these hedonic price indexes are broadly similar. While the traditional aggregate demand price index in table 12.8 averages about 1.30 in 1995, the corresponding hedonic quality-adjusted demand price index is 1.44; if one takes the antilog of the 1995 parameter estimate in table 12.9 minus one times the robust standard error, one obtains a 1995 price index of about 1.34, not much different from that in table 12.8. We conclude, therefore, that traditional and hedonic approaches to price index measurement yield broadly similar results.

12.9 Discussion

Our goal in this research project has been to extend previous research aimed at constructing CPI- and PPI-like medical price indexes that deal with prices of treatment episodes rather than prices of discrete inputs, that are based on transaction rather than list prices, that take quality changes and expected outcomes into account, and that employ more current expenditure weights in the aggregation computations. Although we have made considerable progress in achieving this goal, we believe a number of caveats are in order.

First, the results reported here differ considerably from those reported earlier in Frank, Busch, and Berndt (1998) and Frank, Berndt, and Busch (1999); there we reported substantial supply and demand price declines over the 1991–95 period. Although we are still examining why the differences occurred, we believe that the primary difference is that in the new data set we bring in many more patients. The evidence suggests that over time the new data set has an increasing share of patients with (1) more complicated conditions, (2) greater severity of illness, and (3) elements of longer term treatments such as continuation phase care. While the older data set may have corresponded with episodes more closely approximating the pristine world of clinical trials, the larger, new data set involves patients with more typical complicated illnesses.

It is therefore of interest to examine how robust are our new data set findings when one relaxes the strict guideline-compatible standards we imposed in defining episodes of care. We have created yet another data set, where we relaxed the definitions of the seven bundles. Bundles which consider drugs alone as treatment remain unchanged at 30 to 180 days of treatment. Definitions of bundles which include psychotherapy have been expanded such that the cost of up to twenty psychotherapy visits is now included in the cost of the episode. Furthermore, for the treatment "psychotherapy alone" we previously allowed for a minimum of five visits. This constraint was relaxed to include episodes treated with three or four visits. Appendix table 12A.1 shows that with the broader definition of standards of care the price indexes are largely unchanged. Specifically, they are rather flat, not falling below 2 percentage points in comparing 1991 and 1995.

It is also useful to comment on implications of our research findings. Using alternative index number procedures, we find that over the 1991–95 time period, the nominal supply price of acute phase treatment for depression is essentially unchanged, while the real supply price (relative to GDP deflator) has declined. Note that this may well create an upward bias in estimated price movements for acute phase treatment of depression. Recall that we showed that the percentage of episodes meeting guideline standards has increased over time. The price indexes reported above do not account for this apparent move toward the production frontier. Improved compliance with standards of care implies greater benefits are being generated over time, thereby understating price reductions of effective care. The demand price index revealed a steady 2 to 3 percent per year increase from 1991 to 1994, which is then followed by a sharp 20 percent increase in 1995. Since the demand price encompasses only consumers'/patients' direct OOPPs, and since the supply price is the sum of consumer plus insurer payments, it follows that from 1991 to 1994 there was steady 2 to 3 percent annual *decrease* in insurers' expenditures, and that in 1995 a very substantial 20 percent *decrease* took place. While the nominal supply price of acute phase treatment for depression was apparently unchanged between 1991 and 1995, the compositional burden shifted from third-party insurer to patient. The change in incidence of payment, in large part due to increased patient copayments and deductibles, likely reflects efforts by insurers to deal with moral hazard via design of mental health benefits and tightening of the size of provider networks used in managed care.

Our research findings based on index number procedures are broadly consistent with those based on simple hedonic price methods, particularly with the supply price. On the demand side, the hedonic price index increases more rapidly up to 1994, and then increases more sharply in 1995 than do the traditional index numbers. Note that what we call "traditional" here, however, represents a substantial departure from current BLS practice, in that we have used as elementary building blocks the transaction prices accompanying alternative treatment bundles, and not the (list) prices of fixed set of inputs. Nevertheless, it is interesting that, as in Berndt, Cockburn, and Griliches (1996), the marginal impact of incorporating hedonic pricing methods is not that significant, once one defines output quantities carefully. Our hedonic research could have gone several steps further, allowing for changing parameters over time and integrating the estimated hedonic price equations with index number procedures, but we leave those nuances for further research.[44]

Finally, it is worth commenting on implications of this research for procedural revisions currently under consideration at the BLS. The BLS is responsible for constructing and publishing PPIs and CPIs for a very large number of medical-related services and commodities. Our research has focused on but one disorder—major depression—albeit one whose output measurement presented considerable challenges. We believe that economies of scope and scale are undoubtedly available, and we have experienced a steep learning curve in working with the MEDSTAT data. We also believe that extension of the treatment episode approach to other illnesses and disorders is feasible. Nevertheless, we are struck by how difficult, time-consuming, and expensive this research has been for us. If a treatment episode approach is to be implemented efficiently at the BLS (or elsewhere, such as at HCFA), considerable care needs to be exercised in choosing a set of illnesses/disorders for which treatment bundles can be well defined, for which quality comparisons can readily be made (facilitated by AHCPR or other published professional guideline standards), and for which claims data can readily be employed.

12.10   Concluding Remarks

We have implemented an approach that employs transaction data from a publicly available retrospective medical claims database of almost half a million lives, annually from 1991 to 1995. Based on a review of the clinical research literature dealing with the acute phase of treatment for depression, we identify seven alternative service bundles that combine varying types and quantities of prescription drugs, medical management, and psychotherapy. We construct data on episodes of treatment and their cost.

---

44. See Berndt and Griliches (1993) and Berndt, Griliches, and Rappaport (1995).

Because the treatment bundles are viewed by the medical community as being therapeutically similar in terms of ex ante efficacy, our linking of treatment bundles provides an important step toward incorporation of expected medical outcomes. We distinguish a supply price index, similar to the BLS PPI, that represents the total receipts received by providers of medical treatment (from the insurer and the patient), from a demand price index (similar to the CPI) that incorporates only the out-of-pocket payments (via copayments and deductibles) by the patient/consumer. Finally, we employ a variety of traditional aggregate index number formulas, consistent with varying assumptions concerning the ex ante substitutability among the seven treatment bundles, as well as hedonic price procedures in computing price indexes.

For the supply side price index, the various price indexes all point to a flat and essentially unchanging price over the 1991–95 period. Because the BLS's various producer price indexes all indicate a significant increase over the same time period, our results suggest that in real terms, the supply price for treatment of acute phase depression has fallen over time. On the demand side, however, the indexes show a total increase in price of about 10 percent between 1991 and 1994, and then a very sharp 20 percent increase. The usual welfare interpretation of the CPI is not possible in this case. The price increase largely reflects increased cost sharing arrangements which are certain to reduce welfare losses stemming from moral hazard. This is especially the case in MEDSTAT data, which generally cover plans with substantially lower cost sharing for mental health care than is typical in the economy as a whole (20 percent versus 50 percent).

Our research can be extended in a number of ways. Two issues are particularly important. First, although we have experimented with use of both strict and somewhat relaxed guideline criteria to define episodes of care, in each case we have assumed an "all or nothing" treatment. The implicit production function therefore involves a steep step or cliff in which treatment either is or is not effective. An alternative is to consider some subguideline treatment bundles as having a lower probability of being efficacious than are those meeting guideline criteria, and therefore to assign the subguideline episodes a lower quantity weight. Together with a group of clinicians and psychiatric researchers, we are currently initiating an effort to more completely define the specific depression treatment production function.

Second, we have adhered rather closely to the notion of defining output in terms of episodes of acute phase treatment. This involves a somewhat arbitrary delineation of an output that often does not correspond well to the reality of clinical practice. Because depression is often a chronic recurring illness, continuation and maintenance phase care are part of the overall treatment of the disorder. Unfortunately, because the bulk of clinical research has focused on the acute phase of treatment, our links to outcomes were tied to a somewhat imperfect characterization of care. It is therefore important to more completely specify treatment in this context.

Finally, and perhaps most surprisingly, all of our results point to the fact that given a budget for treatment of depression, much more could be accomplished in 1995 than in 1991. That is, real prices of care have fallen. This runs counter to most public and expert perceptions. The implications for interpreting spending changes are enormous. For years the view has been that spending increases on mental health care (of which depression is 50 percent in private insurance) was due to provision of increasing low benefit services and higher payments to providers. Our results point to a different story where spending increases are due to a larger number of "effective" treatments being provided. These treatments represent a shift toward new treatment technologies that are provided under a new set of organizational arrangements.

Appendix

Table 12A.1   **Aggregate Producer ("Supply") Price Indexes Calculated Using Broader Standard of Care Definitions**

Price Index	1991	1992	1993	1994	1995
Fixed weights					
Laspeyres	1.000	1.015	0.984	0.929	0.997
Paasche	1.000	1.029	1.000	0.968	1.010
Chained weights					
Laspeyres	1.000	1.015	0.981	0.941	0.985
Paasche	1.000	1.017	0.986	0.952	0.993
Fisher ideal	1.000	1.016	0.983	0.946	0.989
Törnqvist	1.000	1.016	0.983	0.946	0.988

References

American Medical Association. 1990. *Current procedural terminology (CPT)*, 4th ed. Chicago: American Medical Association.

American Psychiatric Association (APA). 1993. Practice guidelines for major depressive disorder in adults. *American Journal of Psychiatry* 150, no. 4 (suppl.): 1–26.

———. 1994. *Diagnostic and statistical manual of mental disorders*, 4th ed. Washington, D.C.: American Psychiatric Association.

Armknecht, Paul A. 1996. Improving the efficiency of the U.S. CPI in the future. Washington, D.C.: International Monetary Fund. Unpublished manuscript.

Armknecht, Paul A., and Daniel H. Ginsburg. 1992. Improvements in measuring price changes in consumer services: Past, present and future. In *Output measurement in the service sectors,* ed. Z. Griliches, assisted by Ernst R. Berndt, Timothy Bresnahan, and Marilyn E. Manser, 109–56. NBER Studies in Income and Wealth, vol. 56. Chicago: University of Chicago Press.

Armknecht, Paul A., Brent R. Moulton, and Kenneth J. Stewart. 1994. Improvements to the food at home, shelter and prescription drug indexes in the U.S. Consumer Price Index. CPI Announcement—Version I, 20 October. Washington, D.C.: U.S. Department of Labor, Bureau of Labor Statistics.

Beach, S. R. H., E. E. Sandeen, and K. D. O'Leary. 1990. *Depression in marriage.* New York: Guilford.

Beck, A. T., A. John Rush, B. F. Shaw, and G. Emergy. 1979. *Cognitive therapy of depression.* New York: Guilford.

Berndt, Ernst R. 1991. *The practice of econometrics: Classic and contemporary.* Reading, Mass.: Addison Wesley.

Berndt, Ernst R., Iain Cockburn, and Zvi Griliches. 1996. Pharmaceutical innovations and market dynamics: Tracking effects on price indexes for antidepressant drugs. *Brookings Papers on Economic Activity, Microeconomics,* 133–88.

Berndt, Ernst R., Richard G. Frank, and Thomas G. McGuire. 1997. Alternative insurance arrangements and the treatment of depression: What are the facts? *American Journal of Managed Care* 3 (2): 243–50.

Berndt, Ernst R., and Zvi Griliches. 1993. Price indexes for microcomputers: An exploratory study. In *Price measurements and their uses,* ed. Murray F. Foss, Marilyn E. Manser, and Allan H. Young. NBER Studies in Income and Wealth, vol. 57. Chicago: University of Chicago Press.

Berndt, Ernst R., Zvi Griliches, and Neal Rappaport. 1995. Econometric estimates of price indexes for personal computers in the 1990's. *Journal of Econometrics* 68 (1): 243–68.

Broadbent, W. Eugene., Dan G. Blazer, Linda K. George, and Chiu Kit Tse. 1990. Depression, disability days and days lost from work in a prospective epidemiologic survey. *Journal of the American Medical Association* 264: 2524–28.

Busch, Susan H., Richard G. Frank, and Ernst R. Berndt. 1996. Effectiveness, efficacy and price indexes for depression: A review of the literature. Boston: Harvard Medical School, Department of Health Care Policy. Unpublished manuscript.

Cardenas, Elaine M. 1996a. The CPI for hospital services: Concepts and procedures. *Monthly Labor Review* 119 (7): 34–42.

———. 1996b. Revision of the CPI hospital services component. *Monthly Labor Review* 119 (12): 40–48.

Catron, Brian, and Bonnie Murphy. 1996. Hospital price inflation: What does the new PPI tell us? *Monthly Labor Review* 119 (7): 124–31.

Croghan, Thomas W., Catherine A. Melfi, Deobrah G. Dobrez, and Thomas J. Kniesner. 1999. Effect of mental health specialty care on antidepressant length of therapy. *Medical Care* 37 (suppl.): AS20–23.

Crown, William E., Robert L. Obenchain, Luella Englehart, Tamra Lair, Don P. Buesching, and Thomas W. Croghan. 1996. Application of sample selection models to outcomes research: The case of evaluating effects of antidepressant therapy on resource utilization. Cambridge, Mass.: The MEDSTAT Group. Unpublished manuscript.

Cutler, David, Mark McClellan, Joseph Newhouse, and Dahlia Remler. 1998. Are medical prices declining? Evidence from heart attack treatments. *Quarterly Journal of Economics* 113 (November): 991–1024.

Diewert, W. Erwin. 1976. Exact and superlative index numbers. *Journal of Econometrics* 4 (2): 115–45.

———. 1981. The economic theory of index numbers: A survey. In *Essays in the theory and measurement of consumer behavior in honour of Sir Richard Stone,* ed. Angus Deaton. Cambridge: Cambridge University Press.

Elkin, Irene, T. Shea, J. T. Watkins, S. D. Imber, S. M. Sotsky, J. F. Collins, D. R. Glass, P. A. Pilkonis, W. R. Leber, J. P. Docherty, S. J. Fiester, and M. B. Parloff. 1989. National Institute of Mental Health treatment of depression collaborative research program: General effectiveness of treatments. *Archives of General Psychiatry* 46: 971–82.

Ellis, Randall P., Gregory C. Pope, Lisa I. Iezzoni, John Z. Ayanian, David W. Bates, Helen Burstin, and Arlene S. Ash. 1996. Diagnosis-based risk adjustment for Medicare capitation payments. *Health Care Financing Review* 17 (3): 101–28.

Feldstein, Paul J. 1979. *Health care economics,* 1st ed. New York: Wiley.

———. 1983. *Health care economics,* 2nd ed. New York: Wiley.

———. 1988. *Health care economics,* 3rd ed. New York: Wiley.

Fixler, Dennis, and Mitch Ginsburg. 1997. Health care output and prices in the Producer Price Index. Slides from presentation to the NBER Summer Institute, Franco-American Seminar, Cambridge, Mass., 23 July.

Ford, Ina Kay, and Daniel H. Ginsburg. 1997. Medical care in the CPI. Paper presented to the NBER Summer Institute, Franco-American Seminar, Cambridge, Mass., 23 July.

Frank, Ellen, David J. Kupfer, J. M. Perel, Cleon Cornes, D. B. Jarrett, A. G. Mallinger, Michael E. Thase, A. B. McEachran, and V. J. Grochocinski. 1990. Three-year outcomes for maintenance therapies in recurrent depression. *Archives of General Psychiatry* 47: 1093–99.

Frank, Richard G., Ernst R. Berndt, and Susan H. Busch. 1999. Price indexes for the treatment of depression. In *Measuring the prices of medical treatments,* ed. Jack E. Triplett. Washington, D.C.: The Brookings Institution.

Frank, Richard G., Susan H. Busch, and Ernst R. Berndt. 1998. Measuring prices and quantities of treatment for depression. *American Economic Review* 88 (2): 106–11.

Frank, Richard G., Thomas G. McGuire, and Joseph P. Newhouse. 1995. Risk contracts in managed mental health care. *Health Affairs* 14 (3): 50–64.

Getzen, Thomas E. 1992. Medical care price indexes: Theory, construction and empirical analysis of the US series 1927–1990. In *Advances in health economics and health services research,* ed. R. Scheffler and L. F. Rossiter. Greenwich, Conn.: JAI Press.

Gilbert, Milton. 1961. The problem of quality change and index numbers. *Monthly Labor Review* 84 (9): 992–97.

———. 1962. Quality change and index numbers: A reply. *Monthly Labor Review* 85 (5): 544–45.

Goldman, William, Joyce McCulloch, and Roland Sturm. 1998. Costs and use of mental health services before and after managed care. *Health Affairs* 17 (2): 40–52.

Griliches, Zvi. 1962. Quality change and index numbers: A critique. *Monthly Labor Review* 85 (5): 532–44.

———. 1988. *Technology, education, and productivity.* New York: Basil Blackwell.

Griliches, Zvi, and Iain Cockburn. 1994. Generics and new goods in pharmaceutical price indexes. *American Economic Review* 84 (5): 1213–32.

Hays, R. D., K. B. Wells, C. D. Sherbourne, W. Rogers, and K. Spritzer. 1995. Functioning and well-being outcomes of patients with depression compared with chronic general medical illnesses. *Archives of General Psychiatry* 52 (1): 11–19.

Kanoza, Douglas. 1996. Supplemental sampling in the PPI Pharmaceuticals Index. *Producer Price Indexes Detailed Price Report* (January): 8–10.

Katon, Wayne, Michael von Korff, Elizabeth Lin, Terry Bush, and Johann Ormel. 1992. Adequacy and duration of antidepressant treatment in primary care. *Medical Care* 30:67–76.

Keeler, Emmett B., Kenneth B. Wells, Willard G. Manning, J. David Rumpel, and Janet M. Hanley. 1986. The demand for episodes of mental health services. Santa Monica, Calif.: RAND Report R-3432-NIMH, October.

Keller, Martin B., Gerald L. Klerman, Philip W. Lavori, William Coryell, Jean Endicott, and John Taylor. 1984. Long-term outcome of episodes of major depression. *Journal of the American Medical Association* 252 (6): 788–92.

Keller, Martin B., Philip W. Lavori, Gerald L. Klerman, Nancy C. Andreasen, Jean Endicott, William Coryell, Jan Fawcett, John P. Rice, and M. A. Robert. 1986. Low levels and lack of predictors of somathotherapy and psychotherapy received by depressed patients. *Archives of General Psychiatry* 43 (5): 458–66.

Keller, Martin B., Philip W. Lavori, John Rice, William Coryell, and Robert M. A. Hirschfeld. 1986. The persistent risk of chronicity in recurrent episodes of nonbipolar major depressive disorder: A prospective follow-up. *American Journal of Psychiatry* 143 (1): 24–28.

Kelly, Gregory G. 1997. Improving the PPI samples for prescription pharmaceuticals. *Monthly Labor Review* 120 (10): 10–17.

Kendler, K. S., E. E. Walters, M. C. Neale, Ronald C. Kessler, A. C. Heath, and L. J. Eaves. 1995. The structure of genetic and environmental risk factors for six major psychiatric disorders in women: Phobia, generalized anxiety disorder, panic disorder, bulimia, major depression, and alcoholism. *Archives of General Psychiatry* 52 (5): 374–83.

Kessler, Ronald C., Katherine A. McGonagle, Marvin Swartz, Dan G. Blazer, and Christopher B. Nelson. 1993. Sex and depression in the National Comorbidity Survey I: Lifetime prevalence, chronicity, and recurrence. *Journal of Affective Disorders* 29:85–96.

Kessler, Ronald C., Katherine A. McGonagle, Shanyang Zhao, Christopher B. Nelson, Michael Hughes, Suzann Eshlerman, Hans-Ulrich Wittchen, and Kenneth S. Kendler. 1994. Lifetime and twelve-month prevalence of DSM-III-R psychiatric disorders in the United States: Results from the National Comorbidity Survey. *Archives of General Psychiatry* 51 (1): 8–19.

Kupfer, David J. 1991. Long-term treatment of depression. *Journal of Clinical Psychiatry* 52, no. 5 (suppl.): 28–34.

Kupfer, David J., E. Frank, J. M. Perel, C. Cornes, A. G. Mallinger, M. E. Thase, A. B. McEachran, and V. J. Grochocinski. 1992. Five-year outcomes for maintenance therapies in recurrent depression. *Archives of General Psychiatry* 49:769–73.

Langford, Elizabeth A. 1957. Medical care in the CPI: 1935–1956. *Monthly Labor Review* 80 (9): 1053–58.

Levit, Katharine R., Helen C. Lazenby, Brandley R. Braden, and the National Health Accounts Team. 1998. National health spending trends in 1996. *Health Affairs* 17 (1): 35–51.

Ma, Ching-to Albert, and Thomas G. McGuire. 1998. Costs and incentives in a behavioral health carve-out. *Health Affairs* 17 (2): 53–69.

Manning, Willard G., and M. Susan Marquis. 1989. *Health insurance: The trade-off between risk pooling and moral hazard.* Publication no. R-3729-NCHSR. Santa Monica, Calif.: RAND Corporation.

Marion Merrell Dow. Annual. *Managed care digest: HMO edition.* Kansas City, Mo. Marion Merrell Dow.

McGuire, Thomas G. 1989. Financing and reimbursement for mental health services. In *The future of mental health services research,* ed. Carl A. Taube, David Mechanic, and Ann A. Hohmann. Rockville, Md.: U.S. Department of Health and Human Services.

Mechanic, David. 1989. The evolution of mental health services and mental health services research. . In *The future of mental health services research,* ed. Carl A. Taube, David Mechanic, and Ann A. Hohmann. Rockville, Md.: U.S. Department of Health and Human Services.

Newhouse, Joseph P. 1989. Measuring medical prices and understanding their effects. *Journal of Health Administration Education* 7 (1): 19–26.

Newhouse, Joseph P., and the Insurance Experiment Group. 1993. *Free for all? Lessons from the RAND health insurance experiment.* Cambridge, Mass.: Harvard University Press.

Papolos, Demitri F., and Janic Papolos. 1992. *Overcoming depression.* Rev. ed. New York: HarperCollins.

Prospective Payment Assessment Commission. 1995. *Report and recommendations to the Congress.* Washington, D.C.: U.S. Government Printing Office.

Schulberg, Herbert C., Marjorie Saul, Maureen McClelland, Mary Ganguli, Wallace Cristy, and Ellen Frank. 1985. Assessing depression in primary medical and psychiatric practices. *Archives of General Psychiatry* 42 (12): 1164–70.

Scitovsky, Anne A. 1964. An index of the cost of medical care—A proposed new approach. In *The economics of health and medical care,* proceedings of the Conference on the Economics of Health and Medical Care, 10–12 May 1962. Ann Arbor: University of Michigan.

———. 1967. Changes in the costs of treatment of selected illnesses, 1951–65. *American Economic Review* 57 (5): 1182–95.

Trajtenberg, Manuel. 1990. *Economic analysis of product innovation: The case of CT scanners.* Cambridge, Mass.: Harvard University Press.

Triplett, Jack E. 1990. The theory of industrial and occupational classifications and related phenomena. In *Proceedings of the Bureau of the Census 1990 Annual Research Conference.* Washington, D.C.: U.S. Department of Commerce.

U.S. Department of Health and Human Services. 1980. *International classification of diseases (ICD-9-CM),* 2d ed. Washington, D.C.: U.S. Government Printing Office.

———. Public Health Service. Agency for Health Care Policy and Research. 1993. *Depression in primary care,* vol. 2. Rockville, Md.: U.S. Department of Health and Human Services.

U.S. Department of Labor. Bureau of Labor Statistics. 1992. *Handbook of methods.* bulletin 2414. Washington, D.C.: U.S. Government Printing Office.

———. 1995. Improvements to CPI procedures: Prescription drugs. Washington, D.C.: U.S. Government Printing Office.

———. N.d. A description of the PPI hospital services initiative. Washington, D.C.: U.S. Government Printing Office.

U.S. Senate Finance Committee. 1996. *Final Report from the Advisory Commission to Study the Consumer Price Index.* Washington, D.C.: U.S. Government Printing Office.

Weiner, Jonathan P., Allen Dobson, Stephanie L. Maxwell, Kevin Coleman, Barbara Starfield, and Gerald Anderson. 1996. Risk-adjusted medicare capitation rates using ambulatory and inpatient diagnoses. *Health Care Financing Review* 17 (3): 77–100.

Wells, Kenneth B., Wayne Katon, William Rogers, and Patti Camp. 1994. Use of minor tranquilizers and antidepressant medications by depressed outpatients: Results from the medical outcomes study. *American Journal of Psychiatry* 151 (5): 694–700.

Wells, Kenneth B., Anita Stewart, R. D. Hays, M. A. Burnam, W. Rogers, M. Daniels, S. Berry, S. Greenfield, and J. Ware. 1989. The functioning and well-being of depressed patients: Results from the Medical Outcomes Study. *Journal of the American Medical Association* 262 (7): 914–19.

Wells, Kenneth B., Roland Sturm, Cathy D. Sherbourne, and Lisa S. Meredith. 1996. *Caring for depression: A RAND study.* Cambridge, Mass.: Harvard University Press.

Wilde, Michelle I., and Paul Benfield. 1998. Fluoxetine: A pharmacoeconomic review of its use in depression. *Pharmacoeconomics* 13 (5): 543–61.

Wingert, Terence D., John E. Kralewski, Tammie J. Lindquist, and David J. Knutson. 1995. Constructing episodes of care from encounter and claims data: Some methodological issues. *Inquiry* 32: 430–43.

Comment   Darrel A. Regier

This paper by Berndt, Busch, and Frank offers a new and important paradigm for evaluating the costs of providing and obtaining mental health treatment services in a rapidly changing "defacto mental health service system" (Regier et al. 1993). It is an ambitious effort to use the Bureau of Labor Statistics (BLS) Producer Price Index (PPI) and Consumer Price Index (CPI) conventions to describe market changes in the cost of treating major depression over a five-year time frame (1991–1995). The authors attempt to go beyond the usual CPI approach of assessing the average price of a "fixed market basket of goods and services," such as the average cost of a mental health visit, bed-day, or medication/day, to examining the cost of an episode of care that meets American Psychiatric Association treatment-guideline standards for major depressive disorder in adults. (APA 1993). Although such an approach to assessing "the average costs of the complete treatment of individual illnesses" was recommended as early as 1962 by Scitovsky, very few have advanced beyond pricing health care inputs to obtaining the price of health care outcomes.

Within the mental health field, there have been very few published studies that attempt to assess the cost effectiveness of mental disorder treatments by using comparative treatment outcomes in the analysis. A notable exception is the study by Rogers et al. (1993), which evaluated the relative cost of treatment outcomes of depression in different service systems. In this landmark study, psychiatrists in an HMO practice offered ostensibly less expensive treatment for depression with fewer visits and a lower use of antidepressant medications than were provided for comparable patients in fee-for-service settings. However, when outcomes were factored into the cost estimates, the more intensive treatment was shown to be a more cost-effective approach.

Darrel A. Regier is executive director of the American Psychiatric Institute for Research and Education and director of the Office of Research of the American Psychiatric Association.

With this background in mind, the authors are careful to review the epidemiological literature to assess the potential true prevalence of major depressive disorder in contrast to the treated prevalence reported for the MEDSTAT population used in this paper. There is a significant gap between the reported 10.3 percent annual prevalence of major depression cited from the National Comorbidity Survey (Kessler et al. 1994) and the 18,920 episodes of acute care for major depression from 428,168 enrollees during the five-year study period. If every episode represented a different patient, this would represent only 4.4 percent of the population or an average of less than 1 percent of the population receiving such care each year. The obvious discrepancy between ostensible prevalence and treatment rates raises important questions about the clinical significance of the prevalence rates (Regier et al. 1998), barriers to treatment demand, assessments of "medical necessity" for care (Regier et al. 2000), and the cost of failure to provide treatment (Rupp 1995). However, such larger public health issues remain somewhat outside the scope of this important paper.

The authors do take advantage of a large volume of clinical trials literature on treatment efficacy and the synthesis of this information into treatment guideline standards. They are able to use these well-accepted standards to define "treatment bundles" of specific antidepressant medications and psychotherapies, which are considered comparable in effectiveness for either severe or less severe forms of depression. Since only administrative data sets are available for this study, these treatment bundles of known effectiveness (under ideal research conditions as expressed in treatment guidelines) serve as outcome proxies for price comparisons that are attempting to take episode outcomes into account. Seven different bundles included psychotherapy or antidepressant medication treatment either alone or in various combinations for treatment guideline-determined duration and level of intensity or dose.

The authors note that the proportion of guideline-compatible treatment episodes rose substantially over the five years of experience with the treatment system from 35 percent in 1991 to 56 percent in 1995. The quantities and prices of each treatment bundle were assessed with the finding that the average supply price (PPI equivalent) of the treatment bundles decreased slightly over the five-year period even as there were major shifts in the relative proportions of treatment modalities over this time period. In contrast, the consumer demand price (CPI equivalent) increased by more than 22 percent in a single year (1994–1995) as a result of benefit design changes which increased copayments and deductibles for mental health treatment. The net conclusion from these findings is that the improved compliance with treatment guideline standards in the face of supply price reductions implies a gain in production efficiency within the mental health system. However, the increase in consumer costs to control the "moral hazard" that patients will overuse services beyond their most effective level has other equity implications. The rise in political support for legislation which would mandate parity in benefits for mental and physical disorders has been propelled by the perceived inequity that is reflected in the reported rise in CPI-equivalent costs for treatment of mental disorders (Zuvekas, Banthin, and Selden 1998; National Advisory Mental Health Council 1998).

The authors are to be commended for their creative analytic approaches to mainstreaming health services in general and mental health services in particular into the PPI and CPI framework. The availability of such a well-respected economic framework for evaluating the production of mental health services could be of considerable value to policymakers in their assessment of the relative cost and value of investing greater resources in mental health services, research, and system development.

As a practicing clinical psychiatrist, I am impressed by the care with which the authors have reviewed the clinical treatment literature and have attempted to model the practice guidelines with administrative claims data sets. They also have recognized the limitations of these claims data for capturing the full picture of treatment for major depression, which has both acute treatment requirements for all, and chronic maintenance treatment requirements for many others. However, the shift in treatment styles from a predominance of psychotherapy alone to antidepressant medication alone or in combination during this time frame does have a clear face validity. The shift to the newer SSRI antidepressant medications is also adequately mirrored in this data set. However, before this model is ready for prime time implementation as a component of published PPIs and CPIs from the BLS, it would be important to have a few replications and refinements.

As an epidemiologist with a great deal of interest in the policy applications of such research data, I am impressed by the potential benefits of obtaining mental disorder prevalence rates which would more accurately reflect the need for specific types of treatment (e.g., treatment bundles). The current movement in psychopathology assessment is to obtain more specific measures of clinically significant impairment and symptom levels (routinely used in treatment efficacy studies) in addition to existing diagnostic criteria. If such fine-grained diagnostic criteria could be reflected in epidemiological studies as well as in the diagnostic codes recorded in claims records, the value of the indexes proposed in this paper could obviously be advanced.

Although many other health policy issues are touched on by this paper, including the issue of the optimal cost-sharing for patients seeking mental health services, the most important policy emphasis is the focus on outcome or quality of care rather than simply cost of care. With the current managed care industry competition "race to the bottom" on per-member-per-month costs, it is most important to have cost measures which are adjusted for quality as determined by the outcome of treatment episodes. It is somewhat unexpected to have economists leading the way by identifying methods which would tilt the industry toward quality competition when clinicians and clinical research investigators have been so slow to respond to this challenge. I hope that the obvious benefits of collaboration between economists, clinical investigators, epidemiologists, and other health services researchers will result in refining the outstanding work represented in this paper to the point where it will become a standard economic index for the field.

References

American Psychiatric Association (APA). 1993. Practice guidelines for major depressive disorder in adults. *American Journal of Psychiatry,* no. 150, no. 4 (suppl.): 1–51.

Kessler, R. C., K. A. McGonagle, S. Zhao, C. B. Nelson, M. Hughes, S. Eshlerman, H. U. Wittchen, and K. S. Kendler. 1994. Lifetime and twelve-month prevalence of DSM-III-R psychiatric disorders in the United States: Results from the National Comorbidity Survey. *Archives of General Psychiatry* 51: 8–19.

National Advisory Mental Health Council. 1998. *Parity in financing mental health services: Managed care effects on cost, access, and quality. An interim report to Congress by the National Advisory Mental Health Council.* NIH Publication no. 98–4322. Bethesda, Md.: National Institutes of Health.

Regier, D. A., C. T. Kaelber, D. S. Rae, M. E. Farmer, B. Knauper, R. C. Kessler, and G. S. Norquist. 1998. Limitations of diagnostic criteria and assessment instruments for mental disorders: Implications for research and policy. *Archives of General Psychiatry* 55: 109–15.

Regier, D. A., W. E. Narrow, D. S. Rae, R. W. Manderscheid, B. Z. Locke, and F. K. Goodwin. 1993. The de facto U.S. mental and addictive disorders service system. *Archives of General Psychiatry* 50: 85–94.

Regier, D. A., W. E. Narrow, A. Rupp, D. S. Rae, C. T. Kaelber. 2000. The epidemiology of mental disorder treatment need: Community estimates of medical necessity. In *Unmet need in mental health service delivery,* ed. G. Andrews and S. Henderson. London: Cambridge University Press.

Rogers, W., K. Wells, L. Meredith, R. Sturm, and M. A. Burnam. 1993. Outcomes for adult outpatients with depression under prepaid or fee-for-service financing. *Archives of General Psychiatry* 50: 517–25.

Rupp, A. 1995. The economic consequences of not treating depression. *British Journal of Psychiatry* 166, no. 27 (suppl.): 29–33.

Scitovsky, Anne A. 1962. An index of the cost of medical care: A proposed new approach. In *The economics of health and medical care: Proceedings of the Conference on the Economics of Health and Medical Care,* 10–12 May. Ann Arbor: University of Michigan.

Zuvekas, S. H., J. S. Banthin, and T. M. Selden. 1998. Mental health parity: What are the gaps in coverage? *Journal of Mental Health Policy and Economics* 1: 135–46.

IV

Extensions of the Frontier

13

The Value of Reductions
in Child Injury Mortality
in the United States

Sherry Glied

One of the bright spots in the changing circumstances of American children over the past three decades has been the significant decline in child mortality. The mortality rate among children ages one through four fell 57 percent between 1960 and 1990, and the rate for children ages five through fourteen fell 48 percent over those thirty years (U.S. Department of Health and Human Services 1963, 1994). In percentage terms, these declines are steeper than those experienced by any other age group.

Many of the improvements in child health stem from revolutionary developments in medicine. Congenital anomalies of the heart, many infectious diseases, and several childhood cancers, important causes of death in 1960, no longer threaten children. Further improvements, even into the 1990s, have come through vaccination campaigns, which have nearly eradicated several childhood infectious diseases (most recently meningitis). A growing share of the reduction in child mortality, however, stems neither from medical advances nor from immunization campaigns. Rather, the most important contributor to reductions in mortality since 1970 has been a sharp decline in the rate of child mortality from unintentional injury or accidents. Among children under five, that rate dropped from 44 deaths per 100,000 population in 1960 to 18.6 deaths per 100,000 population in 1990. Among children ages five through nine, the rates dropped from 19.6 to 9.8.

Sherry Glied is associate professor of public health at the Mailman School of Public Health of Columbia University and a faculty research fellow of the National Bureau of Economic Research.

The author thanks James Schuttinga, NBER conference participants, and participants at the 1997 Association for Public Policy Analysis and Management conference for useful suggestions, and Sangheet Gnanasekaran for research assistance.

Despite these large declines in mortality, unintentional injury remains the leading cause of death among children ages one through fourteen, and most of these deaths are, in some sense, avoidable (Rivara and Grossman 1996). Today, virtually all excess mortality among children in the United States relative to other industrialized countries is due to unintentional injury and violence (Centers for Disease Control 1990). Understanding the reasons for the decline in injury mortality is important to further reduce these rates. Furthermore, understanding the mechanisms that brought about the decline in child injury mortality may also inform the design of public policies aimed at reducing violent deaths among children and reducing unintentional injuries in other groups. Finally, like other improvements in health, this decline in the riskiness of childhood should figure in an assessment of changes in the cost of living. The purpose of this paper is to examine the determinants and assess the value of the decline in childhood unintentional injury mortality.

13.1   A Model of Child Mortality from Unintentional Injury

The recent decline in child injury mortality in the United States is characterized by two features: its pervasiveness and its timing. Accidental injury rates have declined sharply in almost every category in the International Classification of Diseases (ICD-9). Childhood mortality rates remained quite steady across most causes through the 1960s and began to decline sharply in the 1970s. The rate of decline actually accelerated over time. In both percentage terms and absolute magnitudes, declines in accidental injury rates were generally greater in the 1980s than in the 1970s.

Epidemiological literature on changes in childhood accident mortality has focused on specific steps taken to avoid injury—whether children wear seatbelts, whether pools are fenced, whether smoke detectors are installed in homes (Office of Technology Assessment 1988). These and similar interventions have been shown to be effective, but epidemiologists generally agree that at current rates of use, these interventions cannot explain a very large proportion of the change in mortality. Furthermore, the pervasiveness of these declines across disparate categories suggests that the decline in unintentional injury mortality cannot be attributed exclusively to a small number of interventions. For example, while car seats and childproof prescription bottles may have contributed to declines in automobile and poisoning deaths, specific regulations of this type cannot explain the equally substantial declines in pedestrian deaths (Rivara and Grossman 1996; Rivara 1990).

The analysis presented here takes a more general approach to trends in childhood injury mortality, relating mortality to characteristics of families and to the overall level of technology. In this approach, a decline in injury mortality from automobile accidents could be a consequence of an improvement in automobile design, a decrease in the number of children the average driver must supervise, a reduction in the number of auto rides taken by children, an increase in seatbelt use, or better trauma care for children. This approach is analogous to that in most health production models (e.g., Auster, Levenson, and Sarachek 1969).

Mortality from injury in childhood can be viewed as the product of two (largely) distinct processes:

(1)   Mortality $=$ Accident $\times$ (Mortality|Accident).

The first process leads to the occurrence of an accidental injury to a child. The second process generates a death as the outcome of that process.[1] Improvements in childhood mortality may be a consequence of reductions in the rate of accidents or improvements in accident outcomes.

Following Grossman (1972), we can describe the first process, child safety (the absence of an accident), as the output of a household health production function.[2] In the Grossman-type model, parents use technology to combine time and money inputs and produce child health:

(2)   Accident $= H(T, M; E)$,

where T represents parental time, M represents parental investments in goods related to childhood safety, and E represents the technology used in home production.

$$H'_T < 0, \quad H'_M < 0, \quad H'_E < 0$$

In this model, improvements in the level of child safety (reductions in accidents) may be a consequence of increases in the amount of time or money devoted to child health. These increases in time or money inputs may reflect increases in family endowments, changes in family preferences about the disposition of these endowments, or changes compelled by regulation. Alternatively, improvements in child health may be a consequence of improvements in the technology used to produce child health.

As I discuss in detail in the data section below, there were no general and substantial improvements in the resources available to families over the 1960–90 period. Family incomes did not increase substantially, family size fell slightly, and more mothers worked. While family preferences over the disposition of resources may have changed, there is no compelling rea-

---

1. The processes are not completely distinct in that the severity of an accident will affect health outcomes.

2. Note that this model assumes that the parental utility value of child safety has not changed over the 1960–90 period. This assumption is violated to the extent that improvements in other aspects of child health led parents to value children more. Such adjacent complementarities are unlikely to be substantial in this context because the absolute rate of childhood mortality, even in 1960, was very low.

son to believe that preferences changed substantially over the period. Instead, we focus on changes in regulations and in information.

13.1.1   Regulation

The late 1960s and early 1970s were the heyday of the U.S. consumer protection movement. Child protection was an important goal of consumer protection efforts and several major federal and state legislative initiatives passed in this period focused on child safety (table 13.1). At the federal level, the Consumer Product Safety Commission produced a range of mandatory and voluntary standards designed to increase the safety of products with which children might come in contact. Products affected by the legislation included toys, children's furniture (such as cribs and changing tables), and products intended for adults that children might use. In the mid-1970s, a separate set of legislative initiatives altered the packaging of drugs to reduce the risk of child poisoning and required that children's sleepwear meet flammability standards (Consumer Product Safety Commission 1993).

At the state level, the most important initiatives focused on highway safety. Between 1977 and 1984, all states passed legislation requiring children (usually those under five) to be in a child safety seat when in an automobile (the details of the regulations vary considerably among states). A few states also required older children to wear seat belts in the front seat (Office of Technology Assessment 1988). Three states, however, rescinded laws requiring use of seat belts (among older children) during the late 1980s (Agran, Castillo, and Winn 1990). Use of vehicle restraints increased sharply during the 1980s, especially among infants but also among older children (Johnston, Rivara, and Soderberg 1994; Agran, Castillo, and Winn 1990).

Several studies have examined the effectiveness of a few of these regulatory initiatives. The most convincing results have been found for child safety seats, which, when used properly, have been shown to reduce the risk of child mortality by about 35 percent (Office of Technology Assessment 1988).

13.1.2   Information

The regulatory environment of the late 1960s and early 1970s followed from, and often encouraged, the development of information about child safety. Prior to the mid-1960s, most research on child health had focused on diseases. As childhood disease mortality declined, epidemiologists' attention turned to injury and accident risks. The subfield of injury epidemiology began in the mid-1960s (Robertson 1992). The Consumer Product Safety Commission, and similar organizations, encouraged further research in these areas.

Table 13.2 provides data about the increase in the production of infor-

Table 13.1   **Public Health Legislation Affecting Children**

1957	National Clearinghouse for Poison Control Centers
1960	Federal Hazardous Substance Act (FHSA)
1965	Voluntary packaging for aspirin
1966	Child Protection Act amendment to FHSA
1966	National Traffic and Motor Vehicle Safety Act—required that cars include safety features (e.g., shoulder belts, energy-absorbing steering assemblies)
1967	Flammable Fabrics Act
1969	Child Protection and Toy Safety Act amendment to FHSA
1970	Poison Prevention Packaging Act (PPPA)
1972	Packaging regulations for aspirin under the PPPA
1972	Consumer Product Safety Act—issues standards; bans and recalls products; informs consumers; researches product hazards through the National Electronic Injury Surveillance System (NEISS) of sixty-four hospital emergency rooms.
1974	Packaging regulations for prescription drugs
1975	Automobile Fatal Accident Reporting
1976	Bicycle regulations—bicycle must have reflectors, hand brakes that pass a pressure test, and frames that pass strength tests
1977	First law passed requiring children to be in an infant or child seat when riding in motor vehicles
1980	CPSC emphasizes voluntary rather than mandatory standards
By 1984	All 50 states required children to be in an infant or child seat
1986	Injury Prevention Act—to promote research and collaboration between agencies to prevent injuries

mation about childhood injury. The table lists the number of publications indexed in Medline, the main medical search index, whose subject was childhood injury in the United States. As the table suggests, publications on childhood injury have been growing steadily, both in absolute terms and as a share of all publications on children in the United States.

Injury epidemiology led directly toward injury prevention in four distinct ways. First, epidemiology led to regulation. In the mid-1960s, for example, epidemiologists in the New York City Department of Health began to examine the characteristics of child injury mortality. They found that an average of thirty to sixty children under five were dying in New York City (mainly Manhattan and the Bronx) each year because of falls from apartment buildings. This information led to a campaign to inform parents of the risk of falls and to encourage (and eventually require) landlords to install window guards. By 1980, the number of children dying because of falls in New York had declined to four (Office of Technology Assessment 1988).

Second, epidemiology provided a basis for lawsuits alleging that a defective product had led to injury. Litigation, and the fear of potential litigation, may have been a motive for the development of voluntary product safety standards in several industries.

Table 13.2   Publications on Childhood Injury in the United States

	1966–75	1976–80	1981–86	1987–92	1993–97
Annual publications	19.1	24.8	35	50	58.4
Percentage of all United States references	0.39	0.36	0.55	0.54	0.59
Percentage of all references to children	0.11	0.12	0.15	0.21	0.26
Percentage of all references to wounds and accidents	0.21	0.27	0.33	0.38	0.46

Source: Medline 1966–97.

Third, epidemiology led to the development of new products. As the relative risks of different causes of injury became better known, manufacturers developed a host of childproofing products to respond to the risk (Office of Technology Assessment 1988; Spock 1992).

Finally, epidemiology provided information to parents that enabled them to better allocate the resources they devoted to child health. One way to see how parents obtained this information is to compare the content of child development books over time. Table 13.3 contrasts the safety information contained in the 1957 second edition of the best-selling Dr. Spock manual of baby and child care to the information contained in the fourth edition (1976) and sixth edition (1992). Clearly, the emphasis on safety, the level of detail, and the conformity of the recommendations to epidemiologic evidence all increased substantially over time.

13.1.3   Trauma Care

Rates of mortality after injury vary considerably among causes of mortality. There are about thirty-two near-drowning incidents (including hospitalizations) for each child who drowns (Wintemute 1990). About 1 in 100 children who are passengers in a motor vehicle that is in an accident suffers fatal injuries (Rivara 1990). Pedestrian injury death rates are much higher. About 4 in 100 children struck by a car dies, and the rate is higher among younger children (Rivara 1990).

There were substantial increases in the availability of childhood trauma care during the 1980s. Trauma care is likely to have led to improvements in outcomes from burn and motor vehicle accidents (Rivara and Grossman 1996). Nonetheless, childhood trauma care lags well behind adult trauma care in saving lives. According to the medical literature, trauma care can contribute less to saving children's lives than to saving adults' lives (because children are more likely to suffer from head trauma; Office of Technology Assessment 1988). Furthermore, for several of the principal causes of death among children (particularly drowning, choking, and falls from more than three stories), most victims die before reaching a hospital (Wintemute 1990; Office of Technology Assessment 1988).

Table 13.3 Dr. Spock on Injury Prevention

	Spock 1957 (2nd ed.), 15 million copies sold	Spock 1976 (4th ed.), 28 million copies sold	Spock 1992 (6th ed.), 40 million copies sold
Section title	"Avoiding Accidents and Fears"	"Avoiding Accidents"	"Preventing Injuries"
Location	"One Year Old" section	"One Year Old" section	Entire chapter
Length	3 pages	5 pages	13 pages + 1 paragraph in "One Year Old" section
Preamble	One year is a dangerous age. Parents cannot prevent all injuries. If they were careful enough or worrisome enough, they would only make a child timid.	Accidents are now the biggest cause of death. (1957 preamble appears later)	"Injuries now cause more deaths in children over the age of 1 year than all illnesses combined. The three leading causes of these injuries are motor vehicles, fire . . . , and drowning." Two basic principles: awareness and supervision. (1957 preamble appears later)
Cautions	high chair	high chair	high chair
	baby carriage	baby carriage	baby carriage
	stairs	stairs	stairs
	windows	windows	windows
	pot handles	pot handles	pot handles
	small objects	small objects	small objects
	bath temperature	bath temperature	bath temperature
	cover wall sockets with tape	**outlet covers**	**outlet covers**
	tools	tools	tools
	medicine and poisons	medicine and poisons	medicine and poisons
		car seats	**car seats**
		seat belts	seat belts
		pedestrian safety	pedestrian safety
		fire extinguisher	fire extinguisher
		clothes **flammability**	clothes **flammability**
		tub drowning	tub drowning
			bicycle helmets
			hot water heater
			smoke detectors

13.1.4   The Relationship between Regulation, Technology, and Postaccident Care and Family Resources

Table 13.4 categorizes the range of changes in the child health environment over the 1960–90 period. Some new information was transmitted entirely through private actions (such as Dr. Spock's books; see table 13.3). Other information was transmitted through regulations requiring safety labeling. Product quality improvements followed regulations and informational developments. Finally, regulations also imposed requirements on parents and others to make use of available safety equipment.

These different environmental changes are likely to have had different types of effects. Furthermore, the effects are likely to have differed across different types of families.

In the context of the child health production model, information that leads parents to recognize risks of which they were previously unaware (or better responses to risks), can lead to reallocations of time and money that allow the production of better health at the same cost. That is, this information improves the technology for production of health. If information is conveyed through voluntary mechanisms, better educated parents are more likely to have access to it. Labeling requirements may convey information to both more educated and less educated parents.

Regulation, by itself, will not have a substantial effect on child health in the standard health production model. In the case of behavioral regulations, if families are required to increase certain inputs for child health beyond what they would otherwise choose, they are likely to reduce other inputs accordingly. Furthermore, behavioral regulations can have perverse effects (Peltzman 1975). For example, requiring small children to use car

Table 13.4   Types of Interventions

Class of Change	Purpose	Examples
Nonregulatory information	Awareness of hazards	Hot dogs, grapes, balloons
Regulatory information	Labeling	Toy labels, plastic bag labels
Regulatory and nonregulatory improvements in product quality	Reduce risks of existing products	Refrigerator and freezer door standards, crib slat design standards, clothing flammability standards, safety caps for pharmaceuticals
Regulatory and nonregulatory development of safety technologies	New products to reduce risks	Smoke detectors, window guards, car seats, outlet plugs, rail guards, bike helmets, scald guards
Behavioral safety regulation	Requirements that consumers comply with standards	Seat belt laws

seats may reduce the mortality of these children, but it could lead to increases in the mortality of older children if parents now drive faster.

Regulations that increase the cost of products, such as rules requiring toys and child furniture to meet new standards, will favor higher-income children. High-income children will benefit when their parents purchase the new products. Low-income families, however, may delay purchasing new products or may purchase secondhand products, potentially increasing the risks facing their children. These regulations may also favor lower birth order children if parents purchase new products for their firstborn children and then pass them along to younger siblings.

Regulation can be effective, however, if it serves as a means of conveying new information to parents. To the extent that regulations substitute for information that would otherwise be available in the private market, they may reduce the production advantages of better educated parents.

Better trauma care is likely to improve outcomes for all children. While high-income children may have better access to physician services, trauma care is provided through emergency rooms that must take all patients. Higher-income children and children outside rural areas may, however, be more likely to be located near a pediatric trauma center.

13.2   Empirical Strategy and Data

In principle, the model described in equation (1) should be tested in two stages: the probability of accident and the risk of mortality conditional on accident. Unfortunately, there is little data on the rate of accidents generally. Instead, I examine the determinants of mortality.

The theory of health production suggests that changes in mortality may be a consequence of changes in time or money inputs or changes in technology. I conduct two (closely related) sets of analyses to examine the roles of changes in inputs and to assess the nature, and role, of changes in technology. First, I estimate a model of the production of child injury mortality by cause in the 1960s as a function of family time and money inputs in that period. I then use the estimated production function to project child mortality by cause in 1980 and 1990 given the characteristics of children and their families in these later years. I compare the projected and actual mortality figures to assess the role of changes in measured inputs over this period. The residual is an estimate of the role of changing health production technology.

Second, I reestimate the model of health production using data from 1980 and 1990. I then compare the coefficients of key variables to assess how technology altered the production function for child health. The changes in the coefficients provide an indication of how the empirical changes in the production of child health conform to those predicted by a health production model.

Third, I assess the value of these changes in child health. I measure this value by imputing a value to the lives of children saved through improvements in technology.

13.2.1   Data

Even in 1960, childhood injury mortality was (thankfully) a rare event. In consequence, standard data sets that include children do not contain enough observations on serious childhood injury or mortality to serve as the basis of an empirical investigation of its determinants. Longitudinal mortality databases focus on mortality in the adult population and, in the few cases that include children, contain too few children to assess the covariates of mortality. Furthermore, these databases do not allow us to examine changing patterns in child mortality over time. Instead, I construct a database by combining data from the National Mortality Detail Files with data from the Current Population Survey.

The National Mortality Detail Files contain a record of every death recorded in the United States. Information in the file includes the state of residence of the decedent, the decedent's age, and the cause of death. I use data from the 1968, 1969, 1970, 1978, 1979, 1980, 1988, 1989, and 1990 detail files. I select all deaths among children ages one through twelve that occurred because of unintentional injury (E codes). I then group these causes into several broad categories and focus my analysis on total unintentional injury mortality and on the four most common causes of childhood injury mortality: automobile accidents, pedestrian accidents, fires, and drowning. I also examine mortality due to falls among children ages one through five. I group deaths into two categories: preschool-age children (ages one through five) and elementary school age children (ages six through twelve). I combine data for 1968–70, 1978–80, and 1988–90 to increase the cell sizes.

The Current Population Survey (CPS) contains demographic and economic information on adults and children in the United States. CPS data before 1968 do not contain information on children so I begin my analysis with the 1968 sample. In each CPS year, I identify all families that contain a child aged one through twelve. I then measure (separately) the average characteristics of families with children ages one through five and ages six through twelve in each state in the United States. Prior to 1973, the CPS combines states into thirty regions, so my analysis is limited to these regions. After 1973, I use data at the state level. Sample sizes for children are quite small, especially in the smaller states. To reduce variability in the data, I compute averages of each variable in each state over the three-year periods above (weighted by the number of observations for that year in that state).[3] Because of the high sampling variability in the CPS, I obtain

---

3. I analyzed the data both using and not using the CPS weights. I report unweighted results here, but use of the weights makes no substantial difference to the results.

counts of children in each age group in each state from the decennial censuses (1970, 1980, and 1990).

The health production model suggests that parental time and money, and technology are the principal inputs in the production of child health. I proxy parental time inputs with five variables: whether the mother is currently married, whether the mother works, how many infants (birth to one year) are in the family, how many preschool-aged children (ages one through five) are in the family, and how many older children (ages six through twelve) are in the family. I expect that married mothers and non-working mothers are likely to be able to devote more time to their children. Mothers with infants are likely to have less time to devote to their older children. The existence of more children of the same age as the index child within a family may improve health, to the extent that there are economies of scale in child safety. Older children may be able to help out and reduce injuries among their younger siblings; alternatively, they may expose their siblings to additional hazards, especially if safety equipment is handed down from child to child in a family. Changes in safety regulations aimed at younger children, however, may increase the hazard to older siblings.

In a very small number of CPS families, no mother is present in the household. In these families, I code the head of household, regardless of sex, as the "mother." A variable for the average percentage of households in a state without a mother present was never large or significant in any of the analyses.

Table 13.5 provides data on the characteristics of families in 1968, 1978, and 1988. In the period since 1968, parental time variables have moved in different directions. More mothers are working and fewer are married. Families are smaller, however, and children are much less likely to have older or younger siblings in the later years than in the early data.

The second set of inputs in the health production model is money spent on child safety. I use two variables to measure these money inputs. First, I measure average family income for families with children ages one through five and families with children ages six through twelve (note that, as discussed above, I also control for the number of children one through twelve in these families). Family income, measured in 1968 dollars, declined in the middle period and returned to just above 1968 levels in the later period. Second, I measure the physical environment of children in each age group. I include variables for the fraction of children who live in central cities and the fraction who live in Standard Metropolitan Statistical Areas (SMSAs). Changes in children's physical environments are likely to have important effects on their well-being. The types of accidents that occur are likely to be different in cities than in rural areas. For example, drowning deaths are rare in central cities, more common among younger children in suburban areas (where private swimming pools exist), and more common among older children in rural areas (where natural bodies of wa-

Table 13.5   Characteristics of CPS Families

	1970	1980	1990
Characteristics of Families of Children 1–5 (state averages)			
Census count of children (1,000s)	17,479	15,869	18,445
Family income (1968$)	8,434.67	7,602.14	8,608.74
Children under 1	0.14	0.12	0.12
Children 1–5	1.65	1.51	1.51
Children 6–12	0.95	0.61	0.58
Mother's education	11.12	11.59	11.65
Mother works	0.26	0.38	0.47
Currently married	0.88	0.81	0.74
Central city	0.27	0.22	0.25
SMSA	0.38	0.27	0.33
Nonwhite	0.16	0.20	0.22
Characteristics of Families of Children 6–12 (state averages)			
Census count of children (1,000s)	28,835	24,509	24,870
Family income (1968$)	9,722.65	8,725.90	9,610.22
Children under 1	0.06	0.05	0.05
Children 1–5	0.58	0.41	0.43
Children 6–12	2.24	1.80	1.72
Mother's education	11.05	11.53	11.93
Mother works	0.36	0.49	0.57
Currently married	0.87	0.79	0.75
Central city	0.26	0.21	0.23
SMSA	0.39	0.29	0.32
Nonwhite	0.15	0.19	0.22

Note: $N = 29$, 1968–70; $N = 50$ thereafter.

ter pose a hazard). Families have moved out of central cities, and, to a lesser extent, out of SMSAs over this period.

I include the average level of mother's education as a measure of the technology for producing child health. Finally, I include a measure of the percentage of a state's child population (in each age group) that is nonwhite as a control. I exclude observations for the District of Columbia, leaving a data set with twenty-nine observations in 1968–1970 and fifty observations in 1978–1980 and 1988–1990.

13.2.2   Statistical Method

The data set constructed by combining CPS and Vital Statistics data contains counts of child deaths (by cause), counts of children from the census, and average values of family characteristics, each measured as state averages. Because the dependent variable data are measured as counts, I use negative binomial regression methods for the analysis.[4]

I constrain the coefficient on the (log of the) count of children from the

---

4. I reject the hypothesis that the data are distributed as a Poisson for every analysis.

census to be equal to 1.[5] I estimate this regression separately for the 1968–70, 1978–80, and 1988–90 data. I use the estimated coefficients from the negative binomial regression to predict the expected number of deaths in subsequent years using the values of the independent variables in those years.

The coefficients from the negative binomial regression describe the effect of increasing an independent variable by one unit on the log of deaths from a particular cause. As an easier-to-interpret alternative, I simulate elasticities of response of cause-specific deaths to changes in the independent variables. I increase the value of each independent variable for each observation in turn by 1 percent (holding all other independent variables at their original values) and then compute the percentage change in the predicted mean for that cause of death. For example, I compute the percentage effect on pedestrian deaths among one through five year olds by increasing the average family income of families with one through five year olds by 1 percent.

13.3 Results

I initially estimate the mortality regressions using data for 1968–70. Coefficients and standard errors from these specifications are reported in table 13.6 for each cause of death and each age group.

Among younger children, average family characteristics explain 5–10 percent of the variation in childhood mortality at the state level. Parental time variables are important contributors to child mortality for some causes of death in 1968–70. States with more working mothers tend to have greater rates of all causes of child mortality than do those in which fewer mothers work. These states have significantly higher rates of automobile deaths and pedestrian deaths. Based on the simulation results (not reported in table), a 1 percent increase in the proportion of mothers working would increase the count of child automobile and pedestrian deaths in a state by 0.7 percent and 0.5 percent, respectively. The presence of older or younger children also tends to raise the risk of mortality for several causes of injury. Increasing the average number of infants in a family by 1 percent raises pedestrian deaths among those ages one through five by about 0.5 percent. There is some evidence of economies of scale in child safety production. States where the average one- to five-year-old has more preschool-age siblings have substantially and significantly lower rates of mortality among those ages one through five.

Family income is a significant predictor of childhood mortality only for automobile mortality among one- to five-year-olds in 1968–70, and for

5. In a separate set of regressions in which I did not constrain the coefficient, I can (almost) always reject the hypothesis that this coefficient is significantly different from 1.

Table 13.6   Production of Mortality, 1968–70

	Auto	Pedestrian	Falls	Fire	Drowning	All
			Children 1–5			
Constant	−9.019*	−5.140*	−15.138*	−9.691*	−6.331	−5.271*
	(3.047)	(1.580)	(3.532)	(1.959)	(4.976)	(1.499)
Income	−0.0002***	0.00003	0.00001	−0.00005	−0.0001	0.0001***
	(0.000)	(0.000)	(0.000)	(0.000)	(0.000)	(0.000)
Babies	2.278	4.610**	−1.687	−2.815	6.791	1.295
	(3.337)	(1.828)	(4.176)	(2.169)	(5.577)	(1.673)
1–5 years	−3.388**	−1.368***	2.648	0.106	−2.729	−1.587***
	(1.738)	(0.807)	(1.890)	(1.064)	(2.965)	(0.850)
6–12 years	0.862	0.533	−0.778	−0.080	0.748	0.455
	(0.613)	(0.332)	(0.748)	(0.383)	(1.123)	(0.306)
Mom's education	−0.040	−0.144	0.062	−0.288**	0.495	0.094
	(0.189)	(0.097)	(0.221)	(0.120)	(0.329)	(0.093)
Mom works	2.281***	1.623**	−2.392	−2.459*	2.653	0.778
	(1.370)	(0.674)	(1.606)	(0.842)	(2.186)	(0.669)
Mom married	6.934	−1.904	1.490	6.085**	−5.736	−0.322
	(4.747)	(2.198)	(4.972)	(2.769)	(8.304)	(2.274)
Central city	1.404**	0.123	−0.454	−0.689**	0.654	0.625**
	(0.583)	(0.284)	(0.634)	(0.352)	(0.924)	(0.283)
SMSA	0.308	0.559***	0.137	−0.395	1.173	0.145
	(0.640)	(0.302)	(0.695)	(0.392)	(1.019)	(0.308)
Nonwhite	1.630	−0.241	0.270	2.907*	−0.837	0.875
	(0.996)	(0.511)	(1.115)	(0.611)	(1.531)	(0.476)
R^2	0.07	0.10	0.05	0.16	0.04	0.06
Z	n.s.	0.08	n.s.	0.07	n.s.	n.s.

Children 6–12

Constant	−11.193*	−5.395*	−12.013*	−10.434*	−8.019*
	(1.956)	(1.704)	(2.356)	(1.758)	(0.926)
Income	−0.0002**	(0.0001)	0.000	−0.0002**	−0.0001*
	(0.000)	(0.000)	(0.000)	(0.000)	(0.000)
Babies	9.596***	6.717	7.841	4.374	5.344**
	(5.203)	(4.744)	(6.136)	(4.560)	(2.503)
1–5 years	−1.257***	0.160	−0.630	−0.046	−0.399
	(0.750)	(0.675)	(0.932)	(0.703)	(0.361)
6–12 years	1.593*	−0.642	−1.002	1.668*	0.930*
	(0.590)	(0.526)	(0.733)	(0.547)	(0.283)
Mom's education	0.228***	−0.380*	−0.047	0.194	0.148**
	(0.137)	(0.130)	(0.179)	(0.126)	(0.067)
Mom's works	1.206	0.639	−1.379	1.724**	0.643
	(0.850)	(0.752)	(1.049)	(0.771)	(0.406)
Mom married	−2.552	0.375	6.637***	−4.464***	−2.670***
	(2.931)	(2.709)	(3.695)	(2.660)	(1.422)
Central city	0.262	−0.908**	−0.772	−0.092	−0.170
	(0.455)	(0.403)	(0.555)	(0.403)	(0.217)
SMSA	−0.104	0.364	1.096***	0.015	−0.020
	(0.488)	(0.429)	(0.589)	(0.438)	(0.233)
Nonwhite	−0.138	−0.046	2.041**	0.180	0.242
	(0.675)	(0.620)	(0.851)	(0.601)	(0.325)
R^2	0.08	0.10	0.10	0.12	0.11
Z	0.09	n.s.	0.10	0.03	0.04

Notes: Coefficients from negative binomial regression. Population coefficient = 1. Standard errors in parentheses. n.s. = not significant.
$*p < 0.01$; $**p < 0.05$; $***p < 0.10$.

some causes of death the coefficient on income is small and positive. Overall, a 1 percent increase in income is associated with a 0.8 percent decline in mortality rates. The geographic distribution of children has varying effects depending on the particular cause of death. Overall, children in states that have more population in central cities have higher rates of mortality.

Mother's education has small, often negative, but rarely significant effects on preschool mortality in the one through five year age group. The proportion of children who are nonwhite greatly increases the risk of fire deaths, but does not contribute substantially to death from other causes.

Table 13.6 reports results for elementary school children ages six through twelve. In general, patterns of results are quite similar across the two age groups. Parental time variables, as a group, are important contributors to child mortality for all causes of death except pedestrian mortality. In states with more working mothers, childhood mortality rates from most causes are higher, sometimes significantly higher. The presence of infants also consistently increases the risk of childhood mortality among elementary school children. A 1 percent increase in the average number of infants in families of six- to twelve-year-olds raises mortality rates in this group by about 0.3 percent.

Family income is a more important determinant of childhood mortality among this older age group. For all causes, automobile accidents, and drowning deaths, children in states with higher average family income are at lower risk. A 1 percent increase in average family income reduces the risk of death from these causes by 1.6 percent. The geographic distribution of families has limited and inconsistent effects on mortality outcomes.

Mother's education has an unexpectedly positive effect on mortality for all causes, automobile accidents, and drowning deaths. This result may reflect unmeasured characteristics of families with more educated mothers. The nonwhite proportion again increases the risk of fire deaths but has little correlation with other causes of death.

13.3.1   Predicting Mortality

The results of the 1968–70 study suggest that changes in the living circumstances of children over the 1968–90 period may have contributed to changes in child mortality. In particular, the decline in the number of infants in households should have reduced mortality, while the increase in the proportion of mothers who work would have been expected to lead to an increase in mortality. Other changes may also have affected mortality outcomes.

To assess the role of these changes, I use the 1968–70 coefficients to predict rates of mortality given annual average living circumstances for 1970, 1980, and 1990. Actual counts of deaths; extrapolations for all causes, automobile accidents, and pedestrian deaths; and extrapolations based on constant rates of mortality are shown in table 13.7.

| Table 13.7 | | Counts of Deaths, Extrapolations, Predictions, and Errors, by Cause and Age Group | | | |

Cause	Actual	Extrapolation	Prediction	Extrapolation Error (%)	Prediction Error (%)
Children 1–5					
Auto					
1970	1,066	1,066	1,124	0	−5
1980	859	969	1,161	−13	−35
1990	722	1,121	764	−55	−6
Pedestrian					
1970	963	963	1,037	0	−8
1980	575	875	1,032	−52	−79
1990	374	1,013	1,569	−171	−320
Total					
1970	5,696	5,696	6,253	0	−10
1980	4,228	5,175	7,552	−22	−79
1990	3,365	5,989	8,706	−78	−159
Children 6–12					
Auto					
1970	1,379	1,379	1,298	0	6
1980	1,019	1,173	1,179	−15	−16
1990	816	1,192	1,185	−46	−45
Pedestrian					
1970	1,223	1,223	1,191	0	3
1980	702	1,040	965	−48	−37
1990	465	1,057	1,021	−127	−120
Total					
1970	5,522	5,522	5,308	0	4
1980	3,420	4,698	5,047	−37	−48
1990	2,409	4,774	5,385	−98	−124

Note: Predictions based on regressions in table 13.6. Extrapolations constructed by holding death rate constant and adjusting for size of population at risk.

For children ages one through five, the prediction regressions substantially overpredict total mortality in the later years. Actual mortality is less than one-third as high as expected. A simple linear extrapolation of death rates overpredicts mortality by about 80 percent.

Differences in mortality counts are relatively small for automobile deaths. This close correspondence is rather surprising because automobile safety was the primary subject of child safety regulation during the 1970s and 1980s. These results suggest that improvements in child safety because of regulations and design changes were offset by increased use of automobiles by children, or that such safety measures had a relatively minor impact on child mortality. The finding is consistent with epidemiologic studies that find surprisingly little correlation between the time series of safety restraint use rates and the time series of automobile fatalities (Agran, Castillo, and Winn 1990).

By contrast, the results of the prediction analysis for pedestrian mortality are sharply higher than actual pedestrian mortality rates. By 1990, the prediction estimates are more than four times as high as the actual figures. The prediction estimates are higher than extrapolations based on constant rates mainly because of the substantial increase in labor force participation rates among mothers of young children. The prediction regressions thus show that pedestrian mortality was expected to increase somewhat over this period. In fact, pedestrian mortality declined by 65 percent. Epidemiologists have noted the large declines in pedestrian mortality but have not been able to explain the observed patterns, especially in this younger age group (Rivara and Grossman 1996).

The prediction regression for deaths from falls (not shown in the table) almost precisely predicts the actual death rate. The prediction for deaths from fires (not shown in the table) strongly underpredicts the actual death rate.[6] Together with motor vehicle accidents, these two areas are those where improvements in pediatric trauma care might have been expected to have substantial effects. The finding that there was relatively less overprediction for these rates than for other causes suggests that improvements in medical care were not the primary reason for reductions in death rates in this age group.

The second panel of table 13.7, presents results for older children. Again, predicted all-cause mortality is more than twice as high as actual mortality. Differences between extrapolations and predictions are quite small for older children. In general, the prediction errors are slightly larger than the extrapolation errors.

The decline in automobile passenger mortality among children ages six through twelve was much steeper than among younger children and was not predicted by the initial regression. In most states, children ages six through twelve were not required to use auto safety restraints during the period under study. Most children did use such restraints, but use of restraints was less frequent in the older age group than among younger children (Johnston, Rivara, and Soderberg 1994). In combination with the results for one- to five-year-olds (who were affected by the regulations), the results for six- to twelve-year-olds whose behavior was not governed by child safety regulations suggest that regulatory changes aimed at child safety seat use are not as important an explanation for declines in mortality as might have been expected. Improvements in trauma treatment may have been an important factor in reducing mortality in this group.

Declines in pedestrian mortality were also steep among older children. Since younger children have very different walking patterns than older children, the combination of results for younger and older children sug-

6. The prediction for drowning deaths is unrealistically high for unknown reasons (the prediction error is 640 percent).

gests that greater use of school crossing guards or similar interventions cannot explain most of the change in pedestrian mortality. One explanation for the lower rate of pedestrian injury in older children is that they are less likely to walk to school alone now than they were twenty years ago (Rivara and Grossman 1996). This explanation is consistent with the pattern for older children, but does not explain the similar decline in mortality among younger children.

13.3.2   Changes in the Production of Child Safety

The discrepancies between the predicted and actual estimates of child mortality suggest that the decline in child mortality is not simply a consequence of a change in the inputs to health production. There is also likely to have been a change in the technology for producing child health. To investigate this possibility, I reestimate the regressions using data for 1968–70, 1978–80, and 1989–91. I include interaction effects for years after 1968 and for years after 1988. To simplify the comparison, table 13.8 reports coefficients for selected variables of interest.

We first examine the changing role of parental time in producing child safety. The effect of mothers' working on child mortality declines over time for most causes of death. The decline is stronger for older children than for younger children. By 1990, the proportion of mothers working in a state has essentially no effect on all-cause mortality for school children. The results for the presence of infants in the family (not reported in the table) show a similar declining pattern for both age groups. This result suggests that products and services (including formal day care) are increasingly valuable alternatives to parental time in the production of child health.

The role of family income varies over time but does not become important over this period for most causes of death in either age group. A growing role for family income is likely to occur when regulations mandate improvements in product quality or when new costly safety-improving technologies are introduced. For example, higher family income may reduce automobile passenger deaths if safer cars are more costly than less safe cars.

Mother's education plays a much greater beneficial role in reducing childhood injury after 1970 than in the early period, especially among younger children. This finding is consistent with the considerable expansion in information about childhood injury that became available in the 1970s and 1980s. Increases in information are likely to widen the gap between less and more educated families.

I had hypothesized that the presence of older siblings in a family might reduce the safety of younger children to the extent that families made time investments in safety technology. I assess this hypothesis by comparing the effect of the presence of older siblings on mortality among one- to five-

Table 13.8 Changing Production Function for Childhood Mortality

	Auto	Pedestrian	Falls	Fire	Drowning	All
			Children 1–5			
Income	-0.0002**	0.0000	0.0000	-0.0001	-0.0001	-0.0001
	(0.0001)	(0.0001)	(0.0001)	(0.0002)	(0.0002)	(0.0001)
Income 80/90	0.0002***	-0.0001	0.0001	0.0000	0.0002	0.0001
	(0.0001)	(0.0001)	(0.0002)	(0.0002)	(0.0002)	(0.0001)
Income 90	-0.0002***	0.0001	0.0000	-0.0001	-0.0001	-0.0001
	(0.0001)	(0.0001)	(0.0002)	(0.0001)	(0.0001)	(0.0000)
6–12	0.8692	0.5436	-0.7586	-0.1066	0.7679	0.4561
	(0.5543)	(0.3428)	(0.6916)	(0.7389)	(0.9263)	(0.2987)
6–12 80/90	2.0782**	0.7227	-0.3511	0.8055	3.4039**	1.7120*
	(0.8797)	(0.6534)	(1.3537)	(1.1766)	(1.3590)	(0.4790)
6–12 90	-2.4317**	-0.4978	2.0790	-0.9368	-2.9832**	-1.5431*
	(0.9964)	(0.9020)	(1.6260)	(1.3980)	(1.4565)	(0.5197)
Mom's education	-0.0437	-0.1452	0.070	-0.2790	0.4954***	0.0944
	(0.1710)	(0.1005)	(0.2042)	(0.2330)	(0.2709)	(0.0904)
Mom's education 80/90	-0.2732	-0.1201	-0.0358	0.2184	-0.7840**	-0.2199**
	(0.1984)	(0.1228)	(0.2533)	(0.2731)	(0.3068)	(0.1047)
Mom's education 90	0.2278	-0.0381	-0.0276	0.2819	-0.0606	0.0390
	(0.1408)	(0.1001)	(0.2030)	(0.2011)	(0.2012)	(0.0734)
Mom works	2.3615***	1.6306**	-2.3586	-2.5598	2.8559	0.7855
	(1.2352)	(0.7037)	(1.4814)	(1.6735)	(1.8204)	(0.6525)
Mom works 80/90	0.1112	-1.0149	0.1404	1.4320	0.3807	0.2902
	(1.4550)	(0.8929)	(1.8614)	(1.9416)	(2.1336)	(0.7630)
Mom works 90	-0.2358	-0.1918	1.0931	-1.1243	-0.1007	-0.5804
	(1.1152)	(0.9001)	(1.6543)	(1.4397)	(1.6249)	(0.5734)
Constant	-9.0677*	-5.1774*	-15.0997*	-9.3117**	-6.5121*	-5.2743*
	(2.7636)	(1.6386)	(3.2433)	(3.8089)	(4.1237)	(1.4636)
Year 80/90	-2.0693	-3.2933	4.2757	4.6924	-5.0039	-2.6649
	(3.1403)	(2.0717)	(4.3428)	(4.2997)	(4.6108)	(1.6589)
Year 90	3.1103	0.3436	4.1090	-0.2863	3.6294	1.3448
	(2.3071)	(2.0515)	(4.0584)	(3.0838)	(3.3591)	(1.2181)
R^2	0.13	0.21	0.13	0.07	0.08	0.15

			Children 6-12			
Test*90	0	0	0.08	n.s.	0	0
Test*80/90	0	0	n.s.	0.10	0	0
Income	−0.0002**	0.0001		−0.0001	−0.0002**	−0.000**
	(0.0001)	(0.0001)		(0.0001)	(0.0001)	(0.0001)
Income 80/90	0.0001	−0.0003*		0.0003***	0.0001	0.0002*
	(0.0001)	(0.0001)		(0.0002)	(0.0001)	(0.0001)
Income 90	−0.0001	0.0001		−0.0002***	−0.0001	−0.0002*
	(0.0001)	(0.0001)		(0.0001)	(0.0001)	(0.0000)
Mom's education	0.2297***	−0.3797*		−0.0347	0.1920	0.1524***
	(0.1412)	(0.1265)		(0.2204)	(0.1352)	(0.0862)
Mom's education 80/90	−0.3390***	0.2563		−0.0549	−0.4649*	−0.3596*
	(0.1775)	(0.1621)		(0.2714)	(0.1747)	(0.1066)
Mom's education 90	0.1248	0.0956		0.2530	0.0473	0.2605*
	(0.1491)	(0.1429)		(0.2212)	(0.1627)	(0.0851)
Mom works	1.1963	0.6358		−1.3299	1.6653**	0.5975
	(0.8738)	(0.7290)		(1.2932)	(0.8181)	(0.5195)
Mom works 80/90	0.3948	−0.9409		−2.7658***	0.4811	−0.4439
	(1.1209)	(0.9660)		(1.6572)	(1.0945)	(0.6535)
Mom works 90	−1.0140	−0.5357		2.9847***	−1.0725	−0.0046
	(1.0475)	(1.0179)		(1.5457)	(1.2331)	(0.6018)
Constant	−11.2132*	−5.3732*		−12.0159*	−10.4250*	−8.1155*
	(2.0089)	(1.6519)		(2.8952)	(1.8770)	(1.1827)
Year 80/90	1.8186	−2.4933		10.4299*	4.0610	2.2501
	(2.4867)	(2.2303)		(3.7284)	(2.4806)	(1.4536)
Year 90	1.2403	0.1273		−5.2572	0.9406	−1.0017
	(1.8478)	(1.9095)		(2.9122)	(2.1776)	(1.0664)
R^2	0.10	0.16		0.09	0.17	0.14
Test*90	n.s.	n.s.		n.s	0	0
Test*80/90	n.s.	0.03		0.03	0.05	0.03

Notes: Analyses also include all terms in table 13.6 and their year interactions. "80/90" interactions combine data for 1978–1980 and 1988–1990. "80" interactions combine data for 1978–1980. p value for Test*: likelihood ratio test of joint significance of 1990 and 1980/90 interaction variables. Standard errors in parentheses. n.s. = not significant.

*$p < 0.01$; **$p < 0.05$; ***$p < 0.10$.

year-olds over time. I find that the presence of older siblings placed younger children at increasing risk between 1968 and 1978, but this result disappears completely by 1988–1990.

Finally, we examine the hypothesis that regulations aimed at reducing injury in one group led to increased rates of injury in a different group as parents adjusted their behavior to maintain a constant level of safety (e.g., Peltzman 1975). We examine the effect of younger siblings (who are most affected by new regulations) on the mortality of older siblings (six- to twelve-year-olds). The presence of younger siblings never has a substantial or significant positive effect on the mortality of older children (not shown).

In the regressions estimated here, changes in the efficacy of trauma care would be expected to lead to overall reductions in childhood mortality, regardless of changes in family characteristics. In almost all of the cases examined, however, we find no significant change in the regression intercept after 1970 or after 1980.

Finally, I perform likelihood ratio tests to assess whether the set of interaction coefficients is jointly significant. I test whether the post-1970 coefficients are significant and whether the post-1980 coefficients are significant. The likelihood ratio tests confirm that the production functions for most causes of death changed significantly between the late 1960s and later and between the late 1970s and late 1980s.

13.4   The Value of Changes in Child Injury Mortality

I next estimate the value of the changes measured here. I apply a conservative estimate of $100,000 per life year, or about $3 million as the value of a life lost from injury to the differences between forecast (extrapolation and prediction) and actual mortality (value of life from Cutler and Richardson 1998). This estimate suggests that the total value of savings for young children amounts to between $8 and $16 billion each year or $430–$870 per child per year. The value of total savings for older children amounts to between $7 and $9 billion each year, or $280–$360 per child per year.

13.5   Discussion

My analysis suggests that there have been several profound changes in the production of child safety over the past three decades. Formal regulatory interventions, including mandatory car safety seats and fire alarms, can explain relatively little of what has happened. Rather, the results suggest that changes in parents' information about child safety are a more probable cause of the observed declines in mortality. This is not to say that regulations have been unimportant. They are likely to have played an important role in providing information to parents and I find no evidence whatsoever to suggest that they have perverse effects.

Economic theory suggests that information is usually a public good. One type of information is information about the nature and causes of injury and illness. This type of information is often produced by publicly funded epidemiologists and statisticians who simply examine patterns in the occurrence of events. In many cases, the conclusions of these analyses seem so straightforward that they hardly seem to present new information at all. Yet the history of child safety suggests that identifying quite obvious causes of injury, and ranking their relative importance, is a task that cannot readily be performed by parents. It would not seem necessary to do a study to show that falling out of windows is bad for children, but the New York City experience suggests that without such a study few parents recognize the magnitude of the risk.

Once epidemiological information about the risks of injury and the options for responding to these risks become available, it is disseminated widely (through vehicles such as Dr. Spock and corporations that sell child safety equipment) and consumers appear to act rapidly to make use of this information. The potential of such apparently basic information is important to recognize when assessing the role of technological change in social well-being and the role of government in promoting such technological change.

As information becomes available, it is easier for better educated parents to respond to it. While my results confirm the importance of information in improving child health, they also provide an illustration of how socioeconomic differences in health can be produced through the socially desirable production of valuable information.

References

Agran, P., D. Castillo, and D. Winn. 1990. Childhood motor vehicle occupant injuries. *American Journal of Diseases of Children* 144:653–62.

Auster, Richard D., Irving Levenson, and Deborah Sarachek. 1969. The production of health: An exploratory study. *Journal of Human Resources* 4:411–36.

Centers for Disease Control. Division of Injury Control. 1990. Childhood injuries in the United States. *American Journal of Diseases of Children* 144:627–46.

Consumer Product Safety Commission. 1993. Compilation of statutes administered by Consumer Product Safety Commission. Washington, D.C.: U.S. Government Printing Office.

Cutler, David M., and Elizabeth Richardson. 1998. The value of health: 1970–1990. *American Economic Review* 88 (2): 97–100.

Grossman, Michael. 1972. On the concept of health capital and the demand for health. *Journal of Political Economy* 80:223–55.

Johnston, Carden, Fredrick P. Rivara, and Robert Soderbergh. 1994. Children in car crashes: Analysis of data for injury and use of restraints. *Pediatrics* 93 (6): 360–65.

Office of Technology Assessment. 1988. Healthy children: Investing in the future.

Office of Technology Assessment Document no. OTA-H-345. Washington, D.C.: U.S. Government Printing Office.

Peltzman, Sam. 1975. The effects of automobile safety regulation. *Journal of Political Economy* 83:677–725.

Rivara, Frederick P. 1990. Child pedestrian injuries in the United States. *American Journal of Diseases of Children* 144:692–96.

Rivara, Frederick P., and David C. Grossman. 1996. Prevention of traumatic deaths to children in the United States: How far have we come and where do we need to go? *Pediatrics* 97 (6): 791–97.

Robertson, Leon S. 1992. *Injury epidemiology.* New York: Oxford University Press.

Spock, Benjamin. 1957. *The common sense book of baby and child care.* New ed. New York: Duell, Sloan and Pearce.

———. 1976. *Baby and child care.* 4th ed. New York: Hawthorn/Dutton.

Spock, Benjamin, and Michael B. Rothanberg. 1992. *Dr. Spock's baby and child care.* 6th ed. New York: Pocket Books.

U.S. Department of Health and Human Services. Various years. *Vital statistics for the U.S.* Washington, D.C.: U.S. Government Printing Office.

Wintemute, G. J. 1990. Childhood drowning and near-drowning in the United States. *American Journal of Diseases of Children* 144:663–69.

Comment   James A. Schuttinga

The paper by Glied is an interesting, unique contribution to this conference volume. It affirms the value of information produced with publicly sponsored research. It illustrates a methodology for evaluating the contribution of epidemiological research to prevention of mortality from childhood injury. And it provides an example of the contribution of research and development (R&D) to health, when the new information (or technology) is not embodied in a new pharmaceutical, device, or medical procedure. In fact, it demonstrates that R&D information can substitute for medical care by preventing injury or illness.

As an economist employed by the National Institutes of Health, I am particularly interested in the implications of this paper for two closely related topics—understanding the contribution of medical R&D to health, and the calculation of a true cost-of-living index.

Review of Findings and Methods

Something good happened between 1960 and 1990—a 50 percent reduction in mortality rates for children from unintentional injury and an estimated $15 billion to $25 billion per year in the value of life years saved. Glied specifies a model and examines the effects of several observable variables as possible explanations for the reduction in injury mortality. She

James A. Schuttinga is an economist in the Office of Science Policy, National Institutes of Health.

attributes the unexplained residual to the effect of epidemiological information on injury prevention. It would be more satisfying to specify a model that includes the instrument of interest and find that the estimated coefficient is statistically significant. That approach does not appear to be an option for this study.

However, Glied is able to tell a credible story. The reduction in injury mortality cannot plausibly be explained by improvements in family resources. Family income did not increase over the period and the share of single mothers and working mothers increased.

She suggests why the epidemiological information was developed. The activities of the Consumer Product Safety Commission stimulated interest in injury epidemiology and well-trained epidemiologists were available. The need for research on infectious diseases was diminishing and injury provided a new opportunity.

The paper provides an explanation of how information is dispensed: through regulations (seatbelts and infant car seats) and threat of product liability, by equipment manufacturers who advertise the benefits of their products, and through guidance books by Dr. Spock and others. It is interesting that a for-profit book was an important instrument for dispensing information.

Glied correctly recognizes that the value and the public goods nature of R&D information justifies public support of certain types of R&D, including epidemiological research on causes of injury. We must also recognize the implications of the costliness of producing, disseminating, and using R&D information and the evolutionary nature of the R&D process. New information may not be used if people do not know about it or it is deemed too costly. Individuals may find the behavioral changes too onerous or the side effects of a pharmaceutical or other intervention too adverse.

The costliness of using R&D information on injury has implications for Glied's analysis of the reduction in injury mortality. While she does not dwell on it, the information on injury is costly to use. It requires purchasing and using new safer products at an obvious and identifiable expense. Even more important, it involves behavioral modification. These costs are not usually expressed in market transactions and can be manifest in unanticipated ways. For some activities, like turning pot handles over the stove and using seat belts and infant car seats, the costs are modest. For other behavior modifications, the costs may be more onerous and may be resisted.

I suspect that many childhood activities now deemed risky are simply prohibited without replacement. Slides and jungle gyms, common on school yards in the sixties and earlier, have disappeared today. Children are not allowed to ride bicycles on streets to school, on errands to stores, or simply for recreation. Some of the cost is borne in increased parental chauffeuring. But I suspect that children bear much of the cost in terms of a more sedentary, less adventuresome lifestyle. Recent news reports suggest that children spend more time on sedentary activities, particularly video games, and are becoming more obese.

I also suspect that part of the reduction in injury mortality is the side effect of a change in life styles, rather than a conscious choice to avoid risky behavior. The design of suburban communities, the busy two-paycheck families who substitute auto travel and supervised day care for time with children, the slow behavioral adjustment to smaller families, and the fear of child abduction and molestation (rather than fear of injury), all conspire to reduce children's risk exposure as well as their opportunity for exercise and adventure.

For all these reasons, more research on how parents and children respond to the relative costs of alternative behavior modifications is needed. It would be informative to develop a more direct story of the intervention mechanism for information on injury epidemiology (perhaps documented with representative case studies or surveys). How did the parents actually receive the information? How did they modify their behavior? The relative costs of proposed modifications might also explain which behaviors were adopted and which were resisted. The response probably varies by family and person. By analogy, we know that some parents, and prospective parents, are not willing to give up behaviors that put children and fetuses at risk (for illness or injury)—alcohol abuse, smoking, aggressive driving, poor food selection and preparation. The public reaction to the recent revision in obesity guidelines illustrates public distrust of public pronouncements and reluctance to modify pleasurable behavior.

It is not likely that the next 50 percent reduction in injury mortality will result from more epidemiological research on injury alone. Information on which recommendations parents have accepted and what they have resisted is important for designing future interventions.

Implications for Evaluation of the Contributions of Biomedical Research

Reflection on Glied's paper suggests a number of implications for the evaluation of the contributions of research. She evaluates the contribution of research-generated information that is not embodied in a specific product or device (or, at least, not completely embodied in new, safer products). NIH cannot take much credit for the reduction in mortality rates, because it did not fund most of the underlying epidemiological research on childhood injury. But NIH does fund analogous research that provides information on beneficial behaviors that can improve health and prevent disease. Examples include the "Back to Sleep Program"—placing infants on their backs to sleep to reduce sudden infant death syndrome (SIDS); information on the benefits of folic acid dietary supplementation to prevent neural tube defects; and information on the effect of alcohol abuse on health—cirrhosis of the liver and fetal alcohol syndrome. Glied's methods might be useful for evaluating the contribution of this type of information also.

Rather than tracing the impact of a single intervention or piece of information, Glied examines the cumulative impact of a broad class of related interventions—in this case, information on injury prevention. Variations on that approach might be useful to examine the contribution of R&D to health: when there are multiple, interrelated risk factors (e.g., multiple genetic and behavioral causes of birth defects) or when multiple interventions are available to control a disease or risk factor (e.g., pharmaceuticals and diet to control hypertension) and an intervention can be tailored to the particular needs or preferences of individuals or subpopulations.

I noted that the costliness of using information on injury epidemiology may inhibit use. More generally, the costliness of producing, disseminating, and using R&D information has implications for the R&D process and for evaluating the contribution of R&D for health. Because of public budget constraints, not every project can be funded immediately. As a result, the available information on injury or disease prevention will initially be incomplete. The most effective products/interventions will not be available immediately. The public's lack of knowledge of new information, the less than complete effectiveness of proposed behavioral modifications or interventions, and inconvenience or adverse side effects will all conspire to limit the use and value of R&D-generated information. Over time, refinements will be developed to improve effectiveness and diminish side effects and costs of use. Partly because public funds will never be sufficient to support all R&D opportunities or to effectively disseminate all available information, private agents are instrumental in the production, dissemination, and use of R&D information. Private firms often take the lead in development and refinement of pharmaceuticals or devices that embody the research-generated knowledge. The products or procedures may make it more convenient to use. For example, a pharmaceutical or dietary supplement may deliver the therapeutic benefits without the need for dietary or behavioral adjustments. But private firms may shy away from the process of transforming knowledge developed from basic research into commercial applications if they perceive the process to be too risky or the market too small.

Health care providers, in general, and physicians in particular, are an important intermediary for disseminating R&D based information. They prescribe pharmaceuticals and procedures and provide information on healthy behavior and risk avoidance. They may be slow to learn about and adopt new procedures and pass on new information when there is not a clear advantage or incentive for them to do so.

A major implication of the costliness is that the benefits of publicly funded R&D-generated information may require years to be completely manifest and will depend on institutional arrangements that influence private agents to develop, disseminate and use R&D information.

Implications for Cost-of-Living Index

Glied's analysis of the contribution of information to injury prevention and more general reflection on the evaluation of R&D contributions suggests a number of implications for the construction of true cost-of-living index for medical care—an index that nets out increased benefits against the increased costs registered by price changes.

First, nonmedical interventions may substitute for medical interventions. The prevention of injury or disease with improved nonmedical products (safer furniture and clothing, smoke alarms, and safety belts) or behavioral modifications can reduce expenditures on medical care. The nonmedical costs and benefits should be netted against changes in medical costs.

Second, the costs of behavioral modifications are not always manifest in prices of market transactions. But such costs should be included in a true cost-of-living index if the associated benefits or reductions in medical expenditures are included.

Third, the costs and benefits of an intervention or a behavioral modification often are not realized during the same period (hospital episode, week, month, or calendar year). As sketched above, because of the evolutionary nature of the R&D process, the benefits of R&D information may be fully manifest after several years. A true cost-of-living index must consider the benefits and costs over the complete time horizon.

Final Thoughts

Glied identified ways that R&D information contributes to injury prevention (and health improvement generally). It motivates safety regulations, encourages development of new products (partly from threat of lawsuits for defective products), and provides information to parents that enables them to better allocate the resources they devote to child health. I would add another way. R&D information, especially epidemiological information, generates hypotheses and stimulates new research that contributes to improved information, products, and procedures. I hope that the research reported in this paper will stimulate Glied and others to continue to examine how R&D information motivates behavioral changes and contributes to improved health.

Patient Welfare and
Patient Compliance
An Empirical Framework for
Measuring the Benefits from
Pharmaceutical Innovation

Paul Ellickson, Scott Stern, and Manuel Trajtenberg

14.1 Introduction

The pharmaceutical industry's innovative output consists primarily of a small number of new drugs, each of which is required to receive FDA approval. While substantial social value is often attributed to pharmaceutical innovation, there have been only a small number of actual evaluations of the welfare gains stemming from the introduction and diffusion of new drugs (Lichtenberg 1996). In the absence of a measurement framework to assess the patient benefits arising from new product introduction, regulation of the pharmaceutical industry and other institutions of the health care system turns on an incomplete vision of the relevant costs and benefits of different public policy choices.

The main goal of this paper is to develop an empirical framework for evaluating the patient welfare benefits arising from pharmaceutical innovation. Extending previous studies of the welfare benefits from innovation (Trajtenberg 1990; Hausman 1997), this paper unpacks the separate choices made by physicians and patients in pharmaceutical decision making and develops an estimable econometric model which reflects these choices. Our proposed estimator for patient welfare depends on (1)

Paul Ellickson is assistant professor of economics and management in the Simon School of Business Administration at the University of Rochester. Scott Stern is assistant professor at the Sloan School of Management, Massachusetts Institute of Technology, and a faculty research fellow of the National Bureau of Economic Research. Manuel Trajtenberg is professor of economics at Tel Aviv University, a research associate of the National Bureau of Economic Research, a fellow of the Canadian Institute of Advanced Research, and a research fellow of the Centre for Economic Policy Research, London.

The authors are grateful to Ashoke Bhattacharjya, Judy Hellerstein, Alison Keith, Ariel Pakes, and Tom Hubbard for useful conversations. This research was supported by Pfizer and the MIT Program on the Pharmaceutical Industry.

whether patients comply with the prescriptions they receive from physicians and (2) the motives of physicians in their prescription behavior. By focusing on compliance behavior, the proposed welfare measure reflects a specific economic choice made by patients. Moreover, because physicians act as imperfect agents for their patients, physician prescription behavior reflects both the consequences of agency as well as an evaluation of which drug yields the highest benefits for a given patient. The key contribution of this paper resides in integrating the choices made by both patients and physicians into a unified theoretical framework and suggesting how the parameters of such a model can be estimated from data.

Relying on recent advances in the study of differentiated product markets (Berry 1994; Trajtenberg 1990), we develop a discrete choice model that lends itself naturally to the evaluation of welfare gains from pharmaceutical innovation. The model highlights two important aspects of pharmaceutical markets. First, pharmaceutical therapies are discrete in nature; for most diseases, one drug regimen is given to each patient to the exclusion of substitutes. Second, patients are heterogeneous in ways which may be either observed or unobserved by the investigator. Examples include the severity of their illness, their price sensitivity, or their sensitivity to the side effects associated with specific drugs. As a first step, we propose a "baseline" model of pharmaceutical choice which abstracts away from the institutional details of pharmaceutical decision making. In this model, fully informed patients are assumed to hold authority over their pharmaceutical choices and bear full financial responsibility for their decisions. Extending past characterizations, we present a computationally straightforward method to calculate patient welfare under this baseline model.

We then turn to the heart of the paper—the development of an estimable model of pharmaceutical choice which accounts for the most salient institutions of pharmaceutical decision making. The key problem lies in the fact that the prescription decision is vested with the physician rather than with the patient. While physicians are more informed than their patients about the relative benefits of different therapies and have some incentives to attain an "optimal matching" between patient and drug, a wedge may yet exist between the interests and preferences of the patient and the actual behavior of the physician. Specifically, physicians may be less sensitive than patients to the effective prices of drugs and may underinvest in gathering the types of information about patients and/or drugs which yield the best fit (Stern and Trajtenberg 1998).[1] As a result, the exclusive use of physician prescription patterns to infer patient welfare is

---

1. This phenomenon may have significantly changed in recent years: the rise of managed care may have increased the incentives of physicians to respond to the true prices (e.g., through a capitation system) while managed care may have reduced the effective price-sensitivity of many patients (by offering more generous pharmaceutical insurance than many fee-for-service plans).

at best problematic. Such a calculation would of course capture patient welfare to the degree that physicians act as a filter for patient preferences, but prescription-level analysis cannot reflect the economic choices made by patients directly.

In order to address the problems stemming from the wedge between physician and patient preferences in the context of drug choice, we redirect our analysis toward the choices that patients do make—whether or not to *comply* with prescriptions. After receiving a prescription from a physician for a specific drug, patients choose whether or not to fill the prescription (purchase compliance), whether or not to maintain the regimen once purchased (use compliance), and whether or not to maintain the prescription over the life of refills and follow-up (sustained compliance). Accordingly, variation in compliance rates across drugs reflects different valuations of the incremental utility afforded by drugs as compared to a common baseline, namely no pharmaceutical therapy (the "outside good"). Of course, welfare analysis based on compliance must account for the fact that, since physicians act as informed and interested agents for their patients, patients who choose whether to comply with a prescription for a given drug have been selected into that choice by their physician.

Clearly, if nearly all patients comply (or if there is little variation in compliance across drugs), the fact that patients face choices still would leave little room for the actual measurement of patient welfare. We therefore present a review of evidence from the clinical medical literature suggesting that compliance both within and across drug therapies is an important empirical phenomena, providing a basis for empirical work in this area. While medical researchers focus on different issues and frame them in different terms than economists might (for example, most assume that noncompliance is irrational on the part of the patient), the evidence is compelling. First, noncompliance rates are astonishingly high, reaching up to 70 percent. Second, there is substantial variation in the compliance rate, depending on the type of drug and disease being treated.

With this evidence as motivation, we introduce our alternative model and corresponding welfare function. Two important issues are addressed: First, patients vary in the degree and nature of their insurance and in their unobserved costs of complying with their physician's approved therapy. Second, because compliance is *conditional* on the prescription behavior of physicians, we account for the selectivity of patients into drugs, induced by physicians responding to patient characteristics which are not observed by the econometrician. To address this selection problem, we specify a general model of physician behavior and identify the distribution of idiosyncratic utility *conditional on prescription.* This conditional distribution is a simple function of the parameters of the physician behavior model and can be calculated analytically for special classes of distributions. Thus, our model provides a way of controlling for the fact that physicians match patients to drugs, for any set of assumptions about how that matching process unfolds. With such a control in place, we are able to propose a consistent estimator for patient welfare for any set of pharmaceutical products available in the market. This estimator is a function of the vector of compliance rates for individual drugs in a therapeutic category, as well as of the characteristics of those drugs and of the underlying patient population. Our estimator can be used to perform counterfactuals such as the welfare loss associated with a year of delay in regulatory approval, or the incremental returns from "one-a-day" pills which increase compliance versus a completely new form of treatment for a particular pathology.

Our analysis suggests that there are high returns to understanding how patients respond to choices in the health care system, even if most of the system involves the delegation of authority to their agents (primarily physicians). Currently, there are few systematic data-gathering efforts by the government (or by private data-gathering sources) aimed at collecting this type of information, limiting both our understanding of the benefits from pharmaceutical innovation as well as the welfare impact of physician authority.

14.2   A Baseline Model of Pharmaceutical Choice and Welfare

We begin by restating the commonly held assumption that consumer welfare can be measured by the revealed preferences of consumers through their observed choices. In the market for a single, homogeneous good, only those consumers who value the good above its price purchase the good.[2] Under these conditions, the consumer welfare (surplus) in this market is measured by the area between the demand curve and price; further, the incremental welfare from product innovation requires a comparison of the difference in the area under the demand curve before and after the innovation has been introduced into the market. In this sense, the welfare benefits from technological change result from the diffusion of new technologies rather than their mere invention (Griliches 1958).

While many studies have attempted to gauge the producer returns to innovation, both in the pharmaceutical industry as well as elsewhere (Hall 1995), the difficulties associated with estimating demand have limited the calculation of the consumer welfare implications of innovation. These difficulties arise in part because product innovation occurs mostly in product differentiated markets, and hence new goods do not simply augment the prevalent market demand curve but provide an imperfect substitute for older goods. When consumers substitute the new (innovative) good for

---

2. Or, alternatively, each consumer purchases the good until her marginal utility equals the price of the good, making her indifferent between and additional unit of the good and its expense (the price).

the old, the consumer welfare benefits from the innovation are composed of two parts: The first consists of the incremental value placed on the new product by those who substituted (a direct effect), and the second captures the impact of the introduction of the new product on the prices and utility earned by consumers of the old product (which will yield a set of indirect effects). Thus, the calculation of consumer welfare arising from the introduction of a new differentiated product requires an estimate of the degree to which the new product replaces older goods, an estimate of the incremental value gained by those who switch, and finally, an evaluation of the competitive impact of innovation on the market prices of existing products.

Consider the introduction of Zantac by Glaxo in 1982. Zantac provided a differentiated substitute for Tagamet, which had been introduced about five years earlier. While Zantac was believed to be superior to Tagamet along some therapeutic dimensions, Tagamet remained the preferred product for a portion of the market (though Zantac eventually achieved a majority market share). In order to calculate the incremental welfare arising from the introduction of Zantac, we need to estimate a demand system which allows us to calculate consumer surplus when Zantac was both in and out of the market. With such a demand system, it is possible to calculate the impact of Zantac as it diffused into the market. After all, the bulk of consumer benefits from Zantac did not arise upon Zantac's introduction (at which time it achieved only a small market share), but only as patients substituted over time out of Tagamet (or no therapy) into the newer drug.

While estimating the welfare impacts associated with these market dynamics is challenging, several methods which have been developed in recent years allow for accurate measurement (Bresnahan 1986; Trajtenberg 1990; Hausman 1997), most notably the discrete choice framework which forms the basis of our current approach. The basic notion in these models is that competing products in a given market can be thought of as consisting of different vectors of characteristics (or performance dimensions), selling for different prices. Consumers derive utility from these characteristics (disutility for price), and choose their preferred product by comparing the various options available in the market in terms of the overall utility that different products provide. The econometric estimation of demand models of this sort yields the parameter estimates needed to compute the welfare gains from innovation: the marginal utility of the attributes of the products, the degree of substitutability between new and old products, and other parameters pertinent to the diffusion process of new products. We can exploit our estimate of the value that consumers place on attributes to compute the incremental surplus associated with the introduction of new products incorporating superior characteristics.

Trajtenberg (1989, 1990) applies this framework to the case of computed tomography (CT) scanners, one of the most remarkable medical innovations of the last few decades. Even though CT scanners are complex systems from a technological viewpoint, there are just a few attributes that characterize their performance (primarily scan speed and resolution). In the decade following the introduction of the first scanner by EMI in 1973, a tremendous amount of entry and innovation took place in the CT scanner market, leading to dramatic improvements in those attributes (as well as the introduction of new features). For example, scan time dropped from five minutes to one to two seconds, and spatial resolution improved to less than one millimeter. Each year, buyers of CT scanners faced much-improved choice sets; the question is how valuable those improvements were. Using detailed data on the prices, attributes, and sales of each model in the market each year, Trajtenberg (1989) estimated a discrete choice model of demand for these systems. The estimated demand parameters were used to compute the (substantial) welfare benefits stemming from the innovations introduced year after year. These calculated gains were then used to compute the *social* rates of return to investments in R&D and examine the pattern of those gains over time.

In view of the peculiarities of pharmaceutical markets, this methodology needs to be extended and modified in order to apply it successfully to the study of innovation in pharmaceuticals. In particular, while Trajtenberg abstracted away from the institutional details of hospital decision making, our approach tackles these issues head on. In particular, our preferred framework (developed in section 14.4) assesses patient welfare from the analysis of *compliance* behavior, rather than simply relying on observed prescriptions, since compliance is a choice made by patients, while prescription is a choice made by physicians acting as agents for patients. However, in order to fix ideas we first abstract away from the institutional context and agency problems, and introduce a baseline model of pharmaceutical decision making predicated on the assumption of optimal prescribing and purchasing behavior by informed patients with authority over their treatment choices.

Our point of departure is a simple discrete choice model, as in Berry (1994). Each patient maximizes the utility derived from pharmaceutical purchasing by choosing among $J_t + 1$ alternatives (J_t marketed products in year t and the option of no purchase [$j = 0$]), as follows,

$$(1) \qquad \max_{j \in \{0, \ldots, J_t\}} V_{ij} = X_j' \beta_i + \alpha_i \text{PRICE}_j + \xi_j + \varepsilon_{ij} = \delta_j + \mu_{ij},$$

where V_{ij} is the value of drug j to patient i, β_i the marginal valuations of the observed characteristics of drug j, α_i the disutility associated with price, ξ_j the utility associated with unobserved (to the econometrician) characteristics, and ε_{ij} an idiosyncratic patient-drug specific effect. Berry (1994) suggests rewriting such a value function in terms of the mean utility accruing to a representative consumer, δ_j, and the deviation from that mean valuation for an individual consumer, μ_{ij}, where the joint distribution of idiosyncratic utility, $F(\mu; \sigma)$, is parameterized according to σ.

The choice problem in equation (1) determines the probability that a patient of a given type chooses the jth drug, that is, $\Pr(V_{ij} > V_{ik} \ \forall \ j \neq k) = \Pr(\delta_j + \mu_{ij} > \delta_k + \mu_{ik} \ \forall \ j \neq k)$. Moreover, by considering a population of such patients, it is possible to estimate the demand for each drug (i.e., its market share, s_j) as a function of its own price and characteristics (conditional on the prices and characteristics of alternatives). Product-level demand depends both on the average utility level, δ_j, and the degree of substitutability with other products (i.e., whether μ_j is correlated with other elements of μ). The empirical characterization of the demand system therefore requires estimates of the elements of δ and σ. As discussed in Berry (1994), estimating distributional parameters may require the repeated evaluation of a $(J_t + 1)$-dimensional integral, a computationally intensive task in many circumstances. Prior research has overcome this challenge by drawing upon distribution functions from the generalized extreme value (GEV) class, allowing for the analytical computation of the market share function (and, as will be seen below, of the welfare function). Our proposed baseline model of pharmaceutical demand follows this methodology, and hence we develop the calculation of welfare under the assumption that the distribution of idiosyncratic utility follows a GEV distribution. In this context, it is useful to recall that the logit function for market share, $s_j = (e^{\delta_j})/(\Sigma_{j \in J} e^{\delta_j})$, results from the imposition of an independent type I extreme value distribution, the simplest distribution function in this class (McFadden 1978). While our framework is flexible enough to accommodate more general distributional assumptions (including semiparametric models), our focus on GEV and variants allows us to sharpen the issues associated with welfare calculation in the context of a computationally feasible model.

While the maximization problem in equation (1) abstracts away from agency and learning problems, it does highlight important elements of pharmaceutical choice. First, the model makes it clear that the benefits from new pharmaceutical products arise from substitution out of old therapies (or no therapy) into the new drug; second, the model highlights the centrality of patient heterogeneity. By specifying that the parameters which govern the value placed on each drug be patient-specific, the model accommodates heterogeneity along several dimensions, including differential sensitivity to price and to therapeutic characteristics of the drug (such as side effects, dosing regimens, or bioavailability). This patient-drug interaction captures the idea that pharmaceutical choice involves "matching" each patient with the drug which is most appropriate for his or her specific condition (Melmon et al. 1992; Stern and Trajtenberg 1998).

As suggested above, the parameters of the baseline model can be estimated from the relationship between observed market shares and the prices and characteristics of different drugs available in the market. With the aid of these parameters, one can then characterize the incremental benefits associated with expansions in the choice set or changes in the characteristics of particular choices (such as changes in prices or dosing regimens). Concretely, as shown in Trajtenberg (1990), W_t can be computed just as the summation of the consumer surplus associated with each product, conditional on the prices and characteristics of available substitutes:

$$(2) \qquad W_t = \sum_{j=0}^{J_t} \int_{p_j}^{\infty} s_j(q_j | q_k = p_k \forall k < j, q_k = \infty \ \forall \ k > j) dq_j.$$

It is useful to note that, even in this general formulation, the incremental welfare from a new good depends on the level and steepness of the slope of the demand curve for it. To the extent that the new product is a close substitute for old products (and thus faces a flat demand curve), the welfare gains from its introduction will be less dramatic than if existing products are poor substitutes for the new good.

Calculating each element of equation (2) requires integrating the J-dimensional integral which determines market share,

$$s_j = \int_R \int_{-\infty}^{(\delta_j - \delta_k + \mu_{ij})} dF(\mu_k | \mu_j, \forall \ k \neq j; \sigma) dF(\mu_j; \sigma_j).$$

However, as mentioned above, if μ is drawn from the generalized extreme value distribution, then this computational complexity is substantially eased, and it is feasible to calculate the market share function analytically (McFadden 1978; Bresnahan, Stern, and Trajtenberg 1997). Here we extend this prior result and show that the welfare function is also an analytically defined function of the GEV distribution function and depends only on estimating the parameters of the discrete choice model. This can be seen most clearly in the case where price sensitivity is constant.

PROPOSITION 1. *Under the maximization model in equation (1) and* $\alpha_i = \alpha$, *if* $G_t: R_{J+1} \to R^1$ *is a nonnegative, homogenous of degree one function satisfying certain restrictions,[3] then* $F(\mu_{i,0}, \ldots, \mu_{i,J_t}) = \exp - G_t(e^{-\mu_{i,0}}, \ldots, e^{-\mu_{i,J_t}})$ *is the cumulative distribution function of a multivariate GEV distribution and*

$$(3) \qquad W_t = \frac{\ln[G_t(\delta_0, \ldots, \delta_{J_t})]}{-\alpha}$$

---

3. The limit of $G(\cdot)$ as any argument goes to ∞ must be equal to ∞, mixed partials of $G(\cdot)$ alternate in sign, and first derivative with respect to each argument is nonnegative (McFadden 1978).

is the per capita expected utility (or average level of consumer welfare) from participating in the market.

PROOF. By Roy's identity, we know that $\partial W/\partial p_j = -s_j$. From theorem 1 of McFadden (1978),

$$s_j = \frac{\partial G(\delta)/\partial \delta_j}{G(\delta)}.$$

Assume that

$$W_t \neq \frac{\ln[G_t(\delta_0, \ldots, \delta_{J_t})]}{-\alpha}.$$

Then,

$$\frac{\partial \left(\dfrac{\ln[G_t(\delta_0, \ldots, \delta_{J_t})]}{-\alpha} \right)}{\partial p_j} \neq -s_j.$$

establishing a contradiction.

The functional form for the choice probabilities in a GEV model makes calculating patient welfare particularly straightforward. As additional products are introduced into the market (or the features of existing products are enhanced), the value of G_t increases, and so does the welfare function W_t.[4] Proposition 1 also suggests a useful way to conceptualize the measurement and meaning of patient welfare: It is the monetary amount a patient would pay to be faced with the choice set J_t prior to observing the realization of idiosyncratic utility (μ_i).

Extending proposition 1 to accommodate heterogeneity in α is immediate. When patients differ in their price sensitivity, *total* patient welfare requires the calculation of just a single-dimensional integral over the distribution of price sensitivities, as follows:

$$(4) \qquad W_t = \int \frac{\ln\{G_t[\delta_0(\alpha_i), \ldots, \delta_{J_t}(\alpha_i)]\}}{-\alpha_i} dF(\alpha_i; \sigma_\alpha).$$

Under this framework, calculating the incremental welfare benefits from innovation is straightforward, involving just the difference $\Delta W =$

---

4. For example, in the simplest case of logit probabilities,

$$W_t = \frac{\ln\left(\sum_{j=1}^{J_t} e^{\delta_t} \right)}{-\alpha}.$$

$W_{t+1} - W_t$, which captures the gains in consumer welfare as the product set changes between the two time periods.

14.3 Economic Implications of Physician Authority and Patient Compliance

Two related features of pharmaceutical decision making suggest that the baseline model presented above may lead to a biased and potentially misleading assessment of the welfare gains arising from pharmaceutical innovation. First, there are strong reasons to believe that physician authority over the prescription decision may lead to systematic biases in prescribing patterns. Because information asymmetry is at the heart of any expert relationship, physicians may have the opportunity to take advantage of their informational advantage in their prescription behavior. For example, several recent studies point to the presence of strong habit effects, whereby some physicians tend to prescribe in the same way across patients, even though the heterogeneity of patients' conditions may call for matching different drugs to different patients (Hellerstein 1998; Stern and Trajtenberg 1998; Coscelli 1998). To the extent that individual patients find it difficult to monitor such behavior, physicians may earn an information rent through underinvestment in "matching" individual patients to drugs. As developed in related work (Stern and Trajtenberg 1998), this would manifest itself in a high degree of concentration in the physician's prescribing portfolio and a tendency to prescribe drugs which are most appropriate for an "average" patient.[5]

Second, to the extent that patients choose not to comply with prescribed therapies, a gulf may arise between physician prescribing patterns and realized patient welfare. Although patients may have relatively little control over the medication prescribed, they are free to ignore their physician's recommended regimen. In fact, since compliance rates reflect patients' valuations of particular therapies, we can take advantage of this observed behavior to infer welfare. By approaching welfare in such a way, our analysis builds on a growing literature aimed at acknowledging the information value inherent in patient decision making and the effect of patient choice on health care outcomes (Philipson and Posner 1993; Meltzer, chap. 2 in

---

5. On the other hand, the impact of agency in pharmaceutical decision making should not be overstated. In contrast to other areas of health care which are subject to physician inducement (Gruber and Owings 1996), physicians receive no direct pecuniary benefit from prescribing one drug over another. Of course, to the extent that the patients can choose their physician, there exists a practice-building incentive to provide high-quality care; however, this practice-building has the effect of ameliorating the agency problem rather than exacerbating it. The presence of induced demand considerations may impact the *overall* level of pharmaceutical demand, as physicians may order expensive (and revenue-producing) procedures and substitute away from pharmaceutical therapy. In other words, while direct pecuniary-based incentive issues may shape the overall substitution between drugs and other therapies, agency within prescription behavior should arise from sources other than induced demand.

this volume). In particular, our methodology complements the work of Philipson and Hedges (1998), who argue that the statistical evaluation of clinical trials must account for the active role that subjects play in evaluating treatments. Specifically, a patient's decision to withdraw from an experiment reflects his or her evaluation of the effectiveness of the therapy (which the patient knows may be simply a placebo). Those patients who receive the greatest disutility from being placed on the placebo may opt out of the clinical trial, leading to a downward bias in the measured effectiveness of the drug as calculated by a difference between the (ex post) treated and control groups. Our model extends these prior analyses by focusing on the implication of compliance for the doctor-patient relationship itself, using the observed compliance share to quantify the wedge between physician and patient valuations.[6]

The degree of observed patient noncompliance is truly surprising. Several studies put overall patient noncompliance at around 50 percent (Sacket 1979), indicating a sizable difference between the benefits perceived by physician and patient. The problem of patient noncompliance has garnered sustained interest in the medical literature for the past twenty-five years. One study has estimated the cost of noncompliance as a result of hospital readmissions and lost productivity at $100 billion annually (National Pharmaceutical Council 1992). Patient noncompliance extends to a variety of chronic conditions, cuts across demographic categories, and covers a wide range of gravity of cases (Dunbar-Jacob et al. 1995). From a clinical perspective, noncompliance involves a variety of costs above and beyond the simple reduced effectiveness of the medication, including reduced ability by physicians to assess drug regimen effectiveness, increased drug resistance, and a higher probability of the onset of a more severe condition. In addition, overestimation of compliance on the part of physicians (given that noncompliance is hard to detect) may lead to inadvertent increases in dosage, decreased incentives to consider alternative therapies, and discontinuance of effective therapies which are simply not implemented by the patient.

A primary concern of the clinical medical literature is simply measuring compliance. Patients choose whether to comply with a prescription in two stages: first, whether to purchase the medication (purchase compliance) and then whether to follow the prescribed regimen (use compliance).[7] Measurement of compliance has been attempted using patient interviews,

---

6. There are a host of additional issues that arise in the context of compliance and constitute interesting lines of investigation: How does the principal's (patient's) reluctance to truthfully reveal their pharmaceutical consumption impact the prescribing behavior of the agent (the physician)? Does optimism regarding compliance on the part of physician lead to inefficiently high levels of medication? Can this problem be mitigated through the development of compliance-enhancing one-a-day medications?

7. Although this difference is not always clearly spelled out in the literature, studies have found noncompliance to be around 20 percent in purchase and 50 percent in use (Beardon et al. 1993).

pill counting, urine and blood tests, and, most recently, electronic and chemical monitoring. Studies using more sophisticated methodologies (such as monitoring) tend to find higher levels of noncompliance (McGavock et al. 1996). Use noncompliance has been found to vary significantly across therapeutic categories: 36 percent in hypertension (Dunbar-Jacob et al. 1991), 40 to 60 percent in arthritis (Belcon, Haynes, and Tugwell 1984; Hicks 1985), 15 to 43 percent among organ transplant recipients (Didlake et al. 1988; Rovelli et al. 1989), and 18 to 70 percent in the treatment of depression (Engstrom 1991; Myers and Branthwaite 1992).

The medical literature has also established a strong link between noncompliance and adverse medical outcomes. Indeed, it is estimated that more than one-third of hospital readmissions for heart failure result from noncompliance with dietary and medication regimens (Ghali et al. 1988; Vinson et al. 1990), while among patients who sustain myocardial infarction, those with poor compliance records were 250 percent more likely to die within a year of follow-up (Horwitz et al. 1990). Another study suggests that "actual compliance . . . might reduce stroke risks by about one half and coronary heart disease by about one fifth within a few years" (Collins et al. 1990). In insulin-dependent diabetes, 39 percent of single and 31 percent of multiple admissions have been attributed to poor compliance (Fishbein 1985), while in tuberculosis and HIV infections, there is an established link between noncompliance and drug resistance (Bloom and Murray 1992). At the extreme, Rovelli et al. (1989) estimate that the probability of tissue rejection (or death) can be as much as four times higher as a result of noncompliance by patients.

These studies can be usefully framed within a health care production function framework: How does noncompliance impact the production of health? Not surprisingly, decreasing a key input reduces overall output. What is missing from this analysis is a discussion of patient welfare. Are the long-term health benefits of compliance outweighed by more immediate concerns? In other words, do patients substitute decreased long-term health prospects for an immediate reduction in negative side effects or other inconveniences associated with drug therapies? Is noncompliance a problem of information or a response to the true psychic and other costs associated with maintaining a drug regimen? Addressing these questions requires understanding how patient and drug characteristics affect the compliance decision.

Indeed, a growing literature focuses on identifying the patient and drug characteristics associated with noncompliance. Perhaps surprisingly, simple demographic characteristics (sex, income, etc.) have not been consistently linked to compliance (Royal Pharmaceutical Society of Great Britain 1998). On the other hand, regimen features such as complexity, number of medications, and duration have been associated with the compliance rate (Goodall and Halford 1991; Col et al. 1990; Parkin et al.

1976). The patient's evaluation of effectiveness or the severity of side effects are also significant (Conrad 1985; Basler and Weissbach 1984). This suggests that patients are responding to perceived costs, both monetary and psychic, when choosing whether or not to comply. The economics of compliance are particularly salient in asymptomatic conditions, where patients are trading off a reduction in immediate and noticeable side effects for an increased risk of future pathology. In the case of insured patients, there is an additional incentive to discount future costs of health care.

Traditionally, health care researchers (particularly noneconomists) have treated noncompliance as the result of irrational or at best misinformed behavior. However, in response to findings that compliance is responding to such factors as the level of side effects, the health care community is reevaluating the rationale for this type of patient behavior. This new approach stresses the importance of factoring the patient's beliefs into the determination of appropriate therapies (Royal Pharmaceutical Society of Great Britain 1998) and emphasizes education for both patients and practitioners and giving patients greater control over health decisions. While these policy recommendations seem eminently sensible, it is quite clear that both economists and health care professionals have yet to develop a clear understanding of the causes and consequences of imperfect compliance.

In sum, the evidence clearly indicates that patient compliance is an important empirical phenomenon, with far-reaching economic and productivity measurement consequences. Two specific examples may shed further light on such issues. First, most prior studies of health care productivity and health care production have abstracted away from the reformulation of drugs (such as one-a-days), assuming that such formulations simply pose an aggregation problem. However, to the extent that compliance is increasing in one-a-day formulations, a revealed preference perspective suggests that there may be substantial incremental welfare gains associated with such therapies.[8] Second, failing to account for patient compliance behavior can also lead to biased measures of the welfare gains arising from the introduction of generic brands. In many instances, the choice between the generic and branded versions of drugs resides at least in part with the patient in consultation with the pharmacist (Ellison et al. 1997). No extant study has examined how the availability of a generic formulation impacts the purchase compliance associated with a drug. Such an exercise could provide direct evidence about patient sensitivity to price conditional on prescription. Motivated by these measurement concerns, we now turn to an estimable empirical model of patient welfare, which focuses on the pa-

---

8. This underestimation of welfare is similar to the concerns raised by Hausman (1997), who suggests that even relatively small changes in the product set may have large absolute welfare consequences in the presence of consumers who are sufficiently sensitive to the degree of the match.

tient compliance decision while fully incorporating physician prescription substitution patterns.

14.4   An Empirical Framework for Measuring Patient Welfare Based on Patient Compliance

The two principal insights to be drawn from section 14.3 are that physician prescription patterns may not reflect patients' preferences, and that patient compliance represents an economic choice which should allow for identification of the incremental benefits of a given drug over the alternative of no drug at all. The goal of this section is to incorporate these insights into an estimable model of patient welfare. We start out by expanding the framework of section 14.2 and consider a two-stage sequential decision process. In the first stage, the physician chooses one drug regimen among J_t available regimens. In the second stage, the patient chooses whether or not to comply with the prescription (see fig. 14.1).[9]

Two key issues arise in such a model. First, the welfare function needs to be modified to reflect the nature of the choices facing patients. Second, to obtain a consistent estimate of the appropriate welfare function, the model must account for the selection by physicians of patients into particular drugs. To the extent that there exists positive dependence between the physician's evaluation of idiosyncratic patient-drug utility, and the underlying (true) patient utility, the sample of patients who are prescribed a particular drug will be biased toward patients who have particularly high valuations for that drug. We start by specifying a simple model of physician choice over drugs:

$$(5) \quad \max_{j \in \{0, \ldots, J_t\}} V_{ij}^{MD} = X'_j \beta_{MD} + \alpha_{MD} PRICE_j + \xi_j + \varepsilon_{ij}^{MD} = \delta_j + \mu_{ij}^{MD}.$$

As will be seen below, a tractable version of the physician behavior model is key to ensuring estimability of a welfare formula based on patient compliance but controlling for physician selection. Consequently, we repeat our suggestion from section 14.2 and resort to a tractable distribution drawn from the GEV family, yielding prescription shares for the total population equal to

$$s_j = \frac{\partial G(\delta; \sigma)/\partial \delta_j}{G(\delta; \sigma)}.$$

Conditional on the physician's prescription in equation (5), each patient chooses whether or not to comply with that choice. If patients respond to

---

9. Of course, one could expand the compliance model to incorporate dynamic elements such as the hazard rate of noncompliance. For example, the clinical literature distinguishes between complete noncompliance and partial noncompliance or "drug holidays."

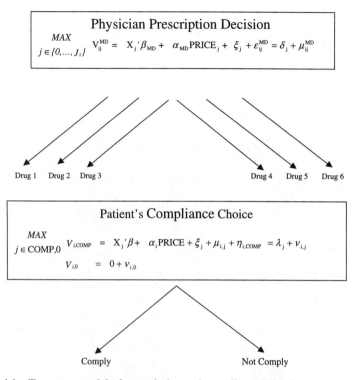

Fig. 14.1   **Two-stage model of prescription and compliance behavior**

exactly the same factors which determine the solution to equation (5), the compliance rate would of course be equal to one. To the extent that the physician chose a particular drug over the outside good in the first stage, then the patient would also choose that prescribed drug over the outside good in the second stage. In order to have a meaningful compliance model, then, the patient's decision model must include elements observed by the patient but not accounted for by the physician:

$$(6) \quad \max_{j \in \text{COMP, 0}} V_{i,\text{COMP}} = X_j'\beta + \alpha_i \text{PRICE} + \xi_j + \mu_{i,j} + \eta_{i,\text{COMP}} = \lambda_j + \nu_{i,j}$$

$$V_{i,0} = 0 + \nu_{i,0}.$$

Patients choose whether or not to comply according to their valuation of observed product characteristics (X_j), their disutility for price, idiosyncratic valuation which was both observed and responded to by the physician (μ), and an additional element of idiosyncratic valuation unobserved by the physician (η). Note that potentially important components of η are the opportunity and attention costs associated with compliance.

The maximization problem in equation (6) characterizes the fundamental economic decision faced by individual patients in the context of pharmaceutical treatment. Other features of the health care environment can be incorporated easily into this framework (insurance, demographics, a dynamic specification specifying the hazard rate for noncompliance rather than a single discrete decision, etc.). From the perspective of calculating welfare, however, the most subtle element in equation (6) concerns the overall distribution of random utility, v, which is a function in part of the draw observed by both the patient and the physician (μ_j). Note that this overall random term, v, cannot be mean zero if physicians skew their prescription behavior toward patients with particularly high valuations of this drug. In the particular form of selection suggested by equations (5) and (6), the distribution of μ_j is the distribution of μ_j from the physician's multinomial choice equation, conditional on having prescribed j. To see the implications of this selectivity, consider repeated trials of equation (5), and, for each drug j, select out the μ_j of those trials for which $V_{i,j} > V_{i,k} \; \forall \; j \neq k$ (i.e., drug j is chosen in that trial). The distribution of μ_j in equation (6) is then simply the distribution of these selected trials.

PROPOSITION 2. *Let* $g^*(\mu_j) = f(\mu_j \mid V_{ij} > V_{ik} \; \forall \; k \neq j)$ *be the distribution of the selection effect in equation (6). Then* $g^*(\mu_j) = (1/s_j) f(\mu_j; \sigma_j) \; \Pi_{k \in Jt, k \neq j}$ $F_{\varepsilon_k} (\delta_j - \delta_k + \mu_j; \sigma)$, *where* s_j *is the overall share of* j *in the physician portfolio, and* $F(\mu; \sigma)$ *is the assumed distribution of idiosyncratic utility in equation (5).*

PROOF. By Bayes's theorem,

$$f(\mu_{ij} \mid V_{ij} > V_{ik} \; \forall \; k \neq j) = \frac{\Pr(V_{ij} > V_{ik} \; \forall \; k \neq j \mid \mu_{ij}) f(\mu_{ij})}{\Pr(V_{ij} > V_{ik} \; \forall \; k \neq j)}.$$

The denominator is simply s_j, and $\Pr(V_{ij} > V_{ik} \; \forall \; k \neq j \mid \mu_{ij}) = \Pr(\delta_j + \mu_{ij} > \delta_k + \mu_{ik} \; \forall \; k \neq j \mid \mu_{ij})$, which can be rewritten in terms of the product of the distribution functions associated with each k evaluated at $\delta_j - \delta_k + \mu_{ij}$.

The distribution of $g^*(\mu_j)$ is therefore simply a function of the distribution of the maximum realization when J_t random variables are drawn from the unconditional distribution $F(\mu; \sigma)$. It is important to note that proposition 2 holds for any $F(\mu; \sigma)$ and so calculating $g^*(\mu_j)$ only requires the ability to calculate $F(\mu; \sigma)$ for any particular point in the distribution. When $F(\mu; \sigma)$ is drawn from the GEV class of distributions, calculating $g^*(\mu_j)$ is a simple analytical function of observables and of the (estimated) parameters of the model. To see the statistical logic behind proposition 2 more clearly, consider the case where the draws are independent and $\delta_j = \delta_k \; \forall \; j, k$. In this extreme case, proposition 2 reduces to the distribution of the Jth order statistic of an i.i.d. random variable, $g^*(\mu_j) = J_t f(\mu_j; \sigma_j) [F(\mu_j; \sigma)]_t^{J-1}$ (Larsen and Marx 1986).

Proposition 2 is crucial to our ability to calculate patient welfare because the realized sample selection distribution depends on the choices available for physicians to prescribe. For example, as new drugs enter the market, physicians will tend to substitute the new drug for patients with relatively low valuations of the older drugs. Consequently, the realized average utility for the older drug (conditional on prescription) may be increasing in the offered product set. Note that this increase is not due to any change on the part of the drug itself but on how the portion of the population which is prescribed this drug is changing as new drugs enter the market.

We can now establish a patient welfare measure in the context of pharmaceutical prescription and compliance. Recall that in our earlier discussion, we suggested that the welfare measure can be conceptualized as the maximum monetary amount that a risk-neutral individual would be willing to pay to access the prescription decision tree (fig. 14.1) prior to observing their individual draws (μ, η). In the current model, this is simply the expected welfare from any prescription conditional on having received that prescription, times the probability of receiving that prescription, that is,

$$(7) \qquad W_t = \sum_{j \in J_t} w_t^j \cdot \Pr(\text{MD prescribes } j),$$

where w_t^j is the expected patient welfare from drug j *conditional* on having been prescribed drug j by the physician.

To illustrate equation (7), we consider two cases under the assumption that η is also distributed according to the extreme value distribution. First, consider the case where physicians allocate patients randomly among drugs and so there is no selectivity in the distribution of individuals facing the compliance decision associated with any one drug. In that case, w_t^j is calculated to be the average welfare over the entire population of potential patients,

$$w_j^t = \frac{\ln G(\lambda)}{-\alpha} = \frac{\ln(e^{\lambda_j} + 1)}{-\alpha} \approx \frac{\lambda_j}{-\alpha}.$$

To estimate such a model, all that would be required is to regress the log-odds ratio of compliance on observed drug characteristics (including price):

$$(8) \qquad \ln \frac{cs_j}{(1 - cs_j)} = \lambda_j = X_j'\beta + \alpha_j \text{PRICE}_j + \xi_j,$$

where cs_j is the compliance share associated with drug j. Consistent estimation of equation (8) can be achieved using ordinary least squares (OLS) (under the assumption that price is exogenous), or, as Berry (1994) suggests, using instrumental variables for price which reflect the marginal cost of j or elements of competition facing j which are unrelated to ξ_j. To evaluate ΔW in this case, we would calculate the predicted values for λ_j resulting from estimation of equation (8) and plug these values, along with therapeutic category prescription shares, into equation (7) for the two periods under consideration.

Calculating welfare in the presence of patient selection into drugs by their physician is somewhat subtler. We must account for selectivity in two distinct ways, first when estimating the parameters determining underlying compliance and second when calculating the average utility received by patients. Consider the following procedure:

1. For any set of products and assumptions about physician behavior, calculate the set of conditional densities, $g^*(\mu)$. Under equation (5), this requires estimation of δ_{MD} and $F(\mu; \sigma)$, which is feasible using data on overall physician prescription behavior.

2. For each drug, solve for λ_j, the average valuation for that drug over the entire patient population. To do this, invert the compliance share equation accounting for the selection distribution g^* from proposition 2:

$$(9) \qquad \ln[cs_j/(1 - cs_j)] = \int_{\mu_j} (\lambda_j + \mu_j)g_j^*(\mu_j)d\mu_j.$$

Note that equation (9) involves the functional relationship (one-to-one mapping) between the compliance share for drug j and λ_j, conditional on the derived distribution, $g^*(\mu)$.

3. Over the drugs in the sample, regress λ_j on observed drug characteristics, prices, and measures of compliance cost, instrumenting for factors which are associated with unobserved patient compliance (such as price).

4. If the distribution of $F(\mu; \sigma)$ is estimated, minimize the GMM objective function of the regression in (c) over σ. This minimization yields the parameter vector $\{\alpha, \beta, \sigma\}$ as well as the predicted values for λ.

5. To calculate welfare for a given product set, one must calculate the expected welfare for patients who receive a prescription for a given drug:

$$(10) \qquad w_t^j = \int_{\mu_j} (\lambda_j + \mu_j)g_j^*(\mu_j)d\mu_j.$$

Note that equation (10) yields a higher estimate of welfare than the estimate based on no selectivity $\lambda_j/-\alpha$, because equation (10) accounts for the fact that those patients who actually receive a prescription for drug j tend to have higher valuations for that drug than the average patient in the overall population.

6. Calculate equation (7) using the vector of conditional welfare estimates from equation (10) and the therapeutic category prescription shares.

This procedure yields consistent estimates for the average value of all drugs in the market, the substitutability between those drugs at the physician level, and the parameters of the distribution allowing for correction of sample selection due to physician maximization. All that is required to perform this calculation is data at the individual or the product level on prescription compliance, along with characteristics of the drugs and their prices. For individual data, insurance information can be directly modeled as an interaction with price; in the case of product-level data, all that is required is information about the distribution of insurance by product category. It should be noted that while our model is general enough to accommodate any specific model of physician behavior (exploiting proposition 2), the welfare measure will depend on the model chosen for physician behavior. In other words, by focusing on compliance data, our model frames a relevant economic decision for the patient; however, a model of substitution between drugs at the physician level is still required in order to understand the diffusion process and its welfare benefits.

14.5   Concluding Remarks

The basic intuition driving this line of work is easy to state: The welfare of any given economic agent cannot be properly assessed when the choices that determine its actual consumption are made by other agents with different information or incentives. This is clearly the case with pharmaceuticals, where physicians retain authority over the choice of which drug to prescribe. Attempts to evaluate the welfare gains from pharmaceutical innovation cannot simply rely on the shares of each drug in the market. Estimating a discrete choice model based simply on prescription shares would confound the preferences of physician and patient in the resulting welfare measure. This basic conundrum has seriously hampered efforts to conduct systematic studies of welfare in this all-important area.

This paper suggests that the patient's compliance decision may provide a key ingredient in addressing the wedge between physician choices and true patient welfare. Incorporating the compliance decision into an augmented two-stage discrete choice model may indeed provide a way of uncovering the true preferences of patients, and hence the means to compute the "correct" welfare benefits accruing to patients. Furthermore, this approach may be usefully applied to other areas in the economics of health care where similar problems occur, namely examining those specific margins where patients do exercise choice. For example, the behavior of patients who refuse treatments of various types reflects information about their preferences; evaluating the welfare benefits from invasive health care technologies could focus around such decision making.

However, the implementation of the approach put forward here requires detailed data on prescription compliance at either the individual or the product level. We are currently exploring several options in this regard. Unfortunately, most data sources examine patient or physician behavior individually but not in concert; as a result, there are no public data sources which "track" prescriptions from the physician's decision through the patient's compliance. We are therefore investigating proprietary data sources collected by private firms for use in the health care sector, which may allow us to carry out the analysis outlined in this paper. However, given the potential importance of this line of research for the evaluation of public policy, we urge and would like to strongly encourage the systematic gathering and publication of data on prescription compliance by public institutions; such data efforts should significantly foster innovative research in this area.

References

Basler, H. D., and I. Weissbach. 1984. Dianostik der Medikamenten—Compliance Durch Befragung des Patienten—Eine Untersuchung an essentiellen Hypertonikern. *Psychotherapie, Psychosomatik, Medizinische, Psychologie* 34:331–335.

Beardon, P. H., et al. 1993. Primary non-compliance with prescribed medication in primary care. *British Medical Journal* 307:846–48.

Belcon, M. C., R. B. Haynes, and P. Tugwell. 1984. A critical review of compliance studies in rheumatoid arthritis. *Arthritis and Rheumatism* 27:1227–33.

Berry, S. 1994. Estimating discrete choice models of product differentiation. *RAND Journal of Economics* 25 (2): 242–62.

Bloom, B. R., and C. J. L. Murray. 1992. Tuberculosis: Commentary on a reemergent killer. *Science* 257:1055–61.

Bresnahan, T. 1986. Measuring the spillovers from technical advance: Mainframe computers in financial services. *American Economic Review* 76 (4): 742–55.

Bresnahan, T., S. Stern, and M. Trajtenberg. 1997. Market segmentation and the sources of rents from innovation: Personal computers in the late 1980s. *RAND Journal of Economics* 28 (special issue): 517–544.

Cardell, N. S. 1991. Variance components structures for the extreme value and logistic distributions. Washington State University. Working paper.

Col, N., et al. 1990. The role of medication noncompliance and adverse drug reactions in hospitalization of the elderly. *Archives of Internal Medicine* 150:841–45.

Collins, R., et al. 1990. Blood pressure, stroke, and coronary heart disease. *Lancet* 335:827–38.

Conrad, P. 1985. The meaning of medications: Another look at compliance. *Clinical Therapy* 15:595–606.

Coscelli, A. 1998. Entry of new drugs and doctors. London: University College. Mimeo.

Didlake, R. H., et al. 1988. Patient noncompliance: A major cause of late graft rejection in cyclosporine-treated renal transplants. *Transplantation Proceedings* 20 (3): 63–69.

Dunbar-Jacob, J., et al. 1991. Compliance with anti-hypertensive regimens: A review of the research of the 1980's. *Annals of Behavioral Medicine* 13:32–39.

————. 1995. Clinical assessment and management of adherence to medical regimens. In *Managing chronic illness,* ed. P. M. Nicassio and T. W. Smith. Washington, D.C.: American Psychological Association.

Ellison, S., et al. 1997. Characteristics of the demand for pharmaceutical products: An examination of four cephalosporins. *RAND Journal of Economics* 28 (3): 426–46.

Engstrom, F. W. 1991. Clinical correlates of antidepressant compliance. In *Patient compliance in medical practice and clinical trials,* ed. J. A. Cramer and B. Spilker. New York: Ravens Press.

Fishbein, H. A. 1985. Precipitants of hospitalization in insulin-dependent diabetes mellitus (IDDM): A statewide perspective. *Diabetes Care* 8 (1): 61–64.

Ghali, J. K., et al. 1988. Precipitating factors leading to decompensation of heart failure: Traits among urban blacks. *Archives of Internal Medicine* 148:2013–16.

Goodall, T. A., and W. K. Halford. 1991. Self-management of diabetes mellitus: A critical review. *Health Psychology* 10:1–8.

Griliches, Z. 1958. Research costs and social returns: Hybrid corn and related innovations. *Journal of Political Economy* 66 (5): 419–31.

Gruber, J., and M. Owings. 1996. Physician financial incentives and cesarean section delivery. *RAND Journal of Economics* 27 (1): 99–123.

Hall, B. 1995. The private and social returns to research and development. In *Technology, R&D and the economy,* ed. B. Smith and C. Barfield. Washington, D.C.: Brookings Institution.

Hausman, J. 1997. Valuation of new goods under perfect and imperfect competition. In *The economics of new goods,* ed. T. Bresnahan and R. Gordon. Chicago: University of Chicago Press.

Hellerstein, J. 1998. The importance of the physician in the generic versus trade-name decision. *RAND Journal of Economics* 29 (1): 108–36.

Hicks, J. E. 1985. Compliance: A major factor in the successful treatment of rheumatic disease. *Comprehensive Therapy* 11:31–37.

Horwitz, R. I., et al. 1990. Treatment adherence and risk of death after myocardial infarction. *Lancet* 336:542–45.

Larsen, R. J., and M. L. Marx. 1986. *An introduction to mathematical statistics and its applications.* Englewood Cliffs, N.J.: Prentice Hall.

Lichtenberg, F. 1996. Do (more and better) drugs keep people out of hospitals? *American Economic Review* 86 (2): 384–88.

McFadden, D. 1978. Modelling the choice of residential location. In *Spatial interaction theory and planning models.* Amsterdam: North-Holland.

McGavock, H., et al. 1996. *A review of the literature on drug adherence.* London: Royal Pharmaceutical Society of Great Britain.

Melmon, K., et al. 1992. *Clinical pharmacology,* 3rd ed. New York: McGraw Hill.

Myers, E. D., and A. Branthwaite. 1992. Out-patient compliance with anti-depressant medication. *British Journal of Psychiatry* 160:83–86.

National Pharmaceutical Council. 1992. *Emerging issues in pharmaceutical cost containment.* Reston, Va.: National Pharmaceutical Council.

Parkin, D. M., et al. 1976. Deviation from prescribed drug treatment after discharge from hospital. *British Medical Journal* 2:686–88.

Philipson, T., and L. Hedges. 1998. Subject evaluation in social experiments. *Econometrica* 66 (2): 381–408.

Philipson, T., and R. Posner. 1993. *Private choices and public health: The AIDS epidemic in an economic perspective.* Cambridge, Mass.: Harvard University Press.

Rovelli, M., et al. 1989. Noncompliance in organ transplant recipients. *Transplantation Proceedings* 21:833–34.

Royal Pharmaceutical Society of Great Britain. 1998. *From compliance to concordance: Achieving shared goals in medicine taking.* London: Royal Pharmaceutical Society of Great Britain.

Sacket, D. L. 1979. *Compliance in health care.* Baltimore, Md.: John Hopkins University Press.

Stern, S., and M. Trajtenberg. 1998. Empirical implications of physician authority in pharmaceutical decisionmaking. NBER Working Paper no. 6851. Cambridge, Mass.: National Bureau of Economic Research.

Trajtenberg, M. 1989. The welfare analysis of product innovations, with an application to computed tomography scanners. *Journal of Political Economy* 97 (2): 444–79.

———. 1990. *Economic analysis of product innovation.* Cambridge, Mass.: Harvard University Press.

Vinson, J. M., et al. 1990. Early readmission of elderly patients with congestive heart failure. *Journal of the American Geriatric Society* 38:1290–95.

Comment   Jonathan Skinner

Professors Ellickson, Stern, and Trajtenberg have produced a sophisticated blueprint for the integration of physician drug choice and consumer drug compliance into the more familiar field of discrete consumer choice. Actually, they do more than that—they also suggest a method for estimating welfare benefits of new drug developments, taking into account the prescriptive decisions of the physician and the compliance decisions of the patient. As the authors recognize, the complicated interaction between physician prescription and patient compliance with that choice is considerably more difficult to model theoretically and econometrically than the consumer's choice of breakfast cereal.

It is useful to reiterate the novel complications of this problem. First, the physician is assumed to choose the specific drug best suited to the patient, although this choice could be less than optimal ex post, either because of normal prediction error (i.e., the patient reacted adversely with the drug in a way that could not have been predicted a priori) or because of habit persistence or inadequate knowledge on the part of the physician. And second, the patient may or may not comply with the prescription,

Jonathan Skinner is the John French Professor of Economics at Dartmouth College, professor at Dartmouth Medical School, and a research associate of the National Bureau of Economic Research.

either because he or she tosses the prescription and never bothers buying the drug, or because he or she doesn't use the drug (or prematurely stops taking the drug) after purchasing it.

The authors have taken on a very important topic and have not hesitated to confront the difficult modeling problems head on. In my comments, I will try to peer into the future of their innovative empirical research and foresee issues in the interpretation of their results.

The most pressing issue relates to the interpretation of the observed behavior as providing information about "true" consumer welfare. The authors' emphasis on the literature relating compliance to whether the intervention is actually helping the patient is welcome here, especially in light of so much research in the medical literature that views noncompliance simply as a public health problem. In the revisionist view (for example Philipson and Hedges 1998), patients may rationally noncomply, in that their decisions reflect the appropriate trade-off between the costs of treatment—including side effects as well as costs—and the potential benefits. In this view, when patients cease to comply with prescriptions provided by their physician, it is a failure of the drug (or the doctor), and not of the patient's rationality.

In many cases, these issues of "optimal" noncompliance are important. To illustrate, I use data from a study of the benefits from following a regime of drugs that either lower low-density lipids (the "bad" cholesterol) or blood pressure (Grover et al. 1998). The benefit in terms of reduced strokes and cardiovascular events is expressed in terms of average additional life years. These benefits vary between as little as 0.2 life years to as much as five years, depending on the patient's condition (high cholesterol or hypertension), and risk factors such as smoking, hypertension, age, and sex. For example, consider the choice facing a woman with low levels of risk factors (nonsmoker, normal blood pressure, moderate cholesterol) at age forty. The estimated extension of average lifespan is 0.6 years through age 75 as a result of following a regime of cholesterol-reducing drug treatment (Grover et al. 1998; they use age seventy-five as the endpoint in all their calculations). Assume the extra years are gained at age seventy, and that she values the extra life year at $50,000, a bit low but within the range of cost-effectiveness benchmarks (e.g., Fabian 1994; also see Zerbe and Dively 1994, chap. 19). Then from the point of view of the patient, the value of taking the cholesterol-reducing drugs is $12,630, assuming a discount rate of 3 percent. So to justify the extra benefit of the drug, the costs cannot be larger than $48 monthly (the $12,630 amortized over the thirty-five years of taking the drug). Aside from the inconvenience or side effects of taking the drug, it is entirely possible that the cost of the drug would exceed $48 per month. Should we observe such a woman in the data, and observe that she did not comply with her prescription, we would be comfortable thinking that she is optimal in not complying. Explaining why the drug was prescribed in the first place is a harder question, since we are unlikely to know whether the prescription reflected a mistake by the physician or a simple ex post mismatch.

What about the other end of the spectrum, where the benefits are large from complying with the drug regime, but the individual still fails to comply? For example, consider a fifty-year-old man in the high-risk category (e.g., a smoker with hypertension and existing cardiovascular disease), who is prescribed a drug for high blood pressure. Here the benefits of taking blood-pressure-lowering drugs are much larger, about 3.6 years (Grover et al. 1998). If the individual values his life at $50,000 per life year saved—as noted above, a rather low valuation on a life year—then the individual would optimally comply with the drug regime as long as the *monthly* cost (direct plus indirect) of taking the cholesterol-lowering drugs until age seventy-five is under $480. This is a much higher hurdle, and one would wonder about the dynamic consistency of such a person who chooses not to comply.[1]

How might the Ellickson, Stern, and Trajtenberg (EST) model deal with such a noncomplier? According to the utility function and the demand equations that result, this individual is presumed to make an optimal decision. Now the EST model does handle error terms; if some people undercomply, others overcomply, but on average they should get the right answer. But suppose there is a larger problem with noncompliance than with overcompliance. For example, individuals may make dynamically inconsistent choices, as in the hyperbolic discounting approach of Laibson (1997) or the procrastination model in Akerlof (1991). In the Akerlof model, for example, individuals face a modest cost today of bothering to take their drugs, but a small benefit of starting today instead of tomorrow. So they put off taking the drug today. Tomorrow rolls around, and they make the same (dynamically inconsistent) choice to put off taking the drug until the next day, and so forth. In sum, procrastination results in a suboptimal regime in which the patient never gets around to complying with the drug regime. In dynamically inconsistent models, the idea of consumer welfare may not be well defined, given that it matters so much from what perspective (one's time t self, or one's time $t + 1$ self) consumer welfare is evaluated.

How to handle systematic errors or bias in judgment is a much larger problem that applies to more than drug compliance, so the authors cannot be faulted for not solving *all* the outstanding problems in welfare analysis. But it does suggest the value of including, in the interpretation of the results, some objective information—from cost-effectiveness or randomized

1. It's possible that someone with high income and a high value of time would find a $480 per month cost of following a drug regime too high. In that case, however, it would be likely that such a person would also place a higher value on life years saved.

trials from the medical literature, for example—on the shadow price or implicit discount rate that individuals must be placing on longevity (or lack thereof) when they are making their decisions. Observing people in HMOs with complete drug coverage who forgo a regime that yields $480 in benefits might raise flags about the nature of their utility function.

In sum, this theoretical and empirical estimation approach represents a huge step forward in thinking about health care problems and consumer choice issues more generally. One can never underestimate, however, the ability of people to behave in ways that appear perplexing in the context of economic models of behavior, and it is always best to be prepared for such behavior in advance.

References

Akerlof, George A. 1991. Procrastination and obedience. *American Economic Review* 81 (2): 1–19.

Fabian, Robert. 1994. The Qualy approach. In *Valuing health for policy: An economic approach,* ed. G. Tolley, D. Kenkel, and R. Fabian. Chicago: University of Chicago Press.

Grover, Steven A., Steve Paquet, Carey Levinton, Louis Coupal, and Hanna Zowall. 1998. Estimating the benefits of modifying risk factors of cardiovascular disease. *Archives of Internal Medicine* 158:655–61.

Laibson, David. 1997. Golden eggs and hyperbolic discounting. *Quarterly Journal of Economics* 112 (2): 443–77.

Philipson, T., and L. Hedges. 1998. Subject evaluation in social experiments. *Econometrica* 66 (2): 381–408.

Zerbe, Richard O., and Dwight D. Dively. 1994. *Benefit-cost analysis in theory and practice.* New York: HarperCollins.

15

The Allocation of Publicly Funded Biomedical Research

Frank R. Lichtenberg

In the last century, the average health of the American people has improved dramatically. The mean life expectancy of Americans has increased almost twenty years, or two years per decade,[1] since the turn of the century. Just from 1979 to 1988, the age-adjusted mortality rate declined 7.2 percent.

An important part of this enormous progress in health (which is scarcely reflected in our national accounts) is probably due to large private and public investments in biomedical research. In 1993, health R&D accounted for 18 percent of total U.S. R&D expenditure. Health R&D expenditures, by source of funding, are shown in table 15.1.

The National Institutes of Health (NIH) administer about 80 percent of federal health R&D. The NIH is made up of twenty-one institutes and centers, each with a mission and a separate, annual budget established by Congress. The institutes and centers are listed in table 15.2, along with the year in which each was established and its fiscal year 1998 budget obligations.[2] NIH does not want people to be misled by the names of the institutes; it points out that "research on any disease is not confined to

Frank R. Lichtenberg is the Courtney C. Brown Professor of Business at Columbia University and a research associate of the National Bureau of Economic Research.

The author is grateful to David Cutler and Ernie Berndt for helpful comments on a previous draft, and to the American Enterprise Institute and the Center for Economic Studies at the University of Munich for financial support. He is responsible for any errors.

1. "Buy ten, get two free," could be a fair, if crass, marketing slogan for U.S. health progress.

2. Older institutes and centers tend to receive significantly more funding than younger ones: There is a strong positive correlation ($r = .636$) between an institute or centers age in 1998 and (the log of) its budget obligations.

Table 15.1   **Health R&D Expenditures**

Source of Funding	1993 Health R&D Funds
Federal	12,051
State and local	2,054
Industry	15,711
Private nonprofit	1,215
All sources	31,032

Source: National Center for Health Statistics 1995, table 132.
Note: Figures are in millions of dollars.

Table 15.2   **NIH Institute and Centers**

	Year Established	1998 Obligations (million $)
National Cancer Institute	1937	2547
National Institute of Mental Health	1946	750
National Heart, Lung, and Blood Institute	1948	1,531
National Institute of Allergy and Infectious Diseases	1948	1,352
National Institute of Dental Research	1948	209
National Institute of Diabetes and Digestive and Kidney Diseases	1950	874
National Institute of Neurological Disorders and Stroke	1950	781
National Center for Research Resources	1956	454
National Institute of Child Health and Human Development	1963	675
National Institute of General Medical Sciences	1963	1,066
National Institute of Environmental Health Sciences	1966	330
National Eye Institute	1968	356
National Library of Medicine	1968	161
John E. Fogarty International Center	1968	28
National Institute on Alcohol Abuse and Alcoholism	1970	227
National Institute on Aging	1974	519
National Institute on Drug Abuse	1974	527
National Institute of Arthritis and Musculoskeletal and Skin Diseases	1986	275
National Institute of Nursing Research	1986	64
National Institute on Deafness and Other Communication Disorders	1988	201
National Human Genome Research Institute	1989	218
Total		13,145

Source: http://www.nih.gov/welcome/almanac/index.html.

one Institute, and no Institute is dedicated to a single disease. An Institute's budget is an inadequate measure of support for research on specific diseases. Research into many diseases is often carried on in several Institutes simultaneously, e.g., several Institutes are supporting research on Alzheimer's disease."

While the NIH focuses much of its research on combating specific diseases, and much of its funding supports research projects that are of obvious relevance to specific diseases, the NIH also places a high priority on funding basic research. These basic research projects may appear initially to be unrelated to any specific disease, but might prove to be a critical turning point in a long chain of discoveries leading to improved health. Each of the NIH institutes supports basic research likely to advance particular areas of science that might prove relevant to clinical problems important to that institute's mission. By supporting disease-related and basic research projects simultaneously, the NIH seeks to achieve both near-term improvements in the diagnosis, treatment, and prevention of specific diseases and long-term discoveries in basic science that in time will produce great advances in our ability to understand, treat, and prevent disease or delay its onset.

In this paper I develop a simple theoretical model of the allocation of the applied component of public biomedical research expenditure—the approximately 50 percent of expenditure that is of direct, near-term relevance to specific diseases—and present some empirical evidence about the determinants of this allocation. The implications of the theoretical model are consistent with government officials' descriptions of the allocation process: The structure of expenditure should depend upon research productivity (or "scientific opportunity") as well as on public health need, that is, the societal and economic burden of the disease/condition. Although we lack, at this point, useful indicators of research productivity (i.e., of the cost of achieving research advances), we have a number of measures of disease burden (i.e., of the benefit of achieving these advances).[3] Analysts of technical change typically have data on neither the costs nor the benefits of technical advance. Failure to measure research productivity will not necessarily bias my estimates; if it does, it seems likely to bias them toward zero.

The paper is organized as follows. In the next section I develop the simple model of public research expenditure allocation. I rely on three types and sources of data to estimate the parameters of the model: data on research activity derived from NIH's CRISP (Computerized Retrieval of Information on Scientific Projects) database, premature mortality data

---

3. The disease burden is the *potential* benefit (ignoring all comorbidities), not the actual benefit.

from the Vital Statistics–Mortality Detail file, and data on chronic condition prevalence and severity from the National Health Interview Survey. These are discussed in section 15.2. Preliminary estimates are presented in section 15.3, and a summary is provided in section 15.4.

15.1   A Simple Model of the Determinants of Research Expenditure at the Disease Level

To motivate the discussion and develop a few intuitions, I write down the simplest possible model of research funding allocation. This model is based on the following extremely strong assumptions (some of which are relaxed below): (1) there are only two diseases; (2) the number of people suffering from the two diseases, N_1 and N_2, is exogenous; (3) the average severity of the two diseases is identical; (4) the probability P_i of finding a cure for disease $i(i = 1, 2)$ is a concave (deterministic) function of research funding for that disease, X_i: $P_i = X_i^\alpha$, where $0 < \alpha < 1$;[4] (5) the effect of funding on the probability of finding a cure is the same across diseases; and (6) the total research budget $X = X_1 + X_2$ is fixed.

Suppose that policymakers attempt to maximize the (expected) total number of people cured of both diseases subject to the budget constraint,[5] that is, they choose X_1 to maximize

$$
(1) \qquad \begin{aligned}
J^* &= N_1 P_1 + N_2 P_2 \\
&= N_1 X_1^\alpha + N_2 X_2^\alpha \\
&= N_1 X_1^\alpha + N_2 (X - X_1)^\alpha.
\end{aligned}
$$

The first-order condition implies that relative funding of research on the two diseases should satisfy

$$
(2) \qquad \ln(X_1/X_2) = [1/(1 - \alpha)]\ln(N_1/N_2).
$$

Research funding should increase with disease incidence: for example, $X_1 > X_2$ if $N_1 > N_2$. This is because the benefit of discovering a cure for the disease is proportional to its incidence, but the cost is independent of incidence. Moreover the elasticity of funding with respect to incidence should exceed unity: if disease 1 is twice as prevalent as disease 2, research funding for disease 1 should be more than twice as great as research fund-

---

4. Viscusi (1995, 3) notes that "in the case of biomedical research, the typical outcome will be a change in societal risk levels induced by the biomedical research outcomes."

5. I assume for simplicity that federal policymakers do not pay attention to biomedical R&D funded by other sources; in other words, they are not merely trying to "fill gaps" in other research, nor do they consider the potential impact of public R&D on other research activity. Toole (2000), however, presents evidence that suggests that public biomedical research may have a significant, albeit very delayed, impact on private drug discovery.

ing for disease 2.[6] Equalizing research expenditure per victim across diseases would be inefficient.

One could generalize this model to the case of $I > 2$ diseases, to obtain $I - 1$ equilibrium conditions of the form

$$(3) \qquad \ln X_i = \text{constant} + [1/(1 - \alpha)]\ln N_i,$$

$(i = 1, 2, \ldots, I - 1)$. Given cross-sectional or panel data on research funding and incidence by disease, one could estimate equation (3) to test the hypothesis of diminishing returns to research funding at the disease level and to estimate the parameter α. But this simple model can and should be extended in at least two directions: We should allow for multiple indicators of incidence and for differences in research productivity (scientific opportunity) across diseases.

15.1.1   Multiple Indicators of Incidence

As the director of NIH says, a given disease imposes a number of different kinds of burden on society, and "policy makers will need to consider the relative importance or weight to be placed on each criteri[on] when assessing the overall societal burden imposed by each disease." While the NIH has indicated interest in determining how to measure public health burden, it has also expressed uncertainty about how to do so. I now outline a procedure for doing this.[7] Then I will perform empirical analysis to ascertain how close the actual allocation of research resources is to the allocation that is optimal, according to my framework. The answer appears to be "pretty close."

Suppose that the overall burden of a disease is perceived by policymakers to be a function of K attributes of the disease: $N_i \equiv f(A1_i, A2_i, \ldots, AK_i)$ where, for example, $A1$ is the number of deaths, $A2$ is the number of bed-disability days, $A3$ is the number of hospital stays, and so forth. Further suppose that the functional form of this relationship is

$$(4) \qquad \ln N_i = \beta_1 \ln A1_i + \beta_2 \ln A2_i + \ldots + \beta_K \ln AK_i,$$

where $\Sigma_k \beta_k = 1$. The term β_k reveals the relative "weight" assigned by policymakers to attribute k in the determination of overall disease burden. Substituting equation (4) into equation (3),

---

6. In reality, finding a cure for one of the diseases may increase the probability of suffering at a future date from the other disease. Development of a richer model to account for this and other complications is a challenging task. Given the stark simplicity of my model, it may be best to view it as a set of organizing principles that can be used to interpret the allocative process, rather than as a theory.

7. Recently a National Academy of Sciences panel looked at priority setting at NIH, and recommended using a number of measures to measure burden of illness in a fashion similar to what I propose. See Institute of Medicine (1998).

(5) $\ln X_i = \text{constant} + [1/(1 - \alpha)]$

$$(\beta_1 \ln A1_i + \beta_2 \ln A2_i + \ldots + \beta_K \ln AK_i),$$

Estimation of equation (5) would provide estimates of these ("revealed preference") weights as well as of the technological parameter α. They would indicate the relative weight given to mortality and bed-disability days, for example.

Since disease outcome and incidence data are available by demographic group, we can also make inferences about weights associated with different demographic groups.[8] For example, let us define "adjusted" bed-disability days $A2^* = A2\text{YOUNG} + (1 + \theta) A2\text{OLD}$, where $A2\text{YOUNG}$ and $A2\text{OLD}$ denote bed-disability days of young and old people, respectively. If policymakers' evaluation of the marginal burden of the two groups' bed-disability days differs, θ will differ from zero. This parameter can be estimated by replacing $A2$ by $A2^*$ in equation (5).

15.1.2   Differences in Research Productivity (Scientific Opportunity) across Diseases

The preceding model is based on the assumption that the effect of funding on the probability of finding a cure is the same across diseases. This assumption is clearly unrealistic, and it is desirable to relax it.[9] We can modify the cure-probability equation to include a disease-specific research productivity parameter π_i: $P_i = \pi_i X_2^\alpha$. The objective function policymakers seek to maximize is now $J^* = N_1 P_1 + N_2 P_2 = N_1 \pi_1 X_1^\alpha + N_2 \pi_2 X_2^\alpha$, and the optimal expenditure on research on disease i is now

(6) $\ln X_i = \text{constant} + [1/(1 - \alpha)]\ln N_i + [1/(1 - \alpha)]\ln \pi_i$.

The research-productivity parameters i enter the objective function and the optimal expenditure equation in the same way as the disease incidence measures N_i. Research expenditure should be an increasing function of scientific opportunity as well as of disease burden. This implication is consistent with the views expressed by government officials: "It is vital that the allocation of medical research dollars takes into account several factors, including scientific opportunity, public health need, gaps in knowledge, as well as societal and economic burden of the disease/condition."[10]

---

8. NIH officials acknowledge that "research funding decisions will also reflect concerns about equity among groups of potential beneficiaries of the research as defined in terms of age, sex, and ethnic origin. Certain criteria favor one group over another. For example, mortality rates and measures of the impact on functioning may favor the elderly whereas measures of economic impact, such as lost productivity, would favor younger citizens" (NIH Director Varmus's responses to questions from Senator Slade Gordon, Labor, HHS, Education Subcommittee Hearing, NIH appropriations for FY 1996, 18 May 1995).

9. Henderson and Cockburn (1996) have studied the determinants of research productivity of pharmaceutical firms, using patents and scientific papers as measures of research output.

10. Office of Science Policy, NIH Response to Congressional Questions, June 1996. Garber and Romer (1995) also argue that "federal policy toward research and development should

I believe that the CRISP data can eventually be exploited to obtain indicators of (changes in) the relative productivity of research on different diseases. The data will enable us to determine, for example, the extent to which research related to a given disease tends to be concentrated in rapidly growing and advancing scientific fields (e.g., molecular genetics) as opposed to mature fields. They will also allow us to quantify the extent to which research on a disease utilizes innovative research techniques (e.g., protein engineering), and how much the distribution of techniques has changed over time.

At present, however, we must treat π_i as unobservable. If research productivity is uncorrelated across diseases with disease burden, that is, if differences in supply (or cost of achieving progress) are uncorrelated with differences in demand (or benefits of achieving progress), estimation of equation (5) will yield an unbiased estimate of the relationship between research expenditure and disease burden. It is possible, however, that N and π are negatively correlated: the diseases that impose the heaviest burden do so, in part, because of the low productivity of past research on those diseases (which should also have resulted in relatively low research funding on them). If this is the case, then the omission of π_i from the research expenditure equation would bias the estimated coefficient on ln N_i toward zero. In particular, although the theory implies that the coefficient on ln N_i should be greater than one, we should not be surprised if we obtain estimated coefficients smaller than one; in other words, if we fail to observe this kind of "increasing returns."

In future research, I hope to directly estimate the contribution of medical research expenditure to subsequent progress against disease, by analyzing the correlation across diseases between research investment and indicators of progress, such as reductions in potential life years lost.[11] I recognize, however, that heterogeneous, unobserved research productivity is likely to lead to *overestimates* of the average return to research expenditure. Diseases receiving the greatest research funding are presumably those for which research productivity is highest. The slope of the relationship

---

respond to scientific advances, technology trends, and changes in the political and social environment."

11. The existing evidence on the contribution of medical research expenditure to subsequent progress against disease is rather limited. The National Institutes of Health (1993) have produced estimates of cost savings from thirty-four "examples" of health care advances resulting from NIH support for applied research and clinical trials. Most focus on a single innovation such as a new vaccine, a new diagnostic test, or a particular therapy. But these case studies are not necessarily a random sample of all NIH-sponsored research, so they may not reveal the "aggregate or average" effect of this research on costs. It is possible, for example, that the distribution of cost savings is highly skewed to the right—a few programs confer large cost savings, but the majority confer few—and that the specific examples chosen tend to be concentrated in the upper tail of the distribution. Mushkin (1979) attempted to determine econometrically the contribution of biomedical research to reductions in mortality and morbidity. But most of her analysis was in an aggregate time-series framework and was based on fairly crude measures of biomedical research, such as the number of biomedical Ph.D.'s lagged ten years.

across diseases between research funding and progress exceeds the mean of the slopes of the disease-specific relationships.[12]

15.2   Data Sources and Methods

15.2.1   Data on Government-Funded Research Expenditures, by Disease

We have calculated distributions of government-funded biomedical research expenditure, by disease, from records of research grants contained in NIH's CRISP system. The CRISP database includes records of all research ventures supported by the U.S. Public Health Service since 1972. In fiscal year 1995, there were records of 63,289 grants, the total value of which was $10.1 billion. Most of this research falls within the broad category of extramural projects: grants, contracts, and cooperative agreements conducted primarily by investigators at universities, hospitals, and other research institutions. The projects are funded by NIH and the Substance Abuse and Mental Health Services Administration. A very small number of these research grants are funded by the Centers for Disease Control, the Food and Drug Administration (FDA), the Health Resources and Services Administration, and the Agency for Health Care Policy and Research. CRISP also contains information on intramural research programs conducted by scientists employed by the FDA and the various institutes of the NIH.

Each record reports the name of the investigator, the name and address of his or her organization (e.g., university and department), the title (and in many cases an abstract) of the project, the administering organization (e.g., National Cancer Institute), the award amount (including both direct and indirect costs), the type of award, and a number of (generally about fifteen) indexing terms assigned by Technical Information Specialists in the Research Documentation Section, Information Systems Branch, of NIH's Division of Research Grants. The indexing process is governed by the CRISP thesaurus, which is the "controlled vocabulary used to assign indexing terms for the CRISP System, and to retrieve subject-related information from it."

The number of distinct indexing terms in the CRISP thesaurus is quite large (about nine thousand), but most of these terms are organized into

---

12. The reasoning underlying this is the same as that underlying Gary Chamberlain's (1984) argument that estimation of production functions using data for a cross-section of firms will result in overestimates of the returns to factors of production, such as labor. Firms with exogenously higher productivity (due, e.g., to greater managerial ability) will employ more workers. Chamberlin's point concerns the coefficient of one variable only—labor in a production function framework. If more than one variable is involved, their coefficients will not necessarily be biased toward zero: The direction of bias depends on the entire covariance matrix. Not all the coefficients on all the $\ln N_i$ variables will be biased toward zero.

a small number of hierarchical classification schemes, including one for diseases. Table 15.3 illustrates the disease classification; it is similar to the International Classification of Diseases, the system used for reporting diagnoses in most health-related data. There are thirty-five disease categories at the highest level of aggregation. Within each of these is a series of more specific disease categories. Space limitations prevent us from displaying the entire "tree structure" of diseases (which includes about twentynine hundred items), but to illustrate the classification system we show the second level classification of "nervous disorders" and a branch leading to

Table 15.3   **Classification Systems for Diseases Used in CRISP Database**

Blood disorder
Calcium disorder
Cardiovascular disorder
Communicable disease
Communication disorder
Congenital disorder
Connective tissue disorder
Digestive disorder
Ear disorder
Endocrine disorder
Enzyme deficiency
Eye disorder
Genetic disorder
Hernia
Immunopathology
Infection
Injury
Lymphatic disorder
Mental disorder
Metabolism disorder
Musculoskeletal disorder
Neoplasm/cancer
Nervous disorder
  Autonomic disorder
    Central nervous system disorder
      Brain disorder
      Cataplexy
      Central nervous system neoplasm
      Degenerative motor system disease
      Encephalomyelitis
      Gliosis
      Hemiplegia
      Meningitis
        Infectious meningitis
          Bacterial meningitis
          Viral meningitis
            Lymphocytic choriomeningitis
[Other disorders]

a "fifth level" disease (with no further subcategories), lymphocytic chorio-meningitis.

This disease classification scheme enables us to compute distributions of research grants and dollars by disease, at various levels of aggregation.[13] How accurate will these distributions be? Recently the Office of the Director of NIH prepared a report that included estimates of NIH fiscal year 1994 research support by disease. These figures, based on data provided by NIH institutes, centers, and divisions (ICDs), "reflect NIH-wide resources devoted to research on the listed diseases . . . [and] generally do not correspond to budget figures for the ICD identifying the cost data."[14] For sixteen randomly selected diseases, I compared fiscal year 1994 funding as reported there with the number of fiscal year 1995 grants citing the disease contained in the fiscal year 1995 CRISP database.

The raw data are reported in table 15.4. A scatter plot of the logarithms of these two variables is shown in figure 15.2; their correlation coefficient is .91. Despite differences in timing and unit of measurement, the two estimates of relative research support by disease are quite similar, suggesting that the CRISP data are reasonably reliable up to a first-order approximation.

As NIH officials observe, much NIH-sponsored research is basic in nature and, although "scientific advances would not have been possible without continuing insight and understanding regarding the fundamental mechanisms of life and disease . . . basic research linkages to health care advances are complicated, long-term, and impossible to allocate clearly" (NIH 1993, 3). Therefore, many research grants do not refer to *any* disease (even though the research may ultimately lead to breakthroughs in the treatment of that disease). In other words, the grants fall into two categories: those that have been assigned to at least one disease and those that have not been assigned.[15] My estimates of research activity by disease are based only on grants that have been assigned.[16] Due to the logarithmic specification of equation (6), the validity of my parameter estimates does not require me to reliably measure the *absolute level* of research funding, by disease; their validity is predicated only on reliable measurement of

13. Data on the disease distribution of *private* R&D sponsored by pharmaceutical firms are available from the Pharmaceutical Research and Manufacturers Association's Annual Survey of companies. Unfortunately, the private R&D data are disaggregated into only about seven broad categories. Figure 15.1 shows the percentage distributions of both private and government R&D, by these categories. Public R&D seems to be more concentrated on digestive/genitourinary and neoplasm/endocrine/metabolic diseases, and less concentrated on infective/parasitic, nervous system, and cardiovascular diseases than private R&D.

14. NIH (1995), table 1.

15. This distinction resembles the distinction made in industrial R&D between basic and applied research.

16. When two or more diseases are cited by a grant, I assign the *entire* amount of funding for the grant to *each* of the diseases cited.

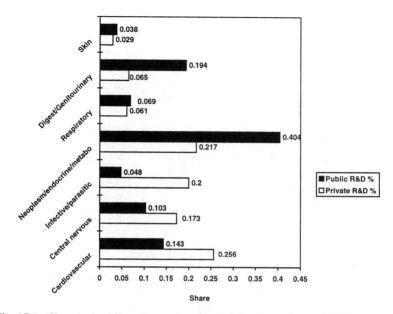

Fig. 15.1   Shares of public and private health R&D allocated to major disease categories in 1982

Sources: Public R&D: 1982 CRISP file; Private R&D: PhRMA Annual Survey.

Table 15.4   Comparison of Fiscal Year 1994 Funding with Fiscal Year 1995 Grants Citing the Disease, for Sixteen Randomly Selected Diseases

Disease/Disorder	FY 1995 Grants	FY 1994 Funds (million $)
Diabetes	1,390	292
Epilepsy	338	52
Asthma	345	66
Arthritis	476	191
Atherosclerosis	650	116
Schizophrenia	458	111
Multiple sclerosis	123	78
Obesity	474	83
Osteoporosis	288	92
Parkinson's	253	68
Psoriasis	53	3
Sickle cell anemia	278	54
Suicide	94	17
Tuberculosis	248	50
Pneumonia and influenza	230	60

Source: NIH (1995), table 1; and CRISP database.

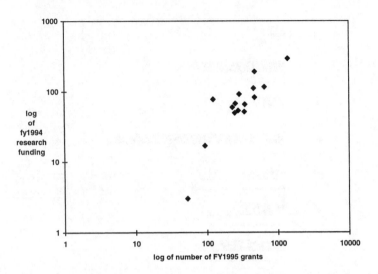

Fig. 15.2   Relationship between estimated NIH research funding, by disease, and number of NIH grants citing disease

relative research funding, or activity. Table 15.5 shows the fraction of 1972 and 1995 research grants whose indexing terms referred to any (at least one) disease and to specific diseases (at the highest level of aggregation) in the CRISP classification. In both years, about half of the grants referred to at least one disease.[17] This is consistent with NIH's statement that "slightly over half, on average, of each Institute's budget supports the best research grant proposals regardless of specific applicability to prevention and treatment of a disease, but in expectation that their results will contribute to advances against diseases within their purview as well as diseases in other Institutes and to our knowledge generally." Relative emphasis on different diseases has been reasonably stable: the correlation across diseases (excluding pathology) between the 1972 and 1995 fractions is .85.

15.2.2   Data on Disease Burden, Prevalence, and Incidence

As indicated in equation (4) above, rather than treating disease burden N (or reduction in the quantity and quality of life) as a scalar, I regard it as an index of a number of disease mortality and morbidity attributes. Data on these attributes are obtained from two sources: the Vital Statistics–Mortality Detail file, a virtually complete census of deaths in the United States, and the National Health Interview Survey, a continuing nationwide survey of households for which a probability sample of the

---

17. The increase in this fraction, from 49 percent in 1972 to 57 percent in 1995, appears to be attributable to the large increase (from 9 to 24 percent) in the fraction of grants referring to "pathology."

Table 15.5   **Percent of 1972 and 1995 NIH Grants Referring to Any Disease and to Specific Diseases**

Disease (Ranked by % of 1995 Grants)	% of 1972 Grants	% of 1995 Grants
Any disease	48.5	56.7
Pathology	8.9	23.7
Neoplasm/cancer	8.6	12.2
Mental disorder	6.5	9.8
Nervous system disorder	6.2	9.6
Communicable disease	2.6	8.2
Immunopathology	4.4	7.8
Cardiovascular disorder	9.4	7.4
Metabolism disorder	6.7	5.4
Blood disorder	7.1	5.0
Digestive disorder	5.2	4.2
Respiratory disorder	3.5	4.0
Endocrine disorder	4.4	4.0
Reproductive system disorder	2.5	3.9
Infection	1.6	3.5
Lymphatic disorder	3.3	3.2
Congenital disorder	3.9	3.1
Musculoskeletal disorder	2.6	3.0
Injury	1.3	2.6
Urinary tract disorder	3.5	2.2
Eye disorder	1.9	2.0
Skin disorder	1.7	1.9
Genetic disorder	1.4	1.3
Communication disorder	1.0	1.2
Connective tissue disorder	0.9	0.7
Ear disorder	0 5	0.6
Pregnancy disorder	0.4	0.5
Nutrition disorder	2.2	0.5
Calcium disorder	0.8	0.3
Enzyme deficiency	0.0	0.2
Postnatal growth disorder	0.2	0.2
Syndrome	0.0	0.2
Orphan disease/drug	0.0	0.1
Nutrient intake disorder	0.1	0.1
Plant disease	0.0	0.0
Hernia	0.0	0.0

civilian noninstitutionalized[18] population of the United States is interviewed by the U.S. Bureau of the Census regarding the health and other

18. It should be pointed out that the restriction of the NHIS to the civilian population not confined to institutions affects the estimated prevalence of chronic conditions. Omission of the institutionalized population reduces the prevalence estimates, especially for the elderly, because the proportion of persons in institutions who have chronic conditions is high. These estimates do not indicate the prevalence in the total population.

characteristics of each member of the household. (The sample for the years 1990–92 was composed of 142,638 households containing 368,075 persons.)

Our use of these two data sources reflects my belief that to obtain a reasonably complete accounting for disease burden, one must consider data on both the dying and the living. Analysis based on only one source will almost surely be subject to considerable sample selection bias.

Premature Mortality Data

The measure of disease burden I computed from the mortality file is potential life years lost before age sixty-five, by disease.[19] The latter is defined as the summation of (65 − age-at-death) for decedents under sixty-five. This is a standard measure of disease burden, or (lack of) progress against disease, in health statistics. It has the drawback of giving no weight at all to deaths of people aged sixty-five and over.

Data on Prevalence of Selected Chronic Conditions

Collins (1997) presents statistics on the prevalence of selected chronic conditions in the United States during 1990–92 by age, sex, race, family income, and geographic region, derived from data collected in the National Health Interview Survey (NHIS). He also reports the percent of selected conditions that cause activity limitation, the percent for which a physician was consulted, and the percent that caused hospitalization.

All information collected during the survey is from responsible family members residing in the household. Methodological studies have shown that chronic conditions are generally underreported in interview surveys. Respondents in health interviews tend to report conditions of which they are aware and about which they are willing to report to the interviewer. Reporting is better for conditions that have made a significant impact on affected individuals and their families. Conditions that are severe or costly, or are being treated, tend to be better reported than conditions having less impact. Methodological studies have also indicated that inclusion of a checklist of descriptive condition titles as part of the interview questionnaire increases the probability that a respondent will recognize the terms and report those of which the respondent is aware.

The current procedure for collecting information on chronic conditions was established in 1978. Currently, six categorical lists of selected chronic conditions are included in the NHIS questionnaire: circulatory conditions; respiratory conditions; digestive conditions; impairments and conditions of the nervous system and sense organs; conditions of the skin and subcu-

---

19. Demographic information on the death certificate is provided by the funeral director based on information supplied by an informant. Medical certification of cause of death is provided by a physician, medical examiner, or coroner.

taneous tissue and of the musculoskeletal system and connective tissue; and endocrine, nutritional, and metabolic diseases and immunity disorders, diseases of the blood and blood-forming organs, and conditions of the genitourinary system. Each family in the NHIS is questioned on only one of these six lists, selected on a predetermined basis. Therefore, each list is administered to only one-sixth of the total NHIS sample each year. For some items, responses are based on the following question: "During the past 12 months did anyone in the family (read names) have . . . ?" For others, responses are based on the question "Does anyone in the family (read names) now have . . . ?" For the rest, responses are based on the question "Has anyone in the family (read names) ever had . . . ?" Estimates for days of disability caused by chronic conditions are based on the number of disability-days reported for the two weeks before interview.

The survey includes data only on persons living in the household at the time of interview. Thus the experience of persons who died prior to the time of interview is excluded from the data. Also excluded is the experience of persons who were institutionalized or who were members of the armed forces at the time of the household interview.

In these data, "prevalence" is defined as the average number of some item existing during a specified interval of time—usually referred to as "period prevalence"—rather than the number of some item existing at a given point in time—usually referred to as "point prevalence." Chronic conditions are defined as conditions that either were first noticed three months or more before the date of interviews, or belong to a group of conditions considered chronic regardless of when they began.

The data presented represent the prevalence of conditions, not the prevalence of persons with a chronic condition. However, for most conditions, the condition prevalence and the person prevalence are almost identical.[20]

15.3   Preliminary Estimates

15.3.1   Premature Mortality

The first measure of disease burden I analyze is potential life years lost before age sixty-five (PLYL). Data on PLYL in 1980 and government re-

---

20. There are some instances in which large variations are present; these occur for two different reasons. The first is that a prevalence estimate of a condition may include more than one of the specified checklist items or a checklist item and a specified "other condition" item that falls into the same International Classification of Diseases category as the checklist item. The second reason is that some prevalence categories shown are a combination of other categories and, as a result, a person may have more than one of the conditions that are added to form the combined category. The concept of condition prevalence is generally used in NHIS because specific health indexes such as limitation of activity and disability days can be ascribed to specific conditions. In addition, prosthetic and pharmaceutical treatment modes are more condition specific than person specific.

Table 15.6   **Life Years Lost before Age Sixty-Five in 1980, and Public R&D Expenditure in 1982, Fourteen Major Disease Categories**

Disease/Disorder[a]	Life Years Lost before Age Sixty-Five in 1980	Public R&D Expenditure in 1982 (million $)
Diseases of the circulatory system (390–459)	2,043,559	117
Neoplasms (140–239)	1,860,531	113
Congenital anomalies (740–759)	760,820	37
Diseases of the digestive system (520–579)	503,531	27
Diseases of the respiratory system (460–519)	434,770	47
Diseases of the nervous system and sense organs (320–389)	294,239	118
Endocrine, nutritional, and metabolic diseases and immunity disorders	223,015	168
Infectious and parasitic diseases (001–139)	162,568	33
Mental disorders (290–319)	124,407	70
Diseases of the genitourinary system (580–629)	86,015	73
Diseases of the blood and blood-forming organs (280–289)	49,814	16
Diseases of the musculoskeletal system and connective tissue	37,403	25
Complicaitons of pregnancy, childbirth, and the puerperium	12,536	8
Diseases of the skin and subcutaneous tissue (680–709)	7,848	21

[a]Numbers in parentheses are International Classification of Diseases codes.

search funding, in 1982, for fourteen major disease categories are shown, in descending PLYL order, in table 15.6. Diseases of the circulatory system and neoplasms are, by far, the diseases with the largest tolls in terms of premature death. While the research funding for these two diseases is among the highest for all diseases, R&D funding for two other diseases with much smaller burdens exceeds the funding for the first two diseases, in one case by a large amount. Nevertheless, as the scatter plot in figure 15.3 and the following regression indicate, there is a very strong positive relationship across the entire sample between life years lost and public R&D expenditure (t-statistics in parentheses):

$$\ln(RD82) = -0.464 + 0.355\ln(LYL80) + e \qquad R^2 = .459$$
$$ (0.34) \quad (3.19) \qquad\qquad N = 14.$$

Life years lost in 1980 explains almost half of the variation across diseases in 1982 research expenditure. However, contrary to the implication of my simple theoretical model of research allocation, the coefficient on ln(LYL80) is significantly less than one. As argued above, this may be due

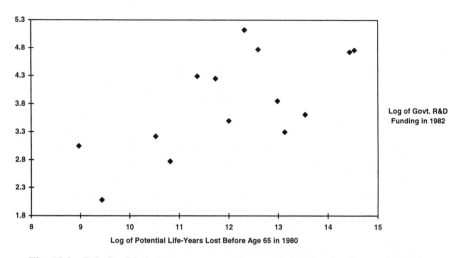

Fig. 15.3   Relationship between government research funding, by disease, in 1982, and life years lost before age sixty-five, by disease, in 1980

to a negative correlation between the regressor and the omitted research-productivity variable.[21]

Life years lost can be classified by sex, race, educational attainment, and other characteristics, so we can investigate whether premature mortality among certain demographic groups tends to be associated with especially high government research funding. Sixty percent of life years lost before age sixty-five are lost by males, and 25 percent are lost by nonwhites (who make up about 10 percent of the population), reflecting the lower life expectancy of these two groups. The proportion of life years lost by men and by nonwhites varies considerably across diseases. Whites account for 81 percent of life years lost to neoplasms but for only 53 percent of those due to diseases of the blood and blood-forming organs. Men account for 81 percent of life years lost to infectious and parasitic diseases but

21. I obtain quite similar results when I use data covering other time periods or when I substitute life years lost before age eighty for life years lost before age sixty-five. (About twice as many life years are lost before age eighty as are lost before age sixty-five; the correlation across diseases between the two is very high—.98.) The correlation coefficient between ln(RD82) and ln(LYL80) is .677. The correlation coefficients between the log of the number of year $t(t = 1980, 1995)$ NIH grants referring to disease i and the log of life years lost before age $j(j = 65, 80)$ to disease i in year t are as follows:

	$t = 1980$	$t = 1995$
j = age 80	.764	.710
j = age 65	.739	.677

for only 28 percent of life years lost to musculoskeletal and connective-tissue diseases.

The matrix of correlation coefficients for four variables—ln(RD82), ln(LYL80), and the fractions of life years lost to men (%MALE) and to whites (%WHITE)—are reported in table 15.7. Public R&D investment is significantly positively correlated with the fractions of life years lost to men and (especially) to whites, as well as with the total number of life years lost. Indeed, %WHITE is more strongly correlated with R&D than total life years lost is. (A scatter plot of ln[RD82] against %WHITE is shown in fig. 15.4.) But as the second column of coefficients reveals, both %MALE and %WHITE are significantly positively correlated with total life years lost: the diseases associated with the greatest number of premature deaths are those for which men and whites account for the greatest

Table 15.7   Correlation Matrix for Four Variables

	ln(RD82)	ln(LYL80)	%MALE
ln(LYL80)	0.67714		
	(0.0078)		
%MALE	0.55375	0.56093	
	(0.0399)	(0.0369)	
%WHITE	0.75643	0.88477	0.50235
	(0.0017)	(0.0001)	(0.0672)

Note: Numbers in parentheses are *p*-values.

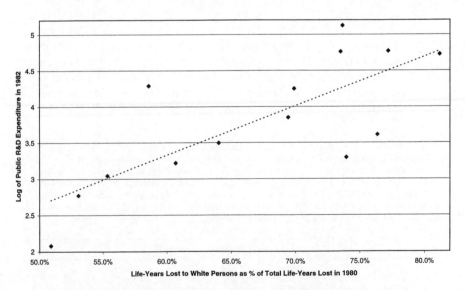

Fig. 15.4   Relationship across diseases between public R&D expenditure and percent of life years lost to white persons

fractions of life years lost. We therefore need to determine whether %MALE and %WHITE have significant effects on public R&D, controlling for total life years lost (although our ability to determine this will be hampered by multicollinearity). The appropriate regressions are

$$\ln(RD82) = -0.164 + 0.280\ln(LYL80) + 1.11\%MALE + e \qquad R^2 = .503$$
$$(0.12) \quad (2.08) \qquad\qquad\quad (0.99) \qquad\qquad N = 14,$$

$$\ln(RD82) = -0.813 + 0.019\ln(LYL80) + 6.56\%WHITE + e \quad R^2 = .573$$
$$(0.64) \quad (0.09) \qquad\qquad\quad (1.71) \qquad\qquad N = 14.$$

The coefficient on %MALE is insignificant and the inclusion of this variable only slightly reduces the coefficient on $\ln(LYL80)$. In contrast, the coefficient on %WHITE is marginally significant, even in the presence of the other regressor, which becomes insignificant (with a t-statistic of only 0.09) when %WHITE is included. We also estimated an alternative functional form of the relationship $RD82 = f(LYL80, \%WHITE)$:

$$\ln(RD82) = 2.29 + 1.35\ln(LYL80 \times \%WHITE)$$
$$(1.14) \quad (1.90)$$

$$-1.30\ln[LYL80 \times (1 - \%WHITE)] + e \quad R^2 = .560,$$
$$(1.44) \qquad\qquad\qquad\qquad N = 14.$$

These estimates indicate that research expenditure is positively correlated with life years lost by whites but not by nonwhites; the coefficient on the latter is negative, but its p-value is only .18. The two coefficients are virtually equal in magnitude and opposite in sign; if one imposes that restriction (which is not rejected by the data), the estimates are

$$\ln(RD82) = 2.72 + 1.47\ln[\%WHITE/(1 - \%WHITE)] + e \quad R^2 = .558$$
$$(8.40) \quad (3.89) \qquad\qquad\qquad\qquad\qquad N = 14.$$

The data are highly consistent with the hypothesis that the amount of publicly funded research on a disease decreases with the share of life years before age sixty-five lost to the disease that are lost by nonwhites. A possible explanation for this finding is that lack of scientific knowledge is a less important cause of premature mortality among nonwhites than it is among whites. Nonwhite premature mortality may be due, to a greater extent, to poor diet, reduced utilization of medical care, or other factors. In other words, it is plausible that the health status of nonwhites tends to be well below the frontier of medical knowledge, whereas the health status of whites tends to be on, or closer to, the frontier. The purpose of biomedical research is to shift the frontier outward, and the allocation or "direction" of research should depend (more) on the distribution of the disease burden of those on, or close to, the frontier. If cures for diseases that impose a heavy toll on minorities have already been found, then the productivity of further research on those diseases may be quite low.

The relative lack of research on diseases borne disproportionately by minorities may also be due to other reasons and may not be efficient. It may reflect the relatively low representation of minorities among the ranks of biomedical scientists. The National Science Foundation monitors the participation of women and minorities in science and engineering and has adopted some policies to increase their participation.

15.3.2 Prevalence and Severity of Chronic Conditions in the (Living) Population

Table 15.8 presents data on the number of FY1995 research grants mentioning chronic conditions surveyed in the National Health Interview Survey and the number of people having, and limited in activity by, these conditions.[22] The condition mentioned in the most (1,807) research grants is diabetes. About seven million Americans suffer from diabetes, according to this household survey; about one-third of them are limited in activity by this condition. Although arthritis is far more prevalent, afflicting thirty-two million Americans, the number of research grants mentioning it (609) is much smaller.

Table 15.9 presents correlation coefficients of the logarithms of these variables and related measures of condition severity. This table indicates that the number of research grants mentioning a chronic condition has a very small and insignificant correlation with the number of people with the condition and with the number who have seen a physician about that condition. Research activity is weakly positively related (p-value = .08) to the number of people who have been hospitalized for a condition. It is very strongly positively related (p-value = .0003) to the number of people whose activities are limited by that condition. Somewhat surprisingly, research activity is significantly positively correlated with the *proportion* of people who have seen a doctor or been hospitalized, as well as those whose activities are limited.[23]

The determinants of the number of research grants citing chronic conditions are further analyzed in table 15.10. The first column presents the regression of ln(NGRANTS95) on a measure of condition prevalence

22. In this section the measure of public research activity I use is the number of grants rather than the dollar value of those grants. For technical reasons, the former is much easier to compute. Substitution of the former for the latter will not affect my results if the average size of grants is uncorrelated across conditions with the number of grants. In the future I plan to compute the distribution of dollars by condition and to integrate the premature mortality and chronic-condition prevalence analyses.

23. This is particularly surprising since, as the second column of table 15.9 indicates, these proportions are significantly inversely related to prevalence per se: conditions that are more prevalent tend to be less severe (i.e., associated with lower probabilities of hospitalization, activity limitation, and physician consultation).

Table 15.8 **Number of FY1995 Research Grants Citing, and Number of People Reporting and Limited in Activity by, Major Chronic Conditions**

NGRANT	N	NLA	Chronic Condition
1,807	6,962	2,416	Diabetes
1,540	27,600	2,926	High blood pressure (hypertension)
671	1,293	374	Diseases of retina
609	31,788	6,739	Arthritis
593	1,513	79	Diseases of prostate
573	3,739	157	Anemias
493	11,482	2,503	Asthma
425	1,243	552	Epilepsy
402	1,562	1,367	Mental retardation
315	8,169	1,291	Blindness and other visual impairments
293	766	130	Liver diseases including cirrhosis
288	3,002	1,078	Cerebrovascular disease
282	23,266	1,280	Deafness and other hearing impairments
258	7,732	2,436	Ischemic heart disease
241	180	125	Multiple sclerosis
241	2,725	556	Speech impairments
216	802	190	Malignant neoplasm of breast
203	6,416	391	Cataracts
195	2,433	326	Glaucoma
119	2,333	161	Enteritis and colitis
118	741	133	Congenital heart disease
118	834	45	Disease of the esophagus
103	322	200	Malignant neoplasms of stomach intestines
99	218	132	Malignant neoplasms of lung bronchus
90	1,984	18	Menstrual disorders
85	2,378	50	Psoriasis
84	1,861	821	Emphysema
84	1,325	46	Kidney infections
84	1,911	134	Tachycardia or rapid heart
83	7,868	504	Heart rhythm disorders
83	344	76	Malignant neoplasm of prostate
80	4,201	328	Ulcer gastric duodenal and/or peptic
74	2,269	88	Malignant neoplasms of the skin
61	2,074	199	Hardening of arteries
59	3,121	240	Gastric ulcer
54	73	2	Benign neoplasm of breast
53	217	7	Cleft palate
50	3,003	30	Gastritis and duodenitis

Notes: NGRANT = Number of FY1995 grants mentioning condition. N = Average number of people (in thousands) in 1990–92 reporting that they have the condition. NLA = Average number of people (in thousands) in 1990–92 reporting that their activities are limited by the condition. Only conditions cited by fifty or more grants are listed.

Table 15.9   **Correlations between Research Activity and Prevalence/Severity of Chronic Conditions**

	LGRANTS	LN	LNLA	LNHOSP
LGRANTS: log(no. of research grants)	1.00			
	(0.00)			
LN: log(no. of people w. condition)	0.04	1.00		
	(0.74)	(0.00)		
LNLA: log(no. w. limited activity)	0.40	0.54	1.00	
	(0.00)	(0.00)	(0.00)	
LNHOSP: log(no. hospitalized)	0.20	0.61	0.74	1.00
	(0.08)	(0.00)	(0.00)	(0.00)
LNPHYS: log(no. seeing physician)	0.07	0.99	0.59	0.66
	(0.53)	(0.00)	(0.00)	(0.00)
LA: % w. limited activity	0.35	−0.26	0.49	0.12
	(0.00)	(0.00)	(0.00)	(0.19)
HOSP: % hospitalized	0.22	−0.46	0.09	0.28
	(0.06)	(0.00)	(0.31)	(0.00)
PHYS: % seeing physician	0.32	−0.43	0.18	0.18
	(0.00)	(0.00)	(0.05)	(0.04)

Note: Figures in parentheses are probability values.

Table 15.10   **Determinants of Number of FY1995 Research Grants Mentioning Chronic Conditions ($N = 54$)**

	Equation 1	Equation 2	Equation 3
$\ln(N)$	0.142		
	(0.73)		
%LA	4.45		
	(2.77)		
$\ln(N \times \text{\%LA})$		0.651	0.369
		(4.12)	(2.39)
$\ln[N \times (1 - \text{\%LA})]$		−0.436	−0.167
		(2.17)	(0.88)
%INCOME < \$10,000			8.61
			(2.17)
%AGE < 18			5.67
			(2.63)
%AGE > 75			7.30
			(2.73)
Intercept	2.09	3.82	0.267
	(1.31)	(2.81)	(0.17)
R^2	0.1317	0.2460	0.4470

Notes: The dependent variable is the log of the number of FY1995 grants. N = Average number of people (in thousands) in 1990–92 reporting that they have the condition. %LA = Fraction of people reporting that their activities are limited by the condition. %INCOME < \$10,000 = Fraction of people with household income < \$10,000. %AGE < 18 = Fraction of people under eighteen years of age. %AGE > 75 = Fraction of people over seventy-five years of age. Numbers in parentheses are t-statistics.

(ln[N]) and severity (%LA). As one might expect given the simple correlations in the previous table, only the severity measure has a significant positive effect on research activity. In the second column, I estimate an alternative functional form of the relationship; the regressors are the logarithms of the number of people with the condition whose activities are ($N \times$ %LA) and are not ($N \times [1 - \%LA]$) limited by the condition. The coefficient on the former is positive and highly significant, indicating that the amount of public research about a chronic condition increases with the number of people whose activities are limited by that condition.[24] Moreover, the amount of public research is significantly *inversely* related to the number of people who have a condition but whose activities are not limited by it. This could conceivably signify that, the greater the number of people who have a condition but are not seriously affected by it, the greater the odds that an adequate treatment for the condition already exists, and the less worthy that condition is of further research. This inverse relation becomes insignificant, however, when we include (in column 3) measures of the income and age distribution of persons reporting the condition. This regression indicates that there tends to be more research about chronic conditions that are prevalent among people living in low-income (below $10,000) households, and that are prevalent among the young (under age eighteen) and the old (above age seventy-five). This suggests that the poor, the young, and the very old may derive disproportionately large benefits from government-sponsored biomedical research. In the previous section I reported that the amount of publicly funded research on a disease decreases with the share of life years before age sixty-five lost to the disease that are lost by nonwhites. Since nonwhites are more likely to be poor than whites, it is surprising that chronic conditions prevalent among the poor tend to be more intensively researched.

15.4 Summary

I have developed a simple theoretical model of the allocation of the applied component of public biomedical research expenditure—the approximately 50 percent that is of direct, near-term relevance to specific diseases—and presented some empirical evidence about the determinants of this allocation. The implications of the theoretical model are consistent with government officials' descriptions of the allocation process: the structure of expenditure should depend upon research productivity (or "scientific opportunity") as well as on public health need, or the societal and economic burden of the disease/condition.

Although we lack, at this point, useful indicators of research productiv-

---

24. As in the analysis of premature mortality, however, the elasticity is significantly less than unity.

ity (i.e., of the *cost* of achieving research advances), we have a number of measures of disease burden (i.e., of the potential *benefit* of achieving these advances). Analysts of technological change typically have data on neither the costs nor the benefits of technical advance. Failure to measure research productivity will not necessarily bias my estimates; if it does, it seems likely to bias them toward zero.

I calculated distributions of government-funded biomedical research expenditure, by disease, from records of all research projects supported by the U.S. Public Health Service; in fiscal year 1995, there were records of 63,289 projects whose total value was $10.1 billion. Some research expenditure cannot be assigned to specific diseases, in some cases because the research being conducted is basic in nature. The distribution of research expenditure by disease that I constructed is quite similar to one calculated by NIH based on data provided by NIH institutes, centers, and divisions (ICDs) designed to "reflect NIH-wide resources devoted to research on the listed diseases" (as opposed to budget figures for the ICD identifying the cost data).

I performed an empirical examination of the relationship of public research expenditure to a number of measures of disease burden. To avoid "sample selection bias," and to obtain a reasonably complete accounting of disease burden, I utilized data on both the dying (from the Vital Statistics–Mortality Detail file) and the living (from the National Health Interview Survey).

The mortality-related measure of disease burden I use is life years lost before age sixty-five. I found a very strong positive relationship across diseases between total life years lost and public R&D expenditure (although the slope of this relationship was smaller than that implied by the theory, perhaps due to failure to measure research productivity). Further analysis indicated that research expenditure is positively correlated with life years lost by whites but not with life years lost by nonwhites. In other words, the amount of publicly funded research on a disease decreases with the share of life years before age sixty-five lost to the disease that are lost by nonwhites. A possible explanation for this finding is that lack of scientific knowledge is a less important cause of premature mortality among nonwhites than it is among whites.

Disease prevalence and severity data for the (living) population provide additional indicators of disease burden. I found that the number of research grants mentioning a chronic condition has a very low and insignificant correlation with the number of people with the condition and with the number who have seen a physician about that condition. Research activity is weakly positively related to the number of people who have been hospitalized for a condition, and very strongly positively related to the number of people whose activities are limited by that condition. Moreover, there tends to be more research about chronic conditions that are prevalent among people living in low-income households, and that are prevalent among the young (under age eighteen) and the old (above age seventy-five).

References

Adams, James D. 1990. Fundamental stocks of knowledge and productivity growth. *Journal of Political Economy* 98 (4): 673–702.

Chamberlain, Gary. 1984. Panel data. In *Handbook of econometrics*, vol. 2, ed. Z. Griliches and M. D. Intriligator, chap. 22. New York: Elsevier Science.

Collins, J. G. 1997. Prevalence of selected chronic conditions: United States, 1990–1992. *Vital Health Statistics* 10 (194): 1–89.

Cutler, David. 1995. Technology, health costs, and the NIH. Unpublished paper prepared for NIH Roundtable on Economics, 19 October.

Garber, Alan, and Paul Romer. 1995. Evaluating the federal role in financing health-related research. Unpublished paper prepared for NIH Roundtable on Economics, 19 October.

Henderson, Rebecca, and Iain Cockburn. 1996. Scale, scope, and spillovers: The determinants of research productivity in drug discovery. *RAND Journal of Economics* 27 (1): 32–59.

Institute of Medicine. Committee on the NIH Research Priority-Setting Process. 1998. Scientific opportunities and public needs: Improving priority setting and public input at the National Institute of Health. Washington, D.C.: National Academy Press. Available at: http://www.nap.edu.

Lichtenberg, Frank. 1996. Do (more and better) drugs keep people out of hospitals? *American Economic Review* 86:384–88.

———. 2000. The effect of pharmaceutical utilisation and innovation on hospitalisation and mortality. In *Productivity, technology, and economic growth*, ed. B. van Ark, S. K. Kuipers, and G. Kuper. Boston: Kluwer Academic.

Mushkin, Selma. 1979. *Biomedical research: Costs and benefits.* Cambridge, Mass.: Ballinger.

National Center for Health Statistics. 1995. *Health, United States, 1994.* Hyattsville, Md.: Public Health Service.

National Institutes of Health. 1993. *Cost savings resulting from NIH research support,* 2nd ed. NIH Publication no. 93-3109, September. Washington, D.C.: National Institutes of Health.

———. 1995. Disease-specific estimates of direct and indirect costs of illness and NIH support. Washington, D.C.: National Institutes of Health.

———. 1997. Setting research priorities at the National Institutes of Health. Working Group on Priority Setting, September. Available at *http://www.nih.gov.*

———. N.d. Stories of discovery: NIH's contributions to progress against disease. Unpublished paper.

Toole, Andrew. 2000. The impact of public basic research on industrial innovation: Evidence from the pharmaceutical industry. Policy paper no. 00-07. Institute for Economic Policy Research, Stanford University, November.

Viscusi, W. Kip. 1995. Valuing the health consequences of biomedical research. Unpub. paper prepared for NIH Roundtable on Economics, 19 October.

Contributors

Aslam Anis
CHEOS, St. Paul's Hospital
620-B-1081 Burrard Street
Vancouver, BC V6Z 1Y6 Canada

Ernst R. Berndt
Sloan School of Management,
E52-452
Massachusetts Institute of Technology
50 Memorial Drive
Cambridge, MA 02142

Susan H. Busch
Department of Health Care Policy
Harvard Medical School
180 Longwood Avenue
Boston, MA 02115

Iain M. Cockburn
School of Management
Boston University
595 Commonwealth Avenue
Boston, MA 02215

Douglas L. Cocks
11715 Fox Road
Suite 400
PMB 115
Indianapolis, IN 46236

David M. Cutler
Department of Economics
Harvard University
Cambridge, MA 02138

Paul Ellickson
Simon School of Business
Administration
University of Rochester
Rochester, NY 14627

Dennis Fixler
Division of Price and Index Number
Research
Bureau of Labor Statistics
2 Massachusetts Avenue, NE, Room
3105
Washington, DC 20212

Ina Kay Ford
Bureau of Labor Statistics
2 Massachusetts Avenue, NE
Room 3260
Washington, DC 20212

Richard G. Frank
Department of Health Care Policy
Harvard Medical School
180 Longwood Avenue
Boston, MA 02115

Daniel H. Ginsburg
Bureau of Labor Statistics
2 Massachusetts Avenue, NE
Room 3260
Washington, DC 20212

Mitchell Ginsburg
International economist
Applied Economics Division
United States International Trade
　Commission
500 E Street SW, room 602-Q
Washington, DC 20436

Sherry Glied
Division of Health Policy and
　Management
School of Public Health
Columbia University
600 West 168th Street, Room 617L
New York, NY 10032

Paul Heidenreich
Section of Cardiology 111C
Palo Alto Veterans Administration
　Medical Center
3801 Miranda Avenue
Palo Alto, CA 94304

Haiden A. Huskamp
Department of Health Care Policy
Harvard Medical School
180 Longwood Avenue
Boston, MA 02115

Darius Lakdawalla
RAND
1700 Main Street
P.O. Box 2138
Santa Monica, CA 90407

J. Steven Landefeld
U.S. Department of Commerce
Economics and Statistics
　Administration
Bureau of Economic Analysis
1441 L Street, NW Suite 6006
Washington, DC 20230

Frank R. Lichtenberg
Graduate School of Business
Columbia University
3022 Broadway, 726 Uris Hall
New York, NY 10027

Mark McClellan
Department of Economics
Stanford University
Economics Building, 224
Stanford, CA 94305

David Meltzer
Section of General Internal Medicine
University of Chicago
5841 S. Maryland, MC 2007
Chicago, IL 60637

Brent R. Moulton
U.S. Department of Commerce
Bureau of Economic Analysis (BE-6)
1441 L Street, NW
Washington, DC 20230

Joseph P. Newhouse
Division of Health Policy Research
　and Education
Harvard University
180 Longwood Avenue
Boston, MA 02115

Tomas Philipson
Department of Economics
University of Chicago
1155 East 60th Street
Chicago, IL 60637

Darrel A. Regier
American Psychiatric Institute for
　Research and Education
1400 K Street, NW
Washington, D.C. 20005

Dahlia Remler
Health Policy and Management
　Division
The Joseph L. Mailman School of
　Public Health
Columbia University
600 West 168th Street, 6th Floor
New York, NY 10032

James A. Schuttinga
Office of Science Policy
National Institutes of Health
Building 1, Room 218
1 Center Drive
Bethesda, MD 20892

Arthur Sensenig
N3-02-17
Health Care Financing Administration
Baltimore, MD 21244

Irving Shapiro
Phillips Eye Institute
2215 Park Avenue
Minneapolis, MN 55404

Matthew D. Shapiro
Department of Economics
University of Michigan
Ann Arbor, MI 48109

Jonathan Skinner
Department of Economics
6106 Rockefeller Hall
Dartmouth College
Hanover, NH 03755

Scott Stern
Sloan School of Management,
   E52-554
Massachusetts Institute of Technology
50 Memorial Drive
Cambridge, MA 02142

Manuel Trajtenberg
Eitan Berglas School of Economics
Tel-Aviv University
Tel-Aviv 69978 Israel

Jack E. Triplett
Visiting Fellow, Economic Studies
The Brookings Institution
1775 Massachusetts Avenue, NW
Washington, DC 20036

David W. Wilcox
Department of Treasury
1500 Pennsylvania Avenue, NW
Room 3454
Washington, DC 20220

Ernest Wilcox
Bureau of Economic Analysis,
   BE-54
U.S. Department of Commerce
Washington, DC 20230

Frank C. Wykoff
Department of Economics
Pomona College
425 North College Avenue
Claremont, CA 91711

Author Index

Subject Index